THE BATTLE OF THE GODS AND GIANTS

STUDIES IN INTELLECTUAL HISTORY

AND THE HISTORY OF PHILOSOPHY

M. A. Stewart and David Fate Norton, Editors

This is a monograph series whose purpose is to foster improved standards
of historical and textual scholarship in the history of philosophy and
directly related disciplines. Priority is given to studies that significantly
advance our understanding of past thinkers through the careful
examination and interpretation of original sources, whether printed or
manuscript. Major works and movements in philosophy often reflect
interests and concerns characteristic of a particular age and upbringing,
and seemingly timeless concepts may vary with the changing background
of knowledge and belief that different writers assume in their readers. It is
the general editors' assumption that a sensitivity to context not only does
not detract from the philosophical interest or rigor of a commentary but is
actually essential to it. They wish to encourage studies that present a
broad view of a subject's contemporary context, and that make an
informative use of philosophical, theological, political, scientific, literary,
or other collateral materials, as appropriate to the particular case.

———————————

Other Books in the Series

Steven M. Nadler, *Arnauld and the Cartesian Philosophy of Ideas*

Catherine Wilson, *Leibniz's Metaphysics: A Historical and Comparative Study*

THE BATTLE OF THE
GODS AND GIANTS

THE LEGACIES OF DESCARTES
AND GASSENDI, 1655–1715

Thomas M. Lennon

PRINCETON UNIVERSITY PRESS   PRINCETON, NEW JERSEY

Copyright © 1993 by Princeton University Press
Published by Princeton University Press, 41 William Street,
Princeton, New Jersey 08540
In the United Kingdom: Princeton University Press,
Chichester, West Sussex

Library of Congress Cataloging-in-Publication Data
Lennon, Thomas M.
The battle of the gods and giants : the legacies of Descartes and Gassendi,
1655–1715 / Thomas M. Lennon.
p.   cm. — (Studies in intellectual history and the history of philosophy)
Includes bibliographical references and index.
ISBN 0-691-07400-3
1. Gassendi, Pierre, 1592–1655.   2. Descartes, René, 1596–
1650.   3. Locke, John, 1632–1704.   I. Title.   II. Series.
B1887.L46   1993
194—dc20   92-26088   CIP

This book has been composed in Linotron Times Roman

Princeton University Press books are printed on acid-free paper
and meet the guidelines for permanence and durability of the
Committee on Production Guidelines for Book Longevity of the
Council on Library Resources

Printed in the United States of America

1 3 5 7 9 10 8 6 4 2

To Robert Earl Butts

Contents

Preface

THIS IS A HISTORY of philosophy that examines the period defined by the death dates of Gassendi and Malebranche. It explores what in my view is most of philosophical interest in the period, namely, the contest between the philosophies of Gassendi and Descartes as the appropriate scientific image of the world to replace the commonsense, manifest image associated with Aristotle and his scholastic epigones. Primarily because of the recrudescence of skepticism and the emergence of the New Science—contradictory circumstances that nonetheless reinforced each other—the world was thought to be other than as it is perceived to be. A main concern will thus be the dialectic of appearance and reality, which, while involving a broad range of philosophical issues, in this period focused on the analysis of space, the things in it, and how we know them. Not often explicit, but almost always implicit at the core of these analyses is the grand metaphysical question of why there exists anything at all.

While the period here studied postdates the death of Descartes, some account of his relevant views is obviously necessary. This is especially so since my overall interpretation, although anticipated by Cousin and perhaps others in the nineteenth century, is highly controversial. Few of the components of this interpretation seem to me problematic, yet no one has quite put them together in this fashion. The key to my idealist interpretation of Descartes is, in any case, that for him the ontological analysis of material things is the same as Malebranche's ontological analysis of the mental representations of material things. Descartes's things are Malebranche's perceptions of things. (Not incidentally, many late seventeenth and early eighteenth-century debates over the nature of ideas saw each side accuse the other of confusing things with our ideas of things.) Moreover, the material things of which our perceptions are representations according to Malebranche turned out to be, as Berkeley most notably argued, ontologically and epistemologically idle. Thus, Descartes's view as I interpret it is, however controversial, most characteristic of Cartesianism. The extent to which Malebranche may be taken as the later standard-bearer of Cartesianism may of course be debated—as it was by Arnauld—but as to the idealism here attributed to Descartes, other Cartesians such as Desgabets and Régis were only more explicit.

This work is not about Cartesianism, however, but its contest with Gassendism. Long neglected, Gassendi is now beginning to approach the prominence he once enjoyed. Translations have made his difficult texts more accessible, and the analyses by Rochot a few decades ago, and more recently by Bloch, Joy, and others, have shown their importance. As with Descartes's philosophy, the concern here is less with the eponymous source of Gassendism than with its subsequent contest against its competitor.

The contest between Cartesianism and Gassendism is a spectacular example of what Plato in the *Sophist* called the battle of the gods and giants—the perennial struggle between the friends of the Forms and the materialists. As Plato also saw, the gravamen of this struggle was the proper exercise of moral and especially political authority. The analysis of space, the things in it, and how we know them—not to mention the grand metaphysical question itself— were all seen to have colossal normative significance. All of these themes are developed in this work, both externally in terms of institutions, personalities, and historical context, and internally in terms of textual analysis. One benefit derived from this study is the recognition that Locke is a prime participant in the struggle and that his *Essay* can be read without exaggeration as an anti-Cartesian polemic from beginning to end.

That Locke opposed Descartes on at least some issues is obvious to his most casual reader. With the larger context supplied here, the anti-Cartesian interpretation of Locke may be extended to all the important questions that have bedeviled Locke exegesis from his own time to ours. Thus this work attempts to provide a uniquely motivated reading of Locke on such issues as ideas, perception, space, substance, qualities, powers, creation, essence, and abstraction.

Nowadays many agree that interpretations and theories carry with them the terms of their own interpretation. Without necessarily committing ourselves to any strong version of the incommensurability of even paradigmatically different theories, we have come to see that the concepts in terms of which we describe the world, if not the world itself, are not independent of those descriptions and explanations. This commonplace is no less true of the account I offer here of philosophy in the late seventeenth century. Indeed, the cause of the giants, which I make no secret of favoring, itself suggests a metalevel philosophy of history. Since my own account is self-consciously written from that metatheoretical perspective, I conclude this work with a chapter that not only illustrates the perspective with material from the period, but also further argues the account on which it is a perspective. Since the perspective is decidedly antirealist, the commonplace above leads one to expect just this sort of bootstrapping support. The thrust of the chapter, in any case, is that if we understand what a history is all about, we shall find less obstacle to accepting that Locke is best interpreted in an Epicurean tradition of the giants that essentially includes tychistic atheism.

In this period of instability in the evolution of critical apparatus, I should say something about my own conventions. Ibid. refers, as usual, to the work just previously cited. Otherwise, I use a short title sufficient to identify it for anyone familiar with it or for anyone who consults the Works Cited. I have tried to preserve original orthography throughout. Except where otherwise indicated, translations are my own; except where some special reason dictates otherwise, titles are untranslated.

Some of the material published here first made its appearance elsewhere. Earlier versions of chapter 4, section 12, were read at the University of Toronto, McMaster University, and the 17th World Congress of Philosophy, and appeared in the *Proceedings* of the latter. Material in chapter 2, section 5, was first used in *Friedrich Ueberwegs Gundriss der Geschichte der Philosophie*. A shorter version of chapter 2, section 7, was read to the History of Science Society, and a longer version of it appears in *An Intimate Relation: Studies in the History and Philosophy of Science Presented to R. E. Butts on His Sixtieth Birthday*, ed. J. Brown and J. Mittlestrass (Dordrecht: D. Reidel, 1985).

Chapter 3, section 11, was read by invitation of the Philosophy Department at Wilfrid Laurier University. A paper read to the Canadian Philosophical Society and my reply to a criticism of it (by F. Duchesneau, to whom I am grateful) was published in *Dialogue* and then eventuated into a much longer treatment in the *Philosophy Research Archives*; this eventually became section 18 of chapter 6. Section 24 of chapter 7 was also read to the Canadian Philosophical Association. Finally, material in chapter 8 was first read at a symposium organized at Waterloo University.

In producing a work of this scope I have perforce accumulated many debts, which I am happy to acknowledge. More specific ones are recorded throughout. More generally, the antepenultimate version of the work was read by members of my seminar, who saved me from many infelicities and outright errors: P. Catton, P. Easton, L. Falkenstein, T. Heyd, B.-H. Jeong, M. Lipson, C. McCurdy, C. Meyer, K. Quartz, C. Simpson, and A. Schneider. The text was computerized no less patiently than skillfully by C. Mabb. Superlative copyediting was provided by M. denBoer. C. A. Hooker early on showed how to think in terms of the big picture. M. R. Ayers was a source of helpful criticism and support during an important stage of the research. Sympathetic and helpful comments on my idealistic interpretation of Descartes came from Frederick Van de Pitte and Alan Nelson. R. F. McRae helped in several critical ways, as did J. W. Yolton, whose *John Locke and the Way of Ideas* set me off on paths of research that often returned me to that seminal work. O. R. Bloch opened the way inter alia to research beyond Gassendi himself. G. Pappas has read more of my material, more closely, than anyone. David Fate Norton offered useful direction at crucial stages. M.A. Stewart meticulously improved much of the ms with many editorial recommendations. Over a long period I have drawn upon sources of inspiration and encouragement; R. G. Turnbull first breathed life into the project and R. E. Butts has sustained my spirit for it. Finally, I am grateful to the Canada Council for the seed grant to help start the project and to the Social Sciences and Humanities Research Council of Canada for a Leave Fellowship to finish it.

Note on Documentation

REFERENCES to Descartes are given first, where available, to the translation by Cottingham, Stoothoof, and Murdoch (CSM) by volume and page, and then, similarly, to the standard edition by Adam and Tannery (AT). My quotations from the text are usually from CSM, sometimes with what I take to be ameliorations, sometimes even from the superseded translation by Haldane and Ross (HR), or by Cress for the _Mediations_, by Miller and Miller for the _Principles_, and by Kenny for the correspondence. Finally, I am grateful to David Behan for showing me his careful translation of _Meditations_ 2, which is a key text for chapter 4.

References to Locke's _Essay_ are to the Nidditch edition, by book, chapter, paragraph, and page number. (2.27.3–6; 328–30, for instance, refers to bk. 2, chap. 27, paras. 3–6; pp. 328–30.)

Gassendi's _Opera_ was first published in 1658 in Lyons, consuming six folio volumes. It is to this edition that my references are made, by volume and page, and occasionally by column. (Thus _Opera_, 2:10a refers to vol. 2, p. 10, col. a.)

The standard edition of Malebranche is the _Oeuvres complètes_, in twenty volumes plus an index volume, under the general editorship of A. Robinet. Reference to this edition will be by volume and page. Translations of _De la recherche de la verité_ are from _The Search After Truth_, of the _Eclaircissements_ from the _Elucidations_. Reference to these works will allow collation with the standard edition and by page number of the translations by book, part, chapter, and section as applicable. Also of use will be the translations of other works by Doney, Buisberg, and Iorio (see Works Cited).

THE BATTLE OF THE GODS AND GIANTS

CHAPTER I

The Philosophical Terrain

§1 THE GASSENDIST FAILURE

The great nineteenth-century historian of Cartesianism, Francisque Bouillier, wrote that "during more than half a century, there did not appear in France a single book of philosophy, there was not a single philosophical discussion which did not have Descartes for its object, which was not for or against his system."[1] Bouillier was a Cartesian historian in two senses of the expression, both of which contribute to the exaggeration of his statement. Even so, he draws attention to what seems to me beyond dispute: that the philosophy of Descartes (1596–1650) dominates the latter half of the seventeenth century in a way that the thought of no one else even approximated.[2] During his lifetime, however, it was not clear that Descartes was to occupy so utterly exalted a position in the history of philosophy. Gassendi (1592–1655) in particular seemed as likely, certainly to many at the time, to enjoy at least as high a place in the philosophical pantheon. Yet the judgment of history has been clear, and it was a judgment that was formed very early. On first view, the question of philosophical importance may not be decidable in terms of whether the candidate has initiated a movement bearing his name, for example, or has succeeded in attracting followers. With the terms given sufficiently broad interpretation, it is even more difficult to argue this with respect to historical importance. I shall have some things to say about these questions. Meanwhile it is clear, in any case, that there were no Gassendists and there was no Gassendism as there were Cartesians and Cartesianism. Those few who were called Gassendists in the latter half of the seventeenth century often were concerned mainly with defending the person of Gassendi against the charge of loose morality rather than with adhering dogmatically to his views.[3]

[1] *Histoire*, I, p. 430.

[2] Spink, *French Free-thought*, p. 188, documents a more temperate version of Bouillier's thesis by listing some ninety-four works from the period whose titles explicitly mention Descartes. But Spink's list is not close to being complete.

[3] Craig Brush, whose translations of Gassendi have done so much to restore Gassendi's importance, rather overstates the case in claiming that "Antoine Adam concluded that at the turn of the century the cultivated Frenchman was more likely to be a Gassendist than a Cartesian" (*Selected Works*, p. xi). If Brush's source is Adam's paper "L'influence de Gassendi . . . ," the point is merely that, by way of correction of Bouillier's exaggerated claims on behalf of Cartesianism, there was between 1670 and 1700 an anti-Cartesian orbit of which an uninterrupted Gassendist *tradition* was a part and which included, for example, Huygens and Leibniz.

Very different was the behavior of the self-styled Cartesians, who debated questions of orthodoxy as vigorously, and as bitterly, as any political or religious movement. It is clear as well that while Descartes is nowadays read by first-year students in philosophy, Gassendi is likely unknown even to graduate students. Conferences on Descartes or Cartesianism are events of ongoing philosophical significance, while the most significant conference thus far devoted specifically to Gassendi has been a provincial event of largely antiquarian inspiration.[4] There is an Equipe Descartes at the Centre National de la Recherche Scientifique, which annually publishes a "Bulletin Cartésien." Although its appearance and disappearance were meteoric, the recent journal devoted to Cartesian studies at least had the opportunity to demonstrate the credibility of its intellectual goals. No such activities have been tried with respect to Gassendi. The eventual downfall of Cartesianism was a momentous collapse still worth writing about,[5] while it is not clear that anything at all called Gassendism ever existed.

This sketch of the relative statures of Descartes and Gassendi has long seemed to me as problematic as it might have to some contemporary of theirs. How could the star of Gassendism, once so much in the ascendancy, have set so definitively when reasons for its former position continued to seem cogent? Leibniz often complained of the weakness or outright lack of Cartesian technology, a sure sign for him of the infirmity of the science on which it should have been based. The main theoretical question here may be framed by asking why history never carried Leibniz's complaint a level deeper to lodge it more generally against the ontology he in fact shared with the Cartesians, namely, that this ontology was systematically at odds with the Galilean-Newtonian axis of empiricist atomism that spanned the seventeenth century. More particularly, the question is why rationalist plenum theories, particularly the Cartesian, should have endured so successfully, on the Continent at least, as the ontology of the New Science. As it stands, the question of course involves gross simplifications. For example, it was not until well into the eighteenth century that Newtonian physics finally prevailed against the Cartesian; and Descartes felt that he was doing more than merely accommodating the undeniable advances of Galileo. That is, during the heyday of Cartesianism the Galilean-Newtonian axis of empiricist atomism was far from apparent; the *Principia* after all was not published until 1687. But the question yet stands as to why in particular the philosophy of Gassendi, the more natural vehicle of atomism between Galileo and Newton, remained, while always a plausible alternative to Cartesianism, an also-ran in the competition with it. Despite his presence and authority recognized in a host of spheres, Gassendi had no discernible school, had very

---

[4] Contrast the *Actes tricentennaire* with the *Cahiers* two years later. (See Sebba, no. 42, p. 11.) But conferences in the Gassendi quatercentenary will have dramatically altered this picture.

[5] See Watson, *Downfall of Cartesianism*.

little exposition of his doctrines by others, and was soon headed for near-oblivion. Why?

My early research on the question immediately suggested a number of hypotheses. Rehearsing them will begin to clarify the questions, or set of questions, I intend to treat. As part of this, the set of philosophical views I have attached to the name of Gassendi will begin to emerge. There are three main hypotheses. One is that Gassendi's position had theological implications that were hopelessly unacceptable; this I treat under the heading, "Opprobrium Theologicum." Under the heading, "A Distinction without a Difference," I insinuate the possibility that Gassendi did not fail at all. "Cleopatra's Nose" is a third hypothesis, which draws attention to the nonrational circumstances affecting the competing positions. Once again, while many factors will be seen to contribute to the Cartesian success noted above, the Gassendist cause will emerge in one circumstance as relatively successful against the Cartesians, namely, in the academies of the period. They will be the topic of this chapter's second section below. In the third section we shall be in a position to focus the philosophical issues at stake between the Gassendists and Cartesians; and in the final section we note that they were not the only contestants in the period.

Opprobrium Theologicum

The major project of Gassendi's philosophical career was the Christian rehabilitation of Epicurus.[6] His aim was to do for Epicurus what Augustine had done for Plato, or, more obviously, Aquinas for Aristotle, namely, to show that a philosopher living before Christ and in ignorance of the Judaic tradition should nonetheless produce a philosophy of use in answering not only profane questions but also those arising from faith. On the face of it this project was exceedingly implausible. As early as Lactantius and Arnobius, and rather continuously thereafter, Epicurus had been roundly condemned as inimical to Christianity; Dante consigns him and his followers to the sixth circle of hell, among the arch-heretics; and the recovery of the complete text of Lucretius's *De rerum natura* in 1417 did not much alter the near-universal perception of Epicureanism.[7]

There were two related kinds of objections. Morally, Epicureanism was regarded as involving hedonism of the grossest and most uncontrolled sort.

---

[6] Brundell, whose work came to me too late to be taken much account of here, argues that Gassendi's principal concern was the overthrow of Aristotelianism. Indeed, he claims, implausibly in my view, that "in making it his life-work to promote Epicureanism to take the place of Aristotelianism, Gassendi was not aware that he might be advocating a philosophy that could be considered dangerous or shocking. Epicureanism was not looked upon in the seventeenth century as an especially offensive philosophy" (*Pierre Gassendi*, p. 138).

[7] For an overview of this history, see Jones, *Pierre Gassendi*, pt. 3, chap. 1.

Horace had branded it "pig philosophy" (*de grege porcum*),[8] a characterization from which J. S. Mill was still explicitly trying to recover it in the nineteenth century.[9] Gassendi tried to argue that hedonism properly understood inclined to asceticism rather than antinomianism, and that contrary to the calumnies of history this inclination had been true of Epicurus himself. But his arguments were increasingly less effective as hedonism came to characterize the *libertinage érudit* that flourished in the 1630s. The significance of this *Lebensform*, as we might call it, has divided historians, but all agree that it combined a freedom of speculation with the pursuit of pleasure. To what extent the pleasure pursued was merely sensual or the speculation went beyond the epistemic bounds imposed by the Church are the questions that divide the historians.[10] Gassendi was in any case a notable part of it all, forming along with Gabriel Naudé, François de La Mothe Le Vayer, and Elie Diodati, the *Tétrade* that Pintard placed at the center of libertinage érudit. It might credibly be argued that the views and conduct of the Tétrade were not necessarily opposed to those required by the Church. The argument is less credible, however, when applied to François Luillier, for example, with whom Gassendi was on terms intimate enough that he lodged with Luillier in Paris in the 1640s. Still less is it applicable to some of those of whom Gassendi was supposed to have been the teacher; especially Chapelle (Claude Emmanuel, natural son of Luillier), François Bernier, of whom we shall have a great deal more to say below, perhaps Molière (at least according to his biography by Grimarest in 1705), and even Cyrano de Bergerac. The moral objection to Epicureanism was based as much on contemporary grounds as historical.

A second objection was based on metaphysical grounds. Historically, Epicureanism had come to signify the two doctrines of materialism, specifically the doctrine that everything is composed of atoms, including people in all their aspects, and, if not outright atheism, at least the rejection of any significant and purposeful divine intervention in human affairs. The one view was read to entail the denial of immortality, and the other, obviously, the denial of Providence. Nor were these viewed as peripheral, dispensable components of Epicureanism. The point of the celebrated *clinamen*, the inexplicable change of inclination in the top to bottom fall of material bodies through the deep void, is that any given order of things is ultimately a product of chance and a fortiori that human fate is not determined by anything divine. As in the case of the moral objection, the metaphysical objection was continuous into and throughout the seventeenth century. Cudworth as late as the penultimate decade of the century was com-

---

[8] Me pinguem et nitidum, bene curata cute vises, / Cum ridere voles, Epicuri de grege porcum (*Epistles*, bk. 1, ep. 4).

[9] Mill, *Utilitarianism*, p. 210.

[10] For a scorecard of the sides, see the notes to chap. 5 of Popkin's *Skepticism*, which makes a convincing case for the consistency between Gassendi's libertinage and his role as a priest in the Catholic Church.

plaining as much of his latter-day sympathizers as of Epicurus himself: "that monstrous Dotage and Sottishness of *Epicurus* . . . [to] make not only the power of Sensation, but also of Intellection and Ratiocination, and therefore all human Souls, to arise from the mere Contexture of corporeal Atoms, and utterly explode all incorporated Substances.[11]

Gassendi had tried to show (1) that the intellectual operations of the soul argued that at least it was not entirely material,[12] and (2) that while void space may be infinite in extent the number of atoms it contained was finite and thus the world-order could not be the product of mere chance. In his view traditional Epicureanism had gotten the connections right among materialism, theism, order, Providence, and the like, but had argued them the wrong way round. To be sure, if the number of atoms is infinite, no appeal need be made to design for the purpose of explaining order, but the argument is *modus tollens*, not *modus ponens*.[13]

In addition to such ad hoc modifications there seems to me a historically more interesting development at stake here. The seventeenth century is perhaps most notable for the rise of the New Science, the mechanico-mathematical conception of the world that replaced the Old Science of Aristotelianism. By giving the New Science a realist interpretation, that is, by regarding its undefined descriptive terms such as 'matter' as referring to what is *real*, one opens up a chasm between the real world and the world we experience (or at least between the real world and the world *as* we experience it). Both Descartes and Gassendi figure as prominently as anyone in the promulgation of the New Science with its realist interpretation. But right from the outset there were important differences in their positions. For one thing, the Cartesian real world is both knowable and in some sense necessary; for Gassendi it is contingent and at best knowable only hypothetically. At a minimum, this difference very usefully characterizes the followers of theirs whom we shall be discussing at some length. In addition, the Cartesian position, for reasons we shall also discuss, invited the inclusion

[11] *Morality*, p. 302.

[12] See Osler, "Epicurean Atomism."

[13] By 1669 atomists even publicly were arguing quite a different line. In *De rerum principiis*, bk. 3, chap. 39, the physician Guillaume Lamy (1644–82) responded to the objection that the chance encounter of atoms could no more produce a world than the *Iliad* could be composed by the random selection of letters. There is only one arrangement from an infinity of possible ones that is the *Iliad*, he said, but any way the atoms come together makes a world. In addition, the significance of the arrangement of letters that is the *Iliad* depends on human institution; but the atoms are independent of human institution and any way they come together will attract human admiration. The quality of argument on behalf of antifinalism was notably stronger at this point as the weak ad hominem response of, for example, Bayle shows (Bayle, *Oeuvres*, 3:110–111). Despite Descartes's proscription of final causes from physics, finalism came to be associated more with Cartesianism than with any philosophy influenced by Gassendi. Malebranche introduced teleological explanations in biology and Bayle argued that chance events are ruled out by natural laws, which must be established by an intelligent cause carrying them out. (This in fact is one of the arguments Bayle gives for his occasionalism.)

among the real things of the world at large nonmaterial elements that both made it more attractive in Christian terms and highlighted its difference from Gassendi's position. Put simply, Gassendi's version of the New Science looked to be more obviously a revival of the old despised materialism.

Now, one response to this danger was to reject outright the theoretical aspects of the New Science. This was the response of the more theologically minded members of the early Royal Society such as Richard Baxter, Samuel Parker, and ultimately Joseph Glanvil, who rejected all such hypotheses and called instead for a crude empiricism, namely, a collection of facts in the fashion supposedly recommended by Bacon.[14] Whether the undeniable advances of the New Science could ever have been accomplished in this fashion is highly doubtful. It was not until Berkeley's instrumentalism restored the reality of the world we experience by reducing the role of theory to predictions about this world that this threat of the New Science to religion was removed. Berkeley is better known for his criticism of certain implications he saw of the New Science; in this regard, however, he was its best champion.[15]

Yet these theological difficulties do not explain, even in the short run, Gassendi's failure against Descartes. For one thing, many included the Cartesians with the followers of Gassendi as advocating materialism. Richard Baxter, for example, complained of those "who in this age adhere to the *Epicurean* (or *Cartesian*) Hypothesis . . . and [who] reduce all to *matter* and *motion* because *matter* and *motion* is thoroughly studied by them."[16] More spectacular is the case of Henry More, who began by viewing Cartesianism as a useful weapon against Epicurean materialism but came to regard it as ammunition for just that view; in the end it was for him "the womb of impiety and godlessness."[17] The Cartesians themselves were not unaware that they were being identified with the new Epicureans. In his *Entretiens* (1666) Jacques Rohault has his antagonist report that "certain people" were saying that the new philosophy was "nothing but a revival of Epicurus's."[18] To emphasize that the principles of these types

---

[14] Kargon, *Atomism*, chap. 10.

[15] Thus the importance of the distinction Garber draws between the two kinds of skepticism Berkeley was concerned to refute. See Garber, "Corpuscular Scepticism." He rebuts skepticism over the nature of things by arguing that what we immediately perceive is the real thing itself rather than a representation of it, that is, by denying that there are real things of which we are in principle ignorant because we do not perceive them. Skepticism over the New Scientific workings, the corpuscular structure and connections of things as Berkeley might put it, is overcome not by denying that there are such things, but by giving them a certain interpretation. To talk of the corpuscular structure is not to talk of imperceivable things and their status, as Berkeley's materialist opponents held, but of the connections between things we do perceive. We may be ignorant of some of their connections but our ignorance is a matter of fact rather than of principle.

[16] *The Reasons of the Christian Religion* (London, 1667), p. 509; quoted in Kargon, *Atomism*, p. 110.

[17] For an extensive treatment of More's changing relationship to Cartesianism, see Gabbey, "Philosophia Cartesiana Triumphata."

[18] McClaughlin ("Censorship," n. 100) identifies the Jesuit René Rapin as among the "certain people" Rohault mentioned.

and those of the Cartesians were "not only different, but even contrary to each other and that between Descartes and Epicurus there is almost nothing in common," Rohault argues that Epicurus advanced important positions completely contrary to both Aristotle and Descartes.[19] Rohault then reads Epicurus as a materialist denying the immortality of the soul. His explanation of why such an antimaterialist philosophy as Cartesianism should be given so mistaken a reading is interesting. He observes that while Epicurus's atomism does not seem contrary to religion, and only his materialist-mortalist view of souls is objectionable, one view can taint all the others. In the same way, he says, Cartesianism has been tainted by Epicureanism because of an alleged similarity between them. Both are said to explain the properties of material things on the basis of the size and shape of their minute parts. But for the Epicureans those parts are indivisible, he explains, while for the Cartesians such parts follow from the infinite divisibility of matter, which they allow following Aristotle.[20] Now, this stance by Rohault is a curious reversal. He began with an attempt to differentiate Epicureanism from Cartesianism but he ends essentially with an apology for it, minimizing its differences from Cartesianism.[21] What this suggests is that theological difficulties do not fully explain Gassendi's failure against Descartes, whose followers were faced with the same difficulties. Indeed, the reversal suggests a rather different attitude toward the whole question of Gassendi's failure.

A Distinction without a Difference

A clear difference prima facie between Descartes and Gassendi is with respect to the ontology of the material world. Gassendi was an atomist, for whom the material world consisted ultimately of invisible, indivisible particles existing in space that was at least partly void of such particles. Descartes was a plenum theorist for whom there was no real difference between the extension of space and the extension of matter and for whom therefore there was no space void of matter, which was infinitely divisible. These seem to be clear differences between them; the relevant texts are prominent, clear, and extensive, and their authors could have written them with each other's views in mind. Yet these differences were not clearly perceived in the seventeenth century. Cudworth, for example, referred to the "*Mechanical* or *Atomical* Philosophy, that hath

---

[19] *Entretiens*, p. 198. On the strategy of this remarkable alliance, more later.

[20] Ibid., pp. 199–203. Rohault cites *Posterior Analytics* 2, 11; 94b 28–30.

[21] Rohault in fact seizes the occasion to argue on behalf of the mechanism common to both. He argues the efficacy of shape with a story about a noblewoman who convinced someone who held the contrary view that on his vew he should never have to trim his pen. (Such was seventeenth-century humor.) Elsewhere Rohault complained, more seriously, in a positivistic vein about the disputes concerning the infinite divisibility of matter; what matters is that it be regarded as sufficiently divisible to do physics (*Traité*, preface).

been lately restored by *Cartesius* and *Gassendus*, as to the main substance of it."[22] Henry More, who took a close interest in Cartesianism, early tried to make a connection between Moses and Descartes, whom he took to be inspired. As part of this he argued (from the premise that a couple of Pythagoreans had dissuaded Plato from burning the works of their master) that the natural philosophy of Pythagoras was atomism (along with a theory of elements, vortices, etc.), "the *Cartesian* Philosophy being in a manner the same with that of *Democritus*."[23] Less fancifully and with greater influence, Walter Charleton cites Descartes as an atomist, who maintained that the material world consists of indivisible, insensible particles.[24] Where he noticed differences between the views of Descartes and Gassendi, Robert Boyle refused to adjudicate them and instead concentrated on the experimental verification of the mechanical philosophy he found in both. Such issues as the infinite divisibility of matter and extension as its essence he took to be of no relevance to the view he described with the catch-all label of 'corpuscular philosophy.'[25] This conflation persisted until the end of the century. In his satirical anti-Cartesian tract *Voyage du monde de Descartes* (1690) the Jesuit Daniel has one of his characters tell Descartes: "as in Spain the name Lutheran was given to all heretics of the last century, whatever sect they might have been, so we indifferently call Cartesian all those who since your time have been involved in subtleties in matters of physics. I have seen more than one hot disputant place Gassendi among your disciples, although you surely were his junior by several years."[26]

In his classic 1950 work, the positivist historian of science Dijksterhuis seized upon the ambiguities reflected above and minimized the differences between Descartes and the atomists. Often their influence was combined, he said, and "hardly any distinction was made between [them]."[27] Despite Descartes's explicit rejection of atoms and the void, Dijksterhuis points to the following important aspects in which Descartes verged toward just this view.

First, space, which though material does not resist the motion of tertiary matter, is mechanically equivalent to the void. (The matter comprising such space seems designed to satisfy the metaphysical requirement that there be no void. Second, some parts of matter though mentally divisible by us are physically divisible only by God; but the same is true for the ultimate particles of the seventeenth-century atomists. (Bayle made essentially the same point with a metaphysical argument. The Cartesians cannot maintain the actual, but only the

[22] *Morality*, p. 55.

[23] *Conjectura Cabbalistica*, p. 104.

[24] *Physiologia*, pp. 85, 88.

[25] For a good account of Boyle along these lines, and for Boyle's likely debt to Charleton and Gassendi, see Kargon, *Atomism*, chap. 9.

[26] *Voyage*, pp. 185, 208. Other critics of Descartes also viewed him as espousing atomism, including Rapin, Duhamel, and Huet.

[27] *Mechanization*, 417.

possible division of matter to infinity; the upshot he pointed out is that having rejected the eternity of atoms and their fortuitous motion, Gassendi differs from Descartes with respect to the principle of material things only in retaining the void.[28]) Third, the lack of motion in the parts of a body with respect to each other is no better an explanation of cohesion than the simple juxtaposition of atoms as proposed by Democritus. (I shall return below to the problem of cohesion, a bugbear of seventeenth-century physical theory.) Finally, Dijksterhuis concludes that "practically the only remaining difference [between Descartes and the atomists] concerns gravity," which for Democritus is primary and for Gassendi is inamissably impressed by God on all matter, but which for Descartes is a mechanical, that is, derived property.

An additional complication was that this coalescence of views was recognized by some Cartesians such as Rohault who tried to resist it, but by others who actively facilitated it. The Cartesian Oratorian Fromentier taught atomism at Angers,[29] and no less prominent a Cartesian than Géraud de Cordemoy was able to advance explicit arguments on behalf of atoms and the void; and even if he drew criticism from other Cartesians, Cordemoy was able to do so while still insisting upon his Cartesian credentials.[30] No less a Cartesian watchdog than Robert Desgabets, who thought the camps of Descartes and Gassendi contrary and the "most considerable" of his time, nonetheless held that on the question of atoms and the void, "the entire dispute [between them] reduced to words rather than things."[31]

Given this emergence of Cartesian atomism *de fait*, a good question is why Descartes frequently, forcefully, and clearly opted for the plenum with his identification of space and matter. Part of the answer is his program of mathematizing nature, which involved not just the application of mathematics to physical phenomena but the understanding of such phenomena as essentially mathematical. Said Descartes to Mersenne, "my physics is [not just geometrical, but] nothing else than geometry." Properly understood this is the whole of the answer as I shall try to show below.[32] But this fuller explanation is prima facie far from apparent. That the essence of material things should be the extension of space may be sufficient for the mathematization of nature, but it is by no means necessary. It would be sufficient (given the privileged place of geometry) to regard extension as an essential property of material things, rather than as their only property, which was the view of the proper atomists. To explain Descartes's stronger claim, one might consider more external, circumstantial motivations. For example, it may have been that by identifying material and spatial extension Descartes was able to fill otherwise unoccupied space

[28] *Dict.* art. Leucippe, rem. D.
[29] Babin, *Journal*, p. 17,
[30] See chap. 2, sec. 8 below.
[31] *Traité*; *Oeuvres*, pp. 27, 29–30.
[32] Chap. 2.

with mechanically irrelevant matter. He might thus have been able to reject the void and thus avoid too sharp a break from the perceived orthodoxy, while yet enjoying the benefits of an atomist physics. This was the explanation offered by Lange,[33] but it fails both as a political stratagem, since Cartesianism was still condemned as atomist, and in conceptual terms, since an additional argument is still required for the physical indivisibility of what are for us ultimate particles.

Along the same externalist lines, one might take seriously the fascinating Rosicrucian connection proposed by Francis Yates.[34] The connection is attractive given the Rosicrucian rejection of the void. The Hermetic writings, with which Rosicrucian doctrine is of a piece, clearly deny the possibility of the void: *Nothing that is, is void.* Furthermore, the place in which the universe moves is said to be an incorporeal intellect.[35] The text here does not identify this intellect with God, but does so later: *All beings are in God.* As a Neo-Platonic text the language anticipates Malebranche in a way that is perhaps not surprising but nonetheless striking. Of greater present interest, however, is the discussion of how things are in God: *However they are in God, they are not in Him as in a place, for place is corporeal; it is an immobile body.*[36] This is all the more inviting as a research program in view of the tie Yates suggests between the mechanico-mathematical Dee tradition and the Invisible College that may have led to the Royal Society.[37] The connection is interesting for the additional reason that, in this early period at least, the Gassendist circle was actively extirpating Hermetic influences. Gassendi himself engaged in a particularly bitter polemic with Fludd, a polemic he took over from Mersenne and eventually passed along to Bernier, and his friend Naudé was among the first to see through the Rosicrucian scare of the 1620s in Paris. This suggests the nice thesis that Gassendi and Descartes were on opposite sides with respect to clandestine influences in the period.

But the thesis will not wash. To be sure there is evidence for Yates's thesis that while seventeenth-century mechanism can be understood as a shift from sixteenth-century magical theories, mechanism was nonetheless made possible by a magical attitude toward nature: Both evidenced a will to operate on nature to suit it to human purposes that contrasts sharply with the fundamentally contemplative attitude toward nature of both ancient science and medieval theology.[38] In addition, Yates at least raises interesting questions about

---

[33] *Materialism,* 1:243–44.

[34] See *Rosicrucian Enlightenment,* chap. 8. For the most recent, informed, and dispassionate account of the connection, see Shea, *Magic* chap. 5, who while denying that Descartes was a Rosicrucian shows possible influences of the Hermetic writings on him, although not particularly on the question below.

[35] *Corpus Hermeticum,* 2, 10–12; Festugière, 1:35–37.

[36] Ibid., 11, 18; p. 154.

[37] Yates, *Rosicrucian Enlightenment,* chap. 13. Alas, the tie can no longer be credited.

[38] *Giordano Bruno,* chap. 8, esp. pp. 155–56.

Descartes's activities during 1618–23, a period crucial to both the genesis of Descartes's metaphysics and the insinuation of Rosicrucianism into Descartes's environment. Whatever the answers to these questions, however, they are not likely to involve any consideration of Rosicrucianism. The only connection that Yates suggests is highly circumstantial and, as she is well aware, Descartes himself explicitly denied any connection. To those who upon his return to Paris in 1623 thought that Descartes might be a Rosicrucian he argued that he could not be one since the Rosicrucians were supposed to be invisible, while he was plainly visible to anyone who might care to enquire.[39] Furthermore, despite his polemic with Fludd, Gassendi's worldview, as indeed that of all the libertins érudits, was never entirely purged of the influence of Italian naturalism and with it a vitalist conception of nature utterly at odds with mechanism. Gilles de Launay, one of the two most important later advocates of Gassendist ideas, was still citing the authority of Hermes Trismegistus in the 1670s, a half-century after the dating and debunking of the Hermetic texts by Casaubon. And by the end of the century the most notorious of the clandestine treatises, *De tribus impostoribus*, was associating Epicureanism with Stoic themes and Spinozist pantheism-atheism in an extraordinary hylopsychistic mélange.[40] Whatever the role of the clandestine literature in the development of the New Science, it cannot be used to distinguish Descartes and Gassendi as our nice thesis suggests.

If anything, one becomes inclined at this point to dissociate Gassendi from the success of the atomist version of the New Science, which in an ironic *volte face* is co-opted by the Cartesians. This is to fall in with Kurt Lasswitz who in the last century argued that "none [*sic*] of the new partisans of atomism, neither Bruno, nor Bacon, nor Basso had showed as forcefully as Descartes that the principle of bodies must be conceived with purely material and mechanical elements. . . . Descartes's great step beyond the ancient atomism was to attempt the qualitative determination of the material corpuscles . . . without which Descartes's mechanics would not have succeeded in conceiving the world as an ensemble of elementary masses in motion."[41] On this line Descartes is not distinguished from the atomist program; on the contrary, he is atomism's most successful champion. Rather it is Gassendi who fails precisely in his role as the vehicle of atomism between Galileo and Newton, and on this ground perhaps the failure of Gassendi can be distinguished from the success of Descartes. What role, then, did Gassendi play in the development of the New Science?

Gassendi's mechanical philosophy is of the crudest sort, no more refined than that to be found in Democritus or Lucretius. He explains the properties of matter in terms of the sizes and shapes of the atoms composing them, and he

---

[39] Baillet, *Des-Cartes*, pp. 91–92; Yates, *Rosicrucian Enlightenment*, pp. 152–54.

[40] Spink, *French Free-thought*, p. 126; for more on this literature, see below.

[41] *Geschichte*, 114; quoted by Prost, *Essai*, p. 19, n. 1.

attributes change in properties entirely to motion, which itself changes only upon collision. But he makes no attempt to explain change in properties in terms of the variation of the motion in the atoms composing them. Gassendi's is a crudely nondynamical mechanism. Such at least is the picture drawn by Marie Boas Hall.[42] In fact, to the extent there is a Gassendist dynamics at all it is incompatible with the inertial physics of the New Science. Classical atomism assigned a property of weight (*pondus*) to atoms as a result of which they fall from an absolute top to bottom through infinite space.[43] The Gassendist cosmology interpreted this property as an inamissable force impressed on atoms by God. Unimpeded particles thus move continuously and come to rest only when, *and only so long as*, impeded by a particle of equal pondus in the opposite direction. Thus while Gassendi is known as the first to have published the modern law of inertia, that law for him applied only to objects at the macroscopic level of compound objects, and not at the microscopic level of atoms.[44] Its nondynamical character does not distinguish Gassendi's mechanism from Descartes's, however. As I see it, the Cartesian system relegates force to divine action. As Leibniz was to complain, kinematics is enough for the Cartesians as far as physics is concerned.

The best case for a clear distinction between Descartes and Gassendi as proponents of the New Science came from Koyré, who said simply that "the Epicurean tradition was not a scientific one."[45] Because of its "extreme sensualism," it was not amenable to a mathematical approach to nature and thus "it has never been able to yield a foundation for physics; not even in modern times: indeed its revival by Gassendi remained perfectly sterile."[46] Even before an audience of compatriots celebrating Gassendi's tricentennial Koyré was unappreciative: "Gassendi was not a great scientist . . . clearly he cannot be compared to the great geniuses illuminating his age: Descartes, Fermat, Pascal or even Roberval or Mersenne. He invented nothing, discovered nothing, and . . . there is no Gassendi's Law. Not even a false one."[47]

This assessment of Gassendi is debatable[48] or at least open to refinement. Koyré himself grants Gassendi, despite his lack of scientific genius, an important place in the history of science. The place he sees for Gassendi is worth outlining. (1) Though preceded by Bérigard, Basso, and others, he said, *no one* did more than Gassendi to promulgate the ontology of atoms and the void and thus to overthrow the Aristotelian substance ontology. (2) His atomism enabled Gassendi to fruitfully interpret the barometric experiments of Toricelli and

[42] "Establishment," p. 434.
[43] Lucretius, *De rerum natura* 92–95.
[44] Bloch, *La philosophie*, pp. 226–27.
[45] *Infinite Universe*, p. 5.
[46] Ibid., p. 278, n. 7.
[47] *Actes du congrès du tricentennaire*, p. 175.
[48] Bloch, *La philosophie*, p. 159.

Pascal. (3) Gassendi was a "professional" astronomer, capable of significant empirical work. (4) He produced an effective empirical demonstration of Galileo's law of fall proportional to time as against Varron's law according to distance. One wonders how Koyré might outline even a comparable case for Descartes in the history of science. As it happens, neither this question nor even that of their relative scientific genius (with respect to the development of the New Science, and in the terms introduced by Koyré) will serve to distinguish Descartes and Gassendi in a way to explain their subsequent reception by history. For, leaving aside the vexed question of the law of refraction, Descartes invented nothing and discovered nothing, and there is not even a false Descartes's Law. Dijksterhuis explained this as follows: "Neither Cartesian nor Gassendist physics, though they recognize as real no other qualities of matter than those which are determined by geometrico-mechanical features, is of a mathematical character in the sense that it attempts to give a mathematical treatment of the corpuscular process. Everything remains in the vaguely qualitative sphere, so there is no question of an experimental verification of the truth of the theories in question."[49]

Much of Cartesian physics, even, and especially, in the hands of Descartes's followers, indeed remained vaguely qualitative and nonmathematical (as in its accounts of phenomena such as magnetism, gravity, planetary motions, and so on). And where it was mathematical, as it was perfectly in its rules of collision, for example, it was inconsistent either with empirical results, or given classical relativity of frames, with itself. What this means is that the area in which Descartes was undeniably an innovator, namely, mathematics, was quite irrelevant to his eclipse of Gassendi. That is, Descartes's superior mathematical ability was not effectively put to the service of a new physics to which he thus would have had greater claim than Gassendi. On the other hand, the inventor of analytic geometry undeniably did far more than Gassendi in providing the means to advance the mathematization of nature, even if that advance was made by others in non-Cartesian terms. This by itself, of course, helps to explain Gassendi's neglect, since it places Descartes in Koyré's class of geniuses that includes "Fermat, Pascal or even Roberval or Mersenne" but that excludes Gassendi. In addition, the failure of Cartesian physics, even in its competition with Newtonianism, was not fully apparent until well into the eighteenth century. As late as the 1720s the Académie des sciences was still awarding its prizes for Cartesian solutions to problems.[50]

Despite his lack of real mathematical genius Gassendi himself was not unaware of the significance of mathematics to the New Science. Part of the rehabilitation of Epicurus was an apology for his failure to cultivate mathematics in the Garden: The relevance of mathematics to a happy, moral life was not

[49] *Mechanization*, p. 430.
[50] Iltis, "Decline of Cartesianism," pp. 358–59.

clear; Socrates, Aristotle, and Zeno were not skilled in mathematics.[51] But even Gassendi was disappointed by Epicurus in this sphere and wished that he had done more. Gassendi himself not only published the modern law of inertia but effectively argued in its behalf by actually performing some of the experiments that Galileo was so certain of without performing them. Gassendi describes how with the help of the Count of Alais, Louis Emmanuel de Valois, he in 1641 experimented in the Bay of Marseille on a galley moving at a speed of sixteen miles per hour. Not only was he able to predict the behavior of stones dropped from the mast, tossed in the air, and thrown from bow to stern and from stern to bow, but more important he was able to give a mathematically accurate and fairly sophisticated account of the results, which he published in *De motu* (1642).

The subsequent treatment of Gassendi's work by his followers is instructive. Discussing projectile motion, Bernier forty years later held that such motion is not surprising in the least, that what would be surprising would be the immediate cessation of a stone's motion upon being released, for nothing prevents it from continuing in its moving state. A stone dropped from the mast of a moving vessel falls at its foot, he says, and does so not in a straight line, but in a parabolic curve, which he tells us can be clearly seen by anyone stationary on the shore.[52] Bernier gives no mathematical account of the phenomenon, nor even an indication that Gassendi himself had given such an account, but only a preposterous empirical report. Such naiveté in mathematics and physics was quite typical of Bernier and in fact of all Gassendi's closest followers.[53]

The main significance of Cartesian mathematics did not lie in substantive arguments on behalf of any doctrine that distinguished Descartes from Gassendi. But this is not to say that it had no role in the contest between them. The new physics was mathematical; Descartes was the premier mathematician; his version therefore of the physical world and presumably of much else was likely preferable to the version of Gassendi, who identified himself with an older, even if mechanical version of the physical world. Descartes was clearly among the *moderns*, Gassendi among the *ancients* for the participants in the *quérelle*, the primarily literary struggle in the late seventeenth century between classical and contemporary models. Such characterizations in terms of progress and

---

[51] *Opera*, 5:235b–36b. For an account of this material, see Jones, *Pierre Gassendi*, p. 241.

[52] *Doutes*, "projectile motion" and *passim*. This work is discussed in chap. 2, sec. 7 below.

[53] Bernier advised Chapelle to avoid as much as possible getting involved in the infinite, a deep and dark abyss that darkens the human mind (*Lettre*, p. 19). The contrast with the attitude toward the infinite of Leibniz or even Malebranche is striking. For those mathematically equipped to deal with it the infinite is a source of metaphysical inspiration; for Bernier it generates only skepticism. Furthermore, his inclination was to emphasize the cleavage between the idealizations of mathematics and physical reality. Mathematical points, lines, and surfaces, "which belong to the understanding only and have no depth," are inapplicable to physical bodies, "which cannot be without all the dimensions" (pp. 18–19). That there cannot be this cleavage for Descartes will be shown at length below.

reaction point to still another aspect of the competition we are studying, namely, the far more effective use of propaganda by the Cartesians.

Cleopatra's Nose

Testimony as to the success of Cartesian propaganda efforts comes as early as Huygens.[54] Writing to Bayle (February 26, 1693) concerning Baillet's *Vie* of Descartes,[55] he said:

> Descartes had found the way to have his conjectures and fictions taken for truths. And what happened to those who read his *Principles of Philosophy* was something like what happens to those who read pleasant novels that make the same impression as true histories. The novelty of the shapes of his little particles and of the vortices was found very charming. It seemed to me that when I read this book of principles the first time, everything went as well as could be, and when I found some difficulty, I believed that it was my fault for not having properly understood his thought. I was only 15 or 16 years old. But having since discovered from time to time things visibly false and others very improbable, I have thoroughly rejected my former opinion and I now find almost nothing I can certify as true in all his physics, metaphysics or meteorology. (p. 403)

According to Huygens, the first thing Descartes had in his favor was that, as opposed to those who talked about qualities and mathematical forms, he could be understood. Not only did he more universally than anyone before him reject the ancient philosophy, but he provided explanations that were readily comprehensible: "The Moderns like Telesius, Campanella, and Gilbert retained several occult qualities just like the Aristotelians, and had neither enough invention nor mathematics to produce an entire system; neither did Gassendi, although he recognized and revealed the ineptitudes of the Aristotelians" (p. 404).

Galileo had both the intelligence and the mathematics to advance physics, though he left much to be done. But he did not have "the boldness and presumption to attempt to explain all natural causes, or the vanity to become head of a school [*chef de secte*]. He was modest and loved the truth too much" (p. 404).

> But Descartes, who seems to me to have been very jealous of Galileo's renown, was very anxious to pass for the author of a new philosophy. This is clear from his efforts and hopes to have it taught in the academies in place of Aristotle's, from the fact that he hoped that the Jesuits would embrace it, and finally because without rhyme or reason he maintained the things he had once advanced, although very

---

[54] Pascal, *Pensées*, 90, ed. Lafuma. A more accurate, if less captivating, image for the Accident Theory of History might be Cromwell's grain of sand (ibid., 203; see pp. 39, 314–15, ed. Sellier).
[55] *Oeuvres*, 1:398–406.

often they were false. He responded to all objections, although I rarely see him to have satisfied those who made them unless as the *soutenants* do at public debates in the academies where they are always left the final word. This would have been obvious had he been able to explain his dogmas clearly; and he could have done so had the truth been found in them. (pp. 404–5)

Huygens continued:

He should have proposed his system of physics as an essay of what might be said with probability in that science by admitting only principles of mechanics and inviting good minds to search on their own. That would have been praiseworthy. But in pretending he had found the truth, as he did everywhere, by relying on and boasting of the succession and fine connection of his expositions, he did something very prejudicial to the program of philosophy; for those who believe him and become his followers imagine themselves to possess knowledge of the causes of everything as far as it is possible to know them. Thus they often lose time supporting the doctrine of their master, and do not apply themselves to penetrating the true explanations of that great number of natural phenomena on which Descartes spun only Chimeras.[56]

On the other hand, it would seem according to Huygens that if Descartes misled some he had a beneficial effect on others, for "it might also be said that in dogmatizing with such assurance and in becoming a celebrated author he excited that much more those who wrote after him to correct him and try to find something better."[57]

At least in one respect, Huygens thus has a mixed judgment on the question of the use of propaganda. Descartes had a stultifying effect on Cartesian true-believers, but a heuristic one on those who could read his views as false but challenging. There are any number of examples falling into Huygens's first category. If it is true that in physics Descartes was hardly a pioneer,[58] the same is true in spades of his followers. Arnauld, Régis, Malebranche, La Forge, Cordemoy, and Rohault hardly figure among the geniuses in the history of science, especially if we adopt Koyré's implicitly realist standard for inclusion. One of the best examples falling into Huygens's second category may have been Huygens himself. Not everyone was taken in by Descartes the intellectual swashbuckler. Huygens by his own testimony is anything but a Cartesian true-

---

[56] Ibid., p. 405. Condorcet complained in a similar way: That madness of believing oneself obliged to explain, well or ill, all phenomena was the sole thing common to the philosophy of Descartes and that of the School; it even increased among the Cartesians, "whose explanations, more plausible and more piquant by their novelty and apparent clarity, were based on the sublime idea of subjecting to the mechanical laws of motion all the phenomena of nature" (*Eloges*, Duclos, p. 67).

[57] *Oeuvres*, 10:406.

[58] This is basically the judgment of J. F. Scott, *Scientific Work of René Descartes*, who nonetheless properly accords Descartes his place in the history of science.

believer; but even this testimony shows that in another respect Cartesian propaganda made Descartes's views an issue in a way that Gassendi's never were.

The Jesuit historian Sortais tried to explain Gassendi's neglect by drawing attention to two points, which contrast with the Cartesian picture above.[59] For one thing Gassendi was intellectually very modest. When he criticizes, Aristotelianism most notably, he is incisive and categorical; but when presenting his own views he is hesitant and timid. As Bernier pointed out, his work abounds with the expression 'it seems that' (*videtur*). How can one inspire confidence in others when hesitant oneself and doubtful of one's own doctrines? Second, all of Gassendi's works, including his main work, the posthumously published *Syntagma philosophicum* (1658), are too long, its arguments, as Sorbière noted also in explanation of Gassendi's neglect, not obviously enough connected, with repetitions everywhere, quotations in the style of medieval glosses, and the whole expressed not just in Latin, but in a dusty, inaccessible Latin.[60]

Gassendi's packaging and marketing procedures did little for the views he espoused and tried to promulgate. To take one example, an important one to which we shall return with a more substantive treatment, Gassendi initially argues for the void without giving an analysis of space and only after addressing at length the Aristotelian arguments for and the Epicurean against the void. In his treatment of this material, Walter Charleton, who was Gassendi's major expositor in England, virtually ignored Gassendi's catalogue of previous arguments and positions, and selected one question "from among those numerous and importune *Altercations*, concerning the *Quiddity* or formal reason of *Place*, in which the too contentious *Schools* usually lose their Time, their breath, their wits, and their Auditors attention."[61] Now, only someone with the text of Gassendi from which Charleton was drawing would realize what perhaps Charleton himself did not realize, namely, that just with his lengthy review of previous positions Gassendi involved himself in "importune altercations" and thus suffers the losses Charleton describes.

All of this was in striking contrast to Cartesian practices. Descartes wrote much shorter, considerably livelier works, with the little space devoted to rival views amounting to not much more than derisory caricatures of them. In addition, of course, he notably wrote in French, and in a French that became a standard of style. His major Latin works were very quickly translated into French (the *Meditations* was published in French six years after its Latin origi-

---

[59] *La philosophie*, pp. 24ff.

[60] Gassendi never published anything in French. His devotion to Latin is seen by Sortais as the reason why Gassendi was never admitted to the French Academy (ibid., p. 182, n. 3). Westfall is right: "[Gassendi's] principal work, *Syntagma Philosophicum* (1658), is an unreadable compilation of everything ever said on the topics discussed, a compilation further which intended to exhaust discussable topics. The work grew like Topsy, . . . in a word, Gassendi was the original scissors and paste man, and his book contains all the inconsistencies of eclectic compilations" ("Newton's Philosophy," p. 39).

[61] *Physiologia*, p. 62.

nal, the *Principles* only three years after its original). Gassendi's work has been translated into French only in the twentieth century, and his magnum opus for the most remains only in Latin.[62] Bernier's *abrégé* of Gassendi's work was not intended to be a translation, not even an incomplete one, and in fact is a paraphrase that is often inaccurate and reflects Bernier's own views. Bayle was one who welcomed Bernier's *abrégé* in the hope, as he put it, that it would save the world from leafing through Gassendi's lengthy tomes; the hope was a false one. We shall return to this below. But even if Bernier had produced complete, accurate, and elegant translations, his efforts coming as they did in the mid-1670s were too late. At least in terms of literary razzmatazz, the Cartesians had the spotlight they have never relinquished.[63] The Aristotelian John Sergeant was one who saw the significance of the Cartesian style: *"He dazzles the Understanding of his Reader with his most Ingenious and Clear Way of Discoursing; a Talent peculiar to himself; and he lays his thoughts together in such an Artificial and smooth-flowing Currency in proper and unaffected language that he captivates it unawares into a complaisant Assent; and his greatest Adversary must be forced to confess that, if his Doctrine be not true, at least Truth was never so exactly and handsomely counterfeited."*[64]

One clientele in particular was appealed to by the availability of Cartesianism in the vernacular and by its nonscholastic, relatively informal literary quality. These were the salons, whose hostesses were generally incapable of reading any Latin at all, much less the Latin of Gassendi. Thus it is not at all surprising that in those of the salons in which philosophy was studied it was especially that of Descartes that was pursued. The salon of Mme. de Grignan was a principal bastion of Cartesianism, as a result of which her mother Mme. de Sevigné was led to a study of it. Mme. de Sablé hosted another center for the study of Cartesianism and Mmes. de Bonnevaux, de Gendreville, d'Outresale, and d'Hommecour were all similarly disposed. Mlle. de la Vigne, another admirer of Descartes, was invited by his niece Catherine to write an account of her uncle's doctrine, and Mlle. Marie Dupré was so identified with the doctrine as to be called *la Cartésienne*.[65]

This success of Cartesianism among women in the period was not unnoticed or even unforeseen. Complaining in an ironic vein against obscurantism, Malebranche at one point claimed that Descartes's philosophy was rejected by

---

[62] See "Note on Documentation." Gassendi's major work, the *Syntagma philosophicum*, occupies the first two volumes of his *Opera* and for the most part has not been translated at all. Modern French translations by Rochot and English translations by Jones and Brush of other works have helped the cause of Gassendist scholarship.

[63] "By their method and clarity, their elegance and grandeur, their grace and spirit many of [the works of Cordemoy, Rohault, Malebranche, et al.] deserve a place not just in the history of Cartesian philosophy, but also in that of French literature" (Bouillier, *Histoire*, 1:443–44).

[64] *Method*, introd.

[65] Reynier, *La femme*, p. 166 n.

some people because its principles are far too simple and easy: "There are no obscure, mysterious terms in this philosophy; women and people who know neither Greek nor Latin can learn it; therefore, it must be something insignificant, and (it must be) inappropriate for great geniuses to apply themselves to it."[66] As Descartes had explained to Vatier, he wrote in French precisely in order that "even women should be able to understand something."[67] Attesting to Descartes's success is the work of F. G. Poulain de la Barre, who argued *The Equality of the Sexes* (1673) on Cartesian principles. Two years earlier, his *Education of Ladies* emphasized the philosophy of Descartes as the best means to exploit the reason and common sense had by everyone; although Gassendi does figure in the curriculum—the bête noire of the piece is Aristotelian Scholasticism[68]—the recommended reading is a textbook course in Cartesianism: the *Port-Royal Logic*, Descartes's *Discourse on Method* and *Meditations*, Cordemoy's *Distinction*, the fourth part of Rohault's *Physics*, and Descartes's *Treatise on Man* with La Forge's notes.[69]

The exceptions to these Cartesian circles gravitating around female personalities were few. Mme. Deshoulières was able to read Latin and may have read Gassendi in the original; she had in her circle Jean d'Hesault, whom Grimarest placed along with Bernier, Cyrano, Chapelle, and Molière in the tutelage of Gassendi. But any circle around her was bound to have been unstable and tenuous, because her preference was for solitude and nature, and she spent much time away from Paris in the Alps. Mme. de la Sablière frequently received Bernier and other followers of Gassendi. In any case, this circle, and especially the other notably Gassendist group, that of the notorious Ninon de Lenclos, did as much to retard as to advance the cause of Gassendi, since to the same extent these people publicized the views of Gassendi they associated them with the morally suspect behavior of libertinage. Another, curious exception arose in respect to the Cartesian doctrine on the bestial soul—the view, to which we shall return below, that nonhuman animals are insentient mechanical automata. No less than Catherine Descartes espoused Gassendi's igneous theory instead,[70] and neither Mlle. de Scudéry nor Mm. de Grignan could accept that

---

[66] *Search* 6.2.4; 454. For a discussion of the Malebranche texts and the references to them, see "Note on Documentation."

[67] February 22, 1638; AT, 1:560. For a discussion of the Descartes texts and the references to them, see "Note on Documentation."

[68] The work is in the form of a dialogue and at one point a participant is asked how he viewed women when as a student he was under the influence of them: "while I was a scholastic I viewed them scholastically, i.e. as monsters and as being inferior to men because Aristotle and some of the theologians I had read considered them as such" (*Education of Ladies*, p. 334).

[69] Ibid., pp. 306–9.

[70] Although Leonora Cohen Rosenfield's explanation of this is not very cogent: "She very likely was brought up in the companionship of domestic animals, for she passed most of her life in the country. And one is never astonished to find a lady somewhat sentimental about animals" (*Animal Soul*, p. 159).

animals were without feeling. Less surprisingly, Mme. Deshoulières was well-known for her theriophilist poetry.

How important hegemony in the salons was in the propagation of Cartesianism is a question difficult to answer and even to formulate. With respect just to the above case, how do we measure the significance of La Fontaine's animal fables in upsetting the Cartesian conception of bestial machines and thus the whole Cartesian metaphysics that sorted everything into sentient human souls or insentient extended matter? Or the significance in this of Mme. de la Sablière, who for some twenty years housed, supported, and nurtured the career of La Fontaine? How do we evaluate these roles against that of the skeptic Foucher who argued against the same metaphysical dualism, but on recognizably more philosophical grounds? This distinction between so-called externalist and internalist questions will be discussed in the final chapter. Meanwhile we can return to the more general externalist question as to how we might understand the propaganda successes of Cartesianism.

At first it seemed to me that the revival of Epicureanism was the victim of misfortune, that with a different role of the die the same traits of personality, language, and circumstance that served Cartesianism could have served the philosophy of Gassendi. To take just the example of the ontology of atoms and the void, Thomas Harriott, who might well have established the view early on in England, suffered misfortune that parallels Gassendi's in France. He was plagued by theological and political vulnerability, ill health, the failure to produce a magnum opus or even anything at all accessible, and followers who failed to properly dispose of his work and who in one notable case ended by strongly arguing against Harriott's own views.[71] The parallel is not exact—Gassendi's *Syntagma* fails as a magnum opus only because it was unreadable and his literary remains, of which the *Syntagma* itself was a part, were carefully attended to and quickly published. But the case of Harriott and others to be discussed below inclines one to look for an explanation other than a bad case of snake-bite.

Part of the explanation, it seems, lies in the very nature of the views of our contestants. In the language of the ancient skeptics, Descartes was a dogmatist: Not only is knowledge possible, but he claimed actually to possess it. In addition, knowledge is *of* eternal fixed essences, again as per the ancient skeptics. In these terms Gassendi is a skeptic; there cannot be such knowledge because there are no fixed essences for it to be about. What this view means is that just as there is and can be no such thing as horseness or squareness apart from the things we call horses and squares, so there can be no such thing as Gassendism apart from the views and people we might call Gassendist. And why we should want to call something Gassendist, or anything else, is a more difficult matter on this view than it may appear to be for the dogmatist,

---

[71] For the Harriott story, see Kargon, *Atomism*, chaps. 3–4.

whose ultimate reason for calling a thing a square, for example, is that it *just is* a square. Furthermore, the people we shall identify as followers of Gassendi were generally consistent in their adherence, or rather lack of it, to Gassendi's views. Their position might be best described as nondogmatic nondogmatism—the "perhaps this, perhaps that" attitude that Malebranche so roundly ridiculed. It is an attitude that helps to explain not only why there was no Gassendist school or movement, as there was a Cartesian, but also why the views that might constitute Gassendism are so difficult to define. If it is frequently convenient here to refer to those either following or influenced by Gassendi as Gassendists, they are Gassendists only in this sense. By their own lights the followers of Gassendi are perhaps skeptics, perhaps not.

All of this is in stark contrast to the history of Cartesianism, where intramural polemics were as bitter, extensive, and consuming as any to be found in religion, politics, or other areas of dogmatic dispute in the period. Consider only the dispute between Malebranche and Arnauld as to the properly Cartesian theory of ideas. Or, to continue the example of atomism, consider the treatment accorded the arch-heretic Cordemoy. Clerselier was a friend of both Cordemoy and Desgabets. He sent Cordemoy's atomist work *Le discernement* to Desgabets, who replied to Clerselier with a long letter criticizing the work for its divergence from the views of Descartes: "Cordemoy thoughtlessly causes a schism [*sic*]," he said, "that is all the more serious since it all of a sudden removes from the true philosophy one of its strongest columns and notably strengthens the camp of Gassendi, which already seems only too likely to support itself and overcome that of Descartes."[72] Such a statement from one follower of Gassendi about another seems to me unimaginable. In addition, the Gassendists were above political intrigue as a matter, shall we say, of both principle and temperament. When, for example, Malebranche's *Traité de la nature et de la grace* was placed on the Index in 1690, it was as a result of the machinations of other Cartesians, particularly Arnauld. And Descartes's being Indexed in 1663 was due to the intrigues of the Jesuits.[73] By contrast, the Gassendists are not to be found either scheming against each other or being schemed against by others. The nearest episode to these imbroglios over the Index, for example, was the harassment of Ninon de Lanclos by the Society of the Blessed Sacrament—a rather pale comparison indeed. Furthermore, the Cartesians were opposed to free-thinking on doctrinal grounds. The sole aim of Cartesian method is to assemble evidence in the perception of essences such that the mind is constrained to accede to the truth of what it perceives. Clarity and distinctness leave it incapable of doubt. The will exercising the freedom of

[72] Quoted in Prost, *Essai*, p. 158.

[73] Much to the chagrin of Arnauld, who complained that Gassendi, who led young people to atheism, got off scot-free (*Oeuvres*, 3:396).

indifference so prized by the skeptics is for the Cartesians a faculty of error and sin.[74]

In addition to the salons there were two other social institutions in which Descartes clearly prevailed, if not against everyone else, at least against Gassendi. These were the schools and the religious orders or societies. The history of Cartesianism in the schools is a long and complex one involving political intrigue, clashes of personalities, and academic bans and subterfuges to avoid them. The most relevant part of this history will best be treated below with respect to the efforts of both Cartesians and Gassendists to accommodate Aristotelianism. For the moment it will be enough to recognize the deeper penetration of Cartesianism in the schools evident from the more intense efforts to resist it. From the Gassendist side there was nothing like the Cartesian infiltration at Leyden and other universities in the Netherlands,[75] the Oratorian schools in France, or even at the University of Paris. When at last the doors were by royal decree closed to Cartesianism, this could only have been if some had gotten in and more threatened to do so.[76]

---

[74] Caton, "Will and Reason."

[75] I have not investigated except peripherally the relative success of Descartes and Gassendi in the Netherlands. Sortais makes a prima facie case for a surprising Gassendist influence here: "Gassendi's trip to Belgium and Holland (1629) began to make him known outside his own country. The penetration of his intelligence, the modesty of his attitude, the agreeableness of his company gained him admirers and friends, several of whom became his correspondents, among the illustrious of the Belgian and Dutch academies: Reneri Erycius Putaneus, J.-B. van Helmont, Aubertus Miraeus, J. Caramuel y Lobkovitz, G.-J. Vossius, D. Heinsius, J. Golius, Is. Beeckman." Most influenced, it seems, were Bornius and Wolferdus Senguerdus in Holland, and in Belgium I. Der-Kennis and de Sluse (*La philosophie*, pp. 242–47) But Gassendi's impact was not nearly as wide (half the medical faculty at Leyden was said to be Cartesian in 1659) or as enduring (Fontenelle complained of Hartsoeker's education from 1674 to 1678 by "obdurate Cartesians") or as visible (there was no Gassendist analogue to the Regius–Voet–Descartes episode at Utrecht). See Spink, *French Free-thought*, pp. 188–89.

[76] Descartes also did better than Gassendi at the celebrated Protestant academy at Saumur. (Prost, *La philosophie*). It began (dedication 1606, royal recognition 1611) with the almost strictly religious aims imposed by its founder Duplessis-Mornay, and was primarily Aristotelian Scholastic in its philosophical outlook. But the academy was too successful, with the result that the Oratorians founded a college in the same town. Eventually relations between them were amicable—they would attend each other's papers, for example—so that still later people like Bernard Lamy, Louis Thomassin, Malebranche for a brief while, and others were able to funnel Cartesianism toward the academy. In addition, La Forge practiced medicine in Saumur from about 1653 and was soon thereafter a strong champion of Cartesianism. (Clair, *Louis de La Forge*, pp. 28–47). Finally in 1664 the Cartesian Jean-Robert Chouet bested the Aristotelian Pierre de Villemandy in a vigorous three-week competition for the vacant chair of philosophy. He befriended La Forge and, after certain initial difficulties due to his defeat of Villemandy, taught with success at Saumur until returning to Geneva in 1669 (where, according to Bayle, both his Cartesianism and pedagogical success continued unabated [Budé, *Jean-Robert Chouet*, p. 135]). Though Villemandy succeeded Chouet, he had by then become an eclectic, explicitly drawing upon Descartes. His *Manuductio ad philosophiae Aristotelae, epicurae & Cartesianae* (Amsterdam, 1685) was an example of the genre called *la philosophie novantique* to be discussed below. He regarded both Descartes and Gassendi

As for the religious orders and societies, Bouillier tries to make the Jesuits out to have been the allies of Gassendi against Descartes by emphasizing their common empiricism. Gassendi was certainly empiricist, as were the Jesuits to the extent they embraced Aristotelian Scholasticism (and to the extent, of course, that Aristotelian Scholasticism can be made out to have been empiricist). But to agree that there is nothing in the intellect that is not first in the senses is one thing; it is quite another to affirm that through the senses the intellect has knowledge of essences, as the Aristotelian Scholastic would affirm and Gassendi deny. The best that Bouillier can do, it seems, is to spell out in some detail what we already know, namely, that practically to a man the Jesuits were unrelenting foes of Cartesianism. If Jesuits like Rapin should argue skepticism against the Cartesian clear ideas of God or of the soul, if the skeptic critic Huet should have a long association with the Jesuits,[77] if Hardouin should actually cite the name of Gassendi against Descartes or Daniel praise him as having as much intelligence as, greater learning, and less obstinacy than Descartes, this does not add up to a Gassendist picture of the Society of Jesus. For the engine of the Jesuit opposition to Cartesianism was not the philosophy of Gassendi or of anyone else, but the threat posed by Cartesianism to their hegemony over the schools. Gassendi posed no such threat. Indeed, the effect of the Jesuit Le Valois's diatribe against Cartesianism as incompatible with the doctrine of the Eucharist was, as we shall see, to make the Cartesians and Gassendists temporary allies.

Apart from the Jesuits there is no questioning of the greater success of Cartesianism among religious orders and societies. Among the Benedictines the Abbaye de Saint-Vannes may have been in opposition,[78] but François Lamy was among the most prominent and Robert Desgabets among the most sectarian of its advocates.[79] The Genévofains also counted their Cartesians, most notably Le Bossu, of whom more below, and Pierre Lallemant, chancellor of the University of Paris, who in 1667 was famously instructed not to give

---

as great philosophers, but complained that their views lead to skepticism and even atheism (*Journal des Savants*, February 1697; quoted by Prost, *Essai*, pp. 125–26). A year later he was back attacking Cartesianism, this time the occasionalism of Arnauld and especially of Malebranche (*Traité des causes secondes* [Leyden, 1686]). Soon after Villemandy the academy went into rapid decline and was finally suppressed. The upshot is that the floruit of the academy was Cartesian, certainly more so than Gassendist.

[77] To whom he left his library as a condition for his pension with them. This collection in fact went to the Jesuits, but upon their expulsion from France, to the royal and later imperial and national libraries. This history is visible from the book-stamps to anyone using Huet's invaluable collection at the Bibliothéque Nationale.

[78] Spink, *French Free-thought*, p. 195.

[79] The recent publication of Desgabets's *Oeuvres philosophiques inedits* will provide much grist for the mill of Cartesian scholarship. Known hitherto primarily for his inapposite defense of Malebranche against Foucher, Desgabets seems to me nonetheless to be no mean expositor of Cartesian metaphysics. See chap. 4, sec. 12 below.

Descartes's funeral oration when his remains were returned from Sweden and buried in St. Geneviève du Mont.[80] At the turn of the century Huet complained: "Quite some time ago the congregation of St. Geneviève declared itself Cartesian. They decided to canonize this doctrine when they received the body of Descartes next to that of St. Geneviève." Even more were the Oratory and Port-Royal known for the infiltration of Cartesianism. The French Oratory was founded by Pierre Bérulle, "perhaps the most important religious thinker of the Counter-Reformation in France,"[81] who was a very strong supporter of Descartes as early as 1628[82] and who according to Baillet placed him under a moral obligation to publish his philosophy. At the end of the century only the name of Malebranche need be mentioned to show how by discharging Bérulle's duty Descartes came to influence his society. As for the Jansenists, Jurieu accused Port-Royal of being more Cartesian than Christian, and Mme. de Sevigné reflected popular perception with her epithet for the Genévofain Le Bossu: "Jansenist, i.e. Cartesian."[83] For political purposes this characterization involved exaggeration, for, after all, Pascal and Nicole were members of Port-Royal no less than Arnauld. Nor was the Oratory without its anti-Cartesians. But neither the Oratory nor Port-Royal had any association with Gassendi at all like that with Descartes. Both were predisposed to Cartesianism by the idealism, among other doctrines, that it shared with their common Patristic authority, Augustine, whose doctrine of illumination, as we shall see, was an obviously more natural tool for the Cartesians than for the Gassendists. (For the Jansenists there was the additional attraction of Cartesian occasionalism, which underlined man's dependence on God.[84]) Finally, Jansenism and, to a less extent, the Oratory were allied by having a common opponent in the Jesuits.

§2   THE GASSENDIST SUCCESS

Descartes predominates against Gassendi in the religious orders and societies (Benedictines, Genévofains, Port-Royal, the Oratory) except for the Jesuits. He predominates in the salons except for that of Mme. de la Sablière. He predominates in the schools. A hitherto unappreciated area in which Gassendi was more successful is in the large number of more or less formal *académies* and *conférences* of the period. These groups of varying sizes (sometimes up to

[80] Since 1819 they have rested in St. Germain des Prés (Bouillier, *Histoire*, 1:58–60). To A. Martin, August 15, 1700, cited after another source by Bouillier (ibid., p. 435).

[81] Popkin, *Scepticism*, p. 175.

[82] Gouhier, "La crise," pp. 45–47.

[83] To Mme. De Grignan, September 16, 1676; *Letters*, 3:334. Like the Oratory, Port-Royal was not a religious order, and thus could count members of religious orders or other religious societies among its members.

[84] Bouillier, *Histoire*, 1:431–33.

several hundred) met on a regular basis, typically weekly, for the purpose of discussing a great variety of topics, especially philosophy and science. Almost always there was a patron who would provide a place to meet and incur expenses, and who in addition would give the group a kind of identity. Conferences were on a smaller scale, less formal, and shorter-lived than academies since they were essentially an occasion for a single individual to make his views public. Academies in principle provided a stage for all members, often had written constitutions, agenda, recording secretaries, and other officers, and were capable of lasting over decades. Among the conferences, those of the Cartesian Rohault, whose "Wednesdays" were celebrated in the period, are not unknown to historians. No less successful according to contemporary observers, however, were the conferences of the Gassendist Gilles de Launay, whom I shall discuss in detail below. Here I wish to look at the academies, especially those that figure in the events that led to the creation of the Académie royale des sciences.[85]

The history of these groups is continuous with the earlier Italian academies and thus with the whole tradition of the patron of learning. The first such important figure in the discrimination of loosely Gassendist ideas is Nicholas-Claude Fabri de Peiresc (1580–1637), patron of learning of all sorts, but especially of experimental science including botany, physics, and astronomy, in which he was no mean participant himself. He was a bridge between the sixteenth-century Italian and the seventeenth-century French academies. In him is found the Gassendist spirit of free inquiry, unrestrained by dogmatic commitments. He was closely associated with Gassendi, who wrote his enormously well-received biography, and was much sought as a correspondent by a remarkable catalogue of the learned.[86] Among them were the brothers Pierre and Jacques Dupuy, whose celebrated *Cabinet* included at various times Luillier, Mersenne, Grotius, Chapelain, Huet, Boulliau, Montmor, Gassendi, and many others. This was a fairly formal (membership was carefully controlled) but flexible group that between approximately 1615 and 1662 discussed a range of topics from science to politics. According to Brown, this was the longest-lived and most influential of the numerous private academies in Paris during the first half of the seventeenth century. The group around Mersenne that met from 1635 to 1648 was of shorter duration but had a rather more impressive concentration of talent: Gassendi, Descartes, Robeval, Pascal, and Girard Desargues among others. Mersenne was a correspondent of Peiresc but also of very many others,

[85] A work needs to be written on the more philosophical organizations of the period. For the more scientific, Brown's *Scientific Organizations* remains the basic secondary source, at least on events leading to the formation of the Académie des sciences. Taton (*L'Académie Royale*, n. 28) expresses some reservations about Brown's work, but in the end these are very minor. Our debt to Brown is great. For example, some of the material in George's important article "Genesis," he acknowledges came from Brown's files.

[86] Brown, *L'Académie*, pp. 3–6.

and although his group cannot be called Gassendist (it was more Cartesian, if anything) this intellectual secretary of Europe was certainly in a position to make known the views of Gassendi, as he did most famously in soliciting Gassendi's *Objections* to the *Meditations*.

Another group into which Gassendism clearly made inroads was the academy of the Abbé d'Aubignac; it helped prepare the way for the Académie des sciences, and because of its connection with the important Gassendist Launay we shall return to it below in another context. Much that can be said of it applies as well to the academy of the Abbé Bourdelot, Pierre Michon (1610–85), sometime physician to Christina of Sweden and Louis XIII. The earliest mention of his academy as such is 1664,[87] but it seems difficult to mark it off from the meetings that Bourdelot was organizing for the Grand Condé, in whose service he also acted twenty years previously. In later years they met weekly and were very popular in two senses of the term, attracting hundreds of people to the point of making communication difficult. Early *invités* of Bourdelot included La Mothe Le Vayer, Montmor, Pascal, François Le Pailleur (?–1654),[88] and Gassendi, although later it also included Rohault and Cordemoy.[89] According to its contemporary chronicler, Le Gallois, no party was embraced: "Aristotle was no less favourably listened to than Descartes or Gassendi; neither Lull, nor Paracelsus nor Hobbes was rejected" (p. 62). This accords rather well with a skeptical spirit of free inquiry, which Le Gallois effectively ascribed to the academy. At the outset of his work he divides philosophy into the three kinds according to Sextus, the third being a mean between the dogmatism of Plato and the skepticism of Arcesilaus, namely, the view that we cannot know the truth "as it is in things," but only what things cause in us; but Le Gallois takes this to be "what the philosophy of Descartes [*sic*] is founded on" (p. 10). How reliable this contemporary observer may have been as to the philosophical stark contrasts, not to say nuances, of the group may be seen from his claim that there is complete agreement between Descartes's and Aristotle's views on the subject of light "as well as in every other matter in physics" (p. 56). It is hard to tell whether this is an instance of novantiquity[90] or of plain ignorance, but the light cast in this context is definitely anti-Gassendist and pro-Cartesian. There are two kinds of philosophy, according to Le Gallois: that of words (the scholastics) and that of things; of the latter kind there is the philosophy of the void (Democritus and Epicurus) or of the plenum (Artistotle and Descartes), and the first of these is not very likely "since there is no inclination that an action can be performed in the void."

What we know of the academy and other activities of Bourdelot suggests

[87] Brown, *Scientific Organizations*, p. 233.

[88] Le Pailleur was himself the host of an academy, which, however short-lived, had a Gassendist flavor. Taton, *L'Académie Royale*, pp. 20–24.

[89] Le Gallois, *Conversations*, pp. 56–59.

[90] See §4 below.

something of an intellectual circus, a largely harmless entertainment, which nonetheless drew the attention of many serious thinkers, and not just those on the scene with a Monday afternoon to pass. For Huygens, Boyle, and Oldenburg among others abroad took an interest. Its crucial years during the 1660s were notably much occupied with the notorious controversies over blood transfusion. While undoubtedly many of the academy's activities at one time or another were well-conceived, many were not. The extreme credulity of the period was allowed by its members to credit reports, for example, of a tooth that when extracted and placed in a box produced three others, or of a woman (to continue the dental theme) who having lost one set of teeth at age thirty grew another at ninety (alas, only to lose them six months later).[91]

A more important academy was that of Henri-Louis Habert de Montmor (?–1679), a member of an important and wealthy Parisian family who used his position to support learning in a number of ways. Baillet relates that he made an offer of his country home at Mesnil-Saint-Denis to Descartes (who did not accept it).[92] Gassendi, however, in May 1653 accepted the offer to live at Montmor's residence in the rue Sainte-Avoye, where he regularly received friends. These meetings would have filled something of a void created by the recent deaths of Mersenne, the abbé Picot, and Le Pailleur for those who were accustomed to gather under their patronage for discussion of science and learning. At least during Gassendi's time there was very little formality, which came in December 1657 with a constitution[93] and the appointment of Sorbière as permanent secretary. Chapelain was also a member of the group but it was not entirely Gassendist or even thoroughly embued with the spirit of its founder. Cartesians, Aristotelians, and truculent types like Roberval also belonged, with the result that no single point of view and certainly no authority dominated. The constitution itself is interesting in this regard; seven of its nine articles are rules of order dealing with procedures for presenting and discussing views, obviously designed to avoid wrangling. The very first rule sets the tone: "the purpose of the conferences shall not be the vain exercise of the mind on useless subtleties."[94] Such rules would have been in response to the kind of situation described by one of its members, Ismael Boulliau, according to whom the Montmorians "dispute with vehemence since they quarrel about the pursuit of

[91] Le Gallois, *Conversations*, pp. 92–94, 122–23. The character of the academy was seemingly struck by that of its impresario, who was regarded as credulous even by Lantin, one of its members: "Bourdelot believed a bit too easily." See Brown, *Scientific Organizations*, p. 244, for his testimony. If Bourdelot's academy was not the most serious at the time, it was far from the most frivolous. Another academy was that of the Venetian Resident, which concerned itself with issues such as which metal composed the chain that bound the winds, and "whether tickling to death or dying for love be the greatest pain" (Le Gallois, *Conversations*, p. 78).

[92] *Des-Cartes*, pt. 2, bk. 8, chap. 2.

[93] Preserved in a letter of Sorbière to Hobbes, February 1658 (Huygens, *Oeuvres*, 4:513; Brown, *Scientific Organizations*, p. 74).

[94] Quoted in Brown, *Scientific Organizations*, p. 75.

truth; sometimes they are eager to rail at each other, and jealously deny a truth, since each one, although professing to inquire and investigate, would like to be the sole author of the truth when discovered. And if anyone in the course of his hunting find that truth, the others will not in the end share in the spoils of their own free will and pleasure, because each one considers that his own fame and glory has lost something if he grant even a blade of grass to the victor and acknowledge him as the real discoverer."[95] Sometime between March and June 1664 the Montmor academy finally expired,[96] the victim of dispute among its members, whose interests, personalities, level of seriousness, and, especially, theoretical orientation were far too divergent. Sorbière wrote that for two years they had sought without success some general principles on which they might reason about natural things, and that there were always a dozen avenging angels ready to destroy in a moment what had cost good minds considerable time and trouble. Sorbière's regret was expressed in 1660, but it remained relevant for the academy's duration.[97]

Before the demise of the Montmor academy, one of its members who was dissatisfied with its disputes and wished to pursue science in a more experimental and less dogmatic fashion formed something of an academy of his own. This was the traveler and amateur of science, Melchésédec Thevenot, around whom gathered other dissidents such as Auzout, Petit of Montluçon, and Martel.[98] According to the best modern summary, "the letters which Oldenburg sent to Boyle during the years 1663–64 consistently group [these three] with Thevenot as the persons in France most appreciative of the advances being made in England. . . . In opposition to the doctrinaire Cartesianism around them, these four stand for the Gassendist spirit of careful and honest observation of nature at work, and for the promotion of such observation by the improvement of instruments."[99] This was likely the group called the *Compagnie des sciences et des arts* for which Auzout asked royal protection in 1664 and whose constitution is preserved in the Huygens papers.[100] This Gassendist group seems to have been

[95] Letter to Heinsius, February 1658; quoted in Brown, *Scientific Organizations*, ibid., pp. 78–79. To be sure, the Gassendists had their innings during these confrontations. Chapelain in a letter to Huygens on July 20, 1661 relates an experiment performed by the group "to the great discredit" of Descartes's doctrine of subtle matter as an account of magnetic attraction. According to Chapelain, a small piece cut from a larger piece of wood failed against Cartesian expectation to undergo the same effect of attraction and repulsion as similar pieces of loadstone (p. 122). On the other hand, Clerselier was able to write to Fermat in the following year that the Montmor group was particularly occupied in clarifying and defending the philosophy of Descartes (Descartes, *Oeuvres*, ed. Cousin, 10:501).

[96] Huygens, *Oeuvres*, 5:41, 70; Brown, *Scientific Organizations*, p. 133.

[97] Taton, *L'Académie Royale*, n. 64.

[98] This academy was very short-lived. By the fall of 1664 the academies of Justel and Bourdelot were the only ones of note since Thevenot was forced to discontinue his and leave Paris because of financial problems (letter cited by Brown, *Scientific Organizations*, p. 136).

[99] Ibid., p. 137.

[100] Ibid., pp. 144–45; Huygens, *Oeuvres*, 4:325–29. Taton wonders whether the document was not drawn up in response to an official request, "if not from Colbert himself, at least from someone

hindered by at least two kinds of circumstance. First, the work itself and hence the prestige of the experimentalists were hampered by insufficient facilities. A letter of 1662 from Petit to Huygens "complains as usual of the shortage of experimentalists, but adds that the difficulty of getting good glass prevents their making advances in the matter of lenses and the provision of tubes and jars for their experiments with the air pump and on the column of mercury and capillarity."[101] (The problem of lenses became particularly absorbing and celestial exploration was sacrificed to testing of lenses by viewing letter cards on St. Paul's, for instance, from the Ile St. Louis.) In addition, the homes in which this group met limited the kind of experimentation and the size of the apparatus that could be used, which in the case of refracting telescopes of, say, forty feet, was an especially serious handicap.[102]

A second kind of problem was generated by the very ambitiousness of the group. Its *Projet*, or proposal, called for "the perfection of the sciences and the arts, and the search in general for everything which can bring utility or convenience to the human race, and especially to France."[103] This was a program that would reflect the grandeur of the Sun King, but which would eclipse the influence of groups like the Jesuits, the Sorbonne, the Faculty of Medicine, and the existing Académie française. The same problem was encountered by the proposal to Colbert from another of his advisers, Charles Perrault, to form a broad group to include sections in literature, history, and philosophy, as well as mathematics. Implementation of Perrault's proposal incidentally could have made Cartesian-Gassendist controversy more likely, more pressing, more extensive, and sharper in focus, for the principles of selection to membership in each of the two main groups would have been different. Admitted to the non-mathematical group would be technicians, with a utilitarian interest in experimentation; to the latter, natural philosophers with broad theoretical concerns.[104] Colbert's intention to aggrandize the monarchy and to subsume as much as possible of the Republic of Letters under its control inclined him to these proposals. But the rivalries were such that when Colbert finally oversaw the formation of the Académie around June 1, 1666, he recognized an institution of much more limited scope, specifically designed to avoid sectarian strife. To the extent that it avoided all dogmatism and especially the Cartesian, this early Académie yet represents something of a triumph for the spirit of Gassendism.[105]

---

else in the ministerial entourage" (*L'Académie Royale*, pp. 32–33). The orientation of the document is important in any case for assessing the orientation of the gestating Académie royale des sciences.

[101] Brown, *Scientific Organizations*, p. 123.

[102] See Sorbière's account of these problems (ibid., p. 127).

[103] Quoted ibid., p. 147.

[104] Hahn, *Paris Academy*, pp. 12–14.

[105] McClaughlin ("Censorship," p. 565) has a different explanation of the exclusion of Cartesians from the Académie, namely, the condemnation of Cartesianism by the university and the government. Certainly there are connections here, but they are more complicated than

Nor was this a surprising development in view of the advice Colbert was receiving not only from Perrault and Auzout, but from Sorbière and Chapelain. Sorbière had read a long discourse to the Montmor academy in 1663, which was then printed and sent to Colbert. In it he argued that there was only one solution to the kinds of problems the academy was experiencing, namely, royal protection, which would allow the work of the group to be conducted on such a scale and with such aims as would be in the public interest. And when the membership of the Académie was to be decided, Colbert turned primarily to Chapelain. The upshot was that when Colbert created the Académie, he yielded to political advice and recognized an institution of more limited scope.

The early official history of the Académie said that it was "born of itself as in a naturally well-disposed soil," but even it recognized its genesis in the academies of Montmort and Thevenot.[106] Chapelain's counsel in establishing the Académie and appointing its members may well be that related by this history in its report of a deliberate decision taken to avoid ideological commitment.[107] It was decided that unlike "public exercises of philosophy, where it is not a matter of elucidating the truth, but only of not being reduced to silence," the Académie would be "simple, tranquil, without ostentation whether of mind or learning . . . and above all, that no system would dominate to the exclusion of others."[108] The appointments came in three groups. First were the mathematicians: (1) Adrien Auzout (1630–91); (2) Jacques Buot (d. 1673; cosmographer and professor of mathematics); (3) Pierre de Carcavy (d. 1684; a friend of both Pascal and Roberval, who was also an advisor to Colbert); (4) Bernard Frenicle de Bessy (1600–75);[109] (5) Huygens; (6) Jean Picard (1620–82); (7) Gilles

---

McClaughlin allows. For the prohibition of Lallement's funeral oration for Descartes, the first setback for Cartesianism according to McClaughlin, came the year *after* the Académie's first meeting and condemnation by the universities of Paris, Angers, Caen, and the religious orders, only in the 1670s.

[106] Fontenelle, *Histoire*, 1:4–5. Fontenelle is known as the historian of the Académie des sciences, but the official historian of the period in question was Duhamel, chosen as secretary according to Fontenelle because of his knowledge of the sciences, his impartiality, his ability in Latin, and the clarity of his style. See Taton, *L'Académie Royale*, p. 41, n. 5. His history was first published in 1698 and was taken over with only slight changes by Fontenelle for his much longer French version in eleven volumes, first published in 1733.

[107] Chapelain recommended to Colbert that he appoint "those who are proficient in experimentation, or those who can extract all useful matters from it, who have the clarity of mind to gather it, and finally those who possess the difficult talents which could make the Royal Academy as sound as it is useful" (quoted in Hahn, *Paris Academy*, p. 15).

[108] Ibid., p. 16

[109] Condorcet's comment about Frenicle is of interest: "Frenicle seems to have anticipated universal gravitation; he attributed weight to a kind of instinct in virtue of which each particle detached from a large mass by an external force seeks to reunite itself to the body it left. The old Academy was very concerned in its first years with the cause of light, which seems to prove that many scientists supported Descartes's system and that few believed it. Almost all our physicists

Personne de Roberval (1602–75). Next the physicists were appointed: (8) Samuel Cottereau Du Clos (d. 1715; an experimental chemist who resisted the application of Boyle's corpuscular physics as "vague and defective"[110]); (9) Cureau de la Chambre; (10) Louis Gayant (d. 1673; anatomist and professor of physics); (11) Claude Perrault; and perhaps at this point, (12) Mariotte.[111] The last group of appointments comprised: (13) Claude Bourdelin (1621–99; chemist); (14) Jean-Baptiste Duhamel (1624–1706—One hypothesis is that a reason why this one-time Oratorian may have been regarded as impartial and thus suitable as the secretary was that before his appointment Duhamel had very little contact with Parisian scientific life. How then he should have been counted among the physicists or nominated at all is unclear); (15) Nicolas Marchand (d. 1678; a botanist trained in Padua who was Director of Plants in the Royal Gardens); (16) Jean Pecquet (1622–74; anatomist); and finally in some auxilliary capacity: (17) Claude-Antoine Couplet (1642–1722; hydraulic engineer and professor of mathematics); (18) Honorat Niquet (d. 1667); (19) Pivert (?); (20) Jean Richier (1630–96; astronomer); (21) Delavoye-Mignot (d. 1684; geometer). The upshot was that the initial Académie was distinctly more inclined toward experiment than theory, an attitude whose description as Gassendist is significantly enhanced when such appointments as Auzout, Perrault, and especially Cureau are considered.[112]

Descartes came eventually to prevail, however. Indeed, the Académie became a bastion of Cartesianism and ultimately its last stronghold, awarding its prizes to Cartesian opponents of Newtonianism well into the 1720s.[113] Nor was it ever explicitly anti-Cartesian. The outset of the official history cites Descartes first "among other great men" as having brought about the successful renovation of physics and mathematics.[114] The groundwork for the later Cartesian character of the Académie may already have been laid in an organizational decision taken at its first meeting. Duhamel's minutes for that meeting on

---

then relied on conjectures and hypotheses when it was necessary to observe and calculate" (*Eloges*, pp. 34–35). According to Condorcet, "Mariotte was the first French philosopher to devote himself to experimental physics" (p. 49).

[110] Ibid., pp. 66ff.

[111] Gauja hypothesizes that Fontenelle just overlooked Mariotte as one of the original members ("L'Académie," p. 47).

[112] It is not quite true, however, that the advice of Chapelain resulted in excluding all Jesuits and Cartesians (Hahn, *Paris Academy*, p. 15). Niquet was a Jesuit and Picard, though interested primarily in astronomy, may be described as a Cartesian.

[113] Iltis, "Decline of Cartesianism."

[114] Fontenelle, *Histoire*, 1:2. The appreciation of this renovation is remarkably like our own standard Whig accounts: "A sterile physics was abandoned which had not progressed for several centuries; principles were established that were understood, were followed and led to progress. Authority ceased to have greater insight than reason . . . and since it was decided to consult nature itself rather than the ancients about natural things, she was more easily revealed."

December 22, 1666[115] report that the company would assemble twice weekly, on Wednesday to discuss mathematics, and on Saturday to discuss physics, and the whole company would meet on both days and not be divided as had been proposed.[116] As the official history explained, "geometry has practically no utility unless applied to physics, and physics has solidity only to the extent it is based on geometry . . . in a word, if all of nature consists in the innumerable combinations of shapes and motion, geometry, which alone can calculate motion and determine shapes, becomes indispensably necessary to physics" (pp. 14–15). Had the two groups been kept distinct, the more qualitative experimental approach of the Gassendists might have held out longer against the more quantitative theoretical approach of the Cartesians.

Another structural proposal that failed to take effect but would have sustained the Gassendist spirit of the Académie came as a suggestion from another of Colbert's advisors, the abbé de Bourséis. He proposed that a group of theologians be admitted for the purpose of Bible studies. This group became the Académie des langues orientales and included the Gassendists Launay and Chapelain among others. But the same problems of turf that doomed the Compagnie des sciences et des arts plagued it as well. The Sorbonne complained that the Bible should not be given over to scientists and Protestants and the group was soon dismantled.[117] In any event it did hold out to some extent for at least a certain period in the 1670s when Gassendism remained a genuine competitor of Cartesianism. My sense is that the situation was accurately enough described in a letter written by George Tullie, a history student from Oxford: "Descartes and Gassendi have each Proselites enough, each publick Assemblies where their Hypotheses are maintained by Ingenious persons, where anybody that looks not like a Beggar or a rogue enters and has ye liberty of discoursing, objecting, &c: a course extremely commendable and to be wisht in our Universities, tho these Assemblies are in ye Citie, for they are both equally exploded by ye Jesuites and ye University here, who are as tenacious as old Aristotle and Mr. Troughere himself though elsewhere I think ye odds goes on Descartes his sides, & one of our Conference ye other day told us of a book lately printed at Venice that explained all of ye Bible accordingly to Descartes, & proved that Moses was a Cartesian."[118]

§3   THE INTERMINABLE BATTLE

Despite the ultimate failure of the Gassendists even in the academies, my research into their relative early success there led me to the realization that in

---

[115] The group was active before this date, however, observing a solar eclipse on July 2, for example, or measuring temperature changes (*Memoires*, pp. 7ff.).

[116] Quoted by Maindron, *L'Académie*, p. 5.

[117] George, "Genesis," p. 396.

[118] Quoted by Brown, who assigned the letter to 1677 (*Scientific Organizations*, p. 167; Bodleian, Tanner 39, ff. 43–46).

the issue of real interest to me, the Gassendists were invincible, even if they were incapable of winning it. For I came to see that the contest between the Gassendists and their Cartesian opponents was an instance of what Plato called "the interminable battle [that] is always going on," a battle between two camps of philosophers whom he calls the gods and the giants. It is worth exploring in some detail Plato's discussion of this battle because his imagery is so compelling, his grasp of the issue so sure, and his statement of the arguments so nearly definitive. In addition I think Plato is right that the battle is perennial. The reason for this is that the set of philosophical issues involved is the most fundamental of all, and in addition, is best expressed in the contest Plato portrays. I believe that in one way or other these issues are always being discussed by philosophers and that this is why if the Gassendist cause represents one side in the contest it is both invincible and incapable of winning.

I shall argue in detail that the above view of the history of philosophy is true generally only by illustrating how it might be true for the latter half of the seventeenth century. I will add, however, that if this view is at all correct, then Plato's martial metaphor is especially apt. I was delighted, indeed, to find it used not much later by Humphrey Ditton (1675–1715; a mathematician and religious dissenter) to describe what I shall argue is an important instance of the same contest. His description of the controversy over thinking matter is worth citing at length:

> To look over this Controversy, as managed by the *Deists*, within the Compass of a few years, gives a man a sort of Image of the Arts of *Defense in War*; where an Enemy retires by degrees from *Outwork* to *Outwork*, and is no sooner dislodg'd from one *Post*, but he takes shelter in another. Our Incredulous People have acted with much such Sort of *Military Prudence*, in the Maintaining their Grand Hypothesis, about *Matter's being a Thinking Substance*. They took care at first to fortify it after such a manner, *that all should not sink and be lost at once*; but that whenever, by superior Reason and Argument, any should happen to be beat out of *one Part of their Scheme*, there should be *another*, like a new *Work*, ready to retreat to; from whence the Dispute might still be carried on.[119]

This language might suggest that the struggle over thinking matter, and more generally between the gods and giants, is a matter of blind sectarianism. Perhaps a philosophically more attractive, and more accurate, way of presenting it is by analogy to the choice of a whole way of life that takes into account as far as possible all of its effects and the principles it embodies without thereby trying to justify either. Though there is and can be no ultimate justification for it, this is not to say that the decision is blind or arbitrary, since it is considered and considered in light of everything relevant to it.[120] But whether blind or con-

---

[119] *Matter*, pp. 1–2.

[120] Hare, *Language of Morals*, pp. 68–69. Hare thinks that the closest specification of such a decision is to be found in "the great religions, especially those which can point to historical persons

sidered, the defense of either position is to the last ditch, for all is at stake. The upshot, as we shall see with respect to the thinking matter controversy, for example, is the familiar display of ingenuity on behalf of a fundamental theory faced by anomaly. And it is precisely to this feature of the controversy, unavoidable if I am right, that Ditton so strenuously objects: "*Censures*, tho' ever so sharp and pointed, won't work thro' Stone-walls, nor make him uneasy, whose only Aim and Business it is *to be safe*. Besides, *Strategems* are allow'd in war, and 'tis a piece of *Policy* practis'd all the world over, for People, by any Shifts, tho' ever so hard, to provide for their own security."[121]

Plato's *Sophist* would here be of interest for many reasons. In it Plato gives his method of division and difference with his whimsical example of angling: the art of . . . capturing by stealth . . . of animals in a fluid . . . by daylight with a stroke from above. But he is also after bigger fish, because he raises the questions of appearance and reality, affirmative and negative statements, and false speech and judgment.[122] The question of appearance and reality arises because the sophist, whose definition is sought by the dialogue, is ultimately regarded as an illusionist; he traffics in images or appearances rather than real things; he is thus a purveyor of falsehood, of what is unreal. But for there to be such sophistic commerce, it must have the unreal as its object; yet how can there *be* what is unreal?

The fundamental constraint on Plato's account of images comes from Parmenides's prohibition of thinking and speaking about what is not: "Never shall this be proved—that things that are not are; but do thou in thy inquiry, hold back thy thought from this way."[123] The way to which Parmenides here refers is described by the goddess who speaks in the proem of his principal work as "the way of how it is not, and how it is necessary for it not to be; this, I tell you, is a way wholly unknowable. For you could not know what is not—that is impossible—nor could you express it." This way is contrasted with the way of Truth, which is "the way of how it is, and how it is not possible for it not to be."[124] The view here expressed—the intelligibility and necessity of being and the unintelligibility and impossibility of nonbeing—appears among the seventeenth-century gods. They are logical plenum theorists, who hold that what can exist must exist. Certainly this view is held by Spinoza, and how others such as Malebranche and Leibniz can avoid holding this is not entirely

---

who carried out the way of life in practice." The way of life I have in mind is both more systematic and more comprehensive than any to be found in religion, which for the most part is concerned with imitative behavior.

[121] *Matter*, p. 5.

[122] 237b–251a, 251a–259d, 259d–264b. In what follows I am much indebted to Cornford for both translation and commentary.

[123] Fragment; quoted at 237a.

[124] Diels-Kranz (hereafter: DK) 28 B2. Robinson, *Greek Philosophy*, p. 110.

clear. Furthermore, if to talk of something it must be possible, at least as an essence, for example, then we cannot talk about what does not exist.

The giants of the seventeenth-century are logical vacuists. They hold that it is possible for there to be some things that are not. The space of possible existence is not entirely filled by what is, much less by what must be. Even to express their view, then, the giants will have to talk about what can exist but in fact does not exist. The most noticed chapter of Locke's *Essay*, for example, is 2.8, in which he sets out his primary-secondary quality distinction. The almost universally ignored context for this distinction is the attempt to show how we can have a positive idea of what in fact is a privation. His famous distinction is part of his explanation of how our ideas of cold, darkness, and rest, for example, which are positive, may be caused by privations in things said to be cold, dark, or at rest. I am convinced that what he is most concerned to explain in this chapter is how we can have an idea of the void, that is, of extension that is the extension of nothing.[125]

Although Plato ultimately finds it necessary to relinquish Parmenides's restriction of speech to *being*, he agrees that we cannot speak of the totally unreal. Through the character in the *Sophist* known as the Stranger Plato argues, first, that 'something' applies only to what exists. To talk about what does not exist in any way at all is to talk about nothing, that is, to say nothing at all (237b–e). This line of argument emerges in the seventeenth century in what might be called the Principle of Intentionality: To think is to think of something; to think of nothing is not to think at all, which according to Malebranche is the first principle of all knowledge. The principle establishes a correlation of sorts between the two senses of idealism, namely, that what is is necessary and that what is is mental. They are both derivable from it. Thus, Parmenides claims not only that what is not cannot be thought and cannot be, but effectively that what is must be thought. "For thought and being are the same." "Thinking and the thought that it is are the same; for you will not find thought apart from what is, in relation to which it is uttered."[126]

A second argument from the Stranger is to the effect that attribution can be only to what exists. This we may call the Principle of Exemplification, associating it with an Aristotelian contention that, ironically, was directed in the first instance at Plato's separated Forms. The idea is that every attribute must be an attribute of something—there are no unexemplified attributes. Strictly speaking, Plato's contention is that it is impossible "for something that exists to be attributed to what has no existence" (238a). He argues that number is to be included among things that exist; indeed, "number must exist if anything does." But we cannot say of the nonexistent either that it is singular ("that which is not") or that it is plural ("things which are not"). But if we cannot speak of it in

---

[125] See chap. 4, sec. 13 below.
[126] DK 28 B3; DK28 B8. Robinson, *Greek Philosophy*, p. 110.

either way, then we cannot speak of it at all (238c). Plato does not consider the attribution of what is not to what is not (or to what is); but this would be another attempt to say what cannot be said. It seems tolerably clear that Plato's is a reference theory of meaning and that reference for him can be made only to what exists. Furthermore, while his argument deals only with the attribution of number, it is expressible in terms of all attributes because the conclusion that "that which just simply is not . . . is unthinkable, not to be spoken of or uttered or expressed" (238c) follows from the prohibition of saying anything at all of it.

Although there are a number of ways in which the Principle of Exemplification might be satisfied—Berkeley, for example, required that qualities occur only in bundles and never alone—the most frequent way is to invoke substance as did Aristotle. There are no unexemplified attributes because all attributes must inhere in some substance that thus supports them. The principle in fact appears in a number of contexts in the seventeenth century. In section 26 of chapter 7 below, Locke will be seen to hold a problematic version of the principle at the conceptual level. For present purposes, the most important appearance of the principle is to be found in Descartes's *Principles* 2, 16: "From the sole fact that a body is extended in length, breadth, and depth; we rightly conclude that it is a substance: because it is entirely contradictory for that which is nothing to possess extension. And the same must also be concluded about space which is said to be empty: that, since it certainly has extension, there must necessarily also be substance in it." The void will be seen to be a crucial issue in the seventeenth-century struggle between the gods and giants. Meanwhile, Descartes here concludes that there is no void from the Principle of Exemplification. The argument needs further investigation, which it will receive below. For one thing, the use of the principle is only hypothetical in the sense that only to the extent that body may thus be regarded as a substance must the alleged void also be substance; Descartes does not say that every body is individually a substance. Also, it is not clear how alleged void relates to substance: Not only every instance of alleged void has extension, but all of its parts have extension and thus would seem to be substances by this argument. The relation between an alleged instance of void and alleged void generally is no less problematic. For the moment the important point is the connection between the two lines of argument based on the Principles of Intentionality and Exemplification. Some commentators think they are the same or at least that Malebranche's Principle of Intentionality is the same as Descartes's Principle of Exemplification. Whether or not this can be established, there is at least the following connection between them. To say of a thing that it is round is to refer to that thing in a certain way. Predication is a kind of reference. There is no other way to understand predication for the Cartesians, according to whom the shape of a thing is, as they put it, just that thing shaped in a certain way, namely, with all its superficial points equidistant from its center. Thus, to predicate of what does not exist at all is to refer to what does not exist at all, which is neither to refer nor to predicate. Thus the contradiction Descartes sees in attributing extension to what does not exist.

Plato is quick to realize that his two lines of argument open the way for the sophist to say that unless he is doing nothing at all, in making images he is making what is real. That is, the sophist might argue from the fact of perception to real existence, that *percipi* is *esse* with respect to what on the Parmenidean dialectic is mere appearance. With this phenomenalism the sophist "with extreme cunning has found an impenetrable working-place" (239c), in which he also seems immune to the charge that he leads us to think and say what is false, that is, what is not (240c). The question then becomes, what counts as proper perception, or perception at all, and what is its object? For the giants there is but one kind of object, the physical, and one kind of awareness, sensory; for the gods there is an additional kind of awareness and object. At 248a the Stranger turns to "the opposite party, the friends of the Forms," asking Theaetetus to act as their spokesman:

> STRANGER: We understand that you make a distinction between 'Becoming' and 'Real being' and speak of them as separate. Is that so?
>
> THEAETETUS: Yes.
>
> STRANGER: And you say that we have intercourse with Becoming by means of the body through sense, whereas we have intercourse with Real being by means of the soul through reflection. And Real being, you say, is always in the same unchanging state, whereas Becoming is variable.
>
> THEAETETUS: We do.

Here we recognize the outline of the theories of perception and of knowledge in the *Phaedo* and *Republic*. But despite the sharp divisions suggested by the simile of the divided line,[127] for example, the distinctions in both Plato and the seventeenth century are far from obvious as more recent debates over the so-called given have demonstrated. Nonetheless, some initial themes can be set out.

To say that a thing can be perceived by the senses is to say at least that it can be imaged; to say that a thing can be imaged is to say at least that it can exist in space and time; and to say that it can exist in space is to say at least that it is a particular, that is, fully determinate,[128] in time at least that it could change. The object of nonsensuous intuition, then, will be an immutable universal.

---

[127] *Republic* 6, 509d–511e.

[128] This is, of course, a problematic notion. A triangle that failed to be either right-angled or scalene, would not be a particular. But it is not clear that determining it in this way is sufficient for particularity, for one wants to know about such qualities as its color. Perhaps the only clear example of a fully determinate particular is a Leibnizean monad, which has one from every pair of simple properties O and not-O. But on this view, properties of shape and color are not simple, and fully determinate particulars are not in space, and perhaps not in time, and are not objects of sensory awareness. For present purposes it will have to suffice for a particular to have one from every range

The primary question is not whether there is intuition beyond that of the senses, but whether there are immutable universals—primary in the sense that, while the answer to each question leads, historically, and, with few additional premises, logically as well, to an answer to the other question, the answer to the ontological question is more tractable. To determine whether we have intellectual intuition independently of the ontological question likely leads to the hopeless sort of introspective tests that Hume seems to have invited. In addition to the contingent variation in imaginative powers from one individual to the next and within the same individual, such a test is useless since the failure to have an intellectual intuition in isolation proves nothing. It might necessarily be the case, as it was according to Aristotle, that thinking is always in terms of imagery, even if the imagery and what is thought in terms of it are quite different (particular and universal). To think of greenness (universal), I may need to image a green thing (particular). The ontological question is more tractable because amenable to argument—nonempirical connections between it and other questions can be established, as they were above. Thus, Plato in *Republic* 6 instructs that the "four affections (*noesis*, *dianoia*, *pistis*, *eikasia*) occurring in the soul [be assumed and arranged] in a proportion, considering that they participate in clearness and precision in the same degree as their objects partake of truth and reality" (511e); that is, the specification of *noesis* as different from *dianoia*, for example, follows upon the difference between *archai* and *mathematika*. But this very pairing of differences in perception with differences in object emphasizes the significance of the sophist's reply that no one can fabricate appearance, or think or say what is false.

To answer the sophist, the Parmenidean dialectic must to some extent be abandoned, that is, we must say that what is, is not and that what is not, is. To show how we can do this, Plato initiates a long discussion of the real (*to on*). Here as elsewhere Plato regards the real as the existent. Thus, what might appropriately enough be rendered in *Phaedrus* as "what is truly good or noble," Plato more literally calls "the good as being or the beautiful as being."[129] More generally, he distinguishes the form of a thing from the appearance conveyed by the instance of it by referring to it as the "what it is." Thus in *Phaedo* (75b) he

---

of properties it *could* have, without an account of its possible ranges. This would allow Forms to be particular, thus inviting the conception of an ideal space to distinguish them from the particulars in physical space. Of this, a great deal more below. Another possibility is to characterize a particular as an Aristotelian primary substance—that which is neither present in nor predicable of anything else. Thus, Dobbin is a particular since while brownness may be present in him and horseness predicable of him, he is not present in or predicable of anything else. While this characterization gives the idea it is only initially helpful, for when the Aristotelian substance ontology is rejected, being present in and predicable of become notions in need of an analysis that is no less problematic than the analysis of a particular. And the philosophers such as Berkeley for whom the particular is most important are just those who reject the Aristotelian substance ontology.

129 Hackforth, 260a.

refers to the "knowledge of the equal itself, what it [really] is" as opposed to belief about this or that instance of more or less equal things.[130] In *Sophist* he catalogues and then criticizes at great length the theories of both the monists who say that reality is one and the pluralists who say that it is many. The details of the arguments need not concern us; they come to the criticism that the monists and pluralists attempt to *identify* the real either with one thing or with many. For Plato, the real must be grounded and not identified, explained and not just picked out; what is called for is not the number of being but a theory of being.[131] Hence Plato (246a–c) turns "to look at those who put the matter in a different way":

> STRANGER: What we shall see is something like a Battle of Gods and Giants going on between them over their quarrel about reality.
>
> THEAETETUS: How so?
>
> STRANGER: One party is trying to drag everything down to earth out of heaven and the unseen, literally grasping rocks and trees in their hands; for they lay hold upon every stock and stone and strenuously affirm that real existence belongs only to that which can be handled and offers resistance to the touch. They define reality as the same thing as body, and as soon as one of the opposite party asserts that anything without a body is real, they are utterly contemptuous and will not listen to another word.
>
> THEAETETUS: The people you describe are certainly a formidable crew. I have met quite a number of them before now.
>
> STRANGER: Yes, and accordingly their adversaries are very wary in defending their position somewhere in the heights of the unseen, maintaining with all their force that true reality consists in certain intelligible and bodiless Forms. In the clash of argument they shatter and pulverise those bodies which their opponents wield, and what those others allege to be true reality they call, not real being, but a sort of moving process of becoming. On this issue an interminable battle is going on between the two camps.

The giants are clearly the materialists, and, it would seem, of whatever stripe. Since Plato is doing philosophy and not its history, according to Cornford, he is concerned with "a tendency of thought, not with one or another set of individuals who, more or less, exhibited that tendency."[132] I agree that Plato is concerned with the materialists just to the extent they are materialists but, as I shall try to show at the end of this work, the distinction Cornford draws involves something of a Procrustean bed. History of philosophy cannot help but deal with philosophical tendencies, indeed can deal only with them. Hence I think it

---

[130] Friedlander, *Plato*, p. 22.

[131] Cf. Socrates's rejection of physicalist theories in *Phaedo* and his decision to have recourse to rational explanations (*logoi*), and to use them in trying to discover the truth about things (99c).

[132] Cornford, *Plato's Theory*, p. 232.

can rather easily be shown that the isolation of history of philosophy from philosophy is wrongheaded. Whether the equation is symmetrical, that is, whether philosophy is intrinsically historical, is a more difficult question I shall have occasion only to speculate about. In either case, it is essential to the thesis of this work that Plato include among his materialists the atomists. Burnet, who regarded this as "one of the most pressing questions in the history of Greek philosophy," argued that Democritus cannot have been meant, since Democritus, who "asserted the reality of the void, could not be spoken of as making impact and contact the test of being."[133] Cornford countered that "the Atomists expressly identified the void with 'not-being' or 'nothing' and atoms with 'being.' You do not refuse to call a man a materialist because he recognizes the existence of empty space, which he calls 'nothing.'"[134] The significance of the void in atomist ontologies is a difficult question, and its difficulty is preserved, as we shall see at length, in the seventeenth century, when the question is raised by Bernier, for example, as to whether empty space *exists*.

It is important to note the language in which Plato contrasts the materialists with their opponents. Note for one thing the pejorative terms in which the rowdy materialists are described and the contrasting honorific description of the friends of the Forms, "who are more civilized." The materialists are "utterly contemptuous" of those who disagree with them and "will not listen to another word." The materialists are "those whose violence would drag everything down to the level of body"; they are "lawless." The argument of *Laws* 10 is that materialism leads to a conventionalist theory of law, which for Plato is relativism ("There is absolutely no such thing as a real and natural right"), and in practice to the result that the stronger prevail amidst general impiety and social chaos (889c). Seen in this light, the materialists in fact represent the danger posed by the sophist, in contrast to whom the philosopher, dealing only in the true and real, recognizes an absolute law that allows right to prevail in a stable society. Even the designations 'gods' and 'giants' and the relative position of their designata indicate Plato's moral and political concerns, not to say biases. The Forms are literally nowhere for they are not in space; yet their friends are placed above the giants, who occupy the nether regions and would drag everything down to their level. The metaphor of the better as superior is as hard to resist as the notion that the intelligible is higher than the sensible.[135]

The materialists are said to define reality as the same thing as body and to attribute real existence only to the tangible. The tactile metaphor is appropriate

[133] *Greek Philosophy*, p. 279.

[134] *Plato's Theory*, p. 232, n. 1.

[135] Consider J. S. Mill defending Epicurean hedonism: "Human beings have faculties more elevated than the animal appetites. . . . Utilitarian writers in general have placed the superiority of mental over bodily pleasures chiefly in . . . their circumstantial advantage rather than in their intrinsic nature . . . ; but they might have taken the other and, as it may be called, higher ground" (*Utilitarianism*, p. 211).

to describe not only the ancient materialists but also their seventeenth-century descendants. In principle, there is no reason why for them the real should be given especially to touch, for the essence of the position is that the real is sensible, that is, available to any of the senses. But touch emphasizes two features of the materialist ontology and theory of knowledge. One is that only in touch is it obviously the case that knower and known must be in contact and stand in a causal relation. For the mechanistic materialist, the one is a condition for the other. By contrast, one need not and, as we shall see Arnauld to have argued, *cannot* be in contact with the object of vision, for we can see things only that are at a distance. This difference from touch was of inestimable importance to the debates surrounding theories of perception in the seventeenth century. In addition, there need be no causal relation between the viewer and the object of vision because sometimes we see things (as if at a distance) that do not exist and thus cannot act as causes of our vision. This relative incorrigibility of touch is crucial. We cannot touch what is not, but we can see what is not.[136] Just to the extent that intellectual intuition is modeled on vision some account of awareness other than in terms of causation must be found.

I am convinced that at the root of the contrast between sensory and intellectual intuition is the difference between passivity and activity understood as creativity. That the mind is passive in sense perception is a familiar theme in the seventeenth century, no less so for the gods than for the giants. Descartes makes this a premise for a proof of the material world in *Meditations* 6, and Malebranche makes the mind passive in all its perceptions as a material thing is passive in the shapes it receives. For Locke we cannot have the simple idea of a pineapple's taste without experiencing it, and Berkeley, having made objects like pineapples mind-dependent, makes the mind's passive perception of them a premise in an argument for an active God's existence. The notion of nonsensory awareness is more problematic. The giants of course reject it. But none of their opponents accepts an intuition that is active in the sense that it creates its object because of its apparent incompatibility with what they require of the object of such intuition, namely, that it be immutable. The *Sophist* exploits this tension in an argument to show that the real must be extended to cover what in some sense changes (248e–250c); but Plato never admits a changing object of knowledge. Instead the metaphor here for intuition is one of a perfectly passive *contemplation*. Nonetheless, I think that a model for intellectual intuition is Descartes's notion of the creation of the eternal truths (which, by the way, are changeless). In this creation, God's will and intellect are one; by willing that twice two is four God knows it to be eternally true. Had He created otherwise, then what God knows to be eternally true would have been different.

---

[136] Strictly speaking, of course, this is not true. There can be tactile hallucinations no less than visual ones, as the much discussed case of the phantom-limb shows. But we are talking here of the suggestiveness of images.

Obviously, lest there be a multiplicity of competing truths, not everyone can have a fully intellectual intuition in this sense, which anyhow requires omnipotency. Peter Browne was a minor figure from the period who was au courant with this notion and the need to restrict its applicability. Discussing how material things might be known he said: "Perhaps this Power of raising up to itself *Ideas*, without the pressure of *Any* Object whatsoever, is a *Privilege* of the Divine Intellect above; and answerable to the Almighty Power of Creation, or producing a Thing out of Nothing."[137] This suggests that innate ideas that the mind is disposed to produce upon occasion of some object might be regarded as an approximation of a fully intellectual version of this intuition. Malebranche rejected the Cartesian theory of innate ideas just because it ran "the risk of claiming that men have the power of creating beings worthier and more perfect than the [material] world God has created."[138] An additional feature of intellectual intuition as creativity is that it gives one the existence of what is intuited. These are the terms in which Kant in the last of the general remarks he added to the second edition of the Transcendental Analytic distinguishes "derivative intuition" (*intuitus derivatus*) from "original intuition" (*intuitus originarius*). The former is a sensory intuition in space and time, and is always passive; it does not itself give us the existence of its object but rather "is dependent upon the existence of the object, and is therefore possible only if the subject's faculty of representation is affected by that object."[139] The latter is, as he says, an intellectual intuition belonging only to the primordial being that does give that being the existence of its object (presumably by creating it). Though he rejected the approximation of intellectual intuition in innate ideas, Malebranche as we shall see anticipated Kant in this with his notion of a direct perception of Being, the perfectly nonsensory version of which is the Beatific Vision. Such are the celestial concerns of the gods. The giants meanwhile reject intellectual intuition, which is why for them the causal relation becomes so important for cognition. The mind has no creativity and hence must be acted upon. And since objects at a distance cannot directly act on the mind, they must do so by proxy, which is why representationalist theories of perception are the order of the day for mechanistic materialism. We shall return to this theme at length in chapter 5.

A second important feature of the contrast between materialism and idealism that is captured by the tactile metaphor is more difficult to express at all literally, namely, that the real is the *gross stuff* of our sensory experience. All the other senses allow a metaphorical grasp by them of the nonmaterial. This is obviously true of hearing (e.g., the word of God) and, as we shall see, especially of vision. It even seems true of smell (the odor of sanctity) and taste (the sweetness of grace). But touch applies only to the material, and those who like

---

[137] *Procedure*, p. 95; see also pp. 382–83.
[138] *Search* 3.2.3; p. 222.
[139] *Critique*, p. 90.

Malebranche in the seventeenth century sought to apply it metaphorically to the nonmaterial succeeded, as we shall see, only in mobilizing materialist lines of argument.

Though it is not employed in the text immediately before us, the visual metaphor is never far from any point in the Platonic corpus. In seeking the definition of the sophist our dialogue discovers dialectic and arrives instead at the definition of the philosopher as one who has mastery of it. The philosopher too may be difficult to see clearly; but the difficulty in his case is not the same as in the Sophist's (253e–254b):

> THEAETETUS: What is the difference?
> STRANGER: The Sophist takes refuge in the darkness of Not-being, where he is at home and has the knack of feeling his way; and it is the darkness of the place that makes him so hard to perceive.
> THEAETETUS: That may well be.
> STRANGER: Whereas the Philosopher, whose thoughts constantly dwell upon the nature of reality, is difficult to see because his region is so bright; for the eye of the vulgar soul cannot endure to keep its gaze fixed on the divine.

The celebrated Platonic allegory of the cave in *Republic* 6 is an extended exploitation of the possibilities of metaphors from vision, that "clearest of our senses, clear and resplendent . . . the keenest mode of perception."[140] Though previously Parmenides, Empedocles, and Epicharmus had spoken of seeing with the mind, it is Plato who first refers to the "eye of the soul," and etymologically, of course, both *eidos* and *idea* are objects of sight.[141]

This imagery is too well-known a part of even an elementary view of Plato to dilate further upon it here. No less well-known is its prominence in the Neo-Platonic tradition. Its vehicle through this tradition into the seventeenth century, especially for the Cartesians, is the obvious one. Augustine was for them the touchstone of Christian orthodoxy in debates on everything from grace to the bestial soul, and his work was reverently studied, even if only in an incomplete and unusual form, as we shall see. His use too of the Platonic light imagery is familiar enough not to require much comment. It is important to note, however, that he emphasizes and makes explicit the contention of *Republic* 6 that the intelligibility, truth, and being of the Forms or Ideas as well as our knowledge of them, depend on something beyond them, namely, the Good, which for Augustine is of course the deity. This is the doctrine of illumination that is seized upon by Malebranche when, for example, he quotes Augustine's commentary on John: "Christ conveys the thought [*insinuavit*] to us that the

---

[140] *Phaedrus* 250d.

[141] Friedlander, *Plato*, pp. 13–31. Significantly, an Epicurean fragment ridicules Plato's "eyes of the soul": "Quibus enim oculis animi intueri potuit vester Plato fabricam illam tanti operis" (Cicero, *De natura deorum* 1.8.19, ed. Usener, *Epicurea* [Leipzig, 1887], frag. 367. Cited in Friedlander, *Plato*, p. 341).

human soul and rational mind have life, happiness and *illumination* only through the very substance of God."[142] There are very many passages from Augustine like this that might be cited, especially in the voluminous polemic with Arnauld, with which Malebranche argues against any of the theories of knowledge, such as espouse innate ideas or ideas as modifications of the mind, which thereby make human reason self-sufficient.[143] The expression 'natural light' found throughout Descartes's work refers to the capacity found equally in everyone to arrive at the truth. It is the common sense (*bon sens*) of the *Discourse* or the intuition (*intuitus*) of the *Rules*. It is a reason that requires for its operation nothing beyond the ordinary divine conservation of things in existence. Against this Malebranche restores the Augustinian notion of reason as an illuminated light (*lumière illuminée*) as opposed to Descartes's and Arnauld's illuminating light (*lumière illuminante*). As he repeatedly reminds Arnauld by quoting Augustine, "say not that you are a light unto yourself."[144]

There are several themes closely linked to these doctrines of illumination. Though its extent and significance for Plato are matters of perennial dispute, the tendency toward *enthusiasm* is unmistakable in his work. The affinity to the Eleusinian mysteries, the insistence on rites of purification and initiation, the ineffability and divinity of the ultimate doctrine, and the ecstasy of experiencing it are all apparent features of both the history of Platonism and the eponymous texts. "There is no way of putting [philosophy] in words like other subjects. Acquaintance must come after a long period of attendance or instruction in the subject itself and of close companionship, when suddenly, like a blaze kindled by a leaping spark, it is generated in the soul and at once becomes self-sustaining."[145] It is hard to distinguish this philosophical knowledge from Christian faith. In *Republic* 532a–b Plato makes the good in itself the ultimate and perhaps only object of knowledge, calling it "the limit of the intelligible." As the sun both makes the colors we see and our eye to see them, so the Good gives both being and intelligibility to the objects of the mind. Taylor was led to regard the Good as other than the Forms, which are but "manifestations or expressions of it";[146] with the apotheosis of the Good in the Christian era, the way is open to Malebranche's theory of the vision of all things in God: in seeing anything we see God.[147]

---

[142] *Tractatus in Joannem* (23.5.1584; Migne, 35). *Search* 3.2.6; pp. 232–33. Malebranche uses the Platonic imagery to make the sensible-intelligible distinction. Those who follow the senses and the imagination gropingly feel their way (*en tâtonnant*) while philosophers are those who *see* (*Dialogues* 1, 9).

[143] See chap. 2, sec. 6 below.

[144] See Jolley, *Light of the Soul*, esp. pp. 7–11, for a contrast in biblical conceptions of man's relation to God between Malebranche on the one hand and Descartes and Leibniz on the other.

[145] *Seventh Letter*, 341c–d.

[146] Taylor, *Plato*, p. 286.

[147] In the seventeenth century Stillingfleet was one who, from a third point of view, was sensitive to the tendency toward enthusiasm and mysticism among the friends of the Forms: "[Pythagoras], from a third point of view, *had learnt*, saith *Porphryry, from the Eastern Magi, That* God *was Light*

Another constant companion of doctrines of illumination is *elitism*. Perhaps this characterization is etymologically rather misleading since the *illuminati* need not be elected, as by the grace of faith, but rather more generally must have some special qualification however it is obtained. Thus the clarity and distinctness of perception that mark Cartesian knowledge are in principle available to all. (Even so, when Malebranche discusses the Reason that he supposes is necessarily the part of everyone, his very orthography suggests the model of faith.) In any case, the essential point is that the proper exercise of the highest faculties remains the exclusive privilege of only a few. In the *Timaeus*, for example, mind is distinguished from true opinion on the familiar bases that what we perceive "through the body" is not to be regarded "as most certain and real" and that there are Ideas unperceived by sense and apprehended only by mind. "Every man may be said to share in true opinion, but mind is the attribute of the gods and of very few men."[148]

Another concomitant of illumination doctrines, this time of a logically closer sort, is *authoritarianism*. By this I mean the view that some people have the right, and in fact the duty, to interfere with others who do not pose a direct and significant threat to them. That is, legitimate interference is not limited, for example, just to protection of life, liberty, and estate. By itself authoritarianism is not very unusual. Many people believe that by gaining a plurality of those voting in civic elections one is entitled to a wide range of interferences, even including those whose only putative benefit accrues to those interfered with. The mark of Plato's authoritarianism is that entitlement to interfere is based on privileged access to knowledge. With the further premise that for all human activity there is a knowably better or worse way of behaving we have the *totalitarianism* of the *Republic*. The following passage from *Laws* 10 gives the gist:

> The principle is this—that no man, and no woman, be ever suffered to live without an officer set over them, and no soul of man to learn the trick of doing one single thing of its own sole motion, in play or in earnest, but, in peace as in war, ever to live with the commander in sight, to follow his leading, and take its motions from him to the least detail—to bolt or advance, to drill, to bathe, to dine, to keep wakeful hours of night as sentry or dispatch carrier, all at his bidding, in the stricken field itself neither to pursue nor to retire without the captain's signal, in a word, to teach one's soul the habit of never so much as thinking to do one single act

---

and Truth; and therefore he look'd on a search after Truth as one way of assimilation to God. But the main thing was in the practice of virtue; of which there is a short Abstract in the *Golden Verses*, and *Hierocles* declares . . . *The design of them all was to bring mankind to a likeness to the Divine Nature*" (*Origines sacrae* 2, pp. 87–88. See chap. 7, sec. 26 below for a discussion of this work).

[148] 51 d–e. See also *Sophist*, 254a: "The Philosopher, whose thoughts dwell constantly upon the nature of reality, is difficult to see because his region is so bright; for the eye of the vulgar soul cannot endure to keep its gaze fixed on the divine."

apart from one's fellows, of making life, to the very uttermost, an unbroken consort, society, and community of all with all.[149]

The context for this passage is a discussion of military preparedness and efficiency, but for Plato the same structure of military discipline is appropriate "in peace as in war."

In these terms, the ultimate significance of the battle of the gods and giants is, as Plato saw, moral and political. What this means is that to the extent it is an element in this contest, Locke's *Essay* must be understood as a protracted plea for a kind of toleration perfectly at odds with the Platonic view. That the *Essay* should be read this way is anything but obvious from the text alone. In his Epistle to the Reader Locke tells us of the inception of the *Essay*. Talking with friends "on a subject very remote from the [*Essay's*]" led to such insurmountable difficulties that it seemed to him necessary first to examine the extent of our intellectual abilities—an examination that ultimately led to the *Essay*. In a marginal note to his own copy of the work, James Tyrrell placed himself among the friends at the original discussion and identified its subject as "the principles of morality and reveal'd religion."[150] But just what those principles are, what Locke's theory of value comes to, especially his political philosophy, and what the connections are between these and the *Essay* have historically all proved elusive questions. His political philosophy has proven chameleon-colored with every imaginable light: asserting and denying natural rights and law; revolutionary, liberal, conservative, anarchist; Hobbist contractarian, egoist.[151] I am committed to a systematic stance with respect to these questions, but I can here only outline that stance on what I regard as its foundations, namely, Locke's argument for toleration, which though explicitly addressed to the question of religious freedom, may be extended, I venture to say, to every sort of freedom.

[149] 942a–c. The passage will be recognized as the second of Popper's epigraphs to *The Open Society and Its Enemies*, with whose view of Plato I am in fundamental agreement. In Popper's estimation, the position that the collective is all-important with the individual counting for nothing (tribalism) is based on the failure to distinguish natural laws from legal or conventional norms (tabooism), a distinction he attributes to Protagoras (p. 61) or perhaps Lycophron (pp. 76–77), in any case to our sophist. Plato's failure here is supported by two factors: (1) his reduction of norms to facts, and (2) the rejection of responsibility for norms. It seems to me that the totalitarianism that follows from Plato's position is content-neutral, however; it need not be reactionary as Popper thinks (for what seem to be historicist reasons: Plato was determined to certain metaphysical views by his psychology and circumstances. One would have thought that if prediction [prophecy] is prohibited then so is postdiction.) That Plato's totalitarianism does not by itself entail any reactionary views is clear from its compatibility with a "moral fact" entailing toleration. That is, the privileged knowledge governing every aspect of human activity might be that toleration is the best policy *tout court*. This raises inter alia the paradox of toleration, namely, whether the intolerant should be tolerated, about which I shall have more to say in chap. 9 below.

[150] Aaron and Gibb, *Early Draft*, p. xii.

[151] For a suggestion that such exegetical variability is of the nature of the beast, see Charles H. Monson, Jr. ("Locke's Political Theory"), who argues that theoretical pluralism makes Locke "the philosopher of democracy."

Locke's advocacy of toleration results from his conviction that religion is not the province of the magistrate. The *Letter Concerning Toleration* argues that the magistrate's power cannot constrain belief: "to believe this or that to be true, does not depend on our will,"[152] thus punishment or its threat can have no effect. Even if the magistrate's power could constrain belief it would be irrelevant and, worse, dangerous. "For, there being but one truth, one way to heaven; what hope is there that more men would be led into it, if they had no other rule to follow but the religion of the court, and were put under the necessity to quit the light of their own reason, to oppose the dictators of their own consciences, and blindly to resign up themselves to the will of their governors, and to the religion which either ignorance, ambition, or superstition had chanced to establish in the countries where they were born?" (p. 12). I think this is a very deep argument. For one thing, a priori there is no more reason to believe that the unconstrained individual will arrive at the one truth; so Locke's argument might best be regarded as intended to establish the *intrinsic* value of the autonomous conscience. Certainly autonomy is necessary for salvation: "No way whatsoever that I shall walk in against the dictates of my conscience, will ever bring me to the mansions of the blessed" (p. 28). But in addition, the argument may well be taken ad hominem: The dictator must assume that there is "but one truth" of the matter over which he dictates, but since that truth cannot be known, as the *Essay* shows, the assumption is insufficient for dictatorship. The assumption is one that in any case Locke himself seems to reject. As I shall try to show, the antirealist semantical theory of the *Essay* is such as to preserve *every* moral and intellectual sphere from the province of *every* authority. In very crude terms, Locke's position is that there can be no philosopher kings. He is the sophist according to whom the nature of knowledge is such that it in principle cannot qualify one better than another to teach and enforce virtue. "Those things that every man ought sincerely to enquire into himself, and by meditation, study, search, and his own endeavours, attain the knowledge of, cannot be looked upon as the peculiar profession of any one sort of men" (ibid.).

Relying on the theory of ideas set out in the *Essay*'s first two books, Locke in the third prepares for the theory of knowledge of the fourth book by setting out a theory of language that would deflate "those huffing Opinions (men) are swell'd with" when they use language improperly. In thus indicating which uses of language are significant, Locke claims to be doing a service to "Truth, Peace, and Learning," a service that if this approach is correct, is rendered not just to the Republic of Letters but through it to the civil state as well. Thus the epigraph of the *Essay*: Quam bellum est velle confiteri potius nescire quod nescias, quam ista effutientem nauseare, atque ipsum sibi displicere![153]

---

[152] *Works*, 5:40.

[153] "How delightful it would be, Velleius, if when you did not know a thing you would admit your ignorance, instead of uttering this drivel, which must make even your own gorge rise with disgust" (Cicero, *De natura deorum*, bk. 1). Gordon Schochet argues that Locke's "religious and

If this history is at all plausible then we should have an indication of Gassendi's motivations in rehabilitating Epicurus. Gassendi's first publication, *Paradoxes Urged against The Aristotelians*,[154] appeared in 1624. The work is directed primarily against contemporary Aristotelianism and sounds most of the main themes heard throughout the rest of Gassendi's work, most notably his nominalism and skepticism. Notably absent is any direct effort on behalf of Epicureanism. In the same year that this work appeared, the Sorbonne, supported by the Parlement, defended Aristotle and condemned the atomism of Jean Bitaud and Etienne de Claves as "false, audacious and contrary to the faith."[155] Was Gassendi showing unusual sensitivity to political circumstances by minimizing or even obscuring the most objectionable aspect of his work? Perhaps so, however indirect the connection between events in Paris and the publishing efforts of this obscure priest in Provence. But even so, the attack on Aristotle is of a piece with the rehabilitation of Epicurus. The *apologia* for the latter was in a sense complete by 1628 and was designed to be appended to the *Paradoxes* of 1624.[156] That this material only appeared two decades later is not to be interpreted as a change in course or in interest or even of subject matter on the part of Gassendi. (Indeed, part of Gassendi's failure as a propagandist is attributable to the consistency of his project. At mid-century he attacks Aristotelianism no less severely than a quarter-century earlier, without fully realizing that the far greater enemy was then Cartesianism.) What binds the negative and positive aspects of Gassendi's single project is a concern over the role of authority. The object of his attack is not the person or philosophy of the historical Aristotle, but the use to which they were being put by his latter-day disciples, for whom he was The Philosopher and who blocked inquiry by slavish and obscurantist deferral to his views.[157] Gassendi was of course not

---

civil concerns were parents to the epistemology," that he moved from his early position of the *Two Treatises* that recognized the autonomy of conscience but rejected toleration to his final position of the *Letter on Toleration* and the *Second Treatise on Government* that declared revolution justified when toleration was denied, and that Locke's empiricism was designed to supply the defects he saw in the consensualist, intuitionist, and nativist bases for these moral and political concerns.

[154] *Opera*, 3:95–210; French translation, B. Rochot, *Dissertations en forme de paradoxes contre les Aristotéliciens.*

[155] Spink, *French Free-thought*, pp. 89–90.

[156] Bloch, *Ueberweg*, 2.b.

[157] Pierre Petit of Montluçon, to be discussed below, was something of a clown; but his *Lettre* reads like a manifesto of the Gassendist spirit of free enquiry: "There is nothing more dangerous in matters of human science than authority and the habit we acquire of acquiescing in the opinion of others *ipsa consuetudo assentiendi periculosa . . .* it is easier to believe than to take the trouble to judge, whence it is that most men cling to what is first taught them, whether bad or good, and as if they had been cast by a storm on an island, desert or fertile, there they remain, *veluti tempestate delati ad quancumque disciplinam tanquam ad faxum adhaerescunt*, without seeking the means to leave. There are also others who so enjoy visions and things they do not understand that they believe them more lofty than those they easily understand . . . *cupititate humani ingenii lubentius obscura creduntur*" (pp. 18–20). The author he cites is Cicero, *Academica.*

alone in this condemnation of this Aristotle. But the grounds for the condemnation by Descartes and the friends of the Forms allowed, indeed encouraged, the substitution of one realism, one dogmatism, one authority for another; their alternative hero would be Plato, to which Gassendi's alternative was the nominalism, skepticism, and rejection of authority advanced by Epicurus.

Despite the ultimate moral and political significance of the battle of the gods and giants, my interest here is largely restricted to its metaphysical infrastructure. For the ground of Plato's doctrine of illumination, his authoritarianism, his enthusiasm lies ultimately, as it does for anyone entering the fray he describes, in the broadest of all metaphysical questions, namely, that of sufficient reason, the grand question, ultimately, as to why there is anything at all rather than nothing. For Plato, as for Greek philosophy almost universally,[158] a beginning of existence from absolutely nothing is inconceivable. Thus, while it is still possible that what exists has always existed by accident, the dialectical tendency for him as for the whole of Greek philosophy and for most of it since, has been to regard at least a part of what is as necessary: What is has always been because it is necessary. Thus, while Plato rejects Parmenides's monism, he accepts his requirements on being. But this leaves unaccounted for the changing, temporal, contingent world of experience, or perhaps better, the connection between this world of appearances and the real, permanent, valuable world of being that we do not experience. Parmenides allows that some opinions are better than others, for he gives an account of appearances "as it seems likely," namely, as one that is minimally false. He also offers a cosmogony which, though in principle impossible, best conforms with the principles of the Way of Truth. But ultimately there can be no account of the connection between reality and appearances because there can be no true account of change, which is utterly false and unreal. Having led Parmenides along the Way of Truth, the goddess turns to the Way of Opinion, however implausibly, only for pragmatic reasons, "so that no thought of mortals shall ever outstrip you."[159] But such otherworldliness is a hard saying, and Plato sought an account of this world and did so in a way that dominated subsequent philosophy. "Let me tell you then why the creator made this world of generation. He was good, and the good can never have any jealousy of anything. And being free from jealousy, he desired that all things should be as like himself as they could be."[160] Historically, this attempt to derive in teleological terms the contingent, changing, temporal world of appearance from the necessary, immutable, eternal world of reality has suffered a severe bipolar tension. Wittingly or not, philosophers have tended either to collapse the contingent into the necessary, or to give up the necessary altogether and to regard the real as in the end a colossal accident. As instantiations of this tendency in the seventeenth century one

---

[158] For some possible exceptions, see Sorabji, *Time*, p. 248, n. 65.
[159] Simplicius, *Physics* 30, 17 & 39, 8 (DK 28 B5); Robinson, *Greek Philosophy*, p. 118.
[160] *Timaeus* 29d–30a.

thinks of the necessitarianism of Spinoza and the pan-tychism of Hobbes. Both Spinoza and Hobbes, however, were pariahs. They were without schools, without followers, without acknowledged influence. They were anti-authorities; they were plagues on their own houses; they were held up as *reductiones* of each other's position. While their views represent the epitome of their respective positions, and while their positions were the logical extremes of the fundamental philosophical issues of their period, they were, as far as our story is concerned, hors de combat.

§4   OTHER WARS

The philosophical contests of the seventeenth century were in many respects multicornered. To forestall confusion and disappointed expectation later, the broader context may be indicated here at the outset. For one thing, the Cambridge Platonists, whom one would have expected ranged among the gods against the giants, in fact occupy a corner distinct from both. But to show this and to show also its significance to my story, I shall first need my chapter on Cartesianism.[161] A second, far more important camp is the Aristotelian, but the question as to what counts as Aristotelianism in the period is an especially vexed one. I confess that my inclination here is whiggish. Not that the Aristotelians were wrong or that they were espousing a doomed cause; they just were not very good.[162] The clearest and most relevant indication of this is their failure to provide new problems to which their program might be applied and by which it might be continually distinguished from its competitors. The result was not a collapse or abandonment of Aristotelianism so much as an adulteration of it by more rigorous programs. In Britain, though people like Thomas White and especially John Sergeant, for example, figure in our story, their

---

[161] Cudworth rejected abstraction on the ground that it would be useless since then ideas would be required to form ideas. He instead held that essences, known through introspection, are ideas in God's mind (*System*, pp. 732–38). This places him very close to Malebranche, but he seems not to have influenced the Oratorian, who did not read Cudworth before 1705. See J. B. DuBos to P. Bayle, March 5 of that year (Malebranche, *Oeuvres*, 10:730). And when Malebranche came finally to know of Cudworth's plastic forms, for example, he thought them words devoid of sense. See his letter to A. Conti, June 14, 1713 (ibid., 19:833). Cudworth, for good circumstantial reasons, was more of an influence on Malebranche's critic, Locke.

[162] What I say of the decline of Aristotelianism may be true generally of Scholasticism. "The most influential and most read scholastic works in the seventeenth century and thereafter were not Aristotelian texts, nor the works of medieval scholastics, but the new textbooks" (Trentman, "Scholasticism," p. 834). These textbooks, by people like Franco Burgersdijck and Bartholomew Keckerman, did not have a firm grasp of Scholastic doctrine and often were original only in giving demonstrably garbled accounts of it (ibid., esp. pp. 835–37). The impression one has is that after Suarez (d. 1617) there is a rather unbroken succession of second-rate minds whose work was sustained by not much more than devotion to a narrow tradition—much like, but without the same justifications as, the formalities and rituals of the universities in which they flourished.

Aristotelianism is only incidental, and the best-known of them is the best example of the Aristotelian loss of identity. Kenelm Digby (1603–65) is nowadays known if at all for his weapon-salve (applied to the weapon rather than the wound caused by it), but in his *Two treatises* (1652) is to be found the best claim to a significant Aristotelian work.

Digby begins his book, however, by taking "Quantity, bulke or magnitude" as the "first and primary affections" of body, and the first author he cites in support of this position is Lucretius. To be sure, he rejects the void, and does so for a reason he attributes to Aristotle, namely, that the void cannot have parts (pp. 21–22). He also propounds the Aristotelian doctrine of four elements based on four qualities but argues to the unexpected conclusion that all operations among bodies "are either locall motion, or such as follow out of locall motion" (p. 36). The upshot is that sensation is mechanical. Indeed, even if Descartes is wrong in attributing the conveyance of motion to vibrations rather than to spirits, he is still the first ever to make "the operations of sense intelligible" (p. 276). Digby subscribes to a mechanical account of gravity and levity. Not surprisingly, therefore, he objected to the illicit use of occult qualities, years before Molière, complaining of some physicians from whom we get "long discourses of a retentative, of an expulsive, of a purging, of a consolidative faculty. . . . And the meaner sort of Physitians know no more, but that such faculties are; though indeed they that are truly Physitians, know also in what they consist" (preface). This perceived champion of Aristotle rejected substantial forms (pp. 39–40) and claimed that only in mathematical matters are demonstrations to be found anywhere in the schools (preface).

By the turn of the century, really only John Sergeant could be regarded as a serious proponent of the Aristotelian cause. As we shall see below, his criticism of Locke's theory of ideas deserves to be taken seriously and was so taken by Locke himself. Indeed, his whole epistemology was a serious piece of philosophizing.[163] Yet even if it has its roots in the *Posterior Analytics*, his epistemology ends by incorporating an atomist theory of sense perception and a theory of dualistic interaction at the pineal gland. Perhaps the most spectacular example of the failure in Sergeant of the Aristotelian program qua Aristotelian is his treatment of the grand metaphysical question. To the Platonic question of why God initiates and maintains our world, Sergeant can find no answer in his Aristotelian scheme and unwittingly, but obviously, ends by denying that the world does have a beginning. (To be sure this was Aristotle's own view, but one that at least since Aquinas had been eliminated from the program by the severest of theological constraints.) In a curious context we need not consider, Sergeant argues that since annihilation involves nonbeing, which can do nothing, not even specify a power, God does not have the power of annihilation, which is no power at all. He does not even have the power of suspending His conservation,

---

163 Wilson, "Lockean Revolution."

"for this takes away from God his *Goodness*, or the Redundancy, Exuberancy or Communicativeness of Being, which is Essential to him, and was the Sole Cause of the *Creation*."[164]

But if His goodness is sufficient for creation then there was no time at which there was no created world.[165] Nor is this an aberrant passage. In another work, he argues that an act of annihilation is impossible to God since to act is to do something and to annihilate is to do nothing, and moreover that God is pure actuality of being and thus never undetermined to act: "Actual Existence being *Essential* to him, his Peculiar Effect is, to *give Existence*, or to *Create* Things; and to Conserve them in Being, which is a *perpetual Creation*, or Creation continued; . . . whence follows, that whatever his Creatures are naturally *disposed* for, he *is actually bestowing* it upon them. Since then the Essences of all Creatures are *Capacities of Being*, the same Goodness that makes the *Sun shine upon The Just and Unjust*; must give them continually to *be actually*."[166] It is worth noting Locke's marginal comment on the first of the passages cited above: "By w(hich) reason t(he) Creation must have been from Eternity (and) consequently t(he) world eternal." What this means presumably is that for Locke Goodness (or anything else) is not sufficient for creation, which thus is accidental.

In France, meanwhile, the ablest defender of Aristotelianism in the latter half of the century, it seems to me, was Jean Baptiste de La Grange, who surprisingly was a member of the Oratory, which for the most part was a bastion of Cartesianism. La Grange argued on behalf of the "ordinary" or "common philosophy taught in the academies of Europe for the previous 600 years," a philosophy he thought best for proving to heretics and nonbelievers that the mysteries of the faith are not impossible.[167] This defense was against all comers, including both Descartes and Gassendi, who he complains did no more than insult this philosophy and dismiss it out of hand.[168] But this does not excuse the Peripatetics from defending it, and he finds it surprising that for twenty years no one has done so. Indeed, it needs, even more than a defense against the new philosophers, a defense and explanation of its principles, for it is vulnerable on substantial forms and suffers from obscurities and methodological problems.

La Grange's critique of Descartes is generally well-conceived. He exposes

---

[164] *Method*, p. 364.

[165] This very way of putting it suggests a possible way of saving Christian orthodoxy, namely, that time begins with the created universe. This is the interpretation of the Platonic ordered world whose beginning is described in *Timaeus* that Philoponus proposed. But this is problematic both as a way of saving orthodoxy and also an interpretation of Plato. See Sorabji, *Time*, p. 268–75.

[166] *Solid Philosophy*, pp. 153–55.

[167] *Les principes*, p. 45.

[168] Ibid., pp. 40–41.

sensitive areas and argues coherently with respect to a range of topics: the creation of the eternal verities, thought as the essence of mind, extension as the essence of body, bestial automata, Descartes's theories of judgment, imagination, method, light and colors, the Eucharist. No less imposing is his critique of Gassendi, who he thinks would have done better to follow his own genius and give his own opinions rather than hanging on the doctrines of Epicurus as if interpreting an oracle.[169] Yet Gassendi on his own hook is still open to criticism, for example, for his two-souls view, his rejection of substantial forms, his account of gravity. But however plausible La Grange's criticisms of Descartes and his followers, of Gassendi and of others, his positive defense of Aristotelianism is vitiated by a naiveté in physics extraordinary even in the 1670s. It may be argued that in its contest with mechanism Aristotelianism has in fact prevailed more recently in an interesting sense;[170] no such case can be made out here. For La Grange dogmatically rejects the earth's movement, both diurnal and annual, for reasons repeated since Ptolemy, blissfully unaware, it would seem, of inertial physics.[171] It is one thing to reject the current literature, even out of hand; it is quite another not to have read it.

There is another, more interesting side to the history of Aristotelianism in France. If in England a tendency was to reshape Aristotle to the New Science, here it was to show that the New Science was not something new under the sun, that in fact it was saying nothing more than what had been said by the ancients, especially Aristotle. The upshot was a more or less popular genre of literature called the *philosophie novantique*. One reason for the appearance of this literature was the close connection between the propagation of the New Science and school curriculum, a connection that did not exist or was much looser in England. Because of it, many of the debates in France were highly politicized and the arguments greatly in need of representation in popular form for purposes of propagandizing for and against them.

Descartes himself helped initiate this development by courting the Jesuits in the hope of converting them and their educational system to his new view of the world. It is clear that he seriously entertained hopes of replacing Aristotle as both the physicist of the natural world and the metaphysician best able to explicate the mysteries of the faith. This strategy was one of philosophical sleight of hand rather than of frontal assault.[172] Thus one of the problematic last dozen paragraphs of the *Principles* is entitled: "Nor does this treatise contain

---

[169] Ibid., pp. 31–37. Curiously, the charge of ocularism abounds in the period. A frequent response to an opposing, and *eo ipso* unsupported, view was that its adherents were either oracles or servants of them.

[170] Ayers, "Locke versus Aristotle," esp. p. 255.

[171] *Les principes*, esp. chaps. 37ff.

[172] Just how clever, or duplicitous, Descartes may have been is a matter of contention. See Caton, "Analytic History."

any principles not received by everyone always, so that this philosophy is not new but the most ancient and common that can be."[173] He claims not to use any principle not received and approved by Aristotle (and all other philosophers), for all he uses are shape, size, and motion, which everyone recognizes. These are clear and distinct, and common to several senses, unlike color, odor, and sound, which are confused and limited to a single sense. Descartes seems here to propose his physics of extension and motion and his theory of clear and distinct ideas as the Aristotelian doctrine of special and common sensibles.

A former tutor of Descartes's at La Flèche who was an eclectic Peripatetic continued this rapprochement of the new and old. In his *Aphorismi physici* (1646), Etienne Noel (1581–1659) aimed, according to the dedication (by Jean Deviennes), "to collect all that might be approved of in philosophy, whether of Aristotle, Descartes or even the chemists."[174] Jacques Du Roure was a one-time Jesuit, doctor of theology, professor of the Académie des sciences,[175] who continued in the same vein, but whose Cartesian sympathies were evident. He wrote that if the followers of Plato and Aristotle read Descartes's work with care, they would find his views not so very different from those of Plato and Aristotle. He produced long arguments to show that the Peripatetics' matter, form, and privation are obscure, false, and anyhow not needed,[176] and claimed that those who uphold such notions follow Aristotle only as night follows day. Du Roure thus employed what became a standard strategy of distinguishing Aristotle's views from those of his disciples and interpreting them in a way compatible with Cartesianism. Thus the doctrine of matter, form, and privation can be understood as the doctrine that there is an extended (ungenerable and incorruptible) substance, that not every material thing has always been as we see it, and that there are particular things belonging to each body.[177] If there is a difference between Descartes on the one hand and Plato and Aristotle on the other, it is that "he did not make a secret of his philosophy and taught clearly

---

[173] 4:200.

[174] Sortais, "Le Cartésianisme," pp. 2–5. The Jesuit Sortais showed that his society was not entirely (if primarily) opposed to Descartes: G. Fourier, F. de la Chaize, R. Rapin, and even Le Valois sang his praises. Descartes's closest friends among them were, of course, A. Vatier and D. Mesland. But the latter left in 1646 for missionary work in the Caribbean and the former left teaching for preaching ("a ministry not lending itself like the professorial post to the propaganda of philosophical ideas" (ibid., p. 19). Bayle's view was that the Jesuit opposition to Cartesianism, and to Jansenism, was explainable primarily, or even solely, in politico-sociological terms: They feared the loss in their influence via teaching that the new new views represented. Even so, Bayle's rejection of ideological considerations seems a bit too hasty. To those entrusted with education for the purpose of salvation, Cartesianism could have threatened the loss not just of students' tuition, but of their souls.

[175] Whose work was obviously not well-received by the Jesuits. See Vissac, *Anthoine du Roure*, pp. 17–18. In addition to the works cited below, he was the author of an *Abrégé de la vraye philosophie . . .* (Paris, 1665). Curiously, he also proposed the rehabilitation of Latin.

[176] *La physique expliqué*, chaps. 30–45.

[177] Ibid., p. 25.

what the others perhaps said, but said obscurely in the oracular fashion of their time and country."[178]

Because of the continued persecution of Cartesianism, the attempted rapprochement with Aristotle continued into the 1670s in important Cartesian texts. In the preface to his *Traité de physique* (1671) Rohault, after asserting that the first obstacle in the way of physics has been its slavish devotion to antiquity, nonetheless claims to have taken from Aristotle all his general notions, of both material things and their properties. In another work of the same year he claimed that neither Descartes nor his disciples reject Aristotle's every view, but only certain ones that even the Aristotelians reject and that certain discoveries made possible only by the telescope, for example, have required. "Otherwise the Cartesians agree with everything Aristotle wrote and differ from the Aristotelians only in that they pass from a metaphysical way of treating things, in which Aristotle was entrenched, to a more particular and physical way."[179] Nor do the Cartesians necessarily differ from Aristotle on matter: (1) Aristotle is obscure on the question (pp. 17ff.); (2) the Cartesian extension or matter in general is without precise figure or determination, which depends on form (p. 22); (3) the Cartesians can agree that there is matter in a different sense, namely, pure potency, because "before a thing may be, in whatever manner it may be, it must be possible for it to be" (p. 23). As for form, another obscure topic in Aristotle, it adds nothing to our knowledge, and hence is no subject for dispute. Anyhow the Cartesians admit the soul to be the substantial form of the body.[180]

If Aristotelianism by this time is intellectually hors de concours and is sustained only by political considerations, then such attempts, however less than straightforward, to deal with it in serious works are largely irrelevant. More important even than, say, Malebranche's attack on sense knowledge in book 1 of the *Search* is a work such as the *Parallel* by René Le Bossu (1631–80), who seems to have been something of a philosophical clown.[181] The

---

[178] *La philosophie diversée*, preface. Du Roure cleverly attributes to Gassendi, Campanella, and Basson the observations that far from being universally accepted, Aristotle was condemned by the early Christians and for a long while was just unknown (p. 256).

[179] *Entretiens*, preface.

[180] Even the most prominent spokesman for Cartesianism, P.-S. Régis, attempts to agree with Aristotle: Though the ultimate subject of material things is extension, one can say with Aristotle that prime matter is the first subject of all forms, the indeterminate subject from which all natural things are made and into which they ultimately resolve themselves (*Système*, 1:284–85). Published in 1690 but completed (and suppressed) much earlier. See below.

[181] 1631–1680. He was also known as the author of a treatise on epic poetry for which he was apparently taken seriously by Bayle, who it must be reminded, took everyone (or perhaps no one) seriously. In a letter to Vincent Minutoli on February 6, 1676, he noted that from Sedan where "we are very poorly located in the Ardennes to know what is happening in the Republic of Letters," Le Bossu's *Traité du Poème Epique* was passing for a very fine piece (*Lettres choisies*, t. 1, p. 84). He seems also to have been taken seriously by Voltaire, who said of him that he "wanted to reconcile Aristotle and Descartes; he did not know that both should be abandoned."

premise of the work is that although there is only one truth, it may be approached by several avenues. But whether Le Bossu himself is on any of them, or intends to be, is not clear. There is an apparent discrepancy between the physics of Aristotle and Descartes, for example, because for Aristotle physics is the method to acquire the science of natural things, or to teach it to the uninitiated, whereas for Descartes it is the science itself, presented to the learned,[182] "which Aristotle doubtlessly had but did not divulge" (p. 314). On the other hand, he is occasionally quite clever, it not entirely convincing. For example, he makes the exegetically valid point that Aristotelian matter as the principle of a material thing, as opposed to the material thing itself, is always relative as the matter of something. A stone may be (part of) the matter of a wall, but as a complete being itself, it has its own matter, say a certain combination of elements, which in turn have their own matter. But as a complete being, it can exist by itself; thus to be matter is only accidental to the stone. Now according to Descartes, "an extended substance occupying all created space would be, before God divided it, the matter of nothing and thus not matter. From which it follows that to be matter is but an accident of the extended substance" (pp. 114–15). As we shall see in chapter 4, this is not an altogether implausible interpretation of Descartes and to that extent offers a plausible reconciliation with Aristotle on issues concerned with individuation.

Generally, however, Le Bossu's reconciliation of Aristotle and Descartes is preposterous. His discussions of matter and form (pp. 128–41) for example, are either patently fraudulent or hopelessly naive (though this is not to say that the work could not have been effective politically on this and other topics). The best philosophical interpretation of the work might be as an instance of crude positivism. For example, he disclaims any intent really to decide whether Aristotle or Descartes arrives at the truth, for this is a matter of physics in which he dares not make a decision. A good instance is the "void," which is actually filled with insensible and dynamically impotent particles; but while these particles are "nothing" in physics, in metaphysics "they are the elements and springs of visible machines"—indeed, they are what philosophers have called the material soul of the world and thus the substantial form of animate things (pp. 154–57).[183] In his attempt to draw the parallel between Aristotle and Descartes, Le Bossu comes close to saying, even if not arguing, that without empirical confirmation, metaphysical claims are translatable across systems.

Still less serious philosophically, but historically more important, is some material from François Bernier, perhaps the best-known disciple of Gassendi, of whom we shall see a great deal more below. In 1670 the Parlement had been petitioned by the Sorbonne to forbid the teaching of Cartesianism, but did not do so, perhaps influenced by a text called *Several reasons for preventing the*

---

[182] *Parallèle*, chap. 1.
[183] And thus, *mirabile dictu*, another agreement between Aristotle and Descartes.

censure or condemnation of Descartes's philosophy.[184] This work of uncertain date and authorship[185] advances the fideistic contention that faith needs to be isolated from philosophical dispute, which can only serve its opponents, particularly the Calvinists, and that in any case only in matters of faith, but not in philosophy, can belief be commanded as readily as was being proposed. History has shown that philosophical allegiance cannot be legislated, as indeed the very saga of Aristotelianism recounted by de Launoy, proves.[186] Thus, with respect to the issue of transubstantiation, on which the anti-Cartesian diatribe often focused, Descartes's view was immunized on the ground that the mysteries of faith are above reason and philosophy, and hence should not be threatened by them (which is true for Cartesianism as much as for Aristotelianism). The Parlement in any case was generally anti-Jesuit, if for no other reason than the Jesuits' ultramontanism, and their decision not to proscribe Cartesianism cannot have been entirely unexpected. To entrench this decision, and for general reasons of propaganda, Bernier under the name of Crotté wrote a *Request of the Masters of Arts, professors and Regents of the University of Paris, presented to the soverign court of Parnassus.*[187] This sendup of philosophical debate premises that poor Aristotle is threatened by reason and experience, which have excited the Cartesians and Gassendists against him.[188] The best defense is to ignore these attacks, hence the request made to the Parlement not to intervene. Meanwhile, "Saturn should be immediately freed from Huygens's rings; . . . the sun should clean its face and no longer appear in public with the ugly spots that indicate corruption and the destruction of Aristotle's celestial quintessence;

---

[184] *Plusieurs raisons pour empecher la censure ou la condemnation de la philosophie de Descartes*, reproduced by V. Cousin, *Fragments*, 3d ed., t. 2, pp. 182ff.

[185] After initially hesitating Cousin attributed it to Arnauld (ibid., p. 181, *Fragments*, 4th ed., t. 2, p. 7, n. 1; 5th ed., t. 3, p. 303). The distinction between *questions de fait* and *questions de droit*, the attack on the Jesuits (especially on the bitter enemy of Port-Royal, Morel) and, from what I can tell, its style, make the attribution quite plausible.

[186] Many of the arguments of this text are to be found in *De varia Aristotelis in Academia Parensiensi fortuna* (1654) by Jean de Launoy (1603–91), academic and ecclesiastical historian. See Lens, "Notice," pp. 32–33. Book 1 of this text is devoted to Gassendi and his anti-Peripatetic polemic.

[187] The publication history of this text is, typically, less than straightforward. It seems to have been first published in 1671 by Gabriel Gueret at the Hague in *La guerre des auteurs anciens et modernes*. It was known in manuscript to Mme. de Sevigné (*Letters*, September 6 and 20, 1671). Sometimes it was attributed to Boileau along with a companion piece that became better known, the *Arrêt burlesque*; but the authorship of this piece too is problematic. Louis Racine attributes it to Boileau, Bernier, and his father. See Lens, p. "Notice," 31; Sortais, *La philosophie*, t. 2, p. 189, n. 4.

[188] The edition of 1715 adds the Malebrancheans and Pourchotists. Pourchot (1651–1734) was a professor of philosophy and rector of the University of Paris who successfully insinuated Cartesianism into the curriculum there (See *Institutiones philosophie*, 1733), just when, as Bouillier points out, its decline was apparent elsewhere (*Histoire*, t. 2, p. 637.) The schools were once again a quarter-century out of date.

. . . the mathematicians [astronomers] should destroy their lenses as faulty and deceptive inventions . . . the air should again become lighter than a feather and the tubes of Pascal and Roberval and others who threaten the interests of the plenum, adversary of the void should be broken; all the beings of reason that fled to Ireland should be recalled and honorably reinstated at the University of Paris, . . . the brain should yield its title as source of nerves to the heart, the objections of Mme. Autopsy to the contrary notwithstanding; . . . Gassendi,[189] Descartes, Rohault,[190] [J.-B.] Denis, Cordemoy, Clerselier, de Launay and their adherents should be led to Athens, there to do public penance for their insults to Aristotle."[191]

The Jesuits meanwhile had carried their cause to a friendlier court and succeeded in having the king order his Conseil d'état to condemn Cartesianism and ban its being taught in the universities. The Oratory was most affected, particularly at the University of Angers, where, despite the genuine and heroic courage of certain individuals like Coquery and Bernard Lamy, at least lip-service had to be paid to the royal order. The situation was complex and various evasions were essayed,[192] but the final, binding, and inescapable order was issued on August 2, 1675. Even so, it took over three years before Sainte-Marthe wrote on behalf of the Oratory to reassure the king. His letter is of interest for its perception of what was at issue between Cartesianism and Aristotelianism. Sainte-Marthe promises that hereafter the following shall be taught: "1) that actual and exterior extension is not the essence of matter; 2) that in every natural body there is a substantial form really distinct from matter; 3) that there are real accidents absolutely inherent in their subjects which are really distinct from every other subject and which supernaturally can be without any subject; 4) that the soul is really present and joined to the whole body and to all the parts of the body; 5) that thought and knowledge are not the essence of the rational soul; 6) that there is no objection to God's being able to produce several worlds at the same time; 7) that the void is not impossible."[193] A curiosity here is that two and perhaps all of the last three were points of agreement between the Cartesians and Aristotelians against the Gassendists. This split may have been a symptom of the growing political tensions.

In 1680 one of the most important tracts in this struggle was published by the Jesuit Le Valois under the pseudonym of Louis de La Ville.[194] Le Valois attacked not only Descartes but also Bernier, whose view although "somewhat

---

[189] "who should be most roughly treated as the most criminal."

[190] Whose weekly conferences Bernier perhaps attended (see Lens, "Notice," p. 29, n. 2) and from whose *Traité* (also published in 1671) Bernier borrows textually when it agrees with his views.

[191] *Requeste*, pp. 6–9.

[192] Cf. the case of André Martin, chap. 2, sec. 6, below.

[193] Bayle, *Receuil*, p. 12; Cousin, *Fragments*, 3d ed., t. 2, pp. 204–5.

[194] *The views of Descartes concerning the essence and properties of bodies, contrary to the Church's doctrine and agreeing with the errors of Calvin on the subject of the Eucharist . . . .*

different from Descartes's was no less dangerous" (pp. 83–84). Sometime after this, Bernier wrote, had printed, and privately circulated an *Elucidation* of Le Valois's book, which was made public by Bayle in 1684 along with other related documents, including Malebranche's anonymous *Reply to La Ville*,[195] which along with the works of Le Valois and Bernier, according to Bayle, showed that Cartesianism was in fact incompatible with the Council of Trent's pronouncement on the Real Presence and that hence the latter must be rejected. As for Bernier, according to Bayle, "he allows the Cartesians to be treated as they may, and declares himself strongly opposed to certain of their doctrines in order the better to make his peace, since he had as many reasons as they to fear being accused of heresy on Transubstantion and did what he could to publicize his innocence."[196] Thus, while ten years previously Bernier was prepared to make common cause with the Cartesians, he now emphasized his differences from them as they had from him. (An additional impetus for Bernier may have come from his work on behalf of Gassendism in the interim, which will be discussed in some detail below.)

The question to which Bernier responds is whether it is theologically permissible to maintain with Descartes simply "that the essence of matter consists in extension," or with Gassendi "that to consider things according to the ordinary laws of nature, the essence of matter seems to consist in solidity, or impenetrability, from which extension necessarily follows." According to *both* views, extension is essential to matter. The difficulty for both is that transubstantiation would allow the extension of bread to remain; thus, extension must be something accidental to matter, that is, "a particular accident, or a certain little thing [*petite Entité*] that makes matter extended and that God by His infinite power might make subsist without matter."[197] Bernier's response to the difficulty exploits the hesitation in Gassendi's position, and emphasizes the distinction between philosophy and theology: As long as philosophers subscribe to what the Church Councils have actually said, it is better to leave them alone. And what Trent has said is that the appearances (*species*) of bread and wine remain after Consecration, which is a miraculous event that should easily be acceptable on the basis of faith. As for the Aristotelian account, would it or his own Gassendist account be more useful in explaining the mystery to the converts he met on his voyage to India?[198] Finally, to show that Le Valois ought not to have treated the Gassendists and Cartesians together, he closes with a catalogue of points on which Descartes differs from Gassendi and is open to objection. (1)"According to Descartes, everything is necessarily full and the void implies a contradiction." The result is that "the world must be eternal, lest before it was created there were empty spaces, that it must be immense or infinitely extended

---

[195] *Receuil*, pp. 91–126; *Oeuvres*, 17-1:506–31.

[196] *Avis au lecteur*.

[197] Bayle, *Receuil*, pp. 46–47.

[198] See chap. 2, below.

in all directions, lest beyond it there be any void, and finally that it must be independent of God, lest should He destroy the least part of it there be any void."[199] (2) Despite their behavior, animals are but senseless machines (a view that Bernier predicted would amaze posterity). (3) Descartes attempts to prove the existence of God, not from order, but from an alleged innate idea of Him. (4) Descartes and the Cartesians make natural causes only instruments or occasions for divine action, which philosophically is a deus ex machina and theologically makes God the author both of good and evil. (5) Descartes gives what we now would call a soft-determinist amount of freedom, which Bernier, perhaps confusing it with fatalist views he encountered in the East, calls the sponge of all religions, wiping them away. (6) The Cartesians with their cogito conclude that "not only is it easier to demonstrate that there are spiritual substances than that there are corporeal ones, but that it is doubtful whether there are any bodies in Nature and that it is even more probable there are not any and that everything is only mind."[200] Thus, although it is often enormously difficult to sort out Cartesian, Gassendist, and Aristotelian elements in the debates of the latter half of the seventeenth century, there are points at which the battle of the gods and giants is tolerably clear. That Bernier's text is one such point will become evident below.

[199] *Views of Descartes*, pp. 81–82.
[200] Ibid., p. 90.

CHAPTER II

The Giants of the Seventeenth Century

§5 DRAMATIS PERSONAE

Biographical, bibliographical, and analytical data on Descartes are either well-known or readily available. The same is true of Malebranche and even of the minor Cartesians. On the other side, Gassendi's situation in this regard has improved considerably in recent years,[1] but for his partisans there is nothing even remotely approaching, for example, Bouillier's work on the Cartesians. It will therefore be apposite, indeed unavoidable, here to discuss in some detail the lives, works, and doctrines of the giants in the latter half of the seventeenth century. What emerges is very much by way of contrast to their divine opponents: As both cause and effect of the Gassendist failure, their lives were from a scholarly point of view relatively more unusual, not to say bizarre; their works were more obscure and inaccessible; and the acuteness, sophistication, and relevance of their philosophical contributions varied far more widely. To put it another way, the lack of a Gassendist cast of characters heretofore, and the difficulty now in constructing one, are in fact illustrations of the thesis set out in the previous chapter about the historical and philosophical differences between the legacies of Descartes and Gassendi. Even so, there is a set of views that the followers of Gassendi defended, with exceedingly discrepant degrees of success, but which distinguished them from the Cartesians: empiricism and skepticism in theory of knowledge, nominalism and tychism as metaphysical views, hedonism in ethics, toleration and anti-authoritarianism in political theory.

Petit

Perhaps the earliest, vaguely Gassendist critique came from Pierre Petit of Montluçon.[2] In 1925 Cornelius de Waard brought to light two manuscripts that he identified as the remains of Petit's objections to Descartes's *Essays* (*Dis-*

---

[1] See esp. the works of Bloch, Jones, and Joy.

[2] 1598 (or 1594)–16?, of whom the biographer of Descartes, Baillet, said: "Petit had much genius for mathematics and excelled particularly in astronomy, and had a special interest in things the knowledge of which depended on experiments" (*Vie*, pt. 1, p. 324). He was employed by Richelieu as royal inspector of seaports; later he became Provincial Commissioner of Artillery and King's Engineer, Supervisor of Fortifications. Said Niceron: "Petit soon left [Fermat's] side to join Descartes's. Not content to become his friend, Petit became his follower and defender, and

course, *Dioptrics*, *Geometry*, and *Meteorology*), which Mersenne had solicited and, in two sections, sent to Descartes. Descartes's reaction to the initial package, Petit's objections to the *Dioptrics*, was moderate and tentative since Petit's work on refraction was not yet published (nor was it ever to be).[3] Those against the *Discourse*, communicated by Mersenne in May 1638, however, evoked Descartes's wrath: Petit was out only to cavort and raise groundless objections. "All he does is jump into a few rotten commonplaces, borrowed from atheists for the most part, that he indiscriminately accumulates, concentrating primarily on what I wrote about God and the soul, of which he has understood not a single word."[4] In the same letter he said that Petit had produced objections only to his metaphysics, an area where "the most ignorant can say many things which pass for probable among those who do not examine them very closely," whereas he hardly dealt with dioptrics, where his ability would be more obviously evaluated. He continued to rail against Petit, saying that he contradicts without understanding and that only the subject matter of God's existence prevents him from replying to Petit with ridicule,[5] that Petit's writings are "so impious that if he were in a country where the Inquisition were more severe, he would have grounds to fear its fires."[6] What could have provoked such a response from the father of modern philosophy?

Having "read each page of Descartes's work as many times as it had lines," Petit advanced a mélange of criticism based on crude empiricism, common sense, and very naive metaphysics. Against Descartes's proofs of the existence of God Petit argued that the idea of God may well be inherited from one's

---

Descartes learned with joy that Petit liked his metaphysics and that he declared himself entirely in favour of his views" (*Mémoires*, 43:187). As we now shall see, this must have occurred early on, or not at all.

[3] Petit complained that Descartes's analogies only explain his theories without proving them. What Petit wanted was an explanation of *why* refraction is proportional to impedance (p. 83). In particular he argued against the view that refraction is proportional to impedance resulting from the hardness of the refracting body: If hardness and weight result from the same cause, compression of parts, Petit thought his experiments with the specific gravity of transparent bodies upset Descartes's claims. In the end, of course, the hardness of a body is for Descartes a result of the common rest of its parts and their inertia, which he claims to have stated in the *Meteorology* (To Mersenne, March 31, 1638). But what we find there is an account of fluidity in terms of the shape of particles, which allows them to move more easily than those of hard bodies, which hook together (AT, 6:233–34).

[4] To Mersenne, May 27, 1638; AT, 2:124. The wells had been poisoned by Descartes's interpretation of an innocuous remark from Petit as an accusation of plagiarism from Kepler (To Mersenne, March 31, 1638). In fact, Descartes seems not to have understood Kepler's position with respect to the hyperbola as a solution to the anaclastic (de Waard, "Les objections," p. 84, n. 1) so the whole affair was a red herring.

[5] To Mersenne, June 29, 1638; AT, 2:191.

[6] July 27, 1638; AT, 2:266. Descartes also complained that Petit's own arguments for God's existence were "so loose that he seems to wish to mock God in writing them," that he would be as ashamed to take Petit seriously as to notice a dog bothering him in the street.

parents like the inclination "to enjoy war, music . . . and other things," and that the reports of missionaries show that to have the idea of a perfect being is not part of man's nature, while our own idea of God is easily accounted for by our early education.[7] He also questioned Descartes's claim that the proof of God's existence is as certain as any in geometry. In one sense, the existence of God is incomparably more certain than anything else. But this is not to say that its proof is as certain; otherwise everyone would agree about God's existence as they now do about certain propositions in geometry. Nor is it true that we can be certain of nothing without knowing the existence of God; all sorts of things can be and are known without the knowledge of God. "How does the evidence of this axiom, things equal to the same thing are equal to each other, depend on the supposition of God's existence; and the knowledge we have of the existence of the sun, the earth, and a thousand other things, does it too depend on it?"[8] To show that he is not opposed to all arguments, however, Petit sent some of his own proofs for the existence of God (concerning which he asked for Descartes's criticism). He thinks that since God has no cause, a priori arguments, which reason from cause to effect, are irrelevant and he thus turns to a posteriori arguments instead. Here Petit, whether intentionally or not, produces some hilarious bits. Because the earth's halves can only be alternately illuminated, each illumination is both preceded and followed by a finite period of time and hence the illumination of the earth is not eternal and must be attributed to the will of God. The same argument is illustrated by the ebb and flow of the tides, which if eternal would mean that "two eternities would precede each other by a short space of time."[9] The maritime theme (recall Petit's first occupation) is continued with the next argument, based on the sea's salinity, which, since it results from a mixture of earth and water, and since what is posterior by nature and in time to something else cannot be eternal, must be due to some first cause. The examples illustrate well the thrust of Petit's argument.[10]

Petit was a member of the Gassendist circle: He early mentions his friendship with Gassendi;[11] he conducts experiments on the pendulum with Mersenne and Gassendi;[12] Gassendi takes note of his observation of a lunar eclipse.[13] etc. In addition, it was Petit who introduced the young Pascal to the Torricelli baromet-

---

[7] De Waard, "Les objections," pp. 70–71.

[8] Ibid., p. 75.

[9] Ibid., p. 78.

[10] Petit has a couple more such arguments that we need not consider. He concludes, however, with a proof based on "an inner reasoning, quite detached from matter," which exhibits a soupçon of philosophical acuteness: It is possible for God to be; but if God were not, He would be impossible since as an infinite being He could not depend on another, nor could He precede Himself as His own cause.

[11] L'usage, preface.

[12] Huygens, Oeuvres, t. 2, p. 255.

[13] Opera, 4:302.

ric experiment on the void.[14] He also showed some dialectical skill in defense of the void.[15] To Pascal's objection that the plenum theorist might claim that the alleged void was filled with air penetrating the pores of the glass, he replied that such an explanation still leaves unexplained the level of mercury.[16] His care for experimental conditions, his imagination in building the apparatus, and his concern to get an accurate account of the results before interpreting them are much in keeping with Gassendi's attitude toward science. He seems to share with Gassendi an almost positivist aversion to metaphysical questions, encouraging dispute in physics as heuristically valuable, but despising questions about universals and individuation, for example, as vain and foolish.[17] And when he does land in nonempirical issues, for example, accounting for heat and cold in terms of specially shaped atoms, he qualifies his explanation as a useful analogy only: "This philosophy of atoms is quite useful although self-contradictory, shape and indivisibility of bodies being unable to subsist together either in physics or mathematics. . . . When a given cold body becomes warm mustn't the shapes of atoms change . . . they are thus neither naturally nor invariably fixed and indivisible with respect to shape, as they say, but chimerically and by analogy in order to explain their action."[18] But whether his early criticism of Descartes can be called Gassendist in any interesting or proper sense is a too-familiar question. However it may be decided, Petit later had a less debatable, intellectually more illustrious contribution that will be noticed below.

Launay

Although now almost entirely unknown, one of the two or three most important Gassendists was Gilles de Launay (1656–77), "counsellor, historiographer of the king and professor of philosophy."[19] His works include *Dissertation de la philosophie en general* (1668), of which a second edition incorporating only very slight changes later appeared as *Introduction à la philosophie* (1675); *Les essaies metaphysiques* (Paris, 1672); *Les essaies physiques* (1667); *La geographie aisee* (?); *La dialectique . . . contenant l'art de raisonner . . .*

[14] Pascal relates that he and Petit followed the description sent from Italy to Mersenne and confirmed it "point by point" (*Expériences*).

[15] He later said that these first experiments in France caused such a stir that it would take him a book to repeat all the arguments for and against the void that he received from the learned of Europe (*Dissertations*, pp. 137–38).

[16] *Observation*, p. 7.

[17] *Dissertations*, dedicatory epistle.

[18] *Dissertations*, pp. 49–50.

[19] *Extrait du privilege du roi. Essais metaphysiques*, p. 136. He should not in any case be confused, as he sometimes is, with Jean de Launoy, who of Gassendi said, "if Ramus, Litandus, Villonius and Clavius had taught in a similar way, what would have been done to them" (*Varia*, chap. 18).

(1673); and *La cosmographie aisée* (1677), a work I have not consulted but which contains the *Géographie* as a part. Finally, there is a curious work entitled *Nouveaux memories pour servir a l'histoire du cartesianisme* (1692), which premised that reports of Descartes's death in Sweden were false and that in fact he was yet to be found in the north teaching philosophy to the Laps. Its actual author was Huet, but it initially appeared bearing Launay's initials.[20] According to Urbain, "Huet, unable because of his dignity to sign his name to so frivolous a book, asked Launay to borrow his," who, according to Niceron, willingly lent it.[21]

Of his life we have only fragmentary clues. Perhaps among the most important is Locke's indication of his having paid in 1677 a Mr. de Launay with whom he lodged during the summer and fall of that year.[22] Arriving from the south of France on June 2, 1677, Locke moved into Launay's almost immediately. If (as is not unlikely) this is the same Launay then a plausible speculation is that Locke was put on to him by people in Montpellier.[23] In addition we know from a journal entry dated June 30, 1678, that Locke possessed copies of the *Essaies physiques*, the *Introduction*, the *Cosmographie*, and two copies, it seems, of one other work he attributed to Launay, *Essaies de logique* (Paris, 1675), which is perhaps the *Dialectique*.[24] But against the inviting supposition of Locke receiving philosophical instruction along with his lodging from Gilles de Launay we have the at least somewhat discomfirming evidence of the *Introduction*, which is dedicated to the Abbot de la Vrilière, just then named bishop of Uzès, and under the protection of whose house Launay says he had been living for fifteen years. Launay, like Gassendi and like Locke in 1677, seems more of a guest than a host. On the other hand, the reference of Launay's dedication may well have been only figurative, as is argued by the sufficiency of Launay's lodging to house an academy (see below). Also, it seems that his works were being sold from *chez l'auteur, rue Mazarin pres le College des Quatre Nations*.

The dedication of the *Dialectique* establishes another potentially important connection. This one is to Huet, who is clearly indicated as a one-time co-student of Launay; perhaps this is the office in which Tolmer, without citing his source, places them together at the Collège du Mont at Caen.[25]

The latest I have been able to trace Launay—and this without much authority—is sometime after 1710. The Bibliothèque Nationale collection R.6684–90 contains a copy of the *Géographie* at the end of which a handwritten note attributes the work to "Mr. de Launay qui professe la Philosophie en

---

[20] A second edition appeared in 1698 and a third, without the initials, in 1711.

[21] *Mémoires*, 41:62.

[22] Lough, *Locke's Travels*, pp. 150, 162, 179.

[23] See chap. 3.

[24] Bonno, *Les relations*, pp. 192, 208; also, Lough, "Locke's Reading."

[25] Tolmer, *Huet*, p. 674. In any case, Launay seems not to have been a member of the academy of physics that later flourished at Caen. Brown, *L'Académie*.

français au faubourg St. Germain." But the same hand also lists on the inside
cover of the collection the table of the other works, the latest of which is
Raphson's *Demonstratio de Deo* of 1710. The earliest I have been able to place
Launay, aside from the scholastic Huet connection, is 1656. According to
Lemaire, he began in that year to give conferences "on all the parts of philosophy to refute the principles of the vulgar philosophy of Aristotle and especially
Cartesian views, which he solidly combatted as contrary to common sense and
in ill accord with the Catholic religion."[26] In an unpublished letter of 1668
Launay thanked Oldenburg for having favorably received "[his] *Essais physiques* that Justel presented to you on [his] behalf" and said that a sequel "will
refute the views of the Cartesians."[27] He is said to have maintained a modified
form of Gassendi's philosophy. He also taught physics, politics, and history for
the benefit of those who were to counsel their sovereigns. Indeed, says
Lemaire, no public conference was attended by such a throng of persons of
letters and quality: French and foreign princes, archbishops, bishops, abbots,
and even several ladies of the court. To Launay's success we also have the
testimony of Bayle, who wrote to his older brother that Launay had for some
time been teaching the philosophy of Epicurus in conferences where his fluency
and eloquence were to be noted.[28]

In addition to giving conferences, Launay was active with the academies of
the period. Le Gallois not only places him among the throng in attendance at the
academy of the abbot Bourdelot, but among those fewer who held forth there.
And Lemaire tells of an academy formed chez Launay under the protection of
the Dauphin, which languished, however, due to the untimely departures of
certain of its members—of d'Aubignac to the next life, and of others to
bishoprics—and because jealous members of the French Academy succeeded
in preventing it from getting *lettres patentes* (which presumably would have
recognized it as a royal academy).[29] This no doubt is the body referred to by Le
Gallois as the well-known academy bearing the name of the Dauphin, which at
that point (1672) had already languished "due to I don't know what fate that
always opposes most of the greatest things."[30] In addition to Launay, whom he
identifies as a celebrated Gassendist and describes as "that great philosopher so

---

[26] *Paris*, 3:444.

[27] Archives of the Royal Society, L.5.117; cited by Bonno, *Les objections*, p. 63, n. 18. Four
years later Launay ended the *Essais metaphysiques* with the following comment: "I feel obliged to
advise the reader at the end of this metaphysics, or general science, before beginning the explanation of natural theology, that my aim here was only to abridge the general principles of this science
in order to make the other sciences intelligible, reserving several large and important metaphysical
dissertations on different matters, but especially to refute the Cartesians" (p. 136). It is not clear
whether Launay felt he had just refuted the Cartesians or was proposing to do so. The *Essais
metaphysiques* is certainly not a systematic attempt to do so and there was no later work published
on the topic. See below.

[28] *Oeuvres*, fol. 1, p. 49.

[29] Lemaire, *Paris*, p. 446.

[30] *Conversations*, p. 42.

renown for his conferences and his works, and even more so for the fine qualities with which his soul is endowed" (p. 48), Le Gallois lists as members the abbot d'Aubignac, Petit ("that Archimedes of our time"), Bailly, the abbot of St. Germain, Gueret and de Villiers ("famous lawyers"), and Vaumolière ("illustrious disciple of Pharamond").

The respective roles of Launay and d'Aubignac (1592 or 1604–73 or 1676)[31] in this academy are unclear, as the importance of each is supported by incompatible chronologies. D'Aubignac himself says that the conferences that he was petitioning to have recognized as a royal academy were two years in progress, thus, if the publication date of the *privilège* for his *Discours*[32] can be accepted,[33] in 1654, and before those of Launay began. This account, which would emphasize the role of d'Aubignac himself, is supported by Sallengre, who places him in attendance at the conferences of Bourdelot, L'Esclache, Rohault, Montmor, and Launay, and then says that "the emulation these sorts of heady assemblies produced among the highminded of his time led him to erect into a Royal Academy the one he had been holding *chez lui* for two years."[34] Sallengre claims, however, that this took place after he had published *Macarise*, which appeared only in 1664; and Sallengre's evidence is further weakened since there was of course no royal academy.

However responsibility for establishing the academy is assigned, we can at least account with some confidence for its characteristics, for it comprised an odd mélange, treating, according to Lemaire, "eloquence and physical experiments."[35] It is clear that d'Aubignac's primary concerns were literary, with a special devotion to theater; thus he is to be found disputing with Mlle. de Scudéry, with Ménange, and in a particularly bitter polemic, with Corneille. He then would have been the motor force in its rhetorical function, which was the subject of a monthly discourse in the Grande Salle of the Hotel de Matignon. Launay meanwhile would have overseen the physical experiments performed in a group each Saturday chez lui.[36]

[31] The circumstances of the "departure" of François Hedelin, the abbot d'Aubignac, from the academy are not certain. One version has it that he lost a suit as a result of which he was deprived of his pension, withdrew from society, and finally died (*Biog. Nouv. Gen.*). Sallengre (*Mémoires*, 1:284 ff.), however, claims that he received the pension, paid by the Grand Condé until his death. Niceron (*Mémoires*, 4:120 ff.) gives the most plausible account: After the death of the Duke de Fronlac (who had been his student and endowed him with a pension), Condé his sole heir at first refused to continue the pension and then did so only as a result of d'Aubignac's *Requète*. This episode, plus the Duke's death, left him with no taste for anything other than retirement to his *cabinet*, where until his death he received only similarly inclined friends.

[32] *Discours au roy sur l'etablissement d'une seconde Academie dans la Ville de Paris* (1664).

[33] As perhaps it cannot, since the *privilège* was valid for only five years, and the book appeared eight years later.

[34] *Mémoires*, 1:308.

[35] *Paris*, pp. 445–46.

[36] A final biographical note comes from A. J. George and relates to an episode referred to in passing in chapter 1 above: "Early in 1667 [Bourséis] had asked Colbert to admit to the [Académie des sciences] a number of theologians whose task would be to interpret and discuss the Bible. After

Classification as a Gassendist is no less problematic for Launay than for anyone else. He tells us that in defending Democritus and Epicurus he will follow Gassendi, "the celebrated and learned, the honor of France and our century." But he "reserves for himself the philosophical liberty of eliminating from [Gassendi] what appears useless, of making such alterations as seem to be improvements, and of adding some new experiments and observations."[37] By itself, such a program not only is consistent with Gassendism, but very much evidences its spirit. Launay faithfully enough adheres to the program as when, for example, he produces further arguments against an infinity of atoms. Whatever their merits as arguments, the contentions that an infinite number of atoms could never be extensively arranged into ordered worlds and that they would moreover completely fill the void thus making motion impossible are plausible extensions of Gassendi's rehabilitation of atomism.[38] There are other instances, however, in which Launay departs from Gassendi's views for non-Gassendist reasons, as when he says that atoms are of two sorts. Some atoms, are "round, igneous and luminous, [and] are in an actual perpetual motion, or a perpetual effort toward motion"; others are "angular or of a shape other than round and are either actually at rest or disposed toward it in order to make up natural things."[39] The reason for this additional kind of atom is so that there might be active and passive principles in the explanation of motion and rest. The passive principle in Gassendi's explanation is not a material principle, but the void.

By far the greatest complication in making out Launay as a Gassendist is his extraordinary eclecticism. His works are much shorter than Gassendi's but they are no less filled with references to classical authors. Thus, as with Gassendi there is a certain problem of digestibility. In addition, a bewildering variety of authors is drawn upon not only, as with Gassendi, as references for staging problems, but as authorities to support solutions. Epicurus, "that great genius of Greece," of course figures prominently; but so do many others, including (most destructively of the Gassendist cause) Aristotle. To take just one example, he argues in the *Metaphysical Essays*[40] that the principles of being in general are essence and existence, act and potency, genus and difference, and

---

some consideration the government agreed to the proposal and magnificently bestowed on those recently enrolled the title of Académie des langues orientales. Bourséis was named president, and under him were placed de Launay, Capelain, LeCoutelier, LaCroix, Derbelot and several others." ("Genesis," p. 395). But the Sorbonne complained to Colbert that "the interpretation of biblical texts should [not] be taken from its jurisdiction and placed within the reach of scientists and Protestants" (p. 396). The group was soon dismantled. It seems to me not unlikely that the Launay here referred to may well have been the Gassendist of interest to us.

[37] *Essais physiques*, preface.
[38] Ibid., p. 19.
[39] *Essais physiques*, p. 112.
[40] *Dissertation* 2, chap. 2.

subsistence (substance) and inherence (accidents). Nor, as we shall see, is this the only source on which Launay draws that is incompatible with Gassendism.

Launay is of course aware of his eclecticism, and he attempts to give a theoretical justification for it. He says he "always thought that all the opinions of the philosophers, and *a fortiori* those universally received, contain some good and that they can often enough be made to agree when favorably explained."[41] Thus even the vilified physics of Aristotle (because it is so general) can be made consistent with other, presumably modern systems. It was Epicurus, however, who explained more things more deeply than anyone else in physics, which is why "after having long examined which sect [he] would more freely embrace, he decided to follow his principles with the learned Gassendi when they conform to Christianity and morals." With a statement that to some extent belies his practice he continues: "My aim is nonetheless not to adhere to a particular doctrine of the philosophers, ancient or modern, because of their authority, but through the weight and strength of their reasons, and for the sincere love I have for embracing the truth and accepting in good faith from all sorts of authors, to seek it by various experiments."[42] Launay's constant appeal to classical sources is perhaps made consistent with this rejection of arguments *ad verecundiam* by what we may call his Golden Age Theory of the source of knowledge:[43] "Philosophy draws its origin and its nobility from God, who is its author and first master, because He is not only the principle of creatures, but the inexhaustible source of illumination and all other perfections they possess."[44] This knowledge was first infused into Adam—how else could he have dominated so many animals and disposed of so many things, even giving them their names? Through paternal love Adam communicated it to his descendants, who more or less faithfully transmit it. One result of this is that there is nothing new under the sun. Thus, there is a certain consistency above, since the truth of every claim, it would seem according to Launay, must be authorized by some author or other, but no author as such is an authority.

---

[41] *Essais physiques*, p. 5.

[42] Ibid.

[43] Roughly, the idea is that we never know as much as we once did. Horton, largely following Popper, takes the view to be characteristic of magical (versus scientific) worldviews. We have seen that Plato held the Golden Age Theory. Not surprisingly, Pythagoras subscribes to the view as well, at least according to Iamblichus: "[Pythagoras] entered the gymnasium, and being surrounded with a crowd of young men, he is said to have delivered an oration to them, in which he incited them to pay attention to their elders, evincing that in the world, in life, in cities, and in nature, that which has a precedency is more honorable than that which is consequent in time. As for instance, that the east is more honorable than the west; the morning than the evening; the beginning than the end; and generation than corruption. In a similar manner he observed, that natives were more honorable than strangers, and the leaders of colonies than the builders of cities: and universally Gods than daemons; daemons than demigods; and heroes than men. Of these likewise he observed, that the authors of generation are more honorable than their progeny" (*Pythagoras*, pp. 17–18).

[44] *Introduction*, p. 70.

There is another twist to this story in the case most of interest to us. Launay says that the Cartesian system can be novel, as its zealots maintain, only "by the quantity of chimerical suppositions thereby introduced which could never have entered the head of Adam or Solomon; but it is not novel with respect to the principles and the greater part of the conclusions—as we shall show when we one day disclose Descartes's thefts and prove that he only turned Epicurus's coat inside out to make believe he had a new one" (p. 74). Given Launay's clear espousal of the ancients in the Quarrel, the charge of old hat is an endorsement, however clumsy, from this supposed advocate of Gassendi.

Another result of Launay's Golden Age Theory is that knowledge is to be found among ancient pagan authors as well as among Christians. Indeed they recognize its heavenly source with their "mysterious fiction" of the birth of Minerva from the head of Jupiter. Thus, Launay effectively sustains a much broader program of rehabilitation than Gassendi's on behalf of Epicurus. The broader program had already been launched by such libertins as La Mothe Le Vayer, who debated the issue whether Socrates, for example, would be among the elect in heaven. This sort of simple-minded question of course was only the vehicle for arguing the relevance and worth of a whole range of literature outside of Scripture that was otherwise beyond the pale. At least on one level La Mothe Le Vayer argued only that some pagan authors were not beyond the pale; Launay supplies an argument that none need be. But there is also a twist to this advocacy of libertinage érudit. Though philosophy yields a perfect freedom, one of the absolutely necessary conditions for a good philosopher is the "guid-ance of a good teacher" (*conduite d'un bon maistre*) (p. 49). This makes sense since the primary aim of philosophy, though it is never stated as such, is to preserve not discover truth. Thus Launay claims that a good memory is neces-sary to the usefulness of all other philosophically relevant qualities of mind (pp. 49–51). The libertine model of rational inquiry as an open conversation among equals seems to give way to a kind of elitism; "as the Greeks said, not all men are allowed to go to Corinth" (p. 51). The contrast with Malebranche, for example, on the epistemic role of memory and history is stark. Given his views on the sufficiency of reason, Malebranche properly condemns "the studious . . . who use their memories more than their minds . . . [and who] admire those things furthest removed from us, the oldest things, those from the farthest or most unknown countries, and even the most obscure books."[45] Although he gives it a different twist to be discussed below, Malebranche accepts Descartes's doctrine announced at the outset of the *Discourse on Method* that we are all equally endowed with the self-sufficient ability to distinguish the true from the false. Despite their theoretical egalitarianism, however, these very Cartesians came to be regarded as the most dogmatic claimants of their own authority.

[45] *Search* 2.2.3.1; pp. 137–39. For the explanation of my Malebranche references, see "Note on Documentation."

In view of these contrasts, therefore, the most spectacular example of Launay's eclecticism is his expropriation of ideas that would have in fact appealed to Malebranche. For he held views very congenial with both components of Malebranche's theory of the vision of all things in God, namely, (1) the causal thesis that only God is a real cause and therefore only God can cause thoughts, and (2) the epistemological thesis that in knowing anything one knows God. As we shall see in chapter 4, the theory is at the core of Malebranche's thinking and thus Launay here typifies the Gassendists' failure, or refusal, to preserve their own doctrinal purity. Given my thesis about the overall failure of Gassendism, or the peculiar nature of its success, Launay's convergence on the two components of Malebranche's later theory bears investigation.

THE CAUSAL THESIS

Launay's analysis of causation is far from clear, but in reconstructed outline at least, it goes as follows. That there are causes should be evident to anyone not deprived of common sense, since creatures no more than anything else do not produce themselves. (That only God is without a cause, Launay just assumes.) "Cause in general is a principle which produces by its own force an effort different from itself and which depends on it for its existence."[46] Though the Aristotelian four causes may be distinguished, properly speaking only the efficient cause is the true cause, since the others in one way or another all depend on it. The efficient cause may be viewed as either "primary, eternal and independent, which is God creator, conserver and mover of all things, or secondary, created and dependent, which is the creature produced, conserved and moved by the primary in all its actions" (p. 102). Efficient causes are also divided into free and necessary. The necessary are those that are determined in the effects they produce; these are material things, which are essentially passive and incapable of moving themselves (p. 120). "All the different bodies composing the universe are, properly speaking, but the instruments of which God as the artisan and sovereign mover makes use to compose the harmony of the universe and thereby manifest His glory" (p. 105). Free causes are able to act or not, without constraint. These are God and all rational creatures, which are essentially active. Despite the essential activity of rational creatures, they no less than necessary causes depend on God's immediate concurrence in order to act. "For although God might have given them the sovereignty of their action, this has always been in conformity with their essential dependence on God, who willed to concur freely with them in the actions they would choose" (p. 116). Launay's account of this concurrence, however, is of a sort to be found in Descartes's *Meditations* 3. Creatures depend on it as much for their conserva-

---

[46] *Essais metaphysiques*, pp. 82–83.

tion as for their production, since "the conservation of a creature is but its perpetual production." Every creature is to God as light is to the sun, that is, perfectly dependent, and would fall back into nothingness if unconserved. The upshot seems to be that, as Launay has defined the notion, only God is a true cause, though as close as he gets to saying just this is his claim that only God has the power to move corporeal beings.[47] His text is unhelpful as to where Launay gets this account, or more important, what the arguments for it might be. It would appear in any case that he did not draw on the Cartesians, whom he criticizes for claiming that matter moves itself on occasion of certain thoughts.[48] But this is an inapposite criticism that would not have put off Malebranche, for example.

THE EPISTEMOLOGICAL THESIS

Launay does not recognize exemplary causes different from the efficient cause, but he raises the topic in order to discuss his theory of ideas. It is a theory that is unique in that the primary foundation for it is purposive action. The argument is that according to Providence, we have dominion over the rest of the universe; but in order to exercise that dominion we must have knowledge of its contents, for which ideas are the only means available since we cannot otherwise know what is outside us. (We shall return in chapter 5 to the argument for the crucial premise that what is outside the mind cannot be known.) The account of ideas is typically eclectic, incorporating an intentional species that while corporeal does not diminish the object producing it; these material images of sensation enter the understanding intelligibly and reduce its potency to act. Explaining how this is done is "the greatest difficulty in animastics" (p. 65). Although the mind's object is immaterial, it resembles the material image in sensation "with respect to representation," the way two statues of different material can represent the same thing. Launay's view, then, is imagist in a way that, as I shall later try to show, Locke's view is. "As long as our soul is in our body it will conceive nothing except by reduction to images of the phantasy" (p. 66). His citation of Paul at this point, *we see now through a glass darkly*, suggests that images are

---

[47] Ibid., p. 113. Furthermore, God is absolutely unconstrained in His action, as is argued by the constant possibility of gratuitous miracles. God is not "some fictitious Jupiter, slave to the fatal necessity of destiny," but, when He wishes to show His glory, He can "establish, continue, interrupt and change nature's course according to His good pleasure" (*Essais physiques*, p. 104). Such a view of course argues radical empiricism, for only through experience can we know what will happen. (For this argument with respect to Charleton, see Osler, "Descartes and Charleton." For its connection with skepticism in the period, see Lennon, "Jansenism.") On the other hand, if miracles are determined by a calculus of divine attributes, then the whole of nature is knowable a priori, at least in principle if not by us. This is an issue on which Malebranche tended to equivocate (Lennon, *Commentary*, esp. p. 824).

[48] *Essais metaphysiques* p. 123.

the appearances of things, whose essence is hidden from us—a view also suggested by Locke.

Launay models his theory of human ideas on a theory of divine ideas. His language is worth quoting at length: "He who would plumb the noble and sublime matter of ideas must consider God as the creator of the universe, in which He has enclosed that great multitude of different creatures that His omnipotence drew from non-being as so many portraits or living images of His divinity, to enable the mind of man to represent to itself in thousands and thousands of ways the infinite perfections that are in Him as the ideas or originals of all creatures" (pp. 59–60). "Objects are the portraits or the living images of the divinity, or better, of the divine Ideas that must be conceived as the noble originals that God contains in the simplicity and perfection of His essence, and that He has imitated in the production of His creatures" (pp. 67–68). All things, whether actually existent or only possible, are represented in God, "because knowing Himself perfectly, He knows the exemplary cause of all things; yet God must not be said to derive His ideas from the creatures He knows, for being simplicity and plenitude itself, He can receive nothing" (p. 70). God knows His divine nature not only as it is in itself, but also "insofar as it can be represented in a different manner by all the creatures He produces as the different portraits of His divinity" (pp. 76–77). "He knows the cause of things' existence and their singularity in His will, the cause of their essence in His ideas" (p. 77). All this is very close to what Malebranche would later hold, except that Launay's theory is a vision of God in all things, not as we shall see it to be for Malebranche, a vision of all things in God. By itself, Launay's Pauline conception is not very extraordinary; what is extraordinary is the Neo-Platonic interpretation given it by a supposed Gassendist.

Given an eclecticism that draws on both Aristotle and the Neo-Platonic tradition, it is not surprising to find Launay's support for nominalism less than straightforward. An indication of his nominalism is that he subscribes to what has been called the localization pattern: To be is to be in some place. "It is inconceivable to the human mind that a being should exist and not be in any place; for everything that is in itself must be somewhere."[49] This is sufficient for the rejection at least of Platonic universals, but, despite chapter 1 above, it is, as we shall see, neither sufficient nor necessary for the claim that only individuals exist.

Another indication of nominalism is the way in which Launay seems to individuate corporeal things. Each portion of matter is "arranged in such a way that all individuals of the same essence have neither the same quantity of matter nor the same arrangement of it"; thus there is no need for the form that empty-headed metaphysicians superadd to matter to account for numerical differ-

---

[49] *Essais physiques*, p. 103.

ences. We might add, however, that the fact that no two things have any same property is *at best* a necessary condition for nominalism, for it may well be contingently true that no two things exemplify the same universal and yet all their qualities may nonetheless be universals.

Launay raises the topic of universals explicitly in his *Dialectic* under the heading of "the universal in general."[50] It is a question that he regards as tortuously complex and thorny, the result of whose treatment will not justify the labor to answer it (p. 67). To neglect in its favour the more important questions of physics, for example, is to leave the roses and gather the thorns. He does, however, mention some benefits, sufficient, apparently, to justify his own treatment: Universals will prevent us from thinking that things separated must be dissimilar; they provide a basis for definition by genus and essential difference; and they are the "principles and the object of the sciences because single things are known [as such] only by experience," and being infinite, can be known only through general notions (pp. 68–70). Of the several senses of universal (in cause, in subject, in significance), the one deserving of attention is its etymological sense. Here three things are involved: "the name expressing several things, the idea representing several things, and the nature which is in several things" (p. 72). The Stoics were the first overtly to combat the last item and have been followed by Nominalists after Ockham, but these are "philosophers in name only," whose theory misses the mark. The universal is the essence "of singular things, it is the object of science, it is necessary, etc., which cannot be said of words or conceptions [alone]" (pp. 73–74). Thus we are not surprised to find that Launay turns to Plato's theory, "one of Philosophy's loveliest views." "What is true and good in this theory so long banished from the Schools is that these Platonic ideas are universal causes to the extent that God makes use of them as divine originals that this great Architect of the universe imitated in producing His creatures, which are copies of them" (pp. 76–77). But Plato's theory is problematic for theological reasons, so Launay comes finally to his own view (he is astonished that the question has raised such controversy): "Who does not evidently know that everything in nature is singular and produced by singular actions? Thus, as the universal is opposed to the singular, it can only be the production of the mind, which unites singular things, insofar as they are alike, under a general idea which rids them of their singularity" (p. 79). The "matter" of the universal is thus the individuals under it, and its "form" is the union given them by the mind, which is the answer to the scholastic dispute of whether the universal is a product of nature or the mind (pp. 78–80). One wonders just how this view differs from that of the despised nominalists.

The empiricism one looks for in connection with nominalism is to be found in Launay's "maxims of a logician." The fourth of them, "contested by the Carte-

---

[50] *Dissertation* 3, chap. 1.

sians [is] that as long as the soul is joined to the body, it does not know anything except through the ministry of the senses, internal and external." And he cites the classic formula: "the understanding which is a white paper, or a blank tablet, can have no natural ideas."[51] His fifth maxim, "dependent on the fourth, establishes for us that ideas that do not pass through the senses are formed from those that do so directly" (p. 56). This is done through (1) composition, (2) division or abstraction, (3) ampliation or diminution, (4) translation and proportion or resemblance. All this would look promising as an empiricist theory had not Launay previously told us that the soul produces ideas as a painter does pictures of things he wishes to represent. We shall return to Launay's theory of perception in chapter 5 below.

The skepticism one also looks for in connection with nominalism is rather less in evidence. There seem to be some things that in principle cannot be known. For example, the size of the created world is beyond our means of measurement since parallax cannot be detected even for Jupiter and Saturn, much less for the stars. Our dominion, and therefore our knowledge, is restricted to our immediate environment, and with respect to the rest of the world the only appropriate attitude is one of humble acceptance of our ignorance. "It has always sufficed for man, who is as small a part of the earth as the earth is of the world, to have used its diameter as a scale or ladder [eschelle] to climb to the planets in order to measure their size and distance. If this ladder is now too short to go any farther, this should inform man of his own baseness and of the weakness of his mind. . . . He will thereby understand that the world is larger than he can imagine, which will give him more veneration for the works of God's hand."[52]

On the other hand, Launay defines physics as "the science of natural things, i.e. a certain and evident knowledge of all the corporeal creatures composing this great universe."[53] Philosophy is "a certain and evident knowledge of things human and divine . . . its certainty comes from infallible principles . . . and its evidence comes from the fact that we must be convinced by the light of reason and sense experience of the truths it makes known to us."[54] In addition, the principles of all the particular sciences are demonstratively proved by a single metaphysical principle that is self-evident and received by all men of common sense.[55] "Of all the things in the world, the first, most general and easiest to know is being; for he who does not know being does not know anything" (p.

---

[51] *Dialectique*, pp. 49–50. See also pp. 53–56, where he argues against the innatist theory of the Port-Royal *Logic*.

[52] *Essais physiques*, pp. 32–38. See also his arguments against Plato and Cicero on the shape of the world (p. 35).

[53] Ibid., p. 1.

[54] *Introduction*, p. 6.

[55] *Essais metaphysiques*, p. 4. However, "philosophers are in great disagreement as to what this principle is" (p. 27).

13). Being cannot be abstracted from; whatever is conceived is conceived as being. Hence the infallible knowledge in which all other knowledge is based is, according to Launay, that being is. Perhaps this view can be retrieved from triviality, but not along Gassendist lines, for according to Launay nonbeing is inconceivable. It is neither true nor intelligible.[56] Alas, this places him on the side of Malebranche and the Cartesians against Locke and the Gassendists with respect to a fundamental metaphysical issue.

A final topic on which Launay's nominalism is both more consistently Gassendist and philosophically more promising is that of truth. Following Gassendi he denies the distinction between essence and existence, even in the case of God. The argument is a bit hazy but seems to be that the supposition of either without the other involves a contradiction. To talk of essence is to say that there exists something of a certain kind and to talk of existence is to say that some (kind of) thing exists. The result is that all essences (but God's) are created and no truths (but those about God) are eternal, although some truths are necessary in that they are independent of time, place, and circumstance. As later for Locke, truth for Launay is of two kinds. Truth of the thing, or metaphysical truth, is the conformity of a thing with its essential principles. In this sense a thing cannot fail to be true, otherwise it would be something else. This is the only sense in which essences are necessary, invariable, and indivisible.[57] This might also be the notion Launay had in mind for his primary metaphysical principle above. A second kind of truth is truth of the sign or logical truth. This is the conformity of the sign with the thing signified, namely, of writing with speech, of speech with thought, and of thought with the object it represents.[58] Presumably these connections are logically all matters of convention, which suggests the intriguing possibility of a Humpty-Dumpty theory of intentionality, namely, that ideas or thoughts mean or are about whatever we want them to mean or be about. Cognitive intention is a species of volitional intention rather than the usual converse.

François Bernier

François Bernier (1620–88)[59] is nowadays the best-known of the Gassendists and was best-known in his own time, even if not primarily as a Gassendist. For he was better known as a traveler. During 1647–50 he traveled through Poland, Germany, and Italy, and in 1656 he embarked upon a thirteen-year journey to

[56] Ibid., pp. 13–14. See also *Dialectique*, p. 43. The first maxim of a logician is to know that the human mind cannot conceive anything "unless it exists as a true being, and consequently that nothingness, the impossible, and all that is not, cannot be known."

[57] *Essais metaphysiques*, pp. 130–32.

[58] Ibid., p. 130.

[59] Lens, "Notice."

the Middle East and then to the Indian subcontinent. His extraordinary experiences during a ten-year stay there are detailed in his *Memoires . . . of the Grand Mogul's Empire*, an enormously popular work that earned Bernier the nickname of "Mogul." The work was regarded as a standard reference work well into the nineteenth century and went through many editions; Dryden based his *Aureng-Zebe* (apparently performed in 1675 and published the following year) on the first of them (1671). Locke, as we shall see, was very interested in the work, taking notes from the original French that are not without philosophical interest. Among others of Bernier's travels was a trip in 1685 to England at the invitation of Saint-Evremond, and to Holland, where he met Pierre Bayle.

Bernier came to know Gassendi personally through Chapelle, whose philosophy lessons from Gassendi in 1642 Bernier shared with such notables as Cyrano de Begerac and perhaps Molière.[60] He also attended Gassendi's lectures on astronomy at the Collège Royal, where he himself eventually did some teaching. In the nasty battle with the astrologer J.-B. Morin it was principally Bernier who took up the Gassendist cause, not without some danger to himself, since Morin had connections in high enough places to seek letters of cachet and excommunication for his adversary. Bernier took a medical degree from Montpellier in 1652 and as physician and friend attended Gassendi during the physical decline of his last years. He is supposed to have closed Gassendi's eyes upon his death. A few months later he left for his famous trip east.

An important aspect of Bernier's career more difficult to pin down is his role in the literary circles through which he moved upon his return. No doubt he was sought after; not only had he been to the most unusual places but he cut an attractive figure. It is hard to find biographical data on Bernier that does not repeat Saint-Evremond's description of him to Ninon de Lenclos as the "pretty philosopher" (*joli philosophe*) because of his physique, bearing, presence, and conversation. He is presumed to have continued relations with Gassendi's old free-thinking circle, for such little time as remained to them, of people like Patin (d. 1670) and La Mothe Le Vayer (d. 1672) and more important with the younger generation of people like Molière and La Fontaine. It would be interesting to know the extent to which Bernier might have facilitated the propagation of hedonism among them, for example, with arguments or suggestions of arguments based on relativity of moral values.[61]

---

[60] *Lettre à monsieur Chapelain*, p. 136. Cf. Lens, "Notice," p. 1.

[61] Said Saint-Evremond, again writing to Ninon de Lenclos, "Bernier, speaking of the mortification of the senses, once said to me, 'I am going to confide in you what I would not to Madame de la Sablière, or even to Mademoiselle de Lenclos and what I yet take to be of a superior order—I shall tell you in confidence that the abstinence from pleasures seems to me a great sin.' I was surprised by the novelty of his system" (Saint-Evremond, *Oeuvres*, 5:321). Against this, however, must be weighed, among other things, Bernier's remonstrations with Chapelle that he "give up that [presumably dissolute] life so displeasing to [his] friends and return to philosophy" (*Lettre envoyée de Chiras*, June 10, 1668).

To Bernier's considerable role in the political battles with the Aristotelians we have already drawn attention. We have also seen the limited extent to which Bernier was prepared to join forces with the Cartesians. For Bernier seems not to have lost sight of the anti-Cartesian polemic of the Gassendists, even while in the East, where he was able to follow events to some extent. Chapelain, for example, wrote to him of the publication in translation of Descartes's *Treatise on Man* (1662), regretting Gassendi's having died; for Cartesianism had many adherents, he said, despite its view that the body is a machine, which he thought to be inconsistent with the immortality of the soul. Bernier while still in the East wrote to Chapelle, setting out his position in the anti-Cartesian debates. According to Bernier, (1) the infinite divisibility of matter was "absurd and unworthy of a philosopher"; (2) bodies are hard, resistant, and impenetrable— properties as essential to matter as extension; (3) through "the concourse, order and particular disposition of these atoms" even so complicated an item as the human body could be formed—"provided that there intervened a directive cause that was sufficiently intelligent"; (4) the sect of Democritus and Epicurus, supposing Providence for them, is able to explain more, and to explain better than all others (pp. 14–26). What cannot be explained solely in terms of atoms, and what leads him "to believe that there is in us something more perfect than everything we call body or matter" (p. 14), are mental operations. Not only are the senses struck (like the eyes of a statue), but we "sense their impressions . . . and are even aware that we sense them."[62] Human consciousness alone defeats what might be called crude (or eliminative) materialism.

Bernier is the most important Gassendist in the sense that he did most to disseminate Gassendi's views. Not just in the latter part of the seventeenth century, but ever since, Gassendi's *Syntagma* has been known to many only through Bernier's account of it in the *Abrégé*. Bernier tells us that his aim was to present an abridgment of Gassendi's philosophy, drawn "not only from his books, but also from the source itself, and from the very frequent conversations he had with him."[63] Bernier's hope was to defend Gassendi against those on the one hand who would make him a mere follower of Democritus and Epicurus, or on the other who would see him as a mere historian or philosophical skeptic. Bernier's initial defense, however, seems only to emphasize the alleged distortions. He tells us that Gassendi made use of all previous philosophers only to draw from them what is best, yet because of our limited vision of first principles and of immediate and proximate causes, Gassendi avoided the presumption of

---

[62] Ibid., p. 33. Other kinds of mental operations that cannot be explained mechanistically are inferences, memory, and introspection. In addition, we go beyond particular impressions, in some unspecified way, "to form the ideas of a thousand things not falling immediately or fully complete as they do under the senses" (pp. 36–37). Finally, human freedom introduces an element of indeterminism beyond mechanical explanation (p. 50).

[63] *Abrégé*, 1674, *au lecteur*; unpaginated. One wonders what source other than Gassendi's books and conversation Bernier may be referring to.

passing beyond what only seems to be the case. As we shall see, this is by no means the only or the most serious instance of Bernier undermining the position he is trying to defend.

The history of the publication and composition of the *Abrégé* is rather complicated.[64] One volume of it appeared in 1674 (hereafter: proto-*Abrégé*) and again, identically except for the title page, in 1675. The first full edition appeared in 1678 in seven volumes. A second edition, "reviewed and augmented by the author," also in seven volumes, appeared in 1684. There are many differences between the two editions (hereafter: *Abrégé* 1 and *Abrégé* 2). There are stylistic changes of no philosophical importance. There are changes in the ordering of the material, some minor, but at least one major. Volume 1 of *Abrégé* 2, on logic, appeared as volume 3 of *Abrégé* 1; volume 2, on metaphysics, and which also contains a set of *Doubts* appeared as volume 2 of *Abrégé* 1; volume 3, on qualities and generation and corruption, and which also contains the *Elucidation of de La Ville's Book*, appeared as volume 1 of *Abrégé* 1.[65] Furthermore, there are important differences in emphasis, one of which (the account of space) I have detailed below. It would seem that Bayle's remark[66] that Bernier's work will dispense us from leafing through Gassendi's huge tomes turns out *not* to be true.[67]

The key to Bernier's treatment of Gassendi's philosophy at this stage is a more rigorous application of Gassendi's own nominalism than Gassendi himself had provided. I think it explains some of the alterations in the *Abrégé*, most important the change in emphasis in the analysis of space. More clearly, nominalism is the key to the doubts Bernier was led to concerning the very material he was abridging.

In 1682 Bernier published his *Doubts about some of the main chapters of the Abrégé*. These doubts were occasioned by a review of the *Abrégé* undertaken by Bernier before translating it into Latin "for the benefit of teachers and foreigners." This translation, which was never completed, would thus have been a curious work consisting either of a retranslation of Gassendi (or perhaps more plausibly the *verba ipsissima*) with Bernier's ordering, condensation, and emphasis. Bernier's skepticism provoked by this project concerned not the faithfulness of his account, but the acceptability of what he had given an account of. His new doubts do not affect the basis of Gassendi's system, "for I do not think that one can reasonably philosophize on any system other than that of atoms and the void." Indeed, the last of the eleven doubts that he publishes is less a worry about, than a reaffirmation of atomism. Quoting Sextus and Lucretius he presents the traditional atomist argument that motion without the void

---

[64] For even more details, see Lennon and Bloch, *Ueberwegs*.

[65] The rest of the volumes follow the same order: (4) astronomy, (5) terrestrial things, (6) psychology, (7) ethics.

[66] To his older brother, June 24, 1675.

[67] As Bernier himself insisted it would not (*Abrégé* 1, vol. 1, *au lecteur*; unpaginated).

is impossible due to resistance on every side. Against the (presumably Cartesian) theory of vortices as an attempt to rebut this argument Bernier retorts that
this theory (1) ignores the question of how motion can be initiated, (2) would
account only for the motion of solid rings and not for free motion like that of a
bird in flight, and (3) does not explain why motion is deflected into a circle.[68]

Despite his disclaimer, Bernier's doubts (especially since they come from
him) do grave damage to the cause of Gassendi's philosophy. He raises substantive questions concerning Gassendi's views on space, time, motion, collision,
and other important topics; presumably because neither Gassendi nor even he
himself has the truth on these topics, he solicits the views of the learned on
them. He claims two purposes. The first is to evidence the poverty of all
philosophy: "I have been philosophizing for more than thirty years and yet here
I am beginning to doubt." The second is to give a general idea of Gassendi's
philosophy, "which after all seems to me the easiest, simplest, most sensible
and most reasonable of all."[69] Whether or not Bernier intended it as such, the
second point can hardly be construed as anything but a proof of the first. In
addition, the wells were poisoned for *Abrégé* 2. Bernier's doubts on space,
place, time, and eternity appear along with the text of what with very minor
stylistic alterations became the chapters on those topics in *Abrégé* 2.

Bernier published a second set of doubts, under the same title, at the end of
the second volume of *Abrégé* 2.[70] These *Doubts* 2 are introduced by a letter to
Mme. de la Sablière in which he emphasizes the reservations he had expressed
in his earlier *Doubts* 1.[71] Now, even worse than doubting the things of which he
had been convinced, he "doubts no longer, having despaired of being able ever
to understand any of them." Immaterial substance, weight, thought, sensation
are all behind the door Nature has closed to us. Even so, philosophy, and
especially that of Gassendi, does reveal enough for us to improve our lot, most
of all by raising us to the ethical ideal expressed by Horace that we should be
amazed by nothing.[72]

Bernier's doubt concerning time is a good example of Gassendist nominalism leading him to reject an important thesis of Gassendi. Rejecting the ontological constraint of late Aristotelian Scholasticism, Gassendi had argued that
beyond the categories of substance and accident we need to recognize two kinds
of extension that are "beings in their own fashion." One is space, "an incor-

---

[68] That this is (or may be) the only way motion is possible short of an infinite displacement for
each motion Bernier seems to regard as just ad hoc.

[69] *Au lecteur*; unpaginated.

[70] This volume contains Gassendi's metaphysics and corresponds to the first volume of *Abrégé* 1.

[71] In one sense Bernier's attitude toward skepticism remains perfectly consistent, namely, that
one should doubt just to the extent that it is appropriate to do so. Thus in 1668 he is able to warn
Chapelle against a gratuitous attitude of "perhaps this is so, perhaps it is not" (*Lettré envoyeé de
Chiras*, p. 5).

[72] Nil admirari prope res est una, Numici,/ Solaque quae possit facere, & servare Beatum
(*Doubts* 2, p. 382; *Epistles*, bk. 1, ep. 6).

poreal and immobile extension in which it is possible to designate length, width, and depth so that every object might have its place." We shall be returning to the Gassendist analysis of space at great length below. The other is time, "an incorporeal fluid extension in which it is possible to designate the past, present and future so that every object might have its time."[73] For Bernier these two categories of space and time represented an ontological extravagance and in their place he proposed an analysis more in keeping with the Gassendist commitment to nominalism. "Everything that exists has some duration, whether great or small; nothing can be generated or perish in a moment, or be produced and destroyed at the same time—that is as repugnant as that a thing should be and not be; consequently, duration must be considered as an essential mode, inseparable from whatever is."[74] The upshot is that there is no real difference between a thing's existence and its duration (to know one is to know the other) and presumably because of this, nothing is better known than duration, which cannot be defined without futility. But as one extension can be measured by another, so the duration of a thing can be measured by the duration of some motion. Hence there is no reason to suppose Gassendi's flux. The measure of duration Bernier calls time: "Time is nothing but some duration determined by motion, which to the extent that it is known and evident, or considered such, can serve as a measure for knowing with precision other durations less well known."[75] A single and immobile existent would thus have duration but would not be in time. Nor can we say, according to Bernier, that "its duration would be long or short, and that this could not be without time. For that it should be such or such in itself does not depend on time, just as that a thing should be of such or such a length does not depend on any measure by which it can be measured. What nonetheless cannot be denied, and what we maintain, is that the duration of this thing would be such that it could have corresponded to finite times, if it has not always been, or to infinite times, if it is supposed always to have been, like God."[76]

In *Doubts* 2 Bernier returned to the notion of a potential time with a long argument in response to the following objection. Suppose God destroyed the world and then reproduced it, but not immediately; between His destroying and re-creating the world, time must have flowed. The objection of course begs the question, the same question Bernier begs in replying that since there was nothing in the interval, nothing could have flowed. That is, the objection assumes that there must be time independent of existents in order for there to be the temporal interval, and Bernier just denies Gassendi's view that time must be distinguished from the world as indestructible. To the objection that, contrary to the supposition, annihilation and recreation would thus immediately follow,

---

[73] *Opera*, 1:220a; *Selected Works*, p. 391.

[74] *Doubts* 1, pp. 108–9.

[75] Ibid., p. 114. "[Time] can only be some arbitrary duration determined by" (*Doubts* 2, p. 458).

[76] *Doubts* 1, pp. 115–16.

Bernier retorts that while there were none, there could have been other events between them. Thus, God's existence is later said to be eternal or infinite, not in the sense that it has been from infinite times—before the world there was no motion and hence no time—but in the sense that had there been infinite times it would have corresponded to them.

Now, it might appear that Bernier here unwittingly reintroduces, if not Gassendi's flux, at least absolute time as God's duration. Certainly the parallel moves were made by others of regarding absolute space as the divine immensity and absolute time as the divine sempeternity. But I think this is not Bernier's move. Instead, just as time is the measure of duration or existence, so potential time is the measure of potential existence. Both are arbitrary in the sense that no measure is privileged. If we choose a certain measure we can say that a certain time has elapsed between annihilation and creation; but some other measure can always be chosen. Bernier considers the objection that just so many events such as the vibration of a pendulum could have taken place, which therefore must be grounded in some flux.[77] His reply that God's duration in the interval is such that it could correspond to such events again suggests an absolute time. But this is to say that, were there to be such events, God would exist at the same time. And this is true of the infinite number of events that could occur between any two others, depending on the measure that is selected.[78]

The problem with Gassendi's flux as Bernier comes to see it is that ontologically it is just plain weird. Time, according to Gassendi, is "a being that can be found nowhere, a being which is neither substance nor accident, nor is capable of any action, a being which is composed of parts which are not, i.e. the past, which is no longer, the present which has never before been able to be nor will ever again be able to be—a strange kind of being! In a word, . . . a being which is in the imagination alone."[79] It seems to me that the point of all Bernier's doubts about time is that it is unintelligible to distinguish it as ontologically something other than the individual things said to be in it. To make this distinction is to treat it as an *abstract entity*, which is how he puts the matter at the outset of his next *doubt* by way of summary of his criticism: "We have rejected time taken abstractly as a certain perpetual and uniform flux independent of every being, motion and rest."[80] His view, I think, is that temporal qualities, like all others, are nothing more than the things that are said to have those qualities insofar as they are considered in a certain way. (For example, a thing is said to be a foot long for Bernier insofar as it measures up to a certain bar in London.) Bernier does not tell us what the temporal way of considering

---

[77] *Doubts* 2, pp. 460–61.

[78] Bernier is not at his very best on this particular point, for he also replies that during the possible pendulum vibrations God might just wait, waiting being a notion with which we are perfectly familiar without reference to any flux.

[79] *Doubts* 2, p. 457.

[80] Ibid., p. 463.

things is, except perhaps by indicating that it is done operationally. The important point would be that the difference, for example, between measuring things spatially and temporally is a difference in what we *do*, not in *what* we measure (although differences between our actions must also be understood operationally). This is to say that things in themselves are not in space or time, and have no qualities at all. Bernier does not arrive at saying this himself, but others of his views, on space and atoms for example, also show him on the way to it.[81]

In making the point that time is "nothing abstract or separated from the motion of bodies," Bernier quotes Lucretius:

> Tempus item per se non est—
> Nec per se quemquam tempus sentire fatendum'st
> Semotum ab rerum motu, placidaque quiete.[82]

But he could as well have cited Descartes, for whom also there is no real distinction between a thing and its duration.[83] "Duration is the mode under which we conceive a thing in so far as it continues to exist, just as order or number are not different from the things that are ordered and numbered but only modes under which we consider these things." And time, as for Bernier, is "a way in which we think" about the duration of things, namely, with respect to some arbitrarily selected regular notion.[84] The difference between them is that what endures for Descartes is something that has an essential property, either thought or extension, which from the nominalist perspective are but ways of considering things that are bare. This is a difference that, as it were, makes all the difference in the world. As we shall eventually see, it is perhaps the deepest issue on which Locke joins company with the Gassendists against the Cartesian gods.

Bernier's nominalism also clearly emerges in his treatment of quantity of motion. *Doubts* 1 sets out three laws of collision. An atom (1) colliding with another at rest in the pure void and thus without resistance carries it with the same motion; (2) colliding with another, invincibly fixed atom stops against it; (3) colliding with another of less than absolute resistance loses its motion to the extent of the resistance and carries it. *Doubts* 2 adds a fourth: Bodies colliding

---

[81] Cf. Plato's assertion in *Theaetetus* (157a) that Protagoras held "that nothing was anything in itself Absolutely, but was always made so to something else, and Essence or Being was to be removed from every thing" (quoted in Cudworth, *Mortality*, p. 39). "Nothing *is* one thing just by itself, but is always in process of becoming for someone, and being is to be ruled out all together" (Cornford, *Plato's Theory*, pp. 47–48). Bernier's is a continuation of the dialectic according to which man is the measure of all things, and what seems to be, is. Especially with his own concern over abstract entities, Berkeley is very much the heir to this tradition.

[82] *Doubts* 2, pp. 457–58. "Likewise time does not exist in itself . . . Nor should it be allowed that anyone senses time apart from the quiet rest and motion of things" (*De rerum natura* 1, 462–63).

[83] *Principles* 1, 62.

[84] Ibid., 55, 57.

with equal but contrary speeds (the case of Descartes's famous first rule) each lose their motion.[85] To the objection that his laws of collision allow for absolute loss of motion Bernier replies that he sees no "absolute necessity that there should always be in the world the same quantity of motion, as if motion were some absolute thing, some substance, some being which could be destroyed only by annihilation."[86] Motion is rather a mode and there is no more reason why it should be constant than that any mode such as curvature should be constant. Alteration in the quantity of motion would mean that there are irregularities in nature, but that is just what we find in the diversity of successive seasons, for example, no two of which are alike with respect to temperature, plants, or insects. Nor is it the case (as Gassendi thought) that motion is an essential and inamissable property of atoms, which in fact require only solidity and extension, and which can thus be indifferent to motion and rest. He grants that many objects apparently at complete rest like molten metal must have extraordinary motion in their parts, but that an atom of marble should have a motion more rapid than the sun's light, "this is in truth a thing, very difficult to believe."[87] For this reason, that is, that atoms should have inamissable motion, the notion of *nisus* was introduced; but this "has always seemed to me a pure defeat and a useless remedy to resolve the difficulty": It is incomprehensible how a body should make an effort and not be in motion or how if at rest it should set itself in motion. Both motion and rest are but modes and are retained by a thing as long as it is unaffected by some other thing. "An atom, you will say, begins to move with a certain force, vigor, energy or inclination to motion natural to it. I hear words, I hear different terms, but I do not understand that in an absolutely simple body, such as an atom is supposed to be, this force, vigor, energy and inclination can be anything else but motion itself."[88]

The problem as Bernier sees it is that motion, which is only a mode, has been abstracted and construed as an entity in itself. In addition to reinforcing the groundless view that the quantity of motion must be constant, it leads to the false view that the degree of slowness of motion depends on intervals of rest. The latter view is dispelled by treating motion and rest like straightness and curvedness. The varying degrees of the curvedness of a stick, for example, are not conceived as produced by more or less straightness interspersed along it. Motion, like curvature, is continuous. To the objection that continuous motions must be equivalent, he replies that it is "of the essence of body, however small it may be, to have length, breadth and depth, an anterior, middle and posterior; as it is the essence of time, however small it too may be, to be successive; that

---

[85] *Doubts* 1, pp. 82–85; *Doubts* 2, pp. 417–18. Bernier mentions no way of determining speed or motion.

[86] *Doubts* 2, p. 432.

[87] For after all, "philosophy is nothing but reasoning about insensible and unknown things by analogy and relation to things which are larger, more sensible, and better known" (pp. 435, 437).

[88] Ibid., pp. 438–39.

being so, it is certain that this difficulty concerns only those who compose the continuum with [mathematical] points and time with mathematical instants, and not those who like us recognize only physical instants and points; so that I answer in a word that while the slow mobile is continuously and successively passing through a physical point, the mobile which is twice as fast, likewise moving successively, continually and without stopping, will pass through a whole one, and so on for the others."[89] Whatever its merit as an answer to the difficulty, Bernier's reply once again involves a clear rejection of abstract entities.

Jean Chapelain

In a work dealing with philosophical influences the case of Jean Chapelain (1595–1674) is particularly interesting. As Chapelain himself clearly realized, he was not in the first rank of those even in the Montmor group. Yet this "impassioned Gassendist"[90] was important because of his energy, his influence, his reputation, his apparently indefatigable interest in all the work of those around him, his service as Huygen's major-domo in Paris, and especially because of his correspondence with leading lights elsewhere.[91]

Chapelain was in the first instance a poet and a man of letters. He was among the first members of the Académie française, was favored by Mazarin and Richelieu, was much sought after as a teacher and advisor (in 1662, for example, he was prevailed upon by Colbert to draw up a list of those literati who were to receive royal pensions). In the formation of the Académie des sciences the role of Chapelain was second to none. Whatever his exact role, Chapelain was clearly very influential in the early days of the *Journal des Sçavants*. Yet on the basis of his written remains it is difficult to justify the position he enjoyed. His major literary effort, a poem about Joan of Arc, was an epic failure, colossally ridiculed by Boileau among others. With respect to the actual practice of science Chapelain seems to have been an amateur in the later rather than the earlier sense of the term. Yet, however puzzling its basis, Chapelain's influence was exercised clearly and over a long period on behalf of Gassendi and contrary to Cartesianism.

Chapelain was a persistent source for Gassendi of praise, encouragement, and constructive criticism.[92] As early as 1633 we find him urging Gassendi to

---

[89] Ibid., pp. 78–79.

[90] Collas, *Jean Chapelain*, p. 329.

[91] As we have already seen, it was Chapelain who was in correspondence with Bernier in the East. The combination of attributes above seems to have suited Chapelain for his collaboration with Denis de Sallo, editor of the *Journal des Sçavants* (see Guy Patin to Falconet, March 20, 1665; *Lettres*, 3:517.

[92] A portrait of Gassendi hung in his study (George, "Jean Chapelain," p. 219). But one of Malebranche does in mine!

return to Paris. At Chapelain's insistence Gassendi undertook his biography of Copernicus, which he dedicated to Chapelain (as he did the expanded version, which included the lives of Brahe, Puerbach, and Mueller). Chapelain was also concerned around 1640 about, and with, the project of rehabilitating Epicurus, specifically the question of whether atoms could plausibly be conceived as the cause of motion.[93]

Chapelain was generally suspicious of intellectual authorities and critical of dogmatism, which he associated with Cartesianism in a way that was typical of many in the period. In a letter to Huet on April 6, 1665, he celebrates the anatomical experiments of Steno, who was able "to compel the Descartists, those obdurate dogmatists, to recognize their patriarch's error concerning the [pineal] gland and its use."[94] Chapelain's skepticism tended toward the fideism often associated with it in this period. A good indication of this is his letter to Balzac (November 18, 1640): "I think none are more temerarious than the dogmatists, nor more wise than the skeptics, and with so much to doubt, I find nothing more appropriate than doubt and irresolution because if in uncertainty we do not enrich our soul with fine knowledge, we at least do not sully it with false opinions and remain always in a state to receive without resistance true illumination."[95] This is the idea, familiar enough in the period, that the soul stripped of the vain pretensions of reason is in a fit state to receive the grace of religious faith.[96]

Finally, manuscript material discussed by Chapelain's last biographer indicates that his interest in scientific matters was very much along Gassendist lines. In a letter to Huygens on April 24, 1662, he attempts to account for hydrostatic effects in terms of atomic properties. In another manuscript, either read at or in some way connected with the *conférences* then in vogue, perhaps the Montmor group, Chapelain discusses the question of rarefaction and condensation, which he attempts to account for along Democritean lines of greater and lesser interstices of void, arguing that any other account would violate the commonsense truths that no place can be occupied by two bodies nor can any body occupy two places.[97]

---

[93] Spink, *French Free-thought*, pp. 87–88.

[94] Quoted in Collas, *Jean Chapelain*, pp. 336–37. There is testimony from the period of Chapelain's perceived anti-Cartesianism: "[Chapelain] knew history, literature and philosophy. That of his dear friend Gassendi thoroughly delighted him; but he thundered mightily against Descartes's, on which he had perhaps not sufficiently meditated due to his former attachment" (Vigneue Marville [Bonaventure d'Argonne], *Mélanges d'histoire et de littérature recueillis* [Rotterdam, 1700]; quoted by George, "Jean Chapelain," p. 219). I am inclined to agree with this (chagrined) judgment of Chapelain's understanding of Cartesianism.

[95] Quoted in Collas, pp. *Jean Chapelain*, 61–63.

[96] Thus it is not surprising to find that in the contest between the Jesuits and Port-Royal, Chapelain, despite some friends among the former, really sympathized with the latter. For the connection between skepticism and Port-Royal, see my "Jansenism."

[97] N.a.fr., 1887 fol. 317; f.fr.12847. See Collas, *Jean Chapelain*, pp. 330ff; letter of July 20, 1661 to Huygens relating the Montmor experiment against subtle matter; quoted by George, "Jean Chapelain," p. 218.

Antoine Menjot

Aside perhaps from the formation of the Académie des sciences, it is extremely difficult at this point to determine with any precision or certainty the success of Gassendism due to Chapelain. A very similar case is that of Antoine Menjot (1615–96), who was known in the period as "attached to the views of Gassendi."[98] Menjot, uncle of Mme. de la Sablière, was a Calvinist until the Revocation of the Edict of Nantes, but despite this near life-long handicap succeeded because of his skill in medicine in moving from the faculty at Montpellier to becoming a royal physician. He seems to have published only medical texts, one of which was the occasion for Bayle's description of him as a very illustrious writer.[99] His *Opuscules posthumes* appeared in 1697,[100] a work consisting of letters and discourses on a variety of topics, primarily theological and philosophical. His work was read and admired by Pascal[101] and Cureau, with whom he exchanged work, at least in his case for criticism before publication.[102] He was widely enough known to have been offered a chair of medicine at Leiden (pp. 60–61). It is hard to say just what his Gassendism would have been. Nor do we know what his influence might have been, since it was primarily oral. Given his position, it could have been significant. What comes across most clearly in the few philosophical remains is his strong anti-Cartesianism.

In a letter to a friend, impossible to date, he criticizes Descartes's physics, discussing four questions from a recognizable Gassendist perspective. The first is the infinite divisibility of matter, which he thinks the Cartesians hold to be actual and not just mental; "this erroneous view derives from the fact that extension is falsely posited as the principle of divisibility" (p. 155), whereas divisibility in fact results from composition of separable parts. Thus a body without composition, such as the atoms of Democritus, "could not be split naturally." The second question concerns the void. Here he argues the unlikelihood of the particles of subtle matter having just the appropriate shape to fill the voids created by their rapid motion, "unless God by His Providence is of assistance, so that instead of, as according to the ancient philosophy, nature abhorring the void, today God opposes it and remedies it as sworn protector of the newly imagined laws of Cartesianism" (pp. 156–57). Then, in an example endlessly debated in the period, he supposes the divine omnipotence to withdraw all the air from a room, which would then be crushed; but "no one would have the temerity to assert that it implies a contradiction that God should be able

98 Jovy, *Antoine Menjot*, p. 97.

99 *Nouvelles de la République des Lettres*, February 1687, art. 6, in *Oeuvres diverses*, 1:756.

100 According to its anonymous editor, at the direction of Menjot. According to Bayle, however, the manuscripts were found in Menjot's office upon his death and clearly were not intended for publication (letter to Du Bos, October 21, 1696; OD, 4:724).

101 Jovy, *Antoine Menjot*, p. 11ff.

102 *Opuscules*, letter to Bazin, pp. 137–38.

to support the walls against the impulse of the air outside, however violent it may be, such that it is impossible for the room to remain void." We shall return to this example at some length in the third section below.

The third question deals, not very effectively, with the Cartesian conception of light as only a sensation. Against it, he argues (1) that contrary to Scripture light could then have been produced only on the sixth day, when men were produced; (2) (in a badly misdirected argument) that some beings, cats, and certain people, have eyes that are themselves luminous; and (3) that pressure against the retina can produce the sensation only of pressure; on the Cartesian theory we should be able to make a man see light just by striking his fingers, since all it regards as important is that the pressure should reach the brain (pp. 157–60). (This result is, alas, precisely the one Descartes had claimed *on behalf of* his theory in the *Optics*.[103])

Menjot's skepticism appears with the fourth question, the mechanical account of bestial animation. His main contention is that the Cartesians have no way of disproving any number of alternative accounts, for example, a corporeal soul with awareness that can approach reasoning. "Surely God in nature, which is His ordinary power[104] has His mysteries, . . . and a part of the true science consists in the confession of our ignorance concerning many natural effects over which it has pleased their Author to draw a veil with the intention of combatting our excessive curiosity or our presumption, so that in Physics as well as in theology, it is better to stay sanely sober and not lose our minds to drunkenness."[105]

Menjot's letter to David Puerari (1621–92; professor of philosophy at Geneva), which can be dated some time after the appearance of Rohault's *Traité de physique* (1671), is anti-Cartesian in a more ad hominem fashion. Descartes invented his subtle matter "only to oppose the tiny voids of Epicurus defended by Gassendi and by this means to become the head of a party instead of resting content to be a disciple of that great man, a role in which many learned people of our century feel honored."[106] Menjot regards it as "the height of temerity to believe that Descartes has unveiled nature with his system."[107] Its accounts of hunger and thirst in animals cause laughter, according to Menjot, who regrets the unavailability of Rabelais to deal with this system. It is primarily Cartesian dogmatism to which he objects, for people both defend and attack Cartesianism with exaggeration. "As for me, I consider [Descartes's views] as games of the mind, and I rank them among those ingenious things which, if not true, are well hit upon. The late Pascal called the Cartesian philosophy the Tale of nature [*Roman de la nature*], roughly like the story of Don Quixote, and yet since that

[103] AT, 6:131.
[104] Menjot's note: cf. Scaliger.
[105] Menjot's note: cf. Paul.
[106] *Opuscules*, p. 119.
[107] Ibid., p. 120.

time his colleagues, the *messieurs* of Port-Royal, have decided to adopt it.[108] It used to be only the pedantic Peripatetics who were sworn upholders of Aristotle's physics; but today certain new Cartesian partisans have arisen who defend all the visions of their sect with an invincible obstinacy. Gassendi, who ought to be regarded as the head of modern philosophers, is known by few people, because his works are too long and we live in an age of laziness where people want to become learned in a flash with hardly any studying. Yet no one can deny that Descartes took from them the foundation, and as it were, the cornerstone of his physics, namely, that all the phenomena of nature depend on certain shapes, and on certain motions of imperceptible corpuscles" (pp. 115–16).

Finally, in a letter to Huet he criticizes the blasphemy of occasionalism (which makes God responsible for criminal acts), the invisible soul as better known than palpable bodies, and the evasion of the indefinite between the finite and the infinite (pp. 136–46). He also lodges a complaint against what he takes to be the lunacy of the Cartesian method of doubt, which is an occasion for Menjot to evidence his empiricism. "Hippocrates includes among the infallible signs of madness the belief that one perceives objects that are not presented to our senses, or not noticing those that are" (p. 139).

Marin Cureau de La Chambre

Marin Cureau de La Chambre (1596?–1669?) was a curiously elusive and yet important figure in the period. He functioned principally as physician to the Chancellor Seguier and also attended both Louis XIII and Louis XIV. He saw Mazarin weekly and enjoyed the support of Richelieu, who in 1635 had him installed in the Académie française, and whose eulogy he later delivered there. He was among the first to write on scientific matters (of a sort) in the vernacular; thus his *New thoughts on the causes of light, the flooding of the Nile* (which he attributed to the rarefaction of nitre in its waters) *and Love by inclination* (1634). He was known most widely for his *Characteristics of the Passions*, which appeared in five volumes from 1640 to 1662. Said Balzac after the appearance of volume 2 of this work (1645), which he says he studied for fifteen full days, "Never has man known the equal of you . . . it might be said without saying too much that you are the philosopher in chief."[109]

---

[108] See also Menjot's letter to Huet (ibid., pp. 145–46), which alleges the Jansenists to have adopted Cartesianism only to cross the Jesuits.

[109] To Cureau, September 15, 1643 (*Oeuvres*, 1:538–40). The letter is beyond hyperbole in its praise, claiming that Aristotle himself would be jealous of Cureau's achievement. Many people praised Cureau's style, including Bayle (*Dictionnaire*, art. Rorarius, n. D).

Some of the literature has tried to make Cureau out to be a Gassendist,[110] though he as much as anyone resists the label.[111] Even so, Cureau clearly advances important positions with respect to three related issues—the extension of the human soul, representationalism, and the bestial soul—in a way that proved to be influential in the anti-Cartesian debates. I shall discuss the significance of his representationalism in chapter 5. Here I shall give a brief indication of his role in the bestial soul debates and then turn at greater length to the issue of the extended human soul.

As we shall see in chapter 6, hardly any Cartesian view captured the popular philosophical imagination more than the conception of animals as unthinking automata. Debate raged around it. The occasion for Cureau's involvement was a contribution from Pierre Chanet (1603?–before 1658?), a Calvinist physician of La Rochelle, about whom very little is known.[112] In his *Considerations* (1643) Chanet anonymously attacked Charron, and Montaigne implicitly, for associating men and animals so closely that both have immortal souls or neither do. Cureau in turn attacked Chanet, without naming him, in *Quelle est la connoissance* (1645), to which Chanet responded with *De l'instinct* (1646), thus prompting Cureau's *Connoissance des animaux* (1648), in which he claims never to have heard of Chanet before *De l'instinct*, thus necessitating Chanet's *Esclaircissement* (1648). As might be gathered, these exchanges were not of great interest. Nor can they be construed as a Cartesian-Gassendist debate. In the very first work, for example, Chanet argued that the senses are much more reliable than the skeptics allowed and in any case are the source of all knowledge. He also insisted upon the knowability and utility of final causes. Even so, Cureau's arguments that animals are sentient were very important in a broad attack on the Cartesian position.

As to Cureau's view of the extended human soul, book 5 of his *System of the Soul (Systeme de l'ame)*[113] is devoted to "the extension, parts, shape and size of

---

[110] Sortais, *La philosophie*, t. 2, p. 183: "La Chambre was readily inspired by the ideas and principles of Gassendi."

[111] The only lengthy biography of Cureau notes that he was criticized by Sorbière and Patin in very unflattering terms (Kerviler, *Marin*, pp. 16, 61) and provides little evidence for Gassendist connections beyond attendance at Mme. de Sablé's (though not frequently enough for her liking [ibid., pp. 85–86]) and a testimonial from Chapelain (pp. 89–90). On the other hand, there is still less basis for the Cartesian connections Balz attempted to make. Certainly Cureau himself would have been surprised at any such connection given just his espousal of skepticism, for example. Though his *Systeme de l'ame* contains the most extraordinary metaphysical speculation, Cureau begins the work "ingenuously confessing that he had only conjectures and hunches to give" (p. 3) In his polemic on the bestial soul he allows himself happy to be classed with Charron and Montaigne (*Connoissance des animaux*, p. 16) and he says later that he "is from conjecture-country" (*L'art*, pt. 3, p. 129).

[112] Patin's letter to Spon, August 17, 1643, in which Chanet is highly praised, is about all we know of him.

[113] Nothing is straightforward with these people. The *Systeme*, a work of 523 pages *in quarto*, is, without indication, the second part of the three-part *L'art de connoistre les hommes* (1657, 1666).

the soul." He has a number of arguments for the soul's extension. One is that only if the soul is extended can it be limited, which it must be by contrast with God. "Every created substance, of whatever order it may be, is limited, because only God is immense and without limits. Now, everything limited must necessarily have an extension, for whoever says that a thing is limited says that it has extremities and these cannot be conceived without there being an extension terminated by them" (p. 338). He distinguishes this extension from corporeal quantity, which makes things impenetrable.[114]

Another argument for the soul's extension is that without it the soul would be just a point; but no point is simultaneously in two separated places, as the soul must be, since it is in all parts of the body (p. 343). In addition, "God is immense because His extension is infinite." Thus, while extension is necessary for limits, it is not sufficient, for God is not limited, yet extended. Cureau's position in fact seems to be that extension is a condition for any kind of being: To be is to be somewhere. This is the localization pattern, noted above in discussing Launay, that typifies the materialism of the giants.[115]

It may well be that at bottom Cureau's concern in these passages is with the issue of individuation. Recall, for example, that spiritual extension is said to "measure" things. The argument with which he concludes his chapter on the extension of the soul seems to explain what he means by this: "If it were of the essence of quantity in general to be corporeal, all of its species would be corporeal, because everything of the essence of the genus is in all its species. Thus number, which is one of its principal species, could not be in intellectual substances without making them corporeal. Yet it is certain that number is a quantity found in spirits, and ten angels make a number as real as . . . ten trees or ten stones."[116] That is, unless nonmaterial things were quantified by extension, there would be no numerical distinctions between them because spatial locations would be confused. This analytic geometry of individuation is complicated, however, by the very feature that distinguishes spiritual extension, namely, its penetrability. Since the soul has extension it has parts;[117] and since

---

[114] "There are two sorts of extension and continuous quantity. One is physical and categorical; the other is metaphysical and transcendent. The first, called quantitative in the schools, makes things impenetrable. The second, called entitative, measures the entity of things and allows penetration" (pp. 341–42). Physical extension is required so that the relation among bodies might be maintained and that the organs of sensation might function properly. Without it there would be confusion in both things and the representation of them. Later, Cureau complicates things still further by distinguishing two sorts of entitative extension, material and immaterial (*L'art*, pt. 3, p. 116). See below.

[115] This may be the basis for the Parisian Pierre Petit's complaint that Cureau's argument commits a *petitio*. See below. Cureau's reply to Petit in any case leaves no doubt that for him God is extended (*L'art*, pt. 3, pp. 35ff).

[116] *Systeme*, pp. 355–56.

[117] He calls these "virtual or assignable" parts as opposed to "real," because the soul is divisible only in imagination, not really. He is not definite as to why the soul is indivisible: "either because its

the whole body is animated, all its parts are united with parts of the soul; but not all parts of the soul are united with parts of it—some are "free." This is because although its shape is ill-defined and changing like that of air or liquid, the soul has a fixed extension (all souls in fact are of the same size); but the extension of the body changes, as when children grow up. These free parts are the basis for the soul's immortality and its intellectual functions. But if they are extended, where are these parts? Cureau's answer is that they are within the body along with the soul's other parts. This is possible due to the penetrability of spiritual extension not only by matter, but by other parts of itself.[118] This makes the sense of its extension problematic; it also means that not even material things are individuated by their spatial location.

It was the *Systeme* that occasioned Pierre Petit's *On the extension of the soul and incorporeal things (De extensione. . .)* (1665). Not to be confused with Pierre Petit of Montluçon, the early Gassendist critic of Descartes, this Pierre Petit (1617–87) was a Parisian physician whose degree was from the university at Montpellier—surprisingly in light of the other names associated with this institution (Bernier, Locke, Régis, and others). Petit of Paris was a staunch defender of Aristotle, who criticized the view that the soul is extended, arguing among other things that if the soul were extended it would not know as it does unextended things.[119] More generally, Petit of Paris attacked the claims of Gassendi and others that to be is to be somewhere, that therefore God is extended, that there are imaginary spaces beyond the world, and so on.[120] This attack led Petit of Montluçon to compose, and publish,[121] his *Letter* to Cureau, urging him to respond to the attack. Petit of Montluçon says that in most metaphysical questions he is a skeptic "until sensible and palpable experience determine [him] to what [he] can no longer deny."[122] He himself is convinced that to be is to be somewhere, for unless a thing is finite, shaped, and limited by the place it occupies, it would be infinite—a truth he takes to be as evident as any his mind has ever comprehended. Montluçon seems to flirt with materialism, claiming that it is nowhere condemned by the Church Fathers or Councils.

---

nature would be destroyed if it could be divided or because there is nothing capable of dividing it" (pp. 351–52).

[118] The bottles may differ, but the genies are all of the same size. It turns out, however, that the soul's extension is greater than that even of elephants' souls (p. 386).

[119] To this Cureau replied that the soul indeed has an unextended *faculty*, but that it does not thereby follow that the soul is extended (*L'art*, pt. 3, pp. 71–73). The soul knows the infinite without being infinite and the universal while being particular. Its species may be extended, but the soul acts on them, compounding, dividing, and abstracting, and thus is able to know things other than as they are first presented to it.

[120] See esp. bk. 1, chaps. 10–12.

[121] Motivated no doubt by the wish to distinguish himself from the author of the attack, a problem for him on a previous occasion that he describes.

[122] *Lettre*, p. 7.

In addition, he springs to the personal defense of Gassendi against what he regards as calumnies in another of Petit of Paris's works, against Vossius. Most notably, he produced the testimonial to free-thinking cited in our first chapter above. Given Cureau's inclinations to publish and to engage in polemic, the urging of the *Lettre* may not have been necessary for him to respond, which he did in any case, quickly and at length. [123] He too springs to the personal defense of Gassendi, taking exception to Petit of Paris's "outrageous words" about him (preface). "He takes Gassendi for a dullard and a fool; and, to the indignation of all those who knew this man, admirable for his knowledge and wisdom, he says that his arguments are worthy of the filth and rubbish heap of Epicurus" (p. 52).

In 1666 Louis de La Forge appears to have replied on behalf of the Cartesians to Cureau's exploitation of the localization pattern. Cureau is not named, but it is clearly his views that are criticized: "I realize that two objections will unfailingly be raised against me; the first, that to be in a place is an attribute of created being as well as to be at a certain time, and thus that what is in no place is not at all. The second, that the mind is finite and cannot be everywhere, hence that even if it were not joined to a body, or even if there were no body in the world, the mind would no less necessarily correspond to a certain determinate part of God's immensity, by reason of which it would be true to say that it occupies a certain place." [124] La Forge thinks the first objection is easily met, for it rests on the common prejudice of conceiving all being in the manner of corporeal extended being, a prejudice that is rejected by Clauberg and Plato, and Porphyry between them, and that is refuted by his own proof that the mind is unextended. The second "more considerable" objection has an answer to each of its two parts: (1) the mind, though finite, is not a quantity, hence need not be limited in space; (2) though the mind, like every creature, corresponds to a part of the divine immensity, that immensity is not any kind of extension but only His omnipotence, by which He is "present to all things," and the sense in which it might be maintained that each thing occupies a part of His immensity is that no thing is "capable of exhausting the fecundity of His omnipotence, and not, as is usually done, by considering His immensity as imaginary spaces." [125]

Six years later, in another reply to a view whose source is unnamed but clear enough, Launay defended the localization pattern against La Forge. "The infinity of divine perfections and of His omnipotence is not this infinity of extension or His immensity," which is a limitless tridimensional magnitude. [126] "It is one thing to be most perfect in nature and in power, and another to be extended everywhere infinitely, which is immensity. . . . Just as one can readily con-

---

[123] *La deffense de l'extension et des parties libres de l'ame* is a 305-page work that appeared in 1666 as the third part of *L'art de connôitre les hommes*. I suspect that *Le systeme de l'ame* became the second part only at this point.

[124] *Traité*, pp. 201–2.

[125] Ibid., p. 203.

[126] *Essais physiques*, p. 102.

ceive that a drop of milk is very white and sweet without having the extension necessary to fill a large vase, so will we conceive that the Divine essence is very perfect and infinitely powerful without conceiving that it is immense, and that it fills every kind of place and space."[127] Even aside from the hopeless analogy, however, Launay's reply is misleading. As we shall see, an important argument for Launay based on the localization pattern requires a cause to be where it acts, so that immensity is at least a condition for omnipotence.

Finally, to return to Cureau by way of conclusion, his theories of light, however fantastic, are noteworthy as vaguely atomistic criticisms of the Cartesian theory. In his work called *Light* (*La lumiere* [1657]), he objects that Descartes's theory has no evidence for it, and that it supposes things "which besides being difficult to admit do not agree with the phenomena of light," for example, that light is but a sensation without correspondence to the truth of the object "and would not be if there were no eyes" (p. 175). In these matters Cureau is an empiricist: Only if we allow ourselves to be led by the senses can we get around difficulties raised by the nature of light.[128] Furthermore, if light were transmitted by means of the subtle matter that Descartes supposes, it would have to be firm like the stick Descartes uses to illustrate its transmission. But light is not firm and the motion communicated along it is from one particle to another, thus involving "a true locomotion which can never be instantaneous" (p. 178). That Cureau rejects the Cartesian identification of matter and extension that requires instantaneous propagation of light is clear also from his account of transparency, which he thinks varies inversely with weight and thus has the same cause, namely, quantity of matter in relation to volume.[129] Though he calls it a quality, Cureau in fact treats light as a substance, since while "attached" to the luminous body, it is yet independent of both that body and, especially, the bodies through which it passes. In fact, in this as well as its indivisible extension, light is not unlike spiritual substances (p. 194).

The upshot is that while not classifiable among the Gassendists except in a loose sense, Cureau was of great value to them in their anti-Cartesian campaigns. Only a fraction of his significance has been noted above. Even in the ontological importance that he attached to spatiality, for example, the localization pattern tells only part of the story. In chapter 5, we shall see that how one interprets spatiality requirements determines the two patterns separating the gods and giants with respect to the analysis of ideas, and that in this interpretation Cureau has more than a minor role to play.

---

[127] Ibid., p. 103.

[128] Ibid., p. 48—particularly the sense of vision, "which is the surest and most faithful that philosophy can have in its most subtle researches."

[129] Ibid., pp. 67ff. The transparency of heavy bodies such as glass is also partly due to their structure.

Walter Charleton

A fair amount is known and available about Walter Charleton (1620–1707).[130] He was a student of John Wilkins at Oxford. Wilkins was later to figure prominently in the Invisible College of Robert Boyle in London, became Warden (1648–59) at Wadham College, Oxford, and played a role in the founding of the Royal Society. Wilkins undoubtedly predisposed, if not actually introduced, Charleton to the new philosophies. He received an M.D. in 1643 and practiced medicine, prominently if without distinction, for most of the rest of his life. He was one of the first members elected to the Royal Society. He published a great deal, on a variety of topics, most celebratedly a theory about Stonehenge. The first of his publications (1650) shows him caught up in Helmontian animistic hermeticism,[131] but by 1652 his sympathies clearly had shifted to the new mechanical philosophy, particularly that of Gassendi.[132] In *The Darkness of Atheism Dispelled by the Light of Nature: A physico-theological treatise* Charleton enlisted his efforts in the attempt to rehabilitate Epicurean atomism. Two years later he published the *Physiologia Epicuro-Gassendo-Charletonia, Or a Fabrick of Science Natural, Upon the Hypothesis of Atoms, founded by Epicurus, repaired by Petrus Gassendus, augmented by Walter Charleton.*

By his own testimony Charleton is not a Gassendist. At the outset of the *Physiologia* he divides philosophers into four classes. (1) Those whom he calls the Female Sect "because as women constantly retain their best affection for those who untied their Virgin Zone; so these will never be alienated from immoderately affecting those Authors who had the Maiden head of their minds" (p. 2). Among these philosophically faithful wives figure most prominently the Aristotelians, but also the Scotists, Lullists, and Paracelsists. (2) Those "whose brests being filled with true Promethean fire, and their minds of a more generous temper, scorn to submit to the dishonourable tyranny of the Usurper, Authority, and will admit of no Monarchy in Philosophy, besides that of Truth." To this "Order of the Assertors of Philosophical liberty" belong Brahe, Kepler, Galileo, Scheiner, Kircher, Harvey, and, "the Epitome of all," Descartes (p. 3). (3) Those who "addict [*sic*] themselves to research the Moniments of the

---

[130] For further biographical information on the period of his life most of interest here, see Sharp, Kargon (introd. to *Physiologia*), and Osler.]

[131] See Gelbart, " 'Charleton."

[132] Little is known about the crucial period 1650–52 in Charleton's life. The literature speculates on various possible influences on Charleton: Hobbes, the Newcastle Circle, Evelyn, or Digby as correspondents in France, or a trip to France (Kargon, *Epicurean Atomism*, p. xvi; Sharp, "Early Life," pp. 324–26). I do not see why Charleton could not have been led to Gassendi as Malebranche was to Descartes, just by picking up his book, in this case the *Animadversiones*, published in 1649.

Ancients and to dig for truth in the rubish of the Grecian Patriarchs." These "Renovators" (and their renovations), include Ficino (Plato), Copernicus (Aristarchus), Lucretius (Empedocles), Magnen (Democritus), Mersenne (Archimedes, Pythagoras), and "the greatest Antiquary of them all, the immortal Gassendus" (Epicurus). (4) Those "who indeed above no Authority, pay a reverend esteem, but no implicite Adherence to Antiquity, nor erect any Fabrick of Natural Science upon Foundations of their own laying"; instead, this "electing sect" chooses from others what seems most true on the basis of right reason and experiment. This sect includes Fernel and Sennert, and Charleton humbly asks to be classed among them (p. 4).

Charleton's *Physiologia* certainly draws on Gassendi's *Animadversiones*, but it is far from being anything like a translation of even part of that work.[133] It consists of translation of certain passages, paraphrase and résumé of others, interpolation of material from other authors, and Charleton's own views—all of it presented in a way often difficult to sort out. (In this respect it is very much like Bernier's later *Abrégé*.) Charleton generally rearranges Gassendi's material, constructing four books dealing with the void, atoms, qualities, and change. Thus Charleton deals only with what Gassendi called the "Epicurean physiology, or physical part of philosophy," ignoring the logic "or canonic part," the meteorology, the ethics, and Gassendi's transcription and translation of book 10 of Diogenes Laertius's *Lives of the Philosophers*, on Lucretius. This is to say that Charleton deals with perhaps a third of the work. With respect to the material Charleton does treat, he produces a text perhaps two-thirds as long as Gassendi's, but the discrepancy is greater than the difference in length suggests, since there is a lot of material in Charleton not to be found in Gassendi's text, one reason being that there are authors on whom Charleton draws who do not figure in Gassendi's text either at all or in the same capacity.[134] The most important example of these is Descartes, since it indicates the extent to which Charleton's eclecticism undermines the cause of Gassendism.

The thrust of Charleton's use of Descartes is to minimize his differences from Gassendi and to find as much of value in Descartes as possible. Only at one point does Charleton criticize Descartes without either first praising his wit or pointing out the plausibility of his views, and that is a short comment to the effect that Descartes along with Thomas White was seduced by the substance-accident dichotomy with respect to the analysis of space. Otherwise Charleton goes so far as to assimilate the "insensible particles" of Descartes to the atoms of Democritus and Epicurus—"something so minute and solid, that nothing can be conceived more exiguous and impatible in Nature."[135] Descartes is cited

---

[133] Kargon, *Epicurean Atomism*, p. xiv; Sharp, "Early Life," p. 331.

[134] Given Charleton's rearrangement of Gassendi's material, I am not prepared to say to what extent his text—aside from the chapter on place—is even based on the *Animadversiones*.

[135] P. 85; also p. 88. Charleton cites *Principles* 4, 201. He also relates a Cartesian atomistic theory of magnetic attraction (p. 124), even if its details are later rejected (p. 412).

generally on behalf of mechanism, sometime plausibly as on behalf of the views that all colors are only apparent and that motion and rest are the principal modes of bodies, sometimes less plausibly as when the Gassendist concept of impressed motion is assimilated to the Cartesian concept of conservation of quantity of motion (pp. 188, 435, 445–46). While Charleton rejects the Cartesian theory of vision based on motion rather than on substantial species, he says of it, without irony, that "it is a conceit of singular Plausibility invented by a Wit transcendently acute" (pp. 152, 192). And if he cannot accept Descartes's explanation of the perception of distance in terms of distinctness, strength, and ocular strain, he does allow his connection between perceptions of size and distance.[136] Generally, Descartes is treated as an authority[137] from whom Charleton appears to differ only on intramural questions of details.

The two topics given longest treatment in Gassendi's *Animadversiones* are the immortality of the human soul and the conception of a creating, governing, and provident deity (pp. 549ff., 706ff.). Though they are the topics most closely associated with the Gassendist program of rehabilitating Epicurus, both are ignored by Charleton. Instead, what one finds along these lines is a rather bold list of four Epicurean "Positions to be exploded"[138] appended to the book on atoms along with the comment that he had already "had occasion to examine and refine all the dross either of Absurdity, or Atheism" in the "faeculent Doctrine of *Epicurus*" in a previous work (pp. 125–26). He is referring to the *Darkness of Atheism Dispelled*, particularly the second of its ten chapters in which he attempts to prove that God created the world ex nihilo. Turning to this work we find something of real importance in appreciating Charleton's role in the contest between Gassendi and Descartes.

Charleton's *Darkness* aims to prove that God exists, that He created the world *ex nihilo*, that there is a Providence, and, steering a course between fortune and fate, that man is free. His arguments for Providence come, as he tells us, from Lactantius, Sebonde, Aquinas, Vives, and "chiefly Gassendi [he cites the *Animadversiones*] the Leaves of whose most learned works, we blush not to confesse ourselves to have been so conversant in, that we have sullied them by often revolution."[139] Clearly, Charleton makes use of Gassendi, especially in presenting and "correcting" the views of Epicurus and Lucretius. His

---

[136] Pp. 146, 158, 164, 165. He also relates Descartes's experiment on retinal images with the eye of an ox (p. 178).

[137] In addition to the above topics, on theories of musical harmony, of calorific and frigorific atoms, and a theory of the tides that avoids occult qualities while allowing lunar influence (pp. 225, 314, 349).

[138] "1) That Atoms were Eternally existent in the infinite space, 2) that their Motive Faculty was eternally inherent in them, and not derived by impression from any External Principle, 3) that their congenial Gravity affects no Centre, 4) that their Declinatory motion from a perpendicular, is connatural to them with that of perpindicular descent, from Gravity" (*Physiologia*, p. 126).

[139] To reader, unpaginated.

definition of Providence, however, involves nothing more than the causal principle that sustained Cartesian occasionalism, namely, that there is no real
distinction between creation and conservation in existence, the conservation of
the universe being prolonged or continued creation (pp. 94–95). And indeed the
initial thrust of the work is not Gassendist, but Cartesian. He announces at the
outset that "every man brings into the world with him a certain *Proleptical*, or
anticipated notion of the *Deity*, indelibly impressed upon the very substance of
his mind." The proofs of the existence of God based on this innate idea are
"wholly collected out of the incomparable *Metaphysicks* of that heroicall wit,"
Descartes, whose *Meditations* he says he has closely and frequently read. He
also says that he has weighed them against the arguments of Gassendi, among
others, and found them "to overbalance all the others, in the points of comprehension, perspicuity, profundity, conviction" (note to reader). He proceeds
to elaborate these points in laudatory, not to say extravagant, terms.

The first chapter of *Darkness* is an attempt to prove the existence of God. A
brief opening section concludes with a citation of the "excellent *Rule* of the
School-men nothing of any sort can be known unless God is known first [Nulla
res qualiscunque est, intelligi potest, nisi Deus intelligatur prius.] revived into
an *Axiome* by the incomparable Des Cartes," whom he then quotes. The second
section is a long and accurate résumé of *Meditations* 3, without so much as a
soupçon of Gassendist criticism. Instead, the section clearly approves such
non-Gassendist items as the division of ideas into innate, adventitious, and
factitious; the distinction between astronomical and sensible ideas of the sun;
thought as the essence of mind and extension as the essence of body; the
distinction between formal and objective existence; and clarity and distinctness
as criteria. The third section defines the metaphysical terms of the previous
section that "may be conceived either too *difficult* for the unriper sort of heads,
or at least *ambiguous*" (p. 21). Charleton does not identify it as such, but the
section consists of a translation of all but one of the definitions at the outset of
the geometrical proofs Descartes appended to his *Replies* to *Objections* 2.[140]
The final section consists of six objections to the (Cartesian) proofs of the
existence of God, together with replies. Briefly, the objections are that: (1) the
finite human mind cannot know the infinite; (2) the idea of God is only a being
of reason with no existence outside the intellect; (3) effects can have more
reality than (certain kinds of) causes; (4) the idea of God can be derived from
sensible particulars; (5) ideas (including that of God) can be added to and
perfected; (6) the sense in which the idea of God might be innate is problematic.
Once again Charleton does not identify the source of his material; but each of
these issues was raised by Gassendi in his set of *Objections*. The specific
version of the first objection, more pressing than Gassendi's, is from the scholastic Caterus, however; the response to it is essentially Descartes's supple-

---

[140] Not all of the definitions are completely translated, but all of the material is Descartes's.

mented by Descartes's reply to Gassendi's similar objection.[141] The version of the second objection came explicitly from the theologians who wrote the second set of *Objections*; once again the reply is Descartes's.[142] The rest of the objections are more or less closely culled from Gassendi and Descartes's replies to them.[143] The objections are but a subset of those Gassendi raised against *Meditations* 3, but they are among the most central (particularly the first, fourth, and fifth) and we shall return to these issues below. For now we can note the significance of what Charleton has done. Even in terms of the *Physiologia*, the antidote to Epicurean atheism is not Gassendism, but Cartesianism as defended *against* Gassendism. To say the least, this rather qualifies the sense in which Charleton can be regarded as having upheld the Gassendist cause.

Samuel Sorbière

Another prominent member of the Gassendist circle was Samuel Sorbière (1610 or 1615–70), physician, early member of the Montmor group, Protestant convert to Catholicism (in 1653 he changed his frock, said Patin—as some wags had it—for benefits other than spiritual). From him we have a very few minor works (*Skeptical Discourse on Chyle*, *Discourse on Comets*, letters), for Sorbière did far more to disseminate the works of others than he did to produce anything of his own. He did translations into French (from Latin, he had no English) of More, Hobbes, and others. He also did an abortive translation of Sextus Empiricus, but it appeared only in a letter to Du Bos, and any influence from it in the spread of seventeenth-century skepticism would be difficult to document.[144] As a Gassendist he wrote the biographical preface to the Gassendi *Opera omnia* (1658) and the preface to the 1659 edition of the little *Syntagma*, and he looked after the publication of the *Disquisitio metaphysica* in Holland in 1644. (The preface is a letter to Sorbière from Gassendi that begins by referring to him as *erudito et amico vero*.) Said Graverol in his *Life:* "There was scarce any Body so well versed in the Philosophy of *Gassendus* as *Sorbière*, of whose Sentiments he was tenacious from the time of his first Acquaintance with him; and I have heard my Worthy friend, the late Monsieur *Bernier*, frequently say, that he knew no Body but *Sorbière* was a better *Gassendist* than himself."[145]

Sorbière was exceedingly anti-Cartesian, to the point that Mersenne felt constrained to counsel moderation.[146] At least some of his criticisms of

[141] CSM, 2:69, 81, 253–54; AT, 7:95–96, 113, 368–69.

[142] CSM, 2:88, 96; AT, 7:123, 133.

[143] CSM, 2:201–2, 252; also 88–89, 97–98, 211–12, 255–56; AT, 7:288–89, 366; also 123–24, 135–36, 304–5, 371.

[144] Popkin, "Samuel Sorbière's Translation."

[145] In Sorbière, *Voyage*, p. xviii.

[146] Sortais, *La philosophie*, p. 204.

Descartes, however, are quite penetrating. For example, he complained to Mersenne that Descartes's illustrations often beg the question, as when to illustrate the possibility of motion in a plenum he pointed to fish, which are able to swim in water. Whether there are no void spaces in water that allow this motion is precisely what needs proof, according to Sorbière.[147] In addition, Sorbière was in the Netherlands in 1644 and in contact with Descartes, to whom he conveyed arguments from Gassendi concerning the void. Specifically, Descartes was asked what the analysis was of what there would be between the walls of a room all of whose contents had been destroyed, whether the walls would have to move in order for there to be nothing between them as Descartes claimed—enormously important thought problems that were to be argued between Gassendists and Cartesians for the rest of the century. Sortais thought Sorbière philosophically naive not to have thought of such arguments himself against the Cartesian plenum and to have expected them to convert Descartes.[148] But Sorbière was so convinced of the truth of Gassendi's position that I think he may be excused from any naiveté in staging this confrontation with respect to so important an issue.

On the other hand, Sorbière was rather an eccentric, whose grasp of Gassendi's views might have been less than perfect. (Chapelain was to criticize his understanding of Gassendi's account of comets, for example, that he was supposed to be presenting in his *Discourse on Comets*.) As for his eccentricity, Sorbière had the bright idea, for example, to publish a work by Gassendi with a dedication to Princess Elizabeth in a prefatory letter. The project seems to have been a ruse designed to indicate waning support on Elizabeth's part for Descartes. The work was a translation of the little *Syntagma* and was already in press when Gassendi himself intervened (as he did when Bernier was similarly carried away defending him against Fludd) and called the project to a halt. Another example, directly relevant to the Gassendi–Descartes contest in England as well as to an important question of influences to be raised below, concerns Sorbière's trip to England in the mid-1600s and the account of it he published. On this trip Sorbière met Hobbes, whom he had seen fourteen years earlier in France, Oldenburg, and many others. He also attended meetings of the Royal Society. Relating its motto, *Nullius in verba*, he commented: "it cannot be discerned that any Authority prevails here; and whereas those who are mere Mathematicians favour *Descartes* more than *Gassendus*, the *Literati* on the other side are more inclined to the latter."[149] But neither group, he says, is less than moderate; both pursue the same ends. Sprat took great offense at this comment and at Sorbière's whole account of his trip: "neither of these two men bear any Sway amongst [the members of the Royal Society]: They are never

---

[147] December 23, 1647; cited in Sortais, *La philosophie* pp. 207–8.
[148] Ibid., pp. 202–3.
[149] *Voyage*, p. 38.

nam'd there as Dictators over Mens Reasons; nor is there any extraordinary Reference to their Judgments."[150] Sprat's response strikes me as downright silly jingoism. Sorbière had given only a mixed review of his hosts and their country, but it was at least a mixed review and hardly as bad as to require Sprat to have "pleaded for a Great, a valiant, and a Vertuous People," as he concluded the work, or to do so just by contradicting nearly everything Sorbière said.[151] However that may be, Sprat seems clearly to have misunderstood Sorbière's report on the Royal Society. Sorbière had given a quite valuable description of the actual conduct of the meeting, the seating arrangements, and the rules of procedure, all of which Sprat thought contemptible. "Is this not a shameful Sign of His Weakness, that he has insisted so long on such mean Circumstances, while he was describing a Subject that might have yielded him so much Noble matter for his Pen?"[152] Perhaps it would be too much to expect Sprat to appreciate the value of such social history. Less excusable is his failure to comprehend Sorbière's comment about the relative significance of Descartes and Gassendi. Sorbière does not claim that they are "named as dictators over men's reasons"; rather, he does just the opposite. Having cited the motto of the society, Sorbière says that "in short, it cannot be discerned that any Authority prevails here,"[153] and then *illustrates* this with his comment about Descartes and Gassendi. Perhaps the contretemps is attributable to Sorbière's failure to communicate with his hosts. After all, he spoke no English. On the other hand he may have invited the misunderstanding, for this was the sort of episode to which he was only too liable. One has the impression of Sorbière as an energetic but peripheral participant in the Republic of Letters, an intellectual groupie whom many refused to take seriously. Had Sorbière been its only advocate, the Gassendist cause would certainly have been without promise.

Cyrano de Bergerac

Savinien de Cyrano de Bergerac (1619–55) was one of the more colorful characters among the generally colorful Gassendists. He was certainly a close friend of Chapelle, but whether, as the story goes, he along with Molière and Bernier shared the philosophy lessons Gassendi gave Chapelle is an altogether different question. He seems to have passed a part of his life impoverished—as I picture him, a café intellectual—and died young.

His most, and really only, important work, *L'autre monde* (*The Other World*), was published only posthumously in 1657. The work consists of two

---

[150] Sprat, *Royal Society*, p. 165; Sorbière, *Voyage*.

[151] For Sprat's response to his comments on English cuisine, for example, see Popkin, "Samuel Sorbière's Translation," p. 107.

[152] Sprat, *Royal Society*, p. 165; Sorbière, *Voyage*.

[153] "En effet, l'on ne remarque point qu'aucune authorité preuaille" (Sorbière, *Relation*, p. 192).

parts. The first is the more important and deals with a trip which, after an abortive effort that landed in Canada, eventually reached the moon and the most extraordinary adventures. The second part, which was never completed, deals with events no less fantastic on the sun. In addition to this work there are a tragedy called "La mort d'Agrippine" and, among lesser works, some letters of interest.[154] A number of factors complicate the interpretation of Cyrano's views and the evaluation of his significance. For one thing, the principal influence of Cyrano would have been in the dissemination of libertine ideas; yet it was just the most extreme of these ideas that his editor Lebret for political reasons expurgated from the edition of *L'autre monde* published in 1657. Ridiculing religion in print was still far from being acceptable. In addition, there is a variety of characters in this work such that it is generally impossible to determine when, if ever, Cyrano should be taken as speaking *in propria persona*. Add to this the fantastic contexts and barely imaginable goings-on, plus a frequent tone of irony and satire, and the exegetical task becomes formidable indeed. At best we can point to the significance of the appearance of certain views in print, whatever their wrapping. Thus, however Cyrano's attitude may have been regarded, one could not have missed his expressions of relativism in moral matters, a rejection of all authority in the formation of opinions, of hedonism as a theory of value, and so on for the themes generally associated with libertinage érudit.

Another role into which the work of Cyrano might be cast is that of popularizing the Gassendist version of the New Science. The evaluation of this project (the French term *vulgarisation* captures the additional sense it had for Cyrano) is even less straightforward than Cyrano's dissemination of libertine ideas because it raises the additional question of whether Cyrano understood his own material. For example, only by ignoring the Gassendist conception of inertia does the motion of the earth show the abortive trip to the moon to leave Paris and by an "almost perpendicular line" return to Canada.[155] And while Cyrano convincingly rejects the Aristotelian theory of weight in favor of a theory of universal homogeneous matter, he does not, as has been suggested,[156] really approach the law of universal gravitation, for according to the law of falling bodies he proposes, size determines rate of descent.[157]

Finally, on the level of propaganda for classical atomism, the advantages of Cyrano's presentation are at least offset by its disadvantages. His treatment of the bugbear topic of chance, for example, is quite sophisticated. He ignores Gassendi's arguments on behalf of Providence and instead argues (anticipating G. Lamy, for example) that any state of affairs is no more unlikely than any

[154] See Bloch, *Ueberwegs*, "Schüler."
[155] *Voyage*, p. 34.
[156] Juppont, "L'oeuvre scientifique," p. 338
[157] On this and on other related topics, see Alcover.

other, all being extremely unlikely, but that since some state of affairs must obtain, something extremely unlikely must and does occur. The occurrence of just this arrangement, therefore, need not be ascribed to design.[158] Second, the laws of this world are such that, not the occurrence of design, but its failure to occur is what should be ascribed to a divine intervention. The risk incurred by these bold arguments might be justified by the premium they consequently place on the search for mechanical causes. That is, the program is theologically suspect but at least scientifically promising. This is not the case with the arguments he advanced on behalf of the eternity of the world. Though an eternal world is inconceivable, he argued, attributing the world to an eternal god is like jumping in the river to avoid getting wet in the rain, for the same problem arises concerning an eternal god, with the additional problem that creation is inconceivable. Now, whatever the premium gained from an eternal world, it need not have been purchased at such a theologically extravagant price, as the Cartesian position had already demonstrated: If there are eternal truths the world may necessarily be eternal, but that is not to say that either it or they are uncreated. Cyrano's position here is (by contrast to his view on chance) gratuitously bold. In conclusion, Cyrano by his work no less than life did much to cast libertinage in just the theologically and morally questionable light from which Gassendi has sought to shield it.

Some Lesser Lights

We might close this catalogue of Gassendists by either recalling, or at least once drawing attention to, the names of some who were close to Gassendi and who, with more documentation or with a history written from a different perspective, might figure more prominently in the catalogue. François Luillier (ca. 1600–51) was the intimate friend of Gassendi who took him to the Netherlands for nine months during 1628–29 and at whose house Gassendi lodged later in Paris. Gassendi dedicated his life of Epicurus to him. Of Antoine de la Potterie, Gassendi's last secretary, we know virtually nothing, not even birth or death dates. The libertin érudit Guy Patin (1601–73) was still another of the many Gassendist physicians, alas to the misfortune of Gassendi, whose death was likely hastened by the bleedings prescribed by Patin. Abraham du Prat (1620–60), also a physician, was one of the principals in attendance at the Montmor academy, and was a friend of both Gassendi and Sorbière. In physics, however, he was in one obvious sense more of a Cartesian than a Gassendist, opting for the plenum and the infinite divisibility of matter. On the other hand, unlike Descartes, he was an experimentalist on such questions as the circulation of the blood, and may have rejected atomism on more or less empirical grounds. Such

---

[158] *Voyage*, p. 98.

was the case later with Claude Perrault (1613–88), who in his *Essais de physi-que* adopts a vortex theory of weight involving three kinds of matter that fill all of space, but whose plenum is based on other than metaphysical considerations. Spherical drops of water and mercury would flatten out in a genuine void; yet they retain their shape when all the gross air is removed from a container. Their retention of shape has the same cause, he argues, as that of the spherical shape of oil drops in water, for example. More generally, Perrault's work sets out a skeptical, incipiently instrumentalist philosophy of science. The main task in physics, he says with rhetorical flourish, is to explain as least badly as possible the cause of things, and in doing so we have complete freedom in making even the wildest supposition, as long as it is not contrary to established facts (*faits averez*) and does not involve presumption of truth. It seems that for Perrault phenomena in principle allow of many explanations, none of which can ever be the true one. The upshot is that even in adopting a Gassendist view of knowl-edge that precludes the metaphysical sort of knowledge of material things the Cartesians claimed to possess, Perrault or du Prat may nonetheless have arrived at Cartesian rather than Gassendist physical theories. This possibility calls into question the status of Gassendist atomism. On the one hand it looks as though the Gassendists regard their ontology of atoms and void as a competitor with the Cartesian metaphysical plenum of extension; but on the other it looks as though they want to argue that the essence or being of the material world cannot be known to be extension or anything else and then to argue for the void, for example, only on physical considerations such as the possibility of motion. This of course is an enormously complex question; we have already raised it above with respect to Bernier's atomism and we shall return to it below. For the moment the moral of the story is the complexity it suggests in cataloguing those influenced by Gassendi.

§6 MIND VERSUS FLESH

Early on Descartes had taken Gassendi to be, if not an authority, then at least someone to be regarded seriously in optics, astronomy, and other matters.[159] With Gassendi's *Objections*, however, Descartes's attitude changes dra-matically. On June 23, 1641, he returned to Mersenne Gassendi's objections along with the advice to have them printed without showing them to Gassendi, who when he saw how bad his objections were would want them "suppressed." Descartes meanwhile was loathe to see his time in replying wasted or the possibility realized that some would think that it was he who, unable to answer

---

[159] See letters to Mersenne, December 18, 1629, AT, 1:97; January 1630, ibid., pp. 112–13; March 4, 1630, ibid., p. 127; May 6, 1630, ibid., p. 148; or even as late as December 1638, AT, 2:464–65.

the objections, had them suppressed. He concludes the letter: "you will see that I have done all I could to treat Gassendi honorably and gently; but he gave me so many occasions to despise him and to show he has no common sense and can in no way reason, that I would have done too much less than my duty had I said less, and I assure you I could have said much more."[160]

A month later Descartes again wrote to Mersenne, saying that Gassendi had no grounds for complaint at his treatment, for he gave only equal in kind despite what he had always heard, namely, that the first blow is worth two and that thus to be really equal the reply should have been doubled. "But perhaps he was affected by my replies because he recognized their truth, while I was not for an entirely different reason; if so, it is not my fault."[161] Two years later Descartes could still muster respect for Gassendi's empirical astronomy,[162] but by then he could tell just from the index of Gassendi's letters that they contained nothing he needed to read.[163] The literature has tended to fault Gassendi for failing really to engage Descartes's views; the converse seems no less true. For the most part Descartes treated his would-be adversary as beyond contempt. Discussing why criticism of his work is no burden Descartes wrote that Gassendi's *Instantia* did not displease him as much as he was pleased by Mesland's judgment that there was nothing in the work not easily answered.[164]

As for Gassendi's attitudes, there are two versions of the story. One has it that he was no less than livid with Descartes and no less than he in his acrimony and petulance. But this version is based on the testimony of Jean-Baptiste Morin, an eccentric to say the least, who on other grounds was concerned to besmirch the reputation of Gassendi. Thus, for example, Descartes's calling Gassendi "Flesh" in his *Replies* would be understood only as justified retaliation for having been referred to as "Mind" in the *Objections*. More credible is the account of Bernier, who portrays a rather more detached, long-suffering response from his teacher. In any case, the personal differences between the great antagonists were finally repaired in 1648 following a dinner arranged for them by the Abbé d'Estrées. As it happened, Gassendi was unable to attend because of illness; but after the dinner, the assembled party visited Gassendi, who was embraced by Descartes.[165]

Gassendi's *Objections* may well be regarded as unique.[166] Among other

---

[160] AT, 3:388–89.

[161] July 22, 1641; AT, 3:416.

[162] To Colvius, April 23, 1643; AT, 3:646.

[163] To Mersenne, February 23, 1643; AT, 3:633.

[164] To Noel, December 14, 1646; AT, 4:585–86.

[165] The episode is recounted in Bougerel, *Pierre Gassendi*, pp. 306–8. See Jones, *Pierre Gassendi*, who gives more details on these personal relations (pp. 66–69) and also gives the substance of Gassendi's criticisms of the *Meditations* (pp. 135–88).

[166] For the outline of my account, I have drawn heavily on the work of O. R. Bloch, to whom my debt will be apparent. Bloch first dealt with the topic in "Gassendi critique de Descartes"; he later

objectors, Arnauld, who really asks only for clarifications, and the Scholastic theologians share important metaphysical presuppositions with Descartes. Hobbes does not engage Descartes so much as merely juxtapose his own views to those of Descartes, with Descartes replying in kind. In the case of Gassendi, however, we find an elaborated and systematic metaphysical confrontation. The length of his exchanges with Descartes thus reflects their relative importance. The *Fifth Objections* (1641) are more than twice as long as any other set, and if Descartes thought them "not the most important"[167] he nonetheless replied to them at greatest length. Within a year Gassendi had responded with his *Rebuttals* (*Instantiae*: literally, follows-up) which with the *Fifth Objections* and *Replies* were published in 1644 under the general title of *Disquisitio metaphysica*, totaling some 150 pages *in folio* of the *Opera omnia*.

At the core of Gassendi's critique of Descartes is the notion of representation. There are arguments from Gassendi against Descartes, as there were later to be from Locke and Foucher against Malebranche,[168] to the effect that an idea to represent a square would have to be square. At one point, for example, Gassendi poses the following dilemma, designed to argue that the mind of which Descartes claims to have an idea is essentially extended. Only if an idea has extension can it represent extension; only if it has shape and location can it represent what has shape and location, for an idea must be like what it represents. But only if an idea has no extension, shape, or location can it be joined to the essentially unextended, unshaped, unlocated thing that the mind is alleged to be, for the essence of the mind is supposed to be thought, which excludes properties of extension.[169]

The dilemma may be released, as Gassendi urges, by denying that the self is an essentially unextended, unshaped, unlocated thing. But this does not explain how Gassendi, or any imagist, deals with the first horn of the dilemma. There seem to me three possible answers to the problem of imagist ideas representing extension. Historically they overlap. One is the skeptical answer, to which Gassendi is certainly inclined, namely, that the idea of a square, for example, just does not represent at all; we do not know the real. But this response by itself is insufficient. Even if the idea does not represent a real square, it is a different idea from the idea of a circle, and it is not clear that the problem of distinguishing them is any more tractable than the problem of how an unextended idea can represent an extended thing. In fact, it might be argued, these are versions of the same problem. It is not surprising, then, that the skeptical answer is to be found combined with others among the philosophically more astute.

---

elaborated many of these themes in *La philosophie de Gassendi: nominalisme, materialisme, et métaphysique*.

167 CSM, 2:268; AT, 9:198.

168 Richard A. Watson takes Foucher's argument to be one of two major reasons for "the downfall of Cartesianism." See his book by that title.

169 CSM, 2:234; AT, 7:337–38.

A second possible answer, one emphasized by Locke, is to give an account of resemblance that would allow the unextended to resemble and thus to represent the extended. I do not have in mind here the realist account in terms of the same thing existing in different ways—a mental, nonspatial square being qualitatively identical to, and thus representing, a material, spatial square. Many agree that this is the account advanced by the orthodox Cartesians, and we shall return to it in chapters 4 and 5. It is also the account advanced by Leibniz, according to whom even ideas of secondary qualities resemble. The idea of pain resembles, although confusedly, a certain motion in the body, for example.[170] There are many reasons, however, why this account is inimical to the tradition whose view of ideas I am discussing here. The one of immediate relevance is that this realist account is incompatible with the skeptical answer above, for it grounds knowledge of the real. Far from cutting us off from the real, this account of ideas gives us immediate access to it. As Arnauld put it, the idea is the thing itself insofar as it exists in the mind.[171]

Instead, the possible answer I have in mind would have it that an unextended idea resembles an extended thing just in case it stands in a certain causal relation to it. Thus we may call it the causal answer. Later there will be a more appropriate occasion to develop Locke's version of this answer. The gist of it is that the idea of a square, and of primary qualities generally, resembles and thus represents its object in that given the corpuscularian hypothesis, the object could produce only that idea. The reality, inseparability, and resemblance to ideas of primary qualities come to the same thing. Given the corpuscularian hypothesis, the world must have certain features in order to appear to us as it does. Secondary qualities, on the other hand, are imputed, separable, and fail to resemble. Even given a fully articulated corpuscularian account, there is no reason why the motion that in fact produces the idea of pain should not produce the idea of redness. That it does not is attributable to the biological utility of the former arrangement. Still, even ideas of secondary qualities are said by Locke to represent and may be said to represent their (partial, remote) causes. However contingent it might be, the fact of the matter is that lemons taste tart and pineapples sweet. And we perceive them in this way at least partly because of their fine structure, between which and our perceptions there is a regular, if mechanistically inexplicable, correlation. Thus, Gassendi's dilemma is generally resolved by denying the crucial premise of the first horn. Representation does not depend on resemblance in the sense that representing idea and represented object both have the same property, but rather on the causal connection between them. The historical irony is that Locke's actual version of the causal answer allows for resemblance in a way that construes ideas as extended and the thing represented as unextended. This is a long story I shall try to tell later on in

[170] *New Essays*, pp. 131–32.
[171] *Des vrayes et des fausses idees*; *Oeuvres*, 38:199–200.

chapter 5. The short of it is that (1) ideas are impressions of which we are aware, that is, corporeal states or motions, and are thus extended, and (2) extension is relational and thus only phenomenal, and hence the noumenal object represented by an idea is unextended.

Ideas are also extended according to the third answer, the materialist answer. According to it, the idea of a square represents a square because it actually is square. This is to embrace the first horn, suitably interpreted, as it is for Locke in the causal answer just given. The historical plausibility of my thesis here will be enhanced by noting that, although essentially materialistic, this tack was taken by Berkeley. Consider, for example, his argument with respect to the intense degree of heat as pain, the very first argument of the *Three Dialogues*. No unperceiving thing is capable of pain; a material substance is unperceiving, hence incapable of pain; but the intense degree of heat is pain, thus material substance is incapable of, that is, cannot have as a property, the intense degree of heat. And, of course, what is true of the intense degree of heat, we later learn, is true of all properties. Given his own analysis of objects as bundles of ideas or sensations, Berkeley is not entitled to the first premise, and he effectively rejects it. More generally, ideas and only ideas have the properties they appear to have, so that when Berkeley takes representation to depend on resemblance in the sense that representing idea and represented object both have the same property, representationalism comes under attack. As Berkeley insists repeatedly, an idea can resemble only another idea. The moral of the story is that the essential element in this approach to ideas is not the invitation to materialism, but the construal of ideas as images. Just how Berkeley distinguishes his view from the materialists is a question beyond the scope of my story. Here it will suffice to show how the imagist conception of ideas ties together the three answers to Gassendi's dilemma.

Taken no further, the dilemma Gassendi poses for Descartes remains at a superficial level. A deeper concern is the whole notion of representation that Descartes employs in extrapolating from ideas to things, or more precisely, from the realm of thought to that of essences. According to one particularly relevant interpretation, the key to Descartes's theory of ideas is his analytic geometry, which provides the model for representation: An idea represents in the way in which the algebraic equation for a curve expresses that curve by giving a rule for the deduction of all its properties.[172] I am not quite convinced that this Leibnizean reading can be wrung from the Cartesian texts. At a minimum, however, it is true that for Descartes an idea is an intelligible rather than sensible representation. As opposed to Gassendist images, which are particular, it is universal. Gassendi has been charged by later commentators with having failed to see how different a theory of ideas he was dealing with, or worse, with having just failed to understand it. But of this Gassendi is innocent,

---

[172] Bloch, "Gassendi critique," p. 232.

for he correctly saw that Cartesian knowledge would be abstract in just the pejorative sense in which Descartes had castigated Aristotelian-Scholastic knowledge as abstract (and in which Bernier, as we have just seen, was to castigate Gassendi's conception of time). Were there Cartesian ideas, Gassendi argued, they might lead to what is true of a thing, but failing to be an image of it, they would not provide *real* knowledge of it. How so?

Gassendi does not object to Descartes's conclusions, at least not to his principal ones concerning the existence of God and the immortality of the soul.[173] Instead, in a way that adumbrates Locke's reaction to Cartesianism, he attacks the arguments for Descartes's conclusions, and especially the *kind* of argument they exemplify. Thus, for example, we find Gassendi taxing Descartes for claiming that his metaphysical demonstrations are more certain than those of mathematics when they do not even get general assent. The following is paradigmatic of the offending sort of argument:

1. Things I consider as conceptually distinct are really distinct.

2. I consider thinking substance and corporeal substance as conceptually distinct. Therefore,

3. Thinking substance and corporeal substance are really distinct.[174]

The first premise expresses a necessary connection between concepts that is apprehended by a metaphysical or intellectual intuition; the second expresses an instantiation of the same concepts apprehended by the same intuition. Now, to be sure, Descartes rejects this syllogized version of his reasoning that Gassendi attributes to him.[175] For Descartes, the conclusion of what is really an intellectual induction is the first premise, drawn on the basis of the second premise and the conclusion. But it is precisely this induction and the intuition on which it rests that Gassendi rejects and that lies at the heart of his critique of Descartes.[176] For Gassendi, as for Locke, experience is the only source of knowledge. For Locke, as for Gassendi, we have no intellectual intuition and thus his rejection of the innate ideas claimed by Descartes and others is of a piece with his rejection of the ideas Malebranche claimed to see in God. Gassendi shows the way, effectively by rejecting the nonsensuous half of *Republic's* Divided Line.

Consider his reaction to the Cartesian method of doubt, a topic on which as a skeptic he is especially sensitive. In the *Disquisitio*[177] he argues that contrary to what is claimed for this method, it is impossible to free the mind from its prejudices. The attempt to do so is, we might say, (1) psychologically, (2) methodologically, and (3) epistemologically futile. Let us consider each of

---

[173] CSM, 2:179; AT, 7:257.

[174] *Disquisitio Metaphysica*; *Opera*, 3:297a.

[175] CSM, 2:100; AT, 7:140.

[176] Bloch, "Gassendi critique," pp. 220–26.

[177] *Opera*, 3:279a.

these aspects, which are important even quite apart from the issue of intellectual intuition.

(1) The *psychological futility* of Cartesian doubt is of a piece with a skeptical position advanced since antiquity. Gassendi's point is that we just cannot avoid making judgments that we are accustomed to making such as that the intersection of two lines produces angles equal to two right angles or that a certain round object shines. And his point perfectly accords with the recommendation of traditional skeptics that we suspend judgment whenever it is possible to do so. For it is possible to suspend judgment in their view only with respect to metaphysical issues, that is, the essences of things. In all other cases, that is, in sense perceptions, nature breaks the skeptic by constraining assent.

Gassendi is often portrayed as having missed, not just Descartes's theory of ideas, but more especially the nature of his method of doubt. Gassendi failed to distinguish, so the story goes, between the intrinsic doubt of convinced skeptics and the instrumental doubt Descartes uses against them, between real and practical doubt on the one hand, and the merely theoretical doubt advocated by Descartes on the other. Descartes did not really doubt he had a body, but only feigned such doubt in order better to support his belief that he did. But in fact Gassendi shows remarkable sophistication in replying to this charge of oversight as it was first raised by Descartes himself. To be sure, "the distinction 'between the acts of daily life and the inquiry after truth' is totally justified."[178] The skeptics reject indifference in questions of daily life (and, we might add, in precisely the same conservative way Descartes did with his provisional morality).[179] With respect to the inquiry after truth they distinguish between *phainomena*, "things which appear to the senses," which they accept, and *noumena*, "the things which are understood by the mind," which they do not.[180] Thus the dogmatist Descartes gets it exactly the wrong way round. This assertion is no argument, but it at least shows that Gassendi understands perfectly well what is at issue.

(2) Gassendi's charge under the rubric of what I have called the *methodological futility* of Cartesian doubt is rather ill-defined.

> Secondly, even if I granted that the mind is liberated and is like a *tabula rasa* on which no judgment has been traced, you assume that "it can deduce some conclusions from principles";[181] but this too appears to be impossible. Clearly if it has no preconceived notions [*praejudicia*], then it does not have any principles; for principles, as they are here understood, are statements [*enunciationes*]; and statements are kinds of judgments in which something is either affirmed or denied. Hence these principles will be judgments, and inasmuch as they are conceived in ad-

---

[178] Ibid., 3:286a.

[179] *Discourse on Method*; CSM, 1:122–25; AT, 2:22–28.

[180] *Opera*, 3:286a.

[181] Cf. Gassendi's syllogistic reconstruction of Descartes's reasoning in *Meditations* 1 (3:279a).

vance, they are preconceived notions. Therefore, if the mind has no preconceived notion in it, neither will it have any principles from which it may deduce something. . .; since no new evidence appears which convinces us that any different relationship than the one above is to be enunciated, it follows that the statements about reality will be neither new statements, nor opposite ones, but the same ones as before, and so the same preconceived notions will crop up again.[182]

Essentially he seems to be saying that even if the doubt Descartes recommends were possible, it could not yield the result he thinks. Gassendi claims that nothing really new emerges from the method of doubt as a deconstruction of all the propositions we have held; that is, having broken down these propositions (enunciationes) into their constituent elements, we then put them together again in exactly the same way. Now, of course we know that the Cartesian restoration of the house of belief may look room-for-room identical; but its novelty is the supposed foundation on which it rests. And it may be to this very supposition that Gassendi objects.

In addition, Gassendi may be arguing "holistic empiricism." Though the mind is initially a *tabula rasa*, and though all knowledge is empirically derived, we need principles to derive principles. We may have here, from the principal source of seventeenth-century empiricism, a prototype of more recent arguments against concept empiricism. Epistemologically, it takes a pair of tongs to make a pair of tongs.

Finally, Gassendi may partially misunderstand Descartes, whose principles are not statements, that is, things *we* put together, but common notions or innate ideas, that is, structures that are *given*. This is the realism to which Descartes, whatever the details of his theory of innate ideas, is clearly committed. In these terms, however, the issue is the very fundamental one we have been discussing of whether we have the intellectual intuition to apprehend these structures that give us the essence of things.

(3) Under the heading of the *epistemological futility* of Cartesian doubt, Gassendi reiterates a point from above and focuses it on a familiar anti-Cartesian theme, namely, that the precious criterion of clarity and distinctness is a psychological phenomenon only.

Thirdly, granted that the mind may retain some principles from which it may draw conclusions, you assume that they are "not obscure and uncertain, but very evident and certain." But, finally, this too is impossible, namely that there should be different principles from the ones that already were, that is to say some that are self-evident and certain, and the majority obscure and uncertain . . . after this liberation from preconceived notions, it remains equally inclined to assent to false principles as to true ones in the event that the former should turn up first and appear to be fact; and you cannot induce any reason why in this state of equal inclination

---

[182] *Opera*, 3:279b; *Selected Works*, p. 166.

false principles must come to the mind seeming only apparent and obscure and therefore uncertain rather than seeming evident and therefore certain. For the mind will be as it were at a crossroads, and it will be a matter of chance whether one set of principles offers itself, or another, and whether it accedes to the first, to the ones that make a stronger impression by the mere fact that they appear to be real, rather than to the others.[183]

For Gassendi, the conviction reached by the Cartesian method of doubt is only psychological, with no guarantee of objective validity for either his concepts or his reasoning. For all we know, clarity and distinctness may be reliable, but how do we even know, asks Gassendi, which ideas are clear and distinct?

Gassendi's answer to the skeptical challenge he poses is a naturalistic empiricism. Thought has an empirically derived structure. It consists solely of material images produced in the brain, stored in the memory, and processed by analogy, composition, division, augmentation, and division.[184] The argument for the central role of these images and against the Cartesian intellectual intuition of essences is one found often enough in the materialist tradition. People affected by drugs or dreaming are furthest removed from the senses and least dependent on corporeal memory, but they are also least capable of thought.[185] Locke was to raise the same consideration as part of his argument against the Cartesian thesis that the soul always thinks: "This I would willingly be satisfied in, Whether the Soul, when it thinks thus apart [i.e., when we are asleep], and as it were separate from the Body, acts less rationally than when conjointly with it, or no: If its separate Thoughts be less rational, then these Men must say, That the Soul owes the perfection of rational thinking to the Body: If it does not, 'tis a wonder that our Dreams should be, for the most part, so frivolous and irrational; and that the Soul should retain none of its more rational Soliloquies and Meditations."[186] The rest of Locke's argument will be discussed below.

Whatever Gassendi's arguments against Cartesian intuition, the question might plausibly be raised as to why images would be epistemologically inadequate to the Cartesian task. However ideas are produced, why do they not give us the essences of things? The crucial consideration here is Gassendi's nominalism, found explicitly in his first work, the *Exercitationes* of 1624,[187] and controlling his thought thereafter. In stating it, Gassendi is as blunt as Locke was to be in stating his: "nothing can be found that is not a unique thing."[188] Nor at this level of philosophical analysis can there be much by way of argument apart from an appeal to parsimony. To invoke or ignore universals is the first

[183] *Opera*, 3:280a; *Selected Works*, p. 167.

[184] Bloch, "Gassendi critique," p. 227.

[185] *Opera*, 3:299b.

[186] 2.1.16; 113.

[187] *Opera*, 3:95–210.

[188] 3:159a; *Selected Works*, p. 43. Cf. Locke: "All Things, that exist, being Particulars" (3.3.1; 409).

step of a research program for which the confirmation or disconfirmation is very remote. The upshot, in any case, is that ideas qua images are particulars and contain no essences. They can contain only what by experience and reasoning we put into them. Gassendi clearly saw the importance of this difference from Descartes, which is worth pursuing textually in some detail.

Descartes in *Meditations* 3 had argued that the idea of God must be innate since (1) it is not derived from the senses; (2) "nor is it likewise a fiction of my mind for it is not in my power to take from or add anything to it."[189] Gassendi objected to this, claiming that in fact the idea of God was partly derived from the senses and partly composed by the mind, for obviously an idea can be added to. Indeed, this is precisely what we do in coming to know God more fully.[190] Locke gives a similar account of our idea of God. The mind "enlarges upon" ideas of existence and duration, knowledge and power, which are ultimately derived from experience, making them "boundless," that is, (potentially) infinite.[191]

In his response to Gassendi, Descartes invoked "the common philosophical maxim that the essences of things are indivisible. An idea represents the essence of the thing, and if anything is added to it or subtracted from the essence, then the idea automatically becomes the idea of something else."[192] To rebut Descartes's response, Gassendi turns against him another of his own responses. Recall the moral of the piece of wax story from *Meditations* 2. We know the piece of wax, not through the senses, nor through the imagination, but by the mind alone (*mentis inspectio*). Gassendi reads this to mean that we are supposed to know the wax itself, the substance of the wax or its essence, and objects that all that we know of it are its accidents, that in fact we cannot conceive of the wax apart from any extension, figure, and color.[193] Similarly, we do not know that the self is essentially thinking, only that it as a matter of fact thinks. In his reply, Descartes seems to give up the game: "I wanted to show how the substance of wax is revealed by means of its accidents. . . . I have never thought

---

[189] CSM, 2:35; AT, 7:51.

[190] CSM, 2:212; AT, 7:304.

[191] 2.23.33–35.

[192] CSM, 2:255–56; AT, 7:371.

[193] CSM, 2:189–90; AT, 7:271–72. See also CSM, 2:190–99; AT, 7:273: "When you go on to say that the perception of colour and hardness and so on is 'not vision or touch but is purely mental scrutiny', I accept this provided the mind is not taken to be really distinct from the imaginative faculty. You add that this scrutiny 'can be imperfect and confused or perfect and distinct depending on how carefully we concentrate on what the wax consists in.' But this does not show that the scrutiny made by the mind, when it examines the mysterious something that exists over and above all the forms, constitutes clear and distinct knowledge of the wax; it shows, rather, that such knowledge is constituted by the scrutiny made by the senses of all the possible accidents and changes which the wax is capable of taking on. From these we shall certainly be able to arrive at a conception and explanation of what we mean by the term 'wax'; but the alleged naked, or rather hidden, substance is something that we can neither ourselves conceive nor explain to others."

that anything more is required to reveal a substance than its various attributes, thus the more attributes of a given substance we know, the more perfectly we understand its nature. Now we can distinguish many different attributes in the wax. . . . And there are correspondingly many attributes in the mind."[194] This seems to mean both that ideas can be enlarged upon, that the essences of things are not indivisible, and that our knowledge is limited to the accumulation of accidents or appearances. And Gassendi is quick to exploit this opening to full advantage.[195]

The opening seized by Gassendi is only an apparent one, however, for Descartes's substance-attribute language cannot be understood in the Aristotelian terms Gassendi clearly assumes. Instead, individual things like the piece of wax are modes of extension in the sense of being instantiations of it, that is, ways that extension can exist (thus the French *façon d' être* as the translation of *modus*). And the better we know extension, the one essence of the material world, the better we know individually extended things like the piece of wax. The connection between extension (*extensio* or *res extensa*) and extended things (*extensa*) is the connection between the axioms and the theorems of geometry; it is the deductive connection that replaces the connection of inherence in the Aristotelian substance ontology.[196] Thus can Descartes claim in response to Gassendi's original objection that by coming to know God better we alter our idea of Him: "once the idea of the true God has been conceived, although we may detect additional perfections in him which we had not yet noticed, this does not mean that we have augmented the idea of God; we have simply made it more distinct and explicit, since, so long as we suppose that our original idea was a true one, it must have contained all these perfections."[197] The process of making explicit what is only implicit in an idea is that of deduction, the possibility for which, as we shall see in chapter 7, qualifies the idea as both innate and distinct.

Gassendi just denies that there are such ideas:

> As for you, when you say that "the idea represents the essence of a thing," it seems that I may infer not incorrectly that if there are any things whose essence you do not know, you do not have an idea of them. Therefore I ask you: do you know the essence of the sun, of the moon, or of some other star? I suspect that you will not say that you do. For what do you know about them besides their size, shape, movement, distance, light, brightness, heat, their power to generate growth, to warm, to move, and other such things, if there are any. But the very essence, the nature, the inner substance which lies underneath these is totally hidden from you.[198]

[194] CSM, 2:248–49; AT, 7:359–60.
[195] *Opera*, 3:352b–353a.
[196] Bracken, "Problems of Substance."
[197] CSM, 2:256; AT, 7:371.
[198] *Opera*, 3:352a; *Selected Works*, p. 222.

To be sure, there are ideas, but from the nominalist point of view they are of a very different sort.

> Actually, you do have ideas of things, but not the kind you claim to have. In fact ideas of things exist only to the degree that we know them. And since we know their accidents with a distinct knowledge, but not their essences, which we divine as it were or conceive indistinctly as lurking under them, therefore, there is a distinct idea of their accidents, but not of their essences, which we comprehend indistinctly underneath them. From which it results that the clearer and more precise idea we have of something, the clearer and more precisely we know several of its accidents. Since experience shows that the ideas in our minds are like images of things, and the images are not of a thing's essence, but of its accidents, it follows that just as the image of a certain man reproduced in a picture is all the more perfect if the symmetry, the arrangement, and the representation of a great number of parts is more elaborately worked out, and each of the individual traits which are in the separate parts is more carefully reproduced, so the idea of any thing becomes all the more perfect if it portrays more of its accidents, or more of the things surrounding it, as it were, in a more ordered fashion, with greater skill, and more lifelike.[199]

§7   GASSENDIST THEORIES OF SPACE: APOTHEOSIS AND ANNIHILATION

Gassendi's account of space and time begins with an attack on the received view that all being is divided into substance and accident.[200] Although it is primarily Aristotle who receives Gassendi's attention, Pythagoras, Epicurus, Lucretius, and others[201] are noted as well, since Gassendi is concerned with a range of views based on the principle that all being is either in itself or in another.[202] With the additional premise that all being is either corporeal or incorporeal, space and time could plausibly be regarded on the Aristotelian view only as corporeal accidents, so that if there were no bodies there would be no space or

---

[199] 3:353b; *Selected Works*, p. 223. Among those who have been sensitive to Locke's debt to Gassendi, François Duchesneau has produced perhaps the most extensive treatment of the question, but one that resulted in a conclusion precisely opposite to that drawn here. He emphasizes Gassendi's rejection of intellectual *pictures*, basing his case on texts from Bernier, Digby, and Gassendi's theory of vision. On this view, the perception of an idea is for Gassendi the mind's act of grasping the intelligible in the sensible given. I am rather persuaded by Bloch, who argues just the opposite from the model of Gassendi's theory of vision: "Vision is in no way the intuition of a cognitive content given in sensation, but a reconstruction by the mind of the reality of things from a content which is, not the [intelligible] translation of that reality [in the mind as per Duchesneau's interpretation according to the Aristotelian tradition], but the [causal] effect of it" (*La philosophie*, p. 20). Thus ideas are not intellectual, but they are yet pictures, which ceteris paribus are caused by what they picture. Of this difficult issue, much more below.

[200] *Syntagma*; *Opera*, 1:179 ff; *Selected Works*, pp. 383ff.

[201] 1:180b.

[202] 1:179b.

time. Gassendi's contention is that even without body there would be unchanging place and flowing time,[203] and that therefore a category beyond substance and accident must be admitted.

Space (*locus*, i.e., unspecified place) is a "quantity or some sort of extension,"[204] an incorporeal tridimensionality: "the length, width, and depth of the walls of some water contained in a vase would be corporeal; but the length, width and depth of the walls of the vase if the water and every other body were excluded from it would be spatial."[205] Note that the corporeal quantity is not the water itself, but its dimensions. One wonders how these corporeal dimensions differ from the incorporeal dimensions of the space it occupies. The distinction itself that Gassendi wants to draw is clear enough, and we shall turn to it at length below. What is unclear is the motivation for the distinction. A thing might be said to be extended either because it is in space, in which case corporeal extension is superfluous, or because it has corporeal extension, in which case its space is superfluous. Gassendi's text thus suggests two, more parsimonious views, each of which was later picked up and developed by his followers.

One view tended to emphasize space and time as conditions for existence—affections as Gassendi called them[206]—and then to use some quality other than extension such as solidity or impenetrability to distinguish body from space. This is the active view of space[207] that dominates the Neo-Platonic tradition and to which Gassendi himself clearly is inclined. There are strategic reasons that make this route attractive to him, but quite independently of these he subscribes to a localization pattern. "There is no substance and no accident for which it is not appropriate to say that it exists somewhere, or in some place, and exists sometime, or at some moment."[208] Cureau is an obvious proponent of this view, and Launay notably arrives at it. In order to secure divine immutability, argues Launay, God must be conceived as in space; besides which, "it is impossible for the human mind to conceive a being that exists and that is not in any place; for everything that is in itself necessarily is someplace."[209]

The other view suggested by Gassendi's text tended to reject spatial dimensions as primitive and instead to derive them from corporeal dimensions. This represents the passive view of space that traces to Democritus.[210] Bernier, for

---

[203] *locum constantem, & Tempus decurrens* (1:182a).

[204] *Quantitatem, extensionemve quandam* (1:182a).

[205] 1:182a–b; *Selected Works*, p. 385.

[206] 1:179a.

[207] Sambursky, "Place and space."

[208] 1:182a; *Selected Works*, p. 384. See *Abrégé* 1, vol. 1: "it is inconceivable that a substance should be and that it should not be in some place" (p. 21). See also p. 19: Space must be uncreated since nothing is created unless in a place, and "it would be ridiculous to say that place is created in another place since this would go on to infinity."

[209] *Essais physiques*, p. 103.

[210] Sambursky, "Place and Space."

example, may have been led to it by considerations such as those just raised. Why must a body be in space in order to exist, he asked, when space is not its "productive cause" and is "of an entirely different nature"? If space can exist without body, why should body not be able to exist without space?[211] If a body has corporeal dimensions different from spatial dimensions, he may be arguing, there is nothing to preclude that a body should exist and yet not be in space. We shall return to both of these tendencies, and the views they embrace, below.

Meanwhile, because these Gassendist views on space are sometimes difficult to sort out, a roadmap through the two tendencies may be of use here before journeying through them. Both tendencies were initially driven by a theological problem that had already been raised by Gassendi himself, namely, that if space is uncreated and independent of God, as it is on his view, then God is not the author of all things. Each is inclined to its own solution. Launay's solution, on the one hand, was obvious. Roughly put, spatiality is a feature of God, not something different from, and rivaling Him. This view may be called the apotheosis of space. In this, Launay was preceded, if not influenced, by Cureau. With Bernier, on the other hand, the tendency was to minimize, and finally to eliminate altogether, the ontological status of space and thus any theological problem it posed. This view may be called—literally, as we shall see—the annihilation of space. An additional contribution of the proponents of either the apotheosis or the annihilation of space was to advance the dialectic beyond anything in Gassendi's text. They each did so in two ways: (1) by giving far greater emphasis to the importance of views on space, and (2) by applying the theological objection to the Cartesians' views on space. In this, both Launay and Bernier were preceded, if not influenced, by Charleton. Bernier's views in particular were anticipated by La Grange's *novantique* criticism of the Cartesian views of Rohault. In turn, Bernier was attacked in Régis's defense of those same Cartesian views. To conclude this section, finally, two reflections will be offered in an effort to establish the contest for the historical and philosophical importance of these views on space. It is important to begin sorting out who may have influenced whom on space as absolute or relative, and to indicate that the stakes concerned no less than the principle of sufficient reason itself. But first, Gassendi's view and his attempt to answer the theological objection to it must be investigated.

Gassendi's View and the Objection to It

To distinguish corporeal and incorporeal extension, Gassendi asks us to imagine that God has annihilated everything below the Aristotelian lunar sphere, the result of which would be the preservation of its original dimensions without any

---

[211] *Abrégé* 2, 2:399–400.

corporeality. For example, a point on the sphere would be a certain distance from the one opposite it, namely, the diameter of the sphere. He next imagines that God creates and then destroys an infinitely large world. The space that remains—in truth, actual space—would have three properties: (1) immensity—space is without limit, although the world occupies only a part of it; (2) immobility—the world or any part of it may be moved without the space it occupies; (3) incorporeality—the space occupied by an object offers no resistance to bodies penetrating it or abiding with it (*corporeis penetranteis . . . compatienteis*). This way of expressing its incorporeality distinguishes space from incorporeal entities such as God, intelligences, and the human mind, the last of which, at least, is a "real and genuine substance with a real and genuine nature."

With the characteristics he has given it, Gassendi's space is indeed liable to the theological objection that it is a thing uncreated and independent of God with the result that He is not the author of all things. To this Gassendi had three kinds of reply. One was to minimize the ontological status of space. As opposed to positive incorporeal things like minds, space cannot act or be acted upon and is characterized only by its penetrability. One wonders how Gassendi can have it both ways. Indeed, the tendency among those who like Cureau and Launay made space and time conditions for existence was to resolve the problem by making space and time properties of God.

A second reply from Gassendi was the argument that he meant by space nothing more than what was admitted as the imaginary spaces by the "majority of sacred doctors," who are undeterred by the objection, "alleging that it is nothing positive, neither a substance nor an accident, under which heading all things created by God are subsumed."[212] These spaces are called imaginary, he insists, not because they depend on the imagination as do chimeras, but because we imagine their dimensions as we do the dimensions of bodies falling under the senses. The way in which these imaginary spaces are apprehended is crucial to their status, but it is just this that Gassendi left unclear. Nor was it made any clearer by Bernier, who at first gave as the reason these spaces are called imaginary that we are unable to conceive of them according to their whole immensity.[213] Later he gave as the reason that we conceive their extension or dimensions in the fashion of corporeal dimensions.[214] But then he tried to reply to the Cartesian argument, to which we shall return below, that if there were nothing between the walls of an empty room they would touch.[215] Here, Bernier interpolates a remark not to be found in Gassendi, namely, that indeed there is nothing between them, that is, "nothing corporeal, nothing that falls under the senses." So either Bernier contradicts himself, or imaginary space is some-

---

[212] 1:183b–184a; *Selected Works*, p. 389. Also, 1:189b. Brundell points out that Gassendi here clearly drew upon the Jesuit *Conimbricenses* (*Pierre Gassendi*, p. 66).

[213] Proto-*Abrégé*, p. 7.

[214] *Abrégé* 1, 1:13.

[215] *Principles* 2, 18; CSM, 1:231; AT, 8:50.

how imaginable but not perceptible.[216] Nor had Charleton offered any improvement: "not that they are merely *Phantastical*, as Chimaera's; but that our imagination can and doth apprehend them to have Dimension, which hold an analogy to the Dimensions of Corporeal substances, that fall under the perception and commensuration of the sense."[217] All of this sounds suspiciously like an important Cartesian view to which we shall also return, at great length, below. Descartes, Malebranche, and others held that we can perceive, not just extended things, but extension in general and that we can do so independently of any sense perception of it. As we shall see here, this is why Bernier came finally to reject the notion.

John Sergeant also rejected it, but for a different reason. He thought that the notion of real imaginary space was either incoherent or contradictory and that what its proponents were talking about existed only in the imagination. In his view they ought to have said that it is the imagination that is infinitely extended beyond the world; "but this is so notorious a Banger, that they say not this neither."[218] That is, if imaginary space is real, the mind is extended. This is not the last of the bangers over the mind's location with respect to its object that will be encountered. The imagination does extend beyond the world in the same sense, according to some, that things beyond the world are in the mind. Indeed, in chapters 4 and 5 we shall see Arnauld argue that Malebranche makes both God and the individual mind materially extended in order to explain perception of things at a distance. We shall also then see that the question of perception at a distance distinguishes the theories of ideas of the gods (Malebranche) and giants (Locke).

In a third reply to the theological objection, Gassendi argues that space as he conceives it with its three characteristics poses less of a threat than those essences admitted as eternal, uncreated, and independent of God and that are the eminence (*praecipuum*) of substances and accidents. This is the problem in spades that Gassendi saw in allowing space as an element of things, for a doctrine of independent essences puts the intelligible component of things beyond divine control. As Charleton put it, "To hold [an essence] uncreat and independent, is obliquely to infer God to be no more than an *Adopted Father* to Nature, a *titular* Creator, and Author of only the material, grosser and unattractive part of the World."[219] Gassendi does not have this problem since he denies the distinction between essence and existence, as much for created things as for God, with the result that no essence is eternal except God's, which is eternal but not essentially so. Thus God according to Gassendi is freer and more powerful even than according to Descartes. For the latter, all truth, including eternal truths, even such as $3 + 2 = 5$, depend on the divine will; but the Cartesian God

---

[216] *Abrégé* 1, 1:13–14. The remark is dropped from *Abrégé* 2.

[217] *Physiologia*, p. 68.

[218] *Method*, p. 42.

[219] *Physiologia*, p. 69.

is constrained by His own immutability. While He could have willed that $3 + 2$ be other than 5, once having willed so He cannot will otherwise. Whether immutability is sufficient to the constraining task that Descartes sees for it is a question to be considered in chapter 4. Meanwhile, we can say that the Gassendist deity is under no such constraint.[220]

Apotheosis

The simplest way of resolving the problem of space as a competing divinity is the way taken by many of those for whom an eternal essence loomed as a competing divinity, namely, by making it an aspect of the single divinity. To this solution Gassendi himself showed more than passing partiality. The localization pattern found in Cureau, however problematic, certainly suggests it. Launay commits himself to the view, though not without a certain ambivalence. He follows Gassendi's characterization of place (*lieu, locus*) as an incorporeal tridimensionality allowing penetration by bodies, and then immediately describes it as nothing other than the virtual or eminent (*eminentielles*) parts of God's immensity.[221] He realizes that "to admit real spaces [*espaces*] that preceded the world and that will follow it as an uncreated being if it is annihilated is a "difficulty" (*inconvenient*)—presumably the theological difficulty above—but he immediately replies to it that spaces so conceived accord quite well with God's immensity.[222] The way such spaces accord with divine immensity, it would seem, is that they just *are* the divine immensity, that is, space is actually a feature of God and the virtual or eminential parts of it that are distinguished by their capacity to receive different bodies are what he calls place. Here Launay uses an image that dates to a pseudo-Hermetic text of the twelfth century, the *Book of Twenty-four Philosophers*: God is a sphere whose center is everywhere and whose circumference is nowhere.[223]

However unclear this conclusion might be throughout Launay's essay on space, none other is possible by the end. Launay repeats the argument that God could create innumerable worlds or enlarge this one and that, to place these worlds, ultramundane spaces must be admitted.[224] These spaces must be infinite, otherwise we would be unable to conceive or represent the divine immensity (p. 102). But Lauany slides from its conception or representation to immensity itself. We must be careful not to make God material, he says, but there is no danger in making God spiritually extended (p. 203). This gives us the signifi-

---

[220] See Heyd, "Philosophy"; Osler, "Providence" for the significance of voluntarist theology in this period.

[221] *Essais physiques*, p. 76.

[222] Ibid., p. 79.

[223] Launay actually says "immense being" (p. 102). Gassendi, *Opera*, 1:190b.

[224] *Essais physiques*, p. 101.

cance of the problem in seeking whose solution Launay had "stirred all the dust in the colleges," namely, how to make place immobile, as it must be in order to mark the beginning and end of locomotion; for otherwise a thing could change place without moving or move without changing place (p. 80 *passim*). His answer was divine immobility: Because God is by His nature incapable of change and hence immobile, space as a system of virtual places is immobile (pp. 80–81). Conversely, this conception of space shows how God is immobile and unchanging even if He should move the world or create others elsewhere— unlike "our adversaries" (unnamed) who are forced to say that God must move in these instances as the soul moves when the body does (p. 103).

At this point, however, it is not clear whether for Launay God *is* space or is *in* (all of) space. Despite his clear adherence to the localization pattern, Launay's conception of space effectively undermines the active, absolutist alternative, for in the final analysis Launay must deny that space is independent of the things it contains. As for Gassendi, so for Launay, not only are matter and space different, but corporeal and incorporeal dimensions are different. They are specifically different kinds of being, as he says: "Extension is the genus of occupied [*plein*] and void place," the specific difference between them being, as Lucretius pointed out, tangibility (p. 97). Thus, Launay may be able consistently to maintain that time (or the virtual parts of God's eternity) endows things with their duration and continuation in existence, but not that space grounds their extension. If anything, corporeal extension is prior to incorporeal. As we have seen, Launay thinks that without an infinite incorporeal extension there can be no account of immensity; similarly, without it there would be no account of "the sphere of activity of an angel or a rational soul, which act only in determinate spaces because their power is limited. To make one thing coexist with another, to render it closely present to all the parts of an extended body without giving it extension is a thing inconceivable and impossible."[225] Two lines of argument thus converge in the conception of immensity. God to act everywhere must be everywhere; and since He is everywhere He is immobile (there is nowhere else for Him to go) and thus the reference with respect to which other things move. But this is to give up the absolutist conception of space, not just in the trivial sense that space as a feature of God is no longer an independent being *suo modo*. For God is *in* space in the sense that He stands in all possible spatial relations. He is to the left of everything and to the right of everything, and He *is* space in the sense that with respect to those relations all other spatial relations can be defined. There is no space apart from things in spatial relations. On this reconstruction of Launay's position, then, he eliminates Gassendi's extra set of dimensions in favor of a relational theory of space. Indeed, we shall see in chapter 4 that the only difference between it and

---

[225] In fact, the incorporeal extension of the soul is somewhat greater than the corporeal extension of the body that imprisons it, since the soul of a dwarf can fill the body of a giant.

Malebranche's relational theory is the difference between real and intelligible extension. This is the enormous difference, however, that places them on opposite sides of the *grande bataille*. However eclectic he may be, Launay does not for a moment flirt with the Cartesian theory that makes extension the essence of matter.

A striking feature of Launay's treatment of space is his unabashed application to the Cartesians of arguments that he takes from Gassendi and elaborates. For, in identifying space, matter, and extension and thus eliminating the void, the Cartesians hold a view that is "much bolder and more dangerous than that of the Peripatetics, who at least do not claim that the void is inconceivable," which amounts to denying divine omnipotence. Affirming omnipotence gives Launay his principal argument, which takes two forms. First, God can destroy all that He has created (pp. 76–78); He can also destroy a part of what He has created, such as the contents of some container whose walls He keeps immobile. *Ex hypothesi* there will not be body between the walls of the container, yet there will be extension between them because they are immobile and would touch only if they moved. Even if as a result of God's act they did move, they could do so only over time, and since God could destroy the contents instantaneously, there would be at least an interval during which there would be extension without body. This form of Launay's argument of course does not really address the Cartesians, for whom the void is not just a physical, but a conceptual impossibility.

A second form of the argument is better in this regard since it involves or at least adumbrates the independence principle that was to figure so importantly in the vacuum-plenum debates. The principle, to be found already in Descartes's *Principles*,[226] is that what is conceivable apart is really distinct as an individual. As we shall see, just what is conceivable apart, with respect to space and its contents and to many other issues, was very much a matter of debate. For the present argument, at any rate, we are again asked to consider an emptied container, for example, a triangular room. Its inner surface "is distinguished only by the mind from the exterior (surface), with which it makes the same body,"[227] and must therefore have the same shape that the exterior surface has. But in order for the inner surface of the room to be triangular, there must be some extension between its sides. That is, the triangle requires the void in order to be preserved as the individual that it is. Perhaps another way we can put this issue for the Cartesians is that if God were to destroy a part of extension as Launay supposes, He would falsify geometry, for the perpendicular drawn from the base to the apex would not have the extension required by Euclid, but none at all. Thus, those Cartesians who save omnipotence in Launay's sense do so only by making geometry depend on the divine will, for if the altitude of a given

[226] HR, 1:242–43; AT, 8:24.
[227] *Essais physiques*, p. 75.

triangle is equal to its area divided by half its base, this is only because God wills to create the space between its apex and base, that is, to create that particular triangle.

That a ground for geometry is the interesting issue here is suggested by a pair of arguments Launay raises that Bernier later picked up in the *Abrégé*. This time God is supposed to create three contiguous worlds in a row and then to annihilate the one in the middle while keeping the two others immobile. The Cartesians would have to say that though they are at a distance these worlds touch and moreover that God could re-create the world between them without moving them. Second, if God were to create a pile of spherical worlds, the Cartesians would have to say that they all touch each other not just at one point, but at all points in the way a pile of cubes would, which "seems to me so contrary to common sense and the demonstrations of mathematics" that the void must be admitted (pp. 101–2). Even these arguments do not get at the core conceptual issue, however, since they assume what for Descartes is unintelligible, namely, that God could create only three extended objects. As we shall see in chapter 4, for Descartes there is only one really extended object—what he called *res extensa*. It is infinite, and cannot be conceived otherwise without doing violence to geometry. For Descartes, the globes Launay is talking about are, if anything, phenomenal entities that depend on *res extensa* for their essence. With respect to them the relevant question is whether they could be conceived without any extension at all or whether they must have an extension that satisfied just the Euclidean requirements that Launay cites. That is, the issue is whether things have essences (of a certain sort) as the Cartesians held, or are bare as the Gassendists held. As we shall see, here and in the next section, Bernier offered arguments that relate more obviously to this issue.

Annihilation

Bernier's account of Gassendi's views on space is problematic in the extreme. There are three versions (the proto-*Abrégé*, *Abrégé* 1, *Abrégé* 2) and there are significant differences among them as to the material from the *Syntagma* that Bernier chooses to include or omit, the ordering and emphasis of the material, and the material of his own that he interpolates. Although it is impossible to spell out the historical details, it seems clear that Bernier was responding to Cartesian arguments on the topic whose general thrust can be made out. These arguments may well have had the additional result of changing Bernier's own views. Whatever its source, in at least one case the change in Bernier's own views altered the way in which he presented Gassendi's. Whether driven to it by the Cartesians or not, Bernier came to a view of space that was more Gassendist than Gassendi's own view.

The most obvious departure is the emphasis given the topic of space by its placement at the very outset of the proto-*Abrégé* and *Abrégé* 1. For Bernier space is of primary importance. "The first thing we must do in turning our eyes toward the universe is to conceive a vast and immense space, infinitely extended everywhere in length, depth and breadth, the field[228] of the Almighty's works and the general place of all that is or may be produced."[229] Gassendi's treatment of space, however, had occurred only in the second of the seven books that comprise the first of three parts of the physics, which occurs between the logic and the ethics; that is, it is rather buried away.[230]

Indeed, Gassendi seemed not to have recognized the significance of his views on space. The *Animadversiones* initially plumps for the void on the basis of physical arguments concerning motion, rarefaction and condensation, and saturation, but connects it to an analysis of space only by way of a worry about the substance-accident dichotomy (pp. 169–77). The account of space, which is actually quite close to what later appeared in the *Syntagma*, figures only as a digression, as Gassendi calls it, from the discussion of time, which space is used to explain since it is a parallel concept (pp. 610–22). Indeed, the account of space is separated from the discussion of atoms and the void by over four hundred pages of text. It was Charleton, six years before the *Syntagma*, who picked out this material and coupled it with the earlier topics and other related material in the first book of his *Physiologia*. This chapter follows the material in the *Animadversiones* fairly closely, consisting of translation, paraphrase, and summary. Occasionally Gassendi does not quite get the argument right, as when he seems to think that it follows from the possibility of God's annihilating and then re-creating the world that the space in which He does so must be immense (p. 67). The crucial premise of the argument, made explicit by Gassendi but ignored by Charleton, is that the world God might create could be infinitely larger than the present one He might annihilate (p. 615). But generally, Charleton's espousal of the Gassendist cause, although ruinous in other respects, undeniably advanced it in the case of the analysis of space. For one thing, Charleton included Descartes in his rebuttal of an argument that Gassendi had attributed only to the Aristotelians, namely, that the sides of a container whose contents have been annihilated must touch since there is nothing between them.

The principal thrust of Charleton's argument for the void is that all the

---

[228] In the heraldic sense: *la table d'attente*.

[229] Proto-*Abrégé*, p. 4: "The first thing a physicist must do . . . is . . . to consider this space as the general place of all that has been produced . . . and that God may draw from His omnipotence." See *Abrégé* 1, 1:7–8; *Abrégé* 2, 2:1–2.

[230] Bernier explains in *Abrégé* 1 that Gassendi thought that logic, the traditional first part of philosophy, was, if harmless, without great use: "if the eye sees, the ear hears . . . without any precepts, the understanding can reason well, seek the truth, find it and judge it without the aid of logic" (*au lecteur*, unpaginated). *Abrégé* 2 returns the logic to be outset of the work, although the treatment of space remains at the beginning of the physics.

arguments against it fail. The argument in particular from Descartes, White, and the other Aristotelians fails because the substance-accident dichotomy is gratuitously restrictive. "When any Cholerick Bravo of the *Stagirites* Faction shall draw upon us with this Argument . . . we need no other buckler than to except Place and Time."

Gassendi's arguments in the *Syntagma* on behalf of the void are aimed directly against the Aristotelians and, if at all, only indirectly against Descartes to the extent that the identification of matter and space, and thus the elimination of the void, relies on an ontology of substance and accident. Like Charleton, Bernier picks up these arguments and turns them specifically against the Cartesians, elaborating them beyond any warrant in Gassendi's text. The clearest example of this is the argument with which he closes the chapter on space: "I might add that those who are unwilling to recognize space in the way in which we allow it seem reduced to an extreme predicament, which is to allow a body of infinite extent that is perhaps eternal, independent and incapable of being destroyed—space, body and extension being the same thing in their view— which is no cause for concern on our view because on it space is neither substance, nor accident, nor anything capable of action or passion . . . and is but a pure capacity for receiving bodies. But I would be ashamed to pause further on this."[231]

Four years later, in 1678, Bernier's shame had vanished and, even if he does not name them as such, he directly attacks the Cartesians. Those who confuse space and body are reduced to the extreme predicaments of "allowing a corporeal substance that fills all possible spaces, or rather, which is itself space and which is consequently of infinite extension, and of maintaining (for fear of being obliged to allow any void) that God with all His power would be unable to destroy or annihilate the least part of that substance and that it is therefore independent of God."[232] But even this he thinks gives them too much attention. By 1684, however, a separate section is devoted to the predicaments of these "moderns" as he calls them. Not only are they taxed with the above theological objection, but Gassendi's objection that the Aristotelians reject the void only by relying on an ontology of substance and accident is now directed against the Cartesians as a great predicament in physics. If God were to empty a room of its contents while preventing both anything else from entering and its walls from moving, they would say that since there was nothing between them the walls would touch.[233]

An additional feature of Bernier's treatment of the above argument shows him to have been involved in the polemics of the period. In all three versions of the theory of space, he argues that the existence or the mode of existence of one

[231] Proto-*Abrégé*, p. 14.
[232] *Abrégé* 1, 1:25.
[233] *Abrégé* 2, 2:5, 10–11.

body cannot "absolutely" depend on the existence of another body, that the shape of the room cannot depend on air or anything else that it may contain. The result is that God might begin by producing the air that the room will contain and then the room; but He might equally well produce the room first and then the air it contains.[234] This of course is the independence principle invoked by the Cartesians, among others, that we soon shall see Cordemoy to have used against them in just this way on behalf of atomism.

An important question is raised by Bernier's attack on the Cartesians. How is it that he thinks the Gassendist theory can avoid the difficulties he aims against the Cartesians? For although the Cartesian extension is corporeal, it does not satisfy the Gassendist condition for being something positive, namely, that it have the power of acting.[235] On the contrary, active matter of the Gassendist sort ought not to have been and was not intelligible to any Cartesian. Indeed, as I shall try to show, for Descartes and some of his followers, the matter identical to extension is incapable even of real motion. Even for those like Malebranche who thought matter capable of real motion, matter had no dynamical properties. It was this conception of matter that figured so prominently in arguments for occasionalism, for example. The most basic dynamical property of impenetrability was necessitated for the Gassendists because they distinguished matter from extension. Bernier's argument, therefore, that the Cartesians introduce a "positive nature capable of acting" because it cannot be destroyed by God[236] either is no objection at all or tells at least as well against the Gassendist theory. In addition, by appealing to the independence principle, Bernier threatens to make not just space independent but bodies as well. If the room and the air it contains can exist apart because they are individuals, then they can exist apart from God. To this the alternative seems to be Spinozism: They are not individuals because they cannot exist independently of God, of whom they must be a feature or a part. Why would Bernier subject Gassendi to the contagion of these issues?

At first Bernier seems to ignore, or at least minimize these difficulties. The proto-*Abrégé*, for example, does not raise the theological difficulty at all as far as Gassendist space is concerned. Instead, Bernier there advances two arguments that space need not be created. One is an argument from the pseudo-Archytas modified to read that everything must be created in some place, but that place cannot be created in some other place since this would open an infinite regress.[237] The other is the argument that if the earth were withdrawn from the place it occupies, there would be no need to create that space in order to replace the earth, and thus there was no need to create its space in order

---

[234] Proto-*Abrégé*, p. 13; *Abrégé* 1, 1:17–19; *Abrégé* 2, 2:12–13.

[235] :See *Syntagma*; *Opera*, 1:184b.

[236] *Abrégé* 2, 2:10.

[237] Archytas had argued that everything is in some place, hence because of the same regress, place must be nothing. See Samburskly, "Place and Space."

originally to create the earth. (Neither argument figures as such in *Abrégé* 1 or *Abrégé* 2.) In *Abrégé* 2, however, the objection is raised in no uncertain terms. Bernier at length applies Gassendi's worry with respect to eternal essences directly to the Cartesians. On behalf of Gassendi's theory, meanwhile, he is content merely to counter with the reply that space thus conceived is no more problematic than the sacred doctors' imaginary spaces.

A clue to the evolution of Bernier's reaction to this problem is his growing reservation over Gassendi's theory of space. Consider the characterization of the void as imaginary space, which differs markedly in *Abrégé* 1 and *Abrégé* 2. To be sure, both make the point that it is so characterized by the theologians not because it is chimerical, depending only on the imagination, but because we imagine its extension or incorporeal dimensions "after the fashion of corporeal dimensions." But, following an ambiguity of emphasis in Gassendi's text, *Abrégé* 1 makes the point in order to emphasize the existence of this space lest having been distinguished from incorporeal *substance* it be thought of as nothing at all. *Abrégé* 2 makes the point in the course of an apology for Gassendist space vis-à-vis Omnipotence; all that is admitted is what the theologians meant by imaginary space, which was uncreated and independent of God and which they yet allowed as orthodox. The change seems explained by the threat expressed in *Abrégé* 1 to the reality of space, which by 1682 becomes the full-blown doubt that space seems properly to be "a pure nothing": "only with difficulty could a being other than God be admitted which is eternal, immense, independent, indestructible . . . penetrable, and immobile, which are nonetheless the properties [that had been] attributed to space."[238] What I am suggesting, then, is that Bernier felt free to attack the Cartesians on a point on which Gassendi's theory was no less vulnerable since he himself was hesitating about just that problematic aspect of it.

Indeed, Bernier's reservation becomes a penetrating nominalist critique of Gassendist space. In addition to the theological difficulty, it is objected that space (1) is incorporeal yet has parts; (2) is imperceptible hence should not be admitted except for very strong reasons; and (3) when imagined as empty is not imagined as a being, whether corporeal or incorporeal.[239] The criticism is sharpened in *Doubts* 2, where such a space is described as the chimera of those who delight in deceiving themselves, and where the characterization of space as a being "in its own fashion" is ridiculed as both obscure and useless against the above objections. The root difficulty, clearly expressed in both sets of doubts, is that the Gassendist space is an abstract entity. To the argument that between the walls of an empty container there must be some distance Bernier now replies that if that distance is "a certain line, or spatial, invisible and incorporeal length which makes the walls distant from each other, it is a pure fiction"—to be dis-

---

[238] *Doubts* 1, p. 25.
[239] Ibid., pp. 25–27.

tant they need only not touch.[240] What is true of equality is true of distance; "they are abstract terms, which like all others of this sort, lead us to error if we conceive something abstract or separated from the concrete" (pp. 387–88).[241] For two things to be equal there need not be some "distinct entity which is the equality" to make them equal. They need only each have a certain size. And when one measures the distance between two things, there is no *thing* that is being measured any more than there is a capacity in an empty room that can receive things. Space in fact is nothing at all: "I maintain that [these allegedly infinite, etc.] spaces are not, do not exist, are not a being, are not a thing" (p. 386). Empty space is best referred to by a negative judgment (p. 385). For example, nothing is in this room, where 'nothing' functions as a "particle" (p. 392) or syncategorematic term, just as there need be no thing called "darkness" spread out in a room in order for it to be dark—there just need be no light in it.

It was not likely that this radically nominalized space, despite its drawing near a relational view, would be found congenial by the Cartesians, who in one way or another take a position of extreme realism with respect to space. Nor was it. Régis for one agreed that the void as a room from which God has removed the air should be conceived by the same kind of negative judgment by which the dark is conceived; but just as the dark is a lack of light in air capable of being illuminated, so the void is a lack of air in a room capable of having it, and since the void has some quantity it is some matter or other.[242] Régis goes on to argue against "others" (presumably, than Bernier) who nonetheless seem to hold his view of the void. They maintain that since space as a mere negation or privation would presuppose some subject, it might be viewed as pure nonbeing (*pur néant*). Régis's main argument that pure nonbeing has no properties, while the void has extension, fails against Bernier, for whom nothing *has* extension. There are things that are extended and qualified in other ways, but apart from which there is no extension or anything else. The distance between two things is not itself a thing but a property of the things distant that is not different from them. Thus, Régis just begs his realism against Bernier, just as he begs the question against Gassendi who rejects the substance ontology.

Bernier's conception of space as a pure nothing was anticipated by La Grange, who in his criticism of the Cartesians departed from Aristotle to allow not only the absolute but the natural possibility of the void.[243] In particular he is concerned with the views of Rohault, the natural sense of whose expression of them, according to La Grange, is that matter is infinite, uncreated, and indepen-

---

[240] *Doubts* 2, p. 387.

[241] The Cartesian Antoine LeGrand later argued that "that which is Nothing can never constitute the Distance of *Bodies*." Nor could distance be "founded in the *Bodies* themselves," for then relations of distance would never change (*Entire Body*, pt. 2, p. 2).

[242] *Système*, 1:286.

[243] *Les principes*, p. 410.

dent of God. But he is also concerned with Descartes's view, which he sees as in effect coming to the same thing, namely, that a plurality of worlds is impossible because there is no place for another beyond the actual one (chap. 28). To combat both Rohault and Descartes, he thinks that either real, extraterrestrial space must be denied, which is not easy, or space though real (*veritable*) must not be something positive (*rien de positif*) or have real extension. The latter is supposed to become plausible when we realize that there is no space between things that touch, but that there is between those that do not because a third thing can be placed between them. "Thus space, properly speaking, is a certain capacity for receiving a body because there is no space in which a body cannot be put" (p. 403). So far this sounds like the Gassendist passive container. Indeed, the space now occupied by the world was the same before the world was created, and is neither substance nor accident. But it is not a being suo modo—"it is not a being at all. It is nothing [*ce n'est rien*]" (p. 404). The line he takes in explaining this view, however, is not at all as clear as Bernier's. Like Bernier, his inclination is to talk of space in terms of relations of distance. Thus he supposes that beyond the created world God could create a stone at a certain distance from it and then, without any real extension between them, alter that distance, and so on. But he gives distance a status Bernier clearly wants to deny it. Although space is nothing, "this nothing is real in its fashion, i.e. it is something that is such as it is imagined to be and thus is not imaginary." (And therefore those who call it imaginary space are badly mistaken.) If we were to imagine real extension where there is none, he explains, it would be imaginary. But space is imagined as it is, that is, not as a being but nonetheless real. He sees two senses of the term 'real': real in the nature of things and real in representation. Space is real only in the latter sense, or can be as when we conceive space between two things that are not in contact. (By contrast, the space imagined between things that are in contact is imaginary.) Space thus conceived as nothing can be uncreated, infinite, indestructible, and immobile (pp. 407–8).

La Grange's rather Hobbist theory of space perhaps gives us a reading of another of Bernier's texts of obvious relevance to his account of space, namely, his chapter on place. The basic structure of the chapter remains unchanged throughout the three *Abrégés*. The problem Bernier deals with, as well as his eventual solution to it, is at least partly linguistic. Place must be immobile otherwise a thing might move without changing place or change place without moving. Thus the place of a thing cannot be the immediate surface of what surrounds it. This Aristotelian view has the additional inconveniences that a tower in the wind, for example, must move, and that the universe as a whole has no place. Place, then, is just occupied space, which when unoccupied is the void. Thus the basic structure of the three *Abrégés*. The tone and detail of the arguments, however, differ markedly. *Abrégé* 2, for example, compresses the material, treats it rather less enthusiastically, and suppresses two rebuttals appended to the earlier editions. One rebuttal replies to the Aristotelian argument that place is not a volume occupied by a body because, as the body itself has volume, two volumes would then occupy the same place. The other replies to the argument that space must be regarded as material since it is a divisible quantity. Both arguments are rebutted with the distinction between divisible corporeal and indivisible incorporeal extension. Once again, these changes in *Abrégé* 2 are explained by Bernier's *Doubts*.

In his *Doubts* Bernier is prepared to endorse the Aristotelian view of place as more plausible than Gassendi's view, at least to the extent that it reflects the commonsense conception of place and melds with his own nominalist conception of space. Place as the surface of a surrounding body seems clearly known, he thinks, by everyone, including children and even animals (a room is the place of a bed, a trunk the place of some gold, etc.). To the objection that such a view leaves the world without a place, Bernier with Aristotle grants the objection as harmless and then argues that the space in which we make distinctions beyond the world is *only* imaginary. It is a pure fiction that is regarded as real, seemingly in La Grange's sense, only because it is formed through constant experience of things that really are in place. The reality is only in the representation. Properly speaking, the void itself is (a place where there is) nothing. Thus neither this world nor some world God might create beyond it are contained *in* the void.[244]

Part of Bernier's worry over place is merely linguistic insofar as the representation or description of motion as change of place is concerned. But part of it would seem to hinge on the deep ontological question of the status required by what is described. And it is here that Bernier's nominalism becomes obvious and perhaps obviously problematic. He tells us that it came to him while thinking about modes that most if not all of them are indefinable, being themselves what enter into definitions of things. What Bernier has to say suggests that modes are known only on the basis of acquaintance: (1) modes are clear and evident by themselves and one need only have eyes to see what they are (p. 408); (2) this is plausibly true of some (e.g., pain) but perhaps not all (e.g., action) of Bernier's examples (p. 407); (3) modes are primitives that cannot be defined without circularity or synonymy (p. 406). Consequently, motion and rest, qua modes of bodies, cannot be defined and are known perfectly and definitively in the fashion of Diogenes. The upshot is that the basic objection to the Aristotelian view of place, viz. that it allows a thing to move without changing place and to change place without moving, is overcome, for it is based on a definition of motion as " a successive application of a body to the parts of the bodies surrounding it" (pp. 401, 410). In fact, only to allow the possibility of motion as "the passage of a body from one place to another" did Gassendi, following the

---

[244] *Doubts* 2, p. 398. With this conception of place Bernier can also answer the puzzle about Archytas's arrow: It would indeed go beyond the world but not *into* the void. With it he can also restore Archytas's argument to its original intent, which he does in effect arguing against Gassendi's view: How must everything be in a place when space, supposedly a real being, has no place?

ancients, admit space—that strange entity now viewed by Bernier as virtually contradictory—"a being which [though] incorporeal has parts . . . which subsists in itself and is not a substance, a being which is everywhere and is nowhere" (pp. 410–11). Better, then, to accept the commonsense view of place and refuse all definitions of motion and all the paradoxes with them.

Bernier thus in a sense avoids difficulties at the linguistic level, but it is not clear just what else he has done. It is one thing to deny to space any independent ontological status. It is quite another to provide an account that without it nonetheless grounds everything that Bernier must regard as true of material things and their motion. After all, the void was admitted, not to provide a definition of motion *in vacuo*, as it were, but, for among other reasons, to avoid the difficulty of the plenum vis-à-vis motion. For Bernier to reject the void and regard motion as a primitive is, at least historically, an unusual procedure. For he not only regards the space in terms of which motion is conceived as merely imaginary, but he rejects every definition of it because "definitions explain the nature of the thing" defined. Those who define motion treat it as a thing that is passed from one moving thing to another, a mistake that he thinks lies at the root of their mistaken view about collision and conservation of motion and of the difficulties they see in projectile motion. Although he never quite puts it in these terms, Bernier's procedure is to move the problems from the level of things to the level of how we talk about them. The procedure may be fair enough, except that the move as effected by Bernier converts nominalism from an ontological view into a lexicographical one. Even if, as some have come to believe in recent years, the world is the language we use to describe it, there is still a difference between physical or metaphysical problems and merely linguistic ones. It is one thing to say there is nothing to talk about; it is another to refuse to talk about it.

Further Reflections

I shall conclude this section with two further reflections. One has to do with the principle of sufficient reason, which in the end will restore the larger context for the philosophical significance of these Gassendist analyses of space. The other, with which I shall begin, concerns the question of historical influences. Toward the end of his chapter on space[245] Gassendi has an argument for the existence of space *suo modo* that may be important in sorting out who was influenced by whom on the question of space. The argument is intended to rebut the view that all being must be substance or accident and that space, since it is dependent on what is in it, must be an accident—a thing can change place as it can change color; hence place like color is an accident of it. Gassendi responds that though place can join and separate from (*accedat*, & *abscedat*) the thing located

---

[245] *Opera*, 1:184a–185b. The text is taken verbatim from the *Animadversiones*, p. 614.

without the destruction of that thing, and hence may seem to be an accident of it, place in fact does not approach or recede (*neque accedere*, *neque abscedere*) but is immobile; it is the thing located that moves. That is, what remains through change in the case of motion is space, not the thing in it which ex hypothesi has changed place. Thus, once again it is the absolute impassivity of space that emerges as crucial in Gassendi's analysis. In this instance, however, either Gassendi just begs the question on behalf of an independent space or what he says is true of all qualities. When a thing changes color, *it* changes, not its *color*: The apple, not greenness, becomes red. Thus, he says that, if anything, substance should be attributed to space insofar as it is successively occupied by bodies (presumably as a thing successively can have different colors). But space cannot be a substance either, "which ordinarily is understood not only as what exists through itself, but also and especially as something corporeal and material, or what has the faculty of acting and abiding, which surely are incompatible with place."

The proto-*Abrégé* and *Abrégé* 2 ignore this argument altogether. *Abrégé* 1 perhaps hints at it, arguing that place has properties not generally attributed to substances: immobility, incorporeality, and inability to act.[246] It is tempting to attribute Bernier's lack of attention to the argument to his own disenchantment with the conception of space as a separate being.[247] Whatever the explanation, Bernier cannot have been anyone's source for the argument. Launay has a version of the argument, but one that is even less successful than Gassendi's in motivating the rebuttal: "If our adversaries say that place [*lieu*] is an accident, because it can be or not be without its subject, *viz.* the thing placed."[248] That is, Launay *begins* with a characterization of space according to which it is, if anything, a substance. Charleton, on the other hand, has a version very close to Gassendi's text that he uses "to authenticate this our Schism."[249] Whether it was from him, or more probably Gassendi himself, that Newton picked it up, is difficult to know. But it does emerge in his *De gravitatione et aequipondio fluidorum*.[250] Having proposed to overthrow the Cartesian philosophy with respect to extension, Newton rejects the trichotomy that extension be substance, accident, or nothing at all. It is not substance because it is not absolute in itself and is not active, and since it is conceivable without body and would not perish with a body that God might annihilate, it is not an accident; indeed it thus

---

[246] 1:21.

[247] He also adds that (1) nothing can be its own place, because a body that moves does not carry its place with it, but leaves one and moves to another; (2) common sense tells us that place is different from the thing placed, and that since place is what receives bodies, it is both prior to and supposed by them.

[248] *Essais physiques*, p. 79.

[249] *Physiologia*, p. 66.

[250] Which its editors date between 1664 and 1668 (p. 90).

"approaches more nearly to the nature of substance." Using Gassendi's term (*affectio*) he calls it a disposition of all being.[251]

Locke has a celebrated passage in which he too rejects the substance ontology, and which, occurring where it does in his account of space, suggests that his source(s) would lead him to the absolutist conception. Despite the suggestion, I shall try to show in chapter 6 that it is Bernier whose views here shed most light on Locke. By contrast to Bernier's line on space, the absolutist view is for a commonsense empiricist like Locke plainly a priori unsatisfactory. It is weird (the soul of dwarfs in the bodies of giants),[252] ill-defined (the question whether God is *in* space), and extravagant not just in being unparsimonious but in admitting the kind of entity it does. If substance and accident are unintelligible, a fortiori are space and time as a third category.

Finally, the Gassendist analysis of space raises a question with respect to the principle of sufficient reason. If space is infinite and homogeneous, and if this world occupies only a part of that space,[253] then why does it occupy the part of space that it does rather than some other; why does God create where He does rather than elsewhere? This is a very old problem with an enormous and difficult literature,[254] to which Leibniz's argument against the Newton–Clarke version of Gassendi's view is only the best known contribution. There are several philosophically plausible ways an upholder of the view might deal with the problem. One of them, however, is not through an appeal to a distorted authority. But I am afraid this is what the Gassendist position comes to, if there is a Gassendist position at all.

On behalf of ultramundane space Gassendi quotes, and Bernier translates, two brief texts from Augustine's *City of God* that deal with the topic. An argument is insinuated to the effect that unless space is infinite, the divine substance is limited by its ubiquity; that is, because God is everywhere, His place must be an infinite extension or He is not infinite. Limited space limits God. The upshot is that the divine substance must be conceived as though it were extended and diffused throughout infinite space.[255] The qualification *as though* is included "lest we imagine that the divine substance is extended in the manner of bodies." But the difference seems only to be that bodies are spatially

---

[251] *Unpublished papers*, pp. 99–100; trans. pp. 131–32. cf. *Syntagma, Opera*, 1:179a. The term does not appear in this connection in *Animadversiones* and therefore not in Charleton's account of space. I am thus inclined to agree with Westfall's contention that Newton here "drew his discussion of space and time directly from the *Syntagma*" ("Foundations," pp. 172–73, n. 5).

[252] Locke of course is interested in metempsychosis (see his notes on Bernier) but only for purposes of thought experiments. He does not say that the soul of Castor in fact is ever in the body of Pollux, but only asks what we would say if it were.

[253] *Opera*, 1:182a.

[254] It has been systematically treated and made remarkably tractable by Sorabji.

[255] praeter eandem concipimus infinitatem quasi extensionis, (*Opera*, 1:191b); comme diffuse & d'étendue (proto-*Abrégé*, p. 7).

(and temporally) limited. "As corporeal extension is said to be extended because it is not merely in a single point but is spread out through several parts of space, so the divine substance is held to be as it were extended [*quasi extensa*] because it exists not merely in a single place but in many, or rather in all places."[256] In these texts, at least, God is not said to be space, but only to be in space.

The context for the Augustinian texts on which the above dialectic is based is a discussion of God as creator. The immediate problem is the creation of the world in time: Why did God create at one time rather than another? This question was raised theoretically by the Epicureans[257] to show that God did not create at all. The problem is over mutability in God and sufficient reason. That God should act at one moment rather than at another indistinguishable from it means either He acts because of some change in Him or for no reason at all. To avoid what seems to be the only alternative to the Epicurean impiety, namely, that the world is created by God but without a beginning in time, Augustine argues that the question is no more legitimate than the question why He creates here rather than elsewhere. "For if they imagine that there were infinite stretches of time before the world existed, an infinity in which they cannot conceive of God's being inactive, *they will*, on the same showing, *imagine infinite stretches of space; and if anyone says that the omnipotent could not have been inoperative anywhere in that infinity, it will follow* that they are compelled to share the Epicurean fantasy of innumerable worlds."[258] Gassendi quotes and Bernier translates only the italicized material. The second text is also taken from its context: "Will they [who acknowledge that God is everywhere in His immaterial presence] say His substance is absent from those spaces beyond the world, that He is enclosed in the space of this world, which is so small in comparison with that infinity?" Augustine's point is that if God were in these infinite spaces, then the plurality of worlds would follow; hence He is not because as the very title of the chapter indicates, there is no space outside the world.[259]

Gassendi and Bernier do not attempt to legitimate infinite and homogeneous space by direct appeal to Augustine, because they themselves do not even raise his problem of sufficient reason. Their distorted texts are cited to show, independently of that problem, that Augustine found the notion of infinite ultramondane space intelligible, acceptable, or whatever. This is reflected in the various uses to which Bernier puts the texts. The proto-*Abrégé* follows Gassendi more or less closely as above. *Abrégé* 1 seems to use Augustine's texts less to argue that space is in fact infinite, or that beyond the occupied space of the world there is unoccupied space, than just to make the distinction between corporeal and incorporeal extension. It also ignores the problematic attempt to distinguish the

---

[256] Ibid.

[257] Cicero, *De natura decorum* 1.9.21.

[258] P. 434, corrected.

[259] *De Civitate Dei*, p. 638. Augustine's points are faithfully conveyed by André Martin, however (*Philosophia*, 3:95).

senses in which bodies are in space and God is in space. *Abrégé* 2 merely reproduces the texts, introducing them with a remark about support for the view of the divine substance as spread out as it were in the imaginary spaces beyond the world, which is a view Bernier thought was held by Democritus, Epicurus, Lucretius, Nemesius, and the theologians.

What, then, to make of the distortion? Outright dissimulation is prima facie implausible, of course, and in any case unnecessary given the availability of acceptable ways of dealing with the problem. Just a mistaken reading is also improbable, but perhaps accounted for by the conceptual improbability, or difficulty at least, even in seeing a problem concerning sufficient reason. For the radical empiricist creation is a matter of sheer, unconstrained volition, or in nontheological terms, existence is fortuitous. Ultimately there is no reason why now and not earlier, why here and not there. That the sphere of what is not—of where God could have created but did not—should be infinite only serves to emphasize the ultimate lack of reason for the finite sphere of what is, of what He did create.[260] At this point the contrast with the Cartesian position is sharp. Here too extension is infinite, but here it is also real, whether material as for Descartes or intelligible as Malebranche would have liked it to be. If extension were merely finite, God would be less than God. In Platonic terms the world would be less than full and God would have been jealous and less than good. In Cartesian terms He would be a deceiver and the Euclidean picture of the world would be false. Given that He is not a deceiver, the existence of extension, whether created or uncreated, is far from fortuitous. Thus the significance of the Cartesian identification of matter and extension, which was sufficient but hardly necessary for the mathematization of nature. For with this identification the question, why here and not there, does not arise; for matter is everywhere it could possibly be. Before turning to the Cartesian position, we must first complete the Gassendist alternative by setting out its analysis of matter.

§8 PHYSICAL AND METAPHYSICAL ATOMISM

For the nominalism typical of the giants, difference is given and sameness is constructed. Since the basic contention is that only individuals exist, the numer-

---

[260] As Launay put it, except for contemplating and loving Himself, God is inactive in those times and places in which He does not create, and if what He creates does not have the full temporal and spatial extension it might have, this is because He is "free and independent and consequently master of His actions" (*Essais physiques*, p. 104). Curiously, Launay initially gets the point of the Augustinian texts right when he argues that there *are not* innumerably many worlds. But later he falls in with the Gassendist interpretation when he argues that God *could* create innumerably many worlds or enlarge this one as it pleased Him, and since He cannot create a world without a place to put it in, ultramundane spaces must be admitted (*Essais physiques*, pp. 16,101). The latter text raises the problem of sufficient reason at least obliquely. God must be where He acts, according to Launay, thus must be beyond the world in order (to be able) to create there.

ical difference between them is taken as primitive in the sense that no ontological category beyond that of individuals is required to explain numerical difference. Individuals just are things that are numerically distinct. Even if, for example, a localization pattern is invoked as part of an account of how things differ, difference between places occupied by *eo ipso* different things is still taken as more primitive than the qualitative sameness of things. In a nominalist world consisting only of individual things, the qualitative sameness of things must be constructed from the primitively given individuals, for example, in terms of our perception of them or the language we use to describe them.

For the realism typical of the gods, sameness is given and difference is constructed. Kinds are taken as the primitive ontological category in that they simply make numerically different things to be qualitatively identical. Although kinds may be accounted for in terms of, for example, Forms, how we are to understand that there are individuals that exemplify them is a further problem. The clearest example of this ontological priority is from Leibniz, who, it might be argued, uses kinds to individuate: Numerical nonidenticals are *eo ipso* qualitatively discernible. In an example of greater relevance to our story, Descartes poses *res extensa* to account for the one kind of material thing in his world, but then, as I shall argue, needs motion and the sensory perception of *res extensa* to account for the numerical diversity we perceive in that world.

The nominalist and the realist are impressed with either the difference or sameness perceived in the world, which each then canonizes with a primitive ontological category. For both nominalism and realism, however, the primitive category is not introduced without a story. Thus, extension is construed by the Cartesians as the ground for geometry, itself the ground for our explanation of the material world. In this section I want to introduce our period's nominalist story about individuals and its surprising connection with Cartesianism. What we find is a groping away from physical atomism toward metaphysical atomism.

Physical atomism is the thesis that the infinite divisibility of matter is a physical impossibility. The laws of physics are such that the integrity of certain quantities of matter cannot be upset. Thus, one might hold, for example, that while matter is conceptually divisible to infinity, only God could effect its division beyond a certain point. It seems to me, however, that physical atomism in this period is itself a conceptual impossibility, at least given the conception of homogeneous matter universally accepted by those who were scientifically *au courant* in this period. The principal attraction of the concept of universal homogeneous matter was that according to it the same set of physical laws is sufficient and necessary for the explanation of all material states. If matter is physically divisible at one level then it should be physically divisible at all levels, no matter how microscopic. Within the eye of a mite we should find worlds containing, if not mites with eyes containing further worlds, then at least nothing essentially different from our own divisible world. Size can make no difference.

Metaphysical atomism is perhaps a more intelligible thesis. One expression of it is the denial that there are internal relations; it is the claim that the existence of a thing and its attributes are independent of everything else. It is, if you will, the ontological version of twentieth-century logical atomism. But this statement of the view, that things are independent, is not quite sufficient, for then with Descartes's definition of substance, any substance ontology including Descartes's would be atomist. Another way to put it might be to say that not everything that can exist does exist. The obvious image, historically very important indeed, is of discrete particles of matter randomly dispersed in the void. The discreteness suggested by this image, however, can only be a physical accident. Instead, a stronger account is required and thus we have to think of the individuals in nonmaterial terms and as located in logical space. What this comes to in its extreme form is a binary system of bare particulars and bare nonexistence. This is by way of obvious contrast with the Cartesian monist picture of space necessarily filled with matter identical to it, with every part or bit of it being necessarily what it is because of its essential mathematical structure.

The early Gassendists were no more than physical atomists. For the purposes of doing physics, they said, let us assume that beyond a certain point matter will in fact never be divided. Such was the attitude of Pierre Petit of Montluçon, who, as we saw, took an unusually sophisticated instrumentalist view of the whole matter. Despite certain anticipations of metaphysical atomism noted below, it seems to me that Gassendi's too was nothing more than physical atomism.[261] Even so, Gassendi's atomism is not without interest by way of contrast to the Cartesians. The following sketch, especially of the Cartesian contrast, is exceedingly schematic, but I hope it will suffice as background to the case I shall present in more detail.

Gassendi's aim of course was to rehabilitate the atomism of Epicurus by correcting its theologically unacceptable features. The principal corrective Gassendi makes in Epicurean atomism is to regard atoms as created. He also reduces the number of atoms and their shapes to a finite (if incomprehensibly large) number, which thus makes atoms by themselves incapable of explaining the order in the world. Finally, while weight (*pondus, seu gravitas*) is for

---

[261] I think it fair to say that Gassendi's atomism generally takes the form of a crude physical theory invoked to explain certain phenomena. Thus, for example, he supposes on the basis of his observation of the formation of salt crystals that gross bodies are "by some sort of necessity" composed of similarly shaped bodies and these of others until atoms of the same shape are reached (to Pieresc, July 6, 1635; cited in Rochot, *Les travaux*, pp. 66–67). Rochot, however, draws attention (pp. 174–78) to one point in the *Syntagma* where Gassendi, in response to difficulties with respect to the divisibility and size of atoms, may be offering a rather more sophisticated theory than anything he resurrected from the ancients. I am none too certain of the interpretation of *Syntagma*; *Opera*, 1:268a, but it may go something as follows. In the *minimum visibilium* there must be perceptible parts, for example, the top, the bottom, each of the sides, that yet are not further *visibilia* and do not upset the *minimum* as a *minimum*. Similarly, atoms may have *conceptual* parts that account for their differences in size but that are themselves not separable as further atoms.

Gassendi as for Epicurus a property of atoms, this notion is given a radically new explanation that rejects the picture of atoms falling primordially downward through the void. Instead, an atom that would otherwise be inactive is created with "a natural and internal faculty or force" that it cannot lose and by which, unless it is inhibited by a similarly grounded motion in some other atom(s), it moves itself and moves others.[262] Thus the law of inertia, for the first publication of which Gassendi has been given credit, is true for him, as we noticed in chapter 1, only of objects at the observational, or at most the molecular level, where bodies at rest remain at rest only as a result of exactly equal and opposed motorforce. The upshot of created, quantitatively and qualitatively finite, and intrinsically, if not natively, inactive atoms is an argument for God as a provident creator.

The contrast with the Cartesian picture that I shall draw in chapter 4 is sharp and dramatic. For Descartes there is but a single real individual, res extensa, which is capable of (and, according to the *Discourse's* fable version of the world, actually assumes) an infinite number of shapes. That is, the one intelligible object of the *mathesis universalis* can be perceived as an infinite number of sense-instantiated corporeal things, which can be regarded as the objects of mathematical theorems. Motion is an essential feature of corporeal things only insofar as it individuates them; it is not a feature at all and a fortiori not a natural force of the real. Regardless of the ontological status of motion, however, the law of inertia obtains at all levels of moving objects and quantity of motion is conserved in all instances of collision. Finally, though God has His purposes, they are irretrievably hidden from human view and play no role in either physics or metaphysics. The only intelligibility is the mathematical intelligibility of what God creates from one moment to the next. Malebranche later altered this picture somewhat. What are corporeal things for Descartes are for him representations of corporeal things, which things are real, multiple, and mobile. But it is just this departure that he had difficulty sustaining in a way that preserves both Cartesian and Christian orthodoxy. He also admits teleological explanations, but only with respect to a restricted range of phenomena that does not argue the existence of God. In short, Malebranche essentially preserved the Cartesian contrast with Gassendism.

Ironically, the metaphysical atomist challenge to Cartesianism first came, not from the Gassendists, but from within the Cartesian camp itself. Gerauld de Cordemoy (1626–84) was a practicing lawyer who was an *habitué* of the leading salons (Mme. de Bonnevaux), *conférences* (Rohault), and academies (Bourdelot) of the 1660s. As suggested by some of the circles he frequented, he was regarded as a Cartesian and in fact was among the anointed Baillet lists as attending the Descartes funeral jamboree of June 29, 1667.[263] His principal

---

[262] *Syntagma*; *Opera*, 1:273a–274a.

[263] For more on Cordemoy, see the introduction by Clair and Girbal to his *Oeuvres philosophiques*.

work entitled *The Distinction between Body and Soul in Six Discourses, intended as a clarification of physics* appeared in 1666. The review of it for the *Journal des Savants* of June 7 of that year thought that its author "generally followed the principles of Descartes, but (that) he was not so attached to them that he did not relinquish them in certain places."[264] In certain places indeed, for Cordemoy argued in no uncertain terms an ontology of atoms and the void. His Cartesian critic Desgabets credited him with being the first to advance metaphysical arguments, however faulty, for the ancient doctrine he espoused.[265]

Cordemoy announces right at the outset of his first *Discourse* that "bodies are extended substances." And, "1. Since there are many bodies, the extension of each of them must be limited, this limit being what is called shape. 2. As each body is but a self-same substance, it cannot be divided—its shape cannot change and it is so necessarily continuous that it excludes every other body, which is called impenetrability."[266] He goes on to argue against the Cartesians' divisibility of matter that (1) the indefinite divisibility they assert really means that it is infinitely divisible, and this is inconceivable; (2) a body at rest among others at rest but different from them in fact is conceivable but on Cartesian grounds is not conceivable; (3) on Cartesian grounds there can be no fixed shape for any body, each of whose parts ad infinitum would be acted upon by a different body ad infinitum; (4) the Cartesians anyhow assume atomism in their actual explanations. He thinks the Cartesians assert the divisibility of body because they confuse body with *matter*, which they take to be a substance, but which in fact is only an aggregate of bodies (p. 98).

Cordemoy argues that because individual bodies are substances, that is, things independent of all other things except God, unoccupied space is not inconceivable as the Cartesians think. It may be that a vase emptied of all its contents would be crushed by the matter surrounding it unless its contents were replaced. But to say that its sides would ipso facto touch without any external pressure, is no argument, he thinks. For no given body depends upon any other (pp. 103–4). Each, including those composing the edges of the vase, is an individual extended substance and not a mode of extension, Descartes's single material substance. This obviously anti-Cartesian thesis of Cordemoy's is reinforced for him by his perfectly Cartesian occasionalism. No body is able to move another, he argues;[267] a fortiori no body can cause another to exist.

---

[264] Ibid., p. 33.

[265] Incipient metaphysical arguments were not the only nonphysical arguments being advanced for atomism. Maignan earlier (1653) had argued atomism on theological grounds. Creation is possible, he thought, only if the continuum is composed of determinate parts, which as the object of creation, must be simple. See Prost, *Essai*, pp. 59–60. The idea seems to be that a limited creation must terminate in limited individual objects. An unlimited creation such as Cartesian extension presumably would be a rival divinity, although I do not know that Maignan ever made this charge as such.

[266] *Oeuvres*, pp. 95–96.

[267] For the details of his argument, irrelevant here, see my "Occasionalism."

Indeed, these two operations come to the same thing. To create bodies is to create them in a certain place, that is, with certain relations among them; and to move them is to re-create them with different relations. Both operations belong only to God.

Cordemoy's book was sent by Clerselier to Dom Robert Desgabets, who responded with a letter whose sectarian reaction of indignation rather typifies intramural debate among Cartesians in the period.[268] To extirpate the atomist heresy so supportive of Gassendi's camp, Desgabets undertook a refutation of Cordemoy's principal theses. For one thing, according to Desgabets, his atomism is based on a false conception of the continuum and infinite divisibility. The alleged atoms have extension, hence parts and thus are divisible at least by God. In every one of them we can conceive an entire world and so on to infinity, argues Desgabets, using the imagery of what is found in a grain of sand, the eyes of mites, and so on—imagery extensively used by Malebranche and others in the period, and made all the more compelling by contemporary discoveries in microscopy. In addition, as Gassendi had argued that infinite divisibility was a mathematical concept that was not physically applicable, so Desgabets accuses the atomists of confusing mathematical points with the real, or at least of trying to construct the latter from the former, which in his view cannot be done.[269] A similar response is made to Cordemoy's advocacy of the void, a response that is worth developing since it leads directly to the issue of individuation raised at the outset of this section.

We have a natural inclination, according to Desgabets, to form ideas of genera, species and "other universals," which he thinks can be true. But what happens is that we have become so accustomed to such ideas that we begin to treat them as real, existing outside individuals, and to regard them in the fashion of Plato as eternal, ungenerable, and incorruptible essences. This is what has happened in the case of the void. It is a reified abstraction—it is only real, that is, material, extension considered in general, just as human nature is nothing but particular men conceived perfectly.[270] Desgabet's criticism is hard to make out in orthodox Cartesian terms, for Descartes's space/extension is while created nonetheless an essence and one the idea of which logically precedes all ideas of individually extended things. This is the doctrine of *Meditations* 3 according to which "there is more reality in infinite substance than in a finite one, and hence my perception of the infinite, that is, God, is in some way prior to my perception of the finite"—a doctrine that was made so much of by

---

[268] The letter remains unpublished in the library of Epinal. It is noted by Rodis-Lewis in *Analecta Cartesiana*, 3:xxxi. Excerpts from it appear in Prost, *Essai*, pp. 156ff.

[269] Interestingly, when Desgabets replies to Cordemoy's contention that the infinite divisibility of matter is inconceivable, it is the mathematical notion to which he appeals: "geometers know perfectly well what they [mean by infinite divisibility]" (Prost, *Essai*, pp. 166–67, n. 1).

[270] Prost, *Essai*, p. 172.

Malebranche in the explication of his notion of intelligible extension.[271] If anything, individually extended things are the abstraction on this view.

Another critic of Cordemoy, Régis, argued at least vaguely along the more orthodox Cartesian line.[272] He distinguished between body, which is indivisible, and quantity, which is infinitely divisible: "There is no one who does not know that there is a substance extended in length, breadth and depth called *body*, for besides the fact that its existence is demonstrated in metaphysics, its idea is so comprised in all those that the imagination can form that necessarily either we know it or we never imagine anything" (1:279–80). Size "in itself" as a necessary result of extension is an essential property of body; a given size, quantity, is not. "Quantity is nothing else but body itself considered as such or such according to size" (p. 280). The distinction between quantity and body is only one of reason, but this distinction is sufficient for them to have different properties. (It is the kind of distinction there is between numbers and things numbered, which have different properties.) (Infinite) divisibility (into proportional parts) is an essential property of quantity, but not of body. If body were divisible, then "since all division brings a change to the thing divided," its essence would be changed, which is contrary to reason (p. 282). Thus after division each part still has the whole essence of body. (The properties of having some shape or other and of impenetrability are also essential properties of actually divided quantity.) "The failure to distinguish body and quantity is the paralogism of those who following Epicurus maintain that atoms are indivisible because they are substances" (p. 282).

Régis now gives what I take to be a fair approximation of the view that I attributed to Descartes. "From this doctrine it follows first that having some quantity or other [*la quantité indeterminée*, as Régis perhaps misleadingly puts it] is of the essence of particular bodies . . . and second that quantity is not an interior mode of body, but an exterior mode consisting in a certain manner in which body is conceived in relation to a given size. Whence it follows that quantity is not distinct from body by a formal or modal distinction, but by a distinction of reason, such as is found between substance and exterior modes" (p. 283). Now, this notion of an exterior mode is what Descartes called an extrinsic denomination. Régis explicates it as typically relational and as depending on how things are conceived (p. 3).[273] The upshot is that *particular* extended things depend on *us*.

---

[271] CSM, 2:31; AT, 7:45. Descartes is referring to the perception of God, but his doctrine applied to the perception of extension as well, as Malebranche showed.

[272] Arguably the best-known Cartesian of his time, Régis published his *Système de philosophie* only in 1690 but, according to Bayle, he had written it some eighteen years before and delayed its publication due to political problems.

[273] Alas, he gives shape as an example of an *internal* mode, that is, as being conceived *in* the substance rather than as depending on something outside it. Perhaps he can be made consistent on this; but perhaps not.

I shall turn now to a more orthodox atomist theory, as presented by François Bernier. Bernier's presentation of atomism in the *Abrégés* seems to me essentially to follow Gassendi's physicalist theories. Typically, for Bernier's own views we must look to his *Doubts*, which, atypically, do not reject Gassendi's view so much as extend it. While his doubts may raise substantive questions concerning Gassenidi's views on space, time, motion, collision, and other important topics, Bernier claims not to question the basis of Gassendi's system, for "[he does] not think that one can reasonably philosophize on any system other than that of atoms and the void." *Doubts* 1 contains a section, curiously lacking in *Doubts* 2, called "Whether the response I give here to the great and ordinary objections made against the existence of atoms is acceptable." In this section Bernier does not question or reject Gassendi's views as he does throughout the rest of the work. Rather, he provides arguments that go beyond them. For Bernier, perhaps guided by Cordemoy, with whom he was later to be associated by the Spinozist Dortous de Mairan,[274] was edging toward metaphysical atomism.

Bernier's treatment is notable for its presentation of atomism as both a physical theory about the arrangement and behavior of matter, and as a metaphysical theory about why ultimately it exhibits the arrangement and behavior it does. The section begins with two arguments, "which among others demonstrate the view of atoms" (p. 28). The first argument, which is found in many previous authors, is that infinite divisibility is incompatible with the finitude of things. The second argument Bernier draws specifically from Lucretius: Only if there are absolutely solid, hard, and impenetrable bodies with more or less void between them can the relative hardness and softness of bodies be explained. To these Bernier later adds a third argument: Only if there are indivisible bodies can there be the resistance called impenetrability. The second argument, concerning hardness, seems more clearly physical than metaphysical, while the other two, concerning finitude and impenetrability, are ambiguous. In Bernier's consideration of objections to atomism, however, the metaphysical comes to prevail.

The first objection is one that Desgabets had raised against Cordemoy, namely, that parts of an alleged atom can be distinguished that are thus really distinct and separable. But for Bernier, "the sign, reason or cause of the separability of any body whatsoever is that it give way, not resist, not be perfectly hard" (p. 136); if all bodies were such, there would be no hardness whatsoever. He does not quite state it, but the generalized version of his argument is that there would be no *body* whatsoever. That is, if all bodies were perfectly soft there would be no difference between them and the void. Thus, in order for there to be separable bodies there must be something that is inseparable, something whose integrity is assured, for example, by its conceivability apart from

---

[274] Malebranche, *Oeuvres*, 19:902.

everything else.[275] So what we are talking about here are not real but conceptual parts. This is an explanation, it seems to me, of Leibniz's cryptic argument later in the *Monadology* (pars. 1–2): If there are composites then there must be (absolute) simples. A problem this dialectic raises among others is to explain how it is that parts that are inconceivable apart are nonetheless known as different. I shall return to this at least briefly at the end.

Bernier argues further that impenetrable solid bodies cannot be considered as composed only of perfectly contiguous but separable parts, for if there are no continuous, inseparable parts, there are no finite bodies, which can have only a finite number of parts. The worry, it seems to me, is not that otherwise bodies would be too big, namely, infinitely large because of their infinite number of parts, but again that there that there would not be any bodies at all. This gives the sense of the physical considerations Bernier cites. The point is that the physical explanation at the macrolevel depends on metaphysical explanation at the microlevel. Thus he argues that ties or hooks of the sort to which Gassendi had appealed are of no use here (Bernier would not have had to look to Malebranche, nor Newton to either of them, for the obvious objection that the coherence of ties still needs explaining) and that motion, to which the Cartesians appeal, is of no use either: "for it is not the idea of motion or of rest that gives us the idea of separability; let diamond powder be as moved and disturbed as you wish, each individual grain will be no less hard and difficult to divide" (p. 142).

The conclusion of Bernier's *Doubt* underlines the metaphysical character of his atomism. Here he raises the bugbear of whether God can divide an atom. "It is true that nothing opposes divine omnipotence, that the human understanding often sees only obscurely what does not imply contradiction, and that thus it must not inconsiderately determine what is or is not possible; so that we can only say here that if God [were to divide an atom] He would do so in a way no less supernatural, nor less inconceivable than the penetration [of bodies], and consequently in a way beyond the consideration of physics, which considers things only according to the ordinary course of nature" (pp. 143–44). Bernier does not draw the comparison, but were God to divide an atom He would do something that was metaphysically no less impossible than if He were to separate a thing from its qualities.[276]

---

[275] As it was for Descartes (*Principles* 1, 60); this shows why for him the whole of extension is a single entity: None of its parts can be conceived apart from the whole.

[276] See below. This of course was generally how the miracle of the Eucharist was described. Gassendi early on came close to elaborating a doctrine of bare individuals with respect to the problem of the Eucharist. The essence of quantity he took to be "external extension," the tridimensionality perceived by the eyes that is commensurate with place. To distinguish "internal extension" from this as consisting of the relations among nonspatial or entitative parts is either to make no distinction or to introduce something that cannot have any relation at all among parts. But Gassendi thought the notion of internal extension incoherent ("how can there be a relationship between the

The conceivability of the different parts of an atom is no more problematic for the atomist than the conceivability of the distinction between a thing and its shape or between its size and its shape should be for the Cartesian. The problem is that what is distinguishable should be distinct and separable. Thus for Berkeley, instantiated qualities such as this blue are ultimately the only physical individuals, which I think is the real significance of his well-known claim that primary qualities vary as do secondary. Thus, too, the use to which Hume puts his famous principle about distinguishability—even if he cannot get clear on just what it is that is no longer further distinguishable. (Is it such items as color or shape, or is it things that have color and shape?[277]) These subscribers to what we might call phenomenalist atomism still require that there be qualitative differences that are *given*. But as we shall see in just a bit, in our period the view was already emerging that only *numerical* differences are given.

The distinction above, in any case, between the (unobservable) microlevel and the (observable) macrolevel cannot be made out as the distinction between metaphysical and physical accounts. This was argued as a reductio of atomism by Desgabets in his criticism of Cordemoy, who as we have seen also relied on considerations of metaphysical independence in plumping for atoms and the void. Desgabets argued that Cordemoy's claim that each body qua substance cannot be divided was true only formally; materially it is false. Desgabets's distinction here is not altogether clear; it seems to be between the thing as nominally defined and the thing as having the constituents necessary for it to satisfy that definition. The constituents can exist apart, but not as such, as when a part is removed from a watch. With this distinction he replies to Cordemoy's contention that contrary to Cartesian doctrine a body at rest amidst others at rest is at least conceivable. According to Desgabets, bodies may be formally distinguished independently of motion in the way in which an army is independent of its members.[278] The entity formed by two drops, for example, is formally indivisible; but this is not to say that one drop cannot be separated from another. This shows in what sense Cordemoy's alleged atoms are indivisible. But it also

---

parts where there is no relationship at all between up and down or any other position"—that is, apart from absolute space). Instead he opted for a fideistic response to the problem: "since this mystery surpasses the capacity of the human mind no matter how you consider it, it is best to refer anything miraculous and inconceivable in it to divine will and omnipotence" (*Exercises against the Aristotelians* 2.3.10–11; see *Selected Works*, pp. 58–64).

[277] "Whatever subjects are different are distinguishable, and . . . whatever objects are distinguishable are separable by the thought and imagination. And we may . . . add, . . . these propositions are equally true in the *inverse*" (*Treatise*, p. 18). But consider: "Tho' a particular colour, taste, and smell are qualities all united together in this apple, 'tis easy to perceive they are not the same, but are at least distinguishable from each other" (ibid., p. 2). This is Hume's view when discussing the simple-complex distinction; when he discusses the distinction of reason he says: "we consider the figure and colour [of marble] together, since they are in effect the same and undistinguishable" (ibid., p. 25).

[278] Prost, *Essai*, p. 167.

shows, according to Desgabets, that unless they confuse mathematical and physical points, atomists have no reason for thinking that atoms must be imperceptibly small.[279] Drops could become indefinitely large.

Desgabets is right, it seems to me, that with respect to the kind of atomism that emerges in Cordemoy and Bernier the size of atoms is an irrelevant consideration. This is not the crude physicalist atomism of Gassendi, whose atoms were in principle imperceptibly small, or of Boyle whose view of an atom, one of the *minima* or *prima naturalia* as he called them, was that it was that which, "though it be mentally, and by divine Omnipotence divisible, yet, by reason of its smallness, and solidity nature doth scarce ever actually divide it."[280] For the problem is not that because of the size of atoms we cannot find knives thin and small enough to cut them. Instead it is a kind of atomism that at this historical juncture is groping its way toward an account of numerical differences in terms of bare individuals that have *no* properties and therefore no size at all.[281] This is the metaphysical atomism discussed at the outset, according to which things just are (as opposed to the void). Such properties as things are said to possess are a function of our perception of them. To use the traditional language, they are accidents, which here means they are only phenomena or the appearances of things. This, I believe, is the view that emerges more clearly in Locke.

With this view, finally, we can see how an answer might go in response to two problems we have raised: (1) Bernier's problem of how it is that parts that are inconceivable apart are nonetheless known as different and (2) Berkeley's and Hume's problem of how it is that the color and shape of a thing, which are inconceivable apart from the thing, are conceivable apart from each other. Both are answered by the most general form of Bernier's argument concerning separability: All predication may depend ultimately on us, but every predication requires a metaphysically integral subject. Of any subject we can (within causal constraints) conceive anything we want, including that it has different parts; but that subject qua subject is metaphysically indivisible. (And what is true of parts is true *mutatis mutandis* of color and shape.) To this extent Desgabets's distinction between material and formal divisibility rather advances the cause of the metaphysical atomists. The difference between his view and theirs is twofold. First, the atomist (formal) definitions of things will be merely nominal, while the Cartesian definitions will be real. This difference is

---

[279] Ibid., pp. 159ff.

[280] *The Origin of Qualities and Forms*; *Works*, 3:29.

[281] More's atomism represents a curious half-way house in this regard. His "perfect parvitudes" or *minima corporalia* have no shape. As the infinitely large has no shape, so the infinitely small has none. An infinitely small cube in fact is a contradiction for him. But they do have extension because finite extensions are composed of them (*The Immortality of the Soul*, bk. 1, chap. 6, pref., sec. 3). Nor are they bare individuals: "the subject, or naked Essence of a thing, is utterly conceivable to any of our faculties" (bk. 1, chap. 1, axiom 8). All things have one from each of two pairs of "immediate properties": penetrability/impenetrability; "discerpibility/indiscerpibility."

due to a second difference, namely, in what is here defined. For the realist Cartesians it is the single res extensa, the essence whose mathematical structure grounds a system of internal relations. Régis gets this exactly right in distinguishing between the (merely) conceptual entity he calls *quantity*, which may change, and *body*, which could not change without a change of essence. (This could happen only if, for example, God were to falsify Euclidean geometry.) For the nominalist Gassendists on the other hand, what is defined is one from a multiplicity of bare particulars, for there is no essence apart from such things, of which they are a part, or in which they participate. The real essence of a thing, as the atomists put it, just is that thing. So a thing cannot be essentially divisible or indivisible, or anything else. Classification of things is entirely a matter of how we classify them. This view too begins to emerge more clearly in Locke as it had already emerged in Hobbes.

CHAPTER III

Locke: Gassendist Anti-Cartesian

IN A WELL-KNOWN but ill-heeded passage of the *New Essays*, Leibniz said of Locke: "This author is pretty much in agreement with M. Gassendi's system, which is fundamentally that of Democritus: he supports vacuum and atoms, he believes that matter could think, that there are no innate ideas, that our mind is a *tabula rasa*, and that we do not think all the time; and he seems inclined to agree with most of M. Gassendi's objections against M. Descartes" (p. 70). My thesis in this chapter will be that Leibniz gets the picture of Locke exactly right. In the first section I shall begin, but only begin, investigating the grounds for placing Locke in the Gassendist camp. In a brief second section I shall begin, but again only begin, the case for his opposition to Cartesianism. The full story on each of these will emerge only over the course of three later chapters below. Finally, in a third section here I shall set out what I take to be Locke's moral and political objection to Cartesianism. Despite its being the infrastructure for the whole of his anti-Cartesianism, I shall return to the theme only en passant in the final chapter of this book. As I indicated in my opening chapter, my main interest here is in the metaphysical superstructure.

§9 LOCKE AND GASSENDI

Suppose someone never read Plato or any account of his dialogues or even heard of him, but argued nonetheless for the theory of Forms, the immortality of the soul based on its imperishability, a geometrical account of the material world, and the like. Do we call such a person a Platonist? As we shall see over the course of this work, the question is an exceedingly complex one. I shall raise a version of it with respect to no less a figure than Descartes himself. The sense of the question I wish to invoke here, however, is a different one. It focuses at the metalevel of how we understand such classification rather than at the object-level of how we are to classify and understand a given philosophy. On one model philosophies are themselves Forms, more or less well instantiated in the efforts of individual philosophers. Philosophers are atemporal with the result that in understanding the propagation of a philosophy we need attend only to its inner logic. The search for what are called influences between philosophers, for example, becomes of secondary importance or vanishes altogether. On this model, in fact, no great harm would be done in describing Plato as a Cartesian.

Another model regards the propagation of philosophies as like the spread of contagious disease: There must be contact. This model comports better with nominalism, inviting us (if I might change the metaphor) to take ideas as things that are passed from hand to hand. Influences thus appear as the main desiderata in explaining the propagation of a philosophy. Someone ignorant of Plato in the way described above could hardly be called a Platonist.

As it happens, I believe that both of these conceptions are misguided and I shall try to explain why I believe this when in chapter 8 I discuss the two conceptions of history they generate. Nonetheless, here it will be useful if we proceed as if the latter conception were appropriate. Looking for specific Gassendist influences on Locke will provide a context for what I take to be the more interesting picture of Locke as a Gassendist that I shall be setting out in the next three chapters.[1]

The influence of Gassendi on Locke is, although widely unexamined by the literature, nonetheless widely acknowledged by it. Leibniz was not the only one of Locke's contemporaries to associate him with Gassendi. Another was Henry Lee,[2] although he did not do so along the party lines that Leibniz did. Hence I do not wish to make a great deal of Lee's testimony. He argued that reflection for Locke comes to nothing but knowing or the power to know thus leaving Locke only sensation as a source of ideas; "and therefore, if it had not been for the commonness of the Expression, he might as well have said, in Gassendus's words, *Nihil est in intellectu quod non prius fuit in sensu*; for it comes all to that even according to his *own* Principles."[3] The designation of 'Gassendist' in the respect intended by Lee would thus be of too wide an extension to be of great significance here. In addition, Lee's syntax indicates that the designation is applied contrary to fact, or at least to usage, that is, the sense is that while Locke may well have been a Gassendist, he actually was not. Later, Thomas Reid drew attention to Gassendi, "from whom Locke borrowed more than from any other author,"[4] and more recently Aaron among others has made the connection. Certainly, there are obvious themes, positions, arguments, distinctions, and terminology to be found in both Gassendi and Locke. But a distinction must

---

[1] These two conceptions of the relation between historical figures have recently been argued specifically with respect to the relation between Gassendi and Locke. David Fate Norton has recently proposed that "The empirical aspects of Locke, Berkeley and Hume are neither original to Locke, nor simply the effect of Bacon and Hobbes on Locke. The seminal figure of 17th- and 18th-century empiricism was not British, but French. . . . The most likely candidate for the title, Founder of Modern Empiricism, is Pierre Gassendi" ("'British Empiricism,'" p. 334). Richard W. F. Kroll objects to Norton's morphological method whereby influence is asserted merely on the basis of similarity of views. Kroll sees a Gassendist connection with Locke through Thomas Stanley's *History of Philosophy*, to be discussed below. For more on this topic, see Milton's "Locke and Gassendi," which is the most recent examination of the whole issue.

[2] Of Lee, more below.

[3] *Anti-scepticism*, p. 41.

[4] *Works*, 1:226.

be carefully made between an influence from Gassendi on the one hand, and a mere favorable climate, sympathetic ambience, or independent agreement, on the other. Sortais, for example, notes that Gassendi's name is mentioned only once by Locke (in the *Second Reply* to Stillingfleet) and then only incidentally.[5] He thus finds Locke's silence too systematic to allow Dugald Stewart's explanation that Locke had so assimilated Gassendi's views as to be unable to distinguish them from his own.[6]

Another difficulty is distinguishing Gassendi's direct influence on Locke (i.e., the influence of Locke's reading of Gassendi) from the influence of Gassendi's followers, some of whose views depart quite radically from those of Gassendi. Distinguishing the latter is further complicated in that there was likely a mutual influence, a cross-fertilization, between Locke and the Gassendists, which in at least one important case may have had Locke as its primary source. For reasons of health Locke traveled in France during the 1670s, and from the journal he kept we know that he was in Paris for two extended periods, from May 1677 to June 1678 and from November 1678 to April 1679, during which time he was in contact with Gassendists such as Bernier and Launay. To establish the influence of Gassendi himself, therefore, it would seem necessary first to isolate what might be called overlap material in Locke, namely, material whose occurrence might be explained as a direct adoption of material in Gassendi, or more problematically, as a clear modification or rejection of it. The task then would be to determine how much of this material might be traceable to Locke's reading of Gassendi. Finally, this material must be sorted out from that resulting from Locke's contact with Gassendist views, both the orthodox and especially the deviant, during the 1670s and later. Of indispensable aid here are Locke's commonplace books and his journal. I shall discuss seven Gassendist connections had by Locke.

Gassendi

The *Essay* was first published in 1689, postdated 1690, but it is significant by itself that in a work begun even as early as 1670 Locke should have followed Gassendi's already archaic division of the sciences into (1) physics or natural philosophy ("in a little more enlarged sense of the word"—in fact, one including much of metaphysics), (2) ethics, and (3) logic, or the doctrine of signs.[7]

---

[5] *La philosophie*, 2:179, n. 2.

[6] Stewart also refers to Hobbes, Bacon, Montaigne, Malebranche, and Descartes (*Works*, 1:212–13). On the other hand, only eleven names appear in the *Essay* and a case needs to be made that the mention of any name indicates or would indicate a genuine and significant influence.

[7] See also Launay: "The most exact, most perfect and most authorized [division of the sciences] that I have been able to borrow from the ancients" (*Introduction*, p. 24; and *Dissertation*, p. 10). These are essentially the same work; Locke possessed it in its later version (Harrison and Laslett,

The division in any case provides convenient headings for an initial discussion of the kinds of influence Gassendi may have had on Locke.

PHYSICS

There are a number of topics classified under this rubric on which, given the debates of the third quarter of the seventeenth century, an influence beyond a congenial ambience might plausibly be attributed: the bestial soul, the issue of whether matter can think, the mechanics of sensation, and the like. Any such attribution, however, must be preceded by a general caveat. In his chapter "Of the Abuse of Words," Locke classifies the "*endeavour towards Motion*" that "the *Epicureans* [have] in their Atoms, when at rest" among the "Gibberish, which in the weakness of Humane Understanding, serves so well to palliate Men's Ignorance, and cover their Errours."[8] Although Locke is an atomist, the distinction between his own atomism and what he refers to as the Epicurean version appears rather more than intramural. His outburst is clearly aimed at Gassendi, whose atoms have, as a universal property, gravity or weight (*gravitas seu pondus*), "which is nothing but the natural and internal faculty or power by which the atom is able to stir and move itself, or if you like, an inborn, innate, native and inseparable propensity to motion, an intrinsic propulsion and impetus [*ab intrinseco propulsio, atque impetus*]."[9] This dynamical property of atoms finds no place in Locke, for whom matter cannot be the source of its own motion (4.10.10). Nor can motion be, as the "atomists" meaninglessly define it, "*a passage from one place to another*" (3.4.9; 423). While Locke might accept Gassendi's principle that all change is change of motion, [10] his conception of motion will be radically different, and thus there will be a second crucial difference in the principles most basic to the accounts, on a variety of topics, common to Locke and Gassendi. Locke's own view of motion is controversial because his view of space is controversial; yet it is on this topic that Gassendi's influence on Locke is historically and structurally most important—structurally in that a view on space in this period determines a host of other metaphysical views, and historically in that Locke seems in fact to have been led to them by a consideration of space. A whole chapter below will be devoted to these topics.

ETHICS

To be sure, both Locke and Gassendi are hedonists; both subscribe to psychological hedonism—people are determined in their actions by pleasure;[11] both

---

Library, p. 170). Launay cites the arguments for, and the illustrations of, this division of the sciences in Augustine and Aquinas among other authors.

[8] 3.10.14; 497. *Essay* 2.27.3–6; 328–30. See "Note on Documentation."

[9] *Syntagma*; *Opera*, 1:273.

[10] *Opera*, 2:338b.

[11] Cf. 2.7.3–4 and 2.21.33–34; *Syntagma*; *Opera*, 2:695.

tend, at least, to embed their hedonism in a utilitarian theory of obligation;[12] both have a view of pleasure as common to body and mind[13] and rank the kinds of pleasure in the same way.[14] But their interests in hedonism, as well as the versions of it they defend, differ significantly. The result is that while Locke's reading of Gassendi may have provided a support and even an inspiration for his ethical views, it cannot properly be described as a source of them.[15]

Consistent with his apologetic reconstruction of Epicurus, Gassendi's main concern with respect to hedonism is to defend it against the traditional charge of its being "pig philosophy." Thus while his arguments tend to show that *only* pleasure is intrinsically good, Gassendi is content with the conclusion that all pleasures are good. Thus also does he treat virtue, obligation, and the highest pleasure (the happiness of *ataraxia*) as concepts to be shown analyzable in terms of pleasure, that is, as moral notions consistent with hedonism.

Locke, on the other hand, having rejected innate practical principles, is concerned to show how there can nonetheless be moral knowledge that is universal and necessary. Perhaps to this end he claims, not that pleasure is of intrinsic value, but, "that we call *good*, which is apt to cause or increase pleasure, or diminish pain in us; or else to procure or preserve in us the possession of any other good or absence of any evil" (2.20.2; 229). If anything, Locke's source here is rather Hobbes: "Every man, for his part, calleth that which *pleaseth* and is delightful to himself, good."[16] With this notion Locke can distinguish between moral and natural good: A natural good will naturally produce pleasure, while a moral good will do so only as a result of the intervention of the will of an intelligent agent.[17] Consideration of divine reward and punishment thus introduces the possibility of an a priorism in ethics after which Locke clearly hankers.

LOGIC

Under this heading would be comprised most notably Gassendi's influence on Locke's view of the origin of ideas and their epistemological role. I shall take up this influence in chapter 5. Of the three headings, Logic is the most important

---

[12] Cf. the texts published by King, *Life*, 2:95; *Syntagma*; *Opera*, 2:710.

[13] Cf. 2.8.2; *Syntagma*; *Opera*, 2:682.

[14] King, *Life*, 2:120; *Syntagma*; *Opera*, 2:706–15.

[15] It would seem that we have a case of Locke and the Gassendists contributing to a mutually favorable climate, one that in this instance was enjoyed by a wider population. One is immediately reminded of the secret, noted above, that Saint-Evremond confided to Ninon de Lenclos concerning Bernier's views on hedonism. But such a secret would have been shared by a spectrum from the most exaggerated libertin to the puritanical Malebranche. In short, hedonism in the seventeenth century was the property of no special group. Driscoll, on the other hand, has argued that Locke's hedonism dates from his period in France and that Gassendi's views were crucial in the formation of it. Given my overall thesis, I should like Driscoll to be shown right and myself wrong on this point.

[16] *Human Nature; The English Works*, 4:32.

[17] King, *Life*, 1:128; also 2.28.5.

and it requires extensive treatment. First, however, I shall turn to connections of a different sort.

What of Gassendi's do we know Locke to have read? We know that he at least possessed the *Objections* to the *Meditations* and therefore could have read Gassendi's detailed, point-by-point criticism of the central document in Descartes's metaphysical writings.[18] Turning to Gassendi's objections, Locke would have found arguments for the materiality of the soul: Only if the soul is moved, for example, can it move the body; but, presumably, only if the soul is material can it be moved.[19] Locke would have found a positivistic distinction between real and nominal essences: Gassendi likens Descartes's characterization of himself as a thing that thinks to the common knowledge of wine as a liquid, compressed from grapes, red or white, by contrast to the explanation of its internal substance in terms of spirits, tartar, and the like.[20] Locke would have found arguments against Cartesian innate ideas[21] and for the sensory source of such ideas.[22] He would have found a rejection of Descartes's *esse formale–esse objectiva* distinction and a clear assertion of a representationalist theory instead.[23] He would have found a clear and coherent nominalist critique of Descartes's view of the eternal verities.[24] He would have found a rejection of the ontological argument.[25] Perhaps most important, Locke would have found a clear expression of free thinking, of tolerant reaction to Descartes's intolerance of anything contrary to what he was calling reason. Gassendi concludes his objections, or observations (*adnotanda*) rather, by rejecting their absolute validity: "I repeat that you have no reason to worry about them since my powers of judgment are so meagre that you should not regard my views as of any value at all. When some dish pleases my palate but I see others do not like it, I do not defend my taste as being more perfect than anyone else's; and similarly, when an opinion appeals to me but is unwelcome to others, I am very far from

---

[18] Harrison and Laslett, p. *Library*, 105.

[19] CSM, 2:182; AT, 7:261. See also HR, 2:192; AT, 7:331: "You [Descartes] add that when the mind imagines, it turns toward the body, but when it understands it turns towards itself and to the ideas it has within it. But what if the mind cannot turn to itself or to one of its ideas without simultaneously turning to something corporeal or something represented by a corporeal idea?" Also, by way of summary of the problems regarded as inherent in Cartesian dualism, see CSM, 2:239; AT, 7:345: "the general difficulty still remains of how the corporeal can communicate with the incorporeal and of what relationship may be established between the two."

[20] CSM, 2:192–93; AT, 7:276–77.

[21] CSR, 2:196; AT, 7:281. See also CSM, 2:214; AT, 7:307: "There is no idea [of God] which He has imprinted on us; for if there were, if one and the same idea were always imprinted on everyone, then everyone would conceive of God in terms of a similar form and image [*sic*], and would give Him the same attributes and have exactly the same view of Him, whereas, notoriously, the opposite is true."

[22] CSM, 2:197; AT, 7:282–83.

[23] CSM, 2:201–3; AT, 7:289–91.

[24] CSM, 2:221–24; AT, 7:318–22.

[25] CSM, 2:224–25; AT, 7:323.

supposing I have managed to come closer to the truth. I think it is more correct to say that everyone is satisfied with his own views, and that wanting everyone to have the same view is as unfair as wanting everyone's taste's to coincide."[26]

Of the works of Gassendi himself the library of the bibliophile Locke possessed but a single one: Gassendi's *Life* of Peiresc.[27] Given my thesis, this is very disappointing since one would have expected it to contain more and the biography of the polymath-patron-amateur it did contain is not of much interest beyond its exemplification of crude empiricism, rejection of intellectual authorities, and many curiosities: weights and measures, physiology and pharmacology, geography and rates of exchange—the sort of reading in which Locke clearly delighted but which could hardly have formed the basis of his philosophy in Gassendi.[28] For greater indication of that one must look elsewhere, to the Locke manuscripts.

Already by 1666 at the latest, Locke in his first commonplace book shows signs of disagreement with the metaphysical core of Cartesianism. He is interested, as were so many in the period, in the interrelated problems of cohesion, solidity, motion, and space. Without comment he quotes Descartes, in Latin, on fluidity (*liquiditas*) from *Principles* 4,118: "To be fluid is nothing other than to be composed of particles which are separated from one another and which are in some motion."[29] Then in three entries he later takes up the issue under *vacuum*. He argues in a way none too clear—for one thing, the Latin manuscript is difficult to make out—that Descartes's account of solidity lands him in the following trilemma: "if contact is the cause of stability, which it is according to [Descartes's] principle, no body will be fluid, or there will be some vacuum, or something else will be required for the firmness of bodies in addition to motion and bare contact" (p. 75). This nest of issues is ultimately focused on the contrast between Descartes and Gassendi with respect to space, which Locke draws under the entry place (*Locus*). He summarizes *Principles* 2, 13 and follows this with an accurate enough citation of Gassendi's *Syntagma* concerning space: "And we must admit that place is a quantity, or some sort of extension, namely the space or internal place made up of the three dimensions length, breadth, and depth in which it is possible for a body to be held or through which it might travel. But at the same time it must be said that its dimensions are incorporeal quantity. Therefore, two sorts of dimensions are to be distin-

---

[26] CSM, 2:240; AT, 7:346.

[27] *Viri illustris Nicolai Claudii Fabrieii de Peiresce . . . vita*, 1655 (Harrison and Lazlett, *Library*, p. 140). Twenty-five questions from it in MS Locke f. 27 show Locke to have been reading this *Life* in 1664. See Milton, "Locke and Gassendi."

[28] Lynn Joy has argued, however, that this biography was very significant indeed since it forced Gassendi to confront historiographical problems the solution of which is crucial to the interpretation of the whole of his thought. So perhaps I have underestimated its significance for Locke's connection with him.

[29] Brit. Library Add. MS 32554. p. 17 in Locke's hand, p. 11 of renumbered MS.

guished, of which the first may be called corporeal and the second spatial."[30] Quite apart from Locke's understanding of the analyses of matter and space in Gassendist versus Cartesian terms—a question I shall return to at length below—what this text shows is that Locke had access to Gassendi's *verba ipsissima*.[31] But given the thesis that I shall try to make out below, namely, that Locke is best understood as prosecuting on a massive scale the case begun by Gassendi against Descartes, in short, that Locke is a Gassendist, we should expect many more references, citations, and noddings, at least, to Gassendi than are to be found even in Locke's manuscripts.[32] If we are to take seriously, for any reason, the requirement of influence for such designations as 'Gassendist,' the *direct* influence here is far too weak to sustain my thesis. For all the reasons discussed in chapter 1 above, Locke himself may have been typical of his period in reading Descartes far more extensively and closely than he did Gassendi. For Gassendi's influence on his reading of Cartesianism, we must look to *indirect* connections.

Charleton

Aside from the texts themselves of Gassendi, we might most naturally turn to Walter Charleton's *Physiologia* as Locke's most likely source for Gassendi's views. Locke possessed four works by Charleton, two encyclopedias of natural history and two medical texts (on menses and scurvy),[33] but seems not to have possessed the *Physiologia*. Nor have I found any reference to it in Locke's published work, correspondence, journals, or notebooks.[34] If Locke is con-

---

[30] *Opera*, 1:182a; *Selected Works*, p. 385. Bloch first drew attention to this very important entry. He also pointed out that the Bodleian MS Locke 14 of the Lovelace collection dating from ca. 1667, cites the *Syntagma* some half-dozen times, in every instance the book on space and time (*La philosophie*, p. 198, n. 115). Milton specifies eight citations and dates the entries 1660–61 ("Locke and Gassendi").

[31] I would take this to be the key premise of the argument recently published by Fred S. and Emily Michael. Relying on what the literature calls the morphological method, that is, similarity of doctrine, they plausibly argue that "the whole content of the account of ideas in *Institutio Logica*, I, is incorporated somewhere in Locke's *Essay* or in the early drafts" ("Theory," p. 395). The aspect on which they focus is the role of ideas in empiricist epistemology and their conclusion is very strong: "A comparison of the two theories leaves little room to doubt that Gassendi's theory was Locke's starting point" (p. 398). They also suggest an influence of Gassendi on Locke's *Essays on The Law of Nature* of 1664 (p. 385).

[32] This conclusion is sustained, alas, by the most thorough analysis to date of Locke's remains. See Milton, "Locke and Gassendi."

[33] *Exercitationes de differentiis & nominibus animalium . . .* , 2d ed. (Oxford, 1677); *Onomasticon zoicon . . .* (London, 1668); *Inquisitiones medico-physicae: de causis catameniorum et de fluore albo* (1686); *De scorbuto liber singularis* (London, 1692). See Harrison and Laslett, *Library*, p. 105.

[34] Although Charleton is quoted obscurely, on Gassendi. See medical commonplace book. Brit. Library Add. MS 32, 554, p. 22.

nected with Charleton and through him with Gassendi, there is likely an indirect connection between Locke and Charleton, perhaps through Newton.[35]

Bernier

It has been argued that Bernier cannot have been a formative influence on Locke since the latter's main views are to be found already formed in the drafts of the *Essay* written in 1671, before he met Bernier.[36] While it is true that the first indication of Locke's connection with Bernier is in 1672,[37] the history of the *Essay*'s composition is very complicated. Roughly speaking we can say that the drafts contain Locke's rejection of innate ideas, his insistence on experience as the source of knowledge, his philosophy of language, and his epistemology generally. Missing, however, are the key ontological doctrines most of interest here. There is at most only a soupçon of the primary-secondary quality distinction or of the corpuscularian hypothesis in connection with it.[38] In Draft A Locke tells us that "when I speak of simple Ideas as existing in things I would be understood to mean such a constitution of that thing which produces that idea in our mindes."[39] Yet the only distinction he here draws between qualities is a curious one between actual and potential qualities. In Draft B we find that "white or sweet, etc., and many other sensations and ideas be caused in us by particles of certain figures,"[40] which is a feature of the later distinction, but hardly the distinction itself. This draft does distinguish special from common sensibles, but only to explain why "some" have made extension the essence of body.[41] Nor is there anything in either draft corresponding to the *Essay's* chapter on solidity (2.4). In fact, even when setting out the position of "an other" (i.e., someone other than Descartes) on extension and body, Locke speaks only of resistibility: "the Idea of Body being the complex Idea of Extension and resistibility."[42] As for the analysis of space, Draft A raises the

[35] According to Westfall, "more than anything else, [Newton's] *Questiones* seem to be a dialogue between the Cartesian philosophy and Gassendist atomism—a dialogue from which the Cartesian philosophy emerges, rather consistently, second best" ("Foundations, p. 173). Westfall notes that Newton repeats Gassendi's conception of motion from *De motu* and that Newton's titles repeat the tactile qualities Gassendi discusses in *Philosophiae Epicuri syntagma*, but that Newton quotes Charleton verbatim rather than Gassendi (pp. 172–73, n. 5).

[36] Kroll, "Question," p. 341.

[37] John Strachey wrote to Locke on January 19, 1672, thanking him for Mr. Bernie[r] (*Correspondence*, 1:364).

[38] Draft A dates from 1671, Draft B from the same year, but later. Bolton argues that three main features of the distinction are absent from the drafts: inseparability of the primary, secondary as mere powers, and resemblance to ideas of primary only ("Origins").

[39] Aaron and Gibb, *Early Draft*, p. 73.

[40] Rand, *Essay*, p. 209.

[41] Ibid., pp. 80–81.

[42] Aaron and Gibb, *Early Draft*, p. 43.

issue of the void but only to show that a priori reasoning cannot settle it; depending on how 'body,' 'extension,' and 'space' are defined, the possibility or impossibility of the void may be demonstrated. "Yet neither of those . . . demonstrations prove to us or can prove that Body doth exist or what it is as it exists, but for that we are left only to our senses to discover to us as far as they can."[43] Draft B at least takes a relational stance with respect to place, calling it a relation, namely, "extension in relation to some other bodies,"[44] but Locke does not proceed to call space a system of places. The point he emphasizes is that the idea of place is got from the senses, specifically sight and touch. Draft B in fact deals with extension as such only in the context of its treatment of the potential infinite as an empirically derived idea, where it figures far less prominently than does duration.

The result is that such ontology as appears in the drafts is very peripheral to the epistemology. This can cut at least two ways. It can mean either that ontology just was not important to Locke (consider the disclaimer in the *Essay* itself) or that its importance was later indicated to him, perhaps by the Gassendists. Given just the later reversal of the relative importance of space and duration, it is worth pursuing Locke's connection with Bernier.

Locke arrived November 24, 1674 in France (having been there briefly in 1672), where he would spend almost five years. We know a great deal of what he was up to in this period from the journal he kept.[45] He made his way south through Paris and Lyons to Montpellier, where he arrived January 4, 1676 and where he would be headquartered for the next fifteen months. Locke naturally had contact with the celebrated medical faculty there.[46] A week after his first documented contact there appears the first of his journal entries on space; previously there had been nothing at all of philosophical interest (however marvelous his entries may be as a chronicle detailing the olive industry, prices noticed or paid for many things, customs, recipes, the weather, etc.) On April 28 Locke made the first of his journal entries on Bernier's travel works. Over the next two-and-a-half months there would be entries on eight additional days from four different works of Bernier.[47] There is a great variety of topics covered

---

[43] Ibid. Locke here shows the influence of Boyle. See below.

[44] Rand, *Essay*, p. 283.

[45] Bodleian MS Locke f. 1–3, British Library Add. MSS 15.642. Parts here have been available in King, Aaron and Gibb, Lough, and Dewhurst. The whole is being transcribed for publication by Shankula.

[46] Even if he was not impressed with its ceremonial aspects (February 27, March 18, 20; Lough, *Locke's Travels*, pp. 50, 57–59). He was impressed, however, with the plants they grew and their methods for growing them (January 15 and *passim*; ibid., p. 2). Montpellier specialized in the treatment of phthsis, which Locke mistakenly believed he had (Cranston, *John Locke*, p. 160).

[47] *Voyage de Kachemir* (1672, 192 pp.) April 28, May 6, 7, 8; *Histoire de la deniere revolution des estats du Grand Mogol* (Paris, 1671, 182 pp.), May 12; *Suite des mémoires* (The Hague, 1671, 252 pp.), May 13, 15; *Evenemens particuliers des etats du Mogul* (Paris, 1671, 201 pp.), June 8. All of these works appear in Locke's library (Harrison and Laslett, *Library*, item nos. 285, 286, 286a,

by these entries: techniques for the refrigeration of water, currency exchanges, calendars, physiology, metempsychosis, the use of opium, moral and religious questions. Locke may well have been put on to these works by friends of Bernier in Montpellier, where Bernier had taken a medical degree and where in any case he had friends. Whether Bernier himself was there[48] or had met Locke the previous year in Paris we shall perhaps never know. The first documented meeting between them occurred only later in Paris, on October 8, 1677. The common (really the only) theme in Locke's reading from Bernier and in his documented conversations with him is Bernier's expertise on the orient.[49] Although Locke possessed the *Abrégé* (inscribed: *Ex Dono Authoris humaniss. juxta ac doctissi)* and the *Doubts*,[50] there is no record of any philosophical conversation between them. Nevertheless, given Locke's interests, given that Bernier published the first complete edition of the *Abrégé* in 1678, and given the more than casual relation between the two,[51] it would be extraordinary if Locke did not both discuss philosophy with Bernier and read his works.[52] In any case, Bernier seems to have stimulated Locke's interest in travel literature.[53] On May 15, 1676 Locke entered in his journal a transcription from the *Suites des memoires* in which Bernier refers to four orientalist authors, at least three of whom were to figure in Locke's library.[54] This concern with travel literature is

---

289) but all are in different editions, thus again showing that Locke's library is not an infallible guide to his reading.]

[48] Bernier habitually spent several months a year in the region (Castonnet des Fosses, *Lettres*, pp. 7–8).

[49] Journal October 8, 1677, June 20, 1678 (Lough, *Locke's Travels*, p. 200; Dewhurst, *John Locke*, p. 127), March 28, 1679 (Lough, *Locke's Travels*, p. 282); *Notebook* (mainly 1678–79, some entries up to 1685), Bodleian MS Locke f. 28 (entry for 1679), p. 60.

[50] Harrison and Laslett, *Library*, item nos. 283–84. Locke also owned Bernier's work on transubstantiation, *Eclaircissement sur . . . de La Ville*, published in Bayle's *Receuil*, item no. 1008. He also owned and read the *Doutes* (1682). See Milton, "Locke and Gassendi," sec. 3.

[51] Writing to Toinard (Nicholas Thoynard), Locke asks to be remembered to Bernier (letter of July 16/26, 1678, from Orleans, *Correspondence* 1:597). Locke had just left Paris for his second trip south. See also his letter from Angers, August 10/20, 1678 (*Correspondence*, 1:603). Writing after his return to England Locke refers to Bernier as "our good friend" (June 6, 1679; *Correspondence*, 2:32). On May 26, 1679 Locke had sent Bernier a gift via Romer.

[52] For a nuanced version of this claim, see Milton, "Locke and Gassendi," sec. 3.

[53] As Cranston claimed (*John Locke*, 170).

[54] Bodleian MS Locke f. 1., pp. 257–58. One is Athanasius Kircher, whose work is identified: *China . . . illustrata* (Amsterdam, 1667; Harrison and Laslett, *Library*, item no. 1641). Another is "Lor"; this no doubt is Henry Lord, whose work may be *A display of two forraigne sects in the East Indies* (London, 1630; Harrison and Laslett, *Library*, item no. 1807). Another is Roa (unidentified). Finally there is Rogerius. On July 26 and August 2 Locke made journal entries on Rogerius, of whom we shall have more to say (edition of Amsterdam, 1671; Harrison and Laslett, *Library*, item no. 2496). The entries concern Eastern geography and the calendar. Locke also refers to this edition in a notebook he kept between June 30, 1677 and June 30, 1678 (Bodleian MS Locke. f. 15, p. 16). For a list of over a hundred items, comprising only those published in French, to which Locke refers, see Bonno, *Les relations*, pp. 192–99. According to Harrison and Laslett (*Library*,

of some philosophical importance. In the case of Bernier's work Locke was very interested in the question of religious psychology. On May 14, 1676 he made two entries referring to the *Suite* on the topics of pretensions to revelation and religious ecstasy.[55] The phenomenon described here Locke will later call enthusiasm, returning to travel literature, and Bernier in particular, for an explanation and illustration of its nature, criteria, causes, and the like. Locke's interest in enthusiasm during his stay in Montpellier is noteworthy for the additional reason that at the same time he was in contact with Pierre-Sylvain Régis, the great popularizer of Cartesianism.[56]

Launay

Aside from Bernier, and perhaps not excepting even him, Launay may have been the most important conduit of Gassendi's ideas to Locke. As we have already seen, it is not altogether unlikely that Locke actually lodged with Launay in 1677. We have also seen, more certainly, that Locke by 1678 possessed important works by Launay. Ultimately, Locke's library was to contain no less than seven items from Launay, one of which, the *Cosmographie aisée*, was a gift from Launay himself.[57] Despite this accumulation of evidence, our

---

pp. 27–28), Locke seems to have bought all the travel books he could lay his hands on. They also point out that of the sixteen authors quoted in the *Essay's* final edition, all but one are authors of travel books.

[55] One of the entries is developed at some length. "Whether extasie be anything else but dreaming with the eyes open or how it can be distinguished from it. Also whether dreaming be anything else but the appearance of Ideas in the minde without knowing the cause that produces them there as we doe waking. For in waking we generally finde out one of those causes. 1 External objects actually producing them by our senses" (rest in shorthand). These references are also noted in 'Lemmata Ethica, Argumenta et Authores, 1659,' a commonplace book kept by Locke until 1701 (Bodleian MS Locke 2.42, pp. 41, 82). The latter entry also contains references to Chrysostom, Basil, Isidor, and Chillingworth.

[56] The journal entry for March 22, 1676 notes (in French) the results of an experiment, tried by Régis and reported to have failed, concerning ashes that were supposed to rise in water the instant of equinox. This is followed by a note: "the new philosophie prohibited to be taught in universities schools & Academies." A marginal note identifies "cartesiana philsophia." Régis is also mentioned on June 16, and August 1 (Bodleian MS Locke f. 1., pp. 259, 286, 377).

[57] Harrison and Laslett, *Library*, p. 286: *Cosmographie Aisée*, 12 (Paris, 1677). Ex dono Authoris. Liber Johannis Lock; *Physique universelle*, not identified; *La dialectique . . .* 12, Paris, 1673; *Essai de logique*, 80, Paris, 1678; *Essais logiques*, 12, Paris, 1657; *Essais logiques*, 120, Paris, 1663; *Introduction à la philosophie*, 120, Paris, 1675. The first two are indicated as entries in Locke's Hyde catalogue. The first item is indicated as then being in the Mellon Library, Oak Spring, Virginia, where it had arrived due to having been part of the moiety left to Locke's cousin, Peter King. The rest of these books—left neither to King, Francis Cudworth Masham, Lady Masham, nor Anthony Collins, who received some few specified items—are lost. The last three items figure in the list of books cared for by James Tyrrell between November 1684 and October 1691 during Locke's exile in Holland. The two other items come from Ms. Locke b.2: "Lists of books acquired by Locke, bills, letters and other papers about the purchase, storing, and dispatch of books 1674–1704."

expectations of finding Launay's work cited in Locke's journals or notebooks are not fulfilled. One therefore looks to the published work for influences nonetheless. As we shall see, on very specific issues like the analysis of space it was Bernier's position rather than Launay's that likely influenced Locke. There are other, more general issues such as the causal argument for intermediary ideas or the localization pattern where Launay is the more likely source. These may not be strongly documentable connections, but *faute de mieux* they serve at least to suggest an interpretation of what Locke may have been about.

Stanley

A possible connection between Locke and Gassendi may have been through the *History of Philosophy* by the poet and classical scholar Thomas Stanley (1625–78). His *History* went through four editions (London, 1655–62, 1687, 1701, 1743) and was translated into Latin[58] and, part of it at least, into French (Paris, 1660). Locke possessed the second edition (1687), too late to have influenced the *Essay* with respect at least to the themes here treated, which do not appreciably change, I venture to say, between Draft C (1685) and the *Essay*'s first edition (1690).[59] Nonetheless, it is not impossible that Locke read someone else's first edition of this clearly popular book.

The first three volumes, appearing in 1655, 1656, and 1660,[60] were on Greek philosophy; the fourth volume appeared in 1662 and was on Chaldaic philosophy. The third volume is of special interest. It has five parts. The fourth part deals with the Sceptick Sect, and contains a translation of Sextus Empiricus's *Outlines of Pyrrhonism*.[61] The fifth part deals with the Epicurean Sect and consists of two main sections. One is a translation of Gassendi's *De vita et moribus Epicuri* (1647), books 1 and 2, to which Stanley adds a chapter in vindication of Epicurus taken from Diogenes Laertius (10:3–12), and which he ends by referring to the (next and) last six books of the *Vita*, where the vindication of Epicurus "is more fully and rhetorically handled by the learned *Gassendus*" (p. 128). The second section, much longer, is a translation of Gassendi's *Philosophiae Epicuri syntagma*, which first appeared in 1649 as an appendix to *Animadversiones*.[62] The last chapter is again taken from Diogenes Laertius.[63]

---

[58] By Godfrey Olarius (Leipzig, 1711; Venice, 1731). Part of it had been translated by Leclerc (Amsterdam, 1690).

[59] Harrison and Laslett, *Library*, item no. 2275. Locke also possessed Leclerc's translation.

[60] Only part 1 of the third volume bears this date; the title page of the four following parts bears the date 1659

[61] This might be of real importance. As far as works of Sextus, Locke otherwise possessed only the *Liber de medicina ex animalibus* (Harrison and Laslett, *Library*, item no. 2640).

[62] Lyons; pp. xcvii–cclxii. *Opera*, 3:1–94.

[63] R. T. Kroll is to be credited for the recent discovery of Stanley in this connection, and most important, for identifying Stanley's texts as translations of Gassendi. Kroll argues that the whole

Stanley cannot have been Locke's principal source for his Gassendism, however, at least not for the ontological views most of concern here. In addition to the lack of evidence for Locke's having read the first edition,[64] there is only the vaguest empiricism, and not much more, to be found in Gassendi's two works.[65]

Boyle

The influence of Boyle on Locke was by any measure considerable.[66] With respect to the battle of the gods and giants and Locke's role in it, however, Boyle's role is negligible. There is no question but that Boyle read both Descartes and Gassendi,[67] and thus may well have provided Locke's first exposure to the works of both; but Boyle took no sides between them and, concentrating instead on their common enemy, Aristotelianism, tended to ignore the differences between them, referring indifferently to both as "corpuscularians." He saw that the Cartesian subtle matter had no dynamical properties and was thus inclined to ignore the issue of the void as empirically undecidable and therefore irrelevant to the establishment of the mechanical philosophy.[68] The question of atomism, the finite divisibility of matter, was similarly metaphysical, according to Boyle, even by Descartes's own testimony. Similarly, with respect to the analysis of space, Boyle was au courant with the Aristotelian, Cartesian, and Gassendist positions and the arguments for and against them; but aside from disfavoring the Aristotelian, he maintained

---

enterprise of Stanley's *History* "is apparently conceived along Gassendist lines." One obvious line is the translation of Gassendi. But another is historiographical. According to Kroll, Stanley follows Gassendi's use of historical material as a mythopoeic vehicle for dealing with contemporary concerns. Roughly, the idea is that only through history are philosophical problems intelligible. This methodological position melding skepticism and empiricism is to be found expressed in the epigraphs of vol. 3 taken from Montaigne and Bacon.

64 The only reference I have found in the MS material is to the second edition (Bodleian MS Locke c. 42, pt. 2, p. 71). Nowhere that I know of is Stanley mentioned in the published work.

65 In addition, as Fred S. and Emily Michael point out, the *Philosophiae Epicuri syntagma* "contains the views not of Gassendi but of Epicurus. Stanley's *History* . . . deals only with the sects of ancient philosophy, and Gassendi's *Epicurean Syntagma* is included just because it is an accurate account of the philosophy of Epicurus" ("Theory," p. 383).

66 A curiosity is that although Boyle and Locke were together in Oxford from 1661 until 1668 save for a year (1665–66), there is no evidence that they had any philosophical discussion. See Rogers, "Boyle, Locke and Reason," pp. 206–7. Yet, that Locke was influenced by Boyle has been denied by no one; their relationship was close and remained so until Boyle's death in 1691. See Stewart, "Contacts."

67 Fred S. and Emily Michael make an interesting comment on the seriousness of Boyle's reading in this regard ("Theory," 380, n. 9).

68 *New Experiments Physico-mechanical, touching the spring of the air and its effects* (1662); *Works*, 1:37–38.

a studied neutrality.[69] To be sure, such positivism should argue the Gassendist cause at least in general terms; but this general consideration is offset by details such as, for instance, Boyle's acceptance of the ontological argument,[70] which is incompatible with Gassendi's basic nominalism.

Other Bridges

An intriguing possibility for the bridge between Gassendi and Locke is Sorbière, who on his trip to England went to Oxford, where he met Wallis (whom he thought a great mathematician, but ridiculous), Lockey (the Bodley librarian), and other noteworthies, and visited the Duke Humphrey library and all the colleges. (He noted the brazen nose at Brasenose College, reporting that it commemorated the nose of John Duns Scotus, who had taught there.) While in Oxford he lodged in Christ Church. An intriguing possibility (for which there is no other evidence but circumstance) is that Sorbière might then have encouraged Locke in his reading of Gassendi, which was already underway, or discussed it with him, or who knows what else. But as we have seen, Sorbière's trip to England, like his career generally, was of inconsistent value to the Gassendist cause. A priori there is as much reason to believe that the sober Locke would have been turned against it by such a character. Other possibilities for a Gassendist connection, finally, might be Pascal, whose work Locke purchased and commented upon,[71] or Auzout, Cassini, Thévenot, Justel, Thoynard, all of whom Locke knew in Paris.

§10 LOCKE AND DESCARTES

The relation of Locke to Descartes has been a matter of some dispute from his own time to the present.[72] We all know the testimony of Lady Masham: "The first books (as Mr. Locke himself has told me) which gave him a relish of philosophical studies were those of Descartes. He was rejoiced in reading of these because though he very often differed in opinion from this writer, yet he found what he said was very intelligible; from whence he was encouraged to think that his not having understood others had, possibly, not proceeded alto-

---

[69] *Advices in judging of things said to transcend reason*; *Works*, 4:459–60.

[70] Ibid., p. 461.

[71] For an account of the influence of Pascal generally, Bonno, *Les relations*, pp. 59–62.

[72] There may be important methodological similarities between Locke and Descartes (Schouls, *Method*). Shankula, however, has defeated the Aaron–Roth thesis that the quasi-rationalist Locke owes to Descartes his notions, inter alia, of certainty, intuition, deduction, and the like; indeed, even Lady Masham's testimony that Locke was awakened from his dogmatic slumber by Descartes must be viewed differently. See Shankula, "Science of Nature."

gether from a defect in his understanding."[73] Then there is the letter[74] from Tyrrell to Locke, March 18, 1689–90: Tyrell had heard secondhand that Locke was viewed as having "taken all that was in [The *Essay*] good from Des Cartes divers . . . modern French Authours, not only as to the notions but the manner of connection of them." But this testimony is not unequivocal. 'Des Cartes' is deleted in the manuscript in favor of 'modern French Authours,' the referents of which might as well have been Bernier or Launay as Arnauld or Malebranche.

Locke himself offers at least some help in this regard. Locke of course possessed the works of Descartes—notably the *Meditations*, *Principles*, *Discourse*, *Passions of the Soul*, *Letters*, and *Objections and Replies to Meditations*[75]—and was a close and serious reader of them as evidenced, I shall try to show, by both his manuscripts and published work, most important, the *Essay*. Not only did Locke possess and read the works of Descartes, but he made a study of how to study them. In his journal on March 7, 1678 he entered (in a French that invites speculation) "a method for the proper study of Descartes's doctrine," including the Cartesian secondary literature, critics not excepted. It is a methodical and fairly extensive account. One begins with Descartes's method (supplemented by Poisson's commentary), then moves on to his logic (supplemented by the Port-Royal *Logic*, Duhamel, and Clauberg), his metaphysics (again Clauberg, C. Van Hogelande), his physics (Rohault, D. Lipstorp, Pardies), his physiology (La Forge, again Van Hogelande).[76]

By his own testimony the work of Descartes played a crucial role in Locke's philosophical development. From Descartes he claims to have got, however, not the substance of his philosophy, but rather the realization that there were alternatives to the Aristotelian Scholasticism to which he was first exposed. As he wrote Stillingfleet, "though I must always acknowledge to [Descartes] the great obligation of my first deliverance from the unintelligible way of talking of the philosophy in use in the Schools in his time," such imperfections as the *Essay* contained (and presumably its perfections as well) were "spun barely from my own thoughts."[77]

Locke goes on explicitly to deny the Cartesian discipleship Stillingfleet attempted initially to attribute to him. Locke specifically rejects Stillingfleet's insinuation that for him as for Descartes certainty consists in clear and distinct ideas: "I do not remember that I have any where said, that we could not be convinced by reason of any truth, but where all the ideas concerned in that conviction were clear and distinct" (p. 42). Clarity and distinctness of ideas may

---

[73] Amsterdam, Univ. Lib., Remonstrants' MSS J57a; quoted by Cranston, *John Locke*, p. 100; Fox Bourne, *John Locke*, 1:1–2.

[74] To which Ware first drew attention ("Influence," p. 210).

[75] Harrison and Laslett, *Library*, pp. 101–2.

[76] There are other references of interest that might be investigated in other histories of the period and of Cartesianism in particular.

[77] *First Letter*; *Works*, 4:48–49.

contribute to clear and distinct reasoning and discourse about them, but we can have certainty about obscure ideas as in the case of the idea of substance. Locke distinguishes himself from "another who has said 'clear and distinct ideas are the sole matter and foundation of all our reasoning'" and finally disclaims any borrowing from Descartes concerning certainty, explicitly naming him (pp. 42–49). He rejects the notion of being "the scholar of so great a master."

A schematic, more extensive picture of Locke's opposition to Cartesianism would contain at least the following elements. Against the view that there are two metaphysical natural kinds is Locke's thoroughgoing *nominalism*, which in him, as historically before him, is dialectically inclined toward *materialism*. Because there are no essences of the Platonic-Cartesian sort they cannot be known, so that, epistemologically, *skepticism* is the result. Indeed, even the essences of a sort that Locke allows are not known. Methodologically, skepticism is a means to dogmatism for Descartes; for Locke it is a permanent state of affairs. Rejecting essences is of a piece with rejecting necessities *de re*, with the result that things ultimately can be known and known to exist only through experience. This *empiricism* not only precludes innate ideas but inclines toward *tychism* in response to the grand metaphysical question. It certainly rules out the ontological argument.[78] I shall attempt in the next three chapters to detail and argue for the more contentious elements of this schema as they relate to the battle of the gods and giants. To conclude this introduction to Locke's role in the battle, I shall focus on the hitherto unappreciated parry of Locke's *Essay* against the metaphysical core of Cartesianism, namely, the view that everything partakes of either of two essences: thought or extension.[79]

Locke's rejection of extension as the essence of body is abundantly clear. By arguing for vacuum as space that is unoccupied by body he rejects the Cartesian identification of body, space, and extension. In due course we shall closely investigate these arguments, for which Gassendi was the most likely vehicle from antiquity. Here I wish to give some indication of how the void, which might appear to lie at the periphery of the *Essay's* concerns, in fact is among those at its center.

Locke is nowadays known for nothing if not for his distinction between primary and secondary qualities. Even more than his theories of personal identity, substance, ideas, and so on, this distinction has drawn and continues to draw the attention of historians and philosophers, especially the analytically minded. Its fascination is perennial. Yet nearly no one notices the context for

---

[78] In the *Essay* Locke leaves open the soundness of the argument, complaining only of those who would make it the only proof "and out of an over-fondness of that Darling Invention, cashier, or at least endeavor to invalidate all other Arguments" (4.10.7; 622). The *First Letter* to Stillingfleet and a paper of 1696 expressly reject it. See Gibson, *Locke's Theory*, pp. 168–69.

[79] F.H. Anderson has been one of the few to have seen that Locke was not only an opponent of Cartesianism, but was opposed specifically to its Platonism. But his account of the matter is far too oracular to be of much use here.

the distinction in the first place. Many pick up Locke's comment that in explaining the distinction he has "been engaged in Physical Enquiries a little farther than, perhaps, [he] intended," that his main concern was to explain the nature of sensation somewhat and to distinguish qualities in bodies from ideas in the mind (2.8.22; 140). But Locke's specific problem with sensation is typically ignored because the first six paragraphs of his chapter are ignored.

Perhaps surprisingly, Locke no less than the Cartesians is under the spell of the Parmenidean dialectic at least to the extent that for him thought requires an object. To think without there being an object immediately before the mind, which object Locke calls an idea, is not to think at all. (As we shall see in detail, Locke's concern is not with the problem of intentionality—to think of nothing is not to think. Rather, his concern is with a causal problem—what the mind thinks of must act on it, and what is not cannot act at all.) And what is true of thought is true mutatis mutandis of categorematic terms as well. Unless there be ideas for words like 'motion,' 'elephant,' and 'drunkenness' to refer to, such words are meaningless. Hence in discussing "words or language in general" Locke is concerned to show that while presumably significant words like 'nihil,' 'ignorance,' and 'barreness,' are *negative* or *privitive*, they "cannot be said properly to belong to, or signify no *Ideas*; for then they would be perfectly insignificant sounds; but they relate to positive *Ideas*, and signify their absence" (3.1.4; 403). How it is that such negative words relate to positive ideas is the problem to be solved by Locke's distinction between primary and secondary qualities.

"Whatsoever is constituted in Nature, as to be able, by affecting our Senses, to cause any perception in the Mind, doth thereby produce in the Understanding a simple *Idea*; which, whatever be the external cause of it, when it comes to be taken notice of, by our discerning Faculty, it is by the Mind looked on and considered there, to be a real *positive Idea* in the Understanding, as much as any other whatsoever; though, perhaps, the cause of it be but a privation in the subject" (2.8.1; 132). Thus, of contrary ideas such as the ideas of light and darkness, motion and rest, while both are *positive* ideas (that is, I take it, both are ideas and not in one instance the lack of an idea), it is possible that one of the ideas should be *caused* by a privation. The explanation of such ideas involves an inquiry into the sort of "Physical Consideration of the Mind" that Locke foreswore in the second paragraph of the *Essay*. He nonetheless here enters into the "natural Causes and manner of Perception" to explain that, our sensations being caused by various motions conveyed to our perceptual systems, any increase or decrease in such motion, presumably such as would be caused by a privation, would result in a different idea (2.8.5; 133). Particles moving in a certain way will cause the sensation of light, their ceasing to move the idea of darkness; and "thus one may truly be said to see Darkness" (2.8.6; 133).

This corpuscularian explanation of sensation is systematically appealed to over the next twenty paragraphs, which set out the primary-secondary quality distinction. Locke's arguments in these paragraphs are not, as sometimes believed, arguments on behalf of the distinction, except by way of a bootstrap. By making the distinction and explaining sensation in corpuscularian terms we are able to deal with the classical problems of relativity of sense perception represented by Locke's examples of manna, porphyry, and pounded almond, which are thus illustrations of a distinction within a larger theory, itself invoked by the chapter to an independent purpose. That purpose is clearest with respect to the explanation of how the same water can cause the idea of hot when I place one hand in it, and of cold when I place the other hand in it. This explanation is easy if we assume along the lines above that the "Sensation of Heat and Cold, be nothing but the increase or diminution of the motion of the minute Parts of our Bodies," since the antecedent motion in each hand may be different (2.8.21; 139). The purpose, it seems to me, is to explain how we can have an idea of, and thus talk meaningfully about, what in fact is nothing. For Locke here in effect returns to the motivating issue set out at the beginning of the chapter, namely, how it is that contrary ideas can both be positive insofar as one of them might be caused by a privation. The most crucial case of this, unstated by an author abhorrent of controversy, is the literal case of the void, which is thus at odds with the first claim at the metaphysical core of Cartesianism. Locke not only shows that unoccupied space is not inconceivable, but suggests the mechanism whereby we come by such ideas. (His elaboration of ideas of secondary qualities as ideas of "nothing but Powers" may be regarded as to the same effect.) If the *Essay* is the anti-Cartesian document I take it to be, then we can read Locke as setting down here the basis for a very strong case. Later we shall see that not only are we not forced to reject the void on conceptual grounds, but as a matter of fact what exists in space does not exhaust what could exist in space. Even beyond his rejection of the physical plenum, Locke is in a position to reject metaphysical plenism. For, contrary to the first principle of Malebranche's epistemology, we can think of what is not and we do so by means of the idea of *nihil*, which is positive insofar as it denotes the absence of being (2.8.5).

As for the second core claim of Cartesianism, Locke's rejection of thought as the essence of mind is, if anything, better known than his rejection of extension as the essence of body. Again the issue is one to which we shall return, in greater length and in greater detail; the occasion will be one of the most raucous disputes of the period, namely, that concerning the bestial soul. Meanwhile I want to indicate just how central to the *Essay* is the rejection of this core claim of Cartesianism.

Having spent the whole first of his *Essay's* four books arguing that the mind is not the source of its own ideas, Locke answers the question as to where it does get them: "in one word, From *Experience*" (2.1.2; 104). He devotes eight paragraphs of the important first chapter of book 2 to outlining this empiricist thesis in terms of his distinction between ideas of sensation and ideas of reflection, and then spends all but the concluding two of the chapter's remaining seventeen paragraphs arguing against what is clearly the Cartesian thesis that the soul always thinks. Among the points that emerge are the following:

1. Whether the soul always thinks is a matter of fact to be decided only by experience. Those who appeal to thought as the essence of the soul beg the question and run contrary to ordinary ways of thinking and speaking (2.1.10, 19–23). Later, in discussing maxims, Locke similarly complains of the Cartesian a priori identification of body as extension: "He that with Des-Cartes, shall frame in his Mind an *Idea* of what he calls *Body*, to be nothing but Extension, may easily demonstrate, that there is no *Vacuum*; *i.e.* no Space void of Body, by this Maxim, *What is, is*. For the *Idea* to which he annexes the name *Body*, being bare Extension, his knowledge, that Space cannot be without Body, is certain." But the principle here proves no such thing, any more than the principle that it is impossible for the same thing to be and not to be proves that extension and body are different. "For that we are left to our Senses, to discover to us as far as they can" (4.7.12–14; 604–5).

2. To explain apparently dreamless sleep (as Descartes did in reply to Gassendi's objections) as a failure to remember is plainly implausible (2.1.11, 14).

3. The appeal to failure of memory also devalues the soul thus conceived since, among other things, it makes memory and coherence of thought depend on close union with the body (2.1.15–16).[80]

4. That the soul should always think is incompatible with the soul as the ground of personal identity. Those who would make the soul in sleep think apart from what is remembered awake in fact make two persons, and thus "every drowsy Nod shakes their Doctrine" (2.1.11–13). The long treatment of personal identity in the chapter on identity, a treatment that is longer by far than that of any other relation, is thus given point, not just as a topic of independent philosophical importance, but as part of the anti-Cartesian polemic.[81]

5. It is clear that Locke regards the Cartesian view of thought as the essence of

[80] Locke's earliest (at least according to von Leyden, editor of Locke's *Essays on the Law of Nature . . .*, p. 265) criticism of the Cartesian view that thought is the essence of the mind occurs in a journal entry for July 16, 1676. He claims that thought is like motion (both are properties), but that of which each is a property is indifferent to it and may be without it. His view at this point seems to be that the primary and inseparable "affection" of body is extension, and that of the soul is a power to produce motion in the body and thoughts in the mind (von Leyden, pp. 271–72).

[81] The *Essay*'s chapter on identity was added to the second edition. Locke's letters to Molyneux on August 23, 1693 and March 3, 1695. His position on the connection between thought and personal identity is adumbrated by his journal entry for February 20, 1682. See Aaron and Gibb, *Early Draft*, pp. 121–23. Commenting on an argument for the immortality of the soul, Locke opined that both its advocates and opponents argue an irrelevancy. What matters is not duration or substantial existence, which is had by body as well, but sensibility, which is not the soul's indivisible and immutable constitution and essence as is demonstrated by dreamless sleep. (To the rebuttal that the soul thinks but does not remember, Locke here rejoins that we might as well say the bedpost thinks but does not remember.) Locke here effectively reverses the *Phaedo's* order of moral *demonstranda*; the question is not imperishability but immortality.

the soul as of a piece with the doctrine of innate ideas. If the soul always thinks then those thoughts it has before or just at its union with the body are not derived from it. But since the ideas remembered at least by a waking man all have a "tangue of the Cask" in being derived from union with the body, the nativist doctrine must be false unless either the soul of a sleeping man remembers ideas that the waking man does not or innate ideas just are not remembered at all (2.1.17).

§11 ENTHUSIASM

Locke typically figures among the seventeenth- and eighteenth-century deists as at most a fellow-traveler, as one who sympathizes with many of their views and supports them with important arguments, but not as one of their principal members. I think this view of Locke is fundamentally correct. Indeed, as we shall see momentarily, Locke's *The Reasonableness of Christianity* is, despite its title, an avowedly antideist tract. Because his influence was far deeper and more extensive than any English deist, however, it seems to me that his importance in this regard wants elevating. That is, although Locke did not fully embrace deism, his sympathy for it and his arguments, explicit and implicit, in its behalf did more to promulgate deism than the efforts of someone like Toland who did fully embrace it. As part of this case, it has long seemed to me that the antepenultimate chapter of the *Essay*, entitled "Of Enthusiasm," which is of a piece with at least the four chapters preceding it, was a key, and perhaps the key, chapter to that work.[82]

As we know, knowledge for Locke in some sense consists in the perception of agreement or disagreement of ideas. Later I shall try to show that this amounts to a theory of predication based on something like a model of class inclusion not unlike the more familiar version of it we find in Berkeley. To say of a die that it is white is to say that the idea of whiteness is included in a class that also contains the ideas of hardness, squareness, and the like, and to know that the die is white is to know that this inclusion obtains. Sometimes the inclusion is indubitable and the perceived agreement or disagreement is as certain as the possession of the ideas themselves, as when it is seen that the arc of a circle is less than the whole circle. This is what Locke calls intuitive knowledge. But the relevant inclusion or its lack is not always apparent to perception, and so in addition reason is required, namely, the faculty of inference that supplies middle terms or ideas, displays them in appropriate order, perceives their connection, and draws the right conclusion. The exercise of this

---

[82] In the final chapter below, I shall return to Locke's *Reasonableness* for an argument at the metatheoretical level for my interpretation of Locke. We shall find Locke advocating just the toleration expected of one with his views on enthusiasm. We shall also find that such an attitude of toleration can be extended to interpretations themselves.

faculty that yields certainty is called rational knowledge; its exercise yielding probability only is called judgment (4.1–2; 4.14–17).

Different from reason, but apparently not opposed to it, is faith, which is "the Assent to any Proposition, not thus made out by the Deductions of Reason; but upon the Credit of the Proposer, as coming from GOD, in some extraordinary way of Communication. This way of discovering Truths to Men we call *Revelation*" (4.18.2; 689). Locke's tendency is to restrict the relevance of faith. Revelation, for example, cannot communicate any new simple idea not had previously from sensation or reflection. Whatever he learned "when he was rapp'd up into the Third Heaven," St. Paul was only able to report that what he experienced was such "as Eye hath not seen, nor Ear heard, nor hath it entered into the Heart of Man to conceive" (1 Cor. 2:9). We believe that Paul had certain experiences, but because we have never had them or anything like them, he cannot tell us what those experiences were. Second, truths such as those of Euclid *could* be revealed, but in "all Things of this Kind, there is little need or use of *Revelation*, GOD having furnished us with natural, and surer means to arrive at the Knowledge of them" (4.18.4; 690). Finally, Locke gives an argument to the effect that no proposition contrary to knowledge can be accepted as revealed and therefore true. The argument is simple: What is divinely revealed must be true; but to accept a proposition for having been revealed we must know that it is revealed; hence no revealed propositions can be any more acceptable than what we know. A version of this argument was later to be attributed by Hume to John Tillotson in section 10 of his *Enquiry Concerning Human Understanding*. Tillotson (1630–94), archbishop of Canterbury, pitted reason against Catholicism, for example, in his argument against the real presence of Christ in the Eucharist. The authority of both Scripture and Tradition with respect to such things, he argued, is founded in the sense experience of those who claimed to witness miracles. But this experience of miracles, even if interpreted to argue the doctrine of the Real Presence, is weakened by being transmitted to us and hence is weaker than our own sense experience, to which the doctrine of the Real Presence is contrary. Hume's generalized version of this argument in his *Enquiry Concerning Human Understanding* is that a miracle, by definition a violation of the laws of nature, has by definition the full proof of uniform experience against it (pp. 114–15).

Locke was speaking for many in the deist camp when he argued that to admit propositions contrary to knowledge on the basis of Revelation "would be to subvert the Principles, and Foundations of all Knowledge, Evidence, and Assent whatsoever; and there would be left no difference between Truth and Falshood, no measures of Credible and Incredible in the World, if doubtful Propositions, shall take place before self-evident; and what we certainly know, give way to what we may possibly be mistaken in" (4.18.5; 692). But Locke stops short of the Humean conclusion, for he allows that there may be some propositions whose truth value cannot be known or can be judged only with probability. In these cases the proposition is purely *"Matter of Faith, and above Reason,"* to the point that "evident *Revelation* ought to determine our Assent even against Probability." It is difficult to know what to do with this position. A recommendation for suspension of judgment or rejection of the alleged revelation would have been expected. For one thing, this is just the conclusion that was being drawn by people like Tillotson. For another, it would have been supported by what Locke says elsewhere in his classic statement of one of the main views in the ethics of belief issue: "The great Excellency and Use of the Judgment, is to observe Right, and take a true estimate of the force and weight of each Probability; and then casting them up all right together, chuse that side, which has the over-balance."[83] It is hard to find a clearer statement than this that belief should vary directly with evidence: Of two competing views always accept the one that is more probable, that is, with more evidence, and entrench the acceptance to the degree of the probability. But the conclusion should be that acceptable Revelation can never be improbable. It is worth elaborating on this point since it bears on Locke's relation to deism.

Locke makes it clear at the outset of *The Reasonableness of Christianity* that his aim is to avoid the extremes of those who make Christianity "almost nothing" by rejecting the transmission of original sin and thus the significance of the Redemption. He is concerned with those who were arguing that it was morally impossible for Adam to have done anything to make a Savior necessary for anyone else and that therefore Jesus Christ was "nothing but the restorer and preacher of pure natural religion."[84] For the deist, both those against whom Locke was arguing and those of the eighteenth century, Christianity is *reasonable* (a code word for them) in the sense that Revelation contains much that can be established by reason alone (the existence of God, the moral code, etc.). But what it contains, or seems to contain, contrary to reason either in fact cannot be there at all or must be false, and thus in either case must be rejected. The upshot is that Revelation is in principle dispensable in favor of reason. For Locke, on the other hand, Christianity is reasonable only in the (rather Pickwickian) sense that Scripture reasonably read belies this deistic position and requires only the belief that Christ was the Messiah. His intended position would seem to be that, if Revelation is accepted at all, then at least one belief must be held on faith beyond reason, and thus deism is upset. But if Revelation is accepted on the basis of reason, then it looks as if nothing revealed will be beyond reason and faith will be dispensable. Thus, even in attempting to distance himself from the deists Locke enhances the plausibility of their position.

William Carroll was one who in the period read Locke's treatment of faith and reason in these terms, and who additionally saw the threat to authority that it represented. He criticized Locke for having followed Spinoza and Toland,

---

[83] 4.17.16; 685. Also 4.17.24; 687–88.
[84] *Works*, 7:4–5.

and the author of *The Rights of The Christian Church*[85] for having followed Locke. What they all did, according to Carroll, was to subvert the nature and use of Revelation and faith by substituting reason for faith. "And whereas they find [reason] common to all Men, they endeavour to make out, that in Matters of Religion, all Men are equal, that none in that respect ought to have any Superiority or Authority, one above another; especially that Clergy-Men neither have nor can have any Authority at all above others, in these matters."[86]

And indeed, even in rejecting deism Locke is careful at the same time to reject religious authoritarianism. His view is that the belief in Christ as the Messiah is necessary and sufficient for eternal life: "this is the sole doctrine pressed and required to be believed in the whole tenor of our Saviour's and his apostles' preaching."[87] "I allow to the makers of systems and their followers to invent and use what they think fit. But I cannot allow to them, or to any man, an authority to make a religion for me, or to alter that which God has revealed" (pp. 101–2). The complication here is that (in response to problems about election) Locke inclines toward fideism. "We know very little of this visible, and nothing at all of the state of that intellectual world, wherein are infinite numbers and degrees of spirits out of our ken, or guess; and therefore know not what transactions there were between God and our Saviour, in reference to his kingdom" (p. 134). God's wisdom and Providence are simply beyond our understanding. In addition, "the greatest part of mankind have not leisure for learning and logic, and superfine distinctions of the schools" (p. 157). Thus, there is a necessity for Revelation, and one that is simple. The problem raised by this restriction of the claims of reason in favor of faith is that it represents precisely the strategy employed by Erasmus on behalf of the authority of Rome against Luther's reformation based on private revelation to the individual reading Scripture. If we take reason to be any individual attempt such as Luther's (or, later, Descartes's) to arrive at a criterion of all belief, and if reason in this sense is humbled by the arguments of skepticism, then the only recourse in practical matters is, as the classical skeptics had urged, reliance on the tried if not true ways of doing things, namely, Tradition, which at this point in history rather clearly was the property of Rome. Such was the strategy of Erasmus, and in such terms it could hardly have been more inimical to the taste and purpose of Locke. Even so, if Locke's commitment to the necessity of faith at all commits him to the dilemma of Erasmian authority of history or Lutheran private revelation, it is the latter he would more vigorously eschew as the very paradigm of enthusiasm.

Whatever the extent of the province of faith, to accept a proposition in its

---

[85] Identified as Samuel Hill, author of *The Rights, Liberties and Authorities of the Christian Church . . .* (London, 1701) by Halkett and Laing, *Dictionary*, 5:124.

[86] *Dissertation*, p. 279.

[87] *Works*, 7:102. Repentance and obedience elsewhere seem also to be required, perhaps as a consequence, or the content even, of this belief.

favor contrary to reason is to succumb to enthusiasm. For Locke, it seems to me, the ultimate danger of enthusiasm is moral and political: He who does violence to his own reason is likely prepared to do violence to others. Its immediate and necessary consequence is the destruction of both reason and revelation: "he that takes away *Reason*, to make way for *Revelation*, puts out the light of both, and does much what the same, as if he would persuade a Man to put out his Eyes the better to receive the remote Light of an invisible Star by a Telescope" (4.19.4; 698).

A curious feature of Locke's chapter on enthusiasm is that while it caps the arguments and distinctions of the four previous chapters, its first appearance is in the fourth edition (1700), the last in Locke's lifetime. What occurred between that date and 1690, the date of the first edition, if not 1694 or 1695, the second and third editions?

The question is related to another: Who were the enthusiasts whom Locke had in mind? Aaron begins his book with the claim, plausible enough, that "Locke might well have regarded the passage of his own life as a passage from an age of Enthusiasm to an age of Reason."[88] He relates enthusiasm to the "emotionalism of the Civil War period." Similarly, Campbell Fraser points to "the extravagance of the sects under the Commonwealth, which vexed and disturbed his early years";[89] and Cranston looks to the "Protestant extremists who claim to have private illuminations from God."[90] These commentators are certainly right as far as they go, for none of these concerns was far from Locke's mind in any period. But the fuller story, it seems to me, is that Locke is attacking what they say he attacks, not as it is found in groups over a quarter of a century previously, but as it is represented by the new authoritarians, the Cartesians. That is, previous commentators have failed to explain why it is that Locke writes a *philosophical* work, of such length, if his concern is only with *religious* radicals. Only if the object of Locke's attack is in his view a doctrine that is both philosophically significant and politically/morally dangerous does the *Essay* seem motivated. As I shall try to show, Locke and others saw Cartesianism as just such a doctrine.

There is some evidence that Cartesianism may have been viewed in these terms in Oxford even before Locke began his *Essay*. We know that Boyle was no anti-Cartesian, but the first historian of the Royal Society and some of its members may well have been. From Spratt we have a very valuable description of the first meetings of the group at Oxford that eventually became the Royal Society: "Their first purpose was no more, than onely the satisfaction of breathing a freer air, and of conversing in quiet with one another, without being ingag'd in the passions, and madness of that dismal Age." As a result, accord-

---

[88] *John Locke*, p. 1.
[89] *Essay*, ed. A. C. Fraser, 452, n. 2.
[90] *John Locke*, p. xx.

ing to Spratt, not only was the university largely saved, but also the next generation, exposed to this atmosphere, was "invincibly arm'd against all the inchantments of *Enthusiasm*."[91] The best defense against such "spiritual Frensies" and "thick deceits" is a "deep skill in Nature" and much converse with "the subtility of things" (p. 54). Spratt does not here identify the enthusiasts, but given his remedy against them, they cannot have been exclusively, or even primarily, religious enthusiasts. Empirical experimentation is an antidote to philosophical enthusiasm, and for this reading there is also good textual evidence. Previously (pp. 28ff.), Spratt had defined five objectionable new ways of philosophizing that may supply his target: (1) modern dogmatists, the new "Tyrants" who, disdaining the ancients, pretend to "public liberty," but who in fact terminate inquiry and foster strife; (2) the reviewers of ancient sects who substitute one tyrant for another; (3) the experimentalists, the followers of Bacon, whose problem was that he took everything indiscriminately; (4) the Chymists, who are "downright Enthusiasts" in their pursuit of the Philosopher's Stone; (5) the specialists who handle (only) particular subjects such as astronomy, geometry, and anatomy—presumably in the fashion of the Académie des sciences. Of the two unidentified groups, the second is likely the Gassendists, who substitute Epicurus for Aristotle. Their wells had been unwittingly poisoned for Spratt by Sorbière's account of his trip to England. But who are the modern tyrants who dogmatically stir up strife? Who else but the Cartesians, who were excluded from the Académie des sciences for the same reason.[92]

We know from his correspondence that Descartes sought consciously to replace Aristotle, not with some other ancient, but with himself as the Philosopher.[93] He set out to produce a comprehensive explanation of the world that not only explained its physical aspects but also the truths of the Faith to the extent they were amenable to reason. As Aristotle had been the authority of the old world-system, Descartes would be the authority of the new—quite literally the only author of its textbooks. Whether or not Locke knew of this correspondence, we can understand how he might have seen what he regarded as evidence for the hopes it contained. For Locke, the Cartesians are no less sectarian and

[91] *History*, p. 52.

[92] Spratt was not the first to identify philosophical enthusiasm. Henry More explicitly referred to the chemists and theosophists, and especially Paracelsus, in such terms (*Enthusiasmus triumphatus*, secs. 42–50). He also described political enthusiasm and discussed at length the case of David George (secs. 32–40). By enthusiasm he understands "a full, but false, persuasion in a man that he is inspired" (sec. 2). His cure was temperance, humility, and reason (the principal feature of which is caution). More's views on witchcraft in book 2 of *Antidote against Atheism* should also be read in this regard, especially his criticisms of Johann Weyer, who had attempted to deal with the phenomenon in naturalistic terms. The three works by More referred to in the text—*Antidote against Atheism* (190 pp.), *Conjectura Cabbalistica* (184 pp.), and *Enthusiasmus triumphatus* (48 pp.)—all appear in *A Collection of Several Philosophical Writings* (London, 1662). The pagination begins anew with each independent work.

[93] For a controversial account of this, see Caton, "Analytic History."

dogmatic, and, because intolerant, politically no less dangerous than the Aristotelians had been. And the basis for the danger of each is the same mistaken view, namely, that endowed with intellectual intuition we can know the essences of things. Claims to know essences run contrary to evidence and right reason, and in this sense are a form of enthusiasm. This is the argument made by Molyneux in correspondence with Locke:

> I should very much approve of your Adding a Chapter in your Essay, concerning Malbranches Hypothesis. As there are Enthusiasmes in Divinity, so there are in Philosophy; and as one proceeds from not Consulting, or misapprehending the Book of God; so the other from not reading and Considering the Book of Nature. I look upon Malbranches Notions, or rather Platos, in this particular perfectly unintelligible; and if you will Ingage in a Philosophick Controversy, you cannot do it with more advantage than in this matter. What you lay down concerning Our Ideas and Knowledge is founded and Confirmed by Experiment, and Observation, that any man may make in himself, or the Children he Converses with; wherein he may note the Gradual Steps that we make in Knowledge. But Plato's fancy has no foundation in Nature, but is merely the Product of his Own brain.[94]

[94] April 18, 1693; *Correspondence*, 4:668. See also Molyneux to Locke, March 8, 1695: "I have also examined P. Malebranche's opinion concerning all things in God, and to my own satisfaction laid open the vanity, and inconsistency, and unintelligibleness of that way of explaining humane understanding" (5:287). On March 26, 1695, following a paragraph on the feasibility of adding to the *Essay* a section on enthusiasm, Molyneux wrote: "I must freely Confess that if my Notion of Enthusiasme agrees with yours, there is no necessity of adding anything concerning it more than by the by and in a single section in Chap. XVIII.L.IV. I conceive it to be no other than a Religious sort of Madness and Comprises not in it any Mode of Thinking or Operation of the Mind, Differ[en]t from what you have treated of in your Essay. Tis true indeed, the Absurditys Men imbrace on account of Religion are most Astonishing, and if in a Chapter of Enthusiasme you indeavour to give an Account of them, 'twould be very acceptable, so that (on second thoughts) I do very well approve of what you propose therein, being very desirous of having your sentiments on any subject. Pere Malbranche's Chapter of *Seeing all things in God* was ever to me absolutely unintelligible; and unles you think a Polemick Discourse in your Essay (which you have hitherto avoided therein) may not be of a Piece with the Rest, I am sure it highly deserves to be exposed, and is very agreable to the Business of your Work. I would therefore humbly propose it to you to Consider of Doing something therein. Pere Malbranche has many Curious Notions; and some as Erroneous and absurd; tis a Good while since I first read him, but I am now turning him over a second time. He is Mostly Platonick, and in some things almost Enthusiastical" (p. 317). And Locke replied on April 26, 1695: "What I shall add concerning Enthusiasm, I guess, will very much agree with your thoughts, since yours jump so right with mine, about the place where it is to come in. I having designed it for *chap*. 18 *lib*. iv. as a false principle of reasoning often made use of. But, to give an historical account of the various ravings men have embraced for religion, would, I fear, be besides my purpose, and be enough to make an huge volume. My opinion of P. Malbranche agrees perfectly with yours. What I have writ concerning seeing all things in God, would make a little treastise of it self. But I have not quite gone through it, for fear I should by somebody or other be tempted to print it. For I love not controversies and have a personal kindness for the author. When I have the happiness to see you, we will consider it together, and you shall dispose of it" (pp. 352–53). I am grateful to J. P. Wright for drawing these texts to my attention.

Those who are overcome by enthusiasm and thus do violence to their own reason in the name of reason introduce a tyranny. Instead of the communal model of knowledge arrived at by public experiment that is always open to scrutiny and criticism, the Cartesians—like Plato—propose an individual model of privileged access, of a private and thus irrefutable authority. Instead of the external and intersubjective authority of experience, the Cartesians propose the introspective authority of intellectual intuition or, as Malebranche was calling it, Reason.

As we shall see in the next chapter, there is a sense in which for Malebranche we are able to perceive God through pure intellection. And he understands this perception in personal, religious terms. Whenever we know truth that is infinite, immutable, and universal, we are in contact with—we consult, to use his term—Reason, which is infinite, immutable, and universal. This Reason is not some subjective faculty of ours, as it is for Locke or even Descartes. Nor is it an impersonal emanation from the One. However much the Plotinian *logos* may have been the model in the Christian Neo-Platonic tradition on which Malebranche draws, his Word is the second person of the Blessed Trinity. It is the Word who was made flesh and dwelt among us (John 1). When we know a truth such as the Pythagorean theorem, or rather, come to know distinctly what we previously knew only confusedly, it is Jesus Christ who speaks (*sic*) to us. Perhaps Malebranche in the many places in which he talks in such terms only picks up the language of Augustine: "I entered into my innermost self and found the light of the Lord . . . whoever knows the truth knows it, and who knows it knows eternity. O eternal truth . . . you are my God, I sigh for you [*tibi suspiro*] night and day."[95] Whether Augustine intended the view that nothing can be known without knowing God, André Martin used this and other texts of Augustine to prove this point.[96]

Malebranche himself leaves no ambiguity in his identification of Reason, the ground for all intelligibility and truth. He says in *Elucidations* 8: "[God] is able not to produce anything external to Himself; but if He wills to act, He can do so only according to the immutable order of wisdom that he necessarily loves. For religion and wisdom teach me that he does nothing without His Son, without His Word, without His Wisdom" (p. 587). In the *Search* he says that "Jesus Christ, as external wisdom, as interior truth, as intelligible light, inspires us in the most secret recesses of our reason" and that this is the *same* Jesus Christ of the Gospel (p. 272). In his *Meditations* Malebranche begins with what he himself calls a prayer. It is an invocation of the eternal Wisdom, the only

---

[95] *Confessions*, 7, chap. 10.

[96] *Philosophia Christiana*, p. 172. See Gouhier, "La crise," pp. 290–91. The question whether Malebranche successfully rejects Martin's Jansenist tinge hinges on how well he is able to distinguish the orders of nature and grace, and natural from supernatural illumination (ibid., pp. 293–94). The tendency of his system is to make everything natural (Spinozism) or everything unnatural (Jansenism).

universal Reason and illumination, which he explicitly identifies as Jesus Christ,[97] who then becomes an interlocutor with the naive Malebranche throughout the rest of the work, promulgating the informed Malebranche's own views. Malebranche thus has his views on the infinite and ultimately his whole philosophy from the mouth of Christ, exactly as it is supposed to be derived according to that philosophy. *Meditations* 1 argues the familiar case that material things by themselves are not intelligible, that the soul's own modifications are not sufficient for knowledge of them. Then, in *Meditations* 2, having seen that the mind's proper object is eternal, immutable, and necessary truth, the Wisdom of God, Malebranche recognizes in a paroxysm of adoration that it is Jesus Himself who speaks to him in the most secret recess of his reason. Not just in particular instances of religion (private revelation), or even religion generally (Scripture and Tradition), but in all instances in which anyone knows the truth, speculative and moral alike, it is Christ who speaks.[98] It is not surprising that Locke should contemptuously, but carefully, refer to the supporters of Malebranche as "these sons of light"—"geniuses who think they either are not or ought not to be ignorant of anything."[99]

It is important to note that André Martin was not the only one to have cited the authority of Augustine on behalf of the Cartesian cause. The connection is to be found as well among Arnauld, Cordemoy, Gibieuf, La Forge, Mersenne, and Poisson.[100] For the Cartesians, of course, the connection legitimates their struggle against Scholastic Aristotelianism; there is no question of the orthodoxy of Augustine against that of Suarez, for example. But from the perspective of one like Locke on whom the constraints of orthodoxy are less severe, the connection might mean that all of Cartesianism is tarred with the brush of enthusiasm found in the Augustine of Martin. For Locke, of course, Malebranche's Reason is a false reason and the philosophical enthusiasm asserting it would be, no less than religious enthusiasm, "founded neither on reason nor divine revelation, but rising from the conceits of a warmed or overweening brain" (4.19.7; 699). According to Locke, the reason we consult is never God's (as Malebranche claims it is in *Elucidations* 10), which is an immediate view of all things. For our reason "is very far from such an intuition; it is a laborious and gradual progress in the knowledge of things [by comparing ideas]. . . . This way therefore of finding truth, so painful, uncertain, and limited, is proper only to men of finite understanding, but can by no means be supposed in God."[101] Malebranche makes knowledge and presumably the claim to govern practical life too easy. Thus, the danger of philosophical enthusiasm, like that of religious enthusiasm, is moral and political fanaticism.

[97] *Oeuvres*, 1:9

[98] Ibid., 23–24.

[99] *First Reply to Norris*; Acworth, "Locke's First Reply," p. 10.

[100] Gouhier, "La crise," p. 295.

[101] *Examination of Malebranche*, par. 52; *Works* 10.

A good example of the kind of Platonist appeal to authority to which Locke might object occurs in the important tenth *Elucidation*, in which Malebranche is expounding his theory of ideas. The point that he wants to make is one that we shall see is very important to him, namely, that eternal truths must be "immutable by the necessity of their nature," else there can be no certainty in either the speculative or moral sciences. His argument, however, is that unless this were so there would be no way to refute the libertine who says that the flesh should dominate the mind (p. 616). That is, because he sees that morality consists in a certain kind of order, Malebranche feels himself entitled to say what that order is. The libertine is wrong because we see—not argue, but see—that the body and its well-being are below the mind and its well-being. Malebranche here uses structural premises about what morality consists in, the logical status of moral propositions, their semantics, and the like, in order to derive substantive conclusions about what in fact is moral and immoral. "Just as there are necessary and eternal truths because there are relations of magnitude among intelligible beings, there must also be a necessary and immutable order because of the relations of perfection among these same beings. An immutable order has it, then, that minds are more noble than bodies, as it is a necessary truth that twice two is four, or that twice two is not five" (p. 618). This supernaturalistic fallacy is typical of his ethical thinking.[102] How very different it is from the thinking of Locke, who also claims that moral propositions have the same certainty as those of mathematics, but who then, far from laying down the law, does not even show how ethics can be any more than empty tautologies. The danger of Malebranche's fanaticism is combatted by the metaphysics of "learned freethinking," which upsets the authority of Reason and encourages the cool moderation of ataraxia.[103]

A good example of what to Locke could not have been anything but philosophical enthusiasm is to be found in Malebranche's thirteenth *Elucidation*. Here Malebranche is responding to the worry that his views on the contributions of the senses to corporeal health and of reason to spiritual health dispense with physicians and directors of conscience. His reply in effect only quickens the worry. He very imaginatively reiterates the Cartesian view of *Meditations* 6 that since the laws designed to maintain the mind-body union must be the simplest possible there will be mistakes where that end is not achieved, but that for the same reason these mistakes will be very rare. To deal with them we may contravene the inclinations of the senses, for example, against bitter medicines, and rely on the experience of physicians; but we should do so only with reluctance, suspicion, and expectation of failure. The case with respect to directors of conscience is exactly parallel: "Only sovereign Reason makes us

---

[102] For an account of Malebranche's attempt to establish a science of ethics, see Walton, *Study*.

[103] I realize of course that this is a controversial reading of libertinage érudit; here I can only indicate my agreement with the general interpretation urged by Popkin.

rational, only Truth enlightens us, only God speaks to us clearly and can teach us. We have but one true Master, Jesus Christ, our Lord, the eternal Wisdom, the Word of the Father in whom are all the treasures of the knowledge and wisdom of God." As with physicians, directors of conscience frequently act in ignorance, from self-interest and with plain bad luck; to rely on them is, as he says, like the blind leading the blind. As a sympathizer with many of the views of Port-Royal, he may well be reacting to the excesses of the Jesuit confessional policies that gave casuistry its bad name, but what Malebranche is arguing for is a revelation that is no less private for being in principle available to all. For its ratification is always by appeal to an inner light. He describes this appeal in terms applicable to the psychology of the most extreme fanaticism: There is no point consulting anyone else when we are certain that the Truth, Jesus Christ, is speaking to us, and there is no mistaking when It/He does so. "We must submit to it without regard for the opinion of other men. We must not take account of custom, or listen to our secret inclinations, or defer too much to the so-called learned. We must not be seduced by false appearances of piety, or be disheartened by the opposition of those who are ignorant of the mind animating them. Rather, we must suffer their insults with patience . . . we must rejoice in the truth that illuminates us" (p. 649). This most royal of all societies has but One member.

Locke must at a certain point make a move at least analogous to Malebranche's appeal to Reason or the more Cartesian appeal to the inner natural light. For I have to say that I believe what I do just because that is the way it seems to me. There is no alternative to saying with Luther, "Hier stehe ich—Ich kann nicht anders." To do otherwise would be irresponsible. Given that he rejects the imposition of religion, Locke presumably also rejects such irresponsibility. No one should accept a proposition only because it has been uttered by a certain other person. Even so, there are important differences between Locke's view and the Cartesians'. For one thing, the assertion of one's own autonomy is never on the basis that it is guaranteed by God, either by having God speak to us directly or by having Him validate the inner light. Such a guarantee is already a violation of that autonomy and one that at least smacks of enthusiasm. Second, there is a difference in the role awarded others in the community in the rational formation of my belief. While I should believe and assert what seems to *me* to be true, on the Lockean communal model I take into account what others believe and assert. To the Cartesian such a procedure is, worse than irrelevant, positively liable to be deceiving.

It is not surprising, therefore, to find the Cartesians as the moderns and the Gassendists as the ancients in the seventeenth-century debates over the value of classical literature. Nor is this just a matter of taste or relative emphasis. The Cartesians are realists: The truth is there to be *discovered*, fully constituted independently of human device. In addition, the whole truth is at least in principle available to each individual starting from epistemological scratch.

This is the case, even if in very different ways, for both Descartes and Malebranche. For neither of them is the classic statement of anything an important value. History itself is a distraction in the search for eternal truth. Their Gassendist opponents, on the other hand, were nominalists and, as I shall try to show even for Locke, were inclined to Hobbist conventionalism. On such a view meaning and truth are nothing apart from a community of language-users whose history is essential in the *production* of truth. Such truth is available only piecemeal to individuals who attend to what others say and traditionally have said. For them, while an appeal to how it seems to me must be the *last* move, it cannot be the *only* move as it is with the Cartesians.[104]

If my general thesis concerning the Cartesians is at all correct, then the occasion for Locke's speaking against enthusiasm was no doubt his controversy with John Norris (1651–1711; a conservative in religion, poetry, and philosophy).[105] This "Malebranche of England," whom Molyneux describes to Locke as an "obscure enthusiastical man,"[106] had in 1690 attacked Locke in his *Cursory Reflexions* and in 1691–92 had a published exchange with Leclerc, who defended Locke. In addition, there was a personal incident: Norris opened a letter he was conveying from Lady Masham to Locke.[107] In 1693, Locke, once the friend and benefactor of Norris, bitterly attacked him in works published only posthumously. In the case of Norris Locke made explicit the intellectual authoritarianism I claim he saw in Cartesianism. Writing to Collins he said, "Men of Mr. Norris's way seem to me to decree, rather than argue. They, against all evidence of sense and reason, decree brutes to be machines, only because their hypothesis requires it; and then with a like authority, suppose, as you rightly observe, what they should prove: *viz*. that whatsoever thinks, is immaterial."[108] But this was only the occasion.[109] If my thesis is correct, Locke took the occasion to make explicit what in fact is the central theme of the *Essay*.

[104] I am grateful to R. Jacobson for encouraging me to clarify my views on this aspect of Locke's relation to the Cartesians.

[105] *British Philosophy*, For details and bibliographical information, see McCracken, pp. 156–79: "of the Malebranchean breed . . . [the] purest British specimen" (p. 179). Norris, who came under more direct influence sometime in the mid-1680s, claimed to have lighted upon the vision of all things in God before consulting Malebranche. While not entirely without foundation, Norris's claims to originality are somewhat exaggerated. Previously he had published works of a Platonic character that offered something like the vision in God as the *goal* of human knowledge. When with *The Theory and Regulation of Love* (1688) and especially *Reason and Religion* (1689) Norris directly defended Malebranche, the vision in God was construed as a *condition* of all human knowledge. McCracken, p. 158.

[106] March 16, 1697; *Correspondance*, 6:41.

[107] For further details of this controversy, see Johnston, "Examination"; Acworth, "First Reply"; *Philosophy of John Norris*, chap. 10.

[108] *Works* 10:283.

[109] "Locke felt that Malebranche's theory was 'an opinion that spreads not and is like to die of itself or at least to do no great harm' [letter from Locke to Peter King, October 25, 1704]. It was because he felt this that he did not publish the *Examination*. Locke would not have written against a

Whatever his point of view, Locke's interest in Descartes would have been expected and in fact is clear. And his interest in Malebranche was anything but *recherché*. For many in England read Malebranche and he had many admirers. They "ranged from a deposed English king who made France his home to defrocked French priests who made England theirs, from London booksellers to Oxford dons, from ladies who wrote essays on divinity to soldiers who had a penchant for metaphysics."[110] Addison, who was one of the many celebrities to visit Malebranche in Paris, thought that he had even more admirers in England than in France, and as late as 1711 thought the *Search* along with Locke's *Essay* and Newton's *Works* the "three modern philosophical works that an English person who aspired to appear learned would keep on his shelf."[111] Nor would Locke's interest in Malebranche have awaited the Taylor translation of the *Search* in 1690, since he purchased that work and others soon after their publication.[112]

We can document Locke's concern with enthusiasm, which predated his correspondence with Molyneux by well over ten years. His journal entry for February 19, 1682 is an extensive and well-developed note on the topic. In it he takes a clear deist stance: "A strong and firm perswasion of any proposition relating to religion for which a man hath either noe or not sufficient proofs from reason but receives them as truths wrought in the minde extraordinarily by god him self and influences comeing immediately from him seemes to me to be Enthusiasme, which can be noe evidence or ground of assurance at all nor can by any meanes be taken for knowledge."[113] This effectively denies all epistemic legitimacy to the order of grace; all that is not based on reason must be rejected as the product of enthusiasm. However clear alleged illuminations may be, he argues, they can be nothing but mere imaginations unless there are proofs and evidence for them, for they should be "parts of reason and have the same foundation with other persuasions in a mans minde and whereof his reason judges."[114] Alleged illuminations are further to be suspected because of how

---

'very groundless opinion' had it not been taken up by Norris and made the basis for a criticism of Locke's own opinion" (Ware, "Influence," p. 557).

[110] McCracken, *British Philosophy*, p. 156. See also his introduction, esp. pp. 2–10.

[111] Ibid., pp. ii, 2.

[112] Locke possessed Malebranche's *De la recherche de la verité* (first edition of 1674–75 and three copies of the fourth of 1678); his *Traité de la nature et de la grace* (1684); his *Défense . . . Contre Mr. de la Ville*; and among polemical works, Desgabets's *Critique de la Critique de la recherche de la verité* (1675), Foucher's *Critique de la verité* (1675) and *Réponse pour la critique* (1675), and Arnauld's *Des vrayes et des fausses idées* (1683). See Harrison and Laslett, *Library*, pp. 75, 182–83. Locke's interest in Malebranche's works, especially the polemical works against Arnauld, has been documented by Shankula.

[113] Aaron and Gibb, *Early Draft*, p. 119. Locke's marginal note says that what otherwise passes for madness is given room in religion, "though indeed it be a more dangerous madnesse, but men are apt to thinke that in religion they may and ought to quit their reason" (ibid., p. 121).

[114] Ibid., p. 119. He further argues that we cannot be assured of what is true in a way that others

they can be induced; fasting, solitude, long meditation, drugs, whirling, all weaken reason and stimulate the imagination. Locke concludes his entry with a remarkable conjecture that enthusiasm is to be found only among those people who, unlike Americans, base their religion on supposed revelation, and who thus suppose that having the benefit of a general revelation they can have that of a particular revelation as well.

This is heady stuff that is at most only hintingly premised in Locke's published work. And, however clear the deist critique of enthusiasm, it here relates only to religion and makes no mention of the Cartesians. To appreciate the significance of this, or the lack of it, we need to look at the context for Locke's journal entry. It may well have been a draft of at least part of a letter Locke later sent to Damaris Cudworth, perhaps on April 6, 1682.[115] Locke was reading John Smith's *Select Discourses*,[116] and she was very interested in his reaction to it.[117] She already knew something of Locke's position, for she knew "not what you may call Vision nor how much you may attribute to the power of Reason"; indeed, it looked to her as if Paul might according to Locke be an enthusiast.[118] Locke responded on or sometime after February 24, 1682 that opinions concerning God and religion not based on reason deserve the name enthusiasm.[119] Damaris Cudworth continued to press the issue on February 27, April 1, and April 20, ending with a citation of Glanvill to the effect that "the Divine Spirit does afford its Sensible Presence and Immediate Beatifick touch to some Persons so and soe Qualify'd,"[120] but Locke seems not to have continued the discussion.

---

are assured of what is false. He gives two examples, in addition to "the most spiritualized Christians," of the false assurance of enthusiasm. One is the Turkish dervishes "who pretent to speak with God and see His face"; Locke's reference is to Paul Ricaut's *L'état presente de l'empire ottoman*. The other example is "the Jangis amongst the Hindous who talk of being illuminated and entirely united to god"; Locke's reference here is to Bernier's *Mémoires*.

[115] *Correspondence*, 2:500–501.

[116] 1660, 2d ed., 1673. Harrison and Laslett, *Library*, item no. 2701.

[117] To Locke, February 16, 1682.

[118] *Correspondence*, 2:484–85.

[119] The draft of the letter appears as a journal entry under this date. The entry is of interest for the additional reason that in it Locke uses Burthogge's analogy of the eye assisted by a glass to make the same point he did, that reason however assisted is still reason: "I thinke of reason as I doe of the sight an ordinary eye by constant imployment about any object may grow very acute in it. The assistance of glasses may make it see things both better and at a greater distance but yet whatever is discerned by the eye however assisted is perceived by and comes under the naturall faculty of seeing, and soe what ever is known however sublime or spirituall is known only by the naturall faculty of the understanding reason, however assisted" (Aaron and Gibb, *Early Draft*, pp. 124–25). The analogy of reason and the eye is not original. It is to be found in Boyle, who, however, proposes as aids to the eye a ruler plumb line or compass, not a glass (*Advice in judging of things said to transcend reason*; *Works*, 4:460). For more on this aspect of Locke's connection with Boyle, see Rogers, "Boyle, Lock and Reason," pp. 213–14.

[120] *Correspondence*, 2:504.

It seems to me that Locke throughout this material may well have been applying to the specifically religious theories of Smith's work a position he had already taken. In the year previous to the exchange with Damaris Cudworth concerning Smith's work, Locke's journal contains an entry which, while it does not use the word, is nonetheless concerned with enthusiasm. Once again the context is religion, but the concern expressed is more general than it was a year later: "inspiration . . . is an opinion in or perswasion of the minde whereof a man knows not the rise nor reason, but is received there as a truth comeing from an unknown and therefore supernatural course, and not founded upon these principles nor observations nor the way of reasoning which makes the understanding admit other things for truths."[121] From this as a general defini-tion of enthusiasm to its application to Cartesianism is a deflection of but a few degrees. Locke's principal criticism of Malebranche's vision of all things in God is that it fails to explain; it is an appeal to an unknown and supernatural cause.

Locke and Molyneux were not the only authors to regard Malebranche and the Cartesians as enthusiasts. Not only was this perception more general, but it was shared by authors with very different moral and intellectual interests. Skepticism, antiskepticism and antifideism, Aristotelianism, empiricism, ide-alism, and Neo-Platonism, not to mention mental health, were only some of the currents stirred by the perception of Cartesian enthusiasm.

Best-known is Berkeley's reference to Malebranche in these terms. On Octo-ber 30, 1710 Percival wrote to Berkeley that Clarke and Whiston thought him a disciple of Malebranche or Norris.[122] In the second *Dialogue*, therefore, Berkeley was at pains to distinguish his own from the view that we perceive all things in God. Before cataloguing the differences between them, Berkeley first points to the superficial, confused, ill-considered views of those who fail to distinguish his view from "the enthusiasm of Malebranche."[123] Despite his denigration of those who made it, the connection is not as implausible as Berkeley makes out given that for him only God is the cause of our perceptions of things, that the things we perceive form the language in which God speaks to us, that he no less than Malebranche strives to show it is God in whom we live and move and have our being. Nor does Berkeley dismiss all of Malebranche's work as mere enthusiasm; he owed too much to him and to Cartesianism for that.[124] But that we should be in God to the extent that in seeing anything we see God was knowledge too directly inspired to be anything but enthusiasm.

It is not unlikely that Berkeley learned to associate Cartesianism and enthusi-asm from Swift. Swift takes up the topic of madness in *A Tale of a Tub* (a work

---

[121] April 3, 1681; Aaron and Gibb, *Early Draft*, p. 114.

[122] *Works*, 9:11–12.

[123] *Works*, 2:214.

[124] Luce, *Berkeley*; Bracken, "Berkeley."

that generally instantiates the concept treated at this point) and takes it to be the source of enthusiasm, without which the world would be deprived of "those two great Blessings, *Conquests* and *Systems*" (p. 169). A very slight difference in their brains is the sole explanation of the different effects of the vapor of madness in Alexander the Great, Jack of Leyden,[125] and Monsieur Descartes. Elsewhere, Swift points to Descartes, but also to Epicurus, Diogenes, Appollonius, Lucretius, and Paracelsus, "who, if they were now in the World, tied fast, and separate from their Followers, would in this our undistinguishing Age, incur manifest Danger of *Phlebotomy*, and *Whips*, and *Chains*, and *dark chambers*, and *Straw*" (p. 166). Even so, the connection among political, religious, and philosophical enthusiasm, with the explicit reference to Descartes, is notable.[126]

Nearly all of Swift's treatment of Descartes was anticipated by a half-century in the work of the Anglican apologist Meric Casaubon, who was the earliest author to have described Descartes in terms of religious enthusiasm. In *A Treatise concerning Enthusiasm* (1655) Casaubon went so far as to associate Descartes with Teresa of Avila among other mystics and religious fanatics.[127] In a text from 1667 that has just been published under the title *On Learning*, Casaubon endorses Gassendi's critique of Descartes in the *Disquisitio metaphysica*, a book that "is to be had everywhere." Although he feels Gassendi to have been misled in his project of rehabilitating Epicurus, Casaubon nonetheless regards him as "the most accomplished Generall schollar we have had of late"; Gassendi "doth lay [Descartes] open, very sufficiently: more need not be said by any man to shew the vanitie, futilitie, nugacitie, of the confident, if not brainsick (in the *Preface* [of the *Meditations*] at lest) undertaker [who goes on] to proclaime himself the Oracle of the world" (pp. 204–5). The procedure of the *Meditations* is that of the "Jesuited Puritans," who first ruin the senses and natural reason of their victims, who then under their total control are raised to heights of credulity as "pure Quacks, or arrand Quakers." "Soe Descartes, after he hath obliged his disciples to forgett and forgoe all former praecognitions and progresses of eyther senses or sciences, then he thinks he hath them sure: they must adhaere to him tooth and nayle. . . . [Given all this and more besides,] would not any sober man, as Gassendus doth well observe, suspect such doctrine, that doth need so much *mountebankisme* to sett it out?" (pp. 205–6).

---

[125] "Johann Bockholdt, a tailor of Leyden, the leader in the final struggle of Anabaptist communism. In Munster, of which the Anabaptists gained complete possession, he was crowned king of the 'New Jerusalem', under the title of John of Leyden. The town was retaken on June 24, 1535, and in January 1536 'Jack of Leyden' was executed" (Editor's note, Swift, *Tale*, p. 170).

[126] Locke's great importance for English literature lasted at least into the nineteenth century. I'm grateful to Christopher Fox for pointing out the significance of Swift. For Kant's psycho-philosophical diagnosis of philosophical enthusiasm, see Butts, *Kant*, esp. pp. 1–15.

[127] Spiller, *Royal Society*, esp. pp. 66–75; I am grateful to Graham Solomon for drawing this material to my attention.

A more expected source for the connection between religious and philosophical enthusiasm is to be found in the Aristotelian John Sergeant. His view was that the Cartesian rejection of the senses as a source of knowledge in favor of the light of Reason amounted to a claim to private revelation. In the preface to *The Method to Science* (1696) he argued as follows: "*Having thus got rid of the Senses giving us notice of outward things, by imprinting Notions in them, which Experience teaches is the* Ordinary *Way of knowing anything; it follows of course, that they must recurr to* Extraordinary *ways by* Inward *means, or to* Inward *Light; which is the Method of Fanaticks in Religion, when they have rejected the Ordinary ways of believing their Proper Teachers.*" Malebranche in particular is singled out for his enthusiasm; after spending several pages criticizing the vision of all things in God, Sergeant concludes with the exclamation, "*Was ever such* Quakerism *heard of among philosophers! Or, plain honest Human Reason so subtiliz'd and exhal'd into Mystick Theology, by Spiritual Alchemy!*"

Two years later Sergeant published his *Non ultra: or, a letter to a learned Cartesian; settling the rule of truth, and first principles, upon their deepest grounds.* Here we learn that while Descartes was not an enthusiast habitually, all his life and in all he did, he was to the extent of "denying his Senses, and devesting himself of all his former knowledges [such that] *he fell, for some few Days,* into a *spice of Enthusiasm*; nay, was *brim-full* of it; and fancy'd he had *Visions and Revelations*; so that he seemed Crack-brained, or to have *drunk a Cup too much*; which are the very Words a *Cartesian*, who wrote his Life, has given us" (pp. 108–9).[128] Malebranche, on the other hand, who makes "all *Humane Science* come by *Divine Revelation*," is a less confined enthusiastiast. The "*Method*, advanced by Malebranche, I saw evidently, brought a kind of *Fanaticism* into Philosophy. For, I believe, no Man doubts, but that the Genius of *Fanaticks* is, to over-leap all *humane Means*, and to pretend that their Light of Knowledge comes to them immediately from God" (p. 110).

A reminder that the battle between the gods and giants was not the only struggle in this period is that Locke in effect tarred Sergeant with the same brush with which he and others were tarring the Cartesians. Sergeant constantly insisted that solid philosophy, as he called it, must arrive at the essences of things. Of one such instance Locke said in his marginal notes to Sergeant's text, "J.S. speaks everywhere as if *Truth* and *Science* had personally appeared to him and by word of mouth actually commissioned him to be their sole defender and propagator"; at another point he calls Sergeant a dictator on philosophy (arguing as he does only by way of repetition).[129] It seems to me that to some extent Aristotelianism represented for Locke the same authoritarianism that Carte-

---

[128] The reference is to Baillet's *Vie*.
[129] Yolton, "Replies," p. 542.

sianism did. He does not call Sergeant an enthusiast, but he might have perceived the grounds for doing so.

Thomas Baker[130] tried to demonstrate the true limits of human knowledge by showing its insufficiency, but without totally discrediting it. His motivation was the service of religion, as he saw it, for when the extravagant claims of reason are dashed, men look where they should not for some other infallible guide, which Baker clearly thinks to be the Church. Thus he was concerned to undo the very strategy of fideism we have seen Erasmus to have employed in the cause of traditional authority. If the claims of reason cannot be sustained, then the only recourse especially in unavoidable practical matters was the traditional way of doing things, which in the circumstance was the way of Rome. In the preface to his *Reflections* Baker thought that if the Papists had consciously set out with this design, they could not have succeeded better. In fact the strategy in many cases was quite conscious.

Whether consciously intending to do so or not, the Cartesians stand accused by Baker of just this exaggeration, which he explains as the result of enthusiasm. The extravagance of the Cartesian Poiret, a "Phanatik in Philosophy" (p. 105), can be attributed only to enthusiasm. Malebranche's vision of all things in God comes in for similar treatment as does the work of Norris, who, according to Baker, having been forced to disengage himself from the Quakers did so only by saying that their views needed merely to be understood properly (p. 107). "These Men of Thought have too low a value of Learning, either as it lies in our common Books or in the Book of Nature, in respect of that light which displays it self from the *Ideal* World, by attending to which, with pure and Defaecate Minds, they suppose knowledge to be most easily had" (pp. 107–8). The Cartesians cheapen knowledge, according to Baker, experience and reasoning become dispensable, and prayer is inappropriately made a condition of knowledge. Baker's characterization of Cartesianism as a form of enthusiasm is notable for its lack of deep philosophical basis. His attitude is one of common sense as far as it goes and skepticism thereafter; he certainly is not among the moderns of interest here since he treats Malebranche's vision in God as the last, disastrous stage of the new way of ideas (p. 5).

Peter Browne, who was born soon after the Restoration and died in 1735, viewed Cartesianism from the perspective of an antideist. This bishop of Cork and Ross, provost of Trinity College (Dublin), had written against Toland as early as 1697, rejecting the new way of ideas at least to the extent that in his view we can go beyond ideas (to which he thought Toland and Locke would restrict us) by means of analogy; in this sense we can go "above reason."[131] In 1728 Browne produced a work that might be described as a philosophical

---

[130] Baker (1656–1740), who as a nonjuror saw his personal fortune suffer, nonetheless had a successful career as a Cambridge scholar, antiquarian, and man of letters. His *Reflections upon learning* enjoyed great popularity and went through many editions.

[131] Yolton, *Way of Ideas*, pp. 122–24.

prolegomenon to Bible criticism. In it he tried to find a proper role for analogy between the two extremes he saw of turning the whole of the Gospel into "mere figure and metaphor" and so literally interpreting it that it becomes absurd and contradictory. Despite Browne's sniping at Locke, his work is essentially empiricist, for he thought all analogy must be based entirely on sensory knowledge. Though he is not explicitly named, Malebranche may well be the object of the complaint against those who dispense with empirically grounded analogy. Those who try "to abstract the Intellect from all Objects of Sense, so as to take a *Direct View* of spiritual things; and work up their Minds to an opinion and belief that they have some degree of *Intuitive Direct* knowledge of them tho' Imperfect and obscure hath proved a fatal Delusion [that] . . . too often ends up in rank Enthusiasm" (pp. 95–96).[132]

Richard Burthogge (1638?–94?; physician and noted advocate of toleration) was a likely source for Browne's doctrine of analogy.[133] He viewed Malebranche as an enthusiast from a fifth perspective different from Locke's and Molyneux's. Very roughly, Burthogge is one of the *novantiques*, and certainly far from the least interesting (or least original) among them. Beyond this rough characterization, it is difficult to find him a niche in this period. Because of this, and because his views have a relevance to our story beyond what he says about enthusiasm, the context for what he says merits some development. In particular, Burthogge is noteworthy for his doctrine of analogical knowledge, which is important both in connection with what Locke will be seen later to say about the same topic and as a premise in the condemnation of enthusiasm.

In 1678 Burthogge published a work with the significant title, *Organum Vetus & Novum: Or, A discourse of reason and truth wherein the natural logic common to mankinde is briefly and plainly described*. First to be noted is its marked difference in spirit from Browne's work, for it shows a clear tendency, at least, toward deism: (1) There is never a conflict between faith and reason; what is contrary to reason cannot even be made sense of, much less believed (pp. 26–27); (2) what can be accepted only on faith (versus what can be accepted only by reason or by either) "may be said to be seen by *Reason above Reason*, by Reason assisted with the light of Revelation, above Reason not so assisted, but onely by the Aids of Nature; but still it is Reason sees in both"—as it is still the eye that sees in sunlight or with a telescope what it cannot see in moonlight or without a telescope. Burthogge's view rather reverses the Augustinian view of philosophy as the handmaiden to theology; here it is not *fides quaerens intellectum*, but, as it were, *ratio quaerens intellectum fide*: "Men are reasonable Creatures, and therefore their Religion must be reasonable: Every Tree must bring forth Fruit of its Kinde. Faith it self is a rational Act" (p. 70).

---

[132] Browne's dispute over analogy became three-cornered when Berkeley argued that in Browne's hands it led to atheism.

[133] This is not to ignore the differences between them or to exclude the influence on Browne of William King.

Another important feature of Burthogge's work is its clear rejection of innate ideas, which he thinks would render experience and observation useless, the futility of which had been demonstrated by the Scholastics: "The Soul in its state of Union and Conjunction with the Body, is so dependent on it in all its Operations, that it exercises none without the Aids of it. Ratiocination itself is an Animal act; not an abstract Action of the Soul, but a (Concrete) act of the Animal; it is the Man that reasons" (pp. 56–57). Burthogge here distances himself not only from the Cartesians, but also from the Cambridge Platonists with whom he might otherwise have been allied.

Burthogge is most important for his doctrine of analogical knowledge, or as he later called it, notional knowledge: We never know a thing in itself, only its appearance, which he calls a sense or meaning. "To understand this, we are to consider that to us men, *things* are nothing but as they stand in our *Analogie*; that is, are nothing to us but as they are known by us; and they are not known by us but as they are in the Sense, Imagination or Minde; in a word, as they are in our Faculties" (pp. 12–13). With this relativism the primary-secondary quality distinction collapses, and all the distinctions we make, all the attributes we apply, relate only to the appearances of things. "Faculties and Powers, Good, Evil, Virtue, Vice, Verity, Falsity, Relations, Order, Similitude, Whole, Part, Cause, Effect, etc. are Notions; as Whiteness, Blackness, Bitterness, Sweetness, etc. are Sentiments: and the former own no other kind of Existence than the latter, namely, an *Objective* (one)." For Burthogge, the things we know do not have two kinds of existence, formal (outside the mind) and objective (inside it), as they do for, say, the Aristotelian Sergeant. We are mistaken when we think, as we generally do, that our notions "have an Existence of their own without the Minde, and though there were no Minde to think of them," but in fact, "they are but *Noemata*, Conceptions, and all the formal being any of them have, is only in it" (p. 15). Burthogge in 1694 published a work called *An Essay upon reason and the nature of spirits*, which he dedicated to Locke; in it he specified a narrow sense of notion as a *"Modus Concipiendi, . . .* a manner of conceiving things that corresponds not to them but only as they are *Objects*, not as they are *Things*" (p. 56). Substance, accident, even *thing* are but ways in which we conceive (pp. 62–65). "The immediate Objects of cogitation, as it is exercised by men, are *entia cogitationis*, all Phaenomena; Appearances that do no more exist without our faculties in the things themselves, than the Images that are seen in water, or behind a glass,[134] do really exist in these places they seem to be" (p. 60). Burthogge failed to move either to idealism by rejecting the thing itself or even to skepticism by concluding that it is unknown and hence that we have no knowledge at all. Instead, he argued that certain appearances, at least, have a ground in the dispositions and textures of the particles of things. How these dispositions and textures might be known other than notionally like

---

[134] These are, as it were, favorite images of Burthogge.

anything else, he left unclear. On the one hand, for example, he wants to be a mechanist: "*Matter* and *Motion* are Real things, and . . . all others that are Corporeal, do result from these." But on the other hand, he earlier explained that "such [cogitatible beings] . . . are called *Real* . . . not that in their own nature they are Realities themselves, but that the things relate to our Faculties; that is, not in the things as they are *Things*, but as they are *Objects*." [135] The tension begs to be resolved into either outright idealism, or a view of things as perfectly bare. The tendency is toward the latter. [136] A further complication is that nothing seems to be merely corporeal, for there is a vital energy throughout the universe. His *Essay* is very concerned with disembodied souls, spirits, witchcraft, and apparitions; like the earlier work its title is of significance. In addition, its professed aim is to "unite and reconcile the experimental or mechanical with the scholastic methods." With such a cacophony of themes, it is not surprising that despite its anticipations of Locke, Berkeley, and even Kant, Burthogge's work fell largely on deaf ears. [137]

The occasion for the *Organum Vetus & Novum*, and thus for the notional theory of knowledge there and as developed in the *Essay*, was a defense of his still earlier work *Causa Dei: or an apology for God* (1675). Objections to this work Burthogge attributed primarily to blind zeal. Zeal with knowledge and wisdom he saw as fire from the altar; without these it is wildfire, "which hath nothing more pernicious than it self to Church or State" (pp. 44–45). He thought there were both theological enthusiasts (H. Nicolls, Father of the Familists) and philosophical enthusiasts (van Helmont and Paracelsus) and enthusiasts of both kinds (Fludd and Bohm). The *Essay upon reason* later defined enthusiasm as "a false conceit of being inspired: [where] to be inspired is to receive immediate notions and instincts from the spirit of God" (p. 40). But as *all* knowledge is only analogical or notional, so is our knowledge of God, which is the sense of Paul's words that we see now as through a glass darkly. Indeed, in the case of our knowledge of God, it could not be otherwise since our eyes are too weak for His pure light. The whole point of Burthogge's epistemology, and the explanation perhaps of why it was unclarified with respect to important philosophical issues, is an argument, or an illustration, that we do not have the Beatific Vision any more than we have intellectual intuition of things apart from their appearances. Now the view that in these terms allows us

---

[135] *Organum*, pp. 16–17. Definitions are said to relate to things, but they are descriptions according to attributes, which in Burthogge's usage are merely ascribed or attributed by the mind. The upshot: "Essential definitions are non-sense. Things are not Explicable, but as they are to us in our Faculties" (p. 36).

[136] See Burthogge, *Essay*, p. 108: Thinking and extension are accidents of substances that are not known in themselves.

[137] For more on the interpretation of Burthogge, see the references cited by Yolton, *John Locke*, p. 20, n. 1. It was Ueberweg who, as far as I know, first pointed out the anticipation of Kant. For the reception of Burthogge's work, see ibid., Yolton, pp. 20–21.

knowledge, not only of the essences of things, but at the same time direct knowledge of God is of course Malebranche's vision of all things in God. Burthogge's attack thus focuses specifically on it and he calls it "mere Enthusiasm" (p. 115). It is mere enthusiasm, presumably, only in the sense that it is *made up entirely* of enthusiasm, not in the sense that it *insignificantly* is, for Burthogge early on pointed to enthusiasm as the ultimate moral and political danger.

The upshot of our excursion among these few British authors is that the perception of Cartesianism, and of Malebranche's version of it in particular, as a form of enthusiasm, was hardly unique to Locke and his friend Molyneux. In one sense this undeniably strengthens my thesis that Locke opposed Cartesianism and that he was opposing what he regarded as enthusiasm and its dangers. For with its wider currency this very reading of Cartesianism thus becomes inherently more plausible and thus more plausible as a reading of Locke's concerns, especially since the same moral and political dangers were perceived in it. On the other hand, the significance of the thesis is diminished by the same wide currency, for Locke's philosophy is no longer uniquely individuated by this opposition to Cartesianism. (It would be as if Locke were to be characterized solely as a mechanist opponent of Aristotelian Scholasticism, a characterization that is true enough but fails to include what on any account is most interesting about Locke, namely, how he differs from other such opponents of Aristotle.) The obvious solution lies between the horns of the dilemma of evidence and interest by showing that Locke epitomized this opposition to Cartesianism and that this is what makes the *Essay* the *Essay*. Before defending this case, however, we must first examine how it was that the Cartesians could have been read in the terms we have seen so far. In particular, we must determine how the systems of Descartes and especially Malebranche could have provided such a perceived contrast with Locke and his tradition. In short, we must first turn to the gods of the seventeenth century.

CHAPTER IV.

The Gods of the Seventeenth Century

§12 DESCARTES'S IDEALISM

The immediate aim of this section is simple, at least to state.[1] I shall try to show that the most important philosopher of the seventeenth century, if not of the entire period between Plato and the present, shared the views Plato ascribed to the gods and that he promulgated them in ways hardly less compelling than did Plato himself. Thus, Descartes will be placed in the venerated tradition according to which the particular as such is unintelligible, that only the universal is a proper object of knowledge, and that the universal is eternal and immutable. Although Descartes is generally regarded as holding important views obviously belonging to this tradition, the significance of the tradition for certain of his other views is in my estimation hardly appreciated at all. Here I wish to argue in light of the tradition that for Descartes (1) the only object of knowledge, or even of thought, is extension; (2) this extension is an unimaginable entity not unlike a Platonic Form; (3) commonsense physical objects, what Descartes calls material or corporeal things, are in part, but at least in part, mind-dependent entities; and, a fortiori, (4) the motion of corporeal things is phenomenal only. The usual view of Descartes would have it that we know all sorts of things, including individual things like minds and bodies, that although space is identical to body it somehow contains body, that physical objects are so many material substances, and that they are capable of real motion.

Even if perfectly realizing my aims, however, the argument will be found defective in at least two respects. The full defense of claims expressed in terms so different from Descartes's verba ipsissima must involve a philosophy of history whose own defense I attempt only in the final chapter below, and then only partially. I will say, however, that I am prepared to defend these claims as historical, as what really happened, "wie es eigentlich gewesen ist" in Ranke's phrase, and not just as counterfactual ruminations about what might have been or what the past might suggest to us.

Second, although my interpretation of Descartes was at least adumbrated in the nineteenth century by Cousin, the interpretation is nonstandard and far from obvious. A full defense of it would, in addition, thus require a systematic elaboration of the claims with respect to the whole of the Cartesian ontology, a great deal of textual examination, a discussion of the relevant secondary litera-

---

[1] See "Note on Documentation."

ture, and consideration of many objections—also a task clearly beyond the present scope. My hope is that, despite these lacunae, enough of an outline can be given, and that the picture thus outlined will itself be of sufficient interest, to make looking at just the sketch of it worthwhile. For in any case, our ultimate interest in the ideas sketched is in how they were instantiated, not in Descartes, but subsequently in Malebranche, who was the gods' chief spokesman in the latter half of the century. The interpretation of Descartes will be found the more plausible as it serves to elucidate the later views of Malebranche (and of other Cartesians) and their contrast with those of the Gassendists (and especially Locke).

Cartesian idealism is perhaps best introduced with the wax example from *Meditations* 2, as illustrative and well-known a Cartesian text as any with regard to the theses I shall argue here. The entrée to the example is the apparent anomaly that corporeal things, which at the point reached by *Meditations* 2 are considered to be doubtful, unknown, and foreign to the self, are comprehended more distinctly than what is true, known, and attached to the self. This anomaly is attributed to the mind's propensity to wander beyond the confines of truth, a propensity Descartes here indulges with the wax example in order better to control the mind later on. A careful reading reveals that the only nonrhetorical question Descartes raises in his repeated inquiries about the wax concerns what there is in the wax that is distinctly comprehended. Clearly it is none of its sensory qualities, since all of these change, including Lockean primary qualities such as shape. It might, however, be a body that appears in these modes of sensory qualities, a body that as apprehended by the imagination is a flexible, mutable, extended thing (*extensum quid, flexibile, mutabile*). Of this thing he asks what can only be the same question: What is it, that is, what is it that is distinctly comprehended? Whatever it is, it is not something imaginable because while the thing is comprehended as being infinitely flexible or mutable with respect to shape and volume, it can be imagined as having only a finite number of shapes and a finite number of volumes. We can fill in Descartes's argument by saying that to imagine is literally to picture; what is known on the basis of imagination must be in the picture; and no picture will contain an infinite number of shapes or volumes. The result is that whatever is distinctly comprehended is comprehended by the mind alone (*mentis inspectio*), a conclusion sufficient for Descartes to dispel the anomaly that corporeal things seem better known than the mind, for even if it is in error about the wax, the mind must exist in order to perceive it.

Notice that Descartes arrives at this result without directly answering the question as to what he distinctly comprehends in the wax. Yet he does say enough at least to adumbrate the answer to this and related questions. He says, for example, that no one would deny that the same piece of wax (*eadem cera*) remains after all its sensory qualities have changed. What remains of the wax cannot be anything else but its essence or principal attribute, since given a change in its extension, in its shape or volume, both of which have changed in this instance, the piece of wax according to an argument I shall detail below would *not* be the same. Meanwhile I wish to emphasize that the extension discussed by *Meditations* 2 is not the principal attribute of body discussed by *Principles* 1, 53. The former, as Descartes's discussion makes clear, is the specific volume of the wax and is on four squares with its shape (or color) as something that is imaginable and liable to change. The latter is immutable and unimaginable in as much as the verities of geometry are eternal and known only by the mind. Of this, more below.

On the face of it by way of proof of the immortality of the soul, Descartes in the Synopsis of the *Meditations* argues that all substances are incorruptible, that what needs nothing other than God in order to exist (*Principles* 1, 51) begins to exist only through creation and ceases to exist only through annihilation, that is, failure of concourse, which from *Meditations* 3 we know is the failure to be conserved or re-created from one moment to the next. Body taken generally is such a substance; so is each human mind. But the human body (and presumably, therefore, each corporeal thing) is not. A mind may have its accidents change— it may now be thinking this, then imagining or willing that—and withal remain the same mind. But "from the mere fact that the shape of certain of its parts should change," an individual corporeal thing is no longer the same thing.[2] Descartes concludes that while the human body may perish, the soul is by nature immortal. Descartes here says that if the shape of *certain* of its parts should change the body is no longer the same thing.[3] What Descartes perhaps has in mind is the kind of change that would make the body incapable of serving as the matter for the hylomorphic unity that is the man. Consider the difference between removing a heart and removing an appendix. Elsewhere he indicates the difference he sees between the human body in this regard and every other body.

> First I consider what the body of a man is, and I find that this word 'body' is very ambiguous, for when we speak of a body in general, we mean a determinate part of matter and the whole of the quantity of which the universe is composed, so that if the least bit of that matter were removed we would judge at once that the body was smaller and no longer whole; and if any particle of that matter were changed we would at once think that the body was no longer totally the same, or numerically the same. But, when we speak of the body of a man, we do not mean a determinate part of matter which has a determinate size, but we mean only all of the matter which is together united with the soul of this man, so that, even though this matter changes and its quantity increases or decreases, we still believe that it is the same body, numerically the same, while it remains joined and substantially united to the

---

[2] CSM 2:20; AT, 7:30.

[3] I am grateful to Paul Hoffman for his article and his correspondence drawing to my attention the fact and the significance of the mistranslation by HR, and I think by CMS, at this point.

same soul; and we believe that this body is entirely whole while it has in itself all the dispositions required to conserve that union. For there is no one who does not believe that we have the same bodies which we have had since our infancy, although their quantity has much increased, and even though according to the common opinion of doctors, and without doubt according to the truth, there is no longer in them any part of the matter which was in them before, and even though they no longer have the same shape; so that they are only numerically the same because they are informed by the same soul.[4]

The distinction Descartes draws is suggestive of Locke's later distinction between the identity of particles and masses of particles (identity in the philosophical sense according to Bishop Butler) and the identity consisting in the organic unity of plants and of animals (identity in a loose and popular sense according to Butler).[5] The idea seems to be that *any* change results in loss of identity in the first sense. I believe that the sense of identity that best applies to substance as defined by Descartes is the identity of a particle. The identity of a piece of wax, which is a nonorganic unity, is like that of a mass of particles, and therefore would ipso facto result in a different thing.

In any case, what is most of present interest is the basis for Descartes's inference in the Synopsis, namely, the view that individual corporeal bodies stand to extension or body taken generally as do thoughts or volitions to the mind—as accidents to substance. One would have thought that the difference between one accident, or set of accidents, and another, between the wax taken fresh from the hive and the wax when heated, must thus be a numerical difference. But usually we take a numerical difference to be the difference between two individuals—what Descartes calls a real difference, for which his criterion is independence or conceivability apart. How then do different *qualities* differ, such as the blackness and roundness of my pupil? They do not differ qualitatively, for it is individuals not having both of them that are said to differ qualitatively. On the other hand we cannot say that they differ numerically, at least not for Descartes, according to whom there is only a *modal* difference both between a substance and one of its modes or between two of its modes.[6] Really the substance and its two modes are all the *same* thing. And, since the substance does not change, there is no real change, numerical or qualitative, in the wax. Only our way of conceiving it changes. Thus, change is confined to the Par-

---

[4] To Mesland, February 9, 1645; AT, 4:166; Descartes, *Philosophical Letters*, trans. A. Kenny, p. 156. This letter was drawn to my attention by Hoffman's article, which argues that in addition to the (strong) sense of substance of interest to me here, Descartes employs a weaker sense of substance as whatever can exist apart from a subject, a sense that does significant philosophical work for him. I owe my views in the next paragraph to this article, although its author may not entirely agree with them.

[5] *Essay* 2.27.3–6; 328–30.

[6] *Principles* 1, 60–61.

menidean Way of Appearance.[7] When there is said to be a change in the color, shape, or volume of the wax, this is a function of our conception of real extension.

The fresh and heated pieces of wax are also said to be the same insofar as they are essentially the same, which here means they are accidents of the same substance. The *same* extension is the essence of both the fresh wax and the heated wax, and both are essentially extended things because they are accidents, or as Descartes usually puts it, modes, of extension or body taken generally. And this object, which is what is distinctly comprehended in the wax, is numerically identical to what is distinctly comprehended in *any* corporeal thing.[8]

It might be noted in passing that this identity of object suggests variability in degree of distinctness in the comprehension of it, with comprehension in the ultimate degree of any corporeal thing amounting to comprehension of *every* corporeal thing. The suggestion is roughly the following. Consider the comprehension of a sugar cube. To the extent that it is known only as white or sweet, the knowledge of it can at best be clear. But if its volume is known to be a certain function of one of its faces, then the knowledge is distinct. This knowledge, expressible as a theorem of solid geometry, is knowledge of the essence of the cube, namely, extension. In a sense it is knowledge of only part of extension, but this sense is *not* that in knowing the cube one somehow gains access to an intelligible particular cube, which with other such particulars (intelligible spheres, etc.) makes up extension. This is because the same extension is known in knowing both spheres and cubes. The relation is better stated by saying that the knowledge of extension expressed by this theorem is indistinct because it is less than the whole of geometry. Distinct knowledge in this sense would be knowledge of all that is true in geometry. Thus, if I knew perfectly the essence of the sugar cube, I would know all there is to know about corporeal things.

Descartes speaks of the sameness or identity of the wax in another sense that prima facie resists the interpretation of the example advanced here, for he tells us that the piece of wax that I comprehend is the same piece of wax that I see, touch, and imagine, that I sense and comprehend the same thing.[9] The resistance is only apparent, however, because for Descartes what I sense is not a

---

[7] At least as far as the substance of the wax is concerned. Strictly speaking, a change in our way of conceiving it is a real change—in us.

[8] That there is but one Cartesian material substance is an interpretation not entirely unknown in the literature. I once argued against it (see "Inherence Pattern"), but see, for example, Keeling, *Descartes*, pp. 129–30: "The whole world tri-dimensionally extended is *one* substance"; for a similar view, see Bracken, "Problems of Substance"; several French commentators, most notably D. Hamelin, have argued the interpretation and its connection to Spinozism (V. Delbos, F. Pillon); for more on them and for an interpretation to which we shall return below, see Rodis-Lewis, *L'individualité*.

[9] *Meditations* 2, CSM, 2:21; AT, 7:31.

sensation à la Berkeley, but as he has just told us, an object such as a piece of wax. Provocatively stated, the view is that I do not see colors at all; instead I see extension colored, or perhaps more accurately, I see extension colorly.[10] The piece of wax is what we shall see Malebranche later to have regarded as the representation of a piece of wax—intelligible extension instantiated by sensory qualities, or alternatively, sensory qualities made intelligible or quantified or "essenced" by extension. And sensing and comprehending are different, though simultaneously possible modes in which I can be aware of it; the former is always materially false, for there are no colors independent of the mind, and I have such a mode of awareness only insofar as something is lacking to the perfection of my nature.[11] Were my mind infinitely perfect, I would only comprehend the wax and my knowledge of it would be perfectly distinct, that is, I would know all of geometry. Given the limited nature of the mind, however, my awareness is never without a sensuous component and my knowledge is only more or less distinct "according as I more or less attend to the things of which it is composed" (prout minus vel magis ad illa ex quibus constat attendo).[12] These "things" are the "simpler and more universal things" of *Meditations* 1 that are true even when I am imagining and that could be false only if I were deceived by the demon.

We might now turn to Descartes's textbook account of these matters: his *Principles of Philosophy*. *Principles* 2, 3 reads: "that the perceptions of the senses do not teach us what really exists in things, but merely that whereby they are useful or hurtful to man's composite nature." Once this principle is accepted, "we will easily lay aside all the preconceived opinions acquired from the senses and in this connection make use of the intellect alone, carefully attending to the ideas implanted in it by nature" (*sibi a natura inditas*). Descartes does say that sense perceptions do not inform us of the qualities in objects *unless rarely and by chance*, thus suggesting they at least sometimes do so. Despite this suggestion, whose full explication I believe is a long story,[13] the thrust of the passage is to rule out sense perception as a source of distinct knowledge about body. The role of the senses as he had just pointed out in *Principles* 2, 1, is but to *stimulate* us to perceive clearly and distinctly a matter that is extended in length, breadth, and depth. He continues in *Principles* 2, 4: "If we do this, we shall perceive that the nature of matter, or body considered in

---

[10] This is what Descartes meant in saying that sensory qualities are the different modes in which body appeared to him—corpus quod mihi apparebat . . . modis istis, which HR misleadingly translates as "body which . . . appeared to me as perceptible under those forms" (1:154; AT, 7:30). Even CMS may mislead: "which presented itself to me in these various forms" (2:20).

[11] *Meditations* 3; CMS, 2:44; AT, 7:44.

[12] CMS, 2:21; AT, 7:31.

[13] Telling the story would involve explaining whether we can arrive at the truth, if only rarely and by chance, by judging with a freedom of indifference, that is, without the constraint of clarity and distinctness (*Principles* 1, 43–44).

general, consists not in its being hard, or something which is hard, heavy or coloured, or which affects our senses in any way, but simply in its being something which is extended in length, breadth and depth." His argument is that if bodies were moved in such a way as never to resist us, we would never feel hardness, and yet they would still be bodies. More generally, bodies could be moved such that we had no sensation of them at all, and yet they would not thereby cease to be bodies. But this argument by itself does not yield Descartes's conclusion, for why can a body not have as real qualities hardness or color that are unperceived? A possible answer is that such qualities, though attributable to individual bodies and constitutive of them as individuals, are in fact modes of perception and are not different from the perception of them. This Berkeleian reply, supported by Descartes's use in *Meditations* 6 of the notorious pain model of perception, fails to explain why these sensory qualities can be only modes of perception, why in addition to the formal reality they have as modes of thought, they cannot have objective reality. A better answer is the enthymeme that despite the lack of sensations, we could, at least in principle, still know body as such; we would know matter or body taken generally as extension only. In short, Descartes is assuming the argument within the argument based on the example of the piece of wax.

There has recently been an important account of Cartesian extension that is superficially similar to the one advanced here. According to it, Descartes in the wax example and in *Principles* 2, 4 and 11, is but analyzing the concept of body. His argument is that a body can lose sense qualities, but not extension, without losing what makes it a body; "as Kant remarks in the *Critique of Pure Reason*, 'All bodies are extended' is an analytic truth, whereas, 'all bodies have weight, is at best a synthetic truth. This reasoning suggests that there is nothing inconsistent in the notion of an absolutely insensible body."[14] The shortcoming of this account, it seems to me, is its failure to distinguish between extension or body taken generally and individual bodies; for while the concept of body or body taken generally involves only extension, it does not follow that there could be an *individual body* that is absolutely insensible. So much seems clear from the wax example and from *Principles* 2, 3 and 4; nor is there any contrary indication from the third text cited on behalf of this account, *Principles* 2, 11. Despite its title, "there is no real difference between space and corporeal substance," Descartes's concern in the text is not with the relation between space and body taken generally, but between an individual body and its space, which he calls internal place. Thus the analysis is for the most part, not of the concept of body, but of a stone qua body. In addition, the concept of extension employed may be incomplete, for Descartes here concludes that "After all this we shall see that nothing remains in the idea of the stone except that it is something extended in length, breadth, and depth. Yet this is just what is comprised in the

---

[14] Wilson, *Descartes*, 84.

idea of space, not only of that which is full of bodies, but also of that which is called void."[15] That is, the concept of extension that Descartes is employing at this point has not been sufficiently developed so as to exclude the possibility of the void. Only later, in *Principles* 2, 16, does Descartes argue that there cannot be space in which there is no substance, for in that case there would be extension that was the extension of nothing, and in *Principles* 2, 18 that if God destroyed the contents of a vessel, there would be nothing between its sides and they would touch, while if there were extension between them, there would be *something* between them and not the void. Finally, the crucial premise in the argument of *Principles* 2, 11 is a repetition of the reconstructed version of the wax example: "We may exclude cold, heat and all other such qualities [*aliasque omnes qualitates*] either because they are not considered as in the stone [presumably Descartes is here thinking of pain, for example], or else because with the change of their qualities the stone is not for that reason considered to have lost its nature as body" (Fr."nous ne pensons point . . . que cette pierre change de nature parce qu'elle nous semble tantôt chaude et tantôt froide"). In short, while it is true that change in the sensible qualities of a stone does not alter its nature as body, this is not to say that it could be a stone with no sensible qualities at all.

This important distinction between extension or body taken generally and individual bodies can be elaborated in terms of Descartes's discussion of space in the early part of *Principles* 2. There he distinguishes two senses of place. One is volume, roughly, and we shall return to it in a moment. The other, external place (*locus externus*) or situation (*situs*), is volume defined in relation to other such volumes (14). Motion occurs when these relations change. Since no volume is absolutely fixed, motion is only relative. How these relations are to be understood is problematic. At one point he is prepared to identify situation with the superficies of the surrounding body (15). This notion of a superficies is not an easy one; the superficies is not part of a body in place or of the body contiguous with it. Rather, it is the surface common to both, which may be the same even if the contiguous body should move, as when wind and water pass by a ship. Depending on what we take to be immobile, the body itself may be said to occupy the same place (given that the volume remains unchanged).

The other kind of place is called space (*spatium*) or internal place (*locus internus*) (10–14). It is said to contain body and is defined by the superficial points of the body; it is, in Descartes's language, a definite magnitude or figure. It is really identical to that body—both are constituted by the same extension— and differs from it only by thought: The extension of body, but not of space, is conceived as mobile and flexible. He tells us that the extension of body stands to that of space as particular to species or genus. Space seems to be an abstracted extension "common to stones, wood, water, air and all other bodies, and even to

[15] CMS, 1:227–28.

a vacuum, if there is such a thing, provided only that it is has the same size and shape, and keeps the same situation relative to the external bodies that determine this space." These too are difficult texts, but they are crucial to a proper understanding of the distinction between extension or *the* extended thing (res extensa) and extended *things* (extensa).

These texts are important for many reasons, not least of all because they recall for us Gassendi's distinction between corporeal and incorporeal dimensions and the two directions in which his followers developed his theory of space. Despite their importance, however, the texts have not drawn much attention from commentators. A recent exception is the following account that explains the distinction between the extension of body and the extension of space in this way: "a stone and a piece of wood can have, successively, the same extension in the generic sense, when the second comes to occupy the place (defined in terms of the shape, size and relative position) previously held by the first. On the other hand, insofar as we think of the extension of the stone as particular to it, it can never be 'had' by any other body. The distinction here is . . . exactly the same as the one we draw on when we say the blue of my shirt, which exactly matches a particular flower, is and is not the same as the blue of the flower."[16]

This does not quite sort out the distinction, however. Because space and the body it contains are *really* the same, and no two bodies are *really* the same, no body *really* occupies the space of another; thus, the distinction amounts only to a way of explaining our way of thinking or speaking, our supposition or the appearance that a body can come to occupy the space of another. Yet on one view of the relation between the two instances of blue, namely, moderate realism, there is something in them that is really the same, namely, the universal quality they share; and on every other view the relation between the instances of blue relates them to a *third* thing—to a word (nominalism), a concept (conceptualism), or a form (extreme realism)—and is thus irrelevant to the explicandum here, which is the successive occupation of the *same* space by different bodies. Thus, to say that a stone and a piece of wood (successively) have the same extension in the sense of moderate realism means that the wood and the stone are the same thing and in every other sense it means that neither is the same as its extension. In addition, the model fails to explain[17] why although two things can be blue simultaneously, they can occupy the same place only successively.

Still, the account is suggestive. It may be that two bodies can token the same space-type, however the type-token relation is understood; and they can do so simultaneously. But not so with respect to situation (situs) or external place (locus externus), which is defined by the relations between a body and those

---

[16] Wilson, *Descartes*, pp. 86–87.
[17] As Wilson realizes.

around it. There cannot be simultaneous tokens of the same situation-type; this type can be tokened by different bodies, if at all, only successively. Descartes seems to argue this on logical grounds, as in his letter to More of February 5, 1649: "in a space, however empty it is imagined to be, one can easily imagine different parts of determinate size and shape, and they can be transferred by means of the same imagination into each other's places; but in no way can two of them be conceived to penetrate each other in the same place, because for that to happen is a contradiction and because no part of space is removed."[18] Perhaps another way of putting this is that relations of situation are precisely what make possible the individuation of bodies; put still a different way, individual bodies are tokens of situation-types. The result of this, as shocking as it is inevitable, is that bodies do not really move at all, for how could they? To move by occupying the place of another, a body would have to drag its own place along and occupying the same place would thus not have moved; or two places would be the same and would be occupied by two different bodies. The difficulties are insurmountable.

It seems to me that to say of a stone and a piece of wood successively occupying the same place that they have the *same* extension in the sense that a shirt and a flower have the same color gets the ontology the wrong way around. The sameness in question is of substance not of quality. *Principles* 2, 16–18, for example, argues against the absolute void. A pitcher may contain now water, then oil. There is no connection between the vessel and the particular body that it contains. But "there is a very strong and wholly necessary connection between the concave shape of a vessel and the extension considered generally which must be contained in the concave shape." The temptation is to consider the extension taken generally as an abstracted particular shape that is successively had by the oil and water. The temptation comes from viewing Cartesian space on the container model—a grid whose parts are regarded as slots that may be successively filled by different objects. The identity of a quality would thus be regarded as the identity of a part of space successively occupied by different objects, and the necessity of which Descartes speaks would be grounded in that identity. But the container model is inappropriate. Descartes goes on to argue that the necessary connection he is talking about is between substance and quality. It would be as contradictory of us to conceive of a mountain without a valley, as to conceive of this concavity without the extension contained in it, or of this extension without a substance: "for, as I have often said, as has frequently been said, nothingness cannot possess any extension."[19] The figure in question, either abstracted or particularized to the oil, water, or vessel, is not a substance. His argument, then, is that because it is a quality it must be the quality of something that is thus contained in it. The

[18] AT, 5:271.
[19] *Principles* 1, 18

containment we are talking about, then, is exemplification: Space/things contain extension by exemplifying it, that is, by conforming to the axioms and postulates of Euclidean geometry. If it failed to contain extension it would fail to be Euclidean. The contradiction that Descartes finds in such a situation is not just the violation of the Principle of Exemplification, but the violation of the very model of intelligibility—geometry, or really the mathesis universalis. If it is false, God is a deceiver, clarity and distinctness are unreliable, and the epistemological chaos of universal skepticism reigns.

Historically, Louis de La Forge was the only Cartesian I know of to have commented in any significant way on Descartes's use of the relation between genus or species and individual to explicate the relation between the extension of space and the extension of body. Body, he tells us, differs from the extension of space insofar as we consider this extension as determinate and singular; but that same extension can be considered as fillable by other bodies having exactly the same shape. "When we say that they occupy the same place, this must be understood in exactly the same way as when we say that the river flowing today is the same as the river that was flowing yesterday, or that it is the same wind blowing or the same fire burning; in all these *façons de parler* the word *same* designates a unity of genus or species, and not a unity of number."[20] Now, of course, rivers do not flow, or move at all,[21] except perhaps in the sense that their *stages* move (to use the language of a more recent theorist who used the same example). What ties the numerically different river stages of the Cayster into the same thing that is the Cayster is, according to La Forge, their being the same *kind* of thing. Applied to the Cartesian picture I have been developing, the account suggests a succession of numerically different objects. But these objects do not move or change at all. As we know from the Synopsis and the letter to Mesland, they cease to be with any change. We can think of the real volume they occupy as a particular having different colors the way an immobile river has successive stages. What then is the status of the successive objects? They depend, as I think Descartes tells us, on our way of conceiving space, namely, in terms of different sensations, apart from which there would be nothing capable of apparent motion and no individuation of physical things.

Before commenting on the Draconian interpretation that denies real corporeal motion, I wish to defuse at least two objections to it. One is based on the obviously many passages in which Descartes speaks of the motion of bodies. Perhaps the most threatening of these is *Principles* 2, 23: "all the variety in matter, all the diversity of its forms, depends on motion." Lest matter be a night of black cows, it would seem that there must be some motion in it. But the text of the principle says that all the properties of matter reduce to *divisibility*, not

---

[20] *Oeuvres* pp. 200–201.

[21] In another sense, of interest to geographers, rivers *do* move, of course, sometimes causing great problems.

actual or real motion, and this is a question of distinguishability of parts, not real separation. Similarly, in *Principles* 2, 20 Descartes had argued against the indivisibility of atoms on the grounds that every part of matter is divisible in thought. To be sure, Descartes in 23 says "if the division into parts occurs simply in our thought, there is no resulting change; any variation in matter, or diversity in its many forms, depends on motion." This seems to say that there must be real motion in extension; but he continues: "This seems to have been widely recognized by the philosophers, since they have stated that nature is the principle of motion and rest. And what they have meant by 'nature' in this context is what causes all corporeal things to take on *the characteristics of which we are aware in experience.*"[22]

The characteristics of bodies that are explained by motion are only *experienced* characteristics. But such experienced characteristics as color are not real, and for us to experience them there need not be a change in the real. This is because Descartes's distinction between division merely by thought and the division or motion that explains the variety in matter need not be a distinction between merely apparent and real division. Volition aside, we can no more cause motion in a thing by our thought than we can cause its color, but its motion may be no less mind-dependent than its color. The "thought alone" whose relevance Descartes here excludes seems to be the "imagination" of his letter to More cited above.

The other objection is based on the very important text in which Descartes defines his notion of real distinction. *Principles* 1, 60 sets out the independence principle: Two things that are clearly and distinctly conceivable apart are really distinct, that is, can exist apart from each other. Strictly speaking, says Descartes, this distinction obtains only between two or more substances: "For example, even though we may not yet know for certain that my extended or corporeal substance exists in reality, the mere fact that we have an idea of such a substance enables us to be certain that it is capable of existing. And we can also be certain that, if it exists, each and every part of it, as delineated by us in thought, is really distinct from the other parts of the same substance." Now, if *res extensa* is infinitely divisible at least in thought, it looks as if we have, more than just a single material substance, infinitely many of them really distinct from each other. At the very end of this chapter we shall find Malebranche arguing, however incoherently, that in fact every part of every part of extension contains infinitely many substances. Three comments should combine to block this as an interpretation of Descartes, however.

First, Descartes may here be willing to use an inaccurate example for heuris-

---

[22] Emphasis added. HR, 1:265 translates the phrase "to become such as they are experienced to be." This translation seems to me a better rendition of the relevant part of per naturam intellexerunt id, per quod res omnes corporeae tales evadunt, quales ipsas esse experimur. See AT, 8:53; Descartes, *Principles.* trans. Miller and Miller, p. 50.

tic purposes. The point of the paragraph is primarily to establish the *nature* of
the real distinction, not to determine its *instances* except by illustration of the
distinction. To the extent that providing accurate examples is important to
Descartes, his concern is with the real distinction, not between material things,
but between "body" (not determined, as it here need not be, whether body in
general or body in particular) and mind, so that the mind, as the rest of the
paragraph makes clear, can exist after separation from (the) body and, presumably, be immortal. Here in this first part of the *Principles*, Descartes's concern is
with the mind and its knowledge; it is only in the second part that he turns to the
principles "of the material world."

Second, it certainly follows from what Descartes says that *if* we could conceive a part of extended substance in distinction from other parts, then that part
would itself be a substance. But he nowhere says or implies, certainly not in this
text, that we *are* able to so conceive a part of extended substance.[23] The
illustration may do its work, that is, even if it is contrary to fact.

Third, there are reasons why Descartes should claim that we are incapable of
conceiving only a part of extended substance. One reason that we cannot do this
is precisely the one that would make that part a substance, namely, that it could
exist by itself. But we know that the extension of the world is not limited
precisely because it cannot even be imagined as such.[24] That is, the argument
for the infinity, or indefiniteness, of the world's extension is, given the identity
of that extension with material or extended substances, an argument for the
uniqueness of material substance. In addition, we know that extension is the
essence or nature of body.[25] But in an important if neglected text Descartes
points out to the empiricist Gassendi, who thinks that the idea of God can be
gradually constructed from experience, "the common philosophical maxim that
the essences of things are indivisible. An idea represents the essence of a thing,
and if anything is added or taken away from the essence, then the idea automatically becomes the idea of something else."[26] Literal and metaphysical divisibility converge here. If *res extensa* were divisible into material substances
on the basis of the independence principle, space would have a different,
presumably non-Euclidean essence. When, therefore, Descartes argues against
atomism, he must be discussing the analysis, not of body (*res extensa*), but of

---

[23] Here HR (1:244), following the approved French translation of Picot, disambiguate the Latin
text in favor of my reading: "if [extended or corporeal substance] does exist, any one portion of it
which we can demarcate in our thought must be distinct from every other part of the same
substance" (Atque si existat, unamquamque ejus partem, a nobis cogitatione definitam, realiter ab
aliis ejusdem substantiae partibus esse distinctam; AT, 8:28). Cf. Alquié's edition, however (vol. 3,
p. 129, n. 1). Notice too the restrictive qualifier in HR, which greatly strengthens my reading. It
would be useful to know with certainty who placed the commas in Descartes's Latin and what they
mean.

[24] *Principles* 2, 21; CSM, 1:200; AT, 8:52.

[25] Principles 2, 4.

[26] CSM, 2:255–56; AT, 7:371.

bodies (*extensa*). "It is impossible that there should exist atoms, that is, pieces of matter that are by their very nature indivisible. . . . For if there were any atoms, then no matter how small we imagined them to be, they would necessarily have to be extended; and hence we could in our thought divide each of them into two or more smaller parts and hence recognize their divisibility. For anything we can divide in our thought must, for that very reason, be known to be divisible."[27] The distinction between body and bodies is the only plausible way to reconcile Descartes's rejection of atomism with his view of the indivisibility of essences, and the only plausible way to make that distinction is by construing bodies as being at least in part mind-dependent.

A final reason why Descartes should deny that *res extensa* is divisible in thought and thus into so many substances is that by calling it a substance he is appealing to the tradition beginning with Aristotle that was to culminate in Leibnizean monads. According to it, substance is indivisible qua substance.[28] Clearly, that it is not divisible is what makes the Cartesian mind a substance (and thus immortal, or destructible only by annihilation). The same may be argued with respect to res extensa. Instead of mounting that historical-plausibility argument, however, I shall take it that at least a prima facie response has been made to the two objections based on the passages in which Descartes speaks about divisibility and the motion of bodies. We may proceed, then, to the following schematic account of Cartesian motion.

1. There is no motion or change at all in extension. Motion is phenomenal only. This is the Parmenidean dichotomy of the ways of being and becoming, except that Descartes gives becoming ontological status by putting it in the mind, which has ontological status.

2. Motion does not individuate material substances, as it is ordinarily thought to do. Indeed, there is but one material substance. Instead, it accounts for the appearance of extension as a multiplicity of bodies. A body will be just as much of extension as appears to move together.[29]

3. Motion itself will occur, or seem to occur, on the model of an automobile's sequential turn signal. A shape distinguished from the visual field by a difference in color will move when qualitatively the same shape is distinguished in an adjacent area of the field by the same color. This is the paradigm case, but there will be others in which with more or less gradual alteration the color and shape will change as well.

4. The Cartesian law of conservation of quantity of motion, both for the uni-

---

[27] CSM, 1, 231; AT, 8:51.

[28] Strictly speaking, physically dividing a substance may for the Aristotelian yield two different substances (e.g. in flatworms). When, more typically, one of the resulting parts fails to have an organic unity, which on the Cartesian scheme is an irrelevant consideration apart from the human body, the previous substance continues identical as, for example, when a tree loses a leaf.

[29] AT, 5:156.

verse as a whole and in individual cases of collision, will govern the rate at which these changes take place. Put another way, laws of motion give the kinematics of qualitative alteration in the visual grid, rather than the dynamics of continuants within a container.

5. Though motion is picked out as change in relations of situation, that is, as locomotion only, motion ontologically is the flow of sensations, and thus Descartes in broadest terms returns to the Aristotelian qualitative conception of change. But despite this, motion takes place against a backdrop of extension, of which it is strictly speaking a mode in the sense that the changing qualities will always have a mathematical structure, namely, volume and relations of situation over time.

6. Individual objects like billiard balls do not exist as such apart from our sensations. Without our sensations there would be only their essence, for without our sensations only unindividuated extension would exist. Physics is thus divided into two radically different, though related, parts. One part, found in the first half of the *Principles*, deals only with the real. It consists of eternal truths about extension as such and allows for certainty based on clear and distinct perceptions. The other part of physics deals with individual objects like magnets, planets, and rainbows that are partly phenomenal since, while their essence is real, their individuation depends on us. This part, found in the second half of the *Principles*, consists of contingent, temporal truths about which all we can ever have, or need, is probability based on coherence. Here we only try to save the appearances because (aside from extension, which is the object of the other part of physics) appearances are all there is to be saved.[30]

7. As we shall see in the following section, Descartes's ontological analysis of material things is, with one qualification, the same as Malebranche's ontological analysis of the mental representations of material things. The qualification, whose importance will also be seen in the next section, is that while for Descartes extension is created, for Malebranche it is uncreated.

Now, it might be wondered why if bodies are in part only phenomenal the *Meditations* has the structure it has. Specifically, if what is ultimately real is not the individual body, but the essence of body, which is elucidated in *Meditations* 5, "The essence of material things, and the existence of God considered a second time," and if the knowledge of extension is guaranteed when clear and distinct perceptions are guaranteed in *Meditations* 3, then does not *Meditations* 6, "The existence of material things, and the real distinction between mind from body," become superfluous? In the refutation of skepticism and the metaphysical vindication of the New Science, *Meditations* 6 seems irrelevant. I shall attempt now to deal with this question in a way that will elaborate and to some extent defend the schematic account of motion and body just presented.

Meditations 6 begins: "It remains for me to examine whether material things exist. And at least I now know that they are capable of existing, insofar as they

[30] *Principles* 2, 36ff.; and 4, 204.

are the subject-matter of pure mathematics, since I perceive them clearly and distinctly. For there is no doubt that God is capable of creating everything that I am capable of perceiving in this manner."[31] This raises two questions: (1) In what sense are material things (bodies) the object of pure mathematics? (2) How are they thus possible existents? Again some help is forthcoming from the most important of recent Descartes commentaries: "Several texts strongly suggest that when Descartes asks whether an idea represents something real, or *rem*, he is asking whether or not in some way it gives him cognizance of a *possible* existent. With a clear and distinct idea there can be no question: 'In the concept or idea of everything that is clearly and distinctly conceived, possible existence is contained.'"[32] As an initial approximation we can say the following. Clear and distinct perceptions of a body qua body are of extension only; material things are the object of pure mathematics insofar as they are extended, that is, insofar as their essence is perceived; insofar as extension is perceived, things could be known to instantiate it, that is, extended things could exist. The crucial text this approach must make sense of is the main argument of *Meditations* 6.[33] "There is in me," Descartes says, a "passive faculty of sensory perception, that is, a faculty for receiving and recognizing the ideas of sensible things," which would be useless unless there were a certain active faculty, either in me or in something else, of "producing or forming these ideas (*producendi vel efficiendi*)."[34] It is not in me: (1) it does not presuppose thought; (2) the ideas are produced without my cooperation and often despite me. We know that the cause of an idea must have as much formal reality as the idea contains objective reality; hence the active faculty can be in a substance which is (1) "body or corporeal nature, in which there is contained formally all that is objectively in the ideas" (thus the ideas under discussion are of extension only, since there is nothing formally in body which is contained objectively by sensory ideas) (2) God, or (3) "some creature more noble than body in which it is contained eminently." God, he says, would be a deceiver in the latter two cases; but in what sense, and why? The answer depends on the notion of causation involved here.

There are at least four notions of causation operative in the *Meditations*. First, there is what was later to be called *real* causation; this is the notion of creation ex nihilo; according to it there is only a distinction of reason between creation and conservation in existence. Only God is a cause in this sense. Second, two events constantly conjoined might be said to be *occasional* cause and effect. Descartes does not use the expression 'occasional cause' and talks of occasions only when there is an essential difference between the events conjoined (thus between a brain-event and a sensation, for example). But no harm

---

[31] CSM, 2:50; AT, 7:71.
[32] Wilson, *Descartes*, p. 108. Text cited is AT, 7:166.
[33] CSM, 2:50–55; AT, 7:171.
[34] CSM, 2:55; AT, 7:79.

will be done in extending the notion to its later more comprehensive use, thus to the connection between motion in one billiard ball and motion in another with which it collides. Third, a substance will be the *material* cause of the modes of which it is the substance. Thus, although its essence is thought, the mind is the material cause of its acts of thinking. A fourth notion might be called *structural* causation. Although the cause of my idea in this sense "does not transmit anything of its actual or formal reality to my idea, it should not on that account be supposed that it is less real. The nature of an idea is such that of itself it requires no formal reality except what it derives from my thought, of which it is a mode. But in order that an idea should contain some one objective reality rather than another, it must without doubt derive it from some cause in which there is at least as much formal reality as this idea contains of objective reality. For if we suppose that something is found in the idea which was not in its cause, then the idea would have it from nothing."[35]

The cause of the *formal* reality of an idea, or more precisely, of the act of thought that is a modification of the mind, might be variously conceived: (1) God as real cause; (2) a brain-event as occasion; or (3) the mind itself as the material cause. The formal reality of the idea is parasitic on the formal reality of this act; construed adverbially it is a way of being aware.

The cause of the *objective* reality contained by the idea is a structural cause: It determines the thought to be of one thing rather than another. The crucial causal principle is therefore that for the mind to be aware, its thought must be adequately structured to its object. An of-an-x thinking cannot be of a y.[36] And the argument Descartes bases on it is that God would be a deceiver if He produced my idea of a body directly, or indirectly via some other creature, without extension as the structural cause of my perception. Now Descartes does say that God would be a deceiver if ideas were emitted from other than corporeal things. But since the atomist effluent view is clearly and repeatedly rejected by Descartes—"nothing reaches our mind from external objects"[37]—this can only mean that such ideas must be materially true, that is, that they are *of* extension.

Were God to deceive me in this regard He would be the demon deceiver of *Meditations* 1. There Descartes argues that even if the general and more universal things of which our dreams and imaginations are confected should like them be false, that is, even if eagles and lions, for example, should be no more real

---

[35] *Meditations* 3; CSM, 2:28–29; AT, 7:41.

[36] Unless x has more reality or is more perfect than y, for a thinking of the more perfect contains the less perfect. Thus God knows all in knowing Himself. Thus also Malebranche's view that the idea of the infinite precedes and is presupposed by all others. See also *Meditations* 3; CSM, 2:31–32. This interpretation of Cartesian ideas, which historically is to be found in Arnauld, however, invalidates the claim that the cause of an act of thinking must contain as much formal reality as it contains objective, and with it the first of Descartes's proofs of the existence of God. Malebranche saw this and used it as an argument against the interpretation (*Trois Lettres*, 1, 3; Oeuvres 6–7: 213–16).

[37] *Comments on a Certain Broadsheet*; CSM, 1:305; AT, 8:359.

than griffins, still the simpler and more universal things, the elements of what we see even in sleep, might be true. "This class appears to include corporeal nature in general and its extension, the shape of extended things, their quantity or magnitude and number, the place in which they may exist, and the time through which they endure, and so on"[38]—in short, the material and common simple natures of *Rules* 12. Haldane and Ross translate Descartes as suggesting that arithmetic and geometry may be true even if these things should not be "actually existent," for even in sleep a square can never have more than four sides. But Descartes in fact indicates that these sciences may be true even if the simple natures are not to be found *in rerum natura* (on our reading, even if there are no corporeal bodies). He does not say they could be true if there is no extension and in fact immediately introduces the doubt of the clear and distinct perceptions of mathematics on the basis of the possible demon who could cause me to have my present perceptions and yet fail to create the earth, heaven, extended thing, magnitude, or place. The crucial item in this list is extended thing (*res extensa*), the eternal and immutable object of geometry that is perceived by the mind alone. The same reading must be given to *Meditations* 5, where to illustrate the existence-essence distinction Descartes says that "when I imagine a triangle, for example, although there may nowhere in the world (*nullibi gentium*) be such a figure outside my thought, or even have been, there is nevertheless in this figure a certain determinate nature, form, or essence, which is immutable and eternal, and not invented by me or dependent on my mind. This is clear from the fact that various properties can be demonstrated of the triangle."[39] The individual triangle, extension instantiated by sensory qualities, may be only imaginary, but its extension, its form, essence, or nature, must exist. Put another way, God in His perfectly unconstrained act of creating extension makes geometry true. This is the sense of Descartes's letter to Mersenne of May 27, 1630 in which he says that God is the *efficient* cause of the eternal verities. He is in the same sense the author of both the essence of things and their existence; as He is free not to create the world, so He is free to make it not true that the lines drawn from the center of a circle to its circumference are equal, and presumably He could do this either by not creating extension at all or by creating a non-Euclidean extension.[40] On the same day eight years later Descartes replied to Mersenne's question whether there could be real space had God not created anything that "not only would there be no space, but even those truths called eternal, such as that the whole is greater than the part, would not be truths, unless God had established it [i.e., space] as such."[41]

Material things or bodies, then, are the object of pure mathematics to the extent that their essence is the object of pure mathematics, and they can thus

[38] CSM, 2:14; AT, 7:20.
[39] CSM, 2:44–45; AT, 7:64.
[40] AT, 1:149–50.
[41] AT, 2:138. Alquié dates this letter ten days earlier (*Oeuvres*, 2:61, n. 2).

exist to the extent that extension exists and can be instantiated by actually existent individuals. But Descartes concludes in *Meditations* 6 that "corporeal things exist."[42] How does it follow that because I clearly and distinctly perceive corporeal things, that is, perceive their extension, they exist? Part of the story is given by what immediately follows Descartes's conclusion: "perhaps they do not exist entirely as I comprehend them by sense, because this comprehension of the senses is in many cases very obscure and confused; but at least all things are in them which I clearly and distinctly understand, i.e. all things which, viewed generally, are comprehended in the object of pure mathematics." Thus, Descartes's saying here that corporeal things exist is only to say that corporeal nature exists.

The rest of the story has to do with things that are "more particular," the size and shape of the sun, and things less clearly and distinctly perceived, such as, light, sound, and pain, in all of which there is *some* truth (*aliquid . . . veritatis*). I seem to be taught certain things by nature, that is, insofar as I am a being composed of mind and body. The means by which I am taught is hedonics, and what I am taught concerns biological utility. This is the theme of *Principles* 2, 3: "that the perceptions of the senses do not teach us what is really in things, but merely what is useful or hurtful to the human composite." Even here there may be deception—the dropsical man desires water—but the occasionally deceptive perceptual system is the best one possible, in the Euclidean world in which simplicity of ways is followed. With all this established Descartes can at last set aside the problem from *Meditations* 1 of nonveridical sense perception, to distinguish dreaming from waking—"I now notice a vast difference between the two,"[43] which of course is coherence.

Descartes has nothing of particular interest to say about coherence, but I think it must ultimately cash out for him in terms of an ability to manipulate the world for practical purposes, and the theory ultimately that allows this is the New Science. This is the science of extension, which, very briefly, for him consists of two parts. The first part is what is true in all logically possible worlds, that is, in all worlds in which clarity and distinctness are reliable; most notable would be the three laws of nature and the seven rules of collision derived from the third; this component is true because of immutable extension. The second part of Descartes's New Science aims at what is true only of this world because of its quantity of motion. One world differs from another because of differences in sensory qualities, the change in which, as we have seen, yields motion. Due to His immutability God must conserve the world with the same quantity of motion, the same rate of change, but what that quantity is can be known only a posteriori, even in a world in which clarity and distinctness are reliable. Objects to be known as objects must be experienced. Thus, in explain-

---

[42] CSM, 2:55; AT, 7:80.
[43] CSM, 2:61; AT, 7:89.

ing particular things like rainbows or magnets we need experiments both to suggest and to test hypotheses, whose only requirement is that the consequences they yield in conjunction with the first component agree with the phenomena. This agreement, I suggest, is just the coherence appealed to in *Meditations* 6. Thus the rest of the story of "how corporeal things" exist is that they cohere. The upshot is a coherence theory of truth with respect to bodies, and a correspondence theory with respect to extension.

To conclude, I would like very briefly to draw attention to the more obvious appearance of many of the views I have attributed to Descartes in the works of Desgabets and Régis. Aside from two opuscules on transubstantiation and blood transfusion, Robert Desgabets (1610–78) published only the *Critique de la critique de la recherche de la verité* (1675) in which he defended Malebranche against the skeptic Foucher.[44] Until recently, his most important work has been in manuscript only.[45] Despite his failure to publish, however, Desgabets had an important influence on Pierre-Sylvain Régis (1632–1707), who did publish, and who aside from Malebranche, Arnauld, and perhaps Rohault, was as visible as any Cartesian in the period. Desgabets and Régis represent an important line of Cartesian development generated by Descartes's doctrine of the created eternal verities. With varying degrees of clarity, relevance, and argumentation they subscribed to doctrines of the indefectibility of substance, the modal status of individual minds and bodies, the individuation of bodies by the mind's perception, the phenomenal status of motion, ideas as forms of thought, eternal truth as correspondence between ideas and indefectible substance and all other, modal truth as coherence.[46] But from the creation of the eternal verities they also argued toward empiricism, going so far as to employ the classic formula: There is nothing in the intellect that was not first in sense. Our interest here is in the line of Cartesian development that went in just the opposite direction.

§13   MALEBRANCHE'S REALISM

The Search After Truth is Malebranche's first, longest and most important work.[47] It is the most extensive and exhaustive exposition of his philosophical thought and also the most accurate in the sense that in its six editions (1674–75

---

[44] Malebranche was less than delighted with the defense, commenting that those who involve themselves in polemics against or on behalf of others should carefully read their works to get their views straight (*Oeuvres*, 2:500).

[45] Known to modern scholars primarily through the work of P. Lemaire and J. Prost. Now we have his *Oeuvres philosophiques inédites*, introd. G. Rodis-Lewis, ed. J. Beaude. Important for an appreciation of Desgabets are Rodis-Lewis's introduction and also Beaude, "Cartésianisme."

[46] For much more on this line, see Lennon, "The Cartesian Dialectic of Creation," forthcoming in *The Cambridge History of Seventeenth Century Philosophy*.

[47] See "Note on Documentation."

to 1712) spanning his career Malebranche incorporated the alterations, refinements, and additions occasioned by his polemics with a number of people on a number of topics. Despite these changes, however, the fundamental position set out in the very first paragraph of the *Search* was never in the least questioned. The themes struck here at the outset provide not just the key for what follows, but its substance and spirit as well.

The mind of man (*l'esprit de l'homme*), says Malebranche, occupies an intermediary position in the cosmological scheme of things. Infinitely above it stands its Creator, while below it is material creation. It has a relation of dependence in both directions. The mind's relation to God is a close and essential relation in that without it the mind could not exist. This union with God "raises the mind above all things. Through it, the mind receives its life, its light, and its entire felicity." The mind's relation to material creation, however, or to that part of it which is the body, "debases man and is . . . the main cause of all his errors and miseries" (p. xix). In explicating these two unions Malebranche draws on two main sources for his philosophy: on Augustine primarily for the mind's relation to God and on Descartes for the mind's relation to the body. But his philosophy is no mere amalgamation of his two sources, because he departs from them, as we shall see, in important ways.

From Augustine Malebranche retained a general theory of illumination but differed from him on just what we see when illumined. The influence of Augustine is one of inspiration in a very general way rather than of doctrinal detail, so that not much dialectic is expended in Malebranche's presentation of this side of his story. Augustine figures primarily as an authority cited on behalf of a certain view of man's dependence on God. Descartes, however, far from being an authority, is cited only to establish that no appeal to authority outside of religion is ever legitimate. What Descartes gives is a certain structure for the epistemic relations between the mind and the material world with the injunction that it be rejected until found compellingly true. In modifying Descartes's own views to satisfy this condition, Malebranche represented himself, plausibly enough, as the true Cartesian.

Malebranche remained an adherent to the metaphysical core of Cartesianism, namely, the doctrine that thought is the essence of the mind and extension of body. The essence of a thing is what is "primary in that thing, what is inseparable from it, and what the properties belonging to it depend on." (3.2.8.2; 243). This is Malebranche's version of the Cartesian doctrine of principal attributes, according to which everything has an attribute on which all its properties depend (*referuntur*).[48] Roughly speaking we can say that the essence of a thing gives what is necessary and sufficient for all a thing's properties. What this means is that no simple thing can have properties of both thought and extension, that if the one is the essence of mind and the other of body nothing can both think and be extended.

[48] *Principles* 1:53.

Related to the mind-body ontological dichotomy is the epistemic distinction between the intelligible and the sensible—in Cartesian terms, between what is clear and distinct and what is not. Again roughly speaking we can say that in repeatedly insisting on the distinction between sensing and knowing Malebranche preserves the Cartesian distinction between kinds of aware-nesses—between apprehension of the wax by the senses and by the mind alone—but that to preserve the distinction he insists on a radically different ontology for his theory of ideas and of their connection with material things. The short version of the story that we shall soon pursue at length goes as follows: "to know [connoître] is to have a clear idea of the nature of (the) object and to discover certain of its relations through illumination and evidence [par lumiere & par évidence]."[49] When we know a triangle, for example, we can make inferences on the basis of what we know about its various properties. Deducibility seems clearly the mark of evidence in this sense, which thus invokes the same notion as Cartesian distinctness. The reason such inferences can be performed is that the object of knowledge is extension, which at least as far as we are concerned uniquely satisfies the Platonic requirement of objec-tivity for knowledge.

By contrast, the sensation of pain, for example, is a particular with no relation to anything else that we can discover. Only by experiencing it through sense can we know what pain is. In a favorite example of Malebranche, color cannot be reasoned into a blind man, but by reason he can come to know the properties of some figure he has never experienced. Sensations are logically isolated. This might be what leads Malebranche to say that the difference between sensations cannot be expressed.(1.13.3) We might say that they can only be named and not described, so that there is nothing about them, no structure or content, that can be communicated. In Descartes's terms, they have no objective reality; their only reality is as modes of the mind, that is, formal reality. Thus, Malebranche would seem inclined to the Cartesian adverbial theory that sensible qualities are modes of awareness, that is, ways of being aware of extension. But instead he draws the inference that since ontologically sensible qualities are modes of the mind, they are awarenesses of the self. The self beyond the present state that is a mode of it is not known. That is, from this or any other awareness, we do not know the essence of the soul, for we cannot deduce from it or any other state what other states the soul may have. Only experience can provide this. Malebranche thus concludes that we have no idea of the self and can know it only through inner sensation (sentiment intérieur). He thus also rejects the conclusion of Meditations 2 that the nature of the human mind is better known than that of the body.

The logical isolation of sensations would also be a reason why Malebranche

---

[49] Entretiens sur la métaphysique et sur la mort (1st ed., 1688; hereafter, Dialogues) 3, 6; Oeuvres 13:66.

claims that even if, contrary to fact, everyone had the same sense organs identically disposed, it could still not be demonstrated that they had the same sensations with respect to the same objects. What one sees as red another could see as green, or feel as hot for that matter. "It is more reasonable to believe" that God always maintains a universal correlation between sensations and their immediate occasions, namely, some brain-event. But that He does not is possible; there is no necessary connection between them.(1.13.5) One result of this is that there is no resemblance between bodies and sensations.[50] Descartes had used this as a premise to conclude that sensations, "apparently" adventitious, are in fact innate. Even in the case of ideas of mathematical properties the brain-events occasioning them are different from them; a fortiori must the ideas of sensible qualities differ. Since a cause in the sense of a source must be like its effect, Descartes argues, the mind itself must be the source of ideas of both sorts.[51] In Malebranche's occasionalism, however, the causal likeness principle is rejected. God as real cause and finite events as occasional causes are, or may be, unlike their effects. Thus, for Malebranche the question of innateness does not even arise with respect to sensations. Instead, we find him closely adhering to Descartes's view expressed in *Principles* that sensations do not teach us what things are in themselves, but only the relation they bear to the mind-body union.[52] Roughly speaking we can say that things closer to us appear larger because they are in a position to affect us; nutritious things seem sweet, noxious things bitter. Strictly speaking, what we sense when we feel pain, for example, "is a modification of our soul in relation to what takes place in the body to which it is joined" (1.13.1; 61)—in this case, to a state that for the good of mind-body union should be changed. Attending to a sensation, then, is attending to the soul itself. About this kind of sensation two points must be insisted upon: (1) We do not thereby know the self except as thus modified—as we have seen, we have no idea of the self; (2) our awareness of the self as thus modified is nonetheless incorrrigible—we are infallible in distinguishing, for example, color from sound.(1.13.2; 61–62) Thus Malebranche effectively invokes the Cartesian technical notion of clarity as what is directly perceived in addition to the distinctness noted above.[53]

Malebranche's account of the sensible essentially involves only emphases of certain points in Descartes's account and inferences from them. But his account of the intelligible, as his long polemic with Arnauld showed, is at least very debatable in Cartesian terms. It may well be that no account of Cartesian ideas as opposed to sensations can be anything but debatable. In his polemic with Malebranche, the skeptic Foucher complained that Descartes held no fixed

---

[50] *Dialogues* 3, 12; *Search* 1, and *passim*.

[51] *Notes Against A Programme*; HR, 1:443; AT, 8:358–59. See Clatterbaugh, "Likeness Principle." This may be regarded as the material cause distinguished above.

[52] *Principles* 2, 3; *Search* 1, and *passim*.

[53] *Principles* 1, 45–46.

theory of ideas and that everything defective in his philosophy stemmed from this failure.[54] Two decades later, a disciple of Malebranche, Henri Lelevel, replied to the same charge from another skeptic, Pierre-Daniel Huet, agreeing that Descartes never explained his notion of an idea very clearly and attributing to this failure Régis's adherence to the interpretation in fact advanced by Arnauld.[55] Nonetheless, at least in recent years the literature has been converging asymptotically on a certain interpretation that regards Arnauld as having championed the orthodox Cartesian cause and Malebranche the heterodox.[56] In the end, Malebranche himself finally decided that Descartes's position on the nature of ideas was just poorly thought through,[57] and that it would be against justice and common sense to ascribe to Descartes the position that Arnauld found in him, for Descartes probably held no fixed position at all.[58] In a rare instance of polemical accord Malebranche thus ceded to Foucher on at least one point. But I think that there is some room for revision. Let us begin with the currently received view of Descartes, which we can summarize in five steps:

1. To say of an object of awareness, such as the sun, that it has formal existence is to say that it exists independently of the awareness.

2. To say of the sun that it has objective existence is to say that it is an object of awareness.

3. The idea of the sun is the sun itself insofar as it is an object of awareness. It follows that:

4. Not ideas, but objects of awareness have objective existence. When I am aware of the sun I am aware of it *simpliciter* and not as an object of awareness. If ideas had objective existence, then in the perception of the sun the idea of the sun would be the object of awareness and the Cartesian theory would be representationalist. In this context, the issue of direct perception *versus* representative or indirect perception is whether the object of awareness is numerically identical to the sun or to some epistemological proxy for the sun.

5. Descartes in *Meditations* 3 says of ideas that they contain (*continent*) objective reality. This can be read, as I think Arnauld did read it, as an invocation of the Aristotelian–Scholastic theory of the intentionality of thought. One and the same

[54] *Réponse*, p. 9.

[55] *La vraye*, p. 49.

[56] O'Neil, *Realism*; Cook, "Representationalism"; McRae, "Ideas"; Lennon, "Inherence Pattern"; and esp. Yolton, "Ideas." For the most cogent account of Arnauld as a direct realist, see Nadler, Arnauld, esp. chap. 5: "There is [for Arnauld] only one relation . . . between the act of the mind and the external object, and this relation is direct and immediate. External things are perceived directly, without the mediation of any third thing (or second relation) standing between the act and its external object. Since 'idea' and 'perception' refer to one and the same thing, to have an idea of an object is to have a perception of that object, i.e. to perceive that object, not some nonphysical proxy" (p. 113).

[57] *Trois Lettres*; Oeuvres, 6:214.

[58] *Réponse*; Oeuvres, 6:172.

thing, the sun, or at least its intelligible component or form, can exist in two different ways. To use Scholastic terms, it can exist materially, outside the mind, or immaterially, as the structure of the awareness in virtue of which it is an awareness of the sun. Thus, since the object "in" the mind is numerically identical to the object "outside" the mind, the Cartesian theory is, despite the generally representationalist language of *Meditations* 3, nonrepresentationalist.

The issue over ideas contested by Arnauld and Malebranche is whether ideas are modifications of the mind (Arnauld) or are independent of the mind (Malebranche), whether the mind's modifications are essentially presentative and thus sufficient for knowledge of material things (Arnauld), or must be supplemented by a special kind of epistemic object (Malebranche). Arnauld in a sense tried to have it both ways. For him a perception is a single thing having two relations. Insofar as it is related to the mind it is properly called a perception; this relation is clearly that of mode to thing modified. Insofar as it is related to its object it is called an idea; this relation Arnauld never made explicit, but given 1–5 above, the relation would seem to be that of identity. The idea of the sun just is the sun existing in an immaterial way.[59]

It seems clear that Descartes does invite this generally Aristotelian Scholastic interpretation of his theory of ideas. In his most explicit definition, for example, he calls an idea the form of a thought.[60] In addition, his several distinctions, most important that between esse formale and esse objectiva in *Meditations* 2, reflect the Aristotelian Scholastic distinction between material and immaterial modes of exemplification. Finally, this interpretation can be argued in terms of Descartes's motivations. For want of a geometry of the mind Descartes might well have adhered to the received account of intentionality; that is, having given the ontology of a mathematicized nature as his principal objective, Descartes might well have desultorily appealed to the available philosophy of mind that would have been best received by the Jesuits whose favor he sought. However that may be, there remains a fundamental inconsistency between the two programs. For the identity of idea and object demands an ontology incompatible with Descartes's mathematical realism, his Platonic account of the material world. An idea and its object are numerically identical on the Aristotelian Scholastic scheme in that one is aware of a form that is common to what is in the mind and to what is outside it; that is, the isomorphism of idea and object is the numerical identity of their common form. But their isomorphism on the Platonic account should be a matter of their relation to a third, ideal thing; there is nothing numerically identical in both. Arnauld was committed to direct realism; the price he paid for it was the above inconsistency. Malebranche was a consistent Platonist; the price he paid was representationalism.

The fundamental issue of the theory of ideas in the seventeenth century may

---

[59] Lennon, *Commentary*, pp.793–809.
[60] *Replies* to *Objections* 2; CSM, 2:113; AT, 7:160.

be put, and typically was put, by asking how it is that things are in the mind. On my account of Descartes, however, things are for him already in the mind. If, unusually, a thing already in the mind is considered just as an object of thought, it may be called an idea; more usually it is considered just as a thing. The difference, as we have seen, is not an ontological but a contextual one. As Descartes puts it in explaining the notion of objective existence to Caterus, it is an extrinsic denomination.[61] The usual correspondence theory regards truth as an adequation of mind to things; for Descartes the adequation is of things (bodies) to extension (res extensa). Our clear and distinct perceptions of bodies (as when we work their geometry) are false just in case the demon fails to create the ideal extension that grounds the eternal truths of geometry. The Aristotelian John Sergeant was on the right track in thinking that Descartes in his *Replies* to Gassendi claimed that truth is a conformity, not of idea to thing, but of thing to idea.[62] Descartes's view may be a rare clear instance of what was called metaphysical truth, the so-called truth of things as opposed to that of propositions.

With this view Descartes remains a realist in the sense that things are directly perceived; but he is an idealist with respect to the existence of those things. The departure of both Arnauld and Malebranche, it seems to me, results from their common assumption that things have a real existence outside the mind. In the case of Arnauld, the result is the incompatible mix of ontologies noted above. In the case of Malebranche, the result is a representational view, which I shall try to show is nonetheless closer to what Descartes was about.

Malebranche's representationalism is clear and unequivocal. It is true that long arguments from Arnauld sanctioned the seventeenth-century usage first clearly specified by Foucher that to represent meant to present; the result of this is that for many authors, including Arnauld himself, it is possible to argue that an idea represents a thing by making it directly present to the mind. No such argument is possible for Malebranche, who in addition to his apparent arguments for representationalism makes clear his use of the relevant term: "strictly speaking, nothing immediately perceived is represented but only presented."[63] Presumably, if something known is not directly perceived it can only be represented.

It might appear[64] that Malebranche gives a number of arguments for representationalism. Thus, for example, he argues that we can imagine a golden mountain, which does not exist; but to be aware is to be aware of something, and what we are aware of even in this case has real existence, because it differs,

---

[61] *Replies* 1; HR, 2:10. Hume was to hold a similar view with respect to what he called perceptions. Bundled one way by the imagination they are constituents of objects; bundled another way the same perceptions may be constituents of the mind.

[62] *Method*, preface, unpaginated. Cartesianism as an antecedent to Kant's Copernican revolution is being investigated by F. Van de Pitte.

[63] Letter to an unknown priest, January 14, 1684(?); Oeuvres, 18:279–80.

[64] As it once did to me (*Commentary*, p. 782).

and thus has properties different from other objects of awareness. He also seems to argue that since minds and material things are essentially different there can be no relation and a fortiori no cognitive relation between them: "Material things . . . certainly cannot be joined to our soul in the way necessary for it to perceive them, because with them extended and the soul unextended, there is no relation between them" (3.2.1.1; 219). It now seems to me, however, that Malebranche offers these not so much as arguments but as consequences, or perhaps illustrations or different expressions, of a fundamental metaphysical position. That position is presented right at the outset of his treatment of the nature of ideas: "I think everyone agrees that we do not perceive objects external to us by themselves. We see the sun, the stars, and an infinity of objects external to us; and it is not likely that the soul should leave the body to stroll about the heavens, as it were, in order to behold all these objects. Thus, it does not see them by themselves, and our mind's immediate object when it sees the sun, for example, is not the sun, but something that is immediately joined to our soul, and this is what I call an *idea*. Thus, by the word *idea*, I mean here nothing other than the immediate object, or the object closest to the mind, when it perceives something, *i.e.*, that which affects and modifies the mind with the perception it has of an object" (3.2.1.1; 217).

This notorious passage has drawn the attention of commentators from Arnauld to the present, who unanimously condemn Malebranche for confusing cognitive presence with local presence. While it may be that things must be cognitively in the mind, they object, it does not follow that things at a distance cannot be (directly) perceived. Arnauld argued that to think otherwise is to be misled by a doubly false analogy to corporeal vision. It is thought that in corporeal vision what is seen must be present to our eyes and that what is seen is an image, but both of these principles are false. We do not see what is in the eye, for what we see, even in the case of reflection, is not an image but the thing itself. In any case, it is not the corporeal eye but the soul that sees, so that even if these principles were true, Malebranche would have no basis other than the confusion of cognitive and local presence for his theory of representative ideas.[65] Malebranche insisted in reply that he was guilty of no such confusion since he rejected the view that the soul can perceive only things that are present to it. That he rejects the condition of local presence is clear, he thinks, from his allowing that we perceive things that do not exist. "The sun that we look at [i.e., with the eyes] is not the one that we see . . . we might see the world such as it appears to us although there may be nothing in creation. . . . Certainly, if I can perceive bodies although there are none, I can perceive them although they are at a distance."[66] Arnauld was no more satisfied with this than with any of Malebranche's replies to his criticisms. He insisted that Malebranche's own

[65] *Des vrayes*; *Oeuvres*, 38:192–94.
[66] *Réponse*; *Oeuvres*, 6–7:95.

reply assumed the very necessity of local presence that he denied, for he makes what we see, namely, the intelligible sun, something that is "intimately joined to the soul" as opposed to the physical sun, which is at a distance.[67]

Arnauld is right that there is a problem with Malebranche's view. But that problem, I think, lies not in a confusion over local presence, but in the use to which Malebranche puts his representationalist theory. An indication of the problem, to which we shall return later, is that Malebranche tells us both that we can perceive what does not exist as in the case of the golden mountain, and that what we perceive must exist since the golden mountain we perceive has proper-ties. If there is a confusion here it is over kinds of perceiving. The perception of an idea of a golden mountain is part of the analysis of the perception of the golden mountain, but as such the object of the former cannot be the object of the latter, that is, the perception of a nonexistent object still lacks an object.[68] The result is that such perception cannot be an argument for representative ideas in such cases. My revisionist thesis is that in fact Malebranche does not argue in this way, that his view on such perception is, along with his view on the lack of relation between minds and material things, the consequence or application of his metaphysics of ideas rather than premises for it.

Only if Malebranche is guilty of fairly grotesque revision of his views ad hoc can we not take him seriously when he says in his reply to Arnauld that his talk of the soul being unable to stroll about the heavens in order to perceive the things there was intended to be taken ironically (*une espece de raillerie*): "But what did I mean . . . ? I meant that an idea is necessary in order to perceive them and my intention was to bring about reflection on a truth with which those whom I was combatting are in agreement but on which they do not always sufficiently reflect. I meant only that something different from the sun is necessary to represent it to the soul."[69] The principle to which he appeals is that particular things as such are unintelligible, which he correctly thinks is accepted by Arnauld when he insists that for a thing to be perceived it must exist objectively in the mind. With respect to particulars, that is, there are no awarenesses that are bare—the mind and its object face to face. The reflection that Malebranche encourages his opponents to make concerns the ontological basis for the principle, which is that particular things are not their own ground of being. They can exist only, as it were, in something else, which is why they can be perceived as if existing when in fact they do not. On the other hand, if there is something we can perceive that is its own ground of being, then it must exist, it is not perceived through a representa-tive idea, and it will be perfectly intelligible. The clarification of these connec-tions yields for Malebranche his whole philosophy of mind: the nature of the

---

[67] *Défense*; *Oeuvres*, 38:493.

[68] "It might be said that we do not so much see the ideas of things as the things themselves that are represented by ideas, for when we see a square, for example, we do not say that we see the idea of the square, which is joined to the mind, but only the square that is external to it" (3.2.6; 231).

[69] *Réponse*; *Oeuvres*, 6–7:95–96.

mind and of its ideas, the relations between ideas and the mind, and the relations between ideas and the things they represent.

To the third edition of the *Search* (1677–78) Malebranche appended a long set of Elucidations on a variety of important topics. The tenth of these deals with the nature of ideas. In it Malebranche claims that it is self-evident that bodies are not cognizable by themselves. He nonetheless proceeds to offer an extended argument on behalf of this important claim, an argument that is based on our possession of knowledge having certain characteristics. The dialectic is the familiar Platonic one that what we know about the objects of sense transcends anything that might be supplied simply by sensation.

That we have such knowledge or even that it is possible is a question that is infected with a certain ambiguity in Malebranche. On the one hand the venom with which Malebranche attacks skepticism shows that he regards it as a serious threat. His long chapter on Montaigne in the *Search* (2.3.25) is a severe and personal attack. In another chapter he describes the position of the Academic skeptics as that "false proposition so hostile to all science and truth" (1.3.1; 13), and he ascribes their doubts to "passion and stupidity, . . . blindness and malice, or simply . . . caprice and the will to doubt . . . a doubt of darkness, never leading toward, but always away from light" (1.20.3; 86). I can see no other way of accounting for such rhetoric beyond regarding it as an epiphenomenon of debate in the period, likely with the Gassendists. For Malebranche's typical position, well-grounded in his philosophy, is that "no one disagrees that all men can know the truth."[70] It is clear Malebranche thinks that not only can men know the truth, but they do know the truth, and furthermore that the truth they know is universal, immutable or necessary, and infinite. He expresses this by saying that man participates in a certain Reason that no man determines. This is not a faculty that all men have—the critique of reason, even of the sort Descartes undertook, forms no part of Malebranche's program. Instead, Reason is the ground for truth; it is the object known when we know the truth. Thus, when he says that Reason enlightens us, he is not referring to the seeing mental eye, the Cartesian *lumen naturale*, but to the object seen. This is why the skepticism that impugns only our powers of vision receives contempt but not philosophical refutation.

The Reason in which man participates is universal in the sense that what is known to be true by one person cannot be contradicted by what is known to be true by another.[71] It is also immutable or necessary; "it is impossible that [the truths men know] should not be as they are."[72] Finally it is infinite in three, not

---

[70] *Elucidations*, 613.

[71] It is not clear what Malebranche means by this. Because of this character of universality, he says, merchants settling their accounts come to agreement, as do geometers reasoning together (*Méditations*; *Oeuvres*, 10:20). They do this presumably because they intellectually apprehend the same objects; so universality seems to be a matter of identity.

[72] *Elucidations*, 614.

clearly distinguished senses: (1) there are an infinite number of truths that can be known, as the infinite number of geometrical shapes demonstrates; (2) the expression of some truths involves an infinite analysis, as in the case of the square root of five; (3) Reason cannot be exhausted in that the truth-value of nothing is indeterminate. Unless Reason has these characteristics, Malebranche says, he can see nothing but "universal confusion."[73] Denying any of them establishes Pyrrhonism—all basis for knowledge, both practical and speculative, is upset.[74] Without these characteristics Reason cannot be appealed to when we condemn (*sic*) the view of the poet, for example, who said that it is impossible to distinguish what is moral from what is immoral.[75]

These reflections on the fundamental principle accepted by the Cartesians that bodies are not known by themselves thus leads Malebranche to reject a number of important Cartesian views. An obvious one is the doctrine of the creation of the eternal truths. Reason for Malebranche is not only independent of men, but of God Himself in the sense that He is constrained to follow it in, for example, the creation and ordering of the material world. God is not free to alter the truth of geometry by creating a non-Euclidean world or to reverse moral relations with the result that a dog has more value than a man. Freedom of indifference cannot be the ground for necessary truth; "God could not have willed certain things, for a certain time, or for certain kinds of beings."[76] From Malebranche's perspective, Descartes's question as to the cause of the eternal truths was misguided, for in recognizing the necessity of the eternal truths we see that they have no cause. There are many philosophical problems that Malebranche opens up here; consider what might be involved in his claim, for example, that if the eternal truths were created "we might be mistaken in claiming that the arithmetic and geometry of the Chinese is like our own."[77] Most important, however, he seems faced with the dilemma either that all truth is necessary, for God could not have willed certain things, for a certain time, or that some truths are utterly accidental, entirely independent of God's will. To this important question that Malebranche was never able to resolve, we shall return below.

The issue of the eternal truths is related to a second important doctrine of Descartes's that Malebranche rejects. According to Descartes all truths are created but for some there is no time at which they are otherwise. To put it another way, they are accidentally true at all times (and thus anything is possible). On the assumption that only eternal truths are proper objects of knowl-

---

[73] *Elucidations*, 617.

[74] *Elucidations*, 620.

[75] Nec natura potest justo secernere iniquum. Malebranche, significantly, identifies the author as Lucretius; in fact, it is Horace (*Satires* 1, 3, v. 113).

[76] *Elucidations*, 615. Cf. Jolley, *Light of the Soul*, p. 11: "The desire to avoid Cartesian voluntarism and to defeat skepticism in a way that Descartes could not is one of the major motives for Malebranche's whole theory of ideas."

[77] *Elucidations*, 615.

edge, we can come to know them only if there is some constraint on our knowledge independent of that knowledge, only if God includes among the eternal truths one that is a handle on all the rest. This the benevolent God does by making it true that what is clearly and distinctly perceived as if true is in fact true. (But since this truth is no less created, whatever problem of circularity generated by the hyperbolic doubt still remains.) Gassendi was the first to raise the objection that clarity and distinctness are useless unless we have some means to determine what is clearly and distinctly perceived.[78] For Malebranche no such psychological criterion is necessary and he is emphatic in his denial of its relevance. Instead of appealing to the clarity and distinctness of the perception, Malebranche looks to the evidence of what is perceived. If anything, the compellingness of clear perception varies inversely with the truth of what is perceived, for the strength of a perception bears on the relation of a thing to us, not on the thing as it is in itself.[79] This is why the celebrated Cartesian method of doubt appears nowhere in Malebranche, for there is, or ought to be, for Malebranche no necessary connection between subjective indubitability and truth about an objective order of reality.[80] Sergeant criticized the Cartesians, particularly Antoine Le Grand, on the ground that a rule of truth is what makes something to be true—and thus a rule of truth precedes clarity and distinctness of perception. He allows that clear and distinct perceptions may be true, but insists as had Gassendi that we still need a means of deciding what is clear and distinct. He points out that people on both sides of disputes often claim clarity and distinctness—as in the very dispute over clarity and distinctness.[81] The issue is worth dwelling on since it represents an important instance of the appearance-reality dialectic.

The appeal to clarity and distinctness might be understood in two different ways. One would be an emphasis à la Ramsay on any perception intended as an assertion. Thus: p is clear and distinct $= p$ is true. Another would be as a justification à la Wittgenstein for a logically first assertion. Thus: p is clear and distinct $= p$ entails everything else relevant to p that I assert. In these terms, the only plausible criticism of Descartes that I can see is that he appeals precipitously to the second, that is, that instead of providing some argument for p he merely asserts p. Whether the arch-deductivist Descartes ever does this is a

[78] *Objections* 5; CSM, 2:193–95; AT, 7:277–79. Sergeant, who was on to Descartes's sense of conformity, later gave the most relevant, if most question-begging, version of the criticism that Descartes's criterion was a useless psychological test; according to Sergeant, Descartes says not that our perception is true because the thing is so and so (as he should) but that the thing is so and so because our perception is clear and distinct (*Method*, preface, unpaginated).

[79] *Dialogues*, 2, 9–11.

[80] To put it another way, for Descartes the mind could have clear and distinct perceptions that were mistaken if the demon deceiver failed to create res extensa; for Malebranche if there were no God and thus no intelligible extension, the mind could not perceive with evidence. I am grateful to Peter Schouls for pressing me to clarify this point, with which I am afraid he will nonetheless still disagree.

[81] *Non Ultra*, pp. 63, 68 and *passim*.

good question. Another good question, however, is whether the two senses can in fact be distinguished. Significantly, Malebranche in framing his rule of evidence slips back into blatantly psychological terms such as the "feeling of inward pain" and "the secret reproaches of reason" we are supposed to feel when we fail to acknowledge what is evidently true. "We should never give complete consent except to propositions which seem so evidently true that we cannot refuse it of them without feeling an inward pain and the secret reproaches of reason."[82] One wonders why this rule, which according to Malebranche is the one most necessary for the speculative sciences, does not read simply: Consent only to what is true. To respond that such a rule does not give us a way of knowing what is true will not do. To respond so would be to slide back into the psychologism of which Descartes was accused, a charge that stands or falls with the appearance-reality distinction, of which the distinction between Descartes's notion of clarity and distinctness and Malebranche's notion of evidence is an instance: The clear and distinct is what appears to be true, the evident what is true.

The rejection of both the criterial role of clarity and distinctness and the view of created eternal truths is tied to a third departure from Cartesian doctrine. As we have seen, Arnauld's mobilization of the Aristotelian Scholastic ontology in his interpretation of Cartesian ideas was at least a debatable matter. Even so, it is undebatable that for Descartes things are in the mind by way of idea, that is, as objects of thought, whatever the ontology thereby involved. For Malebranche, things are not in the mind at all; their only existence is as mind-independent material substances. Indeed, not even ideas for him are in the mind in what is possibly the only clear sense in the period, namely, as modifications of it. This of course was the issue of the protracted debate with Arnauld. The focal point of Malebranche's arguments in that debate is the contention that the nature of what is known has characteristics such as generality, infinity, and objectivity that preclude its status as a modification of the mind. He argues, for example, that we can sometimes have the idea of a circle in general, but that since the mode of a thing is only that thing existing in a certain way, no mode in general can be the mode of a particular thing such as the mind.[83] This returns us to Malebranche's version of the Cartesian distinction between sensing and knowing.

"If it is true that the Reason in which all men participate is universal, that it is infinite, that it is necessary and immutable, then it is certainly not different from God's own reason, for only the infinite and universal being contains in itself an

---

[82] *Search* 1.2.1; 10.

[83] *Réponse*; *Oeuvres*, 6–7:60. See Jolley, *The Light of the Soul*, p. 56: "Perhaps the most basic feature of Malebranche's theory of ideas is its resolute anti-psychologism. Far more than any other seventeenth-century philosopher in the Cartesian tradition, Malebranche insists that logic and psychology must not be conflated. In particular, we need to distinguish carefully between the thought (i.e. thinking of *x* and the concept or idea of *x*)."

infinite and universal reason."[84] This explains why Malebranche can claim with impunity that even God is constrained by the eternal truths, for this amounts to no more than a self-constraint due to His nature, a kind of self-realization that as the exact antithesis to the so-called freedom of indifference is in fact the highest form of freedom. As Malebranche puts it, this Reason is "coeternal and consubstantial with Him." It is the divine essence.

By participating in Reason, however, men do not apprehend the divine essence as it is in itself. In theological terms this would be the Beatific Vision that is reserved to the blessed in another life. For the moment we see only through a glass darkly. In philosophical terms, full apprehension of the divine essence would be immediate knowledge of all truth via an entirely pure intellection, whereas in its present state of embodiment the soul's perceptions always contain some sensation and are limited to individual truths *seriatim*. Instead, we see the divine essence "relative to creatures and to the degree that they can participate in it."[85] Malebranche here sounds a Neo-Platonic theme that was struck by many in response to the problem of how the essences of things might be uncreated and yet not pose the threat of polytheism. The answer that is found throughout the medieval period, including among essentially non-Platonists such as Aquinas, is that the essences of things is actually the essence of God— not by way of composition, as Aquinas puts it, but by way of perfection.[86] There is no multiplicity of essences in God, but the same divine essence as the ground for things having various levels of perfection is the essence of each. The distinction among essences can be drawn only from the bottom of the great chain of being upward, not from the top down. Roughly, the idea is that a single thing of greater perfection can ground a multiplicity of things of lesser perfection. The result is a multiplicity of essences only with respect to the things of which they are the essence.

Malebranche uses the Neo-Platonic account of essences in his explanation of how we know material things. Given that what we know when we are said to know material things is actually their essence, and given that the essence of things is not in things but in God, then in nominally knowing things we in fact know God.[87] The divine essence individuated by such knowledge is what Malebranche calls intelligible extension. This uncreated intelligible extension differs from Descartes's created extension (res extensa) principally in being ideal rather than material. That intelligible extension is in God and is not really different from Him does not mean, as Malebranche repeatedly insisted to

---

[84] *Elucidations* 10, 614.

[85] *Search* 3.2.6; 231.

[86] *Contra Gentiles* 1, chap. 54; Brehier, "Eternal Truths," p. 194.

[87] This leads to the first of Malebranche's two departures from Augustine's doctrine, according to which eternal truths are seen in God. For Malebranche, truth is a relation, in the case of eternal truth between essences or ideas; but since relations are not real—they are beings of reason—we see only the ideas of things in God (*Search* 3.2.6; 234).

Arnauld, that God is really extended. It does mean, however, that Malebranche is able to say with impunity, as Descartes was not, that the extension we know is infinite, rather than merely indefinite.

Epistemically, intelligible extension is the formal cause of our perceptions.[88] This is what we have called the structural cause found in *Meditations* 6. It determines the perception to be of one material thing rather than another. It does this by giving a nonintentional, logically isolated sensation a geometrical structure and thus making it capable of representing a material thing. Consider a perception that consists solely of a sensation—a visual field, for example, consisting of a single shade of green. This perception cannot represent a tree since for Malebranche no tree is really green. But if the visual field is limited such that a green triangle is outlined by some other sensation such as a blue field, then the perception or at least the triangular part of it can represent the tree. How the triangle I see when I look at a tree stands to intelligible extension is an enormously complex affair in Malebranche, but the underlying idea is as simple as I have put it.

The "triangular part" of the perception is what Malebranche calls an idea in the strict sense. The temptation is to construe it in the pictorial terms suggested by the perceptions we have of it in so far as it is instantiated by sensations such as colors. But it would be more accurate to regard this idea as the set of Euclidean theorems applicable to the triangle we perceive. We know less than the whole of geometry just because our perception is limited by the sensations we have. Thus Malebranche's account of intelligible extension so far in no way differs from Descartes's perception of res extensa.[89] A crucial difference between this account and that of *Meditations* 6 is that because Malebranche's formal or structural cause of perception is the divine essence, it would be impossible for God to produce for me an idea of body that was mistaken. This is why Malebranche claims that if the eternal truths were created, that is, other than God Himself, all certainty in the sciences would be upset. What we see according to Descartes is a created, material extension that is no less contingent for being unchanging; according to Malebranche what we see is an uncreated, intelligible extension that is necessarily immutable.

The mind's immediate object, then, in the perception of material things is a particularized instance of intelligible extension. That this idea is something seen in God rather than a modification of the mind is argued by Malebranche in a number of ways. The argument that for polemical reasons is longest and set out in greatest detail, at least initially, is that Malebranche's account suffers none of the defects of what he takes to be its four competitors. What they are need not concern us here; suffice it say that each represents an aspect of the Cartesian theory that he is concerned to refute.[90] As critics like Locke and Régis

[88] *Oeuvres*, 12–13:1900.
[89] Radner, *Malebranche*, n. 11.
[90] Lennon, *Commentary*, pp.783–89.

pointed out, however, Malebranche gave no reason to believe that these were the only alternatives to his theory. His main arguments, however, derive from Augustine. What he calls his strongest argument is a solution to the problem most notably posed by Plato: How can we come to know something without recognizing it as what we are about to know and thus already knowing it? Plato's well-known answer was to recognize recognition: What we call coming to know is really remembering. Malebranche too rejected the simple passage from ignorance to knowledge. We can come to know, as it were, because Being and thus all particular beings are always present to the mind, however confusedly, in the necessary relation the mind bears to God.[91] Malebranche thus enormously elevates the significance of a position Descartes had introduced in *Meditations* 3 only to forestall an objection to his first proof for the existence of God. It cannot be objected, according to Descartes, that God need not exist as the cause of our infinite idea of Him since that idea might be had merely as a negation of the finite. "I clearly understand [*intelligo*] that there is more reality in an infinite substance than in a finite one, and hence that my perception of the infinite, that is, God, is in some way prior to my perception of the finite, that is myself." His position is that despite our language, the finite is more properly conceived as the noninfinite. In response to Gassendi, who had tried through an empiricist via negativa to derive such ideas of God as we may have from a negation of the finite, Descartes insisted that "the infinite is not apprehended by a negation of boundary or limitation, since on the contrary all limitation contains a negation of the infinite." The upshot is that for Descartes the idea of God is "the most true, and most clear and distinct of all."[92] As we shall see, Malebranche denies that we have any idea at all of God; even so, his view on the matter here enjoys its best claim to being properly Cartesian.[93]

There are two other noteworthy arguments that Malebranche directs against Arnauld. He argues in addition that we sometimes know what is abstract or universal, but that what we know in these cases cannot be the modification of a concrete particular like the mind. Finally, in a different kind of argument he claims that only his view adequately reflects man's full dependence on God. Not only is God the only real cause of the mind's perceptions, as Arnauld and practically all the other Cartesians admit, He is its only possible object of knowledge.

The Augustine on which Malebranche drew was the Cartesianized Augustine of André Martin. Under the pseudonym of Ambrosius Victor, this fellow

[91] *Search*, pp. xix–xx.

[92] CSM, 2:31; AT, 7:45–46. *Replies to Objections*; HR, 2:252; AT, 7:365.

[93] Descartes to Clerselier, April 23, 1649; AT, 5:356: "It should be noted that I never use the word 'infinite' to mean only not having limits, which is negative and to which I apply the word 'indefinite,' but to mean a real thing, which is incomparably greater than all those having limits. Now I say that the notion I have of the infinite is in me before that of the finite because from the fact alone that I conceive being or what is, without thinking whether it is finite or infinite, it is infinite being that I conceive; but in order that I might conceive a finite being I must eliminate [*retrancher*] something from this general notion of being which consequently must precede it."

Oratorian published in 1667, and in a second edition of 1671, a *Philosophia Christiana*, which was an anthology of texts taken accurately enough from Augustine but arranged with chapter headings in such a way that Augustine, not altogether implausibly, was made to support Cartesian doctrines on a variety of issues, such as the rejection of sense knowledge, the importance of introspection, the primacy of mathematical truth, and the propedeutic doubt. Even the bestial machine is advanced with the Augustinian imprimatur. The author was a veteran adherent of Cartesianism who avoided the attempted censorship of his teaching at both the college of Angers and later Marseilles by continuing apace with the insistence that what he was teaching was not the doctrine of Descartes but that of Augustine. He thus fostered, even if to an extreme degree, the connection between Descartes and Augustine, and of both with the Oratory, which had been promoted, whether intentionally or not, by Pierre Bérulle, the founder of the Oratory, and by its early luminaries Condren, Gibieuf, and Labarde.[94] With perhaps questionable conviction Malebranche rejected the strong tinge of Jansenism that Martin also insinuated. But he never questioned the Cartesian Augustinianism. Almost all of the many quotations from Augustine that appear in Malebranche are to be found, in the same order, in the *Philosophia christiana*, and to those few that do not appear there Malebranche may have been sent by those that do.[95]

In a preface to the edition of 1667 there appears an argument for the existence of God that is described as the clearest, briefest, and most solid of all:[96] "God is a simply and absolutely immutable nature; now there is such a nature since it is clear that the truth of those standards [*illarum regularum*] commonly called eternal truths is simply and absolutely immutable; thus there is a God." This truth that we know is "incommutable, uncreated, immense, infinite." [97] Malebranche takes over this argument in what he calls the "loveliest, loftiest, most solid and primary proof of the existence of God" (la plus belle, la plus revelée, la plus solide, & la prèmiere):[98] That we are able even to think of the infinite shows that it exists—from the perception of God it follows that He exists. The startling thing is that Malebranche felt that his argument was only an elucidated, emended version of Descartes's ontological argument (4.11.3). In fact, however, it represented a radical extension of Descartes's epistemological views.

The ontological argument of *Mediations* 5 is the fairly standard argument that God must exist since the idea of Him contains existence. There can no more be a nonexistent God than there can be a mountain without a valley. Malebranche's argument, however, is that since nothing can represent the infinite,

---

[94] Bouillier, *Histoire*, 1: chap. 1.

[95] Gouhier, "La Crise," pp. 283–84, 411–20.

[96] *omnium clarissimum, brevissimum, ac solidissimum*

[97] *Philosophia Christiana*, 2:105. See Gouhier, "La crise," pp. 284–85.

[98] *Search* 3.2.6; 232.

when I perceive it I perceive it in itself. In the perception of a finite, created thing I can distinguish between the essence and existence of that thing with the result that from the perception alone I cannot be sure whether that thing exists. So far this is a straightforward rendition of the ontological argument. But for Malebranche, the essence-existence distinction in a material thing means that all I perceive of it is its essence, which represents the thing to me whether it exists or not. Of the infinite, however, there cannot be an idea. If it is perceived, therefore, it itself is perceived, not its representation, and thus it must exist.[99]

Malebranche's arguments for the premise that there is no idea of God are, at least in this context, very sketchy. He says that our idea of God could not be something created,[100] and that the infinite cannot be conceived "simply as a possible being; nothing limits it; nothing can represent it."[101] The background to this is his whole epistemology and its ontological infrastructure. We can know things, both in the sense that we know that they are like our ideas and in the sense that we know necessary truths about them, only if there are ideas after which they are created and we know those ideas. The argument for the existence of God is that without His eternal and immutable essence as the ground there would be no truth with those properties and no guarantee of the likeness between things and ideas. Malebranche thus gives, not an ontological argument, but a transcendental deduction of the existence of God. The same structure in one context is an argument for the existence of God, and in another it is an argument for the vision of all things in God. This is why he is inclined to run together the arguments of Descartes and Augustine. If you like, they are instances of the methods of analysis and synthesis.

In the fifth edition of the *Search* Malebranche added a long excursus to the chapter in which he treats of Descartes's ontological argument (4.11.3). It was obviously designed with an eye primarily to the objections raised by Arnauld to his theory of knowledge. To fill out his argument Malebranche in effect appeals to what we have called the Principle of Intentionality (PI)—To think is to think of something—which he calls the first principle of all our knowledge. Now, when we perceive the infinite, he argues, there must be something that we perceive; but even assuming contrary to fact that the mind acting by itself could know its own modes (Arnauld's view), what we perceive in this case cannot be a mode of the mind (or of any finite thing). For we would then be perceiving something, namely, an infinite, that was not. Malebranche proposes a curious argument here. For one thing, his treatment of PI is perplexing. He says both that its denial is a contradiction (for to think of nothing is not to think) and that it follows from the first principle of Cartesian epistemology, call it the Principle of Clarity (PC), that whatever is clearly conceived as contained in the idea repre-

---

[99] Search 4.11.3; 318 ff.; *Dialogues*; *Oeuvres*, 12–13:53–54.
[100] *Search* 3.2.6; 232.
[101] *Search* 4.11.3; 318.

senting a thing can be asserted of that thing,[102] which is thus dependent on it. For PC is true only if ideas are immutable, necessary, and divine, since God's archetypes in creating the world are His perceptions, not ours. But presumably PC is not a tautology. Even allowing that Malebranche's pre-Boolean use of 'contradictory' indicates only a modal operator, the connection between PI and PC still needs explaining. It seems to me that Malebranche can mean only that if we could think of nothing, a nonexistent infinite, then the ground of immutable and necessary truth would be upset, that is, we would be judging reality according to ideas having no necessary connection with it.

Another difficulty with PI is that it seems much too strong a principle. In Berkeleian terms, it seems to make *percipi* sufficient for *esse*. At one point in the *Dialogues* (1, 4) the interlocuter of Malebranche's spokesman asks, "what, everything that you think of exists?" In response Malebranche distinguishes between the office, desk, and chairs that we see, namely, the ideas of those things, and the office, desk, and chairs that we look at but do not see, namely, the mind-independent material substances; his claim is that percipi is sufficient only for the former. But in that case, Berkeley would ask, in what sense do we ever perceive the latter? That Locke was very concerned with PI and the use to which it had been put by Malebranche is a case that I have already tried to insinuate in some detail. The first six paragraphs of 2.8 of the *Essay*, which draws the primary-secondary quality distinction, effectively explain how we can be aware of nothing, which is no less the metaphysical question of PI than the physical question of the void. However much this reading may have eluded previous commentators, its importance should now be clear if Locke is to be distanced from Malebranche's "first principle of all knowledge."

The conclusion that Malebranche draws, meanwhile, is that it is "as evident that there is a God as it is to me that I am."[103] Elsewhere he says that "the proofs of the existence and the perfections of God drawn from the idea of the infinite are proofs by simple perception. We see that there is a God as soon as we see the infinite, because necessary existence is included in the idea of the infinite, or to speak more clearly, because we can only apprehend the infinite in the infinite itself. For the first principle of our knowledge is that nothingness is not perceptible, whence it follows that if we think of the infinite it must exist" (6.2.6; 481). This simple perception is an intuition that he still elsewhere contrasts with judgment and inference. The difference lies entirely on the side of the object. In simple perception we perceive a single object (e.g., the idea of four); in judgment we perceive objects in relation (e.g., four being equal to twice two); in inference we perceive things in relation to relations between them (e.g., twice two being less than six on the basis of twice two being equal to four and four being less than six) (1.2.1; 7). Malebranche insists that the mind is entirely

---

102 See Arnauld and Nicole, *Port-Royal Logic*, pt.4, chap. 6.
103 *Search* 4.11.3; 323.

passive in these so-called operations. He thus makes explicit what is at best very vaguely implicit in the Cartesian theory of judgment. For Malebranche, and perhaps for Descartes, the active capacity of the will results, not in the synthesis of elements in a logically complex perception, but in the affirmation (or denial) of the complex. The will plays no role in, for example, the perception of the horizontal moon as larger than the meridional moon; only when we affirm that it really is larger does the will enter. This is certainly a part of Malebranche's doctrine of natural judgment and may be suggested by Descartes's theory of vision in the *Dioptrique*. For Malebranche, in any case, our affirmation might be mistaken in three cases: where a relation fails to obtain between objects, as in the horizontal and meridional moons; where a relation fails to obtain between relations, as in the case of the logical paradoxes; or in the perception of a single object whose essence fails to be instantiated. In the perception of a single object that is its own ground of existence, no such mistake is possible, for it is an object allowing no distinction between essence and existence. There is no distinction between appearance and reality.

By proposing a noninferential ontological argument Malebranche is in a position to repair the difficulty known as the circularity of the *Meditations*. The details of the difficulty and of how Descartes attempted to deal with it are a matter of endless dispute in the literature, but its general form is clear enough. The existence of God is proved in order to justify principles of the sort assumed as premises in that proof. In his chapter from the *Search* called "General directions necessary for conducting an orderly search for truth and in the choice of sciences" (6.2.6), Malebranche does not explicitly identify the circularity problem of the *Meditations* as such, but his discussion makes clear that this is what he is talking about, and it is a safe bet that he was familiar with the difficulty from Arnauld's *Objections* to the *Meditations*. All the ordinary proofs for the existence of God are defective, he thinks, in that they involve reasoning, which relies on memory. But if some evil demon exists instead of God, memory cannot be relied upon at all. Hence only through simple perception can the existence of God be known.[104]

§14 MALEBRANCHE'S IDEALISM

The price Malebranche pays for securing PC and avoiding the circularity of the *Meditations* is the threat of Spinozism. Having shown how what we know can be necessary, Malebranche has difficulty making room for anything contingent. The position he argues is the one regarded in the seventeenth century as most orthodox: Though God is under constraint in the way He creates, the fact of

---

[104] See also McCracken, *British Philosophy*, p. 85.

creation is utterly contingent. That this contingency threatens to evaporate from the Malebranchean scheme can be seen in a number of issues.

One indication of Malebranche's Spinozism is his discussion of the motivation for creation.[105] God creates not from logical necessity but from love, which can be only for Himself and which is expressed in His Glory. Now God cannot be glorified, the argument goes, by mere material creation. Creation must be made divine, which is effected through the Incarnation, by God becoming material. (Thus, the Redemption on this account is only incidental; had the Fall not occurred, Christ would have come anyway.) The material world is created in the way best fitted to this end; and the fitness of the infinite number of worlds that God could have created to achieve His ends is judged according to their simplicity. Thus, despite Malebranche's claim that God's act of creation is perfectly unconstrained and indifferent, the existence of this world seems deducible from a calculus of necessary divine attributes. Specifically, it follows from God's goodness (the love He bears for Himself), and His wisdom (the truth He cannot help but know), that He creates and maintains just this world. Theological details aside, Malebranche when faced with the dilemma of tychism or necessitarianism opted, it seems to me, for the latter.[106]

On the other hand, the existence of material things is for Malebranche philosophically idle in the way in which the doctrine of the Incarnation is philosophically idle; neither does a job in the rational explanation of things. It may be true that Christ was both man and God, but this makes no difference in how we understand the world. Indeed, the doctrine itself is in principle incomprehensible to us. Similarly, the annihilation of matter would make no essential difference to the Malebranchean system. Throughout his discussion, says one recent commentator, "Malebranche speaks as if bodies existed; but if bodies did not exist, there would not be a word of his to change."[107] This is an exaggeration, of course. If there were no bodies then changes in the brain, just for example, could not serve as the occasion for the production of sensations. But those sensations nonetheless could occur since there is no necessary connection between them and the brain-events occasioning them. More generally, no necessary truths about the world are upset if bodies do not exist. The twofold upshot is that the ontology of material things begins to look gratuitous and, epistemologically, material things look both unknowable and in any case superfluous since they need not be known. Both amount to the charge that Malebranche can provide no reason for asserting the existence of the finite, contingent realm that he thinks material things constitute. I shall begin with the epistemological side of this story of implicit Spinozism.

In good Cartesian fashion Malebranche regards the existence of a material

---

[105] *Dialogues; Oeuvres*, 12–13:197–222.
[106] Lennon, *Commentary*, pp. 824–25.
[107] Gouhier, "La crise," p. 276.

world as standing in need of argument, which he attempts to support in *Elucidations* 6. There he argues the familiar line that God is better known than material things, that the source of illumination is spiritual, that only in pure intellection does the mind apprehend truth, that the senses are designed only for survival value. The senses seem a compelling witness to material things but, he says, as the New Science shows in upsetting Aristotelian naive realism,[108] the senses must deceive us about the qualities of things and as dreams, madness, and illusion, show, the senses can deceive us about the existence of material things. That material things exist is a possibility, however, and we have a strong inclination to believe they exist. Thus "we have more reason to believe that there are bodies than to believe there are not any."[109] Indeed, "to doubt whether there are bodies would be mad."[110] But Descartes's argument for the existence of bodies based on our inclination to believe in it plus divine veracity is inconclusive because the inclination, though strong, is not irresistible. This means that if there were no bodies God would not be a deceiver, for we would in that case allow ourselves to be deceived. Belief is irresistibly constrained only by evidence and "evidence is found only in necessary relations, and there is no necessary relation between God and such a world."[111]

The result is that it must be through the other channel of divine communication, the grace of faith, that we find assurance of the existence of the material world. This we have in Scripture, which asserts among other things requiring the existence of a material world that the Word was made flesh. The result is that material things are not theoretical entities of natural reason but revealed entities of supernatural faith. In these terms, Malebranche represents the period's most spectacular example of a skeptical fideist, the believer whose program, two centuries before Kant, was to upset the pretenses of reason to make room for faith.[112] In philosophical terms Malebranche's predicament is like that of Descartes with respect to the created eternal truths. Because they depend utterly on the arbitrary will of God, an independent guide to them is needed, which He provides with the no less arbitrary criterion of clarity and distinctness. Malebranche is in a similar position concerning knowledge of the material world, the existence of which also depends on the utterly arbitrary will of God. Since only He knows His own volitions, and since the world is not perceptible by itself, directly, its existence must be revealed to us. Since natural revelation or evidence is insufficient as the failure of Descartes's demonstration demon-

---

[108] *Search* 1.

[109] *Eluclidations* 6, 574. The Cartesian François Bayle thought that sensible things are really distinct from the mind since there is no reason to believe them annihilated when we cease to perceive them. But Bayle was a direct realist who also thought that bodies cause our ideas of them (*System*, pp. 71–72).

[110] *Réponse*; *Oeuvres*, 6–7:82.

[111] *Elucidations* 6, 574.

[112] Popkin, *Skepticism*, esp. preface.

strates, the resolution can be only in supernatural terms through faith.[113] The upshot is that we do not know but only believe in the existence of material things, and that what we know of them, namely, their essence, is known whether they exist or not. This leads to the ontological side of the story.

The Cartesian definition of substance as that which needs nothing other than itself in order to exist [114] leaves the independent reality of finite things in a very tenuous position and leads more directly to Spinoza's monism than the would-be Cartesians of the seventeenth century were prepared to contemplate.[115] Despite, or perhaps especially because of, Descartes's clarification that his definition applies literally only to God, the pressure is to construe finite things as aspects of God, all the more so since for Descartes two things are really distinct only if they are conceivable apart from each other. That things are not conceivable apart from God is the quick argument to Spinoza's conclusion that they are but modes of God. Malebranche is more than flirting with this dialectic when he claims in the *Dialogue between A Christian and A Chinese Philosopher* that "everything of reality or perfection in all beings is contained in God."[116] In addition, a traditionally standard feature of an individual substance is its entelechial activity. Substance typically had been conceived as a principle of change, a feature stripped from it by Malebranche's explicit form of Cartesian occasionalism, according to which all finite things are absolutely impotent. In causal terms as well as the conceptual terms that became the model for the causal relation, finite things stand to God in the traditional relation of modes to substance.[117] A final feature of substance that Malebranche seems to deny individual things is its role as an individuator. This is a crucial issue deserving treatment at length since it bears centrally on the theory of matter in this period and will naturally emerge later at length when we return to Locke's contrasting views.[118]

The problem of the cohesion of bodies became particularly acute when

[113] *Elucidations* 6, 572–74. Malebranche was not the first Cartesian to appeal to faith in this context. Both Régis and Cordemoy had done so previously (Gouhier, "La crise," pp. 277–78, n. 3). Gouhier's long footnote is an excellent introduction to the issues raised here.

[114] *Principles* 1, 51.

[115] Thus the urgency and extent of criticism of Spinoza among P.-D. Huet, P. Poiret, P.-S. Régis, F. Lamy, F. Bayle, F. Fénelon, and H. Lelevel among others. See Moreau, "Le réalisme," p. 103.

[116] *Oeuvres*, 15:3. For the historical circumstances of this work, see Iorio's introduction; for a full treatment of the philosophical context, see Lai, "Linking of Spinoza."

[117] See Alquié, *Le Cartesianisme*, pp. 147–52..

[118] I shall here concentrate on Malebranche's tendency toward monism in his treatment of material, extended things. The tendency is also to be found in his treatment of minds. Bouillier (*Histoire*, 2:61) pointed to a text from Malebranche's *Meditations*: "I feel led to believe that my substance is eternal, that I am a part of the Divine Being, and that all my various thoughts are only particular modifications of universal Reason." Bouillier also points out that Malebranche rejects the view in no uncertain terms, but remarks "one senses that it obsesses him, and seduces him as it were despite himself."

substantial forms were rejected in favor of homogeneous matter. A material thing is not a composite of matter unified by its substantial form, but rather a quantity of matter; it is not substantially different from another such quantity but only spatially different from it. But then how do we account for the difference between A being immediately next to B and C being part of D? Why do some things hang together, literally, and some not?

Malebranche criticized Gassendi's account of cohesion in terms of interlocking, branched, and crooked particles on the grounds that in failing to explain the cohesion of the particles themselves, the account only puts off the difficulty.[119] Nor will it do, he says, to regard the binding particles as essentially indivisible; for their parts are conceivable apart from each other, and hence, as substances, can exist apart from each other. Now, what this means is that contrary to what Malebranche realizes, every extended substance of his contains (actually and not just potentially) an infinite number of substances, because every part of extension is at least conceptually divisible. In chapter 6, in fact, I shall try to show that the possibility of motion for Descartes would require the actual infinite division of extension. I might add too that Malebranche seemed more aware of problems of individuation even for purposes of doing physics when he concluded that there is no difference between continuity, contiguity, and union *in the void*—which is what we have with the Cartesian subtle matter that offers no resistance. Meanwhile, the conceivability criterion Malebranche employs also means that every extended substance is contained by an infinite number of substances. One way to conceptualize this dual relation of containment had by every extended substance is that if it did not obtain there would be holes in space. Or, more spectacularly, there would be a plurality of worlds whose impossibility Descartes infers from the infinite divisibility and extension of the world,[120] and which he avoids with the homogeneous, unchanging res extensa of *Meditations* 2 that only *appears* differentiated into individuals. On the scheme of multiple material substances that Malebranche would like it is hard to see how substances are any longer individuals, why they should be called substances at all. There seems to be only Descartes's single material substance that for Malebranche is superfluous since it replicates the function of his intelligible extension. Arnauld's unrelenting harassment of Malebranche on the failure to distinguish material and intelligible extension was thus the first allegation against him of Spinozism.

One possible way of avoiding the slide toward Descartes's dialectic might be to deny not just the *actual* division but also the *divisibility* of matter to infinity by denying its conceptual divisibility. This is the route of Berkeley and Hume. But with them, at least, it rests on the rejection of what is most fundamental to Cartesianism, namely, the distinction between pure and sensuous intuitions.

---

[119] *Opera*, 1, 403b; *Search* 6.2.9; 511ff.
[120] *Principles* 2, 22.

For them, since infinite divisibility cannot be empirically represented (imagined), it cannot be; for the Cartesians since it cannot be imagined, it must be rationally represented (understood).

Another possibility might be to construe Malebranche's argument against Gassendi in a different way. One part of a quantity of matter, say the alleged binding hook, might be conceivable apart from another part of that hook, but not from every part of matter. This after all is the principal Cartesian argument against the void. We have seen that for Descartes the distinction between a quantity of matter and the spatial extension it occupies is only one of reason. We *conceive of* them as distinct; *really* they are not. Taking this line means that while it is an individual different from other individuals such as minds, *all* of space is a substance. It is also an infinite substance—in Spinoza's language, infinite *in suo genere*—for there could not be an end to it beyond which nothing is conceivable.

So far this might just be, as I have already argued it is, good Cartesianism. But it is not Malebranche's view, or at least not the view he intended. For he asserted the realist view that material things are really distinct from the mind, existing unperceived, indeed unperceivable, as so many individual substances. That he failed to provide a stable ontology for such a view, that in fact what he provided amounted only to the idealism of Spinoza was argued most effectively by a former student of his, Dortous de Mairan.[121]

Malebranche fares badly in this, his last polemic, one reason being that he was old and sick. During the decades of his polemic with Arnauld, Malebranche projects an attitude of prissy insult that anyone would criticize his view, and I for one delight as Arnauld acutely sticks him almost at every turn. With Mairan, however, the Oratorian has my sympathy. He says, and his calligraphy

---

[121] The charge of Spinozism had recently been explicitly made by the Jesuit R. J. Tournemaine in a preface to Fénelon's *De l'existence de Dieu* (1713). But it had also been made three decades earlier. Noel Aubert de Versé (d. 1714) was reared Catholic, took a medical degree in Paris, converted to Protestantism, and moved to Holland where he practiced as a minister; but his theological views got him into trouble even there and he returned to medicine as a livelihood. Like Bayle he had problems with Jurieu. He was finally allowed to return to Paris, on condition that he renounce Protestantism and write against it. His *L'impie convaincu . . .* argued that taking space for a substance (which Malebranche did not do) and the doctrine of continual creation (which Malebranche certainly held) both lead to Spinozism, the view that "there is no other God but nature, or the universe, or matter" (P.1). Calling him a fanatic and a visionary, Aubert takes Malebranche to have advanced Spinoza's views (pp. 144 ff.). He cites Malebranche's view, for example, that we have the idea of the infinite before that of the finite and juxtaposes it with Spinoza's view that all substance is necessarily infinite: "One drop of water is no more like another than is Spinoza's proposition and that of our visionary" (p. 152). Philosophically more important, much of Arnauld's criticism came to this charge as well. As Radner points out, "Mairan tries to give material substance the features of his intelligible extension, viz. infinity, indivisibility, necessity, eternality. Arnauld tries to give his intelligible extension the features of material extension, viz. divisibility, figurability, movability" (*Malebranche*, p. 113). In either case, the distinction between God and creation is threatened.

demonstrates, that his hand trembles a great deal, so much so that it takes him as long to produce a legible line as it previously did to produce a page. "I'm having difficulty regaining my health; I have just been bled again. I'm seventy-six years old."[122] Nonetheless, in response to the insistent, not to say impudent, demands of Mairan (b. 1678) that he produce a geometrically rigorous response, that he not be vague, Malebranche remains courteous and even genial. But his genius had been spent and he was unable to do much more than repeat the very views from which Mairan drew the damnable Spinozist conclusion— which he does vigorously, in detail and, I think, with conviction. Mairan is clearly afraid, given the views he is defending. He refers to Spinoza as *S* in the first instance, as *the author* thereafter, and he indicates to Malebranche that his signature and address should be erased from the letters and that they should be read by no one else.[123]

Mairan begins with the request that Malebranche show him where Spinoza's argument is fallacious because to him it seems "solid and full of good sense"; according to Mairan the chain of Spinoza's argument seems unbreakable and attempts to refute him have so far failed.[124] Malebranche's reply is that Spinoza's reasoning is bad because he equivocates on, for example, the existence of God. The main cause of Spinoza's errors, as he sees it, is that by supposing that things are perceived in themselves he confuses things with the ideas of them, with the result that what in fact is created gets endowed with the eternality, necessity, and infinity of the uncreated.[125] Mairan attempts to rebut both points, claiming that Spinoza's definition of God is the same one from which both Malebranche and Descartes had deduced the existence of God, and that second, the problem of distinguishing things from the ideas of them is rather Malebranche's, since he can see no difference (if he may be permitted a frank admission) between created and intelligible extension. The clearer view he urges on Malebranche is that individual things are not substances but modes of extension. "For there is nothing permanent in them except the extension with-

---

[122] June 12, 1714; *Oeuvres*, 19:882–89.

[123] September 17, 1713; *Oeuvres*, 19:854. Malebranche's second reply was delayed because, as he said, he forgot Mairan's address and lost his note of it. Perhaps so. But perhaps Malebranche was only chiding him for his secrecy. It is a good story either way (December 5, 1713; *Oeuvres*, 19:864).

[124] September 17, 1713; *Oeuvres*, 19:852–54.

[125] September 29, 1713; *Oeuvres*, 19:852–54. Here Malebranche repeats the argument his disciple Lelevel had raised against Régis two decades earlier. According to Lelevel, Régis erroneously held that "the object present to the mind when we contemplate extension is extension itself or matter . . . from which one cannot avoid the excesses of Spinoza who pretended that the substance of the universe was not different from that of God and that all the changes occurring in bodies and minds were only different modifications of matter; or at least one says like Régis that substances have always been produced because one sees that the object present to the mind is inseparable from it and that it has always been and always will be" (*La vraye*, p. 87). Like Malebranche, Lelevel held that the infinite, immutable object present to the mind is God. Lelevel may in fact have been repeating what had been at least suggested by Malebranche in the *Méditations chrétiennes*; this is how Iorio interprets *Oeuvres*, 10:99–101 (*Dialogue*, p. 20).

out which they cannot be conceived." Objects of the senses may be particular and locally extended, but the attribute of extension[126] is itself unextended and is the object of the pure understanding.[127] And surely Mairan is correct in this. Malebranche repeatedly draws the inference that apart from intelligible extension individual things as such are inconceivable just because they are particulars; strictly speaking, then, they should be called modes of that extension.[128] The inference that Mairan draws for theology is devastating. It is a dilemma faced repeatedly by those who have considered extension infinite: If intelligible extension is an attribute of God, "then all the universe and all bodies are but modifications of one of the divine attributes, or are but God modified in a certain way insofar as He is extended; which is the pure doctrine of the author. If extension does not appertain to God, then there is something that is not God and that does not constitute this essence which exists necessarily, is infinite, eternal, indivisible, etc."[129] What is to be made of all this?

Malebranche begins in the *Search* (3.2.8.2; 244) with what looks like the Cartesian view. In discussing the essence of matter he apparently argues from a substance ontology according to which everything is either a substance or a mode: Since extension in matter can be conceived by itself, extension is a substance.[130] "But since matter, because it is but a single being, is not composed of several beings—as is man, who is composed of body and mind—matter clearly is nothing other than extension" (3.2.8.2; 246). But nowhere in the *Search* is to be found the view of motion as the individuator of bodies; in fact, in a crucial text Malebranche seems to make motion extraneous to bodies as such.[131] Presumably, just as it is at least metaphysically possible for there to be a mind without volition, so there might be a body without motion. In the *Dialogues* there is an argument from which Malebranche concludes that "only through the variety in the motion and rest of the parts of matter is there produced that variety of different shapes or bodies that we admire in the world."[132] But the argument is obscure[133] and the context is a discussion of substantial forms

---

[126] Spinoza, *Ethics* 1 def. 4: "By attribute I understand what the intellect perceives of a substance, as constituting its essence."

[127] November 9, 1713; *Oeuvres*, 19:860–61.

[128] September 6, 1714; *Oeuvres*, 19:909: "a substance [i.e., an alleged individual] cannot be conceived without that which constitutes it as substance [i.e., extension]."

[129] Ibid., p. 862; see also May 6, 1714; *Oeuvres*, 19:878.

[130] Actually, Malebranche calls it a being (*un être*). Elsewhere he uses the substance language; *Dialogues*; *Oeuvres*, 12–13:34.

[131] Just as the capacity for receiving two kinds of shape and configuration, gross shape and the array of parts that make a thing the kind it is, stands to the capacity for receiving two kinds of ideas, pure perceptions that do not affect it and sensations that sensibly modify it (*Search* 1.1.2; 2).

[132] *Oeuvres*, 12–13:240.

[133] une étendue indéfinie sans mouvement, sans changement de rapport de distance entre ses parties, ce n'est donc qu'une grande masse de matiere informe. Que le mouvement se mette à cette masse, & en meuve les parties en une infinité de façons, voila donc une infinité de differens corps. Car, prenez garde, il est impossible que toutes les parties de cette étendue changent également de

where the aim is to show how motion of insensible parts can explain what appear to be essential differences between bodies. That is, the concern is qualitative not numerical difference. The same may be true of the description in his letter to Mairan of the "created extension I call material, namely, that of which the world is composed, and which without motion (which is the cause of these different shapes) would be only a formless mass."[134] If anything, it would seem that motion, or at least mobility, is a *result* of shape rather than a condition for it. Replying in the *Elucidations* (10, 626) to the objection that since nothing in God is really shaped or in motion, the shaped and moving material world cannot be represented to us by divine ideas, Malebranche distinguishes between material shape and motion, and intelligible shape and motion: "nothing in God is really shaped and thereby capable of motion, but . . . there are in God figures that are intelligible and consequently, intelligibly mobile." It follows, I take it, that material things are mobile because they are shaped and not conversely.

The difficulty in all this, it seems to me, is that Malebranche wants to individuate real substances but has the apparatus to individuate only representations of them (i.e., what on Descartes's scheme are the things themselves, which exist only phenomenally). For the Spinozist Mairan, individual shaped things are modifications of the attribute extension, and the difference between extension as an attribute and bodies as modes of that attribute is a distinction of reason. It is the difference between something conceived in itself and the same thing conceived through another. It is the exact analogue to Malebranche's distinction between the divine essence as it is in itself and as it is participatable in by finite things. As Mairan puts it, the individual material things that Malebranche distinguishes are so many *abstractions*.[135] That is, it is Malebranche, not Spinoza who confuses things with the ideas of them.

For his part Malebranche insists that he can "conceive, imagine, sense by itself a cubic foot of extension, without thinking of anything else. Therefore this extension [i.e., presumably, the cubic foot of extension] is the substance and its cubic shape is its modification. This cubic foot is indeed a part of the larger extension, but it is not the modification of it."[136] A part of a thing, he says, for example, half of a sphere, is never taken for a modification of the

---

rapport de distance à l'égard de toutes les autres: car c'est à cause de cela qu'on ne peut concevoir que les parties de l'étendue se meuvent, qu'on y découvre une infinité de figures, ou de corps differens. (*Oeuvres*, 12–13:239).

[134] 12 June 12, 1714, *Oeuvres*, 19:884. The same reading can be given to *Search* 4.1.1; 265: "If, in creating the world, God had produced infinitely extended matter without impressing any motion on it, no body would have been different from any other . . . there would not have been the succession of forms and variety of bodies."

[135] May 6, 1714; *Oeuvres*, 19:875. Cf. Spinoza, *Ethics*, pt. 1 defs. 4, 5, prop. 10.

[136] December 5, 1713; *Oeuvres*, 19:865.

whole sphere.[137] Similarly with numbers, both numbering and numbered: Two is not a modification of four, nor two pistols of four pistols, but the half.[138] What is going on here? My thesis is that there is no coherent story to be told on behalf of Malebranche, whose efforts to individuate created things seem doomed. I shall conclude with three comments.

1. Malebranche introduces an infinite number of material substances, for no part of matter is conceptually without parts.[139] This we have seen in connection with Malebranche's criticism of Gassendi's account of cohesion. He also introduces an infinite number of modifications for each substance but one; for a modification is that which is inconceivable apart from that of which it is the modification, and the whole of which any substance is a part is inconceivable apart from its parts. Every substance but one will have an infinite number of modifications, for every substance is a member of an infinite number of wholes except for the substance that is all of extension, which will have no modifications. This line of argument exactly reverses the contention of Mairan. It also shows why the problem of cohesion is so acute when infinite divisibility is combined with the rejection of substantial forms. Substance remains substance in the face of division, or addition, as long as substantial form as evidenced by the organic unity of entelechial activity remains. With organic unity accounted for solely in mechanical terms, the ordinary concept of an individual is no longer relevant.

2. On the other hand, material extension seems to resemble nothing so much as Artistotelian prime matter. Consider: "In intelligible extension I conceive clearly an intelligible infinity, an infinity of intelligible parts, and I conceive that if created extension were only an unformed mass without motion, there would be an infinity of different parts from which there could be formed Paris, Rome, cubes, spheres, which would all be substances of that infinite substance and all of the same attribute, i.e. all extended and of the same nature, all substances of varying size."[140] This, as we shall see, is not unlike Newton's view of the void in which God creates material things by making parts of already differentiated space impenetrable.

3. Mairan raises the issue of individuation in reply to F. Lamy who had claimed that Spinoza was guilty of confusing diversity (*diversité*) with difference (*distinction*).[141] It is just this distinction that Mairan will not allow as a *real*

---

[137] June 12, 1714; *Oeuvres*, 19:885. Also, September 6, 1714; *Oeuvres*, 20:909.

[138] December 5, 1713; *Oeuvres*, 19:865.

[139] June 12, 1714; *Oeuvres*, 19:885. "A cubic foot [of extension] is a substance, or rather an infinity of substances."

[140] June 12, 1714; *Oeuvres*, 19:886. See also *Dialogues*; *Oeuvres*, 12–13:239: "Experience teaches us that in all bodies there is a common subject because they are made from one another." The difference between bodies, he then explains, is not a substantial form, but their configuration of insensible parts. Again, the problem is not numerical but qualitative diversity.

[141] *Le nouvel athéisme*, p. 270.

distinction: "the being or existence of substances is distinguished from their essence only by abstraction, only in the mind."[142] The upshot is that no two things that are really distinct can have the same essence. And here we arrive at the heart of the matter, for Malebranche uses existence itself to distinguish otherwise identical things.[143] It is a brute fact that material things exist. It is a fact for which there is no sufficient reason since it depends entirely on the indifferent will of God. This too is why it can be finite. Mairan had argued following Spinoza that extension must be infinite since to be limited by nothing is not to be limited, and it cannot be limited either by something of the same kind, which would only extend it and not limit it, or by something of another kind, which would still leave extension as such without limit.[144] Malebranche responds to this conceptual version of Archytas's argument by denying the connection of an individual with anything else: "I can conceive ball A and it can exist by itself . . . this is not to say that the ball is infinite but what would limit it? Nothing. To limit it nothing is required; it is enough that it be such as it is. The roundness of the ball belongs to the ball and does not depend on those that surround it."[145] Individuals on this scheme look like bare particulars, which of course are unconnected with anything else.[146] This, however, prohibits Malebranche from saying both that shape is a modification of individual things, and that shape is nothing but that thing existing in a certain way.[147] For, given these two claims, a thing just would not be the same without its shape. The dilemma is released only by construing shape as a modification of extension generally, but this leads back to the charge of Spinozism.

Malebranche thus emerges as the Cartesian epitome of views that are to be associated with the seventeenth-century gods. A crude catalogue of his contrasts with the seventeenth-century giants will be useful as a summary: realism on universals (versus nominalism), a tendency at least toward idealism (versus realism), a similar tendency toward monism (versus pluralism), necessitarianism (versus tychism), plenism (versus atoms and the void), the rationalist's emphasis on reason and the a priori (versus the empiricist's emphasis on experience and the a posteriori, absolutism (versus relativism), enthusiasm (versus toleration). We may now turn, with much greater philosophical and historical precision, to Malebranche's contrast with Locke on representation. This was the issue, as we have seen, that lay at the core of Gassendi's critique of Descartes.

[142] May 6, 1714; *Oeuvres*, 19:874.

[143] June 12, 1714; *Oeuvres*, 19:886.

[144] August 26, 1714; *Oeuvres*, 19:897–98.

[145] September 6, 1714; *Oeuvres*, 19:909.

[146] I take this to be the thrust of Rodis-Lewis's interpretation of Malebranche's position, which she takes to be "profoundly Cartesian." "The individuality of extension is imperfect and contingent, and the principle of the unity and differentiation of individual bodies is appropriately sought in the concrete modalities of matter's existence" (p. 51).

[147] *Search* 3.2.8.2; 244; *Dialogues, Oeuvres*, 12–13:34, and many other places.

CHAPTER V

Ideas and Representation

THE SEVENTEENTH CENTURY witnessed the new *way* of ideas and the way of new *ideas*. That is, both a certain analysis of knowledge and what it was that was thought known were regarded as having first seen the light of day. The new ideas comprised primarily the central theses of the New Science to which nearly everyone—including erstwhile Aristotelians—sought to accede.[1] As an account of how these theses might be known, however, not everyone was on the same new way of ideas, and the divergence of paths on this issue is as philosophically important as any other.

§15 TWO PATTERNS OF IDEAS

There are two general patterns to be found among theories of ideas in the seventeenth century. One pattern is based on the conception of an idea as a particular—typically a material particular. On the other pattern an idea is a universal, whether of the "extreme" Platonist sort, or of the Aristotelian "moderate" sort, and is thus not material. The distinction between these patterns reflects all the most fundamental philosophical differences of the century. But it is not the distinction between representationalism and direct realism. Both of these views are to be found among theories in both patterns, though on the first pattern direct realism is generally to be found only to the extent that ideas are regarded as immaterial, that is, only to the extent it verged toward idealism as with Berkeley. Here I wish to sort out the two patterns, mainly with respect to Locke and Malebranche, both of whom advance representationalist theories. It will be helpful first to distinguish Locke on this question from Descartes's view, at least as Arnauld conceived of that view.

As we have seen, the fulcrum of the debate between Malebranche and Arnauld was the issue of whether ideas were modifications of the mind. On this issue alone it would seem that Locke must side with Malebranche because of the criticism he makes of Malebranche's conception of sensations (as opposed

---

[1] As we have seen in discussing the eclecticism of Launay, however, not everyone thought that the New Science was at all novel. Indeed, Cudworth thought the "Atomical Philosophy to have been antienter than the *Trojan* War" and traced it to Moses (*Morality*, pp. 55–57; *System*, chap. 1, secs. 9–18). But those who were the most successful practitioners of the New Science generally held the view that it really was something new under the sun, and with the success of one went the success of the other.

to ideas) as modifications of the mind. "How," he asks, "can the same unextended indivisible substance have different, nay inconsistent and opposite (as those of white and black must be) modifications at the same time? Or must we suppose distinct parts in an indivisible substance, one for black, another for white, and another for red ideas, and so on of the rest of the infinite sensations which we have in sorts of degrees."[2] Locke here assumes that whatever is in the mind in any way as a modification of it actually qualifies the mind. In Cartesian terminology, what is objectively in the mind is also formally in it; in the Scholastic terminology that Descartes also uses, what is immaterially in the mind is also materially in it. Now, this may be an obviously unfair assumption on Locke's part, as Leibniz was to point out. What is inconsistent in a thing is not inconsistent in the representation of it. At a minimum, however, Locke's assumption suggests very strongly that he cannot hold Arnauld's view of ideas. Furthermore, in his long and detailed criticism of Malebranche's vision of all things in God, nowhere does Locke criticize his definition of idea as an object of thought or, as we shall see, his representationalist theory; nor does he ever assert direct realism. Instead what we find is the complaint, among others, against Malebranche's conception of the immaterial existence of material things. To say as Malebranche does that material things are in God "after a spiritual manner" is something that Locke cannot comprehend. Presumably what is true of such presence in God is true of it in the human mind as well. For had Locke been an advocate of Arnauld's view of ideas, he ought at this point to have argued for that account of immaterial presence as appropriate. But Locke instead finds no meaning in the expression. "This and the like are ways of speaking which our vanity has found out to cover, not remove, our ignorance."[3] Locke's rejection of any such account seems clear: "I understand not what it is to contain a material thing spiritually."[4]

The reason such a view is unintelligible to Locke is that it requires an ontology he regards as fundamentally incompatible with his nominalism. Perhaps nowhere is this clearer than in his reaction to the Aristotelian John Sergeant's theory of ideas, which, like Arnauld's theory, requires things capable of two kinds of existence insofar as they are real and are objects of thought. Sergeant regarded himself as an opponent of the Cartesian theory of ideas, which he took to be representationalist. Yet it seems to me that aside from an alteration of terminology, the only significant differences between his theory and the Cartesian are (1) his doctrine of material species and (2) his clearer assertion of mind-body interaction. The crucial agreement between them is that in perceiving a mind-independent object, the mind is not aware of a *tertium quid*, as it is for the representationalist, but of that object. That object, insofar as

---

[2] *Examination of . . . Malebranche*, par. 39.
[3] Ibid., par. 23.
[4] Ibid., par.45.

it is in the mind, which Arnauld calls an idea, Sergeant calls a notion or a meaning; but for both, what is in the mind and what is external to it as its object are numerically identical: "The same *Ens* or Thing may have diverse *Manners* of Existing; one Corporeal, the other Intellectual or Spiritual."[5]

Locke's view, as I shall try to show, is that ideas and the objects they represent are numerically different. This means that Locke must reject the above theory of ideas. First, Locke rejects Sergeant's view "that a [perfectly] like is the same."[6] The issue is not the identity of indiscernibles, it seems to me, but universals. For the nominalist Locke, the only sameness is in the *numerical* sameness or identity of individuals. Put another way, he rejects the *qualitative* sameness or identity of individuals, for example, of the mind and its object, or the numerical identity of their qualities. This leads to a second objection from Locke. He claims, as he had against Malebranche, not to understand what it is for "a material thing to exist spiritually."[7] If there is nothing identical in different individuals, a fortiori nothing exists both "Intellectual(ly) or Spiritual(ly)" and "Corporeal(ly)," both in the mind and out of it, and thus he must reject Sergeant's (conceptual) distinction between meaning and object, the Cartesian distinction between objective and formal existence, and the Aristotelian Scholastic distinction between virtual (immaterial) and actual (material) exemplification.[8]

For Sergeant, "a Notion is the very thing it self existing in my understanding,"[9] and if it were but an image of the thing, we would then be condemned to skepticism. The claim of Aristotelians to "solid philosophy," and to avoiding skepticism, hinges on this point. "That our Notions, or (as the moderns have

---

[5] *Method*, p. 31.

[6] Locke's *Notes* on Sergeant; quoted by Yolton, *John Locke*, p. 109.

[7] Ibid.

[8] Yolton has developed just the opposite thesis, namely, that Locke's theory of ideas must be read as incorporating this sort of distinction, that ideas are acts and not objects of awareness, and that therefore Locke is not a representationalist in the usual sense. The most relevant of his publications are *John Locke and the Way of Ideas*, chap. 3, sec. 3; *Locke and the Compass of Human Understanding*, chap. 5: "Ideas and Knowledge in Seventeenth-Century Philosophy"; *The Locke Reader: Selections from the Works of John Locke with a General Introduction and Commentary*. Also of interest are his review of François Duchesneau, *L'empirisme de Locke*; "On Being Present to the Mind: A Sketch for the History of an Idea"; "As in a Looking-Glass: Perceptual Acquaintance in Eighteenth-Century Britain." See also, G. A. J. Rogers, who also tries to make Locke out to be a Cartesian on this topic: "Certainly the most important new ingredient in Locke's thinking which is not to be found in Boyle's work is Cartesian in origin. This was the notion of an idea" ("Boyle, Locke and Reason," p. 216). A more thorough treatment of the Locke-Boyle connection on this topic is to be found in J. J. McIntosh. Michael Ayers has argued, however, that Yolton's thesis must be significantly modified because of his failure to appreciate Locke's imagist conception of an idea. ("Are Locke's 'Ideas' Images?" See below.)

[9] *Solid philosophy*, p. 22. See also Digby: "What then can we imagine, but that the very nature of a thing apprehended, is truly in the man, who doth apprehend it? And that to apprehend aught, is to have the nature of that thing within ones self? And that man, by apprehending, doth become the thing apprehended; not by a change of his nature onto it, but by assumption of it unto his?" (*Two*

taken Toy to call them) Ideas, are the very Natures of the Things in our Understanding imprinted by Outward Objects; *without which no Stability of those Notions or Ideas can be, with Evidence, asserted; nor any Solid Knowledge possibly be had of our* Predictions; *nor the true Ground of* Truth *or* Falsehood *be understood; nor consequently, can there be any Firmness in* our Judgements *or* Discourse."[10]

Sergeant gives an argument that shows why he thinks the view that ideas are different from what they represent leads to skepticism. It comes to the sophomore's objection, directed against the Gassendist conception of an idea. "That these *Notions* are the very *Natures* of the Thing, or the *thing* itself existing in us *intellectually*, and not a bare *Idea* or Similitude of it, appears hence evidently, that when we say interiorly, or judge *A Stone is hard*, we do not intend to affirm, That the *Likeness* or *Idea* of a Stone is *hard*, but the very *Stone itself*. And were it not so, the Proposition would be *false*; (for the Similitude of a Stone in our *Mind* is *not* Hard,) whereas yet we are well assur'd that Proposition is *True*."[11] In the margin of his copy of Sergeant's book, Locke wrote: "The Idea then of a stone in our mind is not hard, but the notion of a stone in our mind is hard."[12] Locke no doubt intended to expose an absurdity in Sergeant's view or his reasoning for it; but what Locke wrote of the notion of a stone is true for Sergeant, with the qualification, as it were, that it is *intellectually* hard. For Locke nothing is intellectually hard because he held the Gassendist theory of ideas. Things can be only materially hard, which is to say, as Sergeant had charged, that ideas are material.

Locke seems to take over Gassendi's language in his most direct definition of 'idea': "It being that Term which, I think, serves best to stand for whatsoever is the Object of the Understanding when a Man thinks, I have used it to express whatever is meant by *Phantasm, Notion, Species*, or whatever it is, which the Mind can be employ'd about in thinking."[13] Moreover, he means by an idea what Gassendi does.

First, an idea is an *object* of awareness, that is, the *id quod intelligitur* rather than the *id quo intelligitur*: "that which his Mind is employ'd about whilst thinking, being the *Ideas*, that are there";[14] "I see no Reason, therefore, to

---

treatises, p. 356). Digby tries to say that those who take ideas to be images also hold this view. But his argument for this is that a thing like another in every way is the same, that is, "the thing it self." (p. 357). This in so many words is the thesis that the nominalist Locke denies when he denies that a perfectly like is the same. See above.

[10] Preface unpaginated.

[11] *Method*, p. 2. Sergeant contrasts these notions, which are *intellectual* things expressed by definitions, with ideas, which are corporeal phantasms or resemblances, corresponding part for part with what they resemble (pp.23–24).

[12] Transcribed from the text in Locke's library housed by the Bodleian.

[13] *Essay* 1.1.8; 47.

[14] 2.1.1; 104; see also, 2.1.3–4; 2.1.5.

believe, that the *Soul thinks before the Senses have furnish'd it with Ideas* to think on."[15]

Second, ideas are images. Locke repeatedly refers to ideas as pictures,[16] resemblances,[17] and, using Gassendi's term, images.[18] In an earlier chapter I tried to show that these two features are of a piece and together form the linchpin of Gassendi's anti-Cartesian polemic. I want now to show how Locke engages this polemic,[19] construing ideas in the fashion of Bernier, as material. As to the materiality of ideas, Locke at one point seems to be a skeptic on this question. He argues that we cannot long think of a single thing because our ideas cannot long be kept before the mind; for this relatively rapid succession of ideas he can give us no other proof than experience, "not knowing how the *Ideas* of our Minds are framed, of what Materials they are made, whence they have their Light, and how they come to made their Appearances" (2.14.13; 186). Locke's ignorance, however, is not with respect to the materiality of ideas, but to their mechanistic explanation, which assumes they are material. The thesis I wish to argue is that an idea for Locke is a *material thing (or process of it) of which we are aware*. My thesis is silent on the status of the awareness—an issue that has genereated an enormous literature[20] and to which we shall return under the rubric of the bestial soul in chapter 6. Nor am I unaware that in arguing this case I am addressing an issue that has elicited a no less enormous literature of refined textual analysis,[21] and that it is an issue with respect to

---

[15] 2.1.20; 116; see also, 4.4.3; 4.2.15; 4.2.1; 4.3.6; 2.8.2; 2.8.8.

[16] See, e.g., 3.3.7. An unpublished suggestion from Graham Solomon is that Locke may here mean ideas to be like pictures only in that they uniquely pick out some individual. But, see also 2.24.1; 4.11.1–2; 2.11.17.

[17] 2.11.17; 2.8.16; 2.8.7.

[18] 2.1.15. Fred S. and Emily Michael have recently claimed that ideas are said to be images in the drafts but not in the *Essay* ("Theory," p. 395. But see 2.8.16; 2.14.9; 2.8.7; 2.1.25. A strong defense of the imagist interpretation of Locke is to be found in Michael Ayers, "Are Locke's 'Ideas' Images?" Significantly, Ayers sees Locke's imagist account of number, for example, as "self-evidently a rebuttal of the Cartesian distinction between imagination and intellect" (pp. 9–10). Locke as an imagist is "a member of a highly respectable party consciously opposed to Descartes. Indeed, given its various connections in metaphysics and epistemology, the opposition between 'imagism' and 'intellectualism' might well be regarded as the most fundamental conflict in 17th-century philosophy, at least among proponents of the 'New Philosophy.'" (p. 25). See also Hall, "'Idea,'" pp. 21–22. On grounds very hard to understand, Ayers's account has been criticized by Hinckfuss, who accepts an adverbial interpretation. See esp. pp. 100–101, 105.

[19] It is worth noting with regard to this connection that as for Gassendi, so for Locke, ideas are neither true nor false; a judgment of affirmation or denial must be made before there results a proposition, which bears the truth value. The curious contrast between ideas and propositions (rather than between ideas and judgments, or between words and propositions) also follows Gassendi.

[20] One strand of this literature traces to Wilson's "Superadded Powers." See especially E. McCann, who argues that Locke is a consistent mechanist despite his claims about the possibility of thoughts being superadded to matter.

[21] For an excellent summary of the competing views, see Squadrito, whose "Ontological Status" begins, "No term or theory in the *Essay* has been more criticized and discussed than the term idea

which Locke himself professed no interest. When Norris criticized him for failing to give an account of the nature of ideas,[22] Locke repeated what he had said in the *Essay*, that he was not going to "meddle with the Physical Consideration of the Mind; or trouble [himself] to examine wherein its Essence consists, or by what motions of our spirits or Alterations of our Bodies, we come to have any Sensation by our Organs, or any *Ideas* in our Understandings; and whether those *Ideas* do in their Formation, any, or all of them, depend on Matter, or no. These are Speculations, which, however curious and entertaining, I shall decline, as lying out of my Way, in the Design I am now upon" (1.1.2; 43). My apology for my own meddling is that it would be extraordinary if Locke's position on ideas did not assume some ontology, or if that ontology did not intrude upon his text in important ways. As for the debates in the literature on the topic, I can only suggest that a positive contribution at this stage is most likely to be found with a more global approach such as the one I am suggesting. The best argument is with respect to the whole *Essay*, not a few lines from it.

The long anti-Cartesian argument of the first chapter of book 2 is brought to a head with the question of when a man begins to have any ideas, to which the true answer according to Locke is, when he first has any sensations. "For since there appear not be any *Ideas* in the Mind, before the Senses have conveyed any in, I conceive that *Ideas* in the Understanding, are coeval with *Sensation*; which is such an Impression or Motion, made in some part of the Body, as produces some Perception in the Understanding" (2.1.23; 117). At this point Coste added a sentence of his own (which presumably Locke endorsed in particular since it appeared in the fifth edition of the *Essay*[23]): " 'Tis about these Impressions made on our Senses by outward Objects, that the Mind seems first to employ it self in such Operations as we call *Perception, Remembering, Consideration, Reasoning*, etc." The view seems to be that an object can mechanically cause a change in our body which, if it is strong enough to attract our attention, is perceived as an idea. If anything, the view is clearer in the first three editions: "Sensation . . . is such an Impression or Motion . . . as makes it [i.e., the impression or motion] be taken notice of." That is, to produce a perception is to make a bodily state be taken notice of.

The state, or change in state, is called an impression, language that ulti-

---

and Locke's theory of ideas." Her own thesis in that paper is that the ontological status of ideas cannot be known because we do not know real essences, although she has a reservation about this since for Locke a substance need not be "like" its modes with respect to materiality or immateriality. Later, in "Substance," she argues that for Locke ideas are, with the highest probability, immaterial modes.

[22] Acworth, "Locke's First Reply," p. 10.

[23] Pierre Coste (1668–1747) published a French translation of the *Essay* in 1700 (2d. ed. 1729). Fraser gives the gist of this story: the translation was "prepared at Oates under Locke's eye. 'The author being present,' says Le Clerc, 'he corrected several places in the original, that he might make them more plain.' Coste was Locke's amanuensis, and lived with him at Oates for some years till [Locke's] death" (*Locke's Essay*), 1:24, n. 2).

mately derives from Aristotle's simile of the wax's impression of the signet. For Aristotle, we do not literally have the impression of the signet in sensation, otherwise we would become a signet in perceiving one. We have it, not materially (literally), but immaterially (cognitively). (How the wax literally has the impression of the signet without becoming one shows how difficult the question is even of what a literal impression is, for the impression would seem to be something more than a mere effect.) For Locke, a sense impression is more literal in that it is at least a physical change. "The Sensation of Heat and Cold, [is] nothing but the increase or diminution of the motion of the minute Parts of our Bodies, caused by the Corpuscles of any other Body" (2.8.21; 139).[24] Except for this claim it might have been thought that ideas could be other *bodies* ingested into ours. But as we shall see, Locke elsewhere explicitly rejects simulacra and sensible species views, and more generally any substantival view. In reply to Norris he said, "Ideas may be real beings, though not substances; as motion is a real being, though not a substance." One reading of 'as' in this sentence is 'for instance'; in view of the above, perhaps Locke's meaning is 'because,' that is, ideas are motions, hence real, but not substantival. Locke continues, however: "and it seems probable that, in us, ideas *depend on*, and are in some way or other the effect of motion; since they are so fleeting, it being, as I have elsewhere observed, so hard and almost impossible to keep in our minds the same unvaried idea long together, unless when the object that produces it is present to the senses; from which the same motion that first produced it, being continued, the idea itself may continue."[25] This seems to make the motion the *cause* of an idea, which indeed it is, for the object cannot cause an idea of itself except by motion. But while this makes the ultimate cause of an idea different from the idea, this is not to say that the idea is not a motion, for what else could a motion cause? So even here Locke does not rule out that an idea is a motion (although it may yet be an idea only insofar as it is perceived). The materiality of the idea, that is, what it is that is perceived, seems clear as well from an objection he directs against Malebranche, whose ideas cannot represent things, according to Locke, who cannot see how a spiritual entity "can represent to the mind an extended figure."[26] If material things are extended and are represented by ideas, those ideas must be material.[27]

The same distinction between a mere impression and a perceived impression must be invoked to make sense of what Locke says at the outset of the eighth chapter of book 2, which contains his celebrated primary-secondary quality

---

[24] Locke uses this supposition to explain how one hand (with a greater degree of motion) can feel as cold the same water that the other hand feels as warm.

[25] *Remarks*, par. 17, p. 469.

[26] *Exam.*, par. 18; *Works*, 9:219.

[27] A plausible source for this objection would have been Foucher's skeptical attack on Malebranche, which Locke will have found congenial and with which he would have been familiar. Locke's library contained the relevant works. See Harrison and Laslett, *Library*.

distinction. The context for the distinction is an effort to show that all ideas are real and positive, even those that may be caused by a privation. As part of his argument he says that "whatsoever is so constituted in Nature, as to be able, by affecting our senses, to cause any perception in the Mind, doth thereby produce in the Understanding a simple *Idea*; which . . . when it comes to be taken notice of, by our discerning Faculty, it is by the mind looked on and considered there, to be a real *positive Idea* in the Understanding"[30] (2.8.1; 132). The latter part of this remark suggests that there are ideas previous to their being noticed; but unless Locke contradicts what he repeats so often, against innate ideas for example, that to have an idea is to be conscious of it, causing a perception and producing an idea must be read as the same process. And to produce an idea is to cause a perception of an impression, as is clear from 2.9.4, which distinguishes between ideas, of which there must be an awareness, and an impression, of which there need not be. An object may produce an otherwise sufficient impulse on our organ of sensation and yet a perception might not occur because the mind, occupied with something else, may take no notice of this impression. Lost in thought I fail to *hear* the sound of the bell that would otherwise summon me to dinner.[28]

This conception of an idea might help explicate a striking analogy that Locke seems to be fond of. "Man's Power and its way of Operation [are] . . . much-what the same in the Material and Intellectual World. For the materials in both being such as he has no power over, either to make or to destroy, all that Man can be is either to unite them together, or to set them by one another, or wholly separate them" (2.12.1; 163–64).[29] On my account Locke's ideas *are* material particles, and his simple-complex idea distinction might well be understood as the distinction between awareness of a particle and awareness of an assemblage of particles. It is difficult at this point to give more than the following very rough

[28] Thus the distinction for Locke between an impression and an idea may be precisely that drawn by Gassendi and Bernier between impressed and expressed species. See Duchesneau, *L'empirisme*, pp. 100–101. Also, if an idea is a perceived impression, then Yolton is correct (1) that there are no ideas apart from acts of perception, though not because they are identical, and (2) idea talk for Locke indicates something mental—cognition and cognitive presence—though this is not to say that Locke is a direct realist ("Ideas and Knowledge," pp. 160, 163). It is worth noting, finally, that Hume, who claimed (*Essay*, p. 2, n. 1) to restore the term 'idea' from Locke's perversion of it, perverted the term 'impression' by using it, not for the physical condition for awareness ("the manner in which our lively perceptions are produced in the soul") but for something "for which there is no particular name either in English or any other language, that I know of." These are "the perceptions themselves," which he gets by collapsing the object-act distinction. Locke's impressions ("the manner") are for Hume *conjunctions* among "impressions."

[29] The context is the simple-complex idea distinction. The analogy is also used, to the same purpose, at 2.2.2; 120: "The Dominion of Man, in this little World of his own Understanding, being muchwhat the same as it is in the great World of visible things; wherein his Power, however managed by Art and Skill, works no farther, than to compound and divide the Materials, that are made to his Hand; but can do nothing towards the making the least Particle of new Matter, or destroying one Atome of what is already in Being."

characterization. The simple-complex distinction is a passive-active distinction, and, as I shall argue at length below, the solidity of a particle is the one idea
with respect to which the mind is perfectly passive, with all its other ideas the
result of the perceived relations among rearranged particles.[30] Aside from its
obvious relevance to the issue of Locke's materialism, the principal significance of this conception of an idea is twofold: It indicates why Locke should
have held to a theory of ideas at all, and, as we shall see at the end of this
chapter, it indicates the significance of Locke's main objection to Malebranche's theory of perception.

§16   ARGUMENTS FOR REPRESENTATIONALISM

There are a number of arguments from the seventeenth century that have been
focused on by historians as arguments for representationalism. Perhaps most
prominent among them is the argument from relativity of sense perception. The
usual statement of the crucial premise in the argument is that what we perceive
varies under different conditions, from perceiver to perceiver and in the same
perceiver from one time to another. Thus, what one perceives as green one's
colorblind neighbor will see as gray and, when jaundiced (so the example
goes), one will see as yellow. The locus classicus of this premise is of course the
work of Sextus Empiricus. It has been exploited by many empiricists, including
Gassendi, whose favorite example was the color of a pigeon's neck, which
changes with its movement. When used in the service of representationalism,
however, the premise yields a bad argument, since it commits the sense-datum
fallacy. All that may be concluded from the relativity of sense perception is that
a thing x, which may or may not have a property F is perceived as if it had F,
only if certain conditions are satisfied; we may not conclude that there is
something or some number of things having the properties that appear under
those conditions. (Thus, the example above is a more acceptable statement than
the statement of the premise itself.) To conclude that there is something that has
the properties that appear to us, thus reifying appearances, is the sense-datum
fallacy committed by the representationalist who argues that those properties
are had by our ideas, which represent things insofar as they bear a resemblance
to the properties actually had by the things they represent. Another version of
the argument relies more obviously on the Principle of Exemplification: The
properties we perceive must be properties of something; but because of relativity they cannot be properties of a material thing, which would then have
contrary properties. These properties are thus ideas, which are properties of the
mind, and which represent the properties of things when they resemble them.

It is difficult to find clear instances of this argument—either the version that

---

[30] For Locke's *logical* doctrine, see Ayers, "Locke's Logical Atomism."

makes ideas things or the one that makes them qualities. Locke appeals to relativity of sense perception, but does so only to show either that things are not always as they appear[31] or to suggest an account of why they appear as they do.[32] Nowhere do I find him offering relativity as a reason why we can directly perceive only ideas and never the material things they represent. The appeal to relativity is found frequently enough among the Cartesians. They use it to argue not representationalism, however, but the *denial* of representationalism with respect to sensible qualities. Malebranche, for example, argues in the first book of the *Search* that the sense perception even of primary qualities of shape, size, and motion is relative and thus does not represent bodies as they are in themselves. Sensation at best reveals how bodies might affect us; they are pictures of ourselves if of anything. As far as anything beyond the mind is concerned they are nonintentional. The Cartesians are guilty of reifying appearances, if at all, only when they make sensible qualities modifications of the mind.[33]

A second argument for representationalism is based on scientific realism and goes as follows. The description of the world offered by the New Science in terms of shape, size, and motion (and whatever more or less than this) applies at most to only part of the world as we perceive it—in addition to being shaped, the world is perceived as colored and scented; thus, since the New Science tells us what materially is, or is real, what we perceive is nonmaterial. This argument is related in a number of ways to the argument from relativity of sense perception and like it involves the sense-datum fallacy by inviting us to reify appearances as nonmaterial representations or ideas. Once again Malebranche like the Cartesians uses the premises to argue, not representationalism, but the denial of representationalism with respect to sensations. For Locke, there are two additional reasons for avoiding this argument as an argument for representationalism. For one thing, it at best argues the so-called mixed view, according to which we are directly aware of the primary qualities of things and of ideas of secondary qualities. This interpretation of Locke once was in vogue,[34] but

---

[31] Thus his example of the porphyry (2.8.19).

[32] Thus his analysis of the apparent temperature of water. (2.8.21).

[33] Thus Norris: "sensible qualities have no real existence in Bodies. And yet 'tis as certain on the other hand, that they are not self-subsistent Beings, but must be conceiv'd to depend upon something else as their Subject; that is, they are not Substances, but modes or manners of Being. And since they are not Modifications of Bodies (which if our Ideas of them are true, are capable of no other than Figure and Motion) it follows, that they are indeed modifications of our Minds or *Sentiments*" (*Essay*, 2:250–51). On the other hand, sensations or sentiments are not modes of awareness for Norris in the typical Cartesian sense that they are ways of being aware. Rather they are (inner) *objects* of awareness; he distinguishes the perception of an idea from the perception of a sentiment: "The former being the Perception of some Intelligible Object, distinct from us, and the latter the inward feeling we have of how 'tis with ourselves, or of that particular state, or manner of being, which we are at any time in, sensible perception being not Sentiment itself, but that inward consciousness we have of a Sentiment" (2:212–13).

[34] Around the turn of the century among people like A. C. Fraser and Whitehead. I take it to have been defeated by Jackson ("Locke's Version"; "Locke's Distinction").

nowadays Locke's representationalism seems to be, if anything, the so-called pure version: In the perception of both kinds of qualities we are immediately aware of an idea. "A snow-ball," says Locke, "having the power to produce in us the *Ideas* of *White*, *Cold*, and *Round*, the Powers to produce those *Ideas* in us as they are in the snow-ball, I call *Qualities*" (2.8.4; 134). He in no way distinguishes here the first two ideas, or the (secondary) qualities causing them, from the third idea, or the (primary) quality causing it.

Furthermore, on the view that ideas are material states of which we are aware, an idea cannot be white. At least it cannot be irreducibly white, or white in any way in which the object it represents is not white. Both may be said to be white in the sense that both have a microscopic structure that is a causal condition for our perception of whiteness. (Locke can thus subscribe to a very literal version of a likeness principle governing the connection between ideas and what they represent.) But an idea is not white in the way in which a Cartesian sensation is white, that is, irreducibly and directly perceivable as such. Hence Locke cannot, and does not, appeal to the phenomenological discrepancy between what we perceive and what the New Science says exists in order to establish representationalism. For unlike the Cartesians he does not use the mind as the repository of sensible qualities. Another way to put this is that there is nothing inconsistent between Locke's position and an adverbial theory of sensible qualities: When I perceive the snowball as white I am appeared to whitely, but there is nothing that is white. (By not making sensible qualities modifications of the mind Locke even avoids the Cartesian reification of appearances and the problem it seems to generate of making the mind white when it perceives white.) But what is true of the perception of ideas is true also of the perception of the things they represent. As far as the argument from the New Science is concerned, my perception might as well be directly of them.

Whatever Locke's argument for representationalism, then, it is not the sense-datum fallacy in the argument from the New Science version of it. It is worth noting, however, that when I am being appeared to whitely there is *something* that appears to me. *What* appears to me is not an appearance, namely, the whiteness, for there *are* no such things, but an idea. It is not the object that in veridical perception is represented by this object because, as Locke spends the most celebrated chapter of his *Essay* showing, we can have perceptions without there being this object. This gives a clue as to why ideas are needed at all.

A third argument for representationalism picks up the clue, but as a false lead. The argument from intentionality relies on the premise that all thought or awareness requires an object, a feature of awareness that philosophers especially since Brentano have made the criterion of the mental. Yet sometimes, as in dreams or hallucinations, we are aware of things which, as we ordinarily speak, do not exist. What we are aware of in these cases, the argument concludes, is an idea. Like the arguments above, however, this is a bad argument for representationalism. There are at least two (related) problems with it. First, like them, it reifies appearances: If I am being appeared to there must *be* something of which I am aware. Second, it confuses levels of discourse, or kinds of objects or senses of perception. The perception of an idea is part of the representationalist *analysis* of the perception of what ideas represent, which, in the case of dreams and hallucinations, is nothing at all. The Principle of Intentionality is a principle about the latter kind of perception and cannot be satisfied by the object of the former kind of perception.[35] Finally, even if it were not open to these objections, the argument would fail to establish representationalism, which is the view after all that in *veridical* perception we are immediately aware of something that takes the place of things we are ordinarily said to be aware of.

Once again one looks in vain for signs of this argument cited on behalf of representationalism. To be sure, Malebranche thinks (however confusedly) that his theory of ideas satisfies the Principle of Intentionality; but I have tried to show that this is a consequence or application of his theory and not an argument for it except by proof of the pudding, that is, the way in which for Locke relativity of sense perception is an argument for the primary-secondary quality distinction.[36] In both cases something is subsequently (thought to be) explained by making an assumption—the proof of the pudding is in the eating—but the principal reason for making the assumption in the first place lies elsewhere (in this example, with the corpuscular hypothesis for Locke and a theory of intelligibility for Malebranche). As for Locke, there is at most a *soupçon* of a concern with intentionality in the famous opening to book 2 of the *Essay*: "Every Man being conscious to himself, That he thinks, and that which his Mind is employ'd about whilst thinking, being the *Ideas* that are there, 'tis past doubt, that men have in their Minds several *Ideas*." But there is not the least suggestion here of any problem about nonveridical perception.

A fourth argument for representationalism, almost universally ignored by historians,[37] might be called the *causal argument*. The argument is that there must be a causal connection between the mind and what it knows; but there can be no action at a distance; hence the mind cannot perceive what is not present to it. What it perceives is something that is caused, ultimately, by the thing at a distance and which takes its place as the object of knowledge. To put it another way, if we could know things at a distance directly, there would be occult qualities. Newton was one who was drawing near this connection between Aristotelian theories of perception and gravitation when he turned over the possibility that sensation and planetary action at a distance might occur in the same medium.[38] As long as a causal connection between perceiver and per-

[35] See chap. 4, sec. 13 above.

[36] See chap. 6, sec. 20 below.

[37] A very important exception is Yolton. Since he does not regard Locke as a representationalist he does not focus on the argument in the *Essay*, but traces its later history in great detail. See esp. *Perceptual Acquaintance*, chap. 4.

[38] The General Scholium of the *Principles* at the very least poses "a certain most subtle Spirit

ceived is required, it would seem, representationalism is the only view of perception consistent with mechanism. There are (at least) two sources from which Locke and Malebranche might have gotten this argument. One is Cureau, the other, to which we shall eventually return, is Launay.

The first book of Cureau de La Chambre's *System of the Soul* deals with what he calls intellectual knowledge. The first of its two chapters treats of such knowledge in men and ends with a useful summary. (1) Knowing is an action and the understanding acts when it knows.[39] (2) To act the understanding must be united to its object and this object is the phantasm in the imagination. His previous discussion of this point is worth citing at length: "It must be noted that the objects the understanding needs to know are most often outside it; and as no action can be performed on a distant thing, either the understanding must approach them or they must approach it; the former is impossible because the understanding cannot leave the body to seek them. Thus necessarily the latter. But because no objects have the necessary motion to approach and join the powers of the soul, nature has provided for this with the images that leave those objects and represent them, and which, passing into the organs of the senses, are joined to the imagination; this faculty then acts on them and knows them, after which they are called phantasms"(pp. 6–7). (3) The phantasm is a necessary condition for knowledge, but it is not sufficient, for it cannot represent some things, like universality, which are known. (4–5) The images of things known in the true sense are immaterial and are formed on the model of the phantasms by the understanding, which in forming them becomes the things known. In his discussion of this operation, Cureau explicitly refers to the Aristotelian isomorphic account of knowing, which in view of the rest of the account is an anomaly. Petit of Montluçon complained in his *Letter* (p. 20) that even Cureau was a bit too much a partisan of Aristotle; this may well have been the passage he had in mind. The result in any case is "that we might say that the understanding is to some extent the creator of a new world and that particularly in this is it made in the image and likeness of God who is all things and who produces all things."[40] The understanding ascends gradually from the singular to the universal, "arriving finally at God who is the source and end of all [types of] knowledge" (p. 23).

---

which pervades and lies hid in all gross bodies; by the force and action of which Spirit the particles of bodies mutually attract one another at near distances and cohere, if contiguous; . . . and light is emitted, reflected, refracted . . ; and all sensation is excited" (p. 447). For the possible extension of this subtle spirit to the explanation of gravity at greater distances, see McMullin, *Newton*, pp. 94–101.

[39] His discussion of this point is without present interest: He says that things differ according to their operations and so in order that man may differ from the animals, knowledge must be an operation. Elsewhere he had explained that all things produce images, and some things like mirrors can receive them; but only knowing things produce images within themselves. Knowing is an immanent action (*Quelle est la connoissance des bestes*, p. 8). Presumably, the ability to produce an image from within is a condition for knowing those received from without.

[40] *Systeme*, p. 21.

The latter chapter of this first book of the *System of Soul* deals with the question of how knowledge is acquired by a soul separated from a body. Cureau begins with the observation that even when separated from the body the soul needs images of the things it knows; but without the body to provide the phantasms from which they are derived, or at least modeled on, there is a problem—the very problem theologians have discussed with respect to knowledge by angels. The first theory he mentions is that such beings "see [things] in the Divinity" (p. 29). Though many beings see many things in this way, he says, it does not fully explain angelic knowledge because angels deprived of the Beatific Vision still have knowledge. A second theory, attributed to Aquinas, has it that when He creates angels, God impresses certain general species or images in them. This theory leaves unexplained the knowledge of particulars, however, so Cureau considers a third theory, attributed to Scotus, that species are provided upon each occasion they are needed in order to know "the nature and particular existence of things" (p. 37). A final theory, attributed to Theophile Reynaud, attempts to combine the theories of Aquinas and Scotus: Angels both have innate general species and are provided with an additional one for each thing whose particular existence is known. The problem with this explanation, and therefore with the preceding one, according to Cureau, is that it makes God directly responsible for knowledge of particulars and demons, and that it does not account for knowledge of thoughts, which are not known by images. Cureau's own account, finally, seems to dispense with images altogether: "What prevents the understanding from being able to unite itself [*se . . . unir*] to corporeal objects is that it cannot leave [*sortir*] the body where it is contained to join [*joindre*] them; nor can they enter the head to unite themselves to it. . . . But when the soul is separated, it no longer has any obstacles preventing it from uniting itself to objects, for it is free to move toward them, to join them and to penetrate [*penetrer*] them; and with no need for species or phantasms, it changes and transforms itself into them" (p. 38). Species were needed in the first place only because the object known was at a distance; but a separated soul need not remain at a distance from its object. He says of this *experimental* mode of knowledge that it gets to the bottom of (individual) natures and thus is more perfect than that depending on species, for the senses give us only sensible accidents, which are like the outer covering (*l'escorse*) of things beyond which our notions are vague and confused, circuitously acquired, and often deceptive. Even for separated souls, however, the innate species is required in order to know the (general) essences of things "such as their relations with one another, universal notions and the practical knowledge derived from them" (pp. 39–40).

Malebranche possessed this work by Cureau[41] and it is clear that he drew on it in a number of ways.[42] For one thing, Cureau suggests, at least in outline,

---

[41] *Oeuvres*, 20:260–61.

[42] The Malebranche–Cureau connection was first made by Rodis-Lewis in her comments on a

both the vision of all things in God and the elements of Malebranche's longest argument for that theory. Recall the first theory Cureau considers of how separated souls can know, namely, that "they see things in the Divinity," a theory to which he himself at least partly subscribes. Consider, too, Cureau's conception of the soul arriving finally at the knowledge of God, "the source and end of all knowledge." In addition, each of the alternative theories of perception by default of which Malebranche argues for his theory of the vision in God is found in Cureau—most obviously the view that the soul produces its own ideas as a result of impressions made by things on the body, which is Cureau's own view, but also the views he rejects: that ideas are innate (Aquinas), caused by God as often as they are needed (Scotus), or caused by objects. Cureau also provides arguments for rejecting the views that Malebranche repeated (for example, since ideas are spiritual they could not be produced by a material thing, which is not proportioned to it) even against Cureau's own view (in order to form an idea the understanding would already need the idea as a model for itself, as would a painter in producing a picture). Most important in this regard, Cureau raises what for Malebranche is the Cartesian problem of how an immaterial mind can know a material object and does so in the terms in which Malebranche sought its solution. For it is clear that the ultimate source for Malebranche's alternatives to the vision in God, as well as for elements of the theory itself, is Scholastic angelology, particularly Suarez's discussion of the question of how angels can know,[43] to which Malebranche may well have been sent by his reading of Cureau.[44]

The most important point of contact between the two authors, however, is their view that material things cannot be known directly, but must be represented by ideas. They both hold this view for nominally the same reason:

---

paper by Desmond Connell, "Malebranche et la scolastique." Since then Connell has elaborated the connection in "Cureau de La Chambre, Source de Malebranche."

[43] This was the thesis of Connell's book, which provided the answer to the longest standing puzzle in Malebranche's scholarship. Connell's thesis still stands despite the revelation of the Cureau connection, which as Connell argues in his article, is insufficient to explain, inter alia, Malebranche's criticism of the innatist alternative and the vision in God as a vision of universal being. It might be noted that Malebranche also possessed a copy of Cureau's *Quelle est la connoissance des bestes* (published at the end of *Les characteres*, vol. 2, 1645; Malebranche possessed the 1658 Amsterdam edition, where it is also found, with consecutive pagination, at the end of vol. 2.). In this much earlier work Cureau had already raised the problem of knowledge by separated souls, connected it to angelological discussions, and attempted to solve it with a theory of innate species. See pp. 45–47 (1645), 573–75 (1658).

[44] At the outset of pt. 2, bk. 3 of the *Search*, Malebranche uses a long paragraph to discuss the issue of how it is that angels communicate (and, more important, can keep from communicating) their thoughts to one another. This topic appears rather as a clunker among the work's half-dozen most important pages. That Cureau is a source for Malebranche is argued by this since the topic, "which exercised the Schools," also appears in this context in his work (where nothing seems a clunker). See *Systeme*, pp. 43ff.

Material things are not present to the mind. The very language Malebranche uses to state this premise had been used by Cureau: The soul cannot leave the body to unite or join itself to corporeal objects. This is the notorious imagery employed at the outset of Malebranche's theory of ideas in the *Search After Truth*, imagery that as we argued above has earned the undeserved ridicule of critics since Arnauld. We are now in a better position to see both what Malebranche meant by the argument he expressed with this imagery and why Arnauld was misled by it.

§17 TWO VERSIONS OF THE CAUSAL ARGUMENT

The causal argument is open to two interpretations. The more literal interpretation construes the object as the *efficient* cause of our ideas. As an efficient cause acts only by collision on physical contact, the object must be physically present to the mind if it is to cause an awareness of itself. The same conditions for causal interaction between billiard balls apply to the causal connection that must obtain between the mind and its object. Because things are *spatially* at a distance from the mind they cannot immediately act on it and thus cannot be its immediate object. Thus, Locke argues: "the next thing to be consider'd, is how *Bodies* produce *Ideas* in us, and that is manifestly *by impulse*, the only way which we can conceive Bodies operate in. If then external Objects, be not united to our Minds, when they produce *Ideas* in it; . . . 'tis evident, that some motion must be thence continued by our Nerves, or animal Spirits, by some parts of our Bodies, to the Brains, or the seat of Sensation, there to *produce in our Minds the Particular Ideas we have of them*" (2.8.11–12; 135–36). [45] And later he argues: "For since the Things, the Mind contemplates, are none of them, besides it self, present to the Understanding, 'tis necessary that something else, as a Sign or Representation of the thing it considers, should be present to it: And these are *Ideas*" (4.21.4; 720–21). [46]

---

[45] The point of the chapter in which this expression of the argument occurs is to show how by assuming the mechanical hypothesis, an idea of the void, literally of nothing, is possible. As we shall see below, Reid later thought that Locke gave no argument for his representationalism but merely assumed it. Reid is right at least to the extent that Locke's argument is expressed (1) en passant (2) in an application of a theory that he *assumes* in dealing (3) with a *different* problem. When a position lies close to the core of a system, as this one does for Locke, it is difficult to find a clear expression of it, much less an argument for it. Matthews's suggestion that Locke's representational theory of perception was a "Wittgensteinian . . . 'picture' which 'held Locke captive,'" is right as far as it goes ("Locke," p. 16). My suggestion is that the picture is larger, or rather that the representationalism follows from a more basic ontological picture.

[46] Bayle epitomized an argument that others had used previously; he argued against the Toricelli barometric experiment as demonstrating the void: There must be something in the area vacated by the mercury because we can still see objects through it and "the void would prevent the action of objects on our eyes without which there would be no vision" (*Système abrégé*; *Oeuvres*, 320).

But there is also a more metaphorical interpretation of the argument according to which the worry is over *formal* causation, or, as I called it above with respect to the same problem as it occurs in *Meditations 6*, *structural* causation. The argument is that a material thing cannot inform the mind because a particular thing is as such unintelligible. Things are not spatially at a distance from the mind, because the mind though attached to a body is not at a distance in this sense from anything, for the mind is nowhere (thus the term 'nullibilism,' as the opponents of the view described it). The mind's object is ontologically and therefore cognitively at a distance from it. It is not "proportioned" to the mind, has no "relation" to it, as both Malebranche and Cureau put it. This is an additional reason why Platonism was found so congenial by many giving an ontological account of the New Science. The obvious reason that has been repeatedly noted by historians is Platonism's invitation to mathematize nature. Less obvious but no less important is the Platonist conception of material things as nothing more than individuals. Material things have no intelligible component; they do not have a form as a constituent as they do on the Aristotelian account. Their form is something that transcends the individual. Thus, in what became a slogan repeated again and again by the Cartesians, the shape of a thing is nothing more than that thing shaped in a certain way. Both the mathematization of nature and the conception of material things as by themselves unintelligible were points in principle acceptable to the non-Platonist, atomist conception of the New Science, whose account needed to differ only with respect to the *ground* for the mathematization of nature and the classification of unintelligible particulars into kinds. Here of course the difference is enormous, the former relying on real universals, the latter on concepts or names. In both cases, however, both the atomist literal interpretation of the causal argument and the Platonist metaphorical interpretation, if things could act directly on the mind without the intermediary of ideas the result would be that they have Aristotelian occult qualities. The Aristotelian account does involve ideas; but an idea is *the thing itself* insofar as it is in the mind. According to the literal interpretation of the argument, the thing itself cannot be in the mind because it is spatially at a distance from it; according to the metaphorical interpretation it cannot be in the mind because it is cognitively or ontologically at a distance from it. From both points of view, therefore, the Aristotelian accounts of the causation of an awareness and the causation of an unsupported object to fall involve the same mistake, namely, the sufficiency of individual objects. From the atomist perspective the individual object is insufficient because collision is required both for awareness of it, and for locomotion and thus for the explanation of any kind of change. From the Platonist perspective the individual is insufficient because a transcendent form is required for the same two reasons, namely, knowledge and explanation of change.

At least initially, Arnauld took Malebranche's claim in the literal sense that the soul is unable to leave the body in order to perceive objects directly. Arnauld was led to this interpretation by his inability to find an acceptable sense for Malebranche's notion of intelligible extension. Throughout their long polemic, Arnauld maintained that in distinguishing material and intelligible extension, Malebranche "had without realizing it insensibly passed from the school of Descartes to that of Gassendi."[47] The first mention of the Malebranche–Gassendi connection in this regard is in Arnauld's *Des vraies et des fausses idées*, where he attempts to rebut Malebranche's argument that intelligible extension is not a mode of the mind because we can think of it (as we cannot think of modes of the mind) without thinking of the mind. According to Arnauld, the same argument shows that intelligible extension is not in God either, since we can think of it without thinking of God: "For it is certain that the Epicureans and Gassendists do not think about God when they conceive the space in which their atoms stroll [*se promenent*] as an *infinite intelligible extension*."[48] In his *Defense* against Malebranche's *Reply*, Arnauld argued that Malebranche's intelligible extension was in fact the Gassendist space; both are necessary, immense, eternal, penetrable, and immobile as opposed to material extension, which is created, limited, temporal, impenetrable, and mobile. The only difference he sees is that the Gassendists do not say that their space is God.[49]

Arnauld also complained that despite Malebranche's claim that everything is either a being or a mode of being, his intelligible extension is neither—neither substance nor modification of substance. Now, it has been clear to all of Malebranche's commentators that the ontological status of ideas for him is a vexed question. That they are not modifications of the mind was the main thesis he tried interminably to argue against Arnauld as well as others like Foucher. As we have just seen above, he seems to have argued that they are not modes at all, and yet he also held that they are not substances.[50] I think Arnauld is right at least to this extent that Malebranche like the Gassendists was forced to expand or relinquish the substance ontology; that this by itself should have been problematic (aside from consistency with respect to the principle that everything is either a being, or a mode of one) is far from clear, however, given Descartes's own transmogrification of the substance ontology. Indeed, given his own apparent adherence to that ontology, as well as his refusal to make any distinction at all between material and intelligible extension, it is not clear just how Arnauld's own account might go *in Cartesian terms*. There is another indication of Arnauld's own problems here. Another damning agreement he points to between intelligible extension and Gassendist space is that, in both, shape and motion are imaginary in that they are picked out only by the imagination. What this

---

[47] *Ninth letter; Oeuvres*, 39:146–47.

[48] *Oeuvres*, 38:254.

[49] There was a lot of repetition in this long polemic. These points were repeated in the *Eighth Letter; Oeuvres*, 39:122–23.

[50] "But if it be said that an idea is not a substance, I would agree" (*Search*, p. 223).

means is that for Arnauld shape and motion are, by contrast, real—as they are, we might point out, for Gassendi as far as atoms are concerned. But they are not real for material things on Descartes's account as I have presented it. For once Malebranche's usual indignation at his treatment by Arnauld was justified when, "as an abbreviation," Arnauld proposed calling intelligible extension "Gassendist extension."[51]

The upshot, according to Arnauld in any case, is that with no defensible distinction between formal and intelligible extension, Malebranche makes God formally, that is, really extended when he places intelligible extension in Him.[52] This is a result of his literal interpretation of Malebranche's argument for representationalism. For Arnauld, real extension in God represents a *reductio* of Malebranche's position, since for him, as for Malebranche, there is no distinction between formal and material extension, which is to say that despite his protests to the contrary, Malebranche makes God material. The key move in this argument is to construe God as really extended, which (however successfully) Malebranche denies, but which is asserted by Cureau, the author who, ironically enough, points the way to the metaphorical interpretation of the key argument.

That Malebranche intended his argument in the metaphorical sense and that he did not retract or reinterpret his imagery as a result of Arnauld's ridicule I now take to be obvious. In addition, the Cureau connection removes a curious obstacle to this interpretation. Malebranche says quite frequently that ideas *affect* the mind to make it aware of them in a way that material things cannot affect it.[53] The word Malebranche uses is *toucher*, which means essentially what its cognate does in English. If the mind's object must *touch* it, that is, must make contact with it, then it seems that Malebranche is advancing the literal version of the argument, that he from a Cartesian point of view mistakenly construes the mind as extended, confuses both cognitive presence with local presence, and mental vision with corporeal vision—all as Arnauld had charged. But even this word is no objection to the metaphorical interpretation. In the course of his discussion of the connection between soul and body, where he says repeatedly that the soul affects (*touche*) the body, Cureau offers the following reflection: "There is no need to halt at the word affect [*toucher*], which seems to be said only of bodies. It is general to all things applied and joined [*sic*] to others, for one says that heat and cold affect our parts, that good and evil affect the soul, and when an angel applies and joins itself to some substance, the angel affects it in its own way [*a sa maniere*]; and this affecting is related and analogous to material and sensible affecting."[54]

---

[51] *Eighth Letter*; *Oeuvres*, 39:131.

[52] *Ninth Letter*; *Oeuvres*, 39:143–44.

[53] See Robinet, *Système*, pp. 259–72, for the most extensive treatment of this topic.

[54] *Système*, p. 361. Norris, however, specifically rejected the use of this term in one of his arguments that bodies cannot cause ideas: "Body can act only by Impulse, it can make an impulse

While both Cureau and Malebranche require a causal relation between the mind and its object (and while both are concerned with formal or structural causation rather than efficient), the direction of the relation differs. For Cureau the mind causes its own ideas, however problematically, forming them on the model of the phantasm and thus becoming the object known. This of course is the Aristotelian account of intentionality in terms of a shared form, which is anomalous here not just because it is Aristotelian (see Petit's complaint above) but because is not incompatible with action at a distance. If Cureau is an Aristotelian with respect to embodied soul's perception of ideas or separated soul's perception of material things, he might as well have been an Aristotelian with respect to the embodied soul's (direct) perception of material things. To put it another way, the Aristotelian account obviates the need for ideas of the sort that Cureau espouses. However that may be, Malebranche rejects the account in all its forms. When Arnauld advanced the Cartesian version of this theory according to which an idea is the thing itself existing in the mind, Malebranche claimed (as Locke was to later) not even to understand how a thing could exist in two different ways. Given his Platonism, the Cartesian *esse formale–esse objectiva* distinction that allows the same thing two different modes of existence makes no sense. In addition, Cureau's theory has the defect for Malebranche that it makes our cognition independent of God. Even if Cureau anticipates Malebranche's vision in God in certain respects, he violates the Augustinian dictum that man is not a light unto himself. Thus, he criticizes one of the alternatives to the vision that may be represented by Cureau's own theory. He argues that ideas are real beings different from material things and superior to them because spiritual. Thus, "When it is claimed that men have the power to form such ideas as please them, one runs the risk of claiming that men have the power of creating beings worthier and more perfect than the world God has created."[55] For the view that material things cannot be directly known because they cannot act on the mind Malebranche would have had to look elsewhere. I think it is obvious that Malebranche need have looked no farther than the Augustine at his elbow. An argument that he constantly repeats from the *Philosophia christiana* is that material things cannot act on the mind since a cause must be at least as perfect as its effect and they are less perfect than it. Cureau made Malebranche aware of a certain problem, provided him with the metaphors to describe it, and sent him to Scholastic sources for the structure of a solution. But the two constraints on the solution, that the mind be acted upon and that it be acted upon only by God, came from Augustine.

Reid was another who attributed the literal version of the argument to

---

only upon that which resists it. Spirit cannot resist Body, as being capable of existing in the same *ubi* with it; therefore Body cannot act upon spirit. . . . Besides, Body can act only on Body; for it can act only on what it *touches*, and it can touch nothing but Body" (*An Essay*, p. 223).]

[55] *Search* 3.2.3; 222.

Malebranche. Reid, who notoriously thought that everyone from Plato to Hume subscribed to representationalism, also thought that most of these authors, Locke in particular, just assumed it without argument. He notes several arguments from Norris (see below) but finds them lame, unconvincing, and incomprehensible. The only argument he takes seriously is the causal argument, which he finds is "hinted at by Malebranche, and by several other authors." He found the *same* argument more clearly expressed in Samuel Clarke's *Second Reply* to Leibniz: "The soul, without being present to the images perceived, could not possibly perceive them. A living substance can only there perceive, where it is present, either to the things themselves, (as the omnipresent God is to the whole universe,) or to the images of things, as the soul is in its proper *sensorium*."[56] The basis for the argument was the premise "which Clarke slightly mentions . . . that nothing can anymore act, or be acted upon when it is not present, than it can be where it is not." Reid also draws attention to this argument in Clarke's third *Reply* to Leibniz: "We are sure the soul cannot perceive what it is not present to, because nothing can act or be acted upon, where it is not."[57]

Reid himself rejected the argument that "when we perceive objects either they act upon us, or we act upon them." For Reid, an object does not act at all in so far as it is perceived. "To be perceived, is what logicians call an external denomination, which implies neither action nor quality in the object perceived."[58] He thinks people have been misled on this point, typically, by a false analogy between mind and body: "as a body is put in motion, by being acted

[56] Par. 4; cited by Reid, *Essays*; *Works*, 1:300–301.

[57] Ibid., p. 301. He also notes its queried status in Newton, and quotes its "more confident" expression in Porterfield: "How body acts upon mind, or mind upon body, I know not; but this I am very certain of, that nothing can act, or be acted upon, where it is not; and therefore our mind can never perceive anything but its own proper modifications, and the various states of the sensorium, to which it is present: so that it is not the external sun and moon which are in the heavens, which our mind perceives, but only their images or representation impressed upon the sensorium. How the soul of a seeing man sees these images, or how it receives those ideas, from such agitations in the sensorium, I know not; but I am sure it can never perceive the external bodies themselves, to which it is not present."

[58] In his note to this passage (Reid, *Essay*; *Works*, 2:970) Hamilton argued that here (and below) Reid showed that he is not original in his doctrine of perception, which was the doctrine of Alexander of Aphrodisias and the later nominalists (Ockham, Durandus, Gregory of Rimini, Biel, and others). Hamilton initially disbelieved "that an opinion which had again so completely fallen into oblivion, could have had any influence on the speculations of an author who was so little extensive in his reading." But the occurrence of 'external denomination' in the expression of Reid's doctrine convinced him that Reid had gotten it secondhand from an author whose work he did know. "This philosopher is Gassendi." Hamilton cites, *Opera*, 1:443; 2:373. Hamilton is wrong about one thing. In fact, Reid could have gotten the view from any number of authors. It is found, for example, in Descartes's *Reply to Objections* 1. But the apparent nominalist denial of any physical connection is disturbing—not because it is found prior to Reid, but because it is found among precisely those who should be *asserting* the connection. All I can suggest is the research project that the nominalists cited rejected only a Neo-Platonic, metaphorical connection.

upon by some other body; so we are apt to think the mind is made to perceive, by some impulse it receives from the object."[59] As for the mind acting on the object it perceives, "to perceive an object is one thing, to act upon it is another." To perceive an object produces no effect outside the mind; according to Reid it is what the logicians call an immanent act. To act upon an object is to produce an effect outside the mind; it is called a transitive act.[60]

Even if we should allow these arguments, Reid concludes, we would understand perception no better. "If we should admit an image in the mind, or contiguous to it, we know as little how perception may be produced by this image as by the most distant object" (p. 302). Yet this admission is to be found among those whom Reid criticizes for holding a representationalist theory of ideas. How it is that we see images is something of which both Locke in his criticism of Malebranche and Porterfield in the passage cited both readily confess their ignorance. So what is going on here?

Reid sees the historical importance of the argument but does not really understand it. What becomes clear in this discussion of the argument by one who sees *no* causal connection between the mind and object is that among all of these people it represents an attempt to deal with the problem of intentionality—how it is that the mind is aware of a thing, and of it rather than another. A very plausible opening move is to make a causal connection between them at least a necessary condition, as Locke does. Awarenesses are not random; nor are they voluntary, since, as Malebranche among many others repeatedly insists, they occur independently of our will and often contrary to it. To say that the mind's awareness is determined to an object very naturally translates into its being affected by it. It is not surprising then that Reid who sees no need for a causal connection should fail to see that the argument of Clarke and Porterfield is to be found in Locke, that Malebranche's version of this causal argument involves a notion of causation and presence different from theirs, and that Norris's important arguments on behalf of ideas were an expression of Malebranche's version of the argument. Norris's arguments that "material objects are without the mind, and therefore there can be no union between the object and the percipient," and that "material objects are disproportioned to the mind, and removed from it by the whole diameter of Being," (p. 300), state, however metaphorically, that material things by themselves are unintelligible. As such, his arguments deserved better treatment (along with the causal argument generally) from the usually astute Reid.[61]

---

[59] Reid later observes that the requirement of real presence, or contiguity, has been derived from resolving all essential operations into impressions modeled, however unconsciously, on the sense of touch (p. 302; cf. chap. 1).

[60] Ibid., p. 301. This is a distinction, applied to mind, that Reid could have gotten from Cureau, among many others.

[61] Hamilton's footnote correspondingly shows more astuteness. He thought that Norris's second argument expressed what in recent times has been called the epistemological likeness principle,

So much for Cureau as the source for the causal argument in its metaphorical interpretation and its failure to be understood by Arnauld and Reid. I want now to turn to the other possible source for the argument, which is the work of Launay. As we shall see in a moment, Launay clearly expresses the argument, indeed repeats it, argues for one of its crucial premises, and is a potentially more important source than Cureau for the additional reason that he makes clear that the mind is acted upon in perception. The reason Launay is a good source for Locke is that his argument is the more literal version of the argument, that is, the notion of causation involved is the notion of efficient causation mechanistically understood. For the same reason, Launay would not have been a good source for Malebranche. Yet the connection between them is not to be dismissed out of hand as impossible. Launay's statement of the causal argument is not unequivocally mechanistic and as we have seen a number of his views on ideas, perception, and the mind anticipate Malebranche in startling ways.

I have found no evidence whatsoever for a connection between Cureau and Locke. I have discovered no textual borrowing on Locke's part; none of Cureau's works appears in his library (despite their enormous popularity and Cureau's being the best-known physician in France over a long period); a meeting between them is highly unlikely; and there is no mention of Cureau in any of Locke's published work, journals, or manuscripts. Launay's connection with Locke, however, has been documented at length above. The case for Cureau as a source for Malebranche has a great deal of support, but that for a connection with Launay, on the other hand, is correspondingly weaker. His library contained none of Launay's work, although this is far from an infallible guide to Malebranche's reading since it also contained nothing by Foucher. Also it is far from impossible that Malebranche attended his lectures or knew of his views from others who did.[62]

---

namely, "that the relation of knowledge infers a correspondence of nature between the subject knowing, and the object known." He sees this principle as so generally assumed that "to trace [its] influence, . . . would be, in fact, in a certain sort, to write the history of philosophy. . . . To this principle, in its lower potence—that what knows must be *similar* in nature to what is immediately known—we owe the *intentional species* of the Aristotelians, and the *ideas* of Malebranche and Berkeley. From this principle in its higher potence—that what knows must be *identical* in nature with what is immediately known—there flow . . . the (mental) *ideas* of Des Cartes and Arnauld" (ibid., p. 300). It is worth noting further that Arnauld himself subscribed to the causal argument to the extent that he construes a mediated perception as one whose object is not its immediate cause (*Des vraies*; *Oeuvres*, 38: 222–28; Lennon, *Commentary*, p. 797). Similarly, Leibniz agreed with Malebranche that God is the mind's sole object because only He can act on them ("Remarks"; *Selections*, p. 501). Presumably these are further instances of the metaphorical interpretation, which I think can be generalized for any version of the argument that includes ideas as *universals*.

[62] At a minimum we can say that Malebranche and Launay were reading the same texts from Augustine, perhaps with Malebranche having been put onto them by Launay as he was put onto others by André Martin. The connection beyond this is indirect, very tenuous, and not worth developing at any length, because it seems impossible to establish either Launay or Martin as a

Launay's argument for the necessity of ideas occurs in his discussion of exemplary causes: Without ideas we must remain ignorant and idle, he says, for only through them can we know an external thing or, by imitating them, produce anything. "To prove that ideas are a principle of knowledge, whether in the senses or in the understanding, the argument must go as follows. Knowledge can occur only when the object known is joined and present to the faculty knowing it; for as in order to act it is necessary to be, so in order to act in a place it is necessary to be present to that place where one acts; now, the external things made known to intelligent faculties act on them, therefore they must be present to them; but not being present by themselves because they are outside of us, it follows that they are present by means of their ideas, or images, which are like so many faithful copies or invisible messengers bringing us news of what is outside of us."[63] He later gives an argument for local presence as a requirement for action. Action at a distance is ruled out because "action is a result of being and non-being does not act; thus the agent must be where it acts in order to act, otherwise . . . it could act by its non-being, which is everywhere its being is not." That is, if a thing could act somewhere it was not, there would be no reason why it could not act everywhere it is not. The same principle applies to the First Cause as well; His power is unlimited because He is immense and thus can act everywhere.[64] Launay seems simply to equate the extent of a thing's power with its spatial extension—what it can do with where it can do it. In any case, we have here what is not found very often in the period, namely, an

---

source, or even to determine whether Malebranche was reading Augustine independently. For example, Launay begins his treatment of ideas in the *Essais metaphysiques* (p. 58) with a deviant quote from *De diversis questionibus LXXXIII* to the effect that they are necessary for knowledge: si quidem tanta in eis vis constituitur, ut nisi his intellectis sapiens esse nemo possit (Migne 40, col. 29). This passage is to be found, quoted more fully in *Philosophia christiana* (1667), 3:123–24, followed by the standard Neo-Platonic argument: "who would dare to say that God put things together irrationally?" Though he does so only in the sixth edition of the *Search*, Malebranche refers to the same work in support of his own theory of knowledge; not the eyes of the body but those of the soul, not corporeal sensation but the mind's attention is the means to truth: "because the mind's attention is in effect its return to truth by the manifestation of His substance, as St. Augustine says, without the intervention of any creature" (*Oeuvres*, 1:17–18). Malebranche's quotation of Augustine, also slightly deviant (*haeret enim veritate nulla interposita creatura* [Migne 40, col. 33], is from a discussion of the creation of man in the image and likeness of God. The *Philosophia christiana* discussion of this question is elsewhere (2:363) but concludes with a paraphrase of Augustine's *De diversis questionibus* (Migne 40, cols. 30–31): "the soul is above all of creation and when pure next to God . . . and to the extent it clings to Him in charity it discerns. . . . not through the corporeal [eyes] but through its understanding the ideas of things which are contained in the divine intelligence and which make up the beatific vision [*quarum visione fit beatissima*]" (pp. 366–67).

[63] *Essais metaphysiques*, p. 59. Launay produces the same argument in the *Dialectique*, pp. 44–45.

[64] *Essais metaphysiques*, p. 113.

attempt, however weak, to *argue* the mechanist principle that change occurs only upon contact.[65]

Locke might also have been put on to the causal argument by Cudworth, who argued that we are, at least initially, passive in sensation. "When a Corporeal Object very remotely distant is perceived by us, since it is by some Passion made upon our Body, there must of necessity be a continual Propagation of some Local *Motion* or Pressure from thence unto the Organs of our Sense, or Nerves, and so *unto* the Brain."[66] But if Locke took this lead and concluded that objects at a distance thereby ultimately cause the ideas that represent them, that is all he took. For Cudworth went on almost immediately to argue that sensation also had "something of an Active Vigour in it" (p. 79) and to distinguish sensation from intellection, which reaches the real essences of things by becoming one with them (pp. 93ff.). And later he argued that in addition to "sensible Ideas of Corporeal things . . . there must be also *Conceptions*, or Intelligible Ideas of them Actively Exerted from the Mind it self," (p. 192)—all of which and more is obviously antithetical to the *Essay*. The argument is also suggested by Cudworth at another point: "that which wholly looks abroad outward upon its Object, is not one with that which it perceives, but is at a distance from it, and therefore cannot Know and Comprehend it" (p. 334). But here Cudworth says that things at a distance *are* perceived and his concern is with knowledge of essences (which are known *inwardly*), not causation. It is even less likely that Cudworth was a source for Malebranche, who had a low opinion of his views and read him either very late or not at all, and who would have been far less likely to have seen the *Treatise on . . . Morality* in manuscript.

There is, finally, a better source than Cureau, Cudworth, or even Launay, on whom Locke might have drawn. Whether Reid got his view that there need be no causal interaction between the mind and its object from Gassendi, or from the nominalist theory of perception as Hamilton thought, must remain a matter of speculation. What is less speculative is that Locke may have gotten his view that there must be such a causal connection from the refutation of (what was to be) Reid's view by Gassendi himself, or more plausibly, from Bernier. In his *Abrégé* he considers two sorts of theories of vision. One sort involves an

---

[65] Reid noted Newton's queried expression of the argument against knowledge at a distance and then attributed to him an argument for the crucial premise that a thing must be present to what it acts on. Unfortunately, the argument, at least as expressed by Reid, is, as Hamilton would put it, at best vague and inexplicit. "That nothing can act immediately where it is not, I think must be admitted: for I agree with Sir Isaac Newton, that power without substance is inconceivable" (*Essay*; *Works*, 1:301). It might be granted that every power is the power of some substance; but what remains to be explained is why a substance must be present to that on which it exercises its power. To say that otherwise there would be power without substance is only to say there is no action at a distance.

[66] *Morality*, pp. 76–77. This work was published, posthumously, only in 1731. But that Locke might have been shown the manuscript by Lady Masham is far from impossible.

emission from the eye of spirits, corpuscles, or rays.[67] Among those who hold this view are the Pythagoreans, who thought the eye emitted rays that reflected from the object back to it, the Stoics who conceived of these rays as rigid and thus of vision as a kind of touch,[68] and perhaps Plato.[69] The view is dismissed on several grounds. Given the distance of the stars we see, for example, the eye would soon be depleted of its corpuscles, and the corpuscles or rays would take too long to reach them.[70] Before turning to the view that it is the object rather than the eye that is the source of the causal interagents, *Abrégé* 2 first notes that it is doubtful whether Aristotle should be included among its proponents. For one thing his views are unclear; but in addition, "several Peripatetics have thought that it is not necessary for the thing seen to cause any motion in the eye and that for vision nothing else is needed than for the visible object to be present to the eye, and for it to be illuminated and at an appropriate distance. The Nominalists among others have thought this way, Ockham, Biel, Durandus, Gregory [of Rimini] and the others."[71] Bernier does not "pause over these later [figures]," but when he turns to the second main sort of theory, his arguments on its behalf are effectively arguments against them.

In the first rank of those who hold that vision is a matter of reception of species or images—of something in any case—are Democritus and Epicurus. Both of Bernier's editions argue the view, but the first gives a fuller account of why there must be a transmission from the object to the eye.[72] There are several arguments: (1) by analogy with the other senses, which "obviously" require to be disturbed by something; (2) from reflection in mirrors, which requires something from the reflected object; (3) from the effect of concave and convex lenses, which act on something passing from the object to the eye; (4) from the *camera oscura*, which cannot be explained otherwise; (5) from the fact that we do not see objects in the dark. Now the first four of these argue only that there is *some* causal connection between eye and object, the last two argue it to be of a certain sort (as Bernier thinks, by means of rays of light), and none argues its direction. But his first argument, repeated in *Abrégé* 2, is "from the very nature of the sensitive faculty, which acts only by passively receiving something[73] and does not sense this object rather than another unless the object touches [*touche*] it and determines it, either by itself or by something that it transmits to it."[74]

---

[67] *Abrégé* 1, p.139.

[68] *Abrégé* 2, pp. 105–6.

[69] *Abrégé* 1, p. 141.

[70] Ibid., pp. 139–41. Bernier's treatment of what modern sense-data theorists have called the time-gap between when a thing exists in its presentational state and when we perceive it shows him ignorant of Roemer's demonstration in 1665 of the noninstantaneous propagation of light.

[71] *Abrégé*, 2, p. 106.

[72] *Abrégé* 1, pp. 141 ff; *Abrégé* 2, pp. 108ff.

[73] qui n'agit qu'en souffrant, & en recevrant quelque chose.

[74] *Abrégé* 1, pp. 141–42. *Abrégé* 2, p. 109.

A number of important points are clear from Bernier's texts. For one thing, the causal argument is the more literal version of it. This is true even of the versions of it that attribute the causal action to the eye. Furthermore, an image is required in sensation because what it represents is at a distance. The object or that by which the object acts on the eye must be in contact with it. Finally, it is the perceiver that must be acted upon because of a fundamental passivity that I think is of a piece with empiricism. We must rely on the senses for what we perceive, at least for all the "materials" of what we perceive (to use Locke's expression), because the mind can produce none of its original ideas. The rejection of innate ideas, at least according to certain interpretations that we shall investigate below, thus both supports and is supported by the representationalist theory of perception.

The contrast between the literal and metaphorical interpretations of the causal argument along with the contrast between the relevant notions of causation give the sense of Locke's long criticism of Malebranche in his *Examination of . . . seeing all things in God* and thus to the difference between their views. Locke's principal contention is that Malebranche's theory fails to explain what it purports to explain because of the kind of explanation that it is.[75] Malebranche's contention that we see all things in God comes ultimately to the claim that we perceive things because God wills that we perceive them, which no one would deny. What it comes to, we might say, is a reassertion *that* we perceive. But this does not explain *how* we perceive them, which as Locke might have pointed out, is a requirement that Malebranche himself placed on causal explanation. Recourse to the first cause when explaining why the rivers freeze is inappropriate according to Malebranche, yet this is the mistake that from a Lockean point of view his vision in God is guilty of. What Locke wants is the analogue in the theory of ideas to the change of motion in the river's particles when it freezes.

The best example of this difference in kind between the theory Malebranche proposes and what would satisfy Locke is the criticism of Malebranche that has perhaps most bothered Locke scholars. Malebranche rejected the theory according to which the soul is provided with a magazine of representative ideas on which it draws when perceiving objects external to it like the sun; his ground among others for rejecting it was that such a magazine would be useless since the soul would already have to know the sun in order to choose from its magazine the appropriate idea of the sun to represent it. Locke will have none of this theory, but he criticizes Malebranche's rejection of it as follows (par. 20): "how can [Malebranche] know that there is any such real being in the world as the sun? Did he ever see the sun? No, but on occasion of the presence of the sun

---

[75] Locke's *Examination* is for the most part a series of more or less long comments made by Locke *seriatim* on the second part of book 3 of the *Search* and *Elucidations* 10. For a systematized account of this material, see McCracken, *British Philosophy*, pp. 122–48. References here to *Works*, 9:211–55.

to his eyes, he has seen the idea of the sun in God, which God has exhibited to him; but the sun because it cannot be united to his soul, he cannot see. How then does he know that there is a sun which he never saw? And since God does all things by the most compendious ways, what need is there that God should make a sun that we might see its idea in him when he is pleased to exhibit it, when this might as well be done without any real sun at all?" This sounds very much like the (sophomore's) objection to all representationalist theories: How can we know even that there are physical objects, much less that they are like certain of our ideas, if all we ever perceive are ideas?

Versions of this argument were raised against Locke himself by such early critics as William Carroll, John Witty, John Norris, Henry Lee, and John Sergeant.[76] But this is not Locke's objection against Malebranche. His objection is that Malebranche's theory leaves material things superfluous, presumably in a way that his own theory or an acceptable theory would not. That is, Locke's complaint is not with representationalism as such, but with Malebranche's causal account of it.[77] The vision of all things in God, that is, God's revealing His ideas of things to us, is gratuitous; an hypothesis of representative ideas in the mind caused by objects is not gratuitous because there is independent evidence for the hypothesis, namely, all the evidence there is on behalf of the corpuscular hypothesis, which in two important ways he ties to his theory of ideas in 2.8 of the *Essay*.

First, the primary-secondary quality distinction that he draws there only states the mechanical hypothesis concerning the world's structure and suggests a way that it is compatible with our perception. Supposing that the world has a certain kind of quality X just sufficient to ground the corpuscular hypothesis, we can explain how it is that we perceive it in terms not only of quality of kind X but of Y as well. But aside from considerations of parsimony, this gives us no reason to suppose that the world really has qualities only of kind X. This is perhaps why at 2.8.23 he introduces three sorts of qualities, the last of which is "the *Power* that is in any *Body*, *by* Reason of the particular Constitution of *its primary Qualities*, *to* make such a *change* in the *Bulk*, *Figure*, *Texture*, *and Motion of another Body*, as to make it operate on our Senses, differently from what it did before. Thus the Sun has a power to make Wax white, and Fire to make Lead fluid." These so-called tertiary qualities differ from secondary qualities in that although both are but powers, the effects caused by these qualities, unlike the ideas caused by secondary qualities, are not thought to be resemblances of the powers on which they depend. Locke's argument is the following. Bodies have

---

[76] Yolton, *John Locke*, p. 108.

[77] McCracken gets it exactly right: "What here concerned him was whether or not the assumption that bodies exist can have any explanatory value for an exponent of Occasionalism, not whether that assumption has any epistemological justification for an exponent of a representative theory of perception" (*British Philosophy*, p. 134). Matthews also saw that Locke's worry was a causal one ("Locke," p. 15). See also Yolton, *John Locke*, pp. 98–99.

various qualities. These are powers to cause changes. Some of these are powers to change the qualities in other bodies; these are the tertiary qualities. Sometimes there is a resemblance in these qualities between cause and effect, as when one motion causes another; sometimes there is not, as when the sun makes wax white. Other qualities are powers to cause ideas; once again there is a resemblance in some instances between cause and effect. The primary qualities are those whose ideas resemble them; the secondary those whose ideas do not. And we can distinguish the two on the basis of the distinction between kinds of tertiary qualities. We have evidence, in short, for the kinds of effects bodies have on us from the kinds of effects they have on each other.[78]

The second point of relevance for the corpuscular hypothesis is that it gives the only conceivable way in which ideas could be produced. Locke has a number of comments in his *Examination* and *Remarks* to the effect that it is inconceivable how bodies should cause our ideas. A perhaps natural interpretation of these comments is that Locke is arguing *modo tollendo* that the production of ideas is mysterious because nonmechanistic. My own view is that he is arguing *modo ponendo* that the production of ideas is mechanistic because it would otherwise be inexplicable. That is, the proper inference from the inconceivability of the nonmechanistic account of ideas is not that there is some account we cannot know, but that since ideas are caused they are mechanistically produced (and therefore, we might add, ought to be material).

The interpretation that the production of ideas is nonmechanistic and in principle inexplicable is given no support by Locke's version of 2.8.11, which in fact contradicts it. The first three editions read: "The next thing to be consider'd, is how bodies *operate* one upon another, and that is manifestly *by impulse*, and nothing else. It being impossible to conceive, that Body should operate on what it does not touch, (which is all one as to imagine it can operate where it is not) or when it does touch, operate any other way than by Motion."[79] But in 1699 he wrote Stillingfleet[80] that reading Newton's *Principia* led him to regard the gravitation of matter as an operation of matter inconceivable to him and that he would take care to have this passage rectified. It then read: "The next thing to be consider'd is, how *Bodies* produce *Ideas* in us, and that is manifestly *by impulse*, the only way which we can conceive Bodies to operate it in." His

---

[78] If objects have the power to cause ideas, argues Locke, then we can explain, as the occasionalist cannot, why with an object in the perceptual vicinity a blind man fails to have any visual idea of it (*Remarks*, par. 2). This is a bad objection to occasionalism, according to which anything that would prevent some thing from acting (for example, an inappropriate disposition in its would-be effect such as an opaque cornea) would also prevent it from serving as an occasion. But it would be a good objection to the occasionalist who proposed an analysis of what it is to be a cause as a theory of what the (occasional) cause is in a given case. Historically, however, this was the mistake, not of the occasionalists, but of those who later mistakenly thought that occasionalism was proposed as a solution to the mind-body problem.

[79] Editions 2 and 3 read: "operate without Motion."

[80] *Works*, 4:467–68.

modal terms are a bit fuzzy, but the rectification seems to be this. First he says bodies *cannot* operate other than by impulse; it is impossible, presumably for *anyone*, to conceive nonmechanical operation of bodies. Then he says that they *do* operate nonmechanically, although *we* cannot conceive how they should do so (because all we have is the mechanical hypothesis). But he does not later say, and in fact again denies, that bodies produce ideas other than by impulse.

Even so, Locke makes undeniably clear that there is some aspect of the production of ideas that cannot be explained. My thesis is that what an idea *is* is a motion in the sensory apparatus (an impression) of which we are aware. What cannot be explained is the *awareness* of the impression. A good point at which to begin this case is Locke's treatment of the sensible species view. This is the theory that the objects we perceive emit material likenesses that are picked up by the sensory apparatus. Malebranche had objected against this theory that the materiality of the likeness would make it impossible to perceive simultaneously a multiplicity of objects whose likenesses could not all convene at the same point of perception. In his comments Locke shows much greater sympathy with this theory than he did with the magazine theory, for example. Though he begins by saying that the Peripatetic doctrine "does not at all satisfy [him]" and that it is "not his business to defend what he does not understand, nor to prefer the learned gibberish of the schools to what is yet unintelligible to [him] in" Malebranche, Locke defends a view against Malebranche that agrees with the Aristotelian view that there is a causal connection between object and mind. The crucial (and perhaps only) alteration Locke introduces is the restriction of that connection to corpuscularian mechanisms, which meet all of Male-branche's objections "as far as [Locke's] opinion is concerned in them" (par. 15). Thus, "as to what is said that from one point we can see a great number of objects, that is no objection against the species, or visible appearances of bodies, being brought into the eye by the rays of light; for the bottom of the eye, or retina, which, in regard of these rays, is the place of vision, is far from being a point" (par. 9). As long as the retina has a certain area it can simultaneously accommodate a multiplicity of images, whose information (one might say) is conveyed by various motions to the brain and there perceived in terms of images. Locke professes to understand the entire causal process from object to brain, but the perception itself is not a part of this process. "Impressions made on the retina by rays of light, I think I understand; and motions from thence continued to the brain may be conceived, and that these produce ideas in our minds, I am persuaded, but in a manner to me incomprehensible." In fact, Locke's physiology and optics need differ in no way at all from the Cartesian account. But such an account is insufficient to explain perception—an insufficiency that is not supplied by Malebranche's appeal to the divinity. "The ideas it is certain I have and God is the original cause of my having them; but the manner how I come by them, how it is that I perceive, I confess I understand not; though it be plain that motion has to do in the producing of them" (par. 10).

Locke begins by saying that *ideas* are incomprehensibly produced in the mind, but ends by discussing the "having" of them—"the *manner* how I come by them, *how* it is that I *perceive*"—as problematic. This is not to change what he first said but to explain it: Not the impression but the awareness of it remains unexplained.[81]

Locke reads Malebranche as construing ideas as immaterial substances, which, as we have seen, makes it inconceivable to Locke how they should represent something that is extended.[82] But, "supposing I could conceive an unextended substance to represent a figure, or be the idea of a figure, the difficulty still remains to conceive how it is my soul sees it. Let this substantial being be ever so sure, and the picture never so clear; yet how we see it is to me inconceivable. Intimate union, were it as intelligible of two unextended substances, as of two bodies, would not yet reach perception, which is something beyond union" (par. 18).

That Locke's difficulty lies with the having of ideas is clear as well in his reply to Norris, who had complained that he did not give an account of or define the nature of our ideas. Locke replied that this cannot mean that he failed to make men's ideas known to them, which need not and cannot be done. What Norris calls for, then, is an account of the alteration of the mind upon beginning to see or upon seeing one thing rather than another. But neither can this be done, according to Locke, because the only alteration we can explain is the rearrangement of the particles of compounds.[83] No alteration of simples can ever be explained. This is the issue of supervenience to which we shall return. Meanwhile, what Locke might be saying is that awareness is supervenient and therefore inexplicable, as are *all* simple features. (The only other such feature, I shall argue, is *solidity*.) Whatever the story, *this* feature is inexplicable. "What alteration a man finds in himself when he sees a marigold and sees not a marigold has no difficulty, and needs not be inquired after; he has the idea now, which he had not before. The difficulty is, what alteration is made in his mind . . . the difference between perceiving and not perceiving" (par. 2).

---

[81] Arnauld also took awareness to be primitive. "Given that there can be no thought or knowledge [*connoisance*] without an object known, I can no more trouble myself for the reason why I think about something than why I think, since it is impossible to think without thinking of something. But I can well wonder, why do I think of one thing rather than another" (*Des vraies*; *Oeuvres*, 38:184. In answer to this, more legitimate wonder, Arnauld produced his theory of ideas. Although his was a very different kind of answer, Locke's theory of ideas is in response to the same wonder that elicited Arnauld's. The difference between them is that Arnauld took thought to be the essence of mind and appealed to structural causation to account for its intentionality, whereas Locke, as we shall see, took thought to be an epiphenomenon of matter and appealed only to mechanical causation to account for its production.

[82] See chap.3, sec. 1, above. Nor are ideas as immaterial *modes* any less inconceivable, he continues, for this would be to make them modes of God. The thrust of the passage is to make materiality a condition for representation of the material. See also par. 38.

[83] See chap. 6, below.

The main failing of Malebranche's theory according to Locke is that in the end it relies on an inexplicable revelation or discovery by God of His ideas to us. That there is a problem in perceiving things at a distance is not a point of difference between them. But the discovery Malebranche relies on to solve this problem turns out to be nothing more than the brute fact, we might say, that at one time God wills us to see and at another time not, or that at one time we do see and at another not; but it is just this difference that Malebranche's theory purports to explain.[84]

Locke's criticism of Malebranche and his disciple Norris is no superficial disagreement but reflects metaphysical differences at the deepest level. For Malebranche's account of mind involves two components that are at perfect odds with the ontological basis for Locke's whole way of philosophical thinking. First, he makes the Cartesian assumption that it is of the essence of the mind to think; the mind's consciousness is grounded in its very nature. This doctrine is set out in part of the third book of the *Search*, which was not commented on by Locke in his *Examination*, but which presumably he read. If he did not read it in Malebranche he did somewhere, and probably among several authors, for as we have seen, Locke criticizes this view in the *Essay* at great length. From Locke's point of view, not only is it empirically refuted there, but, as we shall see, it involves an incoherent view of essences. Second, the thesis of what is intelligible to this essentially conscious mind is itself unintelligible to Locke. The infinite, necessary, and universal being that is the mind's only immediate object for Malebranche is for Locke an abstraction,[85] which, far from being the mind's most intelligible object, is the least so, since it has the least content. It is also least real. Malebranche's argument, repeated by Norris, is that because all created things are individuals, the perception of what is universal proves the presence to the mind of God, who as the ground of being makes all beings present to the mind. Of this Locke rhetorically asks, "Are not all things that exist individuals? If so, then say not all created, but all existing things are individuals; and if so, then the having any general idea proves not that we have all objects present to our minds; but this is for want of considering wherein universality consists; which is only in representation abstracting from particulars" (par. 4). Locke here comes close to arguing, Berkeley was to argue against Locke, that the idea of being in general is the idea of nothing at all. "*Being in general*, is being abstracted from wisdom, goodness, power, and any particular sort of duration; and I have as true an idea of being, when these are

---

[84] "He pretends to explain to us how we come to perceive anything, and that is, by having the ideas of them present in our minds; for the soul cannot perceive things at a distance, or remote from it, and those ideas are present to the mind only because God, in whom they are, is present to the mind. This so far hangs together, and is of a piece; but when after this I am told, that their presence is not enough to make them be seen, but God must do something further to discover them to me, I am as much in the dark as I was at first" (par. 30).

[85] *Remarks*, pars. 17–18.

excluded out of it, as when extension, place, solidity and mobility are excluded out of my idea. And therefore, if *being in general* and *God*, be the *same*, I have a true idea of God when I exclude out of it power, goodness, wisdom and eternity" (pars. 32, 34).

From Locke's nominalist perspective Malebranche necessarily has the relation between the particular and the universal exactly the wrong way around. Because our idea of the infinite is of the potential infinite only,[86] the idea of the infinite is not presupposed by all others, but conversely.[87] Furthermore, since even those ideas that in representation are universal are in themselves particular, there is no question either of failing to notice part of the universal content of an idea or of rendering that initially confused content distinct by a process of deduction. Ideas for Locke are as it were perfectly transparent. To have an idea of a thing is to have a picture of it, and all that I know about that thing by means of the idea is in the picture. As Locke had argued at length with respect to innate ideas, to have an idea and not to be aware of it, indeed fully aware of it, is "impossible."[88] Thus, Locke rejects the notion of seeing all things in God confusedly. "If we see them in God, and they are not in Him confusedly, I do not see how we can see them in God confusedly."[89] The upshot is that Malebranche's version gets Paul exactly the wrong way around. Paul says we see the Creator in creatures, not creatures in the Creator: "The invisible things of God are seen by the visible things he has made" (par. 36).

Thus also does Locke reject distinctions between ideas based on the relation of participation in the divine essence. In fact, he could find no other meaning to the notion that ideas are the divine essence insofar as things participate in it than that God can always produce what does not involve a contradiction (par. 10). His nominalism leaves no room as it were for such relations as Malebranche's metaphorical conceptions of the mind's "intimate union" with God and its lack of proportion to the body. According to Malebranche, argued Locke (pars. 4–

---

[86] See chap. 7 below.

[87] Strictly speaking this is true only of the infinite of its kind, that is, the idea of the infinite in extension, for example, presupposes the ideas of every finite extension, no one of which is taken as ultimate. On the other hand, I do not see how Locke can recognize any other infinite but of its kind.

[88] McCracken draws attention to the significance of Locke's objections against the innatist theory of ideas, which Malebranche rejects, but which apply mutatis mutandi to the theory Malebranche accepts. Thus Norris, who does "as little believe there are any such things as Innate Principles . . . as the Author himself," nonetheless tries to counter that Locke's objections are inconsistent with his own theories of attention and memory (McCracken, *British Philosophy*, pp. 140–42). At 2.9.4, however, Locke says only that we sometimes fail to notice *impressions* when contemplating something else. The crucial distinction between an impression, of which we need not be aware, and the awareness of it also sorts out his (more problematic) views on memory as well, but that is a longer story.

[89] *Examination*, par. 22. See also par. 29: "if the ideas I see are all . . . real beings in [God]; and if we see them in him, we must see them as they are, distinct particular things, and so shall not see them confusedly and in general. . . . What I see I see, and the idea I see is distinct from all others that are not the same with it."

7), there is no proportion between the mind and God and yet God is most intelligible; there is no proportion between mind and body and yet they are united (though in any case not in a way sufficient for perception). Nor, of course, does it make any sense to speak of matter being in God "after a spiritual manner." "This and the like are ways of speaking which our vanity has found out to cover, not remove, our ignorance" (par. 23).

Given all this, it is not in the least surprising to find that Locke had problems with Malebranche's distinction between an idea and a sensation. "If by 'sentiment,' which is the word he uses in french,[90] he means the act of sensation, or the operation of the soul in perceiving; and by pure 'idea,' the immediate object of that perception, which is the definition of ideas he gives us here in the first chapter; there is some foundation for it, taking ideas for real beings or substances" (par. 38). But what this means, according to Locke, is that for Malebranche we must see colors and smell odors in God; for when we perceive a violet we smell its odor and see its color as much as we see its shape. For Locke all three are on a par; either all are sensations, in which case none is perceived in God "and so this whole business of seeing in God is out of doors," or, as he clearly believes, they are all ideas, in which case we smell a violet, taste wormwood, and feel cold in God, which "shows a little too plainly the absurdity of that doctrine."

Locke agrees with Malebranche that one who had not seen a color or felt heat could not be given those sensations by words, but insists that the same is true of space or motion (par. 49). Only the pervasiveness of space and motion leads us to think that we could have ideas of them without experience. This is not a simple empirical matter that Locke raises such as the Molyneux problem might be interpreted to be. It is the fundamental issue of the battle of gods and giants, namely, the rational intuition of real essences versus the sensory intuition of individuals that are the referents of nominal definitions.[91] We shall now see that much of importance in Locke's *Essay* can be read in these terms.

---

[90] And which Locke did not know how to translate into English; see par. 42.

[91] Leibniz insightfully commented that to deny the distinction, as Locke did, is to make all ideas *images* ("Remarks on the opinion of Malebranche that we see all things in God, with reference to Locke's Examination of it"; *Selections*, p. 502).

CHAPTER VI

The Untouchable and the Uncuttable

LOCKE'S *ESSAY* is a book about knowledge that forswears ontological questions. Yet, to repeat what was said above, it would be surprising if the author of such a text held no ontological views, or if those views did not frequently intrude upon the work in important ways. I believe that roughly speaking Locke's ontology is an anti-Cartesian one of atoms and the void, designed to avoid what he regards as the pernicious results of the Cartesian version of the New Science.

Locke's chapter on the simple modes of space (2.13), for example, is for the greater part devoted to an extended critique of the Cartesian view. It is clear that Locke is here interested less in the question of the nature of space than in the Cartesian plenum theory, according to which there can be no space unoccupied by body because space or extension and body are identical. The problem with this theory from a Lockean position is that it is inconsistent with empiricism on two related counts. First, Descartes holds that (1) geometry is a priori, (2) the object of geometry is space or extension, (3) for geometry to be true its object must exist, (4) extension and body are identical, and thus (5) geometry gives us a priori knowledge about *existence* of body. For Locke, of course, all a priori knowledge is only hypothetical and existence claims about body must be based ultimately on sensation alone. Second, for Descartes not all *contents* of knowledge would be derivable only from experience; strictly speaking, in fact, none are empirically derivable. In the case at hand of an a priori geometry of space, the contents of knowledge are available *a priori* as an innate idea. For an intuitive image of the contrast here, consider the Cartesian as endowed with an intellectual intuition of what is known, a clear and distinct vision of a nonempirical object. For Locke, however, the appropriate metaphor is not intellectual seeing but physical touching. For Plato he is the sophist who "takes refuge in the darkness of Not-being, where he is at home and has the knack of feeling his way."[1] We must experience the world to determine its shape, so to speak, by feeling about to determine where there is solidity and therefore body, and where not. Intellectually blind in Cartesian terms, we must feel out of sight for the ends of being, if not ideal grace.[2]

An atomist reading of Locke is not new. It was proposed by Leibniz, for

---

[1] *Dialogues*, 254a.

[2] But cf. light metaphors in Locke's *Essay*: 4.3.20; 4.3.21; 4.2.1. Visual imagery is, as it were, hard for anyone to resist.

example, who in the *New Essays* saw Locke as continuing Gassendi's struggle against Descartes on behalf of Democritean atomism.[3] I believe, however, than an articulated atomist interpretation brings to grief a number of the central features of what has come to be the standard view of Locke. It will help in following my interpretation if we first set out in rough terms some of the central features of the prevailing view that it would falsify. (1) *Substance*. Ordinary objects are substances, with the result, among others, that they are mind-independent. (On my interpretation, ordinary objects are indeed substances, but as such they are phenomenal. Substances are ideas. Locke is, if you like, a Kantian [we perceive the world in terms of substance], but a Kantian without a transcendental deduction [we perceive as we do because of our psychology]. In any case, his noumenal world does not contain substances, consisting only of solidity.) (2) *Primary qualities*. Primary qualities are occurrent properties. (On my interpretation only solidity is occurrent; all the other primary qualities are dispositions or powers resulting from the spatial distribution of solidity.) (3) *Secondary qualities*. There is no standard view of Lockean secondary qualities, but each of the following must be rejected: (a) the view of a string of commentators beginning with Berkeley that Lockean secondary qualities are ideas; (b) Mackie's view that Locke's treatment of secondary qualities renders his account of qualities inconsistent; (c) the more recent view that secondary qualities are textures of the microscopic parts of things. (My view will regard secondary qualities as powers.) (4) *Space*. As for Newton, space for Locke is absolute and real. (Though many commentators realize that the *Essay* waffles on this, few realize that Locke's journals clearly reject absolute space, and no one has shown why he should be so disposed. Here the motor force is not Locke's atomism but its attendant nominalism.) (5) *Mind*. Locke is a dualist. (I shall not argue so here, but what is true of objects with respect to substance is true of minds as well. They are perceived only as substances. And the perceptions that are said to be had by minds are epiphenomena of a purely material world. Thus Locke subscribes to the materialism typical of the atomist tradition on which he draws. The result is that this chapter on Locke's atomism is really about the whole of his ontology.)

The rectification of the standard view of Locke is only incidental to my purpose. It falls out indirectly from what I say. So perhaps it will also help if I sketch the topics I shall discuss directly. In the first section of the chapter I shall try to show that while Locke agrees with the Cartesians that space is relational, there are important differences between their views, and in addition that for Locke what stands in spatial relations is solidity only. The second section discusses Locke's simple-complex idea distinction in an effort to show how the mechanism of this distinction allows it to be that there is only solidity in the mind-independent world. An obvious objection can be raised to this claim that for Locke there is only solidity in the real world; for according to Locke there are ideas other than that of solidity that resemble that world. Thus the real world would have, in addition to solidity, shape. The third section attempts to meet this objection and at the same time say something new about the chestnut topic of the primary-secondary quality distinction. This will lead to problems about powers, which will be addressed in the fourth section. The next section ties together a number of issues related to solidity in an effort to provide a proof-of-the-pudding argument for the special status of solidity. Finally, in the last section I turn to an issue that in the seventeenth century captured the philosophical imagination, at least the popular version of it, in a way that few others did. The issue of the bestial soul should here prove to be an historical proof-of-the-pudding argument on behalf of my interpretation of Locke.

§18 SPACE AND SOLIDITY

Locke's analysis of space undeniably evidences a Gassendist spirit and yet departs significantly from Gassendi's actual views. The same departure is found advocated in yet more radical form by the leading Gassendist on the Continent, François Bernier, who might have led Locke to it or been led to it by him. I shall try to show that whatever the provenance of this Neo-Gassendist analysis of space it was advanced by Locke because it was more congenial with the nominalism and empiricism at the core of Gassendism than was Gassendi's own analysis.

The *Essay* is at least superficially undecided about the nature of space, apparently leaving open the possibilities of either the relational or absolute views. This is likely so because Locke's primary concern is with the plenum version of absolute space, although there are texts that suggest that any version of absolute space is unacceptable. In any case, the journals Locke kept during his trips to France in the 1670s clearly argue the relational view. There is a crucial difference, however, between Locke's relational view of space and the Cartesian view, which is also relational. For Descartes, space though relational

---

³ In the English secondary literature, where the realization of this has come comparatively late, Aaron for example, drew attention to Gassendi's influence on Locke (*John Locke*, pp.31–35) and we have seen Norton's more recent comment on Gassendi as the father of British empiricism. Most notably, Mandelbaum's book in its second sentence tells us that "Locke . . . was an atomist." But how Locke was an atomist beyond his nominal acceptance of the corpuscularian hypothesis of the master builders is not altogether clear in Mandelbaum. Specifically, Mandelbaum fails to show how Locke's allegedly mind-independent substances relate to his atomism. Indeed, he seems just to contradict himself on this point: "If we may take 'the unknown essence' to be equivalent to the substratum in this passage [2.23.2]—as I believe the context permits us to do—we have textual evidence in the *Essay* itself for connecting the general notion of a substrate and the atomic constitution of material objects" (p. 38, n.75). "I think it a mistake to regard the notion of a substratum as being connected with the *actual qualities* of an object, rather than as being an indeterminate notion connected with our sensible *ideas* of such qualities" (p. 41, n. 79; emphasis added).

is yet at least quasi-substantival; space or extension (body in general) is independent of the individual bodies perceived to be in space. For Locke, space is relational in that apart from the bodies said to be in space, space is literally nothing at all. In this Locke departs from Gassendi, who was the first source for his views on space.

Beginning probably about 1658, Locke kept a series of commonplace books in which he wrote, among other things, excerpts from authors he was reading; in addition to citing medical texts by Boyle, Sennert, van Helmont, Glisson, and Swammerdam, Locke also copied from Bacon, Descartes, and Gassendi.[4] As we have already seen, in the first of these notebooks, composed between 1659 and 1666, one finds after a résumé of a Cartesian text on space a passage copied almost verbatim from Gassendi's *Syntagma* in which he clearly set out a container view of space as something different from body.[5] This is proof that on space, at least, Locke was in contact first with the primary source, rather than the later versions of the Gassendist theory to be found in, for example, Bernier or Launay.

For Gassendi, space as opposed to the body that may occupy it is neither substance nor accident; it is, in the phrase of Seneca, whom he quotes, a being *suo modo*. He distinguishes between space or the void and body or matter on three grounds: (1) the former is infinite, and exists always, (2) it is immobile, and (3) it is incorporeal, as a result of which it offers no resistance to occupation by matter.[6] The last characteristic, the passivity of space, clearly distinguishes space from body, which for Gassendi, in contrast to the prevalent view of the seventeenth century, is primordially if not intrinsically active. Ultimate particles of matter are inamissably endowed with a propensity to motion he calls gravity or weight. This essentially dynamical conception of matter is already suggested when he reduces the Epicurean *conjuncta* to size, shape, and weight or gravity on the basis that the fourth, resistance, is "less a property than the subject of the three other properties or the substance itself [*subiectam Naturam*], . . . namely solidity, *ex qua est ipsa resistentia.*"[7]

A parallel distinction between solidity and resistance is to be found in Locke, for whom impenetrability is a negative idea, and is only the consequence of solidity, "which has something more of positive in it."[8] But for Locke this is not an indication of a Gassendist *materia actuosa*. Some recent literature has

---

[4] Dewhurst, *John Locke*, pp. 27–28.

[5] Est quantitas extensiove quaedam spati[us] nempe seu intervallum triplici dimensione, longitudinis latitudinis et profunditas constans, in quo corp[us] recipi, aut per q[uo]d transire corp[us] possibile sit at simul dicend[us] ejus dimensiones esse incorporeas atque adeo loc[um] esse intervall[um] spatiumve incorporeum seu incorpoream quantitatem dimensio ig[i]t[ur] 2 x corporea et spatialis Gassendi Phys.S.I.I.2.p.182 C.I. British Museum MS Add. 32554, p. 182; quoted by Bloch, *La philosophie*, p. 198 n. 115.

[6] *Syntagma*; *Opera*, 1:183.

[7] *Opera* 1:276a.

[8] *Essay* 2.4.1; 123.

shown Locke to have been less than a pure mechanist,[9] but not, in my view, to have been so impure as to have admitted active matter. He does, however, retain from Gassendi the notion of solidity as fundamental. "[Solidity,] of all other, seems the *Idea* most intimately connected with, and essential to Body, so as no where else to be found or imagin'd, but only in matter."[10] We shall return to this at great length below.

Locke's chapter on the simple modes of the idea of space (2.13) is for the most part devoted to an extended critique of the Cartesian view. His main argument against the Cartesians, (2.13.11) repeated a number of times, is that the ideas of body and extension are different. The former is "something that is solid, and extended, whose parts are separable and movable different ways,"the latter "only the Space that lies between the Extremities of those solid coherent Parts, . . . which is possessed by them," which includes no solidity, no resistance to motion, and whose parts are inseparable and immovable. Though there can be no solidity without extension, he says, the intelligibility of the dispute over the vacuum shows that the ideas of the two are distinct.

Three other arguments of Locke could have, and likely did ultimately, come from Gassendi. One is the argument of the Pythagorean Archytas conveyed from antiquity to the seventeenth century by Gassendi, though it had in the meanwhile recurred elsewhere.[11] The argument is that space must extend infinitely beyond body since a man conveyed to any boundary assigned to body could either place his hand beyond that body and thus into a space beyond previously without body, or be prevented from doing so, in which case there would be body and thus space beyond the assigned boundary, and so on. Locke's conclusion from the argument is that for the Cartesians body must be either infinite ("though they are loth to speak it out") or else different from space (2.13.20–21). Another argument originated with Gassendi and can be understood as part of his Christian apology for atomism. The divine power of annihilation, he argues, may be exercised with respect to a part of creation without necessitating motion in any other part; the annihilated matter must therefore leave a void in its wake. Locke repeats this argument, adding against the Cartesians' vortex theory of particles simultaneously replacing and being replaced by each other that it begs the question. (2.13.21) Finally, he relates a version of Gassendi's most Epicurean argument, namely, that the possibility of motion depends on there being space without matter; dividing a body so as to make possible the rearrangement of its parts, he argues, requires that there be a void at least as large as the least part of that body (2.13.22). I shall have more to say about this argument below.

---

[9] Wilson, "Superadded Powers."

[10] *Essay* 2.4.1.; 12.

[11] It is found, for example, "in Richard of Middleton's writings in the fourteenth century (perhaps with reference to Simplicius' *Physics* 108a), still before the rediscovery of the *De rerum natura* in 1418 by Poggio" (Jammer, *Space*, p. 11).

However clear its anti-Cartesian thrust, the *Essay* leaves unclear the ontological status of space. "Whether any one will take Space to be only a relation resulting from the Existence of other Beings at a distance [presumably Locke means here any spatial relation, including those of what he variously calls capacity, or extension, in addition to those of distance]; or whether they will think the Words of the most knowing King *Solomon, The Heaven, and the Heaven of Heavens, cannot contain Thee*; or those more emphatical ones of the inspired Philosopher St. *Paul, In Him we live, move, and have our Being*, are to be understood in a literal sense, I leave everyone to consider"(2.13.26; 179). The alternatives he leaves open are (1) absolute space understood as perhaps the divine immensity,[12] or (2) relational space for which, given his nominalism, the ontological status would be minimal.[13]

At one point Locke appears ready to opt for Gassendi's version of absolute space: "Those who contend that *Space* and *Body* are *the same*, bring this *Dilemma*. Either this *Space* is something or nothing; if nothing be between two Bodies, they must necessarily touch; if it be allowed to be something, they ask, whether it be Body or Spirit? To which I answer by another Question, Who told them, that there was, or could be, nothing but solid Beings which could not think; and thinking Beings that were not extended? Which is all they mean by the terms *Body* and *Spirit*" (2.13.16;173). Locke here suggests a third kind of being, namely, unoccupied space. But, "if it be demanded (as it usually is) whether this *Space*, void of *Body*, be *Substance* or *Accident*," Locke instead of opting for space as being suo modo, and thus Gassendi's absolute space, pleads ignorance—"I shall readily answer I know not"—and proceeds to an extended

---

[12] Edward Grant argues contrary to my position (1) that the primary influence on Locke was Henry More, (2) that space is the divine immensity, and therefore (3) that the mature Locke believed "in an absolute, infinite, rather than relative space" (*Much Ado*, pp. 240–41, n. 329). But even if Locke identifies space with the divine immensity (2.15.8: "The boundless invariable Oceans of Duration and Expansion . . . belong only to the Deity."), it does not follow that space is absolute. To the contrary, given Locke's view of the infinite as potential, it follows only that for every place there is beyond it a place with God, which system of places may be entirely relational.

[13] Curiously, Aaron, who rightly regards Locke's theory as non-Newtonian, does not recognize the former as Newtonian: "In stating the alternatives in this passage there is no reference to Newton's theory—so little is the *Essay* Newtonian in its conception of space!" (*John Locke*, p. 157). Instead he sees it as More's view, which Locke cannot accept outright since "first, he was not sure we had a clear, positive conception of God's infinity. Secondly, to assert that the Deity was an extended being might savour in 1690 of materialism or Spinozism" (p. 158). The divinization of absolute space in the General Scholium, however, adds nothing to, but only emphasizes, the characteristics it had all along for Newton. What is important in any case is that either view, relational or absolute, is compatible with the void of interest to empiricism. Even if God fills otherwise empty space, for example, still that space is void of *body*, and thus to determine where there is body and where not, sense experience is needed.

The Locke–Newton–Gassendi triangle remains to be sorted out. McGuire takes Charleton rather than Gassendi to have likely been Newton's source (*Questions*, pp. 198–99). Suffice it to say that clearly Newton also read Gassendi during the decade of 1660, at least according to Westfall ("Foundations").

attack on the intelligibility of the notions of substance, accident, and inherence. (213.17–20).

The rather long discussion of place, (2.13.7–10) on the other hand, suggests a preference for the relational view. "Our *Idea* of Place, is nothing else, but such a relative Position of any thing," namely, "the relation of Distance betwixt any thing, and any two or more Points, which are considered, as keeping the same distance one with another, and so considered as at rest"—such consideration being a matter only of convention based on convenience.[14] On this view, according to Locke, the universe as a whole is said to be somewhere only in the sense that it exists, not that it has a place *sensu stricto*; also, as Locke realizes, the question of whether the universe as a whole moves in the void is without sense. It would seem too that, for reasons to be expanded below, space cannot be regarded as a system of places, as it is for the Cartesians, but at best a system of *possible places*. Finally, Locke has available to him a reading of the localization pattern, namely, that to be is to be some place: "though it be true, that the Word Place, has sometimes a more confused Sense, and stands for that Space, which any Body takes up; and so the Universe is in a Place" (2.13.10; 171). 'Place' here evidently means extension or capacity (see below), for which solidity is sufficient. The question of Locke's materialism, it may be noted in passing, is whether it is also necessary, that is, whether to be is to be solid.

The journal entry for March 27, 1676 expresses a view curiously very close to the Cartesian position:

> 27th Rain. Imaginary space seems to me noe more any thing than an imaginary world for if a man or his soule remained and the whole world were annihilated, there is left him the power of imagining either the world, or the extension it had which is all one with the space it fild, but this proves not that this imaginery space is any thing reall, or positive. For space or extension, seperated in our thoughts from matter or body seemes to have noe more reall existence, then number has (sine re numerata) without any thing to be numbered and one may as well say the number of the sea sand doth exist and is anything after such an annihilation. The space or extension of the sea does exist, or is any thing after annihilation. These are only affections of real existences the one of any being whatsoever the other was of material beings, which the mind has a power not only to conceive abstractedly, but increase by repetition, or addeing one to another, and to enlarge, which it hath not any other Ideas but those of quantity which amount at last but to the faculty of imagining and repeating addeing unites or numbering, but if the world were annihilated one had no more reason to thinke space anything, then the darkeness that will certainly be in it.[15]

[14] Cf. Locke's journal entry for January 20, 1678: Distance "seemes to me to be a pure relation" (Aaron and Gibb, *Early Draft*, p. 100).

[15] ibid., p. 77.

We have already examined this space called imaginary to indicate not that it is unreal, but that its nature is grasped by the imagination on analogy to the experience of material extension through the senses. On Locke's view there cannot be this unoccupied space or extension without body, for it would be a relation without relata, or more generally, a property that was the property of nothing. This is an argument offered by Descartes[16] and later exploited repeatedly by the Cartesians,[17] who of course regard extension as the principal attribute or essence of body. Since, if anything does, solidity plays this role for Locke, he will have a different understanding of the argument.

The key to the argument, and to the whole account of space, is the analysis of place, which is relational because dependent on distance. My thesis is that for Locke as for Descartes, space consists of two systems of relations, namely, those of distance and those of capacity or the extension of bodies, with the analysis of the latter assumed in the analysis of the former—a connection that is obscured by Locke's inconstant terminology. According to the fourth edition of the *Essay*, space "considered barely in length between any two Beings,[18] without considering any thing else between them, is called *Distance*," space considered in length, breadth, and thickness is *capacity*, and 'extension' refers to space however considered (2.13.3). In the previous three editions, however, extension is said to be space "when considered between the extremities of Matter, which fills the Capacity of Space with something solid, tangible, and movable." At 2.13.26 Locke again alters his terminology in the fourth edition; 'extension' is reserved to body and 'expansion' is applied to "*Space* in general, with or without solid matter possessing it, so as to say *Space* is *expanded*, and *Body extended*."[19] I propose to use 'space' as the generic term, 'distance' for the space between specific bodies, and 'capacity' for the space 'between the extremities of bodies.' What is of interest here is the suggestion that capacity in this sense is a relation between the extremities, since it brings Locke close to the Cartesian view of locus internus, which differs from body only conceptually.[20] Indeed, in the journal of January 20, 1678 Locke goes so far as to say that *body* "appears to me to be noething but the relation of the distance of the extremity." "This [capacity] is looked on to be a possessive inhaerent property of the body because it keeps constantly with it always the same and every particle has its share of it."[21]

On June 20, 1676 Locke urged the same view he had on March 27 of that year, that without body there is no space;[22] but he also argued that distance

---

[16] *Principles* 2, 16; *Second Replies*, def. 5; AT 7: 161; to Arnauld, July 29, 1648; AT, 5:223.

[17] Malebranche, *Search*, pp. 217–18.

[18] In 1685 Locke wrote 'Things' and crossed it out in favor of 'Beings.'

[19] See also 2.14.1

[20] *Principles* 2, 10–12.

[21] Aaron and Gibb, *Early Draft* p. 100.

[22] Ibid., p. 77; in the same entry he calls it a *nuda relatio*.

"seems . . . [a] simple relation arising [between] two bodies or beings that doe not immediately touch one an other," which begins to explain that view. While real ("this distance which is not barely an imaginary thing but really a relation between two separate beings")[23], the relation of distance nonetheless does not obtain without its relata: "relation being noething but the result of things in being as they are considerd or compard togeather."[24] On September 16, he continued, "for were there noe beings at all we might truly say there were noe distance."[25] Finally, in the entry for January 20, 1678, Locke argues that for the world to be a foot distant from something beyond it, there must be something real to which it stands in this relation: "it is evident there is always required some real existence to the other terme of the relation."[26] Locke is thus able "to resolve some doubts which have perplexd the learned of this later age about body extension, distance and space . . . distance may be something though it be not body and . . . though it be something it is not yet uncreated which have been the difficultys that have arisen about is matter."[27] He distinguishes the relation from body in Gassendist fashion as not having *partes extra partes*, as being immobile, indivisible, and inseparable even mentally. But the important result, contrary to Gassendi's view of space as a being suo modo, is that while distance between bodies is something, distance where there is no body, "abstract space," is nothing but the possibility of body.

Locke had reached this result by January 24, 1678:

> Space in its confusd and generall sense signifies noething but the existibility of body, when we have a more destinct and precise notion of it and make it the same with distance it is noe thing but the relation of two reall beings and supposes them actually to exist for if we say there is soe much space or distance to make the sentence clear and significative we adde between such a thing and such a thing, for one cannot say nor conceive that there is any such thing as space or distance between something and noething or which is yet more absurd too noethings.[28]

Previously, on September 16, 1677, he said "space in its self seemes to be noe thing but a capacity or possibility for extended beings or bodys to be or exist, which we are apt to conceive infinite."[29] Later in the same year he claimed that

---

[23] Ibid., pp. 77–78.

[24] Ibid., pp. 79–80. See also the entry for July 9, 1676: Space is described as a "real" relation but "in itself really nothing," "being but the result from the being of other things" Locke, *Essays on the Law of Nature* . . . , ed. von Leyden, pp. 258–59).

[25] Aaron and Gibb, *Early Draft*, p. 95.

[26] Ibid., p. 102.

[27] Ibid., pp. 79–80.

[28] Ibid., p. 105. Cf. January 20, 1678: "When we speak of Space in generall abstract and seperate from all consideration of any body at all or any other being it seems not then to be any reall thing but the consideration of a bare possibility of body to exist" (p. 100).

[29] Ibid., p. 94. Here Locke anticipates the container language of the *Essay*, but uses it to refer to the possibility of corporeal existence conceived as lack of resistance of body, which is how he

"Space is just noe thing, and signifies noe more but a bare possibility that body may exist where now there is none."[30] The term 'where' can refer only to place, which therefore seems definable in terms of spatial relations among non-material points independently of bodies (because even if there were no bodies and thus no material points we could still talk of space in this sense); the consequence is of course that space is relational, but also that the points themselves must be possibilities of solidity. On this view, Locke's plumping for the void means that the possibility of some spatial relations fails to be realized because the possibility for some instances of solidity fails to be realized. Strictly speaking, this claim is true only of space *void of body*, not absolutely void. It may be that with space identified with the divine immensity, all spatial relations are realized by God. But this would have no effect on Locke's empiricism, since only through experience could we know which relations are realized by body. To say that one thing is at a foot from another is not to say that there is anything a foot wide between them; it is only to say that there could be a body a foot wide between them without altering their relation of distance. To know which relations are realized and which not, the only recourse is to experience. To put it another way, abstract space is not real space as it is for Descartes. On the contrary, abstract space is nothing but a possibility, which is to say nothing at all. To determine what exists, where there is an existent and where not, we must appeal to experience. Thus Locke's rejection of the plenum is, as claimed above, his crucial stance against the Cartesians for whom all such relations must be realized.

Distinguishing space and body in defense of the void, Locke uses what he finds in Gassendi against the Cartesians; yet in doing so he himself opts for the relational space of the Cartesians against the absolute space of the Gassendists. The dénouement of the story here is in response to this apparent anomaly and is partly structural, partly historical. The historical part of the *dénouement* we have already seen. When Bernier reviewed the *Abrégé* 1 in preparation for a Latin translation of it, misgivings arose about Gassendi's views on a variety of fundamental issues, leading finally to his *Doubts*. So severe were Bernier's doubts about Gassendi's view of space as a being *suo modo* that for him space had become a pure nothing (*un pur rien*). As we have seen, Bernier argued the

---

conceives of it in his statement of the argument from Archytas against the Cartesians: "the Argument is at least as good, that where nothing hinders, (as beyond the utmost bounds of all Bodies) a *Body* put into motion may move on, as where there is nothing between, there two Bodies must necessarily touch. For pure *Space* between, is sufficient to take away the necessity of mutual Contact; but bare *Space* in the way, is not sufficient to stop Motion" (2.13.20; 176).

[30] Ibid., p. 96. On the other hand, Locke here at least adumbrates the absolutist alternative of *Essay* 2.13.26: "or if there be a necessity to suppose a being [where there is only the possibility of body] it must be god whose being we thus make *i.e.* suppose extended but not impenetrable." He concludes, "but be it one or other extension seemes to me mentally seperable from body, and distance noe thing but the relation of space resulting from the existence of two positive beings or which is all one two parts of the same being."

annihilation of space on several grounds; the most fundamental of these is that Gassendi's absolute space is an abstract or ideal entity. Bernier's alternative is precisely Locke's. Spatial relations are given the same nominalist analysis given any relation. It is no more the case that there *is something*, namely, space, between things distant from each other than there *is something*, namely, equality, when they are of the same size. To what extent Bernier's nominalist critique of Gassendi's view of absolute space was the source of Locke's rejection of that view, or was itself derived from that rejection, or perhaps was jointly arrived at with it, is, without further evidence, difficult to say. Given the personal relations between Locke and Bernier and the similarity of their views, however, the connection seems certain.

The second part of the dénouement deals with the structure of Locke's system. Admitting absolute space would be in violation of Locke's empiricism since it would amount to knowledge of an existent of which there was, and could be, no, or only partial, experience. Chapters 13–16 of book 2 (Of space and its simple modes, of duration, of duration and expansion considered together, of number)[31] can be plausibly read as of a piece with the following chapter (of infinity) in which Locke might well have considered a major threat from the Cartesians.

Descartes in *Meditations* 3 tried to disarm an objection to his argument to the existence of God as the cause of his idea of God. We could not be the cause of the idea of the infinite by negating the finite, he says, since there is more reality in an infinite substance than in a finite one. "Thus the perception of the infinite somehow [*quodammodo*] exists [*esse*] in me prior to that of the finite."[32] The way in which the idea of the infinite exists in me is undoubtedly as an innate idea. Thus Descartes concludes the paragraph with the Platonistic argument that I know myself to be imperfect only because I have the idea in me of a more perfect being with respect to which I know my imperfection.

Locke may have had this line of argument in mind in Draft A of the *Essay*: "Finite is that which hath an end, an end is a negation of farther production or extension Infinite is the negation of that negation ergo the Idea of Infinite is positive."[33] It is clear in any case that Locke's concern with the infinite even at this early date concerns the issues of innate ideas and empiricism. Paragraphs 44–45 of Draft A are specifically designed to answer the objection that the idea of the infinite must be innate because it cannot possibly be had from the senses. Locke responds that the idea of the infinite is a negative idea relating only to quantity.[34] And paragraphs 123–28 of Draft B already set out his position on the infinite as potential only. He says, for example, "when we speak of infinite, either duration or extension [in this work, these ideas along with their common

---

[31] As Aaron suggests (*John Locke*, pp. 154–171).

[32] AT, 7:45; CSM 2:30.

[33] Aaron and Gibb, *Early Draft*, p. 70.

[34] Ibid., pp. 69–73.

measure, number, are strictly speaking the only ideas of the infinite], it seems to me that we have not the positive or actual conception of any such thing, but barely the power of adding still any assignable or conceivable length of duration or extension; whereof we have the actual positive idea, to any number of the same lengths."[35]

As we have seen in some detail, Malebranche argued a case even more extreme than the innatist position on the infinite. For one thing, the idea of the infinite is not merely a standard against which finite things are measured. This secures for the idea of the infinite only a heuristically superior status over other ideas, which may be all it has for Descartes for whom all ideas are innate. For another thing, our knowledge of the infinite is for Malebranche a departure from the new way of ideas. Not only is the idea of the infinite not innate, we do not even have such an idea in the first place. In knowing the infinite we know God directly.

Malebranche in the *Dialogues* naturally enough raises the issues of abstraction and induction in this connection. His interlocutor objects that the idea of the infinite may be only the confused perception of many finite things and that the idea of being is only a confused mass of ideas of particular beings.[36] The suggestion is that by viewing several circles of different diameters, for example, one can arrive at the idea of a circle in general. Malebranche responds that while it is true that such a procedure gives rise to the idea of a circle in general, that idea is more than the mass of particular ideas giving rise to it. The general idea represents an infinite number of circles of infinitely many different diameters and thus contains more reality than any finite number of particular ideas. "You, can think of an indeterminate diameter only because you see the infinite in extension and can increase or decrease it to infinity. You could never think of these abstract forms, *viz.* genus and species, unless the idea of the infinite, which is inseparable from your mind, were quite naturally joined to the particular ideas you perceive."[37] This is also why, contrary to Arnauld, ideas and perceptions must be distinguished. We can have many sensations of color or pain, for example, and these are modifications of the mind (perceptions), but these never amount to the idea of a color or pain in general, which cannot be the modification of a particular being[38]. The mind therefore always has available to it, but different from it, the idea of the infinite or being in general, under which it subsumes its particular perceptions. (Malebranche's metaphor here has it that

---

[35] Rand, *Essay*, p. 265.

[36] *Dialogues* 2, ix–x; *Oeuvres*, 12–13:57–60.

[37] Ibid., The notion of a merely indefinite diameter suggests the potential infinite. But earlier Malebranche had raised this possibility only in order to reject it: "The mind perceives an infinite whose end it does not see but it does not see an infinite extension" (*Dialogues* 1, viii; *Oeuvres*, 12–13:43). Malebranche's reply argues for an actual infinite only if we assume, as we must for him, that the certainty he claims we have that infinite extension has no end requires an actual object.

[38] Ibid., p. 59.

the mind spreads [*répandre*] the idea of infinite over its finite ideas. Elsewhere he has it join the two. The result in any case is a representation.)

The upshot of all this is, of course, the vision of all things in God. In perceiving any given thing, what we know is in fact the divine substance insofar as it can be participated in by that thing, i.e. what we know is its archetype. The idea of the infinite, Malebranche concludes, thus precedes the idea of the finite. He follows Descartes in this but extends Descartes's claim that the infinite "somehow" precedes the finite far beyond any warrant of the Cartesian texts. For Malebranche, "in order for us to conceive of a finite being, something must necessarily be eliminated [*retrancher*] from this general notion of being . . . and far from this idea being formed from the confused collection of all our ideas of particular beings . . . , all these particular ideas are in fact but participations in the general idea of the infinite; just as God does not draw His being from creatures, while every creature is but an imperfect participation in the divine being."[39] No such view is to be found in Descartes. It is not surprising, then, that Malebranche distinguishes the way we know finite material things from the way we know God. Finite material things, because they are unintelligible by themselves, are known only indirectly through their ideas. God is known directly[40]. The perception of a material thing, as Malebranche insists at every opportunity, consists of a subjective modification, namely, a sensation, and an idea, namely, the divine substance limited by the sensation. The perception of God, however, is, as Malebranche puts it, by pure intellection.[41]

The argument of both Descartes and Malebranche is from the perception of the actual infinite to a special source for the perception beyond sense experience, and to a special mode of awareness, namely, intellectual intuition. Locke attempts to shortcircuit these Cartesian arguments by allowing a potential infinite only, the preparation for which is his analysis of space. In this he follows the lead of Gassendi, who in his *Objections* and *Disquisitio metaphysica* raised similar objections to similar views in Descartes.[42]

---

[39] *Search*, p. 232.

[40] Ibid., pp. ii, vii. These ways of knowing are also distinguished from how we know ourselves (i.e., by consciousness or inner sensation) and how we know other minds (i.e., by conjecture).

[41] *Search*, p. 322.

[42] Bloch, *La philosophie*, pp. 133–34. It might also be the case that Locke was influenced by Cudworth in this strategy. Though he rejected the inference that "Modern Atheists" drew from it, Cudworth granted their premise that we have neither a sensible phantasm nor an intelligible idea of the infinite, allowing only a potential infinite with respect to space, number, and perhaps time. "*Infinite Space*, beyond the *Finite World*, is a thing which hath been much talked of; and it is by some supposed to be Infinite Body, but by others to be an *Incorporeal Infinite*; through whose Actual Distance notwithstanding (Mensurable by Poles and Miles) this *Finite World* might rowl and tumble *Infinitely*. But as we conceive, all that can be demonstrated here, is no more than this, That how vastsoever the Finite World should be, yet there is a *Possibility* of more and more *Magnitude* and *Body*, still to be added to it, further and further, by *Divine Power*, *Infinitely*; or that the World could never be made so Great, no not by himself, as that his own Omnipotence could not make it yet Greater. Which *Potential Infinity* or *Indefinite Encreasableness* of *Corporeal Magnitude*, seems to

What of the things that are said to be in space? As a first approximation we can say that for Locke what is in space is solid and only solid. "[Solidity] of all other, seems the *Idea* most intimately connected with, and essential to Body so as no where else to be found or imagin'd, but only in matter"(2.4.1; 123). In his treatment of it, solidity seems for Locke to constitute the principal attribute or essence of matter in something like the Cartesian sense—on it all its other properties depend. Insofar as a body is solid it fills space; using the language of the container view of space Locke here presumably attributes even the geometrical properties of body to solidity. Its filling space means two things: Metaphysically, it excludes others from the space it fills, and thus solidity seems to be the principle of individuation, of which I shall say more later; and physically, it resists bodies that would fill its space, that is, it grounds the fundamental dynamical property of bodies. (2.4.2) In addition, the "*Mutual Impulse, Resistance,* and *Protrusion*" of bodies depend on solidity. (2.4.5; 2.13.11) Most important, and most contrary to the Cartesians, space and solidity differ. "By this *Idea* of Solidity, is the Extension of Body distinguished from the Extension of Space. The Extension of Body being nothing, but the cohesion or continuity of solid, separable, movable Parts; and the Extension of Space, the continuity of unsolid, inseparable, and immovable Parts" (2.4.5; 126). In thus viewing solidity as fundamental to matter, Locke again follows the Gassendist lead. Consider Bernier:

> having three or four things in matter, solidity, hardness, resistance, impenetrability and extension, which at bottom are a single and unique thing conceived differently, solidity must be considered as what is primary in matter and as the primitive and original cause of extension. . . . The reason for this is that we conceive that what makes two parts of matter keep their extension or remain outside each other without them reducing one to the other and merging in a single and same place is that they mutually resist each other, and they resist each other because they are hard and solid. From which it must be inferred that rather than extension as the essence of matter, we must establish solidity, which is primary, or if you wish, impenetrability, which follows from solidity, although necessarily.[43]

Notice that Bernier adumbrates even Locke's distinction between solidity, which "carries something more of positive in it," and impenetrability, "which is negative, and is, perhaps, more a consequence of *Solidity*, than Solidity it self" (2.4.1; 123). Notice too the suggestion that solidity is not just the property on which all the other properties of a thing depend, but the *only* property of a thing,

---

have been mistaken for an *Actual Infinity* of *Space*" (*System*, pp. 643–44; see also pp. 765–66). This text was published in 1678, by which time Locke's strategy was already in place, but it received an imprimatur in 1671, so perhaps Locke had access to a prepublication version by which he might have been influenced. The one possibility ruled out by the early imprimatur (as if it needed to be ruled out) is that Locke influenced Cudworth.

[43] *Abrégé* 2, 2:104–5.

and that its other properties are but solidity *conceived* differently. That is, a thing is said to have properties beyond its solidity only in so far as its solidity is conceived in different ways.

To show how for Locke the appearances can be saved by solidity alone, something must first be said of his distinction between simple and complex ideas. For eventually I shall advance the bold thesis that ultimately the idea of solidity is the only simple idea for Locke and that the complexity of all else we experience is a function of our perceptual relation to it. We know just from his classification of it that the idea of solidity is a simple idea for Locke. (2.4) As a quick approximation of my argument that it is the *only* simple idea, consider his later treatment of the other ideas, such as colors and powers, (2.3–7) which are there also classified as simple: "I confess *Power includes in it some kind of relation* . . . as indeed which of our *Ideas*, of what kind soever, when attentively considered, does not? . . . And sensible Qualities, as Colours . . . what are they but the *Powers* of different Bodies, in relation to our Perception?"(2.21.3; 234). Now, if all relations are complex and thus, as we shall see, at least in part the work of the mind, and if only solidity fails to be relational when attentively considered, then (the idea of) solidity will be ontologically and epistemologically most primitive.

§19 SIMPLE AND COMPLEX IDEAS

Locke's attempt to distinguish simple and complex ideas on phenomenological grounds is generally regarded as not very helpful. To say of a simple idea that it is "in it self uncompounded, and contains in it nothing but *one uniform Appearance*, or Conception in the mind" (2.2.2; 119) is to say both too much and too little. The idea of a curve may be uniform but is nonetheless complex; and to call an idea uncompounded is only to call it simple. More promising is the characterization of simple ideas as those in whose perception the mind is entirely passive, and of complex ideas as those resulting from the mind's activity. "Where the Understanding is once stored with these simple *Ideas*, it has the Power to repeat, compare, and unite them even to an almost infinite Variety, and so can make at Pleasure new complex *Ideas*. But it is not in the Power of the most exalted Wit, or enlarged Understanding, by any quickness or variety of Thought, to invent or frame one new simple Idea in the mind, not taken in by [sensation or reflection]". (2.2.2; 119–20). Thus, never having previously encountered a pineapple I cannot have an idea of its taste, but having seen things of the same color and shape, I can combine these and imagine what it looks like. What exactly is this activity and what does it yield?

At 2.12.3 Locke divides complex ideas into modes, substances and relations. (Note for later that he does *not* say *ideas* of modes, substances and relations.) In the fourth edition, however, he adds to 2.12.1 a division according to the mind's acts "wherein it exerts its power over its simple *Ideas*"; the first of these is its power of combining ideas, and from this, he says, result all complex ideas. This poses a terminological problem since relations and general ideas result from two *further* kinds of act, comparing and separating. The problem, at a minimum, is that relations are thus classed both as complex and noncomplex and further, that it is unclear how general ideas stand to substance and mode.

The terminological instability may be an indication of two models of mental activity. (1) On the *production model* a new idea is produced *from the materials* of simple ideas; thus, "though . . . made up of several simple ones put together," "complex ideas may be considered each by it self, as one entire thing, and signified by one name."(12.12.1; 164). There might be various versions of this model. (a) One would be the *creation* version, a theory Malebranche criticizes as requiring a power no less than that of creation ex nihilo. "It is no more difficult to create an angel than to produce it from a stone," and no less difficult to produce an idea from an impression than to create it from nothing.[44] But this is not Locke's position, for it seems precluded by what he says about the production of simple ideas. As in the material world our power is restricted to the rearrangement of particles and never extends to the creation or annihilation of them, so in the mental we cannot create or annihilate simple ideas but only as it were, rearrange them.[45] (b) Another version of the production model might be called the *essentialist* version, whose main idea would be the Aristotelian contention that a house, for example, is more than the sum of its parts. Again we have a view that cannot have been held by Locke, for whom the essence of a thing consists only in its microscopic parts. There are emergent properties for Locke, but these as we shall see, relate only to the production of *simple* ideas of *secondary* qualities. (c) There is a less extreme version of the production model that might be called the *combinatorial* version; here complex ideas are just sets of simple ideas. As an ontological account of complex ideas, this version is not incompatible with the second model of mental activity.

(2) On the *perception model*, complex ideas are merely *results of viewing* simple ideas in a certain way, with no real change in the simple ideas. For an intuitive idea of the model, consider figure-ground shifts; to see now as a rabbit what we just saw as a duck requires no change in what we see. On this model the world's complexity is a function of our perception of it, which is as it should be, given atomism. Substances, that is, perceived things such as calendars and harmonicas, are, like relations and universals, mind-dependent, though through "inadvertency" we may regard this complexity as a simple idea, that is, as given.(2.23.1; 295) Now, a full explication of this model would have to show how in fact *all* perception for Locke is passive—after all, complexity cannot be

[44] *Search*, p. 223.
[45] 2.2.2; 120. Also, 2.26.1–2; 324–5 and below.

a matter of volition, for it is not up to me to see the calendar to the left of the harmonica, or to see them as substances. This is a long story involving the role of judgment in perception, what Malebranche called natural judgments and Hume called natural beliefs, the historical dénouement of which is association-ist psychology. But in any case, I do think that this is the model Locke has in mind when he says that we get relations by "bringing two *Ideas* . . . together; and setting them by one another, so as to take a view of them at once, without uniting them into one"(2.12.1; 163); whereas substances are got by viewing ideas so as to unite them, and modes by viewing ideas so as to separate them. On this model Locke, far from being sloppy, in fact is as precise as he can be when he later says that the nature of relation consists in the *referring* or *comparing* of two things (2.25.5; 321), for relations *are acts of awareness*, not occurrent real properties of things. Nor is Locke guilty of one of the confusions to which he admits between 'idea' and 'quality' when he says (2.23.1; 293) that a substance is a bundle of *ideas* (plus a substrate), rather than a bundle of *qualities*, for substances (apart from the substrate) must be perceived.

That substances are not real, of course, contradicts the classical reading by Gibson, for example, who says that Locke assumes "as axiomatic that reality can consist of nothing but substances and their modifications. For him, as for the Schoolmen, the idea of substance is the 'foundation of all the rest.' "[46] To be sure, the *idea* of substance is the conceptual foundation of all the rest of our *ideas*. But it does not follow from this that substance is found in reality.[47] In the fifth edition Locke appended a footnote to 2.23.2 in which he discusses the notion of substance in general, that is, the subject of inherence. He disclaims any intent to give an account of the idea of substance in general; if I am right, this idea is incoherent, or at least less than serviceable—as Locke makes clear in this section with his analogy of the elephant and the tortoise.[48] He says that his aim was instead to explain how individuals of various kinds (which in fact are complex) come to be regarded as simple and the basis for this, presumably psychological, operation is "the supposed simple *Substratum* or *Substance*, which was look'd upon as the thing it self in which inhere, and from which resulted that Complication of *Ideas* by which it was represented to us" (2.23.2; 295). Locke's doctrine of both individual substances and substance in general

---

[46] *Locke's Theory*, p. 191.

[47] In addition, in the very passage Gibson quotes in support of his interpretation, Locke says that a positive, clear, distinct idea of substance "is concealed from us" such that "the *Ideas*, we can attain to by our Faculties, are very disproportionate to Things themselves" (4.3.23; 554).

[48] "If any one should be asked, what is the subject wherein Colour or Weight inheres, he would have nothing to say, but the solid extended parts: And if he were demanded, what is it, that Solidity and Extension inhere in, he would not be in a much better case, than the Indian . . . who, saying that the World was supported by a great Elephant, was asked, what the Elephant rested on; to which his answer was a great Tortoise: But being again pressed to know what gave support to the broad-back'd Tortoise, replied, something, he knew not what" (2.23.2; 295–96).

thus carries with it no ontology beyond that of *ideas*. It is worth dwelling on this important point.

Consider the two expressions, 'a statue of Caesar', and 'a statue of marble.' The first is a genitive of representation, indicating what the statue is about; the second is a genitive of composition, indicating what it is composed of. One difference between them is that Caesar is really distinct from the statue while the marble is not. My contention is that when Locke speaks of the complex idea of substance he is using the genitive of composition. Only when he uses 'substance' in a loose and popular sense, in the way that substance would be acceptable to Berkeley, for example, is it used as a genitive of representation. When applied to the Lockean idea of substance, however, it is difficult to keep these senses distinct. For both senses distinguish the idea of substance as a *kind* of idea. Thus an of-a-substance idea is the kind of idea in terms of which we perceive, if not substances, at least things *as* substances; that is, each of the genitives is in this case a condition for the other. One might therefore plausibly find two competing strands in Locke's thinking about substance: One is more ontological, regarding substance as a substrate for real qualities; the other is more Kantian, regarding substance as a mental category unifying experience.[49] According to my reading, the substrate for real qualities is nothing more than a mind-imposed category. Thus I am proposing the Kantian reading of Locke, albeit with an empirical theory of categories instead of a transcendental deduction of them.

The strongest evidence *against* this interpretation is to be found in Locke's *Letter* to Stillingfleet, who had charged Locke, along with Toland, with having "almost discarded *Substance* out of the reasonable part of the World."[50] Locke resists this characterization, citing at length his various statements on substance in the *Essay*, which he summarizes as follows: "These, and the like fashions of speaking, intimate, that the substance is supposed always something, besides the extension, figure, solidity, motion, thinking, or other observable idea, though we know not what it is." But notice that Locke says, not that substance *is*, but that substance is *supposed*. He continues: "as long as there is any simple idea or quality left . . . substance cannot be discarded; because all simple ideas, all sensible qualities, carry with them a supposition of a substratum to exist in, and a substance in which to inhere."[51] Here the ambiguity is clearly focused on the kind of supposition carried by ideas and qualities (and Stillingfleet subsequently pressed Locke on just this point). Later in the *Letter* Locke specifically distinguishes the being of substance from its idea; but he gives a weak defense against the charge that he makes the former doubtful by making the latter doubtful and imperfect. He quotes 2.23.29 to the effect that there are many

---

[49] Thus Yolton, *John Locke*, pp. 135–36.
[50] *Discourse in Vindication of The Trinity* (1696), chap. 10; *Works* 3:503.
[51] *Works*, 4:7.

things that exist, angels for example, of which we have but imperfect ideas or no ideas at all, and that sensation convinces us there are solid extended substances as does reflection that there are thinking ones.[52]

The question remains open, however, as to the nature of this conviction about substance and the basis for it. For since sensation and reflection yield only ideas, the appeal can be only to a supposed support.[53] In the key text on this question Locke says: "not imagining how these simple *Ideas* can subsist by themselves, we accustom our selves, to suppose some *Substratum*, wherein they do subsist, and from which they do result, which therefore we call *Substance*" (2.23.1; 295). Stillingfleet very properly picks up on this custom of supposing and wants to know about its basis: "Is that *Custom* grounded upon true Reason or not?"[54] I shall return to this issue in section 26 of chapter 7 below, attempting to show that Locke in fact does not discard substance out of the reasonable part of the world because the only reasonable part of the world is the mental, where substance is to be found. For Stillingfleet, on the other hand, the reasonable part of the world is nonmental; it is found in the real nature of things, which Locke finds incomprehensible and which is why, I think, he is genuine in his claim of not understanding Stillingfleet's charge in the first place of having discarded substance out of the reasonable part of the world.[55] We shall return to this issue at length in the next chapter.

With this nonontic account of substance, meanwhile, better sense might be made of Locke's division of complex ideas. Locke added the problematic classification of ideas according to the mind's different activities to the fourth edition of the *Essay* (1700). This was the first edition to appear after the polemic with Stillingfleet. Whatever the significance of the new classification, I think that there is little doubt it resulted from that polemic. My hypothesis is that Locke as a result of it came to see the inadequacy of his original classification, which was designed for a very limited though important purpose, namely, to give an empiricist account of our knowledge of space, time, and infinity. He ends the chapter, for example, claiming that with the distinctions just made he can do precisely this, and the category primarily used for the task, mode, is treated first and most extensively. But however sufficient for this task, mode, even of two sorts, is otherwise a Procrustean bed. Simple modes are "only variations, or different combinations of the same simple *Idea*, without the mixture of any other, as a dozen or score." Mixed modes are "compounded of simple *Ideas* of several kinds"; thus beauty or thrift (2.12.5; 165). In neither of these sorts do we find the idea of whiteness, for example. The idea of *this* (instance of) white is a simple idea, but the idea of whiteness in general is certainly not, otherwise anyone who has ever seen a white thing would have it,

[52] *Works*, 4:18. See also n. to 2.23.1 of 5th ed.

[53] See p.29, where Locke speaking of the existence of bodily substances confirms this reading.

[54] *Vindication*, chap. 10; *Works*, 3:504.

[55] *Works*, 4:5.

which Locke thinks is false. For him, only through great effort and experience do we achieve such an idea. The issue of kinds was one on which Stillingfleet pressed Locke very hard and for this reason abstraction, for instance, is explicitly recognized as a separate mental activity in the later edition. This is part of a general shift in emphasis from the production model to the perception model. It should be underlined that the two models are not at all incompatible and certainly are not clearly distinguished in the text. What the perception model allows, however, is the clear distinction between ideas and things that enables Locke to respond to Stillingfleet's objection that for him essences are no less arbitrary and all distinctions no less subjective than for Hobbes. Roughly the idea would be that complex ideas are not our creations (creations ex nihilo in one of the extreme versions of the production model) but different ways of viewing a world that is no less objective for being viewed in those ways. Whether this counts as an answer to the charge of Hobbism is a question we shall have a great deal to say about below.

Now, what does all this mean for solidity, and more especially, for space? If space were a mode, or even a relational set of simple modes, we could conclude straightaway that spatial characteristics are mind-dependent. But 2.5, "Of simple *Ideas* of divers Senses," makes clear that the idea of space is a *simple* idea, and Locke repeats the point in a remark that does not appear in Draft C (1685) but only with the first edition, referring to "the *simple Idea of Space*" (2.13.2; 167). Henry Lee was one who found this classification problematic: "*Simple Modes*, in the Author's sense, are a sort of *Complex Ideas*, tho they be only various Modifications of a *Simple Idea*. Thus tho' Time, Space and Number be *simple Ideas* themselves, yet the Parts or Modes of them are complex Ideas: such are the words *Year, Foot*. . . . How proper it is to call the Part of a thing complex, and the Whole a *simple Idea*, I leave others to examine."[56] Since the simple-complex distinction is the passive-active distinction, a simple idea being composed of complex ones need not be paradoxical in the way Lee evidently thinks it is; the mind may be unable to produce its idea of space, but once in possession of that idea it may be able to produce its parts.[57]

[56] Lee, *Anti-scepticism*, p. 70.

[57] Locke was not unaware of the objection raised by Lee. In the second edition of his translation of the *Essay* Coste reports that he conveyed to Locke the objections from Barbeyrac, professor of law at Groningen, that he had failed to define 'simple' and had made the simple idea of space to consist of parts. In a note to the fifth edition Locke insists that he did provide the definition in question and that as indicated at 2.15.9, the idea of extension is simple in the sense that although compounded it is not compounded of ideas of different kinds. But this would make all ideas of which there are simple modes in this sense simple. Locke realizes that there is something unique about the idea of extension, however, when he concludes his note: "But if this is not sufficient to clear the Difficulty, Mr. *Locke* hath nothing more to add, but that if the *Idea* of Extension is so peculiar, that it cannot exactly agree with the Definition that he has given of those *Simple Ideas*, so that it differs in some manner from all others of that kind, he thinks 'tis better to leave it there expos'd to this Difficulty, than to make a new Division in his Favour" (2.15.9; 201–2).

More problematic is the classification of space, or extension, along with figure, rest, and motion (2.5) as common sensibles: "that we get the *Idea* of Space, both by our Sight and Touch . . . is so evident" as to need no proof.[58] A long tradition typically regards the simple as incorrigible, with error being a function of complexity, as contributed by judgment, for example. Locke joins this tradition with his view that truth and falsehood properly apply only to propositions. "*Ideas*, being nothing but bare Appearances or Perceptions in our Minds, cannot properly and simply in themselves be said to be *true* or *false*" (2.31.1; 384). Such ideas as may be called true or false are complex in that they are based on some proposition. *Simple* ideas, meanwhile, are but the effects of powers and thus are *adequate*, that is, they "perfectly represent those Archetypes, which the Mind supposes them taken from; which it intends them to stand for, and to which it refers them" (2.31.1; 375). Now, Locke's and Aristotle's lists of common sensibles are essentially the same; both include rest, motion, and shape, and for Aristotle's number and size Locke substitutes space or extension.[59] But a feature of Aristotelian common sensibles is that we can be mistaken with respect to them.[60] It is tempting to regard Locke as having nodded, then, in classifying space as both simple and a common sensible. Certainly this was the reaction of Berkeley, whose rejection of all common sensibles, the linchpin of his theory of perception, began with a long argument against space as a common sensible. In this regard it is worth recalling that the common-special sensible distinction corresponds to the primary-secondary quality distinction. A reason why special sensibles might be thought incorrigible is that like secondary qualities they are in some sense only subjective. Common sensibles may be thought to be, like primary qualities, mind-independent and thus it may be possible to be wrong about them. Berkeley thus attacks the mind-independence of any sensibles by attacking both distinctions.

I shall have more to say below about the simplicity of the idea of space but meanwhile we might begin answering the difficulty by appealing to the Principle of Exegetical Charity.[61] As we shall see with respect to the idea of power, Locke sometimes describes an idea as simple that in itself is complex because it is simple in relation to other ideas. Among such ideas are just the ideas in question here: "Extension, Duration and Number . . . Bulk, Figure, Texture and Motion of the Parts" (2.21.3; 234). These ideas all include some relation, he

---

[58] 2.13.2; 167. Thus, for example, figure is a common sensible in that it can be perceived by the senses of sight and touch, as opposed to a special sensible such as color, for example, which is specific to sight.

[59] *De anima* 2.5.6; 418a18.

[60] At least according to Aquinas, whose gloss is incorrigible, it seems to me. See *Aristotle's De Anima*, 255.

[61] Ceteris paribus, texts should be interpreted charitably, that is, so as to make them true, interesting, relevant, consistent, etc.

says, and thus are complex. We may provisionally conclude, then, that spatial characteristics are in a radical sense mind-dependent.

The upshot is that a thing's perceived shape is a function of our perception of it. This is not merely a matter of perspective, although problems of perspective are resolved by this thesis: As there is no perceived color that is the real colour of a pigeon's neck, so there is no perceived shape which is the real shape of a penny, both varying with perceptual conditions. For the same conclusion is reached by another kind of argument. At 2.4.5 Locke distinguishes in Gassend-ist fashion between the extension of body and the extension of space: "The Extension of the Body [is] nothing, but the cohesion or continuity of solid, separable, moveable Parts; and the Extension of Space, the continuity of un-solid, inseparable, and immovable Parts." Since atomic particles are by defini-tion inseparable, that is, indivisible, they are without extension, and thus with-out shape.[62]

A similar result is reached at 2.1.3, where Locke attacks the Cartesian plenum with an argument for which Gassendi may have been the primary vehicle from antiquity.[63] The argument is interesting in its own right. Dividing a body so as to make possible the rearrangement of its parts without altering the superficies of the body, Locke argues, requires a void at least as large as the least part of the body even if it be no larger than the one-hundred-millionth part of mustard seed. The situation is illustrated by Sam Loyd's "15 Puzzle"—the two-dimensional rearrangement of square tablets numbered one to fifteen, which requires an unoccupied sixteenth square. The upshot is that because atoms are solid they are inseparable, and because inseparable, without extension.

This is a slightly different argument from that advanced by the ancient atomists. Simplicius tells us that "Leucippus, Democritus, and Epicurus sup-posed [the first principles] to be uncuttable and indivisible and impassive be-cause of their solidity, and without any share of the void. For division, they maintain, takes place because of the void which is in bodies."[64] The argument is that a knife can cut through bread only if it encounters void space and that it will do so only to the point at which it meets the uncuttables, namely, the atoms, which are solid, or as Leucippus put it, "well-kneaded," that is, "without air spaces." Now, this argument, which unlike Locke's does not insist on unaltered superficies, may be rebutted by allowing parts of alleged atoms simply to be moved aside. Division may require motion in the divided, and motion may require the void, but that void may be *outside* of bodies.

The Cartesian might try to use a version of this rebuttal in response to Locke's argument: For a body to move, space void only of *it* is required; thus motion is

---

[62] This was pointed out to me by James Pettit.

[63] The argument is also to be found in Bruno, in Cicero's *De natura deorum* (1.20.50), and in Lucretius. See Koyré, *Infinite Universe*, pp. 283–84, n. 33.

[64] *De caelo* 242,18 (DK 67 A14), quoted by Robinson, *Greek Philosophy*, p. 198.

possible if bodies simultaneously displace and are displaced by others, thus in a circle or three-dimensionally in a vortex. But this solution must be rejected by Locke because it entails that, contrary to the atomist hypothesis, matter is infinitely divisible, which Locke regards as near-contradictory (2.23.31; 313). For Descartes a body is as much of matter as moves together; and motion is relative to surrounding bodies. Thus motion occurs when the relation of the parts of a body to those around them change. But there will be parts of a body only if they have their own motion, which they do not have since the body moves as a whole.[65] To avoid the conclusion, first suggested by Newton, that if Descartes's view is correct no motion is possible, we must suppose motions on motions carousel-style to infinity, and thus the infinite division of matter. This in fact was a view held early on by Leibniz, who concluded against Descartes that, not extension, but motion was the essence of body.[66] And later Leibniz argued that if one takes cohesion to be the essence of body, as he thought Locke had done, then motion in a plenum is impossible.[67] Except for his distinction between extension and body, Leibniz's solution would be acceptable to a Cartesian, since it introduces no nongeometrical properties. But it would obviously not be acceptable to a proper atomist. Some other account, then, must be found for the cohesion of Locke's extensionless atoms.

The problem of cohesion of bodies is very prominent in the period. For example, Leibniz's first criticism of Hobbes was directed to the solution he saw Hobbes as offering to this problem.[68] The problem also lies at the heart of Malebranche's revision of Descartes's rules for the communication of motion and his debates with Leibniz on the topic over a thirty-five-year period. Locke does not know what to make of cohesion, finding it as inexplicable as thinking in the soul. "Since Body is no farther, nor otherwise extended than by the union and cohesion of its solid parts, we shall very ill comprehend the extension of Body, without understanding wherein consists the union and cohesion of its parts; which seems to me as incomprehensible, as the manner of Thinking, and how it is performed."[69] The inexplicable cohesion is not that of bodies composed of atoms. The result of this attachment of parts is hardness, which can be explained in mechanistic terms.

For Locke there can be no mechanical account of cohesion in the sense we are discussing. At 2.23.23 he argues that our idea of body is no less obscure than our idea of spirit. Just as one does not know how he thinks, so he does not know "how he [sic] is extended; how the solid parts of Body are united, or cohere together to make Extension"(2.23.23; 308). An ambient fluid may explain the

---

[65] Grosholz argues that Descartes circularly relies on individual parts of matter to account for individuation in terms of common motion of parts ("Case Study," esp. p. 122).

[66] To Arnauld, November 1671; *Papers and Letters*, p. 148.

[67] *New Essays*, p. 59.

[68] in terms of reaction. To Hobbes, July 1670; *Papers anf Letters*, p. 106.

[69] 2.23.23; 309. Also 4.3.28–29; 558–60; 2.23.28; 311.

coherence of matter whose pores are less than, and whose parts are greater than, the parts of the fluid. Although Locke, typically, does not name him, Malebranche had given this explanation.[70] This solution does not explain the cohesion of the fluid particles, however; or, if this is explained by a still finer fluid, of its particles, and so on. What is more, according to Locke, the much discussed phenomenon of the polished slabs of marble that can be separated only by sliding them apart shows that if the pressure of an ambient fluid were the only cause of cohesion, every body would be separable along every plane intersection just by sliding the parts. Such separation would encounter no more resistance from the fluid than would motion of the whole through it; for both cases would allow accession of the fluid parts to the parts of space vacated by the corporeal parts. The problem is the one Malebranche essentially taxed Descartes with, namely, to account for the ultimate difference between contact and continuity.

What Locke finds incomprehensible is the internal, necessary cohesion of the parts of *atoms*, which along with the production of sensation and the rules for communication of motion, he elsewhere attributes to the "Arbitrary Will and good Pleasure of the Wise Architect" (4.3.29; 560). We are unable to understand what it is that is kept together as opposed to what keeps it together.[71] What Locke feels he cannot explain is the fact, or as he puts it, the creation, of material existence, which just is the indivisibility of solidity, that is, the difference between material space, between body and the void, between being and nonbeing. I shall return to Locke's view on this question in a separate section below. Meanwhile, it is worth noting that, at least early on, Leibniz clearly distinguished the mechanical and metaphysical questions of cohesion. To the former he answered in terms of motion. Things cohere and are distinguishable as bodies in so far as they are composed of particles, that is, disparate motions in the same direction. Given the infinite divisibility of matter, nothing is ultimately coherent.[72] Similarly, nothing is ultimately fluid, that is, utterly without resistance to division. Thus he rejects both Epicurus's atoms and the Cartesian subtle matter.[73] But why there is any cohesion at all, which for Leibniz is the question why there should be any motion, is a *metaphysical* question whose answer entails the existence of God.[74]

Henry Lee in effect tried to collapse the distinction between the mechanical

---

[70] *Search*, p. 520. See also *Oeuvres*, 17:39–44. William Carroll took Locke's chapter to be proof that he had read the *Search*, whence, according to Carroll, Locke took his conception of truth and knowledge (*Dissertation*, p. 285).

[71] Another instance of Locke's distinction between mechanistic and metaphysical questions and his agnosticism with respect to the latter is his claim that we can no more understand the initiation of motion by impulse than we can of it by thought (2.23.28). Mechanics will give us laws of motion but will not explain how impenetrability is sufficient for alteration of motion.

[72] *New Essays*, p. 59.

[73] Ibid., p. 125.

[74] "The Confession of Nature Against Atheists" (1669); *Papers and Letters*, pp. 107–12.]

and metaphysical questions. He claimed that Locke's argument at 2.13.22 concerning the mustard seed fails because the parts might be fluid.[75] The problem as he saw it was not the void but moving parts. But as Leibniz saw, perfect fluidity, absolute penetrability, *is* the void, and to describe this *materia subtilissima* as matter would be (as Lee himself realized) hopelessly ad hoc: "And therefore I always suspected that the conceit [of the plenum] was set up, by the late Masters of the *Mechanick Hypothesis*, only to serve a turn to help them explain, in their way" (p.71). I think Lee just failed to catch the peculiarly metaphysical significance of Locke's notion of solidity, criticizing Locke's account for either inventing a new word or giving a new sense to the old one. By 'solid' Lee thought Locke meant continuity and coherence of parts; his own account in these terms, it might be noted, is incoherent, indeed contradictory, because he goes on to claim that resistance is a matter of filling space or coherence of parts, not solidity. In any case, Lee failed to see that Locke had distinguished solidity from hardness and resistance (p.51).

§20   PRIMARY AND SECONDARY QUALITIES

It might be thought that an objection to the above is found in Locke's representationalist theory of perception, which distinguishes between ideas of primary and secondary qualities on the basis of their resemblance or failure to resemble those qualities. Although they have a representative function, ideas of secondary qualities do not resemble those qualities; but among ideas of primary qualities, which do resemble those qualities, we find in addition to the idea of solidity, the ideas of extension, figure, motion or rest, and number. It would seem to follow that in addition to being solid, what is external to the mind really is extended, figured, and the like, that it is such independently of its being perceived as such. So far is this theory from being an objection to my account of solidity, however, that I am prepared to make it the main post and pillar of the account. To show this, the objection must be developed in further detail.

Recall that for Locke an idea is the object of awareness, the *id quod intelligitur* in the Scholastics' phrase. "Whatsoever the Mind perceives in itself, or is the immediate object of Perception, Thought, or Understanding, that I call Idea" (2.8.8; 134). Or again, "Every Man being conscious to himself, That he thinks, and that which his Mind is employ'd about whilst thinking, being the Ideas, that are there, 'tis past doubt, that men have in their Minds several Ideas" (2.1.1; 104). These ideas are needed because of the problem of action at a distance; objects that are not spatially present to the mind cannot act on it in the way necessary to be perceived. " Bodies produce *Ideas* in us . . . *by impulse*. . . . If then external Objects be not united to our Minds, when they

---

[75] *Anti-scepticism*, pp. 74–5.

produce *Ideas* in it; . . . 'tis evident, that some motion must be thence continued by our Nerves, or animal Spirits, by some parts of our Bodies, to the Brains or the seat of Sensation, there to *produce in our Minds the particular* Ideas *we have of them*" (2.8.12; 136). Or, in an even clearer passage, " since the Things, the Mind contemplates, are none of them, besides it self, present to the Understanding, 'tis necessary that something else, as a Sign or Representation of the thing it considers, should be present to it: And these are *Ideas*" (4.21.4; 720–21). In addition, these epistemological proxies are said to be pictures or images of the things whose place they take. So much is clear from Locke's use of the camera oscura model of the mind: "external and internal Sensation, are the only passages that I can find, of Knowledge, to the Understanding. These alone, as far as I can discover, are the Windows by which light is let into this *dark Room.* For, methinks, the *Understanding* is not much unlike a Closet wholly shut from the light, with only some little openings left, to let in external visible Resemblances, or *Ideas* of things without; would the Pictures coming into such a dark Room but stay there, and lie so orderly as to be found upon occasion, it would very much resemble the Understanding of a Man, in reference to all Objects of sight, and the *Ideas* of them" (2.12.17; 162–63). The objection may now be stated more clearly. The images depicted on the mind's screen, as it were, appear to be both colored and shaped; but on the corpuscular hypothesis we can explain this appearance by assuming that the object causing the image is shaped, both at the macro- and microlevels, but not in any other sense colored. The result is that mental images only partially resemble what they represent, but they do so in a way that extends beyond solidity to shape and other such qualities. The linchpin of the objection is its notion of resemblance, which fairly begs to be explicated. I shall begin with an attempt at explication, which, though unsuccessful in my view, nonetheless has something to contribute to our own story.

It might be thought that the resemblance between an idea and its object is the literal isomorphism of moderate realism, according to which two things that are qualitatively identical share a third thing, the quality that in this sense is universal. In the language of the best-known proponents of this view, qualitatively identical things share the same *form.* On this reading Locke's is not a representationalist theory requiring ideas as objects, but instead ideas for him are the *id quo intelligitur*, the structures by means of which we are aware of the *objects* of ideas. Thus Locke would hold something like the Cartesian theory of ideas whose distinction between objective and formal existence is derived from the Scholastic distinction between the virtual and real exemplification of the same form. As we have seen, the view is that the mind is aware of an object by conforming to it in a certain way, and this is possible insofar as the same thing can exist both as the object and as the act of awareness. On this view it is analytic that an idea and its object resemble, for they are the same thing. An idea does not represent its object by standing for it in the mind but by presenting it to the mind. As Arnauld put it, the idea is the thing itself insofar as it is in the mind.

I believe the case against reading Locke in this nonrepresentationalist way is massive. Part of it we have already seen. The part of it relevant for present purposes is that Locke himself rejects the view, and for reasons lying at the core of his thinking. Sergeant in his *Solid Philosophy* set down the view that intentional awareness requires what he called *meanings*, which, but for the terminology, are indistinguishable from Cartesian ideas. The crucial agreement between Sergeant's and the Cartesian view is that what is in the mind and what is external to it as its object are numerically identical. "The same *Ens* or Thing may have diverse *Manners* of Existing; one Corporeal, the other Intellectual or Spiritual." We saw that in his marginal notes to *Solid Philosophy* Locke objects to Sergeant's view "that a (perfectly) like is the same."[76] As Locke announces at the outset of the *Essay's* chapter, "Of General Terms," "All Things, that exist, being Particulars" (3.3.1; 409), the only sameness for him can be the sameness or identity of an individual. Thus he must reject the qualitative identity of individuals, for example, of the mind and its object, or the numerical identity of their qualities. A fortiori must he reject the view that a thing can exist in two different ways, as the awareness or its structure and as the object of that awareness, and in fact he claims in the marginal notes not to understand what it is for "a material thing to exist spiritually." The important point here is not just that an interpretation of Lockean ideas is wrong, but that an interpretation of the connection between them and their objects is wrong. Just as the direct realist account is wrong because there are no shared forms, so the representationalist account of resemblance in terms of literal isomorphism is wrong because of the same nominalism. Thus it cannot be argued that because some ideas are immaterially shaped and also resemble with respect to shape, things have, in addition to solidity, real shape. The representationalism stands, and it remains true that ideas of primary qualities resemble, but some other account of that resemblance must be found.[77]

The three principal features of Lockean primary qualities are that they are real, they are inseparable and they resemble. My suggestion is that the three features amount to the same thing. Consider their inseparability. A grain of wheat divided until its parts become insensible "must retain still each of them all those qualities [of solidity, extension, figure, and mobility]" (2.8.9; 135), which in fact are "utterly inseparable" from it. Now one commentator after another has pointed out that what Locke says here is true of primary qualities only as determinables, but that in this sense it is true of secondary qualities also. The determinate qualities, both primary and secondary, may vary, but it must

---

[76] Yolton, *John Locke*, p. 109.

[77] For another account of resemblance, which does not regard it as primitive, see Alexander, "Boyle and Locke." According to him, resemblance is a matter of *accuracy*. For reasons why this imaginative account is problematic, see my "Locke's Atomism," esp. pp. 12–13.

have some determinate for each determinable of both kinds, both kinds of which are thus inseparable. This is such an obvious point, it seems to me, that not even Berkeley's Locke could have missed it. To show that in fact he was not guilty of this oversight, let us take seriously in a way that few have what Locke means by 'quality': "the Power to produce any *Idea* in our mind, I Call Quality of the Subject wherein that power is. Thus a Snow-ball having the power to produce in us the *Ideas* of *White*, *Cold*, and *Round*, The Powers to produce those *Ideas* in us, as they are in the Snow-ball, I call *Qualities*" (2.8.8; 134). What is going on here?

The term 'quality' is used in the latter half of the seventeenth century in a way that invokes no theory beyond what is needed to distinguish subject and predicate. For example, the anti-Aristotelian Bernier nonetheless describes his own definition of quality as Aristotelian: "what makes a thing to be called such or so; . . . anything that makes things to be denominated in a certain way."[78] Locke enriches this common currency with his view that what makes us say of a thing that it is of a certain kind is that it causes us to have certain ideas. In Draft B of the *Essay* Locke was already leaning toward a definition of qualities in solely causal terms: "[By 'quality'] I mean any thing existing without us which affecting any of our senses produces any simple idea in us."[79] But he had not yet analyzed them as powers. This specification Locke took not from the atomists Gassendi, Boyle, Bernier, et al., but from the Cartesian Rohault. In his widely read and influential *Traité de physique* (p.24) we find the following: "by the word *quality* we shall hereafter mean what makes a thing to be denominated in a certain way; thus, whatever it might be in fire, that power it has of exciting in us the sensation of heat, insofar as that makes the power be called warm, we call a quality of fire." In the *Entretiens sur la philosophie* (pp. 74–75) Rohault adumbrates the lines along which Locke developed the notion: "We admit these qualities in objects only because we experience that they excite in us various sensations we do not have in their absence. [Thus] it is easy to see that we may define the sensible qualities of objects [as] the powers they have of exciting in us the sensations we experience them to excite. Thus the savour of wine is the power the wine has to make us taste as it does; likewise, the snow's whiteness is the power the snow has to make us see as it does." Later he tells us about these powers: "the nature of all sense qualities, or of all those different powers that various bodies have to make us sense as they do, consists only in the various sizes, shapes and motions of the particles of which these bodies are composed" (p.85). Locke in a familiar passage (2.8.10; 135) says the same thing of secondary qualities, namely, that they "are nothing in the Objects themselves, but Powers to produce various Sensations in us by their *Primary Qualities*, i.e. by the Bulk, Figure, Texture, and Motion of their insensible parts" At one point

---

[78] *denommées telles; Abrégé*, 1, p. 4.
[79] Aaron and Gibb, *Early Draft*, p. 73.

Locke indicates a very strict adherence to Rohault's view when he says that "the simple *Ideas* whereof we make our complex ones of Substances, are all of them (bating only the Figure and Bulk of some sorts) Powers."[80] This seems to say that only secondary qualities—Rohault's sensory qualities—are powers and that figure and bulk and perhaps other qualities are not powers. But Locke's point in the paragraph is to show the inadequacy of our idea of any substance by arguing that because we cannot know all the relations it has to other substances we cannot know all its powers. Thus Locke does not deny that figure and bulk are powers or relations, but only that they are powers or relations defined with respect to other bodies.

With qualities as powers to cause ideas, what is the sense in which primary qualities are inseparable? An easier question to answer concerns the sense in which secondary qualities are *not* inseparable. At 2.8.13, at which point primary and secondary qualities have been distinguished only on the basis of separability, Locke supposes that the ideas of secondary qualities might be caused "after the same manner" as ideas of primary qualities, namely, by the impulse of insensible particles. They might be so caused, "it being no more impossible to conceive, that God should annex such *Ideas* to such Motions, with which they have no similitude; than that he should annex the *Idea* of pain to the motion of a piece of Steel dividing our Flesh, with which that *Idea* hath no resemblance." Secondary qualities, I suggest, do not resemble and are not inseparable in that they have no necessary connection with the ideas of them. The idea of pain could be annexed to the motion that in fact produced the idea of color.

Later, in discussing the extent of knowledge in book 4, Locke tells us that with our present powers of perception we just do not know the primary qualities of the insensible parts on which the secondary qualities depend. But in addition, "there is yet another and more incurable part of Ignorance, . . . and that is, there is no discoverable connection between any secondary Quality, and those *primary Qualities* that it depends on" (4.3.12; 545). We do not know (1) the texture, that is, the configuration of the primary qualities of microscopic parts, (2) the connection between the texture and secondary qualities, or even (3) how there *could be* a connection between them. "We are so far from knowing what figure, size, or motion of parts produce a yellow Colour, a sweet Taste, or a sharp Sound, that we can by no means conceive how any *size, figure, or* motion of any Particles, can possibly produce in us the *Idea* of any *Colour, Taste,* or *Sound* whatsoever; there is no conceivable *connexion* betwixt the one and the other."[81] The result is that a thing might under the same circumstances have different secondary qualities, and yet be the same thing. If I am right, this is the sense in which secondary qualities are separable and have no resemblance.

---

[80] 2.31.8; 381. Bolton draws attention to this text ("Locke's Doctrine").

[81] 4.3.13; 545, See also 4.3.28; 558–59; 4.3.6; 541.

It might be noted *en passant* that secondary qualities are, not the primary qualities of particles, but the powers that result from these. They are "nothing, but powers." And in order to know what these powers are, we must experience the ideas of secondary qualities. Thus, although secondary qualities are, as Locke repeatedly says they are, in the object, they are, as in the tradition, mind-dependent. Take away the mind's power to receive certain ideas, or alter those powers, and the secondary qualities of the thing are taken away or altered. This is the sense in which those qualities are only *imputed* (2.8.22; 140).

Primary qualities on the other hand are *real* or *original*; they are independent of our perception of them (2.8.23; 140). They are inseparable in the sense that because the connection between these powers and the ideas produced is *necessary*, the thing must always have these powers. With microscopical eyes, for example, our ideas of secondary qualities might be unpredictably different or cease altogether; but such is not the case with primary qualities. The upshot is that ideas of primary qualities give us information about the world in a way that secondary qualities do not. In a moment we shall see that ideas of all the primary qualities except the idea of solidity are relational. Thus complex, these ideas must, as we have seen, be a function of our perception of them. But the way we perceived them will be fully constrained by the corpuscularian hypothesis, which will specify a thing to have certain powers.

The distinction between primary and secondary qualities, then, is the distinction between appearance and reality that one would have expected. In the case of primary qualities, what appears, *is*; that is, ideas of primary qualities give us the way the world is. This is why it is possible to have a science of optics that can explain why things appear to have the shape they do when viewed in perspective, for example. But the appearances of secondary qualities are nothing but appearances in the sense that it is in principle impossible for there to be a science of them. Even though there may be a systematic variation between those appearances and microscopic structures, those structures do not explain the appearances. Whiteness adverbially construed cannot be explained, nor, therefore, can the power to cause it. Not only do *we* lack a geometry of the mind, there is *none* to be had.

The rest of this story is a long one, most of it is epistemological. For example, with what we have in hand sense can be made of Hume's otherwise perplexing classification of resemblance among those philosophical relations that yield knowledge. His other relations in this category—contrariety, degrees in quality, and proportions in quantity or number—are unproblematic; but how for a nominalist resemblance can be "discoverable at first sight, and fall more properly under the province of intuition than demonstration,"[82] how it can "depend entirely on the ideas, which we compare together" (p. 69), is more than I can make out except along the lines above. That is, if Hume takes over something

---

[82] *Treatise*, p. 70.

like Locke's account, then we have an explanation of why resemblance is a necessary feature of the world and thus one that yields knowledge. The account works only for ideas of primary qualities, but it is at least arguable that Hume did not mean resemblance between ideas of secondary qualities to be an object of knowledge.

Leibniz too has some interesting things to say about the Lockean connection between qualities and ideas. In the *New Essays* he gives an account of the primary-secondary quality distinction, which in fact is very close to that advanced above as Locke's. He defines qualities for Locke as the "faculties [of things] for producing the perceptions of ideas in us," and then comments that the difference between primary and secondary qualities for him is that the former "power is intelligible and admits of being distinctly explained. [The latter] is merely sensible and yields only a confused idea" (p.130). But for Leibniz there *is* a resemblance or exact relation, and not just the accidental one he sees Locke admitting, between ideas of secondary qualities and those qualities. The connection is like the "expressive" relation between a parabola and the circle of which it is the projection on a plane (p.131). To Locke's argument about the pin and the pain it causes, for example, he responds that "pain does not resemble the movement of a pin: but it might thoroughly resemble the motions which the pin causes in our body, and represent them in the soul, as I have not the least doubt it does" (pp. 131–32). The difference between Locke and Leibniz on this point is crucial for their epistemologies. Locke has the weakly necessary connection between ideas of primary qualities and those qualities (weak because contingent on the corpuscular hypothesis), and only an accidental connection between ideas of secondary qualities and those qualities. But Leibniz has a strongly necessary connection between all ideas and what they represent (strong because the connection is the literal isomorphism of moderate realism); my perception may be confused as it is in the case of color, but *what* I perceive is the same form that is in the object. Thus we find in Locke the skepticism, even with respect to primary qualities, that is so alien to Leibniz. Locke never refers to corpuscularianism as anything more than a hypothesis.

To take stock: We have met one kind of objection only to raise another. While Locke's representative theory of perception does not entail that the world has occurrent properties beyond solidity, it does seem to entail that it has dispositional properties beyond solidity. Purged of extension, the world now seems infested with powers.

§21 POWERS

Locke sometimes says that *qualities* produce effects (2.1.1; 119; 2.23.2; 295), at other times that *powers* produce effects, or that *things* do in virtue of powers

(2.8.24; 141). I propose the following stipulations, on which of course I shall have to make good. Let us say that a power is that the possession of which enables a thing to be a cause (or in the case of passive powers, an effect). To say that *x possesses P* in this sense is to say that *P* is *true of x*, and to say that *x* is *enabled* to be a cause is to say that *x* is *defined* as a cause under certain conditions. The definitions by which power predicates may be eliminated (or introduced) is of the kind that Carnap called conditional, namely, a logical bilateral reduction sentence. On this account, if a thing is viewed under certain conditions, then it has, for example, the secondary quality green, that is, the power to cause the idea of green just in case that idea is perceived. Besides reducing the power predicate, such an account both emphasizes the lack of additional factual content in the statement introducing them, which is very much in keeping with the anti-Aristotelianism of the corpuscular hypothesis, and also suggests the relational character Locke sees inherent in powers.

What is it the possession of which enables a thing to be a cause? On my thesis it is solidity and solidity alone. Recall a passage (2.21.3; 234) to which we have already drawn attention:

> I confess *Power includes in it some kind of relation* . . . as indeed which of our *Ideas*, of what kind soever, when attentively considered, does not? For our *Ideas* of Extension, Duration, and Number, do they not all contain in them a secret relation of the Parts. Figure and Motion have something relative in them much more visibly: And sensible Qualities, as colors and Smells, *etc*. What are they but the *Powers* of different Bodies, in relation to our Perception, *etc*. And if considered in the things themselves, do they not depend on the Bulk, Figure, Texture, and Motion of the Parts? All which include some kind of relation in them. Our *Idea* therefore of Power, I think, may well have a place amongst other simple *Ideas*, and be considered as one of them, being one of those, that make a principal Ingredient in our complex *Ideas* of Substances.

It should be noted first of all that while Locke here calls the idea of power a *simple* idea, thus indicating perhaps that power is nonrelational and primitive in a way contrary to my thesis, he later clarifies this as true only relative to the substances they for the most part constitute: "I have reckoned these Powers amongst the simple Ideas, which make the complex ones of the sorts of *Substances*; though these Powers, considered in themselves, are truly complex *Ideas*" (2.37.7; 299). The powers of Gold, for example, "are nothing else, but so many relations to other Substances; and are not really in the Gold, considered barely in it self, though they depend on those real, and primary Qualities of its internal constitution, whereby it has a fitness, differently to operate, and be operated on by several other Substances" (2.24.37; 317).

But the main point is that among the exhaustive list of ideas said to contain some relation is not to be found solidity. It would seem that solidity is that on which power and all other relations—in fact, all other complex ideas—depend.

This would make solidity the only simple idea, a view that Locke seems early on to have rejected. In a journal entry for August 3, 1676 he wrote: "Simple Ideas cannot be defined, nor can we ever gain any notion of them by words. The simplest of all seems to be Unity, and space pain and pleasure. The Ideas of those tangible qualitys that are produced by immediate contact at least some of them are not simple, as rough and smooth &c. are complex as being soe grosse that the parts that compose them are discernible to our eyes but those that are produced at distance are not soe as heat and cold."[83] Despite the claim about pleasure and pain, which *seem* to be among the simplest ideas, ideas of secondary qualities are complex. They are distortions insofar as they represent as simple what in fact is complex, namely, what is intrinsically relational. Now this is a difficult view, and one that Locke did not explicitly develop in the *Essay*. But what Locke had in mind seems an anticipation of Leibniz's doctrine of *petites perceptions*. Commenting in the *New Essays* (p. 120) on the warmth and softness of wax and the hardness and coldness of ice as simple ideas, Leibniz claimed that these ideas appear simple only because they are confused. Just as a tower that has angles may appear round, or green, which is a mixture of blue and yellow, may appear to be a simple idea, these and all sensible ideas are in fact complex. What Locke says about tactile qualities above can thus be extended on this analysis to heat and cold, pleasure and pain. This leaves unity and space. Space, or rather spatial characteristics, we tried to show above to be complex. If unity were construed as solidity, then space itself might be the void, the lack of solidity. Simple ideas would then be those we get while feeling about to determine the shape of the world, that is, in learning where there is existence and where not. Of this, more below.

The thesis that powers are purely relational for Locke thus includes him among the majority in the seventeenth century who like Descartes, Hobbes, and Boyle took 'powers' in bodies to be ascribable to them only under certain conditions. These conditions are specifiable solely in terms of the relations between bodies; thus, the sun has the power to melt wax, for example, only when wax is present and the wax to melt only when heat is present. In the eighteenth century, however, powers came to be regarded in nonrelational, substantival terms. Powers were thought to be inherent in bodies as part of their essential activities. Curiously, Locke was read by Hutton, Priestly, and others as advocating just this view.[84] This reading seems to me mistaken. Of the two groups of texts that might be cited in its support,[85] one group has appeared to some to deny that the powers inherent in bodies are active and thus to assert that some powers are inherent in them. But the texts deal, typically, only with the

---

[83] Aaron and Gibb, *Early Draft*, p. 83.

[84] This distinction between seventeenth- and eighteenth-century views, along with the suggestion of Locke as the source of the latter, came from Heimann and McGuire, who find textual support where I do not for the substantival reading of Locke.

[85] See the texts cited by Heimann and McGuire, "Newtonian Forces," pp. 248ff.

question of the *source of the idea of power*, not with the question whether bodies are inherently active. The possibility remains, however, that once in possession of the idea from reflecting on the mind's operations, namely, volitions, we might then attribute powers to objects in the way Hutton, Priestly, and others in the eighteenth century did. These texts therefore do not decide the question.

The question then comes down to the other group of texts, which make up the discussion of ideas of primary and secondary qualities in 2.8 of the *Essay*. One recent account of them goes as follows:

> Since secondary qualities are powers barely, and nothing but powers, relating to several other bodies, and resulting from the different modifications of the original qualities, Locke not only designated secondary qualities as relational properties, but also tends to construe them as exemplifying an undefined notion of causation. . . . To say of matter that it possesses the property of being red is the same as to say it is capable of producing under suitable conditions an idea of redness in our awareness. Thus, a chair does not have the color red as well as the power to produce the idea in the mind. To have a causal power is not the same as to have a property like red. With respect to primary qualities, however, Locke holds that they exist absolutely and categorically in the object and also have the 'power' to produce ideas of primary qualities which in the mind resemble those qualities themselves.[86]

The powers inherent in things are the primary qualities, or perhaps the powers resulting from these, for they appear to be different from qualities, and these powers are said to exist absolutely and categorically in the object. Presumably it is the inseparability of primary qualities that would entail that they are substantival. But, as I have tried to show, the inseparability of primary qualities does not entail that there is anything more than solidity in things. To put it a different way, primary qualities are, no less than secondary qualities, *dispositive*, to use Boyle's term, so that what might be said about secondary qualities on the basis of Boyle's example of the key's power to open can be said of Locke's primary qualities as well.[87]

This is not to say that Locke is entirely unequivocal in speaking of powers, for he sometimes does have them dependent on other things and sometimes not. If *all* powers are relational then the explanation of his apparent equivocation is

---

[86] Ibid., pp. 248–49.

[87] "In considering the 'power' that a key has to open a door Boyle points out that there is nothing in the key over and above its shape and size and the fact that it fits a particular lock. This shows three things about Boyle's conception of power (and presumably about his notion of the way things in the absence of sensation are 'dispositively' endowed with colors, tastes, etc.): 1) that it is *relational* 2) that powers are *not* entities distinct from the primary qualities nor are they inherent properties in objects, and 3) that they are distinct from the effects objects have on one another by means of their inherent qualities" (Ibid., pp. 247–48).

an oscillation between a relation considered as (1) the "occasion" for the would-be relation, and (2) the relating, which can obtain only if there exists the other relatum. Relations are acts of relating, thus mind-dependent, but not everything can be related in every way—to use his example, only he who has gone through a certain ceremony can be husband of Sempronia. Thus primary qualities are mainly regarded as relations in the first sense, that is, as the objective occasion. They are had, and given the corpuscular hypothesis, must be had, independently of everything else. Secondary qualities are taken in the second sense; they are nothing but powers, dependent on the perceiver.

Locke's equivocation or oscillation between relational and substantival powers thus seems more apparent than real. But there is a deeper ambiguity relating specifically to active powers, which may be reducible in another sense. Here Locke really does shift his position, perhaps insensitive to the shift because of other, overriding concerns.

Locke's chapter on power is an additional example of a topic treated only in relation to some other, polemical purpose. Of its seventy-three paragraphs, sixty-seven deal with the problem of freedom. It seems clear that his primary aim is less the metaphysical analysis of power than with the moral problem of securing responsibility and freedom within a deterministic framework. The spectre of Hobbes, or rather of the treatment accorded Hobbes and Spinoza as well, looms over the chapter. The result is that Locke's views on active power, or at least the language used to express them, are here and elsewhere less than precise.

Locke seems at various times to have held three different views on active powers.[88] His latest view can be found in the addendum to paragraph 73 published in the fourth edition, the last in Locke's lifetime. The relevant claim here is that "the *Active Power* of motion is in no substance which cannot begin motion in it self, or in another substance when at rest." At this stage Locke is distinguishing between causal powers, which can be had by bodies, and active powers, which can be had only by spirits. "When I turn my Eyes another way, or remove my Body out of the Sun-beams, I am properly active; because of my own choice, by a power within myself I put myself into that Motion. Such an Action is the product of *Active Power*" (2.21.72; 286).

The next earliest view is to be found in the first, and subsequent editions of the *Essay*, and also in the 1685 Draft C. It is expressed by the familiar passage, among others, in which Locke tells us that communication of motion from one body to another "gives us but a very obscure *Idea* of an *active Power* of moving in Body, whilst we observe it only to transfer, but not produce any motion. For it is but a very obscure *Idea of Power*, which reaches not the Production of the Action, but the Continuation of the Passion. For so is motion in a Body im-

---

[88] This has been persuasively argued by Mattern, "Locke on Active Power," whose account I follow very closely here.

pelled by another" (2.21.4; 235). These might be called *degenerate* powers in the sense that the idea we have of them is inadequate in Locke's sense of the term; they are *poor examples* of active powers, but examples nonetheless. Locke's earliest view is found in Draft C: "Power thus Considered is twofold, *viz.* as able to make or able to receive any change the one may be called *Active* and the other *passive power*" (2.25.2).[89] "If we would consider them aright we should I suppose find that one of them is soely [*sic*] in God and not at all in creatures and the other soely in the creatures but not at all in God. For I thinke it is a cleare truth that God alone has power to change all other things but is not capable of any change in himself. And that all the creatures are capable of change but have not in themselves an active power to produce it" (2.25.2). On this view God alone has active powers; but Locke crossed out this passage— perhaps not taking it very seriously because of its blatant proximity to occasionalism. He added a marginal note, which with the first passage above was to appear in all published editions of the *Essay*: "whether Matter be not wholly destitute of *active Power*, as its Author GOD is truly above all *passive Power*; and whether the intermediate state of created Spirits be not that alone, which is capable of both *active* and *passive Power*, may be worth consideration" (2.21.2; 234).

But suppose we consider carefully the *next* sentence: "I shall not now enter into that Enquiry, my present Business being not to search into the original of Power, but how we come by the *Idea* of it." That is, the whole rest of the chapter is intended to deal with how we get the idea of power rather than with what has power and in what sense. Thus, even when Locke suggests that the mind might "receive its idea of *active Power* clearer from reflection on its own Operations, than it doth from any external Sensation" (2.21.4; 236), he *need* not be suggesting that the power whose idea derives from reflection is had by the mind. Indeed, the nicest Lockean view would be that active power belongs only to the Creator, as Draft C states, and that it is only *experienced* in us and, to an imperfect extent, in bodies. Since Locke forswears the question, this is a difficult exegetical position to defend. But it is textually at least plausible.[90] Its best defense will be a proof-of-the-pudding argument—the justification lies not with the recipe but with the result, in this case, an interesting reading of a number of related issues that will show that active power clearly is the power of creation.

§22   MATTER AND CREATION

The chapter "Of Cause and Effect, and other Relations" (2.26) distinguishes two sorts of causes or "Originals of things." One is *creation*, "as when a new

---

[89] Mattern, "Locke on Active Power,"p. 62.

[90] D. A. Larivière is the principal originator of this thesis, in unpublished work.

Particle of Matter doth begin to exist, *in rerum natura*, which had before no Being" (2.26.2; 325). The other sort of causation employs these already existing particles and itself divides into three kinds. One, I think, involves the rearrangement of particles with a resulting organic unity; this Locke calls *generation*. Another kind occurs when the rearrangement of particles results only in a change of primary qualities; this he calls *making*. Finally, when the rearrangement results in a change of secondary qualities, we have *alteration*. Solidity on this scheme seems able to be caused only in the first sense; it must be created, for it does not result from rearrangement of particles, which rather presupposes solidity.

The same conclusion is suggested by the following chapter, "Of Identity and Diversity" (2.27). Here Locke distinguishes a number of senses of identity, the most basic of which is relative to the place and time of origin of the thing individuated. For both bodies *and finite spirits* an individual is just that thing whose history is traceable back to the place and time it began to be. But given the relational view of space and the dependence of relations on relata, place-time cannot individuate. This, of course, is not Locke's argument but Russell's. Still, place-time do not individuate for Locke. "From what has been said, 'tis easy to discover, what is so much enquired after, the *principium Individuationis*, and that 'tis plain is Existence it self, which determines a Being of any sort to a particular time and place incommunicable to two Beings of the same kind" (2.27.3; 330). What excludes every other body from the place-time of a body is its solidity, or the impenetrability resulting from its solidity. But what is it that excludes another spirit from the place of a spirit? Nothing from what I can make out in Locke. Only if there is but one sort of being, namely, solid being, can Locke's principle of individuation be made to work. Creation of any sort, then, is the creation of solidity.

Finally, there is a remarkable passage from book 4 in which Locke speculates about the creation of matter. His contention is that while the creation of matter is inconceivable it is nonetheless possible, because the creation of spirit is also inconceivable yet undeniable since there was a time at which each of us began to exist. "When well considered, Creation of a Spirit will be found to require no less Power, than the Creation of Matter. Nay possibly, if we would emancipate our selves from vulgar Notions, and raise our Thoughts, as far as they would reach, to a closer contemplation of things, we might be able to aim at some dim and seeming conception how Matter might at first be made, and begin to exist by the power of that eternal first being: But to give beginning and being to a Spirit, would be found a more inconceivable effect of Omnipotent Power. But this would perhaps lead us too far from the Notions, on which the Philosophy now in the World is built, [thus] it would not be pardonnable to deviate so far from them" (4.10.18; 628–29). Leibniz picked up on this and actually had a correspondence about it during 1704–5 with Lady Masham, at whose house at Oakes Locke was a guest. But Locke died before Lady Masham got around to asking him about it. In the *New Essays* Leibniz offers a conjecture on what Locke might have had in mind, but it seems to me that he was misled by the translator of the *Essay* he read. Newton too became involved in the story, curiously via the same translator; he too had an explanation of what Locke had in mind. This part of the story has been told in the recent literature[91] and will come out in a moment. But there is more to the story. Reid, for example, was struck by the passage: "There is, indeed, a single passage in Locke's essay (4.10.18), which may lead one to conjecture that he had a glimpse of that system which Berkeley afterwards advanced, but thought proper to suppress it within his own breast."[92] After a not obviously unfaithful reading of the text, Reid compares it with Berkeley's views: "According to Berkeley's system, God's creating the material world at such a time, means no more but that he decreed from that time, to produce ideas in the minds of finite spirits, in that order and according to those rules which we call the laws of nature. This, indeed, removes all difficulty, in conceiving how matter was created; and Berkeley does not fail to take notice of the advantage of his system on that account." In characteristic fashion Hamilton pursued the matter, pointing out that a different reading was given by Dugald Stewart, who said of the passage, "when considered in connection with some others in his writings, it would almost tempt one to think that a theory concerning *matter*, somewhat analogous to that of Boscovich, had occasionally passed through his mind." In Hamilton's view,

The whole arcanum in the passage in question is, however, revealed by *M.Coste*, the French translator of the Essay, and of several other of the works of Locke, *with whom the philosopher lived in the same family, and on the most intimate terms, for the last seven years of his life*; and who, though *he has never been consulted, affords often the most important information in regard to Locke's opinions.* To this passage there is in the *fourth* edition of Coste's translation, a very curious note appended, of which the following is an abstract: - " Here Mr. Locke excites our curiosity without being inclined to satisfy it. Many persons, having imagined that he had communicated to me *this mode of explaining the creation of matter*, requested, when my translation first appeared, that I would inform them what it was; but I obliged to confess that Mr. Locke had not made *even me* a partner in the secret. At length, long after his death, *Sir Isaac Newton*, to whom I was accidentally speaking of this part of Mr. Locke's book, *discovered to me the whole mystery*. He told me, smiling, that it was he himself who had imagined this manner of explaining the creation of matter, and that the thought had struck him one day, when this question chanced to turn up in a conversation between himself, Mr. Locke, and the late Earl of Pembroke. The following is the way in which he explained to them his thought: '*We may be enabled* (he said) *to form some rude*

91 *V.* Bennett and Remnant, "Matter."
92 *Essays on The Intellectual Powers of Man*; *Works*, 1:286.

conception of the creation of matter, if we suppose that God, by his power, had prevented the entrance of anything into a certain portion of pure space, which is of its nature penetrable, eternal, necessary, infinite; for henceforward this portion of space would be endowed with impenetrability, one of the essential qualities of matter: and as pure space is absolutely uniform, we have only again to suppose that God communicated the same impenetrability to another portion of space, and we should then obtain in a certain sort the notion of the mobility of matter, another quality which is also very essential to it.'

The result, according to Hamilton, is that Stewart's hypothesis gains at the expense of Reid's. A. C. Fraser later was led by Newton's account to combine the hypotheses of Reid and Stewart: "This 'dim conception' [how matter might be created], if it means that the material world may be resolved into a constant manifestation of God's power to man's senses, conditioned by space, so far coincides with Berkeley's account of it; he emphasises the sensuous manifestation of divine power in selected spaces, as well as the ultimate dependence of space on sense. Newton, it seems, suggested that 'creation of matter' means, God causing in sentient beings the sense-perception of resistance, in an otherwise pure space—a theory akin to Berkeleyianism in its recognition of the Supreme Power, and to Boscovich in its conception of the effect."[93]

But against this line of interpretation there seem to me two invincible objections. One is that it seems to require an absolute space that is inimical to Locke's conception of space no less than it is to Berkeley's. Newton seems to have had, rather than Locke's, his own view in mind: "There are everywhere all kinds of figures, everywhere spheres, cubes, triangles . . . even though they are not delineated by sight. For the material delineation of any figure is not a new production of the figure as regards space, but only a corporeal representation of it, so that what was first insensible in space now appears to the senses to exist."[94] For Locke, as we have seen, space apart from the things in it is, as it was for Bernier, a pure nothing. But the major objection is that Locke insists that impenetrability, in which matter entirely consists when conceived as the *puncta* of Boscovich, is negative and only the result of solidity. For what it is worth we may note that Coste himself rejected Newton's account on this ground.[95]

The two objections really come to the same thing. Newton's suggestion requires that there be something immaterial ontologically prior to impenetrability. This might be an assemblage of nonspatial things, which either with or without the superaddition of impenetrability might be perceived spatially. Spirits or Leibnizean monads would be examples of such things. But the only historically plausible view would be for space, conceived absolutely, to have its

[93] *Locke's Essay*, ed. Fraser, 2:322 n.
[94] *De gravitatione*; *Unpublished Scientific Papers*, p. 100.
[95] Bennett and Remnant, "Matter," p. 10.

parts endowed with impenetrability. But Locke rejects absolute space. What is ontologically antecedent to impenetrability is solidity, which is what God creates when He creates matter. Nor, it would seem, can solidity be used dispositionally for Locke as a power in the fashion of the other primary qualities. John Sergeant took solidity in its ordinary sense to be hardness, the quality whose contrary is fluidity, and he thought that Locke idiosyncratically meant by the term "*Impenetrability* of the Potential Parts of Quantity."[96] Later in the same work, (p. 375) when Sergeant construes matter in Aristotelian fashion as pure potency, Locke noted in the margin of his copy: "Matter is a solid substance and not a power."[97] This remark may be intended to rule out only the Aristotelian view, but it would seem in any case to make solidity occurrent.

William Carroll had an interesting interpretation of Locke's speculation about the creation of matter. His thesis, about which I shall have more to say below, was that Locke was a crypto-Spinozist, and he contended that Locke's meaning was that matter cannot be created except in what he took to be the Spinozist sense—matter as the eternal, single substance cannot be created, only its modifications that *we call* matter.[98] Carroll thought that Locke was ironical in this passage and that his purpose was to dissuade the reader of the possibility of the creation of matter in the orthodox sense. This was another example of the constant equivocation Carroll saw in Locke between substance in itself and substance as we perceive it, namely, in terms of modifications. To expand Carroll's account we might say that for Locke creation is only an appearance, that what is real is uncreated. How this account differs from the one we have given of Descartes's views on the same topic will be examined in chapter 7.

I have thus far spoken of solidity as a property, indeed as the property on which all the other properties of body depend. This usage is employed by Locke,[99] but is nonetheless misleading. For, although he is not without ambiguity, Locke seems inclined, not just to nominalism, but to *extreme* nominalism. Not only are there no universal properties, but there is not even an ontological distinction to be drawn between properties and things.[100] So Locke is faced with something like a Kantian problem in attempting to say anything at all about solidity, which is for him the real thing-in-itself. The problem is that nothing can be said of it. To predicate for Locke is to express an agreement or disagreement of ideas. Predication is thus limited to complex ideas as when we say of substances that they have certain modes or stand in certain relations. Thus

---

[96] Sergeant, *Solid Philosophy*, p. 129. Locke's note goes on to distinguish his view from Descartes's.

[97] Yolton, "Marginal Replies," p. 558.

[98] *Dissertation*, p. 240.

[99] *Letter*; *Works*, 4:33: "Substance, that has the modification of solidity, is matter."

[100] Loux, *Universals and Particulars*, pp. 7–8.

predication is restricted to the way solidity *appears* to us. Our knowledge of these appearances is, if you like, knowledge by description; but of solidity itself we have only knowledge by acquaintance. I think this is what Locke is telling us when he says:

> If anyone asks me, *What this Solidity is*, I send him to his senses to inform him: Let him put a Flint, or a Foot-ball between his Hands; and then endeavor to join them, and he will know. If he thinks this is not a sufficient Explication of Solidity, what it is, and wherein it consists; I promise to tell him, what it is, and wherein it consists, when he tells me what thinking is, or wherein it consists; or explain to me, what Extension or Motion is, which, perhaps, seems much easier. The simple *Ideas* we have are such, as experience teaches them us; but if beyond that, we endeavor, by Words, to make them clearer in The Mind, we shall succeed no better, than if we went about to clear up the Darkness of a blind Man's mind, by talking; and to discourse into him the *Ideas* of Light and colors. (2.6.6; 127)

Notice too that this reading saves Locke from an error sometimes attributed to him, namely, that in this passage he confuses solidity with impenetrability, for what we *feel* is not solidity but impenetrability. Though he could never express it in these terms, Locke is giving a transcendental argument; We do not *sense* solidity as we would an appearance: we *know* it.[101] If there are phenomenal appearances, there must be noumenal things that appear, and which are thus known in abstraction from anything that can be said of them. Berkeley who was wrong about so much in Locke was right about the fundamental point, namely, that the basis for Locke's realism is an appeal to nonempirical abstraction, which he is thus at great pains to attack.

§23 THE BESTIAL SOUL

An upshot of Locke's rejection of thought as the essence of the mind, or rather of the view that men always think, is that thought may be an attribute of matter (or also of nonhuman matter in case men are material). Since a man does not always think, his thought is accidental to him, and what is an accident of one thing may always be the accident of another. So the difference between men and the rest of their world cannot be their thought, for the world, or part of it, may have thought too. The sensitive premise in this bit of reasoning is the claim about the universal exchangeability of accidents. Commonsensically we would want to say that not every accident can be the accident of just anything. For example, the timbre of a musical note is (unlike its pitch) an accident of the

---

101 This was Leibniz's correction of Locke: "Solidity, in so far as there is a distinct notion of it, is fundamentally conceived through pure reason, though the senses provide a basis for reasoning to prove that solidity occurs in nature" (*New Essays*, p. 124).

note, but nothing having the color yellow as an accident, such as a lemon, could have that timbre. This is the issue that used to be debated under the rubric of the synthetic a priori. In these terms there are for Locke no synthetic a priori propositions. A principal aim of this section will be to show how the exchangeability thesis is nonetheless true for Locke and to do so in a way that further shows his systematic opposition to the Cartesians. Roughly, the idea is that all attributes are accidental and that accidents are the appearances of things.

A good place to begin is with the issue of the bestial soul. The issues whether animals have souls and whether matter thinks are distinct. It is possible that 1) animals have souls and matter thinks (by thinking here let us mean at a minimum consciousness of pain.); in fact, that matter eo ipso thinks was Aquinas's view. (2) Animals have souls and yet matter does not think; this would be, for example, Cartesian dualism extended to include nonhuman minds and bodies—a view held, as we shall see, by certain minor figures. (3) Animals do not have souls and do not think; this was the Cartesian view. (4) Animals have no souls but do think; this might be any of a number of materialist views, including Hobbes's. Although distinct, the two issues of bestial soul and thinking matter are connected. In a journal entry for February 20, 1682, Locke entered a long comment on an argument for the immortality of the (human) soul that was found often enough in the period. The argument is that since matter cannot think the soul must be immaterial; but an immaterial thing cannot be destroyed naturally; hence the soul is immortal.[102] The objection to this related by Locke is that since animals "feele i.e. thinke" they have immaterial and thus immortal souls. "This has by some men been judged soe urgent that they have rather thought fit to conclude all beasts perfect machins rather than allow their soules immortality or annihilation both which seem harsh doctrines."[103] The connection that Locke thus establishes is that there is no need for the Cartesian doctrine of the beast-machine if it be allowed that matter can think.[104]

It is difficult for us nowadays to appreciate the extent to which the issue of the bestial soul captured the imagination of the period. This was a period in which

[102] By natural destruction is meant dissolution, which is precluded by the soul's simplicity. For the relevant history of this argument, see Mijuskovic, *Achilles*, chaps. 1–2.

[103] Aaron and Gibb, *Early Draft*, p. 121. Not every thinker was put off by the immortality of the bestial soul. Witty saw no problem in saying that if animals think, as they give "almost all the outward Evidences" of doing, they are immortal (*First Principles*, pp. 299–301).

[104] A particularly relevant version of the immortality argument comes from Rohault and Malebranche. Rohault argued that "the view that attributes [to animals] a soul that thinks is very dangerous in that it provides freethinkers with the means to avoid the main argument we have for the immortality of the rational soul" (*Entretiens*, p. 175). In the *Dialogues* Malebranche's interlocutor asks to have it proven to him that matter is nothing but extension and thus incapable of thought. "This seems to me necessary in order to silence freethinkers who confuse the soul with the body and maintain that the former is mortal like the latter, because according to them, our thoughts are only modes of that unknown thing called body and all modes can cease to be" (*Oeuvres*, 12–13:73). Locke allows that thought may be a mode of the body, but denies that men must always think.

people depended on animals and lived closer to them. These close and obvious connections help to explain the vehemence of the philosophical debates throughout the seventeenth century and into the eighteenth as to whether animals have souls. Even so, such connections predate and postdate the period; Descartes was not the first to suggest that animals had no soul or even that they were machines. In the sixteenth century Gomez Pereira described a clear-cut version of the beast-machine, and in the thirteenth Aquinas likened the natural functioning of animals to that of a clock.[105] In addition, people thought that there were very deep philosophical differences that divided them on the issue. The Jesuit Gabriel Daniel at the end of the century was prepared to make it the litmus test for Cartesianism: "This single point [of the beast-machine] contains or supposes all the principles and bases of the sect. One cannot think that way unless one has true and clear ideas of body and soul, and unless one has followed the great Descartes's demonstration of the difference between these two kinds of being. With the doctrine, it is impossible not to be a Cartesian, and without it, it is impossible to be one. It is the very spirit and sap . . . of pure Cartesianism."[106]

Should the issue of whether animals have souls, whether they think or sense, prove to be as deep as it was thought to be, it would not be surprising to find the experimental evidence regarded as perfectly arguing the competing views. And in fact it is clear that no datum on the behavior of animals was going to alter anyone's views, and that whether animals communicated or fail to do so, learned or failed to do so, would always be regarded as consistent with one's theory. Consider the anecdote related by Racine *fils* about Pascal. As evidence against his view that animals were machines lacking intelligence, Pascal was shown a frog that repeatedly played dead at the approach of a pike. Pascal's response was that since the frog always acted the same way, it obviously acted only mechanically. More generally, such intelligence as animals exhibited could always be attributed to the design of their mechanism. Voltaire complained of Melchior de Polignac's inference from animal cunning, not to their intelligence, but to that of God and the wonders of mechanism.[107] Much later the abbé N. Montfauçon de Villars would tell of a monkey who beat the king of Poland at chess, a feat the Cartesians attributed to the hand of God.[108] Or consider the case of a horse refusing to transgress the edge of a precipice from the bottom of which rises the smell of oats and hay. What does this show about the bestial soul? In one of the most important anti-Cartesian tracts on the topic, Daniel thought it showed the horse to be more than a machine.[109] The ambigu-

---

[105] Rosenfield, *Animal Soul*, p. 19.

[106] *Nouvelles difficultez* . . . (1693), pp. 5–6; cited in Rosenfield, *Animal Soul*, p. 87.

[107] Ibid., pp. 52–53.

[108] Ibid., p. 95. It should be noted that monkeys beating kings at chess are already found in the sixteenth century.

[109] Ibid., p. 88.

ity in all such cases is reflected, and the more so if unintentionally, by Molière's well-known line: "Les bêtes ne sont pas si bêtes que l'on pense."[110]

Another indication that we are dealing with deep issues is the bewildering variety of terms in which the superficial issue of the bestial soul was contested. That is, the disputants seldom argued their case in terms of its metaphysical roots with the result that ultimately what was at issue was generally far from clear. At least this is a possible explanation of the unclarity on which I shall have to make good by unearthing the roots. Before attempting to do so, however, I wish to turn to the emotive engine of the contest, which is another, philosophically more important part of the explanation of the questions held over the seventeenth-century imagination. As the various views on the bestial soul were in fact the consequences of deeper views, so the views on the bestial soul were perceived to have certain consequences. While the former connection may have received imperfect attention, or none at all, the latter was taken to be of paramount importance. Indeed, differences on the bestial soul were regarded as indicating deep metaphysical differences just because of these consequences. So we have three levels of issue: a metaphysical infrastructure, the level of the issue itself, and the superstructure of moral and political consequences. The last gave the issue its sense, but also was taken as an indication of the first.

A further complication is that far from all of the debate on this issue was between the Cartesians and their opponents. An early important instance of the debate took place between Cureau de La Chambre and Pierre Chanet, the Calvinist physician of La Rochelle of whom very little is known. One thing is clear, however, and that is that Chanet was no Cartesian. In his *Consideration of the Charron's Sagesse* (1643) he attacked Charron, and Montaigne implicitly, for associating man and animal so closely that either both have immortal souls or neither do. But he also argued that final causes are knowable and useful, and also that the senses are much more reliable than these skeptics allowed and are in any case the source of all knowledge. Thus Chanet can hardly be placed in the Cartesian camp, and was likened by Sainte-Beuve, at least, to the Scottish realists.[111] Without naming him, Cureau responded to Chanet in a work called *What bestial knowledge is and how far it can extend*, which he appended to the second volume of his *Characteristics of the Passions*. It begins with an argument from the great chain of being: Nature exhibits an ordered, continuous gradient of perfection. Things have more or less essence up to God. Thus if there is a rational soul, there must also be a (merely) sensitive soul.[112] This

---

[110] Prologue, *Amphitryon*. A similar and similarly relevant ambiguity infects the animal rights issue. We have heard of the horrors of vivisection at Port-Royal, of Malebranche jokingly kicking a pregnant dog before Fontenelle; but is it the Cartesians who are calloused and lack moral sentiment or those who though believing animals to have real sensation nonetheless kill them for food? See Descartes to More, February 5, 1649.

[111] *Pierre Chanet*, Piobetta, p. xvi.

[112] *La lumiere*, pp. 101ff.

instance of the debate over the animal soul therefore was between a non-Cartesian opponent of skepticism and an alleged Gassendist who opens with a quintessentially Platonist argument. The debate drew a lot of ink, with Chanet responding in 1646, Cureau in 1648, and Chanet again in 1648; but at no point did the dispute sort itself out along Cartesian/non-Cartesian lines.

Within three months of the publication of Descartes's *Discourse on Method* (1637), Fromondus (Libert Froi(d)mont) raised two objections that the beast-machine might lead to the man-machine and thus to atheism. His first argument went as follows: "What Descartes said of the animal soul as operating through the heat of the body could be applied by atheists to the rational soul, . . . It is blasphemous to attribute such excellent actions as occur in beasts to such a humble cause as mechanism."[113] His second argument rests on a curious reversal of theoretical parsimony. According to Fromondus, even if rational functions could be explained mechanically, a separate rational soul would be needed, for what can be done with less simplicity must be—a rather strong principle that entails that nothing can be done. But at least this is a recognizable argument, unlike the first effort, which attempts to falsify a view by showing that an argument for it is "dangerous."[114] The danger was that the argument might be used to denigrate man by making him material, that is, mortal and determined, and therefore unresponsible. This contention that the Cartesian view of the bestial machine could be extended to man would be repeated throughout the century and the danger seen in it was always the same moral and political threat. The man-machine was a double invitation to lawlessness, for being mortal it had no prospect and thus no sanction of ultimate reward and punishment, and being determined it could not be held responsible.

The same objection was made against the best-known proponent of the view that animals are *not* mere machines. Locke distinguished the concepts of man and person, and made the identity of a man consist—as it does for plants and animals—in the organization of the body over time. With the concept of a person a forensic concept only, the possibility that matter might think was not an isolated suggestion on Locke's part but the recognition of a consequence of his other views. That is, Locke's suggestion that matter might think was of a piece with his rejection of thought as the essence of man, with his allowing consciousness in animals, and with the above account of identity that he introduced in the second edition of the *Essay*. This suggestion in any case was criticized as dangerous in just the sense that Descartes's view had been. Nor was the criticism less immediately forthcoming or less enduring. People like Stillingfleet, Peter Browne, Henry Lee, John Broughton, and John Edwards had made essentially the same objection while Locke was still alive, and people like John Witty, Samuel Clarke, and Humphrey Ditton continued the objection well

[113] Rosenfield, *Animal Soul*, p. 8; AT, 1:403.

[114] Perhaps this was intended as a reductio. On the significance in this period of arguments by reductio ad absurdum, see chap. 10.

into the eighteenth century. The objection was, as Ditton put it, that around the hypothesis of thinking matter "The Whole System of Modern Infidelity does turn."[115] The infidels "have made the whole *Universe* a mere lump of Matter; and *Man*, the most elegant and lovely creature of all; they have complimented no higher, than to give him the Title of the best and finest Piece of *Clock-work*. They have divested us of all our *Intellectual* Powers, and made up our very *Souls* of *Wheels* and *Springs*; so that we are only a Set of moving prattling machines (pp.23–24). Ditton argues, not very well, that if matter should think mechanism would be upset, and that the appeal by Locke to unknown properties of matter is an argument *ad ignorantiam* (sees. 3–4). But by far his most important consideration is that religion would be threatened (pp.23ff.), and the principal threat is that traditionally seen in Epicureanism. "In short, the Hypothesis is levell'd against *Futurity*: 'Tis a Fence against the Belief of Punishments in a Life to come."[116]

What then was at the root of Locke's suggestion and the opposition to it? As a first approximation we might say that for the materialist there is no reason why in principle nonhuman matter should not think. Since men think and are material, there is nothing about matter as such that precludes thought. Liancourt's frog may truly exhibit more than mechanical behavior; and right across nature (to use a concept to which this view gave rise in the eighteenth century) the apparently conscious or intelligent may really be so. Ironically, it is the materialist who can give richest expression to the great chain of being, for while all is material, the material may be indefinitely graded with respect to these (and all other possible) attributes. Not so for the friend of the Forms, who in this period has seen his friends reduced to at most two, with the result that the chain of being is as great as it can be with but two links. But this division between qualitative monism and dualism, between (let us say) Gassendist atomism and Cartesian dualism, is far too simplistic to categorize the dispute over the bestial soul. On the one hand there is no reason why the atomist must allow that animals think—animals and man too could be no more than atoms organized into machines. On the other hand there is no reason why the Cartesian cannot extend thinking souls to animals—this after all was Plato's view.

The issue is far more complex. For one thing, it is fruitless to try sorting the views according to whether animals are thought to have souls. Even if the strict Platonist view of transmigration of souls can be ruled out as hopelessly heterodox,[117] the soul was an elusive notion in the period, and all the more so since its

---

[115] *Matter*, p. 9.

[116] P. 27. For an account of the earlier material, what he calls "this complex and tedious controversy," see Yolton, *John Locke*, esp. pp. 152–66. For the sequel, which he summarizes: "The force at work in those who reacted against that suggestion [that matter might think] was the fear of the automatical man."(p.45), see Yolton, *Thinking Matter* esp. chap. 2.

[117] Locke was interested in the history of this issue. In his commonplace book *Lemmata physica*, Locke entered three references taken from Rogerius, *La porte ouverte*, p. 194, dealing with the

ambiguities were constantly exploited by traditionalist defenders of religion who sought to locate the bestial soul as an intermediate between material and immaterial substances. Their standard vehicle of exploitation was an essentially Aristotelian concept of soul. But this concept was applicable, and previously had been applied, to everything said to be animate, including plants. To these people, Locke's allowing sense in animals was quite orthodox. The reason his suggestion that matter might think came under such attack was that he allowed that matter might think *rationally*. That is, while the danger in the views of both Descartes and Locke was regarded as the same, namely, the evaporation of all difference between man and mere matter, that danger sprang from opposite sources. Descartes was seen to denigrate matter, Locke to glorify it. The explanatory success of mechanism created an impulse that had to be deflected in one of these two directions.

A greater cause of confusion around the concept of the soul was that the seventeenth-century Aristotelian concept was degenerate. That even the human soul should be regarded as a substance in the primary sense, namely, as an individual, was a corruption of the Aristotelian view of the soul as the highest set of dispositions of a body, the view of the soul as a substance only in the secondary sense, namely, as the form of an individual. Thus, when Locke regards that in virtue of which he is rational (thinking) or a person (consciousness) or a man (the continued organization of his body) to be more like attributes than things, he is much closer to Aquinas than are the so-called Peripatetics who criticized him.

As I see it the fundamental cleavage on this issue is between qualitative monism and dualism. The question is, how many kinds of thing are there? Monistic options in the period before Hume are restricted to materialism. Berkeley opens the way to phenomenalism but leaves it to Hume to chart the path of a consistent monistic alternative to materialism. And there are two materialist options available.[118] One is the reductive materialism whose best known exponent was, and was perceived to be, Hobbes. Thus Cudworth saw Hobbes as maintaining "that *Cogitation*, *Intellection*, and *Volition*, are themselves really Nothing else, but *Local Motion* or *Mechanism*, in the inward *Parts* of the *Brain* and Heart," and that men are "Really Nothing else, but *Machines*, and *Automata*."[119] Eliminative materialism is more difficult to pin down; it would be a universally true version of what Descartes claimed of animals. Descartes sometimes speaks of sensation in animals, thereby suggesting a

---

preexistence of the soul. One reference is to Origen, who according to the footnote in Rogerius was undoubtedly of this opinion; a second is to Mersenne, who relates the Church's condemnation of this view; the last is to Benedictus Pererius, who discusses the question whether Augustine held the view. The entry is undated but follows entries as late as 1698. For more on Locke's use of Rogerius, see below.

[118] See Lycan and Pappas, "Materialism," for the terminology.

[119] *System*, p. 761; see Yolton, *Thinking Matter*, pp. 6–7.

reductionist account; thus he wrote to More: "To no animal do I deny life, inasmuch as I attribute it solely to the heat of the heart; nor do I deny sense insofar as it depends on bodily organism."[120] But it is rather clear that with respect to animals Descartes is an eliminative materialist. To Mersenne he writes that animals feel *no* pain, not that they feel pain, which in fact is nothing but a mechanical state.[121] The second materialist option would extend this account to all things.

On the dualist side there were also two options available. One is what might be called essential dualism: There are two kinds of thing, and things are *essentially* of one kind or the other. Thus, on the Cartesian scheme, a mind would no longer be a mind if it were material. Not only would it no longer be a mind, the same *kind* of thing, but it would no longer be the same *thing*. It would lose its identity and cease to be. Malebranche, for example, claims that it would be no more difficult to create an angel than to make one out of a stone, because making one out of a stone in fact is a matter of first annihilating the stone and then creating an angel instead.[122] In short, numerical identity across change in kinds is impossible. This is not true for the second dualist option, which we might call *bare* dualism: There are two kinds of thing, but the kinds are inessential to things, which may change kinds and remain numerically the same, or for that matter, may exemplify both kinds. I think this is the view Locke holds open as a possibility when he suggests that matter might think. Finally, in these terms the traditionalist attempt to secure a halfway house for the bestial soul would be a version of essential *pluralism*: There are more than two kinds and they are essential to the things exemplifying them. Only with this view could the extremes be avoided either of denigrating matter (Descartes) or glorifying it (Locke).

Locke's bare dualism is a very fragile view. He proposed it only as a possibility—as something that might be true *as far as we can know*. That Locke really meant his suggestion of thinking matter to be nothing more than an unproven suggestion may be gathered, for example, from his critical reaction to William Coward's views. Coward held that the soul is a "superminent" power implanted in matter. Of his *Grand Essay* Collins wrote to Locke: "Dr. Coward has publish'd a Book to show that no such thing as Immaterial substance exists in nature & that all matter has originally a principle of selfmotion in it. His arguments are very far from proving either & are too mean to give you any account of."[123] Locke replied: "by what I have seen of him already I can easily think his arguments not worth your reciting." Locke's statement in the *Essay* is a clearer repudiation of dogmatism on the question: "He that considers how hardly Sensation is, in our Thoughts, reconcilable to extended Matter; or Exis-

---

[120] February 5, 1649; AT, 5:275–79; also, to Regius, May 1641; AT, 3, 369–72.
[121] AT, 3:85.
[122] *Search*, p. 223.
[123] February 16, 1704; February 28, 1704; *Correspondence*, 8:198, 217.

tence to anything that hath no Extension at all will confess, that he is very far from certainly knowing what his Soul is" (4.3.6; 542). As long as we keep the hypotheses of the material and immaterial soul in mind, he says, we shall be able to opt for neither. This Pyrrhonian suspension judgment is borne out by the Locke manuscripts. Writing about 1694 Locke poses the same dilemma: "A thing that hath noe extension we cannot conceive to exist or have any being. And an extended solid we cannot conceive to have life i.e. motivitie & perception. And yet we know and must grant there are thinking beings."[124]

It is not surprising, then, that Locke foregoes the details of the ontology of bare dualism as not within the scope of our understanding. But beyond this skepticism, there is an inherent ontological instability. To see this, consider just one more distinction. Dualism of epiphenomenal kinds is the view that minds and bodies as these kinds are appearances of the real; dualism of real kinds is the view that kinds are real—however the appearance-reality distinction might be drawn. Thus, on any account Descartes would be a dualist of real kinds. But Hobbes might be a dualist of epiphenomenal kinds if mind, which is reducible to body, can thus be regarded as mere appearance. Now, for Locke, *all* qualities are epiphenomena, since the ability even of primary qualities to cause thought cannot be mechanistically explained. Indeed, qualities of mind and qualities of matter may be epiphenomena of the same thing. This cat was not long in the bag, for Locke, as we shall see, was early on accused of Spinozism. The argument from Carroll, for example, was to the effect that bare dualism collapses into eliminative materialism, and that this *qualitative* monism collapses into *quantitative* monism, the most damnable view of all that there is but one thing in the world. As I shall try ultimately to show, the issue turns on whether and in what sense epiphenomena are for Locke real.

The context for Locke's suggestion that matter might think is a discussion of the limited extent of our knowledge. But if Locke's principal aim was to illustrate our limited capabilities in this regard, the significance of his example could not have been fully unintended. For Locke's suggestion was made against a background of related issues and positions on those issues with which he was au courant. Whether animals known to be material might also be conscious and whether humans known to be conscious might also be material were both issues that involved analyses of consciousness and matter. It is a priori very unlikely that Locke did not see this connection. In addition, there is such circumstantial evidence as his reading,[125] and his interest (seen in the *Essay*) in such things as

---

[124] Bodleian MS Locke c.28 fol.115. This has been identified as a note from about 1694 concerning additions to the *Essay*. See Long, *Catalogue*, p. 29.

[125] Locke certainly came to do a lot of reading on these issues late in his life. A series of entries in his commonplace book, *Lemmata physica* deals with topics like the formation of the fetus, the materiality of the sensitive soul in man, the animal soul, the separability of the soul, and its relation to the body. References are to the atomist Sennert, Bacon, Willis (whose *De anima*, pp. 9–10, sets

conversing parrots, mechanical birds, monsters, and the ability of animals to infer, which suggest a familiarity with the bestial soul disputes.[126] But the principal evidence for making the connection is the thrust of the rest of the *Essay's* anti-Cartesian case. That matter might think is fundamentally contrary to Cartesian dualism (and of course that we cannot know whether it does is contrary to Cartesian dogmatism). Even to the extent that animals think this dualism is upset; for Locke animals have at least limited ability to compare ideas, even if none to abstract or to compound ideas, and they can reason concerning particular ideas.[127] Even such limited consciousness is precluded from animals by the all-or-nothing character of Cartesian thought. Such cognitive abilities as Locke would allow animals would be modes of the Cartesian principal attribute, with the result that matter would be essentially a mind.

It would be nice for my thesis if Locke were to be found influenced by and defending the Gassendist line on the animal soul, namely, that it consists in the disposition or organization of the body. This is a line that runs from Gassendi through Cureau, Bayle, and others to La Mettrie, who despite the title of his *L'homme-machine*, recognizes a human soul as dependent on this organization of the body.[128] And Locke does repeatedly insist that for matter to think it must be "fitly disposed." Only to "certain Systems of created senseless matter, put together as he thinkes fit" might God give thought (4.3.6; 541). Yet what I shall try to show is that these appearances of reductivism are misleading.[129]

It is worth noting that Locke was aware of the reductivist view as applied to the human soul as well. In his commonplace book *Lemmata ethica*, which he kept from 1659 until 1701, Locke refers to page 191 of a work by one Roger, which in a most remarkable context sets out a view relevant to this question. Roger turns out to be Abraham Rogerius and the work to which Locke refers is a

---

out the Cartesian-Gassendist contrast on the question), Gassendi, Aristotle and Cicero on other authors, and Cudworth on Philoponus. The entries begin in 1695, however, and may only reflect concerns latterly generated, for example, by the Stillingfleet controversy (Bodeleian MS Locke d.11 p.4).

[126] Yolton points out these examples and their significance (*John Locke*, p. 149). Might Locke have noted the characterization of man as a featherless parrot by the lunar animals in Cyrano's *Voyage*? Locke possessed only his *Satirical Letters* of 1658.

[127] 2.11.5, 7, 10, 11.

[128] See Rosenfield, *Animal Soul*, pp. 114, 125, 191. Rosenfield wonders whether Locke might have been influenced by Cureau, but without evidence or argument. It is noteworthy that despite the popularity of Cureau's works, Locke possessed none of them.

[129] Yolton properly emphasizes the significance of Locke's insistence on the appropriate disposition of matter for it to think and its significance for subsequent British thought of the eighteenth century (*Thinking Matter*, pp. 34, 199, and *passim*), but he interprets Locke as strongly endorsing the Cartesian understanding of animals (p. 35). As I see it, Locke would at most be a reductivist, but he seems not even to go this far, for he rejects the view that animals are *nothing but* machines. The ability of birds, for example, to imitate tunes heard previously indicates (as Yolton himself notes) a memory that according to Locke cannot be explained mechanically.

French translation published in 1670,[130] of a work first published in Dutch in 1651. Abraham Rogerius was a Dutch Protestant minister who spent the years 1631–41 in Pulicat, on the Coromandel coast of India, as chaplain at the Dutch East India trading station. While in India, Rogerius made the acquaintance of a Brahman named Padmanabhan, through whom he was able to make the first translation from the Sanskrit into a European tongue of the *Sutaka*. Upon leaving India he returned, first to Batavia, then to Holland in 1647, and died in Gouda in 1649. With the help of a professor at the University of Leyden, the *Open door* was published in 1651 with a set of notes.[131]

In the view of the annotator, the main value of Rogerius's work is that its account of the religious beliefs of the Hindus will better equip those who would convert them to Christianity. He points out that the strategy would thus be that of the early Church Fathers, whose missionary efforts often built on the foundation of what was already believed. To this end, his notes to Rogerius's text for the most part point out relevant analogies, arguments, and discussions, in Western thought. Much of this material would have been of interest to Locke, quite apart from his general interest in travel literature. The second half of the

[130] By Thomas LaGrue, master of arts and doctor of medicine. It had been translated into German in 1663 (Nuremberg).

[131] At the end of the nineteenth century this work was still regarded as the most complete account of south Indian Hinduism. There is another curious, if accidental, connection between this text and our own story. It was once thought that Rogerius's book was the source for references to the Vedas by a fabrication called the *Treatise of the three impostors*. This turns out to be the most important clandestine tract of the Radical Enlightenment, in which Moses, Jesus and Mohammed are argued to be imposters, and religion a ruse by rulers to subjugate their subjects. In the nineteenth century the legend of its having been composed in the Middle Ages, by Averroes, for example, was to have been exploded in part by the rediscovery of Rogerius's text, which thus dated it no earlier than 1651. Burnell tried to show that information on the Vedas could have been available in the sixteenth century. Most recently, Margaret Jacobs has on the basis of new information definitely traced the *Treatise* to Jean Rousset de Missy (1686–1762), who had written it by 1711, but presumably not much earlier, capitalizing on rumors of its existence during only the previous forty years. Rousset was a member of a Masonic coterie called the Knights of Jubilation, which circulated the text along with a life of Spinoza. Their story (and its context) is a long one; the short of it is that they had combined Renaissance naturalism with the mechanical philosophy in a new religion of nature—a pantheism that was at once materialist and vitalist and that had explosive moral and political implications. Says Jacobs: "This spirit in matter philosophy must be seen, within those circles at least, as the philosophical foundation for republican and even democratic philosophies of government. If the world of ordinary people and daily events is rendered, in effect, sacred, then systems of government justified by recourse to supernatural authority, even if reinforced by contract, lose all validity"(p. 224). Perhaps the principal player in this drama was Toland, whose version of these views was as systematic, undisguised, and widely disseminated as anyone's. The connection through Locke to Rogerius's book, if in fact it was a source for Rousset, is thus not entirely accidental to our story. To Jacobs's account I would add but a small detail, which is another accidental connection to our story. J. B. Morin responded (1654) under the pseudonym Vincentius Panurgus to Gassendi, Bernier, and Laurent Mesme (better known as Mathurin Neuré) who had attacked his *Dissertatio de atomis et vacuo*. Morin called them the three impostors. This suggests that rumors of the *Treatise's* circulation were somewhat earlier than Jacobs claims.

work, for example, begins with a claim of significance to the innate ideas issue, namely, that exploration has shown that no people are so brutal or deprived of understanding as not to believe there is a God. The notes dispute this, citing ancient Greek authors who were atheist, and ending with the wish that Rogerius's claim were true even of those who profess to be Christians.

There are a surprising number of actual references by Locke to this work. We might divide them into two groups. One deals with the question of the world's creation. Among them is a reference[132] to a text relating the Hindu belief in an infinite series of worlds—the same view that Epicurus held, it is pointed out. (The note cites Aristotle's view that no further worlds could be created and Pererius's criticism of this view.) Another[133] is to a text relating the belief that God created Brahma from a leaf and then because of Brahma's gratitude allowed him to create the rest of the world. The note takes exception to this, suggesting that the Hindus thought of Brahma as the Son of God, since almost all peoples have attributed creation to the divinity. Many sources are cited to this effect. The second group of Locke's references deals with the soul-body connection. Thus, Locke was interested in a footnote to Pererius on the body as the prison or sepulchre of the soul,[134] and at another point he notes Rogerius as a source for opinions for and against the immortality of the soul.[135]

Among the latter references, the most important occurs under the heading "Man. Defenders of the opinion that the excellence of man consists in the body."[136] This returns us, after our digression through Locke's source for the reference, to the issue of his awareness of the reductivist view of man. Rogerius relates the Hindus' belief that man is the most perfect creature but that, since he has the same soul as the animals, his perfection lies in his body, "by means of which the soul produces and makes appear all the qualities found in it." They cannot be persuaded that it is his soul in which man's perfection consists. They attribute man's difference from the animals in rationality to the difference in his body from theirs; and they support this with the concomitant variation of rationality and bodily disposition between children and adults. If children have a reasonable soul they reason less well than adults only because of the difference in their bodies, which must be appropriately disposed in order for certain qualities to appear. According to the notes, this shows the Hindus to be true Platonists, as were, inter alios, Parmenides, Empedocles, Democritus, and Pythagoras. This might have been a source for Locke's ruminations about the Cartesian thesis that the soul always thinks and the related question of the

---

[132] Bodleian MS Locke d.10 p.109; Rogerius, *La porte ouverte*, p. 177.

[133] Ibid., p. 23; Rogerius, *La porte ouverte*, p. 142.

[134] Bodleian MS d.11 p.4; Rogerius, *La porte ouverte*, p. 194.

[135] Bodleian MS Locke d.10 p.5; Rogerius, *La porte ouverts*, p. 192. The note mentions, inter alios, Hermes Trismegistus, Plato, Thales, and Pythagoras for, Aristotle and the Stoics against.

[136] Ibid., p. 77. Homo. Excellentiam hominis consistere in corpore huius opinionis propugnatores; Rogerius, *La porte ouverts*, p. 190.

identities of a man and of a person.[137] This text might have shown both what was wrong with the Cartesian view and what the correct view was, for it is ambiguous. The annotator's interpretation is that the soul is a thing different from the body that depends on it for an instrument; the difficulties in this view Locke spells out at great length. But the text might also be read, or slightly emended to read, that the soul depends on its disposition in the sense that the soul just is that disposition (and in this sense the souls of animals and men are the same). How Locke might understand this possibility returns to a final consideration of his view that matter might possibly think. The relevant text is his *Second Reply* to Stillingfleet.

Stillingfleet had objected that by allowing that matter might think, Locke had confused the ideas of matter and spirit. Locke replied in effect that thinking matter might be a kind of matter just as a horse, though more than mere matter, that is, more than solid, extended substance, is nonetheless still matter. If God can superadd motion, vegetation, and substance to matter, as Stillingfleet agrees He can, then He can also superadd thought. The only restriction is that what is superadded not be excluded from the essence involved, and no one has shown thought to be excluded from matter. Our inability to conceive how this may be done is irrelevant, Locke continued, for we know as a matter of fact that God has superadded gravity to matter, and thus action at a distance, which is beyond our ability to conceive. Locke then explains this matter "a little further." He thinks everyone will agree that God can create a substance, material or immaterial, without giving it any activity, including motion or thought, which are activities.[138] "Now I would ask, why Omnipotency cannot give to either of these substances, which are equally in a state of perfect inactivity, the same power that it can give the other?"[139] The answer cannot be that the material cannot have spontaneous or self-motion, for it already has the attribute of gravity; in addition, self-motion is no more conceivable in an immaterial substance. Locke concludes: "That omnipotency cannot make a substance to be solid and not solid at the same time, I think, with due reverence, we may say; but that a solid substance may not have qualities, perfections and powers, which

[137] "waking *Socrates*, has no Knowledge of, or Concernment for that Happiness, or Misery of his Soul, which it enjoys alone by itself whilst he sleeps, without perceiving any thing of it; no more than he has for the Happiness, or Misery of a Man in the Indies, whom he knows not" (2.1.11; 110).

[138] This is not an ad hoc invention on Locke's part. Ayers ("Locke versus Aristotle," p. 230) draws attention in this regard to a journal entry for February 20, 1682: spirit and matter "may both lye dead and unactive, i.e. the one without thought, the other without motion . . . which wholly depends upon the will and good pleasure of the first author" (Aaron and Gibb, *Early Draft*, p. 123) Locke here may be following Malebranche, who viewed motion and volition as kinds of superadditions by God to extension and thought (*Search*, p. 198); but if he is, it should also be noted that Malebranche thought extension may not be the essence of matter. The essence of a thing is what is conceived first in a thing, that is, that on which all its properties depend, and for all we know there may be something more primary on which extension depends (*Search*, pp. 243–44).

[139] *Works*, 4:464.

have no natural or visibly necessary connection with solidity and extension is too much for us (who are but of yesterday, and know nothing) to be positive in."[140]

This view raises some difficulties. One that has been noted concerns Locke's justification for saying that motion is not of the essence of matter if that essence is unknown.[141] Similarly, in a passage of which Locke was not likely ignorant, Digby offered the following reductio ad absurdum. Unless the qualities of corporeal things and of minds can be explained, then any operation of an allegedly spiritual soul can be attributed to the body.[142] A generalized version of this problem led in the period to the charge of Spinozism against Locke: For all we know everything might be this attribute of a *single* substance. Given the use to which Locke's philosophy was later put by Toland and others in the service of pantheistic materialism, this charge deserves closer scrutiny.

By his own account William Carroll was the first to see through Locke's stratagems and to realize that his aim was to establish Spinoza's "hypothesis" that there is but one substance—a material substance—of which all particular things are but modifications. He takes the whole *Essay*, top to bottom, to be a concealed effort to this end. In the final chapter below I shall have more to say about this charge of philosophical subversion. Here I want only to set out Carroll's principal argument that what Locke says about substance commits him to quantitative monism. Carroll focuses on 2.13.18, where Locke appears to be arguing that we have no clear, nonrelative idea of substance.[143] His argument is that if we have the *same* idea as applied to God, spirits, and body, then these will "differ not any otherwise than in a bare different modification of that *Substance*; as a Tree and a Pebble, being in the same sense Body, and agreeing in the common nature of Body, differ only in a bare modification of that common matter; which will be a very harsh Doctrine." If we have *different* ideas, they should be made out and denominated differently; but if this can be done, then a fourth such idea could be made out and, presumably, so on (2.13.18; 174). Carroll takes this to be a disjunctive syllogism involving the denial of the latter alternative. In short, the "harsh doctrine" is Locke's.[144]

Carroll sees Locke's use of the term 'substance' as ambiguous (an ambiguity Locke is charged with exploiting in hiding his Spinozism). When Locke uses the term in the singular he means the (single) support for all modifications; when he uses it in the plural it refers merely to so many collections of modifications. That the "*Support Subject of Inhesion or Substance is One* and the same *every where*" Carroll thinks clear from what we have called Locke's bare dualism—what makes a thing matter or spirit is solidity and thinking, regard-

---

[140] Ibid., p. 465.

[141] Ayers, "Locke versus Aristotle," pp. 229–30.

[142] *Two treatises*, preface.

[143] As he later in fact puts it to Stillingfleet (*Works*, 4:21–22).

[144] *Dissertation*, p. 28.

less of what other modifications it may have (p.31). "For *Solidity*, with Mr. *L.* stands for the same thing that *Extension* does with *Spinoza*; that is, for the primary *Quality* or *Modification* amongst those they call *Body* or Matter" (p.32). Carroll thus makes Locke out to be a materialist, not in the sense that the only kind of thing is material, but in the Spinozist sense that everything is material, whatever other kind of thing it may also be. Even so, this does not secure quantitative monism. For that Carroll provides two further arguments. The one he develops at greater length depends on Locke's doctrine of real and nominal essences. I shall have a great deal to say below on this topic, which incidentally will tend to show Carroll to be right in what he contends, namely, that Locke can account for differences in kind only among *ideas* and not among *things* (pp.36–42). For now, a passage Carroll cites from Locke will give the idea: "The next thing to be considered is, by which of those Essences it is, that *Substances are determined in Sorts*, or *Species*; and that 'tis evident, is by the nominal Essence. For 'tis that alone, that the name, which is the mark of the *Sort*, signifies. 'Tis impossible therefore, that any thing should determine the Sorts of Things, which we rank under general Names, but that *Idea*, which that Name is design'd as a mark for; which is that, as has been shewn, which we call the Nominal Essence."[145] A second argument is to the effect that Locke's direct treatment of identity and diversity (2.27) shows them to be mere modifications—distinctions that we draw but are not real. Locke can have only "nominal differences" between things.[146] Diversity, in short, is only *apparent*. Carroll's argument perhaps successfully makes only this Kantian point and not the charge of Spinozism he intends, but his work nonetheless indicated the significance Locke would have for many important thinkers who found themselves in agreement with Locke thus interpreted.

There is a second difficulty in the view Locke expressed to Stillingfleet, namely, how is a material substance known to be solid and extended? Note that Locke says in his *Reply* that the activity of either substance, material or immaterial, may be added to the other. That is, just as thinking might be added to matter, so might motion (that is, presumably, locomotion) be added to spirit. It would be puzzling, however, to find Locke here reverting to Cureau's or perhaps More's view. A solution is indicated by a letter from Locke to Anthony Collins, in which he is responding to certain Cartesian objections in these matters: "Extension and Solidity we have Ideas of and see, that cogitation has no necessary connection with them nor has any *consequential result* from them, and therefor is not a proper affection of extension and solidity nor doth naturally belong to them, but how does it follow from hence that it may not be made an affection of or be annexed to that substance which is vested with solidity and

---

[145] 3.6.7; 443; Carroll, *Dissertation*, p. 40.

[146] Ibid., p. 43. Carroll uses the Spinozist language of 'modifications' to refer to ideas. The use is not implausible since accidents were typically regarded as the appearances of a substance.

extension."[147] To say that a material substance is *vested* with solidity suggests that it could be *divested* of it, that the underlying substrate is bare, and that Locke's dualism, such as it is, is bare.

On this account, then, *all* attributes are superadded. In the usual language of Porphyry's doctrine of the predicables,[148] there are no *properties* (attributes that flow from the essence of a thing) but only *accidents* (attributes that are incidentally applied). Locke often enough speaks of properties flowing from the essence of things, but this is only to say that there are deductive connections among certain attributes. Thus when he says that if we knew the relevant internal constitution, 'all gold is malleable,' for example, would be as certain as 'the three angles of all right-line triangles are equal to two right ones' (4.6.10), he means *as certain as*. The certainty may be total, but it is a certainty that in both cases *we* invest in the proposition. The difference between the two cases is that there is a constraint on what we say in the first kind of case; but that constraint cannot be essences *in rebus* of which essential claims are true. (This I shall try to show is what Locke rejects as scholastic gibberish.) To put it another way, the only necessity for Locke is *de dictu*. (Recall that the example he gives—his only example—of superaddition that is impossible because excluded by the essence of the thing is a substance that would be both solid and not solid.) The question as to how we might know whether motion is part of the essence of a thing does not even arise. Such essences as sort things into kinds are, as Carroll observed, entirely nominal, entirely of our fabrication, and thus entirely transparent. Apart from these there are only unsorted things.

Yet Locke does refer to the *real* essence of a thing in terms of its internal constitution. He is very insistent that this essence is in everything that exists, that it is identical to the internal constitution, and that it is not something that "flows from" the substance, as Stillingfleet had put it.[149] Again we have intruded upon a longer story to be told below; the short of it is that Locke is drawing out the consequences of his nominalism. A thing and its attribute are only conceptually different: The shape of a thing is the thing shaped in a certain way.

This leads to a certain ambiguity, for on one reading *all* attributes are thus essential. The result would be that superaddition is impossible, for to add any attribute would be to produce an essentially different kind of thing and thus a numerically different thing. This was the criticism of Malcolm Flemyng,[150] who in effect argued a universal nonexchangeability thesis. "Whatever exists

---

[147] March 24, 1704; *Correspondence*, 8:255.

[148] Whose significance here has been emphasized by Ayers ("Locke versus Aristotle").

[149] *Works*, 4:82–83.

[150] This physician and physiologist of some significance was born in Scotland, studied with Boerhaave in Leyden, practiced medicine in Scotland from 1725, then in Hull, did some teaching around mid-century in London, and died at Lincoln in 1764.

really is a concrete Individual, and is possessed of all the Attributes that concur to constitute it the very thing it is."[151] Locke's attempt to distinguish as he did in his *Reply* to Stillingfleet between matter and kinds of matter is a distinction of reason, and 'matter as such' is a being of reason. Locke commits a "Blunder" in speaking "as if the Essence of matter in general were a concrete Substance, and could actually exist naked, as it is conceived, and unfurnished with any other Property" (p.16). Locke is accused of forgetting his own "admirable" theory of abstract ideas. "His Reasonings constantly suppose, that abstract Ideas have Architypes or Models, really existing without the Mind, answering to these Ideas, and divested as much as they are of such Properties as concur to constitute either the inferior Species, or the singular Nature of Individuals" (pp.23–24).Flemynge here argues what was Berkeley's principal case against Locke, namely, that whatever exists is fully determinate.[152] Berkeley's further step, which Flemyng seems clearly not to have followed, was to regard the indeterminate as inconceivable.

The ambiguity in Locke, at any rate, is between a doctrine of bare particulars according to which things are mere individuals but are different from their attributes, and a doctrine of perfect particulars, according to which things just are the unique instances of attributes. This ambiguity, I think, helps explain Locke's slide in the use of 'solidity' between the thing and an attribute of it. The ambiguity is obscured by the construal of attributes as appearances of the thing; the shape of a thing is indeed the thing shaped in a certain way, but this is to say that it is perceived in a certain way. As we have seen, we shape the world. In any case, the ambiguity is harmless enough. For both views preserve versions of the exchangebility thesis. In neither case is any combination of attributes ruled out by the kind of thing; there are no essences of this sort and no synthetic a priori propositions describing them. Also, in both cases the attributes may necessarily be their unique instances and thus nominalism is preserved.

Samuel Strutt[153] held something very like the bare-particularist view I attribute to Locke, and although he himself did not attribute it to Locke and in fact developed it out of criticism of Locke at certain key points. The work is a pamphlet that appeared in 1732 and the occasion for it was the Clarke–Collins controversy over thinking matter. Strutt was a materialist, or at least an antiimmaterialist, who thus took the side of Collins that matter might think. As Strutt saw it, the issue between the disputants came down to the question of

---

[151] Flemyng, *Examination*, p. 14. (Yolton first drew attention to this work [*Thinking Matter*, pp. 26–27].) *Cf.* Spinoza: an attribute is "that which the mind conceives as constituting the essence of a substance" (*Ethics* 1, def. 3). Flemyng later argues that either thought necessarily follows from the disposition of matter or else God in adding thought does not superadd a property but creates an additional substance pp. 25–30).

[152] Flemyng was a reader at least of Berkeley's *Siris*; *A proposal for the improvement of medicine* and extensively contested both Berkeley's tar-water doctrine and his use of the term 'panacea' *Proposal*, pp. 122–47).

[153] For more on this author, see chap. 8.

whether parts individually must have every attribute of a whole, that is, whether a system of matter alleged to think meant that the parts composing it must individually think with the result, as Clarke argued, that the unity of consciousness would be upset. Clarke distinguished between *extrinsical denominations*, such as rotundity, of which this principle was not true, and *inherent qualities*, such as consciousness, of which it is true. The difference is that the inherent quality is real, whereas an extrinsical denomination is "only a mere Idea rais'd in us, by the Situation of an external Object."[154] Strutt's argument is that *no* qualities are inherent and thus consciousness is not. Strutt thus agrees with Collins that matter can think in the sense, but *only* in the sense, that matter is extended. He defines a quality or attribute as "*whatever may be predicated of any Subject, resulting from its Te[x]ture and Frame*" (p.8). On quality Locke was inaccurate and perplexing for "the truth [155] is, that *Bulk, Figure, Number, Situation, Motion* and *Rest*, are no more *really* in the Subject of which those Qualities may be predicated, than colors, Sounds, or Smell are in the Bodies that produce those Ideas in us" (p.10). The upshot is that Locke's distinction between primary and secondary qualities in terms of whether the qualities are "really in the Bodies, whether we perceive them or no" is a "distinction without a difference" (p.12). The absurdity of the reality of qualities can be shown, he thinks, by Locke's talk of the modifications of qualities,[156] for to talk of them in this way is to treat qualities as *substances*. For Strutt, clearly, only individual *things* are real; its qualities are its *appearances*. "The Body of which we affirm such a peculiar *Figure, Bulk, Situation, Motion* or *Rest* only so exists, or under such a Modification, that we collect those Ideas from it: It is true the Subject itself, if it has a terminated Existence must have extream parts; which constitute what we call Figure; and so it must likewise be of such a Bulk, or in such a peculiar Situation, and in *motion* or at *rest*: But these Qualities are only the several *Manners*, under which the Body or the Object presents itself to us, or in which we perceive it to exist; and to say the *Manner* of a Thing's Existence, is IN, the Thing itself, would be very unphilosophical, and yet when Mr. *Lock* says, that *Bulk, Figure, Number, Situation, Motion* or *Rest* are *in* the Subject whether we perceive them or no, it is in effect, only saying this" (pp.10–11).

His view is that "*Every Quality or Attribute, that can be affirm'd of any Subject, must necessarily be the Result of the Texture and Frame of the Subject, of which it may be predicated*" (p.18). Given this, superaddition of thought, for example, of the sort whose possibility Locke proposed is ruled out. "For if every Quality or Attribute must necessarily be the result of the Texture and Frame of its Subject, then it will be impossible to superadd any Quality, unless

---

[154] *Enquiry*, p. 7.

[155] "as difficult as Truth to receive as any of those which Mr. Locke introduc'd in the World" (p. 10).

[156] Secondary and tertiary qualities are only powers that "result from the different Modifications of those primary Qualities" (2.8.23; 141)

something that is material be added to the Subject; in which case no new Quality would be superadded, but that portion of Matter would really be converted into something else, that would be specifically different from all other Matter: It being as inconceivable that any Quality should be actually separated from its Subject (*which the Superaddition of a Quality supposes*) as to conceive the Figure of a Body, actually separated from the Body itself. That God might so modify and dispose the Parts of any System of Matter, as to make it capable of Thinking, might very reasonably have been said by one, who doubted of the natural Capacity of Matter to think, but that a Quality must be superadded for that Purpose, is both impossible and unintelligible" (pp.18–19, n.).

It is clear that what Strutt calls the texture and frame of a thing are not its primary qualities, not even the primary qualities of its minute parts. Qualities are, ultimately, the appearances of a thing or the idea we have of it. For God to superadd a quality would be to generate an appearance in the absence of the appropriate thing. (Strutt does not use the analogy, but what Locke was proposing was just like transubstantiation.) In this Strutt is criticizing not so much the foundation of Locke's philosophy as his failure to be consistent with it. The important difference between Strutt and Locke concerns the connection between a thing and its appearances. For Strutt this is clearly a necessary connection; for a thing to appear differently it must be altered, that is, it must be a different thing. Strutt, then, is a dogmatist of the most radical sort, for he is a naive realist in the sense that things could not appear other than they do. For Locke, as he makes clear both in his letter to Collins and in his *Reply* to Stillingfleet, there are no such strongly necessary connections—certainly not between any arrangement of matter and consequent thought (nor even between an arrangement and any idea of a primary quality, which, as we have seen, depends solely on the truth of the mechanical hypothesis). In this sense all attributes are superadded and thus are fundamentally inexplicable. This may be a skepticism congenial with the tenor of Locke's epistemology, but it is perhaps too much of a welcome thing. For the problem now is to find some basis for kinds in this buzzing blooming confusion of appearances. How is the world we recognize sorted out of a world of mere bare particulars?

Putting the problem in another way might point to its solution. It has not been noticed, as far as I know, that for Locke superaddition is not just a matter of adding otherwise inexplicable attributes to things (as Strutt, for example, thinks); for he says that (as far as we know) it is no more inconceivable that God should superadd a faculty of thinking to matter "than that he should superadd to it another Substance, with a Faculty of Thinking" (4.3.6; 541). That is, one *substance* might be superadded to another. What can this mean? Roughly the idea is that to superadd is *to make true of*. Were God to superadd a thinking substance to a nonthinking one—the Cartesian case that I think Locke in fact rejects—He would make it true that man is a composite (whatever might be the explanation of *how* He might do so that the Cartesians never really supplied).

What is needed from Locke, more generally, are the analogues to (1) the Cartesian God's creation of an object that makes a proposition true and (2) the Cartesian conception of a natural logic according to which "the order and connection of things is the order and connection of thought." That is, what we need from him is a general theory of truth.

CHAPTER VII.

Innateness, Abstraction, and Essences

§24 INNATENESS

A landmark issue of the seventeenth century, certainly of its latter half, was the nativist-empiricist controversy over what, if anything, might be the mind's original baggage.[1] This controversy was exceedingly complicated due to the failure, or inability, to get clear on the crucial terms of the debate, especially the notion of experience on which the mind was said to be dependent, or not, for its knowledge. Consonant with the theme sounded from the outset of this work, my thesis is that the historical controversy is best understood as concerned not with the question whether mathematics, for example, can be *known* independently of sense experience, but rather with what there must *be* in order for there to be mathematical knowledge at all.[2]

Let us begin by distinguishing three theories of innateness that eventually emerge most clearly in Leibniz. The first of these may be called the reflective theory. It is most clearly stated in Leibniz's response to Locke's empiricist dictum that there is nothing in the intellect that was not first in the senses, which he emended to read, except the intellect itself.[3] "It is thus, that in thinking upon ourselves we think of *being*, of *substance*, of the *simple* and *composite*, of a

---

[1] Since its publication nearly twenty years ago, R. F. McRae's "Innate Ideas" in my view remains the best paper on the topic. Here I shall use it as a vehicle to extend discussion to the ontological issues I regard as underlying the historical disputes about innateness. My heavy debt to this article will be apparent and is gratefully acknowledged.

[2] Before proceeding I must first indicate a background assumption of this chapter. It relates to the long-standing exegetical chestnut as to who held the views Locke attacked in his polemic against innate ideas. I take this question to have been conclusively decided by Yolton's *John Locke and The Way of Ideas*, which cogently argued from a battery of historical material that the actual proponents of these views composed a heterogeneous group of Locke's contemporaries and immediate predecessors in England. Their views on innate ideas range from the "naive form [which] claimed that God wrote into or impressed upon the soul or mind at birth certain ideas and precepts . . . even though we do not become aware of these innate principles . . . until maturity," to a modified form according to which "the name innate was meant to apply only to those principles which we easily assent to" (p. 29). Yet if the polemic against innate ideas is *not* directed against the Cartesians, then why in preparation for the remaining three books of the *Essay*'s anti-Cartesian diatribe does Locke attack innate ideas? A background assumption here will be that Locke's aim was directed against the Cartesians though his attack in fact reached views no Cartesian ever held. Descartes by his own testimony held some view of innateness, but what that view was, as we shall see, was far from apparent. To refute Descartes, then, Locke attacked every view of innateness he could find.

[3] *New Essays* 1, ii, 20; quoted by McRae, "Innate Ideas," p. 33.

material thing, and of *God* himself."[4] "The soul comprises being, substance, unity, identity, cause, perception, reason and many other notions which the senses cannot give."[5]

This version of innateness appears in *Meditations*, where Descartes distinguishes a class of ideas that "might be borrowed" from my idea of myself, namely, substance, duration, number, and "anything else of this kind."[6] These may be regarded as categorial concepts that are applicable to every sort of thing.[7] Descartes appeals to this sense of innateness in his defense of the primitive status of the cogito. In correspondence, in the *Conversation with Burman* and in *Replies to Objections*, Descartes insists that the cogito is noninferential but yet allows that our knowledge of it is dependent on knowledge of knowledge itself, of existence, thought, and certainty, and that whatever thinks exists. The presupposed knowledge may be understood on the model of the *Posterior Analytics* (71a7) account of our knowledge of universal principles—the "intuitive induction" whereby we derive demonstrative knowledge by "exhibiting the universal as implicit in the clearly known particular."[8] For Descartes ideas would be innate in this sense if they are implicit in consciousness and available to us explicitly when we reflect on our thought.[9]

That such ideas are termed innate in any interesting sense, however, is unclear to me. Locke, who claims to reject innate ideas in every sense, yet admits ideas of reflection, perhaps even ideas that though derivable *only* from reflection are still portable *beyond* that experience. In his chapter on power in which the concern is "not to search into the original of power, but how we come by the *Idea* of it" (2.21.2; 234), Locke allows that "if we will consider it attentively, Bodies by our Senses, do not afford us so clear and distinct an *Idea* of *active Power*, as we have from reflection on the Operations of our Minds" (2.21.4; 235). Once in our possession, however, this idea can be incorporated into our complex idea of substance, in which it in fact figures as the most prominent component of all. If there is a significant difference in this regard between Locke on the one hand and Descartes and Leibniz on the other, it lies in response to the ontological question of exactly *what* is found upon reflection. In contrast to the nativist view, Lockean reflection yields no more extensive, or less problematic, an ontology than that afforded by sensation: What we say about the being, substance, action, cause, unity, identity, similarity, and duration of the self is on all fours with what we say about body. Put another way, reflection does not get us beyond the contingent realm of sense experience to an order of necessary truth as it does for Leibniz and Descartes.

---

[4] *Monadology*, sec. 30.

[5] *New Essays* 2, i, 2; quoted by McRae, "Innate Ideas," p. 33.

[6] CSM, 2:30; AT, 7:44.

[7] As McRae points out, Descartes says there may be thousands of such ideas (p. 34).

[8] The expression 'intuitive induction' comes from W. E. Johnson.

[9] A great virtue of McRae's paper is its meticulous and convincing account of these connections.

As it is in Aristotle, the notion of 'implicit' involved here is quite vague. We may define the notion somewhat by noting that two sorts of items are said to be implicit: concepts like *thought* or *existence* and propositions like *whatever thinks exists*. The distinction between them is ignored by Descartes and in due course I shall have occasion at least to outline why he should take this horrifying stance. The prologue to that story is the initial distinction between two sorts of implicitness. We might be tempted to say that some concept A, say of figure, is *conceptually implicit* in a concept B, of a triangle, just in case B cannot be had without A. But in addition to its being psychologistic, the claim would be false for Descartes, since with the cogito I need not have the concept of existence, for example—except *implicitly*, of course, which is what needs explaining. Let us say, then, that whatever is true of B depends on what is true of A, where the dependence cashes out as logical deducibility with a relevance condition. Similarly, let us say that a proposition P, for example, 'whatever thinks exists,' is *logically implicit* in a proposition Q, 'I think, therefore I am,' just in case Q is relevantly deducible from P.

A second interpretation of innateness appeals to the Platonic metaphor of reminiscence. In *Meditations* 5, perhaps the only text that actually employs the metaphor, Descartes imagines extension along with the size, shape, situation, motion, and duration of its parts. "Not only are all these things very well known and transparent to me when regarded in this general way, but in addition there are countless particular features regarding shape, number, motion and so on, which I perceive when I give them my attention. And the truth of these matters is so open and so much in harmony with my nature, that on first discovering them it seems that I am not so much learning something new as remembering what I knew before; or it seems like noticing for the first time things which were long present within me although I had never turned my mental gaze on them before."[10] The interpretive key here is Vlastos's explication of Plato's reminiscence metaphor, namely, "any enlargement of our knowledge that results from the perception of logical relationships."[11] These relationships are of two sorts, neatly corresponding to the two versions of implicitness we have distinguished above. One sort involves the intrapropositional relation of analyticity of concepts; the other involves the interpropositional relation of logical deducibility, and to recollect is, on this account, to realize just these connections. In fact, we can extend this account as above so that it is the exact converse of the reflective theory with the result that any two ideas in the sense stated between which there is a relation of relevant deducibility are innate.[12]

---

[10] CSM, 2:63; AT,7:63–64.

[11] "*Anamnesis*", p. 156; quoted by McRae, "Innate Ideas," p. 48.

[12] McRae is committed to rejecting this result since according to him the idea of extension is adventitious. All of geometry because deducible from extension is innate, but the idea of extension itself is derived from sense experience. Thus once again Locke would seem on McRae's account to have held a theory of innate ideas. McRae's view on this is mistaken, it seems to me, for he fails to

The third sense of innateness construes ideas as dispositions built into the soul, presumably in the way Aristotelian potentialities are built into substances. This dispositional theory of innateness is to be found elaborated in the *New Essays* and, some have thought, at least sketched in a passage from the *Comments on a Certain Broadsheet*, in which Descartes says that ideas are innate "in the same sense as that in which we say that generosity is 'innate' in certain families, or that certain diseases such as gout or stones are innate in others; it is not so much that the babies of such families suffer from these diseases in their mother's womb, but simply that they are born with a certain 'faculty' or tendency to contract them."[13] Descartes's concern in this text is the radical dissimilarity he sees between appearances in sense perception and what he takes to be their causal antecedents. This is obvious in the case of secondary qualities such as color and pain, but even in the case of primary qualities such as shape and motion, the way we apprehend them differs from the way they are in the corporeal organs of sense. For reasons we need not investigate,[14] Descartes requires that there be an essential similarity between cause and its effect. He would seem to resolve the tension here by construing the corporeal antecedents to the production of ideas as but occasions, as he specifically calls them, with the mind containing these ideas previous to its production of them as active potencies, as La Forge was later to put it.[15] Without some further qualification, the result of this theory would be that all ideas for Descartes are innate.

Again, however, we have a sense of innateness that is inoffensive to Locke. If all that is argued for as innate is the mind's capacity, says Locke, then all ideas are innate and the dispute about innateness is a verbal one only, "For no Body, I think, ever denied, that the Mind was capable of knowing several Truths" (1.2.5; 50).[16]

---

distinguish between the ideas of material things or bodies and extension, which is the essence of such things, between the particular piece of wax, for example, which can be sensed and imagined, and its extension, which as Descartes insists in *Meditations* 2 can only be intuited by the mind alone (*mentis inspectio*). This is not a minor emendation to McRae's position since, as I shall eventually try to show, the idea of extension is precisely that of deducibility. McRae's thesis that the idea of extension is innate has come under attack from M. Myles, whose argument hangs on a distinction very similar to that between *extensio* and *extensa*. See his article and rebuttal and McRae's reply.

[13] CSM 1:304; AT, 8:358. See also Port-Royal *Logic*, chap. 1; Arnauld, *Oeuvres* 4.

[14] See Clatterbaugh, "Likeness Principle."

[15] *Traité de l'esprit de l'homme* (1666); edition of 1725; quoted by McRae, "Innate Ideas,"p. 52.

[16] McRae denies that this sense of innateness characterizes any Cartesian idea, his main reason deriving from Descartes's reference in *Comments* to his *Dioptrics*: "nothing reaches our mind from external objects through the organs of sense beyond certain corporeal movements . . . ; but even these movements, and the figures which arise from them, are not conceived by us in the shape they assume in the organs of sense, as I have explained at great length in my *Dioptrics*." In this work Descartes had set out a theory of perception according to which the perception of size, for example, depends on the perception of distance, with the former to be read as an inference or judgment based in part on the data provided by the latter. According to McRae, "it is the faculty of judging which is innate to the mind, and if we speak of the conceptions which we form through judgment as innate, it

The three senses of innateness in Descartes will differ according to the different occasions for the mind's own production of its ideas. The anamnesis account seizes upon the deduction characteristic of the Cartesian method of synthesis. The reflective account is mobilized by the Cartesian method of analysis, which shows how these deductive connections are discovered. Finally, the occasion may be, rather than a deductive connection, a brain-event only; these logically isolated episodes will be either the factitious or the adventitious ideas of *Meditations* 3, between which there is the contextual distinction drawn by *Meditations* 6—as against ideas of imagination, ideas of sense will be livelier, more coherent, and of biological utility. Attending to them will have survival value in keeping the soul conjoined with the corporeal machine. Though they may be clear, indeed in some cases must be to fulfill their function, neither of these sorts of ideas may be distinct, since as we know from *Meditations* 1 and 2, they do not get us at the mind-independent essence of things. Distinctness is a title reserved to ideas had through either recollection or reflection, which have characteristics, particularly universality,[17] qualifying them as innate in the narrower sense of *Meditations* 3. These are the ideas comprising "arithmetic, geometry and other subjects of this kind which deal only with the simplest and general things, regardless of whether they really exist in nature (*in rerum natura*)," but which, as we saw in chapter 2 above, may be false if God has not created extension (res extensa).[18] In creating extension, however, God as their efficient cause provides the object of eternal truths.[19] This object, extension, is what makes deducibility relations obtain; it is the object of Descartes's mathesis universalis. It is an entity that can be merely contemplated to yield concepts, but also described to yield propositions—which is why Descartes can with impunity ignore the concept proposition-distinction in what for most would be a gross category mistake.

I am here able only to outline what is a very contentious interpretation of Descartes on these matters. Its full defense cannot be attempted. Instead, I shall

---

is only because they are formed by that innate faculty, not produced by what comes through the senses. It is impossible to read into the *Dioptrics* any conception of ideas as innate active dispositions. They are not potencies prior to acts of judgment. They are products of judgment" (Innate Ideas," p. 53). It seems to me, however, that the *Dioptrics* clearly indicates that color is a simple, non-inferential object of perception on the basis of which perception of size, shape, and the like, occurs. Yet in *Comments* color is said to be innate. The ideas of the *Notes*, therefore, cannot be said to be innate in the sense that they are products of an innate faculty of judgment. See Lennon, "Representationalism."

[17] See ibid.: "I should like [Regius] to instruct me as to what corporeal movement it is which can form in our mind any common notion, e.g. the notion that '*Things which are equal to the same thing are equal to one another*, or any other that he pleases; for all these movements are particular, but notions are universal, having no affinity with movements and no relation to them" AT, 8:359; CSM 1:304–5.

[18] CSM, 2:14; AT, 7:20.

[19] To Mersenne, May 27, 1638; AT, 2:138.

contrast the account with what we find in Locke in such a way that the significant difference between the nativist and empiricist positions I am most interested in will begin to emerge.

In the second chapter of the *Essay*'s book 4, "Of the Degrees of our knowledge," Locke says things sounding very similar what Descartes says in *Regulae*, even to employing the same metaphors. "In [intuitive knowledge], the Mind is at no pains of proving or examining, but perceives the Truth, as the Eye doth light, only by being directed toward it."

> This part of knowledge is irresistible, and like the bright sun-shine, forces it self immediately to be perceived, as soon as ever the Mind turns its view that way; and leaves no room for Hesitation, Doubt, or Examination, but the Mind is presently filled with the clear Light of it. 'Tis on this *Intuition*, that depends all the Certainty and Evidence of all our Knowledge, which Certainly every one finds to be so great, that he cannot imagine, and therefore not require a greater. (4.2.1; 531)

Comparing this to the *Regulae* one cannot help but feel Locke had Descartes in mind:[20] "*By 'intuition'* I do not mean the fluctuating testimony of the senses or the deceptive judgement of the imagination as it botches things together, but the conception of a clear and attentive mind, which is so easy and distinct that there can be no room for doubt about what we are understanding. Alternatively, and this comes to the same thing, intuition is the indubitable conception of a clear and attentive mind which proceeds solely from the light of reason."[21] In addition, Locke follows Descartes in construing deduction, or demonstration as he calls it, as a special application of intuition, the skillful application of which in this instance is called, by both Descartes and Locke, sagacity.[22]

But for Descartes, what is intuited is a structure built into what is known, the essence of the wax that is given to the inspection of the mind alone. "When I considered the matter more closely, I came to see that the exclusive concern of mathematics is with questions of order or measure and that it is irrelevant whether the measure in question involves numbers, shapes, stars, sounds, or any other object whatever. This made me realize that there must be a general science which explains all the points that can be raised concerning order and measure irrespective of the subject-matter and that this science should be termed *mathesis universalis*."[23] As I see it, even measurement is important to Descartes's mathesis universalis only as a vehicle of expressing and establishing deductive relations. However that may be, the essential point here is that

[20] Perhaps as conveyed by the Port-Royal *Logic*. See pt. 4, chap. 6.

[21] CSM, 1:14; AT, 10:368.

[22] "Now, *in every step Reason makes in demonstrative Knowledge, there is an intuitive Knowledge* of that Agreement or Disagreement, it seeks, with the next intermediate *Idea*, which it uses as a Proof: For if it were not so, that yet would need a Proof" (4.2.7; 533; also, 4.2.3; 532; AT, 10:400; HR, 1:28).

[23] CSM, 1:19; AT, 1:377–78.

these relations are part of the real world; in fact, they are all we may properly be said to know. As we have seen in chapter 4, this result, obviously contrary to the putative conclusion of *Meditations* 2, was argued in detail as the proper Cartesian view by Malebranche, for whom there is no clear and distinct idea of the self.

For Locke on the other hand, this structure is mind-contributed. This is clearest in the case of what he calls demonstration, which is essentially a heuristic: "Those intervening *Ideas*, which serve to show the Agreement of any two others, are called *Proofs*; and where the Agreement or Disagreement is by this means plainly and clearly perceived, it is called *Demonstration*, it being *shown* to the Understanding, and the Mind made to see that it is so" (4.2.3; 532). In addition, the heuristic is of our fabrication: "Because between two different *Ideas* we would examine, we cannot always find such *Mediums*, as *we can connect* one to another with an intuitive Knowledge, in all the parts of the Deduction; and wherever that fails, we come short of Knowledge and Demonstration" (4.3.4; 539). The sole function of demonstration is to facilitate intuitions of otherwise too complex propositions. For Descartes, even when by running over the steps of a deduction to the extent that the whole can be viewed in a single intuition, the structure is preserved. For Locke in such a case it would be eliminable as superfluous.

We have seen that the proper object of Cartesian knowledge is an essence available only to nonempirical intuition. For Locke what is known is the difference and agreement of ideas, an instance of predication modeled on class inclusion of the sort later to be elaborated by Berkeley. To say of gold that it is yellow is to say that yellowness is a member of the class yellowness, malleability, ductility, and the like. All predication is thus analytic and its truth value conventional; but the empiricist constraint on meaningful discourse is restored, as I shall try to show, by adding conditions that can be satisfied only by determining how the world is, namely, what exists and how it behaves, and this will always be a matter of experience.

The upshot is that Locke allows innate knowledge in neither the reminiscence nor reflection senses, and while the mind may for him harmlessly be said to have capacities for awareness, these are never dispositions for nonempirical intuitions of mind-independent real essences. The traditionally radical cleavage between nativist and empiricist views is thus intact.

§25 ESSENCES AND ABSTRACTION

My account of Locke's rejection of innate ideas in terms of an anti-Cartesian polemic obviously restricts me to certain interpretations of the major themes in what Locke takes to be the purpose of his book. At a minimum I must show how it is possible for Locke to do what he claims to do without appealing to ideal entities or rational intuition. His inquiry into the origin, certainty, and extent of human knowledge leads Locke into topics like abstraction and essences that have since vexed his readers. These are very debatable topics in the Locke literature. Here I can offer only the outline of an interpretation that fits with my anti-Cartesian story, and which I happen to believe is independently the best account, though I cannot here defend it as such.

A good beginning is what Locke says about the degrees of our knowledge. Intuitive knowledge is the highest degree and occurs when "the Mind perceives the Agreement or Disagreement of two Ideas immediately by themselves, without the intervention of any other." "Thus the Mind perceives That *White* is not *Black*, That a *Circle* is not a *Triangle*, That *Three* are more than *Two*, and equal to *One* and *Two*. Such Kind of Truths, the Mind perceives at the first sight of the *Ideas* together" (4.2.1; 530–31). But notice the second example, which seems to conflict with what Locke says about the Molyneux problem. Locke accepted Molyneux's own answer to the problem—a man born blind and then made to see would not immediately be able to distinguish by sight, though he was previously able to do so by touch, between a cube and a sphere. (2.9.8; 146) Does Locke contradict himself? The paragraph continues: "a Man cannot conceive himself capable of greater Certainty, than to know that any *Idea* in his Mind is such, as he perceives it to be; and that two *Ideas*, wherein he perceives a difference, are different, and not precisely the same" (4.2.1; 531). My hypothesis is that agreement and disagreement of ideas in which intuitive knowledge consists is a matter of their identity and difference or diversity. The first two examples are of difference, the last two, one more plausibly than the other, of identity.[24] When I intuitively know that a circle is not a triangle, I do not know that the one is a *circle* and the other a *triangle*. I know only that they are *different*. This view is not at all implausible and is best supported by the experimental accounts of the Molyneux problem. It is also, of course, consistent with what Locke says about the problem.

If the agreement and disagreement of ideas is a matter of identity and diversity, then we can see why Locke can so confidently claim about intuition that "what we once *know*, we are certain is so: and we may be secure, that there are no latent Proofs undiscovered, which may overturn our Knowledge, or bring it in doubt"(4.16.3; 659). For what could overturn my conviction that two things simultaneously perceived are numerically different? (Knowing that I suffer double vision might lead me to revise at least certain of my judgments, but perhaps not the judgment that what I saw was two; for in that case, it might be argued, I could not have known I had double vision.) On the other hand, that they are qualitatively different might be overturned; that this object I take to be a

---

[24] For a suggestion of how 'more than' might be read along these lines, see Ayers, "Locke's Doctrine of Abstraction", pp. 9–10. 'Equal to' I take to be obviously amenable to analysis in terms of identity. I realize that the first two examples are of qualitative difference; of this, more below. Meanwhile they are *sufficient* for numerical difference as well.

hexagon is really an octagon might have to be proved to me. Demonstration might discover latent proofs, but not intuition.

My hypothesis would mean that for Locke the truth value of all that we might know is analytic. The two extreme versions of this view were held by Leibniz and Hobbes. Truth value is analytic for Leibniz in the sense that in every proposition the *concept* of the subject term "contains" (or does not contain) that of the predicate term; for Hobbes in that the predicate *term* "comprehends" (or does not comprehend) the subject term. In the one case the appeal is to sufficient reason, in the other to convention; thus the realist and nominalist versions of the thesis. Does Locke, anticipating the one or adopting the other, hold either? Given what we know about his theory of ideas, we must expect him to opt for the nominalist version, if for either. Thus we would look for the Humpty-Dumpty theory of meaning and truth: All meaning and truth are invented arbitrarily by the inventors of speech.[25] I believe that Locke does opt for this theory, but that he does so in a way that improves upon Hobbes's excessively illiberal semiotic. For Hobbes, since "*true* and *false* are attributes of speech . . . and where speech is not, there is neither *truth* nor *falsehood*," those who are deaf and mute are incapable, at least of universal truth, and I should think, of any truth at all.[26] For Locke, truth and meaning are properties not just of language, but also, and primarily, of thought (4.5.2; 574).[27]

Our hypothesis is initially upset, however, when we turn to what Locke says about the kinds of agreement and disagreement between ideas, for he tells us that there are *four* kinds, of which identity and diversity compose but one. The others are relation, co-existence or necessary connection, and real existence. But there is less to this division than meets the eye. Real existence, the existence of things independent of the mind, is an obvious anomaly, for it is not a relation of agreement or disagreement since it is not a relation of any sort, and still less a relation between ideas. Thus Locke gives it very little attention in this context.[28] Unless another account can be given of real existence, Locke is in

[25] "Of Logic and Computation," bk. 1, *De corpore; Works*, 1:2.4, p. 36, 3.9, p. 36. See Watkins, *System of Ideas* (p. 104, n.29): "When I use a word," Humpty-Dumpty said in a rather scornful tone, "it means just what I choose it to mean—neither more nor less." "The question is," said Alice, "whether you *can* make words mean so many different things." "The question is," said Humpty-Dumpty, "which is to be Master—that's all" (Lewis Carroll, *Through the Looking Glass*, chap. 6). For a good account of this theory that ties it to Hobbes's moral and political theory, see Krook. Whether the Humpty-Dumpty theory as I shall employ it here accurately reflects Hobbes's position, or even that of Carroll's character, however, is a question I shall leave open. I am grateful to A. Schneider for clarification on this point.]

[26] *Leviathan* 1.4; *Works*, 3:23.

[27] The perception of identity and difference can be understood, as per Hobbes, only in causal terms—human psychology in response to the environment. The only ontology that we need, or can have, for Locke, is existence and nonexistence, that is, a certain distribution of solidity. The theory of knowledge is thus the naturalistic one we would expect from Locke, and the on-off character of identity and difference suggests an information-theoretic account such as Dretske's.

[28] Cf. 4.3.21; 4.2.14; 4.1.7.

trouble. For consider: (1) "if our Knowledge of our *Ideas* terminate in them, and reach no farther, where there is something farther intended, our most serious Thoughts will be of little more use, than the Reveries of a crazy Brain" (4.4.2; 563). (2) "We can have Knowledge no farther than we have *ideas*" (4.3.1; 538). It is hard to avoid the skeptical conclusion, especially given the consistent use of metaphor, unless real existence is known in some other way. As it happens, I think it is for Locke. We know the solid by a special kind of abstraction, of which more below.

What then of the other kinds of agreement and disagreement? Identity and co-existence are actually nothing but relations, says Locke, "yet they are such peculiar ways of Agreement, or Disagreement of our *Ideas*, that they deserve well to be considered as distinct Heads, and not under Relation in general" (4.1.7; 527). But the only example he gives of a relation different from these is equality, which one is hard put to distinguish from identity (4.1.7; 527). What is peculiar, then, about identity (and diversity)? As Locke sees it, unless there were relations other than these, the only positive knowledge we would have would be of individual ideas, "since all distinct *Ideas* must eternally be known not to be the same" (4.1.5; 526). Such immediately identical propositions as 'a fetiche is a fetiche' he describes as a trifling proposition (4.8.3; 609–10). "By [identity and diversity] the Mind clearly and infallibly perceives each *Idea* to agree with it self, and to be what it is; and all distinct *Ideas* to disagree, *i.e.* the one not to be the other" (4.1.4; 526). The only appeal in such instances of knowledge is to the law of noncontradiction. All this is clear; what is unclear is why noncontradiction is insufficient for Locke, unlike for Hume, whose only criterion for a relation between ideas is noncontradiction.[29] I shall pursue this question by raising another: How does identity differ from co-existence or necessary connection? I shall try to show that there is no real difference and that thus identity and its criterion of noncontradiction suffice for Locke's position.

"All Things, that exist [are] Particulars (3.3.1; 409). But Locke thinks that a world consisting solely of particulars would be too complex to be significantly experienced except, at least sometimes, in general terms: We cannot frame and retain ideas of all the particulars we encounter and have to deal with. Communication also requires general terms. Locke's argument for this is that only I would ever know my names for particulars. A better argument might be a version of the first consideration: The world is too complex to be profitably communicated about except in general terms. Finally, knowledge "enlarges it self by general Views" (3.3.4; 410). People are thus led "to consider Things, and discourse of them, as it were in bundles, for the easier and readier improvement and communication of their Knowledge, which would advance but slowly, were their Words and Thoughts confined only to Particulars" (3.3.20; 420).

---

[29] At least in the *Enquiry* (sec. 4).

Though words and ideas are like everything else particular in their existence, they can be general or universal in their meaning. This additional feature of some words and ideas is a product of the mind. "When therefore we quit Particulars, the Generals that rest, are only Creatures of our own making, their general Nature being nothing but the Capacity they are put into by the Understanding, of signifying or representing many particulars." They are "inventions" (3.3.11; 414).[30] The crucial part of this text is the claim that general signification is added by the mind. Contrast this view with the Cartesian view of ideas. Ideas in their existence, that is, formal existence, are particular, but their universal signification is a function of the ideas themselves. For the Cartesian of every denomination, the intelligible component in awareness is given to the mind, not invented by it. God may create the eternal verities, but we do not. This is a fundamental point of opposition between Locke among the giants and the Cartesians among the gods. No less fundamental is the opposition between their objects of knowledge. For Locke what is known is the individual that with other individuals happens to support a generalization; for Descartes it is a universal that happens to be instantiated by individuals.

Granting that the universal cannot exist apart from individuals, we can still ask with Boethius how the universal is conceived. This was the famous question of Boethius that dominated a thousand years of Western philosophy. Boethius's own answer was that the universal can be conceived separately, even though it cannot *exist* separately, as long as the separation is not *asserted*. Boethius's answer contained an ambiguity turning on 'asserted.' One meaning was picked up by the nominalists; thus Abelard: "And when I say that I consider only this one among the qualities a nature has, the 'only' refers to the attention alone, not to the mode of subsisting, otherwise the understanding would be empty. For the thing does not have only it, but is considered only as having it." On this account we do not conceive apart what cannot exist apart, but only partially consider, or attend to only part of, what does exist apart. The other meaning was picked up by the realists; thus Aquinas: "what is joined in reality the intellect can at times receive separately, when one of the elements is not included in the notion of the other." Such is the case with a thing's essence or nature, which has "a twofold act of existing, one in individual things, the other in the mind."[31] Thus we have two views of abstraction: partial consideration and extraction.

Which, if either, does Locke hold? The usual view is that he holds the extraction account[32] and that thus Locke is liable to the principal objection raised by Berkeley against his theory of abstract ideas. Very roughly, Berkeley argued on grounds accepted by Locke that what cannot exist cannot be con-

[30] See also 3.6.6.

[31] Quoted by Weinberg, *Abstraction*, pp. 6–11. This important work deserves more attention than it now receives.

[32] See Weinberg, for example.

ceived, and thus what cannot exist apart cannot be conceived apart; since an abstract idea is a conception apart of what cannot exist apart, we cannot have abstract ideas. To be sure, there are passages that seem to support this reading and thus the criticism of Locke. "The Mind makes the particular *Ideas*, received from particular Objects, to become general; which is done by considering them as they are in the Mind such Appearances, separate from all other Existences, and the circumstances of real Existence, as Time, Place, or any other concomitant *Ideas*. This is called ABSTRACTION" (2.11.9; 159). This same talk of abstraction by separation occurs at 2.12.1 in the fourth edition: "separating them from all other *Ideas* that accompany them in their real existence; this is called *Abstraction*." And at 3.3.6 Locke says that "*Ideas* become general, by separating from them the circumstances of Time, and Place, and any other *Ideas*, that may determine them to this or that particular Existence."

But even in these passages it is not clear that by separation Locke means extraction and not merely consideration as if separated. A crucial text in this regard is 2.13.11–13.[33] Locke here argues against the Cartesian identification of body and extension. While there is no body without extension, the ideas of each are *different* and *distinct*, "*Space and Solidity* being *as distinct Ideas* as Thinking and Extension, and as wholly separable in the Mind one from another." If this is not the extraction view, then what is it? A possible reading of this text is that space and solidity are not *wholly* separable because thinking and extension are not. Locke's sentence begins, "*if* it be a Reason to prove, that Spirit is different from Body, because Thinking includes not the *Idea* of Extension in it; the same Reason will be as valid, I suppose, to prove that *Space is not Body*, because it includes not the *Idea* of Solidity in it" (emphasis added). That is, Locke's argument here may be only ad hominem against the Cartesians. In addition, while being different and distinct is a symmetrical relation, it seems that for Locke being separable from is nonsymmetrical. To say that *x* is separable in the mind from *y* is to say that *x* is conceivable apart from *y*, or as Locke also puts it, that the idea of *x* does not include or require the idea of *y*; and if *x* is conceivable apart from *y*, *x* can exist apart from *y*, that is, *x* is really separable from *y*.[34] But to say that *x* is mentally and really separable from *y* is not to say

---

[33] A generally neglected but not totally ignored text. See Gibson, *Theory*, p. 69; Ayers, "Locke's Doctrine of Abstraction," p. 8, both of whom, as far as they go, get it right.

[34] This connection between mental and real separation seems implied at 2.13.13, where Locke argues that the parts of space, unlike those of body, cannot be separated, "neither really nor mentally." The argument might be that the parts of space are not really separable because they are not mentally separable: "to divide mentally . . . can only be done in things considered by the Mind, as capable of being separated; and by separation, of acquiring new distinct Superficies, which they then have not, but are capable of." Locke does not *say* that mental division can occur only if things are capable of distinct superficies; what he says is that it can occur only if they are *considered* as capable of distinct superficies. The ambiguity is due I think to Locke's syntax; in any case it is resolved by the journals (Aaron and Gibb, *Early Draft*, p. 78: 1676, f.292): "to divide mentally . . . is only to consider things as separate which are not and to ascribe to them superficies which they

that y is mentally and really distinct from x. "Motion can neither be, nor be conceived, without Space; and yet Motion is not Space, nor Space Motion; Space can exist without it, and they are very distinct *Ideas*." Space is separable from motion, but not motion from space. How then do we apprehend motion? We do so in the way we apprehend parts of space, it seems, *namely, by partial consideration*:

> 'Tis true, a Man may consider so much of such a *Space*, as is answerable or commensurate to a Foot, without considering the rest; which is indeed a partial Consideration, but not as much as mental Separation, or Division; since a Man can no more mentally divide, without considering two Superficies, separate one from the other, than he can actually divide, without making two Superficies disjoin'd one from the other: But a partial consideration is not separating. A Man may consider Light in the Sun, without its Heat; or Mobility in Body without its Extension, without thinking of their separation. One is only a partial Consideration, terminating in one alone; and the other is a Consideration of both, as existing separately. (2.13.13; 172–73)

This text also is not without its ambiguity. Consider the possible referents of the last sentence's first word. But I think what Locke is saying is that the apprehension of x that cannot exist apart from y is by a partial consideration of y; y is separable from x, but not x from y. *Separating* (i.e., *wholly* separating or dividing) as distinct from this, is a consideration of what can exist apart each from the other, for example, the parts of body—"a consideration *of both* as existing separately," each is separable from the other.

Now, what happens in what Locke calls abstraction is that whiteness, for example, which cannot exist apart from some thing that is white, is apprehended by partially considering some white thing. Whiteness is not extracted or wholly separated from that thing. And I think this is true of all the abstract ideas of which Locke speaks in the *Essay*, including the notorious one of a triangle that is neither scalenon, nor equicrural, and so on. By only partially considering a scalenon triangle I can ignore that it is scalenon and consider only that it has three angles. But this account is satisfactory *only* of the abstract ideas Locke mentions. What of those ideas, such as space, without which others such as motion cannot be conceived? These ideas too are abstract, but cannot be had by partial consideration. If my account above is correct, it is the idea of solidity that for Locke is ultimate in this sense, for without it space is inconceivable. It seems to me that Berkeley's famous argument against Lockean abstract ideas is against *this* kind of abstract idea, not the kind of abstract idea Locke mentions.

At this point it is worth drawing a contrast with the Cartesian position on abstraction. Descartes does not have much to say specifically about abstraction;

---

really then have not but are capable of." Whether real separability for Locke also entails mental separability is not clear—unless it is clear from what he says about transubstantiation and implies about the Trinity.

instead we must turn to the Port-Royal *Logic*, a Cartesian text whose influence extended to many non-Cartesians including, as we have seen, Locke. There is a passage in it on abstraction that by itself could have been taken over by Locke verbatim: "Although all things that exist are singular, yet by the abstractions we have just explained we can have several sorts of ideas, some representing only a single thing, such as the idea each of us has of himself, others representing equally several things, as when we conceive a triangle without considering anything in it but that it is a figure with three lines and three angles. The idea formed of it can serve for conceiving all other triangles" (pt. 1, chap. 6).[35] This is not an extraction view any more than Locke's is—Aristotelian Scholasticism is rejected—but it is no less different from Locke's view (and thus a three-cornered opposition appears here as elsewhere).

The *Logic* makes it clear, as the first order of business in chapter 1, (1) that ideas are not merely images; for there is no imaginable difference between our idea of a chiliagon and our idea of a myriagon. Without naming them it nonetheless clearly argues against Gassendi and Hobbes, (2) that not all ideas are derived from the senses, for there is no sense from which the idea of thought, for example, comes, and (3) that while the connection between words and ideas is arbitrary or conventional, ideas themselves—at least those that are clear and distinct—are not, for "very real effects" depend on our reasoning with respect to them. (Thus, we know that the round axle will turn freely in the round hole of a mill wheel but that the square one will engage a square hole and turn the wheel. "This effect follows infallibly.") All three views attacked by the *Logic* are held by Locke. The connection among them for the *Logic* is tolerably obvious. If ideas are merely images then as particulars they are fully derivable from experience; but if they are so derivable they can be extended beyond the particular only through convention. We do not arrive at the real essence of things, such as it is, by means of any abstraction on this view. At best we arrive at the nominal essence.

By contrast, the *Logic* regards nominal definitions as having to do only with words (pt. 1, chaps. 12–13). Proper abstraction yields real definitions grounded in the real essence or nature of the things themselves. The reasoning about the mill wheel, for example, is based not just in conventions about assemblages of words, but about the thing itself, about a natured particular. (Thus the suggestion in the quotation above that the idea of the self is abstract. The idea of the self is the idea of the thing that [essentially] thinks.) And by abstraction, which is to say by exposing logical relations, we get at the nature or essence of the thing, the idea of which is in this sense innate.

How then can the *Logic* claim that abstraction occurs when we consider things "by parts"(pt. 1, chap. 5)? Such partial consideration is of three kinds, corresponding exactly to the three kinds of distinction Descartes drew in the

---

[35] Arnauld, *Oeuvres*, 41:144.

Principles. The first is when the parts are integral and really distinct. On this kind of partial consideration depends our knowledge of physiology and arithmetic. Second is the consideration of a mode without attending to the substance of which it is the mode. Such abstraction is performed by geometers in considering lines and surfaces; that such lines and surfaces are not really distinct from substance does not, as the skeptics contend, upset the knowledge geometers claim, for geometers make no assertion to the contrary. Finally there is the abstraction of one attribute from another between which there is only a distinction of reason. Thus, starting from the idea of an individual triangle I can progressively consider it only as equilateral, as triangular, as a plane closed figure, and finally as merely extended and so arrive at the idea of extension. It is clear throughout the discussion that abstraction gives us knowledge of things grounded in their real essence in a strong, realist sense, and not just in nominal essences or ways of talking and thinking about things that are only causally constrained by those things in the weak, nominalist sense.

Locke's view of abstraction combines with his nominalism in his theory of species or essences, as he is prepared to call kinds. He says repeatedly that species or essences *are* abstract ideas with words annexed to them.[36] The upshot is that species or essences, as a kind of universal, are "the Workmanship of the Understanding, since it is the Understanding that abstracts and makes those general *Ideas*"(3.3.12; 415). These are the essences Locke calls *nominal*. Concerning *real* essences, which are not the workmanship of the understanding, Locke thinks there are two opinions: "The one is of those, who using the Word *Essence*, for they know not what, suppose a certain number of those Essences, according to which, all natural things are made, and wherein they do exactly everyone of them partake, and so become of this or that *Species*" (3.3.17; 418). This is the Scholastic view that essences are substantial forms. For Locke it comes to grief on two grounds: (1) There are productions such as monsters that do not fit essences thus conceived as "forms or moulds," and (2) such unknowable essences would be useless in our actual classifications.[37]

"The other, and more rational Opinion, is of those, who look on all natural Things to have a real, but unknown Constitution of their insensible Parts, from which flow these sensible Qualities, which serve us to distinguish them one from another, according as we have Occasion to rank them into sorts, under common Denominations" (3.3.17; 418).[38] For Locke as for Leibniz the nomi-

---

[36] See 4.4.17; 3.3.12; 3.3.15; 3.1.2; and *passim*.

[37] See also 3.6.5; 441: "to talk of specifik Differences in Nature, without reference to general *Ideas* and Names, is to talk unintelligibly." See also, 3.6.14–20. Whether in thus rejecting this first opinion Locke thus rejects every opinion that there are real natural kinds is a question that perhaps can be left open for the moment. Bolton has strongly argued that Locke admits real natural kinds that are not substantial forms ("Locke on Substance").

[38] Fred S. and Emily Michael cite Cranston, who claims that Locke read Gassendi's *Disquisitio metaphysica*, and then argue for it as a source for his position here ("Theory," pp. 384, 387–88).

nal essence picks out a thing as of a kind, and the real essence gives all its properties. (Thus for both Locke and Leibniz we know the real essence only of abstract things, which for Locke is to say only of those things in which nominal and real essences coincide.) From the passage above it is clear that even the Lockean real essence is relative to sorting, for we suppose the nominal essence to flow from the real. We suppose the real essences of things "without precisely knowing what they are: But that which annexes them still to the *Species*, is the nominal Essence, of which they are the supposed foundation and cause." It is important to note that only the nominal essence is "immutable" (3.6.6; 442). The real essence may be altered, and herein lies Locke's key difference from Leibniz: There is no a priori concept of an individual. As Locke puts it, the real essence of a thing is "the very being of any thing, whereby it is, what it is" (3.3.15; 417). The real essence is not a concept instantiated by the individual; the real essence just *is* the individual. (Thus, such concepts of individuals as there would be, even complete concepts, are purely a posteriori.) Another way of stating Locke's view is that there is no distinction, such as the Scholastics had drawn, between properties and accidents, between essential and nonessential qualities.[39] Since a thing just is its real essence, that is, its inner constitution or fine structure, every quality a thing has is in this sense essential to it at that time. But in another, more proper sense as Locke sees it, no property is essential to a thing since given any property it now has, the thing may be without that quality at another time; qualities are relative to *our* sorting of things.

> All such Patterns and Standards, being quite laid aside, particular Beings, considered barely in themselves, will be found to have all their Qualities equally *essential*; and every thing, in each Individual, will be *essential* to it, or, which is more true, nothing at all. For though it may be reasonable to ask, Whether obeying the Magnet, be *essential* to *Iron*? Yet, I think, it is very improper and insignificant to ask, Whether it be *essential* to the particular parcel of Matter I cut my Pen with, without considering it under the name *Iron*, or as being of a certain *Species*? And if, as has been said, our abstract *Ideas*, which have names annexed to them, are the Boundaries of *Species*, nothing can be *essential*, but what is contained in these *Ideas*. (3.6.5; 441–42).

Things for Locke are bare particulars in just the sense Aristotelian prime matter as pure potency is bare. Everything can become every other (kind of) thing.[40] This world of bare particulars, which are the kinds of things they are because of our classifications, is just the ontology that grounds the Humpty-Dumpty theory of meaning and truth.

---

[39] See Ayers, "Locke versus Aristotle," p. 261. Whether Leibniz is able, as he would like, to sustain any accidents in this sense is a matter of debate—one of the debates that evidence the obscurity of his role in the battle of the gods and giants.

[40] Ayers, "Locke versus Aristotle," pp. 269–70. This of course anticipates my answer to the question raised above whether there are for Locke real natural kinds.

An important difference between a nominal essence and what we take to be a real essence is that the latter is unbounded and thus anything we say about it will be uncertain. We just do not know whether what we take to be the real essence is in fact the real essence of anything at all. This difference is the basis for the anticipation of the causal theory of reference that Mackie saw in Locke.[41] Though Locke recommends against doing so, he thinks we can and often do use words to refer to the unknown real essence; thus the anticipation. But the contrary recommendation of the causal theory of reference depends not just on realism,[42] that there are essences, for Locke is a realist, but on dogmatism, that they can be and often enough are known, which Locke rejects. As he argues, any such claim as 'gold is fixed' will always "fail us in its particular application," for while we can define a nominal essence as including fixedness and call it 'gold,' we never know if there is anything to which it applies. In being intended to refer to the real essence of things, the word 'gold' "comes to have no signification at all, being put for somewhat, whereof we have no *Idea* at all, and we can signify nothing at all, when the Body is away" (3.10.19; 501). I take it from this that while we can thus refer to a real thing we call gold if it is present, we could not refer to gold in its absence. A theory of reference that allows us in this way to refer to a thing in ignorance of its essence only when it is present is perhaps a very faint anticipation indeed of the causal theory of reference. And whether even such restricted reference is possible given empiricism is a question that Berkeley was to pursue with a vengeance.

The radically nominalist interpretation of Locke has two main components, namely, that the world both of minds and of things consists of ontologically simple particulars, and that the Humpty-Dumpty theory of meaning and truth is the account of what we say and know about that world. A part of that interpretation as presented here is the hypothesis that the only relation between ideas is that of identity or diversity. The interpretation does not collapse without this hypothesis, for there may be other relations that are compatible with it and sufficient to the epistemological job. I do not know what those relations might be, but whatever they might be, the resulting picture of Locke would be less neat, both historically in terms of the Hobbist tradition and philosophically in terms of the minimal ontological commitments of nominalism. However that may be, I want now in light of what I have said about abstract ideas and essences to complete my case for this hypothesis and to do so in a way that shows how identity might be sufficient to the epistemological job.

Recall that Locke's complaint with identity or diversity as the only relation between ideas was that it precluded all but trifling knowledge as positive. Such would be our plight "if we could not perceive any [other] Relation between our *Ideas*, and find out the Agreement or Disagreement, they have with one an-

---

[41] Primarily at 3.10.17–20, but also at 2.31.6 and 3.9.12 . See "Locke's Anticipation," pp. 177–80; *Problems*, pp. 93–99.

[42] Mackie, "Locke's Anticipation." p. 177.

other, in several ways the Mind takes of comparing them" (4.1.5; 526). While it is comforting to the nominalist thesis to find Locke suggesting that relations between ideas are ways the mind compares them, he nonetheless says that their agreements and disagreements are *found out*. This is a threat, not just to my hypothesis, but to the whole nominalist interpretation. For if these relations are discovered, then perhaps meaning and truth are not at all conventional but are grounded in real natural kinds that are themselves grounded in things with universal components. A lot may come undone.

Nor is this an isolated passage. Elsewhere Locke distinguishes trifling propositions whose truth is purely verbal (e.g., purely identical propositions) from instructive ones, "which affirm something of another, which is a necessary consequence of its precise complex *Idea*, but not contained in it. As that *the external Angle of all Triangles is bigger than either of the opposite internal Angles*" (4.8.8; 614). In such instances of "instructive real Knowledge," notice what is affirmed is not only different from, it is not even *contained in* what it is affirmed of. What is affirmed is simply a *necessary* consequence of what it is affirmed of. Elsewhere, however, Locke uses the same metaphor of containment or inclusion to make an apparently different claim about instructive propositions. "In some of our *Ideas* there are certain Relations, . . . so visibly included in the Nature of the *Ideas* themselves, that we cannot conceive them separable from them, by any Power whatsoever. . . . Thus the *Idea* of a right-lined Triangle necessarily carries with it an equality of its Angles to two right ones" (4.3.29; 559). In the first case, *bigger than either of the opposite internal angles* is a necessary consequence of, but is not contained in, the idea of the external angle of a triangle. In the second case, *equality to two right angles* is included in the idea of the angles of a triangle. Given that these propositions are of the same sort, and that containment and inclusion are synonymous, does Locke just contradict himself with respect to the nature of this geometrical knowledge?

The short of this story, and the explication of identity and its epistemological role, is as follows: (1) An expression of identity *simpliciter* occurs when we use the same name twice. This is the trifling proposition whose form is 'A is A.' (2) A nominal essence is formed when we say that in addition A is B, C, D. The copula now indicates class membership. This is the relationship Locke calls 'being joined to.' "All our Affirmations . . . are only in concrete, which is the affirming, not one abstract *Idea* to be another, but one abstract *Idea* to be join'd to another." Thus we say not that humanity is rationality, but that they are joined (4.8.1; 474). If the class membership is explicit then containment or inclusion is affirmed, as between a triangle and equality of angles to two right angles. If the class membership is only implicit, then there is no containment or inclusion and the connection as between an external angle of a triangle and a size greater than either of the opposite internal angles is established by demonstration. This gives us all of what is known by the relation of agreement or disagreement

Locke specifically labels 'relation.' When he comes to discuss the *extent* of this kind of knowledge, distinguishing it from identity, co-existence, and real existence, he makes it clear that it is only a matter of demonstration. It seems to me that Locke can have nothing else in mind but demonstration when he says, "This, as it is the Largest Field of our Knowledge, so it is hard to determine how far it may extend: Because the Advances that are made in this part of Knowledge, depending on our Sagacity, in finding intermediate *Ideas* that may show the *Relations* and *Habitudes* of *Ideas*, whose co-existence is not considered" (4.3.18; 548). It is modeled on, but not limited to, mathematics. It also includes the ethical knowledge that Locke thought demonstrable (but never demonstrated). (3) Finally, if in addition we experience the members of the class thus demonstrating the possibility of their being conjoined in an object, we have the relation of agreement he calls co-existence (4.4.12). This is "the greatest and most material part of our Knowledge concerning Substances," but withal it is "very narrow and scarce any at all" (4.3.9–10; 544), since what little way we can go toward necessary connections among the members is by means of the corpuscularian hypothesis (4.3.16). At best, then, we have hypothetically necessary connections.

What I have been calling the fundamental relation of identity, then, emerges as class membership. It takes four forms according to the four kinds of agreement and disagreement between ideas. (1) If the class has only one member we have what Locke calls identity. This is a trifling proposition connecting the same name to itself. (2) If the class has more than one member, then we have a nominal essence proper; either the membership is explicit, or can be made so through demonstration. This is what Locke calls relation. (3) If the class has more than one member and can be shown both to be possible and necessarily connected, we have what Locke calls co-existence or necessary connection. (4) Finally, real existence, an anomalous category from the outset, might be regarded a single-member class, so that like identity it involves only a single name, but like co-existence it is tied to existence, namely, to a particular.

But even if class membership can play the role I have assigned it here, there remains the question of how it is established. Specifically, we want to know whether it is an invention grounded in mere convention as the Humpty-Dumpty theory would have it, or whether it is grounded *in rerum natura* and thus discovered as Locke's passage about nontrifling propositions would have it. In short, we want to know whether Locke, despite his insistence that whatever exists is particular, nonetheless admits universals. The question is still open because realists from Aristotle to the present have also insisted on this by requiring all universals to be exemplified. A way then of distinguishing between these moderate realists and nominalists is by asking whether what exists must be complex, consisting of something in addition to a single universal—another universal with which it is bundled, for example, or more typically, a particular. That what exists should be simple, then, will be sufficient for nominalism.[43]

It seems clear that at least at certain points Locke makes co-existence fully dependent on nominal definitions and thus logically conventional: "When we pronounce concerning *Gold*, that it is fixed, our Knowledge of this Truth amounts to no more but this, that fixedness . . . is an *Idea*, that always accompanies, and is join'd with . . . Yellowness [etc.] which make our complex *Idea*, signified by the word *Gold*" (4.1.6; 527). On the other hand, Locke also says that "Nature in the Production of Things, makes several of them alike . . . the Understanding, taking occasion from the similitude it observes amongst them, to make abstract general *Ideas*, and set them up in the mind, with Names annexed to them, as Patterns" (3.3.13; 415) to which things agree and thus are classified. The point of the passage in full context is that despite similarities and our observation of them, kinds are the "workmanship" of the understanding. But how can Locke avoid the view that the abstract ideas set up by the mind replicate, or might replicate, what is found in nature? [44]

Nominal essences are of course "made by Man with some [but only some] liberty" (3.6.27; 454). The constraints on this liberty, however, come not from real natural kinds, but from the way things just happen to behave. The difference between the mechanistic matter Locke admits and the Aristotelian substances he rejects is that explanation by appeal to the substantial forms of the latter is *occult*, whereas explanation by appeal to the former involves mechanical properties that are "totally actual and directly perspicuous to the mind."[45] This *perspicuity* is not a matter of universals, or even a common universal nature as Descartes would have it, but of *perspicuous resemblance*.[46] We pick out this perspicuity for practical purposes in dealing with the world, especially in communicating about it, and the resemblances themselves are nothing more than causal connections. To say that two things are alike is to say that they produce the same idea and why they should do so is just the way the world is—a matter, as Locke puts it, of divine pleasure. Ultimately there is no other reason why it should be the case, as Locke thinks it is (3.6.29), that certain ideas must be emphasized in the construction of certain essences (shape in inanimate things, colour in animate). These are the constraints on our freedom to abstract, or to form nominal essences; they distinguish those whose heads are filled with chimeras and who speak a babel from those who have real knowledge of the

---

[43] Though not necessary: What exists could yet be a bundle of nonuniversal qualities, as it is for the nominalist Berkeley.

[44] Nor is the above an isolated passage. Thus: "*Nature makes many particular Things which do agree* one with another, in many sensible Qualities, and probably too, in their internal frame and Constitution" (3.6.36; 462). And in correspondence with Molyneux, January 20, 1693, the realist suggestion is even stronger: "There are real constitutions in things, from whence those simple ideas flow which we observ'd combined in them. And this I farther say: that there are real distinctions and differences in those real constitutions one from another; whereby they are distinguished one from another, whether we think of them or name them or no" (*Correspondence*, 4:626).

[45] Ayers, "Locke versus Aristotle," p. 254.

[46] In Ayers's felicitous expression, (Ibid., p. 255).

world (3.6.28). It is not surprising, then, given the centrality of communication among the practical considerations in how we carve up the world, that language itself should function as a constraint on where to place the joints. Thus, Locke gives an ordinary-language argument against the Cartesian identification of body and extension (3.6.21): We just cannot *say*, for example, that one extension by impulse moves another. On the other hand, when he comes to criticize the wrangling of Scholastics concerning useless maxims, Locke uses this example to emphasize the constraint of experience. There is nothing preventing us from calling extension body and then proving the "vacuum" by appealing to the maxim that the same thing cannot be and not be. "Yet neither of these Principles will serve to prove to us, that any, or what Bodies do exist: For that we are left to our Senses, to discover to us as far as they can" (4.7.14; 605).

Very different from this is the Cartesian view. According to the Port-Royal *Logic* (pt. 4, chap.6) there is a single principle on which the certainty and evidence of our knowledge of natural things depend and without which an absurd Pyrrhonism is established: "All that is contained in the clear and distinct idea of a thing can be truly affirmed of that thing."[47] To be sure, "we can judge of things only by the ideas we have of them." But as we have seen, the idea of a thing is *the thing itself* as it exists, intelligibly, in the mind. "If the judgments we form by considering these ideas did not concern the things in themselves, but only our thoughts, . . . it is clear that we would have no knowledge of things, but only of our thoughts, and consequently that, of what we believe ourselves to know most certainly of things, we would know nothing; but we would know only that we think them to be of a certain sort, which would destroy all the sciences."[48] The containment of one idea in another is, according to the *Logic*, not conventional, but real inclusion and can thus be asserted categorically and not just hypothetically of things.

§26 THE POLEMIC WITH STILLINGFLEET

Locke's best-known polemic (1696–98), and undoubtedly the one to which he devoted his greatest effort, was with Edward Stillingfleet, bishop of Gloucester. My overall thesis about Locke would be given a great boost if it could be shown that, in attacking Locke, Stillingfleet was defending if not Cartesianism then at least positions in specifically Cartesian terms.[49] While there are some suggestions in his work that Stillingfleet was influenced by the Cartesians, alas, there seems to me little solid evidence to support this reading. Nonetheless, there are,

---

[47] Arnauld, *Oeuvres*, 41:378.

[48] Ibid., pp. 378–79.

[49] Stewart first drew attention to Stillingfleet in these terms in a paper at the Rutgers Locke Conference, June 1983. Stewart showed the importance of Stillingfleet's works, generally neglected, other than those relating to the Locke polemic directly.

as we shall see, a number of good reasons here to examine the issue, the chief one being that Stillingfleet draws Locke out as the giant in the terms in which he has been portrayed here.

Origines sacrae (1662) was Stillingfleet's earliest important work; it was essentially an apologetic tract on a question that was to dominate his thoughts thirty years later, namely, the reasonableness of Christianity. Its aim was to show the consistency of Christianity with history, reason, and philosophy[50]. There are several counts on which Cartesian chords are struck, but each of them seems offset by further notes. (1) Stillingfleet throughout uses the language of clear and distinct ideas; but there is no indication that he is using these terms in the technical Cartesian sense and some indication that he is not, for there are indications, for example, that he rejects the Cartesian ontology on which the notion of distinctness, at least, is based. (2) In good Cartesian fashion he insists that ideas are not just images, but the account he gives of *entia rationis*, for example, seems to be the Scholastic extractionist account of abstraction. This would seem to offset the significance of the strong anti-Epicurean and anti-empiricist bias of the work generally. (3) Perhaps the strongest evidence is that he draws the Cartesian distinction between an idea as a mode of thought and as an objective reality, attributing a truth value only to the latter. He says too that ideas are "nothing else but the things themselves as they are objectively represented to the understanding."[51] But of course this need be no more than a commitment to the Aristotelian account. (4) Stillingfleet subscribes to the ontological argument and does so in specifically Cartesian terms.[52] But Stillingfleet also subscribes to arguments for the existence of God either ignored by Descartes or inconsistent with Cartesian principles. Thus we find the argument *consensus gentium*, a cosmological argument (from the existence of immaterial beings *versus* the Cartesian causal argument from the existence of the self and its ideas), and, treated at great length, the argument from design. (5) While Stillingfleet saw much of value in the New Science, he was far from being a universal mechanist; perhaps some of the appearances might be produced by mere matter and motion, but certainly not all. Natural kinds in particular cannot be anything less than the effect of a "Supreme Governor."[53] The Cartesian mechanism requires God as a creator and mover of matter; whether even that version of mechanism be true is an issue he forswears, claiming interest only in how it might lead to atheism. He concludes the work by saying that he is inclined to Gassendi's view about the particular manner used by God as the

---

[50] Preface to *Works*, 2a.

[51] Ibid., p. 232.

[52] "The clear and distinct perception of the Mind is the greatest evidence we can have of the truth of anything." "That which we do clearly and distinctly perceive to belong to the nature and essence of a thing [read: idea] may be with truth affirmed of the thing." "Necessary existence doth immutably belong to the nature of God" (ibid., p. 249).

[53] Ibid., p. 253.

efficient cause in bringing being to the world: majus est mundus opus, quam ut assequi mens humana illius nolitionem possit.[54]

Various other, decidedly non-Cartesian elements emerged in the course of Stillingfleet's work. For example, his conception of proof evidenced a non-Cartesian conception of both essences and evidence: "When we demand the proof of a thing, our eye first must be to the nature of the thing which we desire may be proved; for things equally true, are not capable of equal evidence, nor have like manners of probation."[55] Despite his affectation of clear and distinct ideas, they do not carry the all-or-nothing character of the Cartesian notions. In addition he in no uncertain terms claims that certainty is not invariably tied to indubitability or the impossibility of being deceived. Against Sergeant's contention that certainty required infallibility, Stillingfleet argued that where this was required historically, as by the Stoics, skepticism was the result, as with the Academic and Pyrrhonian skeptics.[56] Finally, and I think most important, nowhere do we find in Stillingfleet anything like a commitment to the Cartesian ontology of thought and extension.[57]

The upshot is that when Stillingfleet comes finally at the end of his life to criticize Locke, it is, if anything, Stillingfleet who regards Locke as the Cartesian. There was a good reason for this. Toland had begun his *Christianity Not Mysterious* with a provocative paraphrase of Locke on the sources of ideas and the definition of knowledge in terms of the agreement and disagreement of ideas (pp.9–11), and then used the Lockean notions of real and nominal essences in later arguments (pp. 75–89). In between, however, Toland may have led Stillingfleet's interpretation of Locke straight up the Cartesian daisy path. Not only does he use the language of clear and distinct ideas, but he indicates the technical usage. Consider his saying that God has "endu'd us with the Power *of suspending our Judgments about whatever is uncertain, and of never assenting but to clear Perceptions.* [He has privileged us] by placing our Liberty only in what is indifferent, or dubious and obscure; [and] he provides on the other hand, that we should discern and embrace the Truth, by taking it out of our Power to dissent from an Evident Proposition" (p. 20).[58]

Beyond this circumstantial reason for Stillingfleet's view of Locke as joining the Cartesians in the new way of ideas, there was the engine of Stillingfleet's attack on anyone so viewed, that the new way of ideas represented a threat to religion. By the end of his career, Stillingfleet's attitude toward Cartesianism

[54] Stillingfleet showed a very un-Cartesian partiality to Gassendi throughout. It should be noted too that both Stillingfleet's preference for the empiricist version of the New Science and his view of its limitations persisted until the end of his life. See *Origines sacrae* 2; *Works*, 2b:100.

[55] Ibid., p. 241.

[56] Popkin, "Stillingfleet," p. 307.

[57] Although in his most obviously anti-Cartesian work he expresses no objection to this ontology.

[58] He also says that certain ideas of sensible bodies are *occasioned* in us by bodies (p. 17).

was of strong distrust since he felt it contained a strong tendency to atheism. When he died in 1699 Stillingfleet left unfinished what may have been intended as a second edition of the *Origines sacrae*, on which he had been working at the time of his polemic with Locke. In it he sets out at length his objections to Cartesianism. However Descartes's intentions may have been to the contrary, according to Stillingfleet, his philosophy has a tendency toward atheism on two counts: (1) It weakens accepted proofs for the existence of God and Providence, and (2) it attributes too much to the mechanical powers of matter and motion.

Stillingfleet agrees with Gassendi's *Objections* to the *Meditations* that when speaking of God an exception must be made to the exclusion of final causes. Descartes had replied that what had been attributed to final causation must be referred to efficient causation and that God's ends are unsearchable. But Stillingfleet agrees too with Gassendi's rebuttals of these replies: (1) Eliminating final causes reduces the significance of God's efficient causation; (2) God's ends are not entirely unsearchable as is evident from the fitness of human physiology.[59] Mechanism without design "takes away all *Life* and *Spirit and Religion*"[60] In addition, howevermuch Stillingfleet had previously accepted the esse formale-esse objectiva distinction, he now finds the causal argument for the existence of God in which it figures inconclusive. Here Stillingfleet inclines toward the objection of Huet,[61] despite the reply[62] of Régis, that finite ideas cannot prove the existence of an infinite object. Similarly with respect to the ontological argument, there is a standoff between Gassendi and Huet on the one side and Régis and the Cartesians on the other, which shows the mistake in abandoning the argument from design.[63] The reason that Stillingfleet gives for Descartes's exclusion of final causes from philosophy is interesting: "That the immortality of the soul hath been excluded too. For, altho' according to the Doctrine of *Des Cartes* its distinction from the Body be asserted and proved, yet its immortality is pass'd over; under this pretense, *that* God *may fix its duration by His Will*; and therefore unless we know the Will of God in it, we can determine nothing in *Philosophy* about it" (p.88). A final objection to Descartes's rejection of final causes is that it opened the way to Spinoza. This "Person too well known in the World" used Descartes's ontological argument to prove the world to be God, an argument supported by Descartes's own idea of matter as infinite and necessary (p. 93).

As to the dangers of mechanism, Stillingfleet distinguishes between those who proceed "in the way of experiment" and those who produce cosmologies. With the former, as represented by Boyle, he can agree, with two reservations:

[59] *Works*, 2b:80–81.
[60] Ibid., p. 82.
[61] *Censura*, chap. 4, par. 3.
[62] *Réponse*, p. 192.
[63] *Works*, 2b:85–86.

(1) Not all qualities in bodies relate to our senses;[64] (2) not all qualities of bodies can be accounted for by mechanical principles. In a real departure from Boyle, Stillingfleet argues following Sydenham that the composition, diseases, and nerves of animal bodies cannot be accounted for by mechanism (pp. 99–100). But the main objection is to mechanical cosmologies, as represented by Descartes, which tend toward atheism in two respects: (1) They make matter independent of God; (2) they ignore particular Providence. Descartes's "fundamental mistake" in this regard is his notion of matter as extension, which (1) confuses mathematical and physical bodies (Stillingfleet here follows Huet, Petit, and Duhamel)[65]; (2) is inconsistent with his own system, which requires that matter actually be divided; (3) makes matter uncreated because space is; (4) results, as Duhamel pointed out, from Descartes's preoccupation with geometry; (5) makes one inseparable property of body the whole essence of it.[66]

There are some matters to which Stillingfleet does not object in Descartes: (1) "That we cannot take falsehood for truth, if we only give assent to such things as we clearly perceive"; (2) "That the things which fall under our perception are either things and their Properties, or eternal Truths. Of things, the most general are Substance, Duration, Order, Number and such like, which extend to all kinds of things"; (3) "All [things] may be comprehended under these two: Of Intellectual or Thinking Substances; or of Material, i.e. of Bodily and Extended Substances"; (4) "By ['Substance'] we can understand nothing but a thing which so exists, as to need nothing else to support it. There is but one Substance in the World which needs no support, and that is God. All created Substances need his support, and the Notion of them is, that they are things which only stand in need of God's concourse to support them"; (5) "Nothing can be attributed to Nothing. From whence we conclude from any Real Attribute, that there must be a thing or Substance to which it belongs" (p. 103).

But from all this it does not follow—and this is Stillingfleet's main point— "that there must be a Corporeal Substance in Imaginary Space, because there is an Extension there" (p. 103). This imaginary space is only the possibility, or the capacity for, the existence of bodies and has no real extension. Stillingfleet proceeds to argue at some length that the Cartesians' view either is inconsistent with their substance ontology or, more likely, makes matter necessary and independent of God, since it makes it impossible for God to annihilate only a part of matter. In this he sympathetically repeats the arguments of Duhamel, Huet, Bernier, and More, and rejects the replies of Descartes, Régis, and Rohault.

As for the second tendency toward atheism of Descartes's system, that it

---

[64] It is not clear this is a real difference from Boyle. All Stillingfleet argues for is an occurrent structural basis for the dispositions of things to produce sense impressions.]

[65] Duhamel, *De consensu* 1.1, chap. 8, n.9; Petit of Paris, *Dissertationes*,, p. 28; Huet, *Censura*, chap. 8, n.9.

[66] *Works*, 2b:102–3.

ignores particular Providence, Stillingfleet sees the main question as "whether Matter being [by God] put into motion, can produce the *Phenomena* of the World, without any further interposition of Providence, than only to preserve the motion of matter?" (p. 108). Specifically, he wants to know about (1) the nature and laws of motion, and (2) the account they give of the phenomena. He rejects the Cartesian view of motion as a mode (since it would thus be incommunicable) and as a constant quantity (because of resistance); he rejects the Cartesian statement of inertia (and maybe every statement of it) and the rules for collision (primarily on Boyle's authority). He thinks that Descartes's account of the elements is gratuitous, neglects design, is contrary to Scripture, and is impossible on its own grounds (because it cannot account for the real division it requires). Nor is Descartes's derivation of the phenomena any more successful. If for no other reason—and there are other reasons (p. 115) Descartes's whole account is upset if there is a "Principle of Gravitation" in things, which in fact has been fully demonstrated by a "very Learned and Judicious Mathematician of our own" (p. 116).[67]

The upshot seems clear that in the Locke–Stillingfleet exchange we do not have an instance of the battle of the gods and giants, but a reminder that this was not the only contest at the time. The relation among Stillingfleet, Locke, and the Cartesians was in fact a three-cornered contest in which Stillingfleet's only stake was a defense of Anglican Christianity as he understood it. He himself, I venture to claim, had no consistent philosophy, or at least none that was consistently interesting. Thus, while he clearly rejects both nominalism and Platonic realism, the moderate realism in favor of which he may do so is far from clear.[68] No clearer is his alternative to the empiricist theory of ideas; whether he held a theory of innate ideas and, if so, of what kind is a matter of dispute.[69] Perhaps his philosophy is best described as a mixture of Commonsense, Aristotelianism, and Stoicism, supplemented with bits from Descartes, the Gassendists (Gassendi himself, Bernier), and skeptics (Huet, Duhamel).[70]

But Stillingfleet was no moss-backed reactionary with his finger in the dike against the onrush of intellectual history;[71] rather, he accepted the New Science, for example, even if with limitations, and thought that it could be more than accommodated by Scripture. Stillingfleet was no fool; for he foresaw the direction that onrush might take and, as its author did not, the use to which Locke's philosophy might be put in the service of deism, free-thinking, Soci-

[67] A principle that is acceptable so long as gravity is "not inherent and essential to matter, but by a force given and directed by Divine Power and Wisdom."

[68] *Works*, 3:580.

[69] See Yolton, *John Locke*, pp. 36–37; and Carroll, *Stillingfleet*, pp. 91–92. Carroll points out that Locke charged Stillingfleet with holding a theory of ideas that was no clearer than his own. "Locke could have pushed his claim further, however, but either out of ignorance, courtesy or indifference he did not" (Yolton, *John Locke*, p. 97).

[70] Popkin, "Stillingfleet."

[71] Ibid.

nianism, and much else that in fact came to fruition in the Enlightenment. For Stillingfleet this had already been demonstrated by Toland's use of Locke, despite Locke's undoubtedly sincere efforts to disassociate himself from To-land[72] and no less sincere protestations of faith.[73] The result of Locke's new way of ideas was an epistemology that was insufficient to account for our knowledge of immortality, the existence of God, and the Trinity; skepticism on these matters could be the only result from skepticism about substances, na-tures, and persons. Faith was relinquished as soon as certainty was restricted to ideas derived solely from experience. All of this Stillingfleet thought had already been seen in Toland, and he was right. In one of his arguments based on Lockean representationalism,[74] for example, Toland argued that the mysteries of religion that involve contradictions are literally inconceivable. We have no ideas of them, and hence they cannot be a part of religion, which at least in this sense is not mysterious or above reason (p. 27). In a reversal of what would be Stillingfleet's argument, Toland held that belief in contradictions would result in skepticism: "For the Proof of the Divinity of Scripture depending upon Reason, if the clear light of the one might be in any way contradicted, how shall we be convinc'd of the Infallibility of the other" (p. 31). There is no room here for Locke's provision for faith in what might be uncertain. "To believe the Divinity of *Scripture*, or the sense of any Passage thereof, without rational Proofs, and an evident Consistency, is a blameable Credulity, and a temerarious Opinion, ordinarily grounded upon an ignorant and willful Disposition; but more generally maintain'd out of a gainful Prospect" (p. 36). Worse than skepticism, faith in such things as transubstantiation and the Trinity leads to self-interested enthusiasm (p. 173). Another characterization of faith by Toland deserves a final notice because it recalls the principal objection traditionally raised against Epicureanism and the whole skeptical, anti-Platonic tradition: "If we might doubt of anything that is clear, or be deceiv'd by distinct conceptions, there could be nothing certain: Neither Conscience, nor God himself should be regarded: No society or Government could subsist" (p. 67).

Locke's polemic with Stillingfleet is, of course, hardly unknown to people who have worked on Locke and the philosophy of the period generally. But it has not drawn the attention it seems to me to merit. There are some obvious reasons for this. For one thing it is very long (as indeed is the *Essay* itself); it is also repetitive. Here I shall remedy this neglect by looking at least some themes that will tie together some major issues of these last two chapters.

It is difficult in one sense to distinguish Locke and Stillingfleet on substance, since they each use much the same language in stating and defending their

---

[72] Letter; *Works*, 4:43 and *passim*.

[73] Ibid., p. 96 and *passim*.

[74] "We have only Ideas in us, and not the Things themselves" (*Christianity*, p. 16).

views.[75] Locke himself claimed to be at a loss to make out the distinction.[76] Whether this is a ploy on Locke's part, or as I shall suggest is more likely, whether Locke from his point of view really did not understand an important part of Stillingfleet's position, there is an important distinction, and it is one that is clearly indicated by Stillingfleet: Our knowledge of substance for him must have a nonempirical source. Sense and reflection, the experience that Locke takes to be the only source of ideas, are insufficient for a proper idea of substance, which in fact is had from *reason*. I shall now try to show that this thread leads to enormous and systematic differences.

Substance as a substrate, the notion to which both Locke and Stillingfleet appeal, traditionally[77] involves two related notions. One is the notion of an individuator; what makes two things numerically different, as are the identical twins Damon and Pythias, is a difference in substance. The individual substance that is Damon is not the individual substance that is Pythias. The other notion is of a support for qualities. Many who reject Plato's view that there may be qualities that are not the qualities of anything require that all qualities be qualities of substances. The connection between the two notions is that qualities are thus supported by being individuated. To put it another way, substance serves to tie or bundle qualities together. And it does so in three ways: (1) over time, (2) into kinds, and, most basically, (3) at a time. Locke claims not to understand how Stillingfleet conceives any of these three, but does, I believe, have a way of making sense of them in his own terms.

Bundling qualities as qualities of the same thing over time. Stillingfleet was very concerned with the doctrine of the resurrection of the body and how on Locke's view it might be said that the *same* body is resurrected. At issue between Locke and Stillingfleet was the implication of a biblical text that was supposed to illustrate the connection between the body that goes to the grave and the one that is resurrected. "They sow bare grain of wheat, or of some other grain, but God giveth it a body, as it hath pleaseth him, and to every seed his own body" (1 Cor. 15:37–38). Stillingfleet read this to indicate a doctrine of substance in the sense that "the same body" that is the grain sown is the plant of wheat. To Locke this was incomprehensible: "This I confess I do not understand; because I do not understand how one individual grain can be the same

[75] As Yolton points out, "Stillingfleet's description of our idea of substance is, of course, identical with Locke's except that he prefers to call it a necessary or rational idea 'because it is a Repugnance to our first conception of Things that Modes or Accidents should subsist by themselves' (*John Locke*, pp. 133–34). But even this nominal difference seems removed by Locke at one point: "I grant it to be a good consequence that to those who find this repugnance the idea of a support is very necessary; or, if you please to call it so, very rational" (*Second Reply*; *Works*, 4:452–53.

[76] *Letter*; *Works* 4:11, and *passim*.]

[77] I use the term consciously. The tradition begins with Aristotle's notion of substance in the primary sense (*Categories* 2a11).

with twenty, fifty, or an hundred individual grains, for such sometimes is the increase." The relevant sense of sameness or identity is the identity of a particle existing at a given space and time; as I have tried to argue, it is the existence of solidity at that space and time that metaphysically excludes the intrusion of other things on it. But it also excludes other things being taken from it. From Lockean stones comes neither blood nor even other stones. In these terms the growth Stillingfleet is talking about is really creation ex nihilo. What Locke understands from the Pauline text, even if he thinks that no mechanical account of the process can be discovered, is that "in the production of wheat and other grain from seed, God continue[s] every species distinct; so that from grains of wheat sown, root, stalk, blade, ear, and grains, of wheat [are] produced and not those of barley."[78] This leads us to the second way substance bundles qualities.

Bundling qualities, and thus things that have them, into kinds. Stillingfleet claimed that "the general Idea is not made from the simple *Ideas* by the mere Act of the mind abstracting from Circumstances, but from *Reason* and Consideration of the true Nature of things."[79] That individuals belong to the same kind depends, not on a nominal essence we arbitrarily put together, but on a real, common essence that is unchangeable. Another way to put this is that Aristotelian primary substances are also individually instances of Aristotelian secondary instances; Dobbin is an individual, but also an individual horse. For Stillingfleet the same rational necessity that bundles qualities as qualities of things both at a time and over time bundles things into kinds. It is not clear whether Stillingfleet has an extractionist view, a partial consideration view, or some other view on exactly how we apprehend these essences; but it seems clear that we do so in some nonempirical fashion.

Locke responded to this in two ways. Stillingfleet's notion of a real essence he found inconceivable. "This, my lord, as I understand it, is to prove that the abstract general essence of any sort of things, or things of the same denomination, v.g. of man or marigold, hath a real being out of the understanding; which I confess, my Lord, I am not able to conceive."[80] This may mean a number of things. (1) Things have a real essence but it is unknown to us. This *is* Locke's view, but I think his claim here is stronger, for it suggests the reason why Stillingfleet was mistaken in his view that we apprehend real essences; he has a mistaken view of what real essences are. (2) That things should have a real essence of the sort described by Stillingfleet is inconceivable. This too is Locke's view. Things are not classifiable into kinds, as Stillingfleet thinks, because of real essences in which they are grounded. (3) That an abstract general essence should exist outside the mind is inconceivable because abstract general essences are ideas, which exist only within the mind. Thus Stillingfleet

---

[78] *Second Reply; Works* 4:317.
[79] *Vindication*, chap. 10; *Works*, 4:511.
[80] *Letter; Works*, 4:83.

with respect to substance confuses the world with our way of looking at it; he confuses things with ideas.[81]

Locke's second way of responding is of a piece with the first way and in the texts not at all clearly distinguished from it. Stillingfleet had argued that while we do not know what the real essences of things are, rational necessity requires us to recognize that there are such things. Locke responds by carefully reiterating the distinction on which Stillingfleet's position rests. We can know *that* there are real essences even if they are not the sort of thing Stillingfleet takes them to be; but we cannot know *what* they are.[82] Thus, save the important difference as to the nature of real essences, there is no difference that Locke sees between himself and his critic. The two strands of Locke's response then come to the following: They disagree about the kind of thing kinds are (i.e., about the nature of essences), but agree that kinds of things (at least the real essences of things) cannot be known.

The most basic sense in which substance bundles qualities is its *bundling at a time*. On it depend the other two senses. Only if sense can be made of how qualities are qualities of a substance at a time can appeal be made to substance in explaining how qualities are qualities of a thing over time or how things are bundled by their qualities into kinds. The connection here is of inherence; qualities inhere in a substance, which thus supports them. Locke in the *Essay* had already found this sense of substance no more comprehensible than the previous two. Those who say that it is substance that supports accidents give no better account than the Indian philosopher could have given had he said that the earth was supported, not by an elephant and the elephant by a tortoise, but by substance (2.13.19). "Were the Latin words *Inhaerentia* and *Substantia*, put into the plain English ones that answer them, and were called *Sticking on*, and *Under-propping*, they would better discover to us the very great clearness there is in the Doctrine of *Substance and Accidents*, and shew of what use they are in deciding of Questions in Philosophy" (2.13.20; 175).

Stillingfleet objected that such a way of carrying on ridiculed the notion of substance. But Locke rejects this characterization of what he was doing. *Even if* substance did support accidents, philosophers have no clearer idea of substance than the Indian had of what supported his tortoise. Then he says, "Had your pen, which quoted so much of [2.13.19, i.e., the above text] but set down the remaining line and a half of the paragraph, you would by these words which follow there, 'so that of substance we have no idea of what it is, but only a confused obscure one of what it does;' have put it past doubt what I meant."[83] I take this to be an indication that for Locke substances do not really support

---

[81] Thus Locke at the end of the controversy: "Your lordship here, I know not upon what ground, nor with what intention, confounds the idea of substance and substance itself" (*Second Reply*; *Works*, 4:451.

[82] *Letter*; *Works*, 4:26–27.

[83] *Second Reply*; *Works*, 4:448.

qualities (and qualities do not really inhere in them). But the idea of substance (compositional genitive) nonetheless does a job. It is a category in terms of which we organize experience. This is the key, finally, to the systematic differences between Locke and Stillingfleet in everything they say about substance. On the one hand Locke is talking about ideas and the psychological certainty/necessity involved in how we use them in viewing the world. It is a fact, but metaphysically a bare fact only, that we perceive qualities bundled into things and that we perceive those things as of a kind and continuing as the same despite changes in qualities. In response to Stillingfleet's construal of substance as a requirement of *reason*, Locke initially did not see what was required for reasoning beyond the faculty itself.[84] And while he sees that Stillingfleet distinguishes between reason and ideas, he claims not to understand what the distinction is; reason is employed about ideas, making simple ones into complex (pp. 70–71). To Stillingfleet's insistence that general ideas are made from reason and the consideration of the nature of things, Locke responds that while there may be constraints on abstraction (for the mind must notice certain ideas as going together), the constraints are not Stillingfleet's real essences of things.[85] On the other hand, Stillingfleet is talking about things and the metaphysical certainty/necessity grounded in their natures. Thus we are led back to Stillingfleet's original charge that Locke had almost discarded substance out of the reasonable world and his reformulation of it that Locke had no grounds for being certain about substance.

In his *Answer to Mr. Locke's Letter* Stillingfleet tried to sharpen his difference from Locke by shifting the question to certainty about substance. He grants that Locke repeatedly says that substance is *supposed*, but asks what reason there is to make the supposition. Even that we cannot conceive things otherwise is for him insufficient; "Are there not multitudes of things which we are not able to conceive, and yet it would not be allowed us to suppose what we think fit on that account? I could *hardly conceive* that Mr. L. would have brought such Evidence as this against himself; but *I must suppose some unknown Substratum* in this Case" (p.523).

In his last treatment of the issue,[86] Locke distinguished, as he felt Stillingfleet had not, between the questions whether, on his principles, he can have any certainty about the *idea* of substance and about the *being* of substance.[87] The first question is easy, Locke thought, for the burden of proof is on Stillingfleet and he failed to deliver. Indeed, part of the reason for that failure, as Locke saw it, was Stillingfleet's failure to distinguish the two questions. That Newton discarded Descartes's vortices does not mean that he discarded the

---

[84] *Letter; Works*, 4:11–12.

[85] *Works*, 4:86–93.

[86] At least his last treatment as far as Stillingfleet was concerned. Locke completed his text on May 4, 1698 and Stillingfleet died on March 29, 1699.

[87] *Works*, 4:442.

notion of vortices that is necessary even to discuss the issue (p. 451). The crucial issue in any case is the second, and Locke treats it at length. Part of his answer is that Stillingfleet's complaint that he makes substance a mere supposition is a complaint against his own position on substance as well. In Locke's view each has the same claim to certainty: "Your Lordship . . . concludes that there is substance, 'because it is a repugnancy to our conceptions of things . . . that modes or accidents should subsist by themselves;' and I conclude the same thing, because we cannot conceive how sensible qualities should subsist by themselves. Now what the difference of certainty is from a repugnancy to our conceptions, and from our not being able to conceive, I confess, my Lord, I am not acute enough to discern" (p. 445). Locke here overlooks a reasonable enough demand from Stillingfleet for a ground of our inability to conceive sensible qualities subsisting by themselves. He regards as an insulting attempt at humor Stillingfleet's question as to how sensible qualities carry with them the supposition of corporeal substance.[88] The question is, more than legitimate, direct to the point. Yet Locke fails to see it since for him reason deals not with the world but with our way of viewing it; thus his reply is superficial: " 'by carrying with them a supposition', I mean, according to the ordinary import of the phrase that sensible qualities imply a substratum to exist in" (p. 447).

Locke was similarly at a loss to respond to Stillingfleet's linking him with Hobbist nominalism. He insisted that there was a clear distinction between names and ideas but never made clear what that distinction was or what its significance was.[89] Thus Stillingfleet pressed the point: "The Question is not, Whether in forming the Notion of Common Nature, the Mind doth not abstract from the Circumstances of particular Beings; But it is whether there be not an Antecedent Foundation in the Nature of things upon which we form this Abstract Idea? For if there be, then it cannot be called *an universal name* only: or a mere sign of an *Idea*, which we have formed from putting many simple ideas together, which *Name* belongs to all of such a sort, as have those *simple Ideas* united together."[90] Apparently still not able to see any difference between Lockean general ideas and Hobbist names, Stillingfleet pressed on again to link the two. The end of the polemic saw Locke still defending himself against this linkage, lest it made the link between ideas and the word arbitrary and thus all knowledge uncertain. Stillingfleet had argued that if ideas are not representations then they are mere names, to which Locke replied that while some ideas are not likenesses of anything without, yet they are not mere names. "Methinks they might be allowed to be ideas, and that is all they pretend to be, though they do not resemble that which produces them. I cannot help thinking a son something really more than a bare name, though he has not the luck to resemble his

---

[88] "truly that is burden enough for them. But which way do they carry it?"
[89] *Letter*; *Works*, 3:24–25.
[90] *Answer*; *Works*, 3:556.

father, who begat him: and the black and blue which I see I cannot conclude but to be something besides the words black and blue (wherever your lordship shall place that something, either in my perception only, or in my skin) though it resemble not at all the stone, that with a knock produced it."[91] The only connection Locke sees is *causal*, not rational, because our connection to the world is via the senses not reason.

If part of Locke's actual answer to Stillingfleet is thus superficial, there is another part of his answer that goes very deep indeed. It turns on the distinction between the "bare being" of substance and its "subsistency by itself." Stillingfleet seems to think that because he has the clear and distinct idea of its manner of subsistence, that is, as a support, he has a clear and distinct idea of the substance. But since being and manner of subsistence are different, this is a non sequitur. We have only a very obscure and confused idea, as in the case of that whose manner of subsistence is to be supported, both of which we "call by the general name of things that have or have not support."[92] I think that what Locke is saying here is what he says so often: There *is* something, but we do not know what it is. What *is* is the thing in itself, but of this we have no idea. We can only *call* it that which supports. We are like the blind man, says Locke, who says he has an idea of scarlet that is something, he knows not what, supported by another thing.[93] The analogy is apt. We have the senses to have clear and distinct ideas of appearances, but no rational intuition to know noumena. The support relation, then, is the relation of appearing. If we could know the thing that supports we could know the thing in itself and not just as it appears to us.[94] If Locke fails to understand reason as more than a way to view the world (as he must since we are restricted to phenomena), then Stillingfleet fails to distinguish between ideas and things. He oscillates between certainty with respect to the idea of substance and certainty with respect to the being of substance. This is because it is not clear whether for Stillingfleet substance is a being or a category of being. If the latter then it is only an idea, a way of viewing the world; but if the former then we cannot talk about it or even perceive it. The dilemma opens the way to Berkeley, who was later to deny that we have any idea at all of the thing in itself;[95] there are only ways of viewing, or as he put it, the viewing is the being.

---

[91] *Second Reply; Works*, 3:399.

[92] Ibid., p. 450.

[93] Locke thus extends to substance in its most basic sense the metaphor he had used previously with respect to substance as a bundler into kinds: "we in vain pretend to range Things into sorts, and dispose them into certain Classes, under Names, by their *real Essences*, that are so far from our discovery or comprehension. A blind Man may as soon sort Things by their Colours, and he that has lost his Smell, as well distinguish a Lily and a Rose by their Odors, as by those internal Constitutions which he knows not" (3.6.9; 444–45).

[94] This is the relation referred to in the idea of substance as "an obscure and relative" one (2.23.2; 296).

[95] As Stillingfleet pointed out, Locke has almost (but only almost) discarded substance.

CHAPTER VIII

Philosophy and the Historiography of Philosophy

A CRUCIAL THESIS of this work is that Locke needs to be interpreted in light of a certain tradition for which Gassendi was the principal funnel into the seventeenth century. This tradition gives the sense of his empirical-skeptical epistemology and of his nominalist ontology of atoms and the void by emphasizing the centrality of his moral and political views of relativism and toleration. It also systematically places Locke on the opposite side to the Cartesians with respect to virtually every issue of significance in the period. In these terms, Locke engages the Cartesians in Plato's battle of the gods and giants.

However plausible the case developed thus far, there yet remains the following question: Why is the anti-Cartesian defense of intellectual and political toleration not more obvious throughout Locke's *Essay*, especially if as I contend this defense is a key to the work as a whole? In addition, how can we construe Locke's work as an effort on behalf of the materialism of Plato's giants against the friends of the Forms, the gods whose cause was championed in the seventeenth century by the Cartesians? For after all, the engine of the ancient giants' toleration was a tychistic atheism that seems inimical to Locke's theistic providentialism. Locke not only gives arguments for the existence of God but among them one that is quite interesting and original with him. His rejection of tychism too seems clear. Not only the power but the goodness and wisdom of God also are infinite, as demonstrated by the sufficiency of even our limited perceptual powers for making our way in the world (2.23.12–13). The falsity of tychism in fact is Locke's own example of a probability from which assent cannot be withheld. "Whether it be possible, that a promiscuous jumble of printing Letters should often fall into a Method and Order, which should stamp on paper a coherent Discourse: or that a blind fortuitous concourse of Atoms, not guided by an understanding Agent, should frequently constitute the Bodies of any Species of Animals: in these and the like Cases, I think, no Body that considers them, can be one jot at a stand which side to take, nor at all waver in his Assent" (4.20.15; 716). As we have just seen, in fact, Locke consciously fought his longest polemic against an opponent who correctly foresaw the use to which Locke's philosophy might be put on behalf of "a certain tradition." Nor, as we shall soon see, was Stillingfleet the only one to force Locke into a defense against such charges. John Edwards, for example, no less formidably made these charges. In response to him, however, Locke clearly appealed to the concept of toleration at the center of both of his thought and the tradition in which I have tried to place him. What begins as an objection to my interpretation turns out in part to be an argument in its favor.

§27 DISSIMULATION AND MEANING

There are a number of hypotheses that might be advanced to account for Locke's failure to make clearer what I think he was up to. One is the outright dissimulation hypothesis, which, for example, has recently been invoked as an account of Descartes's metaphysics. According to this application of the hypothesis, the *Meditations* was consciously perpetrated as a philosophical joke—a metaphysical burlesque if you like, the obvious futility of whose argument was designed precisely to show the futility of just that kind of argument. The aim of the *Meditations* on this view was not to replace one metaphysics with another, but to announce the end of traditional metaphysics in a hilarious *reductio ad absurdum* of the whole enterprise. The *Meditations*, then, was a parody of the views it generally is taken to express, and the way to fool "the most wise and illustrious, the deans and doctors of the sacred faculty of theology in Paris," to whom the work was dedicated, was through the sophistication of the parody.[1]

Now, it may be that something like this was true of Locke's *Essay*. Even as late as 1690 anyone flirting with materialism lay under the spectre of Hobbes, whose only rival as the century's perfect anti-authority was Spinoza. What better way to propagate the views I have attributed to Locke than by indirectly insinuating them under a more respectable veneer, or in some other misleading way? Perhaps even Locke's comment, for example, about the promiscuous jumble of letters or the fortuitous concourse of atoms is a rejection of tychism only for the unwitting. After all, he says only that our assent is unwavering and does not indicate here or by the context to which side it is given. That Locke may have had such a strategy of subversion would be argued by its very success in later English deism. Certainly there grew up an enormous polemical literature on just this question of the subversiveness of the *Essay*, whether intended or not. In addition, despite the attractions of the fideist interpretation of libertinage érudit, the dissimulation hypothesis is a plausible account of some of its practitioners; perhaps not of Gassendi, on whom Locke directly draws, but certainly of many of his cohorts. That is, the profession of religious faith by the libertins need not have been the expression of skeptical fideism whose possibility we noted above, but rather a camouflage for the atheism thought consequent on skepticism, as it is according to the more standard view.

As an account of the *Meditations*, however, the dissimulation hypothesis seems wildly implausible. How could a twentieth-century historian, indeed

---

[1] Caton, "Analytic History".

only that historian, have been in on Descartes's joke, but not Clerselier, Régis, Arnauld, Malebranche, or anyone else? Only the most fiendish deviousness on the part of Descartes as the perpetrator of the ruse could account for this universal misinterpretation of his work for more than three centuries. Even less likely would be a conspiracy theory according to which the leading lights of Cartesianism were au courant with the supposed intentions of the master. But even if Descartes's premises logically and historically yielded conclusions opposite to those on the face of them intended, such a theory strains credibility in view of the total lack of any other evidence in favor of it. (I cannot imagine how the Malebranche–Arnauld polemic, for example, might be read in light of such a theory.) More was one who as we noted drew attention in no uncertain terms to these prima facie unintended consequences of Descartes's view, but he nonetheless rejected the dissimulation hypothesis and a fortiori the conspiracy hypothesis as well. Stillingfleet was another: "I can by no means suspect that Descartes designed to take away the force of other Arguments for a Deity, that he might secretly undermine the belief of a God, by introducing his Argument from the Idea, which he knew would not hold; (as some have suggested) for I am satisfy'd, that he thought this Argument beyond any other; For, in a Letter to a Friend, he saith, *He had found out such an Argument as gave him full satisfaction* . . . Which being written to his intimate Friends shew[s] sufficiently his own apprehensions of the strength of [his arguments]. But what opinion soever he had of it himself, they have not met with such a reception among thinking men."[2]

But what of dissimulation or conspiracy as an account of Locke? Carroll was certainly inclined toward such an account: "[Locke's] Design was, to establish *Spinoza's* Hypothesis in his Essay, and to print and publish that Book, in order to teach and spread his Doctrine."[3] That doctrine is that all that exists is a single material substance and that all particular beings are but collections of its modifications (p. 23). Yet had Locke used Spinoza's terms, according to Carroll, he would have failed in his purpose; people would have rejected the doctrine from Locke's pen no less than from Spinoza's. Thus Locke disguised his meaning. First publishing only an extract of the *Essay*, in French, for example, was part of his attempt "to convey it in Maskerade" (p. 274).

On the face of it this disguised, atheistic-materialism interpretation of Locke is preposterous, however consonant the allegedly disguised views may be with the tradition into which I have tried to fit Locke. Consider just Locke's relation to Scripture. Locke's *First Letter* addressed to Stillingfleet ends as follows: "The holy scripture is to me, and always will be, the constant guide of my assent; and I shall always hearken to it, as containing infallible truth, relating to things of the highest concernment. And I wish I could say, there were

---

[2] *Origines sacrae*; *Works*, 2:83.
[3] *Dissertation* p. 24. See also p. 49.

no mysteries in it: I acknowledge there are to me, and I fear always will be."[4] Is there any reason to take this statement at less than face value? What Locke produced in his struggles with deism would argue that there is not. The *Reasonableness of Christianity* evidences a quite remarkable knowledge of the biblical text and an apparent attitude that is hardly one of a disinterested scholar. While his aim is to show that the text is compatible with reason, the thrust of the compatibility is to secure the text, not to extend the province of reason. From Coste too we have evidence of Locke's devotion to Scripture.[5] And his interest was not that of an aloof puzzle-solver; explicating the Scripture's mysteries, as Locke calls them, is of importance to one's moral and religious life. In response to Lady Peterborough's solicitation of advice as to the education of her son Lord Morduant, Locke recommended history, geography, and morality. "I mean not the ethics of the schools, [but Cicero, Pufendorf, Aristotle, and] above all The New Testament [wherein] a man may learn to live which is the business of ethics, and not how to define and distinguish and dispute about the names of virtues and vices."[6] There is further evidence of the sort Stillingfleet would have appreciated. Lady Masham reports that Locke was "naturally compassionate and exceedingly charitable to those in want. But . . . one article of his enquiry when any objects of charity were recommended to him used to be whether they were people that duly attended the public worship of God in any congregation of God whatever. And if they did not, but were such as spent their time on Sunday lazily at home, or worse employed in an alehouse, they were sure to be more sparingly relieved than others in the same circumstances."[7] Predicting his own imminent death, Locke asked Coste to be remembered in his prayers and allowed the Masham family to hold their prayers in his bedroom; as he actually transpired Locke may have been having the Psalms read to him by Lady Masham.[8]

So it would seem that Locke cannot have intended the deistic or outrightly atheistic consequences that even in his own lifetime were being drawn from the *Essay* by Toland and others. We can imagine Locke saying,

> That is not what I meant at all;
> That is not it, at all.

Malcolm Flemyng was one who along these lines was prepared to absolve Locke from atheism but not from propagating atheistic views. Locke meant well but did ill, and in fact was culpable for the choice of means to carry out his intentions. Writing about Locke's treatment of the topic of thinking matter,

---

[4] *Works*, 4:96.

[5] Recorded in his obituary that Coste published in *Nouvelles de la République des Lettres*, February 2, 1705, pp. 154–76. See Cranston, *John Locke*, p. 438.

[6] Ibid., Cranston, pp. 427–28.

[7] Amsterdam: Remonstrants' MS J. 57a. See Cranston, *John Locke* p. 426.

[8] Ibid., p. 480.

Flemyng argued that "Great Geniuses, who venture to think and write out of the common Road, and from their own Fund, though at Bottom Friends to Religion, and the Interests of mankind, yet sometimes throw out Singularities and Paradoxes, which may be, and not seldom are wrested by Persons of a loose Turn, so as to do great Hurt."[9] He recommends consideration of the effect, especially when the subject is momentous and the author is young. (Even if he had begun it much earlier, Locke was fifty-eight when he published the *Essay!*) So on this view it was his interpreters who got Locke wrong, with horrifying results. "Free thinkers, spider-like, converted into Poison everything they read and fed their Understandings with" (p. 10). Whether intentionally or not, they failed to convey what Locke ultimately meant.

But how does it matter what Locke meant? By identifying the intentional fallacy we have been taught in recent times that if an author's meaning is fully or even crucially determinant of the meaning of a text, then no text has any meaning, except perhaps one's own for oneself. Still more recently we have been taught the general irrelevance of meanings to theory and understanding. The intentional fallacy against which people have had to inveigh so mightily is but an instance, and a not very special instance, of the irrelevance of meanings. As I shall try to suggest, the meanings of even our own texts are no less elusive, and no more so, than those of Locke or anyone else. John Witty looked for the significance of what Locke said elsewhere than in what he may have intended: "What was the design of Mr. *Locke*, who denys all knowledge of Substances, in his famous *Essay* . . . I won't examine: whether it was writ with an intention to establish Spinoza's material Deity; or whether all he aimed at in it was to enquire after the Fundamentals and Extent of Human Knowledge."[10] Witty claimed rather to be interested in showing that Spinoza's view was false. Similarly, whether Descartes aimed at establishing the mind-body distinction or at undermining it by making it depend on an absurd philosophical system is, according to Witty, irrelevant to the validity of that distinction. But of course distinguishing, as Witty does, between the meaning and the truth of a text, indeed between historical-temporal and philosophical-eternal truth is no less problematic. Of this more below. Here I want to pursue the issue with respect to the questions of influence and traditions in a way that bears on the real meaning of an author.

It is not surprising that in arguments for incompatible conclusions we should find what appear to be common premises, for this is one obvious way in which there can be questions and different sides to the same question. A particularly compelling instance of this is the evolution undergone by reductio ad absurdum arguments in this period. What happened (and perhaps this happens in every period) was that such arguments were often stood on their heads. An author

[9] *Examination*, p. 6.
[10] *First Principles*, p. 100.

offers an argument on behalf of some position P: not-P entails Q, but not-Q therefore P. Along comes another author who thinks that not-P is the case and argues Q by quoting our first author. The historical example immediately brought to mind by this outline is the treatment of the parallel line postulate. That exactly one line parallel to a given line can be drawn through a point outside that line was thought to be sufficiently less obvious than Euclid's other postulates as not to be independent of them. Attempts to prove it as an axiom of course failed, or were thought to have failed, except for sixteenth-century reductiones ad absurdum on its behalf. Questions of the very sort we are here investigating aside, these arguments in the nineteenth century became part of the development of non-Euclidean geometries; the postulate was denied, not to show how the results proved the postulate to be true, but *on behalf of* those very results.[11] A nice example in our period comes from Ignace-Gaston Pardies, who in 1672 published a work called *Discourse on Bestial Knowledge*; in the first part he sets out the Cartesian case for the bestial machine and then in the second part argues the Aristotelian case against it. But the first part was viewed as so strong and the second part so weak that he was thought by many to be a Cartesian—"a liar who in his soul was a Cartesian" (un prévaricateur qui étoit cartésien dans l'ame) as the Jesuit Gabriel Daniel put it.[12] In a more relevant example, Carroll in his attack on Locke drew attention to Jurieu's attack on Bayle, who is charged with the artifice of having given all the arguments impiety can give for the "indifferency" of religions and then having added a brief and equivocal rejection of them.[13] Again setting aside such questions as may be raised by, for example, the dissimulation hypothesis, we might generalize this case to cover a whole range of theological argument in the period. It seems that a main theoretical engine of eighteenth-century atheism was theistic reductio arguments of the late seventeenth century. Competing sides in a given question such as the efficacy of grace would try to show that the views of the other side led to atheism; these arguments were taken over ready-made by those happy with the previously absurd conclusion.[14]

Crucial Lockean texts are expressed so as to be susceptible to a reversal of their significance as reductiones. One notable instance that we have already seen is Locke's stance with respect to the Cartesian identification of body and

[11] Heath, *Euclid's Elements*, 1:202 n.

[12] For a case against his interpretation, see Rosenfield, *Animal Soul*, p. 80 n. She points to external evidence (Pardies was regarded by the journals as an opponent of Cartesianism—thus *The Philosophical Transactions of the Royal Society of London*, the *Journal des Sçavans*, the *Mémoires de Trévoux*; his work was attacked by antischolastics—thus Dilly and Sbaragli) and internal evidence (Pardies clearly gives the Peripatetic position). But on the dissimulation hypothesis, for example, none of this adds up to anything more than a case for the cleverness of Pardies's ruse.

[13] Carroll, *Dissertation*, p. 251; Jurieu, *Tableau du Socinianisme*. Consider also Bayle's reasoning in note E of the article on Rorarius: If man's soul is spiritual, so is the beast's; if the beast's soul is corporeal, so is man's. La Mettrie would agree.

[14] This thesis is defended in great detail by Alan C. Kors.

extension: "If it be a Reason to prove, that Spirit is different from Body, because Thinking includes not the *Idea* of Extension in it; the same Reason will be as valid, I suppose, to prove, that *Space is not Body*, because it includes not the *Idea* of Solidity in it; *Space and Solidity* being *as distinct Ideas*, as Thinking and Extension, and as wholly separable in the Mind one from another" (2.13.11; 172). La Mettrie, for example, would have no problem whatsoever with Locke's argument. An even more important instance is the conclusion of Locke's argument for spiritual substance: "It being as rational to affirm, there is no Body, because we have no clear and distinct *Idea* of the *Substance* of matter; as to say, there is no Spirit, because we have no clear and distinct *Idea* of *Substance* of a Spirit" (2.23.5; 298).[15] Toland picked this up and, quoting it almost verbatim, argued that there are no spiritual substances.[16] Or consider Locke's argument, against Malebranche's theory of perception, that talk of union with or containment in, as the mind is said to be related to God, applies literally only to bodies. Gerdil, an eighteenth-century Italian defender of Malebranche, later pointed out on behalf of Malebranche that Locke himself talks of the soul as united to the body and of ideas as in the mind.[17] Gerdil's point was to disarm Locke's argument against Malebranche; but if my interpretation is correct, Locke's language needs to be taken in just the materialist sense Gerdil offered as part of a reductio on behalf of Malebranche. So who is responsible for the materialism being expressed and spread at the turn of the century? The question smacks of priority debates in the history of science; the intelligibility of both, it seems to me, typically depends on a kind of realism that I along with the tradition whose history I am writing here find unintelligible. Before taking the several more steps to that issue, however, I want to make a general disclaimer about the full significance of reductio arguments in this period.

The full story on such arguments requires more skill and space than I have to examine the roles of satire, parody, irony, and especially the revival in the seventeenth century of the dramatic dialogue as a vehicle of philosophical expression.[18] But even apart from such considerations, the significance of

---

[15] See also 2.23.29–30.

[16] "*We may as well deny the existence of Body because we have not an idea of its real Essence, as call The Being of the Soul in question for the same reason*" (*Christianity*, p. 87).

[17] McCracken, *British Philosophy*, p. 125.

[18] One would like especially to examine Shaftesbury's recommendation of ridicule as a response to enthusiasm, particularly to that of the French Protestants "lately come among us" (*Letter Concerning Enthusiasm* [1708]; *Characteristics*, vol. 1): "For to apply a Serious Remedy, and to bring the Sword, or *Fasces*, as a Cure, must make the Case more melancholy, and increase the very Cause of the Distemper" (p. 16). His comment on Platonism and Epicureanism vis-à-vis enthusiasm especially invites investigation: "Whilst some Sects, such as the *Pythagorean* and latter *Platonick*, joined in with the Superstition and Enthusiasm of the Times; the *Epicurean*, the *Academick*, and others, were allow'd to use all the Force of Wit and Raillery against it" (p. 18). One would like to know, for example, how it is that, as a purely rhetorical device, rational argument differs from either ridicule or the persuasions of enthusiasm. The relation of each to toleration makes this a particularly pressing issue.

reductio arguments in deistic debates over materialism, providentialism, and the like becomes exceedingly complex. Consider once again Samuel Strutt. Strutt develops the case at great length that thought or volition cannot move matter and that a material thing can be put in motion only by another material thing. At the end of his case he turns to Cudworth's consideration of the objection that God being incorporeal could not move matter: "he would run thro' all things, and could not lay hold or fasten upon any."[19] He cites Cudworth's reply that God "must needs have a despotic Power over all," moving matter "*not Mechanically* but *Vitally*, and by *Cogitation* only. And that a *Cogitative Being* as such, hath a natural *imperium*, over *Matter* and *Power* of moving it, without any *Engines* or *Machines* is unquestionably certain, even from our own *Souls*; which move our *Bodies* and command them every Way *merely by Will or Thought*" (p/ 887).[20] But for Strutt, because our soul does not move our body, there is a problem in asserting how God moves matter. (In fact, he takes Cudworth's notion of an imperium to be meaningless and his position to be either contradictory or meaningless (p. 44).) That is, he reverses Cudworth's argument. Not only this, but he realizes what he is doing and what it might mean. "It has been thought indeed, that Dr. *Cudworth* has put some of his Objections too strong, to suppose him not interested in the Defense of them, instead of answering them clearly; and that he did not intend to serve the Cause of Religion by it" (p. 45). Strutt takes this to be only "clamour," as is evidenced by Cudworth's having "laid open and exposed to publick View" (i.e., *presumably* to have refuted) almost all the objections to the existence of God. But to the extent that just one objection of this sort fails to be refuted, its plausibility is enhanced both by Strutt *and* by Cudworth. Strutt's own view is that the divine attributes are better understood by common sense and reason than by abstruse metaphysical speculation, which is shown by "the mysterious manner in which [Cudworth] has answer'd a plain Objection" (p. 43), and which was his reason for considering the Cudworth material in the first place. The mind is staggered, and with it any bare attempt to assign responsibility for the promulgation of atheism.

§28 WHAT LOCKE SAID

Let us return, then, to our original question of why it is that the message of the giants fails to be clearer in Locke's text. A second kind of hypothesis would have it that for whatever reason Locke simply errs when he turns to certain questions. To be consonant with his basic epistemological and ontological views Locke ought to have been an atheist, but fallible philosopher that he was,

---

[19] *System*, p. 886.
[20] Cited by Strutt, *Enquiry*, pp. 42–43.

he wound up on the wrong side of this question. Like Homer, Locke occasionally nods. The problem with this nodding-Locke hypothesis is the threat it poses not just to Locke's *Essay*, but to the whole history of philosophy as worthy of study. On the one hand, it threatens to lose interest as a series of sophomoric errors that the least of us have no trouble identifying; and on the other, it threatens to evaporate as historical study if all we are interested in is that in which a philosopher does not err—that is, we wind up doing only philosophy, not its history. Texts, it seems to me, must be taken much more at face value. The question is whether this can be done in a way that preserves the interpretation I have given Locke. This suggests a third kind of hypothesis, which, if the interpretation is correct, ought to be how I got the interpretation in the first place, namely, that Locke *does* say just what I say he does, albeit with a language whose interpretation is what is at issue. My account of Locke is not a version of what he *ought* to have said had he been more consistent or more philosophically enlightened. Nor is it a creative extrapolation *beyond* what he said. The account is of what he *did* say.[21]

The attitude of this hypothesis approximates that of Berkeley toward several people.

That atheistical principles have taken deep root, and are farther spread than most people are apt to imagine, will be plain to whoever considers that pantheism, materialism, fatalism are nothing but atheism a little disguised; that the notions of *Hobbes, Spinoza, Leibniz,* and *Bayle* are relished and applauded; that as they who deny the freedom and immortality of the soul in effect deny its being, even so they do, as to all moral effects and natural relation, deny the being of a God, who deny Him to be an observer, judge, and rewarder of human actions; that the course of arguing pursued by infidels leads to atheism as well as infidelity. . . . if I see it in their writings, if they own it in their conversation, if their ideas imply it, if their ends are not answered but by supposing it. . . . [then] surely what the favorers of their schemes would palliate, it is the duty of others to display and refute."[22]

---

[21] Part of the explanation of Locke's failure to be more explicit is the fluidity of philosophical language in the seventeenth century to which McMullin draws attention (*Concept of Matter*, pp. 1–2). The longer part of the explanation investigates the source of this fluidity. I might add too that what I here say about the interpretation of Locke applies as well to the interpretation of everyone else, including Descartes. Though I have found my interpretation to have been essentially advanced by Cousin and others in the nineteenth century, and in crucial respects by Desgabets and Régis in the seventeenth, it will likely not have been initially very plausible here to very many. It may be noted, incidentally, that the historiographical views I am now proposing also allow, for example, the rehabilitation of Caton's view of Descartes that I vilified above. That is, they do so in principle, although in practice I cannot see how his view could be made acceptable for the same reasons already given. Finally, many of the historiographical worries here trace to my reading of the work of Louis Loeb, who also claimed to write a book "about what actually happened, as best [he] can tell" (*Modern Philosophy*, p. 17). His notion of a "pattern of argument" deserves attention.]

[22] *The Theory of Vision . . . Vindicated and Explained*, par. 6; *Works*, 1:253–55.

Berkeley is specifically concerned here with more obviously atheistic types like Halley and Collins, but he ought to have been concerned no less with Locke if this hypothesis is correct. For according to it, Locke was, despite whatever intentions he may have had, an atheist.

Consider once again Carroll, who seems to have held the dissimulation hypothesis. Certainly this hypothesis is indicated by the claim that 4.10 ("Of our Knowledge of the Existence of a God") is "the Center of the *Essay* . . . A Book purposely writ, in order to spread and teach the Doctrine established in it," to wit, Spinozism—the eternal existence of the world only. Locke had a "double Design," to advance materialism but to disguise the doctrine from those who "know the existence of the one only true God."[23] But there is another reading, according to which the disguise of Locke's theory amounts only to the impenetrability of its meaning to certain readers. According to Carroll, both Locke and Spinoza really advance the same thesis, but this is difficult to show because both give language an extraordinary sense. And the reason for this is that both thought "the Nature of Things is quite different from what it really is; and from what others know and take it to be" (p. iii). That is, because their view of reality is incorrect their use of language is incorrect, and though they may say the same things as others do, the meaning conveyed is different. When Locke and Spinoza say there is a God, they say "in Sense and Reality, exactly and precisely, what others say when they say there is no God but the world." This is a difference in sound only, but a dangerous one, "For hereby the Writings of those two Authors gain admittance into our Hands, and infect us one way or other, before we perceive it; and indeed undertake to confirm us in Atheism, by convincing us, that *there is a God*" (p. 52).

It is a good question how, if these two impostors are so successful in systematically distorting their language and thus keeping from us their true atheism, they can at the same time "infect us one way or other" with that atheism. Carroll cannot have it both ways. Even so, Carroll does suggest still another hypothesis namely, that what Locke says sounds like one thing but means another) and with it a nest of difficulties that even unsolved will offer some understanding of what history is about. This is the homonym theory, a relevant precedent for which is found in the phrase that Aquinas appended to each of his five ways. Concluding from various premises that there exists an unmoved mover, a first cause, a necessary being, Aquinas added "and this all men understand to be God." But of course not all men understand the unmoved mover or the first cause or the necessary being to be God and those who do can do so only in light of a rather complex theory.

This raises the question of just how much understanding of Him is required of an author in order to say of him that he is referring to the "one only true God." This question had been raised, it will be recalled, in no uncertain terms by

---

[23] *Dissertation*, p. 108.

Descartes in response to Gassendi, who thought that the idea of God was not given innately and all at once, but rather was built up gradually through experience. Descartes appealed to "the common philosophical maxim that the essences of things are indivisible. An idea represents the essence of a thing, and if anything is added to or taken away from it, it is forthwith the idea of something else."[24] The issue is the familiar one of realism and nominalism that divides the gods and giants. Instructive here is Descartes's comment immediately following: "This is how the ideas of Pandora and of all false gods are formed by those who do not have a correct conception of the true God." Descartes here explains how heresy is possible. The heretic fails to have the idea of God at all and is thus really an atheist or an idolator. With such a binary conception, the theoretical basis is clear for the division between those who should be burned and those entitled to burn them. With the Gassendist conception of an idea, on the other hand, while some may have a relatively more perfect idea of God, no one has it perfectly and certainly no one has an idea that represents the divine (or any other) essence. How, then, to burn anyone? Such an attitude of toleration based on empiricism, if not outright skepticism, is clearly in the tradition going back to Sextus.[25] One notable member of this tradition was Montaigne, of course, who in response to the witch-burning craze said, "after all, it is to place a very high value on one's views to cook a man alive on the basis of them."[26]

Now, Locke clearly placed himself in this tradition on just this issue. The Calvinistic pamphleteer John Edwards[27] accused Locke of atheism in the terms above. It was not sufficient to be a Christian, he said, to hold only that Jesus is the Messiah—as Locke had claimed in *The Reasonableness of Christianity*. For the Scriptures hold that Christians must be taught, and presumably must therefore believe in, the Trinity. However much he or they may profess a belief in God, Locke is a member of the Socinian sect and hence an atheist. Locke's replies were chagrined, protracted, and less than candid. But his attitude with respect to the "fundamentals necessary for salvation," as well as the basis for it, were essentially Montaigne's: "why may I not be permitted to follow my guesses, as well as you yours?"[28] The niceties of toleration aside, we are still left with a problem of reference. Specifically, in the tradition above, how is historical reference possible in such a way that, contrary to the dissimulation,

---

[24] HR, 2:220; AT, 7:371.

[25] See Groarke, *Scepticism*, chap. 4, for a defense of egalitarian toleration in skeptical terms, and *Greek Scepticism* for its historical basis.

[26] *Essays*, 3:11; p. 416. Recall from above Gassendi's criticism of Descartes's reliance on clarity and distinctness, that in any case we have no way of determining what is clear and distinct from what only appears to be clear and distinct. His illustration: People are seen to go to the stake, literally, for their clear and distinct perceptions on opposite sides of the same issue.

[27] For more on whom, and on this episode, see Cranston, *John Locke*, pp. 390–92.

[28] Such an attitude also makes religious authority, and thus the authorities themselves, clergymen, all dispensable—the alarming conclusion that we saw William Carroll draw from Locke's work. See chap.3, sec. 11 above, on enthusiasm.

nodding-Locke, and homonym theories, my account of Locke is an account of what Locke said? I shall return to this issue shortly. But first I shall say something about two kinds of views of history according to which it is also possible to give an account of what Locke said. Both require the realism with respect to universals that is rejected by those in the tradition of the giants.

§29 TWO CAMPS OF HISTORIANS

In proposing my interpretation as well as the account I am giving of it, I feel myself squeezed by two familiar camps of historians of philosophy. On the one hand are the analysts, whose guiding thought is that the history of philosophy consists of the discussion of texts having philosophical importance from our point of view. Against them stand the historians, whose guiding thought is that philosophical importance in the period in which it was produced is the criterion of a text's importance. The two camps generally ignore each other despite perfunctory exchanges acknowledging each other's independent value. Since I find myself partly in each and thus partly outside the other, I shall need to say something about this great dichotomy, which will be addressed as the distinction between history of philosophy and history of ideas—terminology beginning to prevail because of the prevalence of the former in the philosophical profession.

History of ideas is concerned with interpretation of texts. Its aim is generally to reconstruct the text in terms of its context, both temporally immediate and subsequent, and to do so in such a way that we are enabled to understand its meaning. The tendency is to reduce text to circumstance—text is what comes with it (context). With this enterprise it is not clear what could be said about a text apart from its circumstances. Thus the reliance of history of ideas on sociology, theology, political history, psychology, and so on. This relativity of perspective may be regarded as an insurmountable obstacle to the real interpretation of the text, with the result that one eschews history of ideas in favor of some other kind of history; or it may be taken to be the very stuff of the enterprise.[29] In either case, there is typically an almost irresistible invitation to

---

[29] Thus Williams finds history of ideas corrupted by hindsight. Our choice of works for interpretation and thus for inclusion in our histories is determined not by the works themselves but by "their subsequent history." Presumably, unless Descartes's work had been found of interest both in his own time and since, including by lesser minds, his work would not now figure as it does in our histories (*Descartes*, p. 10). But for Lovejoy, for example, the subsequent history, often especially as it involves lesser minds, is what is most of interest. A main part of the enterprise here is "to understand how *new* beliefs and intellectual fashions are introduced and diffused, to help elucidate the psychological character of the process by which changes in the vogue and influence of ideas have come about; to make clear, if possible, how conceptions dominant, or extensively prevalent, in one generation lose their hold upon men's minds and give place to others" (*Great Chain*, p. 20).

realism in two senses. For one thing, essences are recognized to the extent that a kind of activity is recognized called philosophizing, which is instantiated at certain times and places and of which the history is an account. That is, philosophy is itself a metaphysically real natural kind. An indication of this realist interpretation is the tendency to treat ideas (or theories or views) as things, at least as spatio-temporal particulars, which tendency is itself indicated by the tendency to regard the relevant mode of explanation in history of ideas as causal. Thus the prevalence of questions of influence in such histories. The second invitation to realism comes from the evaluation of the account. Accounts in history of ideas are naturally regarded as pictures—pictures constructed to show how it really was, "wie es eigentlich gewesen ist" in Ranke's phrase. The fuller and more accurate the picture, the better the account of a past that is obviously taken to be metaphysically given independently of anything we might say about that past. This is why the dependence of the interpretation of a work on the subsequent history of the work is found to be so problematic. Descartes's *Meditations* is a seventeenth-century text, a part of history that is over and done with, fixed forever with the rest of the past, and it is the historian's job to retrieve, reconstruct, or duplicate it as best as possible. But if the retrieval, reconstruction, or duplication depends on the vagaries of subsequent history, there will be a discrepancy from the original. This is a cinematographic view of history, but one that begins to disintegrate as soon as we begin to ask what it is that ideally history should be filming: the writing of the *Meditations*? its reception at the publishers? what Descartes, or anyone else was thinking at the time? Of this, more below.

History of philosophy, as it is coming to be called in a restricted sense, is regarded as a very different enterprise from history of ideas, for it is of a piece with philosophy itself. Here the primary aim is not temporal, historical accuracy; nor is the concern with the actual meaning of an author or text. Rather, the aim is atemporal philosophical accuracy; the concern is with the truth of what an author may or may not have meant. But here too there is a dual invitation to realism. For one thing, different authors can be thought to have the same views in a metaphysically real sense. That philosophical views are themselves natural kinds in fact enables the enterprise to be called historical. Although it may be a historical accident of no ultimate significance to the enterprise, nonetheless there remains at least the possibility that the view the historian of philosophy treats under the description of Cartesian was actually held by Descartes himself. The tendency is thus to treat ideas (or theories or views) as essences and the relevant mode of explanation as philosophical argument. Here too there is a second invitation to realism when we come to evaluate the account. The pictures whose accuracy we measure are not of events in the past but of essences and relations between them. The best example is the familiar blending of the Forms depicted in the *Sophist*, the description of which is said to be true just in so far as the description reflects the Forms and how they are blended. Plato's own analysis of this reflection will now strike many as bizarre, but I am convinced that something like it is assumed by all realist accounts of truth. We shall come to it in a moment. Meanwhile, such an analysis models history only in so far as historical figures happen actually to have dealt with the same essences and the relations between them.

Both kinds of history invoke essences. So much is clear from the tendency of both to speak of the Lockean (or Cartesian, or Aristotelian, or whatever) view as if there were one such view, fixed immutably forever apart from our fleeting attempts to describe it. One kind focuses on the conditions for the instantiation of the view; the other on the view itself. With respect to history of ideas we may well wonder how to determine at what point in his life Locke held the Lockean position. Consider Saul on his way to Damascus. There is a difference between Saul on his horse and Paul, let us call him, struck to the ground. We want to say that on the horse he is a pagan and on the ground a Christian, but in what does his newly acquired Christianity consist? Belief in the Trinity, transubstantiation, the virgin birth, papal infallibility—enough at any rate to keep him from the stake in 1685? We might want to say instead that his conversion consisted not in the acquisition of beliefs (defined faith), but in the acquisition of dispositions to believe (the grace of faith). The determination of what Paul was disposed to believe, however, what he would have believed under later conditions, is the history of much of Christianity with its persecution of heresy. The basis for the persecution of heresy has been the realist conviction that apart from all later attempts at interpretation there was one, ipso facto orthodox set of beliefs to which Paul was disposed.

The sense in which history of philosophy also takes philosophical views to be given and clearly definable is perhaps too obvious to require much comment. This would be the doctrine of fixed discrete essences—the natural kinds Locke impugned by pointing to monsters. I shall, however, draw attention to some consequences of the doctrine for the present inquiry. One might be called the paradox of historical interest. If historians of philosophy were more thoroughly convinced of their realism, they would prize historical texts less for their originality, however great, and more for their alleged truth, however minimal, than they now do. The present canon includes Descartes, most of whose program most of us regard as mistaken, however grandly so, but excludes, say, Cicero, the study of whose work would provide more of what might be taken as true according to both history of ideas as well as history of philosophy. This relates to what might be called the paradox of historical truth. The failure of history of philosophy to yield anything like a consensus on philosophical issues ought to indicate how rare or possibly nonexistent a commodity philosophical truth is in the sense in which it underlies the practice of history of philosophy itself. Plato is right that even the greatest battle is incessant. In the face of this disagreement, joining any philosophical dispute would require the deepest-rooted conviction that one's own position is right—eternally and immutably fixed as such. Skeptical withdrawal seems more reasonable. But instead of the skepticism that realism ought to suggest we find instead the progressive view that history culminates in any given present moment, that understanding or knowledge or whatever always increases over time, that on the whole any given thinker in light of some other thinker's work will do better.[30] I find the success of the view puzzling, for there seems to me no a priori reason for such optimism. In fact, those most inclined toward optimism about intellectual progress, for example Descartes, are inclined to reject the relevance of history; and those in the skeptical tradition, like Erasmus, who most emphasize the significance of history are inclined toward pessimism, viewing history as a holding operation, a means of scraping through. Even with Leibnizean optimism, where everything turns out for the best possible, it may be that our knowledge is diminishing. For we might know as much as we can at any given time, but that might be less than for any previous time. I also find the view disturbing, for it is an essentially conservative, self-justifying enterprise.[31] Historically, such eschatological realism has most frequently been associated with tyrannical persecution and the blockage of research. My citation of Paul is in this regard no less illustrative of the realism assumed by history of philosophy than of that assumed by history of ideas. Beyond what I already said, however, I'll not argue this case and instead turn more explicitly to realism as a philosophy of history.

For one thing, only on the assumption of realism is it at all easy to distinguish history of philosophy from history of ideas. Eternal, immutable, and necessary essences can be the object of the former; a temporal, changing, and contingent realm of the latter. But on the Humpty-Dumpty theory this distinction carries no great epistemic weight. Similarly, the attempt to distinguish them along the lines of the recent internalist-externalist distinction as dealing in the one case with reasons and in the other with causes also rests on the honorific justificatory status of essences. Even granting the distinction in theory I do not see how it can be made in the practice of history. Thus, it may have been that Locke gave

[30] One of course thinks of Hegel as proposing such a view, but it also seems to be the view of less likely recent proponents such as Rorty. See his introduction, with Schneewind and Skinner, esp. pp. 1–2, and his paper "Historiography," esp. p. 31. A more qualified statement of the view is found in Butts, "Methodology," pp. 258–59: "One would hope . . . that such historical work will be deeply evaluative, for one of the things we need to know about science is why, for example, Galilean ways of viewing the world . . . are *better than—are improvements upon*—Aristotelian modes of structuring experience. If [*sic*] we cannot arrive at something like answers to this epistemological/methodological question, there would seem to be little point in regarding the history of science as helpful in understanding science."

[31] Consider Rorty, whose view is that historical knowledge enables us, among other things, to imagine conversations between ourselves and the mighty dead: "We want to be able to see [the history of our race as a long conversational interchange] in order to assure ourselves that there has been rational progress in the course of recorded history—that we differ from our ancestors on grounds which our ancestors could be led to accept. . . . We need to think that, in philosophy as in science, the mighty mistaken dead look down from heaven at our recent successes, and are happy to find that their mistakes have been corrected" ("Historiography," p. 51).

reasons for theism but nonetheless caused others to become atheists. Or conversely. Someone may have repeated verbatim the words we take to express the grounds for theism and yet be caused by them to adopt atheism. Or conversely. It seems to me that those who have invoked this distinction in any of its versions are too inclined to take reasons to be determinants of their own beliefs, or of what they believe would be their beliefs if they held certain other beliefs, and causes to be the determinants of everyone else's beliefs.[32]

Consider a distinction recently drawn that is very similar to that between history of ideas and history of philosophy, namely, historical as opposed to rational reconstruction. In order to do historical reconstruction, which may be philosophically uninteresting but is historically accurate, the following standard must be met: No agent can eventually be said to have meant or done something which he could never be brought to accept as a correct description of what he had meant or done.[33] The idea is that we can attribute to an author only what the author would have accepted in terms of the criteria of description and classification he could have understood. Thus we might historically reconstruct Locke in terms of a Malebranchean, but not a Hegelian, critique of him. But at what point do we draw the line between hypothetically relating the view to Locke or translating it for him, on the one hand, and on the other of offering him a hundred-year philosophy course at the end of which he would understand and accede to the Hegelian description of his view? Or imagine someone who as a matter of fact does not accept an inference, even a very simple one, from what he said. Or who rejects, as G. E. Moore is supposed incredulously to have done on one notable occasion, even a verbatim repetition of what he said. The only difference, it seems to me, between historical and rational reconstruction, or between what Charleton distinguished with respect to our main question as "either downright or oblique and inferrible *Atheistical misapprehensions*,"[34] lies in the relative philosophical sophistication of the latter (a difference due to *our* presumed advances in philosophical argument). The historical-rational reconstruction distinction leads one to take such claims as, given his premises Locke ought to have said there is no God, to be anachronistic in the sense that they are true only for us who realize this is so. From my perspective, however, the claim was true in 1690 of the historical figure Locke. But to make this, *or any other claim about him*, reconstruction or interpretation is necessary. What I

---

[32] Thus I find a bit parochial Laudan's criterion of rationality for the internalist-externalist distinction. Rationality may indeed be defined in terms of progressiveness, that is, problem-solving, but problems are taken, not given, and not everyone takes the same issues to be problems or weights them in the same way. Otherwise, aside from the residual realism in the distinction between history of science itself and writing about history of science (p. 158), which I take to be at odds with the rejection of truth as relevant to problem-solving (p. 24), the account here is much in sympathy with, and I think has benefited from, *Progress and Its Problems*.

[33] This is Quentin Skinner's standard, which Rorty quotes in drawing the historical-rational reconstruction distinction ("Historiography," p. 50).

[34] *Darkness*, to reader, unpaginated.

am suggesting is that there is a metalevel analogue to the battle of the gods and giants. What we say about the historical figure Locke (or anyone else) is like what we say about the world according to Locke. The only constraints in either case are causal as per the tradition of the giants. In neither case are there ontological constraints in the fashion of Plato's Forms that epitomizes the tradition of the gods. At this point philosophy and its history become continuous, and both become continuous with the side of the giants.

§30 HISTORY AND INTERPRETATION

What is it to interpret the past? To reconstruct the whole past, even if it were possible for us to do so, is both too much and too little. Merely to produce the object to be interpreted is not to offer an interpretation of it; *le temps perdu* recovered in its entirety is no more intelligible than *le temps vécu*. But to delete part of the past, to ignore some of the elements known to compose it, as it were, and to interpolate others inferred from what we know, at least partially gives the idea. Not everything that is known to have occurred during the French Revolution is included in every history of it or in any one of them. Nor does every history of the French Revolution assume what is contained in every previous such history. Each is a different version in a sense that no version could ever be complete. But such a conception of history also partially misleads. For it suggests a narrative that depends on a linear ordering of narrative-independent data. Intelligent selection of what to include requires a principle of selection, which constrains the interpretation. But such principles bring with them their own data. The upshot is that history is not a reconstruction of the past; rather, each history is a construction of it de novo.[35]

As literary artifacts there is no difference *at all* between fiction and history.[36] Thus it is not surprising that both appeal to the same canons of credibility. *That*

---

[35] That is, in terms of the absolute ontology of realism. The continuity provided by intertextuality, as people today call the historical dimension of context, is another matter.

[36] For a good discussion of this, see White, *Tropics of Discourse*, esp. chap. 3 and 5. To distinguish history and fiction, White relies on two principles, the latter of which may be a corollary of the former. One is a localization principle: What is real exists at a time and place. The other is an empiricist principle: What is real is perceptible to the senses. These two principles qualify historical but not fictional events as real. "I wish to grant at the outset that *historical events* differ from *fictional events* in the ways that it has been conventional to characterize their differences since Aristotle. Historians are concerned with events which can be assigned to specific time-space locations, events which are (or were) in principle observable or perceivable, whereas imaginative writers—poets, novelists, playwrights—are concerned with both these kinds of events and imagined, hypothetical, or invented ones" (p. 121). But of course novelists also tell us when and where what they describe takes place and what we would have seen had we been there. They may even say that their account is true, that it is a history, that the events it describes are real. In view of this, White's distinction comes to a tautology: History deals with historical events, fiction with fictional ones.

is not the way real people behave (or *think* or *reason*) is an acceptable criticism of a proferred piece of history as well as of fiction. Both must be internally coherent within their own worlds and history must be externally coherent with a larger world as well. But what is written as fiction can cohere, in whatever sense we choose for this term, with the larger world as well. This possibility is but an instance of the general indistinguishability of any two representations that are alleged to differ only in that one is veridical and the other not. Just from the experience itself one cannot tell that one is dreaming or having an hallucination, otherwise one could never be fooled by such an experience. Phenomenologically, as reality is the fiction of which we are a part, so it is also the dream of which we are a part.

This is but another of the many instances that show that history poses no special epistemological problems. The saw that the past is gone and beyond knowing except through theoretical reconstruction cuts (as it were!) against virtually all knowledge. Consider just the time-gap argument. Nothing very likely exists in its perceived state as it does in its actual state because of the time-gap between them. The most spectacular case is that of stars, which we now see as they were millions of years ago, so long ago in fact that when we see them they may no longer exist. It is perhaps another question whether what we now see is therefore some proxy for those stars—sense data, ideas, or whatever that now exist and thus satisfy the requirement of Malebranche and many others that only what exists can be perceived. Less questionable is the, at least minimal, theorizing, or construction if you will, that is going on even in so simple a case as a present sense perception.

The realization that history is not that of which we give an account but the account itself relieves some of the pressure of the main question of this chapter. Whether Locke was *really* an atheist quite apart from any account of what he said is one that invites metaphysical realism. Without realism we can ask the same question, but its import is circumscribed by a certain context. It may be, for example, the query whether all the documents of a certain kind have been examined; but it is not the question whether apart from documents (or evidence of every kind) Locke had a certain characteristic. Thus the biblical injunction *judge not* is very paradoxical: In the metaphysically strong sense neither Locke nor anyone else *can* be judged; in every other sense we can do nothing but judge. I shall not insist on this little piece of exegesis.[37] A more relevant text in any case would be, *by their deeds ye shall know them*, which in the spirit I am proposing it need not be an instance of behaviorism. Once realism is rejected, an author's intentions can harmlessly be reintroduced, for they along with

---

[37] One might consider, however, what the rejection of metaphysical realism does to Arnauld's distinction between *questions de fait* and *questions de droit*. Arnauld held that in condemning the Five Propositions taken to be definitive of Jansenism, Pope Innocent X had acted infallibly, but that what he condemned was always open to fallible interpretation. See my "Jansenism," esp. pp. 303–05.

everything else we may wish to talk about are products of interpretation. (Indeed, we ourselves, no less than the rest of our worlds, are our own creations.[38]) But that intention is not a hidden fact, absolutely given. To see the difference, consider: That the meaning of a text is the author's intention is itself just a theory of meaning. With all intention construed as interpretation, it is not at all paradoxical to say that we can know and express better what Locke meant than he could. Thus too can we often come to know what we mean by something only after we have said it. From this point of view the various hypotheses we have looked at (dissimulation, nodding-Locke, etc.) are not just explanations of Locke's failure to be clearer, but also indications that no text by itself is clear.

Contrary to the nominalist-relativist line here being suggested, the realist distinguishes two senses of history: one is the written version; the other is what is written about. Putting it so of course shows that the issue is the most general one of the relation between thought, theory or language on the one hand and reality on the other. To save, or at least postpone, another book, we can turn again to Plato, whose account is once again quintessentially relevant and compelling.

Cratylus (384d) addresses the question whether "there is no name given to anything by nature; [whether] all is convention and habit of users."[39] Socrates's argument begins with a rejection of relativism. While names may be relative to different peoples or to different individuals, the things they name do not differ as the names do—"they have a permanent essence of their own." "If what appears to each man is true to him, one man cannot in reality be wiser than another." Thus things "are not in relation to us, or influenced by us, fluctuating according to our fancy, but they are independent, and maintain to their own essence the relation prescribed by nature" (386d–c). Actions too are real (cutting, for example), and are performed according to a proper nature with the proper instrument (a knife, for example). Now, speaking, specifically naming, is an action and ought to be done according to a natural process. The instrument of naming is the name, by which we convey information and distinguish things according to their natures. The logically proper name, as we would say, is the work of the legislator who, unlike the arbitrary sovereign of Hobbes's theory, is directed by the dialectician to put the true names of things into sound. For these names truth is a matter of their imitation of, or likeness to what they name. The sound is the material instantiation of the name and may vary from one natural language to another as a suitable knife may be made from either of two different metals. In the cases of both the name and the knife, their suitability as instru-

---

[38] It seems to me that those who have argued the equivalence of act and rule utilitarianism have tended to regard actions as metaphysically real. Overlooked is the Berkeleian point that only what can be conceptualized is relevant for moral evaluation. See my "Rules and Relevance."

[39] This dialogue, it seems to me, is central to Plato's thought and in any case is hardly "a medly of merry pranks." (Friedlaender, *Plato*, p. 32).

ments is grounded in objective, independent essences in so far as the imitation is gotten right.[40]

What this theory means is that theories, including historical accounts, are not invented but discovered, not created ex nihilo but come upon already fashioned. This should cause no surprise; it is the theory of all knowledge conveyed by the doctrine of reminiscence, according to which all coming to know is a matter of making explicit what is already implicit. The historian, like any teacher or seeker after truth, is no more than the instrument of what he brings us to know. In history of ideas we are brought to see the likeness between what we say about the facts composing the past and those facts. The appeal of a cinematographic model here is obvious—the true theory is the accurate newsreel of what happened. What is perhaps less obvious, of course, is why even if we were there at the original rather than at the filmed version of it our understanding of it would be any better. (Even *You Are There* consisted for the most part of interviews with the relevant personages, not bare pictures of what they did.) In history of philosophy, on the other hand, at least this question is answered, for we get delivered to us the essence of what we are inquiring about. True words instantiate, indeed *are* the very essence they denote.[41]

History, so the slogan goes, is the truth about the past. But if we accept the Humpty-Dumpty theory of truth, then the truth about the past comes into being only when we speak it. We must reject the cinematographic theory of truth about the past according to which the past consists of a set of facts from among which it is the historian's job to select those that support the theory answering the questions that pursue him. Too, we must reject the discovery theory of theories about the past, according to which it is the historian's job to *come upon* that theory that answers his questions.[42] Theories, no less what they are about, are our creations.

How then are we to avoid making all history mere propaganda? What is to prevent people from just falsifying the record? In one sense propaganda, indeed political propaganda, cannot be avoided. If any realist thinks that a history can be without practical implications, including specifically political ones, indeed if he thinks that *any theory at all* can be without them, he should consult either of the arch-realists Plato or Marx, who theorized precisely because there always

---

[40] The dialogue is typical in its argument by way of appeal to the moral and intellectual superiority of the interlocutors: Only if value is objective, Socrates and Hermogenes agree, can some people (namely, they themselves) be better than others. Furthermore, the dialogue lays down conditions only for the ideal language. But because the original giver of the names comprising natural language might not have gotten it right, natural language is not to be trusted. It is better to attend to the things themselves, which as far as this dialogue is explicitly concerned, may be fixed or (as Heraclitus thought) flow. Once this detail is made explicit, the dialectician emerges as the only one capable of appreciating the truth of language.

[41] Cassirer's logico-anthropological thesis about the origins of language and myth deserves consideration here. See *Language*, esp. pp. 48–49.

[42] The etymology of 'invent' is misleading us here.

are these implications. The disinterested search for objective truth is a reflection of no more than the attitude of the seeker, whose dispassion leads him to delusion. As to falsification, this even on the realist view happens all the time, at least in the sense that what is false gets expressed, even and especially in the natural sciences, whose history is comprised primarily if not entirely by what is false. The real issue here is the question in agent-morality as to the character of the theorist. Someone who either deliberately ignores or fabricates evidence on behalf of a theory is properly held to be morally reprehensible. But such behavior says nothing, except in a loose and contingent way, about the worthiness of his theory. Indeed, even what is true can be offered in bad faith as evidence on behalf of an indefensible theory. Consider the first mate who when unusually called upon to make the day's entry in the ship's log noticed the specific days previously on which the captain had entered that the mate was drunk; the mate's entry: Today the captain was sober. We do not need an objective fact of the matter to recover the sense in which the mate is having us on. Nor do we in distinguishing history written in bad faith.[43] The moral issue between realism and its rejection is not truth but responsibility. On the nominalist view, people are responsible not just for their choices but for the world in which they make them. This is a terrifying thought. It would be much easier if the world and theories of it were given as Plato thought so that there might be experts with real knowledge of it who could tell us what to believe and do. Thus the perennial lure of Platonic paternalism.

The methodological upshot of this epistemological stance is that this work may well be regarded as a history of philosophy from 1655 to 1715—*a* history of philosophy, not, as such works are sometimes styled, *the* history of philosophy. *The* history of philosophy cannot be, for there are infinitely many such histories. Even so, my own principle of selection and thus the warrant for my history may well be questioned. While just about everyone in the seventeenth century of philosophical interest by our standards is a part of the battle of the gods and giants, not even all the major figures are here discussed at all in detail. The roles of Hobbes and Spinoza, for example, might especially call for elaboration, given the significance of reductio ad absurdum arguments in the period. But so much has been written about them that so much would have to be

---

[43] McCullagh seems to think that realism is the only safeguard of history against degeneration into propaganda. This view is not to be despised; Plato held it with respect to all knowledge claims. But McCullagh should have read White: "if historians were to recognize the fictive element in their narratives, this would not mean the degradation of historiography to the status of ideology or propaganda. In fact, this recognition would serve as a potent antidote to the tendency of historians to become captive of ideological preconceptions which they do not recognize as such but honour as the 'correct' perception of 'the way things *really* are.' By drawing historiographically nearer to its origins in literary sensibility, we should be able to identify the ideological, because it is the fictive, element in our own discourse" (*Tropics of Discourse*), p. 99). It seems to me that White has it exactly right. Realism, rather than its rejection, leads to propaganda, that is, the intolerant imposition of one's views on others by whatever means necessary.

written here to establish anything beyond the obvious place, indicated above, of Hobbes among the giants and Spinoza among the gods. For others, like Pascal and especially Leibniz, there is the opposite problem. Their position depends so much on controversial interpretation that again the reasonable confines of a work such as this would be pressed. His own role apart, Leibniz at least shows up as a contemporary historian of the battle itself. He saw the two camps and their principal leaders, and he saw the systematic significance of their respective stances concerning sufficient reason. But beyond that, I have confined my detailed treatment to those principal leaders on the interpretation of whom hangs the significance of the interpretation of all the rest. To expect much more is perhaps anyway to succumb to the realist temptation of a total picture of an individual or period. On the nominalist view, pictures can be more or less complete, but their difference in value, if there is one, is not with respect to truth but to understanding. I could say more here about the period that I take to be true, but the addenda would likely not improve upon this, my best attempt at conveying my understanding of the period.

With the rejection of realism we seem to sacrifice the basis for both philosophical and historical knowledge as the outcome of a historical approach to philosophy. One may well ask, if history is creation, invention, or construction, rather than discovery, recovery, or reconstruction, then why bother? Indeed, it may well be asked whether in calling a piece of writing history or historical knowledge we are not just deluded. These of course are Plato's questions to the Sophists. At the methodological level, if the Sophists are right, the questions have no point. We go on writing history, and theorizing generally, as before. The interesting sense in which Nature here breaks the skeptic is not that his assent cannot be withheld but that skepticism at this level makes no direct practical difference. I shall return to this in a bit. At the metaphysical level, however, where the stakes are ultimate justification, the realist's questions are as pointed as any. Because there are no Forms we can never arrive at the ultimate truth either about the relations between them or about their instantiations. Both kinds of historical realism go by the boards. To this the only response is that of the traditional skeptic, namely, that history itself goes bail for knowledge of the Forms. This can be understood in two senses. One is a matter of advocating historical knowledge as a substandard surrogate for real knowledge of the Forms. The familiar position is that because we possess only sensory knowledge and such knowledge is relative, we have no knowledge of the proper object of knowledge, which is absolute. To deal with the practical exigencies of life we do best to rely on the tried if not true way of doing things. Moreover, even if the skeptical tradition had to await Berkeley's enunciation of the full extent of this philosophy of living, this applies as much to that part of life called physics as it does to medicine. What we get is not real knowledge but the pale image of truth, namely, probability (*vraisemblance*).

There is a second sense, however, in which historical knowledge emerges as a substitute for real knowledge. Here there is no nostalgic appeal to what cannot be. Instead, history is regarded as the ongoing communal creation, the activity which defines us as a species. History in this sense is ipso facto the history of our kind, by definition the widest possible account of human experience. It may well be that such a sense of history at least partly underlay Gassendi's near maniacal citation of previous authors. (That Gassendi or any giant should be made to advocate the Hegelian view that all knowledge is in principle historical should not, however, lead us to overlook the worlds that separate the different views of history itself.)

This indicates another sense of the two Platonic questions as to whether there is any recoverable sense of a genuine history. Especially in light of such worries as the time-gap argument, what makes a piece of writing historical as opposed to anything else? I am not sure there is an answer to this question. Certainly I have none; nor am I convinced even that it is a very important question. I shall deal with it, however, to the extent of commenting on the relevance of the material from Strutt, Flemyng, Carroll, and other such characters in arguing my case about Locke. What mad manner of modern Gassendism is this, it might be asked, to cite and take seriously such insignificant thinkers? At the object level these citations are illustrations and to some extent arguments for my interpretation of Locke; they are indications of how people were thinking and how language was being used. But the interpretations themselves, despite having been articulated by Strutt, Flemyng, Carroll, et al., are our interpretations. Not, as the realist would have it, in that we along with each of these people discovered or invented or plugged into the same various theories, which were in the theory-magazine waiting for us to come along. Their theories are ours in that it is according to us that each of these people held the theory they did. There are no nontheoretical theory-holders any more than there are particulars existing characterized in a given way apart from any conception of them. This extension of the Berkeleian position to conceptualizers themselves is, as Hume partly showed, a natural one. But a piece of proferred history according to just our theory, which does not include as a part of it the construction of other people's theories, especially those of historical figures, is not likely to be taken as history, even by those who at the metalevel regard historical figures and their theories as constructions. For it is under this rubric that the whole of testimony falls, whether about events such as battles or theories such as Locke's on substance. What beyond this pragmatically necessary condition might be required for history is not clear to me. I reckon that what I have done here suffices for history, but at this point in my argument it does not much matter to me. Despite this attitude, or perhaps because of it, it does matter very much that it be taken in *some* sense, and I shall now conclude with a general argument on behalf of toleration.

Both history of philosophy and history of ideas regard the text as primary—not just in the sense that the text is the principal datum, but that its recovery or reconstruction is the goal. The difference is that the reconstruction in the former domain is in philosophical terms with a philosophical purpose. One takes a text that is for whatever reason obscure and elucidates it in such a way that we learn something of philosophical value from it, either because what it is then revealed as saying is true or, more typically, as false. History of ideas, on the other hand, attempts to reconstruct the text in terms of the historical circumstances of its production, propagation, and reception. The aim is to recover the text in terms of a theory that is true about the past, quite independently of whether what took place in the past is philosophically true or false. In both domains the text is the primary given and is given as metaphysically absolute. According to the one it is a Platonic entity whose meaning is fixed independently of interpretation, and according to the other it is an historical object whose existence is fixed independently of interpretation.

The metaphysically absolute status of the text has been rejected in no uncertain terms lately by a number of literary theorists, largely on recognizable philosophical grounds.[44] Consider the following attempt to draw the fact-fiction distinction, or more precisely, the distinction between serious or normal discourse and fictional or literary discourse, as a distinction between the relationship each bears, not to the world, but to its users. Serious discourse is or pretends to be part of the standard story,

> a story in relation to which we are not tellers (and therefore free to approve or reject it) but characters, simultaneously enabled and limited by the ways of thinking and seeing it constrains. While the world given by the standard story is no less a construed one than the world of a novel or a play, for those who speak from within it (and indeed as extensions of it) the facts of that world will be as obvious and inescapable as one could wish. In short, the standard story and the world it delivers rest on a bedrock of belief, and even if that bedrock were challenged, it would be so from the vantage point of a belief (and a world) that had already taken its place."[45]

This view is very close to that of Carnap in "Empiricism, Semantics and Ontology." Like Carnap's linguistic frameworks, stories here are constituted by rules. The justification of the rules is independent of an order of reality of which the story would be true, for there is never a possibility of such an order. Rather, the stories bring with them their world. For Carnap, to accept the thing world, for example, "means nothing more than to accept rules for forming statements and for testing, accepting or rejecting them" (p. 73). One might then go on to argue that the evidentiary procedures of the standard story cannot be used "to prove its fidelity to some supraconventional reality,"[46] namely, that the procedures themselves are perforce a part of the story. In addition, choice of a story or

---

[44] The people I have in mind here are best represented by Stanley Fish, who argues a relativism very close to that of Nelson Goodman in *Worldmaking*.

[45] Fish, *Interpretive Communities*, p. 199.

[46] Fish, *Interpretive Communities*, p. 239.

of a framework is grounded in pure praxis and the only mechanism of change is persuasion. The difference is only one of interest and degree between, on the one hand Carnap's construal of the phenomenalist-realist debate, for example, as the debate concerning whether a phenomenalist or a realist language better serves the needs of physics, and, on the other hand, the construal of the debates between critics as debates concerning strategies "not for reading but for writing texts, for constituting their properties . . . these [interpretive] strategies exist prior to the act of reading and therefore determine the shape of what is read rather than, as is usually assumed, the other way round" (p. 14). What begins as a problem about texts ends as an implicit but no less fully blown metaphysics, for what is said here about texts can be said about everything: "It is often assumed that literary theory presents a set of problems whose shape remains unchanging and in relation to which our critical procedures are found to be more or less adequate; that is, the field of inquiry stands always ready to be interrogated by the questions it itself contains . . . however, the relationship is exactly the reverse: the field of inquiry is *constituted* by the questions we are able to ask because the entities that populate it come into being as the presuppositions— they are discourse specific entities—of those questions" (p.1).

How does relativizing the text help with respect to my problem concerning the interpretation of Locke? In one sense it does not help at all. Even with a relativized text, it will be primarily by appeal to the text that realists and I will discuss the correctness of my interpretation. That is, even if historical accounts are no longer regarded as pictures of either eternal forms on the one hand or of temporal facts on the other, but instead as effectively creating what they are supposed to picture, there is no other touchstone but the text for the acceptability of a historical account. This is to say that the thesis I have been arguing makes no methodological difference—relativizing the text has no direct relevance to the ways of doing history of philosophy. To think otherwise is to assume the metaphysical absolutism of the realists, namely, that we can reconstruct Neurath's ship at sea, or even provide an argument for doing so, from a position elsewhere than on the ship itself.

On the other hand, the failure of Locke's position to be obvious except in terms of an interpretation, one that incidentally is highly contentious, is not a special problem because nothing is obvious, nothing at all, except in terms of interpretation. More generally, revisions of interpretation at the object-level that do not also involve revisions of interpretive strategies at the metalevel are less interesting. This is the difference between history and chronicle. Thus, altering the metaphysics of the history of philosophy in favor of relativism does have an indirect bearing on how it might be evaluated, for it suggests a certain principle of toleration that may be of great heuristic value. The soundness of arguments with respect to the proper interpretation of a text remains unaffected because unaddressed; this is the methodological indifference of my thesis. But the significance of their soundness, of the arguments themselves, is very much affected. Carnap, in the work just referred to and in his earlier *Logical Syntax of Language*, developed a principle of tolerance, the idea that as long as the speaker speaks clearly, that is, specifies his syntactical rules, no language is intrinsically prohibitable, and that reasons for speaking one language rather than another can be put only in terms of, for example, the efficiency, fruitfulness, and simplicity of doing so. This tolerance is made possible by the lack of a single world specifiable apart from language that would discriminate against all but a single language appropriate to it. And as Carnap and others relativized ontology to language, so has language itself been relativized. What this means for history is that there should be no temptation to specify even a Lockean language L, and still less to justify it once and for all, as that language that, quite apart from our language by which we now realize the fact, Locke spoke. Taking this tack I would advance my interpretation of Locke as simpler, more efficient, and more fruitful, as more *interesting* than the history of philosophy that concerns, for example, only the primary-secondary quality distinction or the history of ideas that wonders whom Locke had in mind in his attack on innate ideas. To be sure, this is a proof-of-the-pudding argument; yet the reason even for considering it is the same toleration at the metalevel that Locke urged at the object level. But if we take toleration seriously in the fashion of the giants, that might be the only kind of reason. More generally, it seems to me the lesson here is that thinking about history, including history of philosophy, raises no special philosophical problems, that the same, and only the same, problems of meaning, truth, and reference, arise concerning it as arise elsewhere.[47]

---

[47] If I read her correctly, this result may be a way of expressing what Joy offers as the view of Gassendi's that opens a reading of the whole of his work.

Works Cited

Aaron, R. I., *John Locke*. 2d ed. Oxford: Clarendon Press, 1965.

Aaron, R. I., and Jocelyn Gibb, eds. *An Early Draft of Locke's Essay together with Excerpts from His Journals*. Oxford: Clarendon Press, 1936.

Actes du congrès tricentennaire de Pierre Gassendi. Digne: R. Vial, 1957.

Acworth, Richard. "Locke's First Reply to John Norris," *Locke Newsletter* 2 (Summer 1971).

———.*The Philosophy of John Norris of Bemerton (1657–1712)*. Hildesheim: Georg Olms, 1979.

Adam, Antoine. "L'influence de Gassendi sur le mouvement des idées à la fin du XVIIe siècle," In *Actes du congrès du tricentennaire*, pp. 5–11.

Alcover, M. *La pensée philosophique et scientifique de Cyrano de Bergerac*. Paris/Geneva: Droz, 1970.

Alexander, Peter. "Boyle and Locke on Primary and Secondary Qualities." *Ratio* 16 (1974). Reprinted in ed. I. C. Tipton. *Locke on Human Understanding*, Oxford: Oxford University Press, 1977.

———. *Ideas, Qualities and Corpuscles: Locke and Boyle on the External World* Cambridge: Cambridge University Press: 1985.

Alquié, Ferdinand. *Le Cartésianisme de Malebranche*. Paris: Vrin, 1974.

Anderson, F. H. "Locke and the Polemic against Cartesian Philosophy: Causality and Cognition." In *Proceedings of the Seventh International Congress of Philosophy*. London: Oxford University Press, 1930.

Armstrong, D. M. *What Is a Law of Nature?* Cambridge: Cambridge University Press, 1983.

Arnauld, A. *Des vrayes et des fausses idées, contre ce qu'enseigne l'auteur de la recherche de la vérité*. 1683. In *Oeuvres*, vol. 38.

———. *Oeuvres*. Paris, 1775–83.

Arnauld, A., and P. Nicole. *L'art de penser (Port-Royal Logic)*. 1662. In *Oeuvres*, vol. 41.

Aubert de Versé, Noel. *L'impie convaincu, ou dissertation contre Spinosa*. Amsterdam, 1684.

d'Aubignac, Abbé François Hedelin. *Discours au roy sur l'establissement d'une seconde Academie dans la Ville de Paris*. Paris, 1664.

Augustine, Saint. *De Civitate Dei*, ed. J. Stoer. Geneva, 1622.

———. *Concerning the City of God Against the Pagans*, trans. H. Bettenson. Harmondsworth: Penguin, 1972.

———. *The Confessions*, trans. Edward B. Pusey. New York: Washington Square Press, 1952.

———. *Opera*, ed. J.-P. Migne. Paris, 1841–42.

Ayers, Michael. "Are Locke's 'Ideas' Images, Intentional Objects or Natural Signs?" *Locke Newsletter* 17 (1986): 3–36.

————. "Locke's Doctrine of Abstraction: Some Aspects of Its Historical and Philosophical Significance." In *John Locke: Symposium Wolfenbuttel 1979*, ed. Reinhard Brandt. Berlin: Walter de Gruyter, 1981.

————. "Locke's Logical Atomism," Dawes Hicks Lecture 1981. *Proceedings of the British Academy* (1981): 211–25.

————. "Locke versus Aristotle on Natural Kinds." *Journal of Philosophy* 78 (1981): 247–72.

Babin, François. *Journal ou relation fidelle de tout ce qui s'est passé dans l'université d'Angers au sujet de la philosophie de Descartes, en execution des ordres du Roy, pendant les années 1675, 1676, 1677, 1678.* N.p., 1679.

Baillet, A. *La vie de M. Des-Cartes.* Paris, 1691.

Baker, Thomas. *Reflections upon learning, wherin is shewn the insufficiency thereof . . . in order to evince the usefulness and necessity of revelation.* London, 1699.

Balz, Albert G. A. *Cartesian Studies.* New York: Columbia University Press, 1951.

Balzac, Guez de *Oeuvres.* 2 vols. Paris, 1665.

Bayle, François. *The General System of the Cartesian Philosophy*, Englished out of French. London, 1670. Published with *A Discourse written to a learned Frier by M. Des Fourneillis* [Cordemoy], *shewing that the system of M. Descartes, and particularly his opinion concerning brutes does contain nothing dangerous*; . . .

Bayle, Pierre. *Dictionnaire historique et critique*, ed. P. Desmaizeaux. 4th ed. Amsterdam, 1730.

————. *Receuil de quelques pièces curieuses concernant la philosophie de Monsieur Descartes.* Amsterdam, 1684.

————. *Lettres choisies.* Rotterdam, 1974.

————. *Oeuvres.* La Haye, 1727–31.

————. *Oeuvres diverses.* La Haye, 1737.

Beaude, J. "Cartésianisme et anticartésianisme de Desgabets." *Studia Cartesiana* 1 (1979): 1–24.

Bennett, J., and P. Remnant. "How Matter Might at First Be Made." *Canadian Journal of Philosophy*, supp. 4 (1978): 1–11.

Bergmann, Gustav. "Synthetic *a priori*." In his *Logic and Reality*. Madison: University of Wisconsin Press, 1964.

Berkeley, George. *The Works of.* ed. A Luce and T. Jessop. Edinburgh, 1947–58.

Bernier, F. *Abrégé de la philosophie de Mr. Gassendi.* Protoversions, Paris, 1674 and 1675; 1st ed., Lyons, 1678; 2d ed., Lyons, 1684.

————. *Doutes . . . sur quelques-uns des principaux chapitres de son Abrégé. . . .* Paris, 1682.

————. *Lettre envoyée de Chiras en Perse le 10 juin 1668. . . .* Paris, 1671.

————. *Lettre à monsieur Chapelain, envoyée de Chiras en Perse le 4 octobre 1667. . . .* Paris, 1671.

————. *Requeste des maistres ès arts. . . .* Delphe [*sic* Paris], 1671.

Bigourdan, G. "Les premières sociétés scientifiques de Paris au XVIIe siècle"; "Les premières réunions savantes de Paris au XVIIe siècle."*Comptes rendus hebdomadaires des séances de l'Académie des Sciences* 164 (1917).

Bloch, Olivier René. "Gassendi critique de Descartes." *Revue philosophique de la*

France et de l'Etranger 156 (1966): 217–36.

———. *La philosophie de Gassendi: Nominalisme, matérialisme, et métaphysique.* The Hague: Martinus Nijhoff, 1971.

———. "Pierre Gassendi," "Schüler und Anhänger von Gassendi (1.Einleitung, 2.Cyrano). In *Gundriss der Geschichte der Philosophie begrundet von Friedrich Ueberweg.* Basel: Schwabe, forthcoming.

Bolton, M. B. "Locke on Substance Ideas and the Determination of Natural Kinds: A Reply to Mattern." *Locke Newsletter* 19 (1988): 17–45.

———. "The Origins of Locke's Doctrine of Primary and Secondary Qualities." *Philosophical Quarterly* 26 (1976): 305–16.

Bonno, Gabriel. *Les relations intellectuelles de Locke avec la France,* University of California Publications in Modern Philology, 38, no.2, (1955) 37–264.

Bougerel, J. *Vie de Pierre Gassendi.* Paris, 1737.

Bouillier, Francisque. *Histoire de la philosophie cartésienne.* 3d ed. Paris, 1868.

Boyle, Robert. *The Works.* London, 1772.

Bourdelot, Abbé. *Conversations de l'Académie de M. l'abbé Bourdelot.* Paris, 1672.

Bourne, H. R. Fox. *The Life of John Locke.* London, 1876.

Bracken, Harry M. "Substance in Berkeley." In *New Studies in Berkeley's Philosophy,* ed. W. Steinkraus. New York: Holt, Rinehart and Winston, 1966.

———. "Some Problems of Substance among the Cartesians." *American Philosophical Quarterly* 1, no. 2 (April 1964): 129–37.

———. *Mind and Language: Essays on Descartes and Chomsky.* Dordrecht: Foris, 1984.

Brehier, Emile "The Creation of the Eternal Truths in Descartes's System." In *Descartes: A Collection of Critical Essays,* ed. Willis Doney. Garden City, N.Y.: Doubleday, 1967.

Brown, Harcourt *L'Académie de physique de Caen.* Caen: C. Le Tendre, 1938.

———. *Scientific Organizations in Seventeenth Century France (1620–1680).* Baltimore: Williams and Wilkins, 1934.

Browne, Peter. *The Procedure, extent, and limits of human understanding.* London, 1728.

Brundell, Barry. *Pierre Gassendi: From Aristotelianism to a New Philosophy.* Dordrecht: D. Reidel, 1987.

Brush, Craig B., trans. *The Selected Works of Pierre Gassendi.* New York: Johnson Reprint, 1972.

Budé, E. de. *Vie de Jean-Robert Chouet.* Geneva, 1899.

Burnell, A. C. "On Some Early References to the Vedas by European Writers." *The Indian Antiquary* 8 (1879): 98–100.

Burnet, John. *Greek Philosophy from Thales to Plato.* London: Macmillan, 1962. First published 1914.

Burthogge, Richard. *Causa Dei: or an apology for God.* London, 1675.

———. *An Essay upon reason, and the nature of spirits.* London, 1694.

———. *Organum Vetus & Novum: Or, A discourse of reason and truth wherein the natural logic common to mankinde is briefly and plainly described.* London, 1678.

Butler, R. J. *Cartesian Studies.* Oxford: Basil Blackwell, 1972.

Butts, R. E. *Kant and the Double Government Methodology: Supersensibility and Method in Kant's Philosophy of Science.* Dordrecht: D. Reidel, 1984.

——. "Methodology and the Functional Identity of Science and Philosophy." In *Pisa Conference Proceedings,* ed. J. Hintikka, et al. Dordrecht: D. Reidel, 1980.

Carnap, R. "Empiricism, Semantics, and Ontology." in *The Linguistic Turn,* ed. R. Rorty. Chicago: University of Chicago Press, 1967.

Carroll, Robert Todd. *The Common-sense Philosophy of Religion of Bishop Edward Stillingfleet: 1635–1699.* The Hague: Martinus Nijhoff, 1975.

Carroll, William. *A Dissertation upon the tenth chapter of the fourth book of Mr. Locke's Essay concerning human understanding, wherein that author's endeavours to establish Spinoza's atheistical hypothesis, more especially in that tenth chapter, are discovered and confronted. To which is subjoin'd; a short account of the sense wherein the titles of, and the reasonings in the following penicious books, are to be understood, viz. The Reasonableness of Christianity. Christianity not mysterious. The Rights of the Christian Church, & c. As also, how that sense and those reasonings are bottom'd, upon the hypothesis establish'd in the said Essay of human understanding.* London, 1706.

Casaubon, Meric, *On Learning.* in Michael R. G. Spiller, "*Concerning Natural Experimental Philosophie,*" pp 195–217. The Hague: Martinus Nijhoff, 1980.

Cassirer, E. *Language and Myth.* New York: Harper, 1946.

Castonnet des Fosses, H. *Lettres de François Bernier.* Angers, 1890.

Caton, Hiram. "Analytic History of Philosophy: The Case of Descartes." *The Philosophical Forum* 12 (1981): 273–94.

——. "Will and Reason in Descartes's Theory of Error." *Journal of Philosophy* 72 (February 27, 1975): 87–104.

Chanet, Pierre. *Traite de l'esprit de l'homme et de ses fonctions.* Paris, 1649.

——. *Esclaircissement de quelques difficultez touchant la connoissance de l'imagination.* La Rochelle, 1648.

——. *De l'instinct et de la connoissance des animaux. . . .* La Rochelle, 1646.

——. *Considerations sur la sagesse de Charon* [sic] Paris, 1643.

Chapelain, J. *Lettres,* ed. Ph. Tamizey de Larroque. Paris, 1880–83.

Charleton, Walter. *Physiologia Epicuro-Gassendo-Charletoniana, Or a Fabricke of Science Natural, Upon the hypothesis of Atoms, founded by Epicurus, repaired by Petrus Gassendus, augmented by Walter Charleton.* London, 1654; New York and London: Johnson Reprint, 1966.

Chaudon, Louis-Mayeul. *Nouveau dictionnaire. . . .* Amsterdam, 1766.

Cicero. *De natura deorum,* trans. H. Rackham. Cambridge: Harvard University Press, 1956.

Clarke, Samuel. *A Discourse concerning the being and attributes of God. . . .* 6th ed. London, 1725.

Clatterbaugh, Kenneth C. "Descartes's Likeness Principle." *Philosophical Review* 89 (1980):379–402.

Collas, G. *Jean Chapelain.* Paris, 1912.

Collins, Anthony. *A Discourse of Free-Thinking.* London, 1713.

Condorcet, Marquis de. *Eloges des académiciens.* Paris, 1778.

Connell, D. "Cureau de La Chambre, source de Malebranche." *Recherches sur le XVIIe siècle* (Cahiers de l'Equipe de recherches 75 du Centre d'histoire des sciences et des doctrines du C.N.R.S., dirigée par A. Robinet), pp. 158–72. Paris, 1978.

————. "Malebranche et la scholastique." *Les études philosophiques* (1974): 449–63.

————. *The Vision of God: Malebranche's Scholastic Sources*. Louvain, 1967.

Cook, Monte. "Arnauld's Alleged Representationalism." *Journal of the History of Philosophy* 12 (1974): 179–95.

Cordemoy, Gérauld de. *Oeuvres philosophiques*, ed. Pierre Clair and François Girbal. Paris: Presses Universitaires de France, 1968.

Cornford, Francis M. *Plato's Theory of Knowledge*. Indianapolis: Bobbs Merrill, 1957. First published 1934.

Corpus Hermeticum, ed. A. D. Nock and A.-J. Festugière. 2d ed. Paris, 1960.

Cousin, Victor. *Fragments philosophiques*. Paris, 3d ed. 1838, 4th ed. 1848, 5th ed. 1866.

Coward, William. *Grand Essay, or a Vindication of Reason*. London, 1704.

Cranston, Maurice. *John Locke: A Biography*. London: Longmans, 1957.

Cudworth, Ralph. *A Treatise Concerning Eternal and Immutable Morality*. London, 1731.

————. *The True Intellectual System of the Universe*. . . . London, 1678.

Cureau de la Chambre, M. *L'art de connôistre les hommes: partie troisième qui contient la deffense de l'extension & des parties libres de l'ame*. Paris, 1666.

————. *Les caracteres des passions*. 5 vols. Paris, 1640–62.

————. *La lumiere*. Paris, 1657.

————. *Nouvelles pensées sur les causes de la lumière, du débordement du Nil et de l'amour d'inclination*. Paris, 1634.

————. *Quelle est la connoissance des bestes, et iusques où elle peut aller*. Published at the end of *Les caracteres des passions*. Vol. 2 Paris, 1645. Also, with consecutive pagination, at the end of the Amsterdam edition of 1658.

————. *Le systeme de l'ame*. Paris, 1664.

————. *Traité de la connoissance des animaux*. . . . Paris, 1662. 1st ed. 1648.

Cyrano de Bergerac, Savinien de. *Voyage dans la lune* (L'autre monde ou les etats et empires de la lune), ed. Maurice Laugaa. Paris: Garnier-Flammarion, 1970.

Damiron, J.-Ph. *Essai sur la philosophie en France au XVIIe siècle*. Paris, 1846.

Daniel, G. *Voyage du monde de Descartes*. Paris, 1711. 1st ed. 1690.

Descartes, R. *Philosophical Letters*, trans. A. Kenny. Oxford: Clarendon Press, 1970.

————. *Meditations on First Philosophy in Which the Existence of God and the Distinction of the Soul from the Body Are Demonstrated*, trans. D. A. Cress. Indianapolis: Hackett, 1979.

————. *Oeuvres*, ed. V. Cousin. Paris, 1824–26.

————. *Oeuvres*, ed. C. Adam and P. Tannery. 1st ed. 1897–1913; 2d ed., CNRS, Paris: Vrin, 1964–75.

————. *Oeuvres philosophiques*, ed. F. Alquié. Paris: Editions Garnier Frères, 1963.

————. *The Philosophical Works*, trans. E. S. Haldane and G. R. T. Ross. Cambridge: Cambridge University Press, 1968. 1st ed., 1911.

————. *The Philosophical Writings*, trans. J. Cottingham, R. Stoothoff, and D. Murdoch. Cambridge: Cambridge University Press, 1985.

————. *Principles of Philosophy*, trans. V. R. Miller and R. P. Miller. Dordrecht: D. Reidel, 1983.

Desgabets, Robert. *Oeuvres philosophiques inédites*, ed. J. Beaude. *Analecta Cartesiana* 2 (1983).

Dewhurst, Kenneth. *John Locke (1632–1704) Physician and Philosopher: A Medical Biography, with an Edition of the Medical Notes in His Journals*. London: Wellcome Historical Medical Library, 1963.

Digby, Kenelm. *Two treatises*. . . . Paris, 1653.

Dijksterhuis, E. J. *The Mechanization of the World Picture*, trans. C. Dikshoorn. Oxford: Oxford University Press, 1961.

Ditton, Humphrey. *Matter not a Cogitative Substance: Or, the True State of the Case About Matter's Thinking: with Considerations and Reflections thereon, tending to the compleat settling of that Point*. Printed in 1713, published as an addendum to *The New Law of Fluids*. . . . London, 1714.

Dourtous de Mairan, J. J. *Eloges des academiciens*. Paris, 1742.

Dretske, F. *Knowledge and the Flow of Information*. Cambridge: MIT Press, 1981.

Driscoll, E. A. "The Influence of Gassendi on Locke's Hedonism." *International Philosophical Quarterly* 12 (1972): 87–110.

Duchesneau, François. *L'empirisme de Locke*. The Hague: Martinus Nijhoff, 1973.

Duhamel, J.-B. *De consensu veteris et novae philosophiae*. Paris, 1663.

Du Roure, Jacques. *La physique expliquée suivant le sentiment des anciens et nouveaux philosophes; & principalement Descartes*. Paris, 1653.

————. *La philosophie divisée en toutes ses parties, établie sur les principes évidents & des nouveaux auteurs; & principalement des Peripateticiens, et de Descartes*. Paris, 1654.

Fafara, R. J. "The Notion of the Idée efficace in the Philosophy of Malebranche." Ph.D. diss., University of Toronto, 1975.

Festugière, A.-J. See *Corpus Hermeticum*

Fish, S. *Is There a Text in This Class? The Authority of Interpretive Communities*. Cambridge: Harvard University Press, 1980.

Flemyng, Malcolm. *A Proposal for the improvement of the practice of medicine*. . . . 1748; 2d ed. London, 1753.

————. *A new critical examination of an important passage in Mr. Locke's Essay . . . to which is added an extract from the fifth book of Anti-Lucretius*. . . . London, 1751.

Fontenelle, B. *Eloges*, ed. F. Bouillier. Paris, 1883.

————. *Histoire de l'Academie Royale des Sciences*. Paris, 1733.

————. *Oeuvres complètes*. Paris, 1818.

Foucher, S. *Réponse pour la critique . . . de la recherche*. . . . Paris, 1679; 1st ed. 1676.

Frankfurt, H. "Descartes' Validation of Reason." *American Philosophical Quarterly* 2, no. 2 (April 1965). Reprinted in W. Doney, *Descartes*. Garden City, N.Y.: Doubleday, 1967.

Friedlander, Paul. *Plato: An Introduction*, trans. H. Meyerhoff. New York: Harper and Row, 1958.

Gabbey, A. "Philosophia Cartesiana Triumphata: Henry More." In *Problems of Cartesianism*, ed. T. Lennon, and J. Nicholas, J. Davis. Kingston/Montreal: McGill-Queens University Press, 1982.

Garber, Daniel. "Locke, Berkeley, and Corpuscular Scepticism." In *Berkeley*, ed. C. M. Turbayne. Minneapolis: University of Minnesota Press, 1982.

Gassendi, P. *Animadversiones in decimum librum Diogenis Laertii.* . . . Lyons, 1649.

———. *Dissertations en forme de paradoxes* . . . , trans. B. Rochot. Paris, 1959. [*Exercitationes*, 1624; *Opera*, 3.]

———. *Opera.* Lyon, 1658.

———. *Institutio logica*, trans. Howard Jones. Assen: Van Gorcum, 1981.

———. *Recherches métaphysiques* . . . , trans. B. Rochot. Paris, 1962. [*Disquisitio metaphysica*, 1644; *Opera*, 3].

———. *The Selected Works*, trans. C. Brush. New York: Johnson Reprint, 1972.

Gauja, Pierre "Les origines de 'l'Académie des Sciences de Paris'". *Academie des Sciences: Troisième Centenaire, 1666–1966*, (1967): 1–51.

Gelbart, N. Rattner. "The Intellectual Development of Walter Charleton." *Ambix* 18 (1971): 149–68.

George, A. J. "The Genesis of the Academy of Sciences." *Annals of Science* 3 (1938): 372–401.

———. "A Seventeenth-Century Amateur of Science: Jean Chapelain." *Annals of Science* 3 (1938): 217–36.

Gibson, James *Locke's Theory of Knowledge and Its Historical Relations*. Cambridge: Cambridge University Press, 1931.

Gouhier, H. "La crise de la théologie au temps de Descartes." *Revue de théologie et de philosophie* 4 (1954): 19–54.

———. *La philosophie de Malebranche et son expérience réligieuse*. Paris: Vrin, 1948, pp. 19–54.

Gousset, Jacob. *Causarum primarum et secundarum realis operatio.* . . . Leovardiae, 1716.

Grant, Edward. *Much Ado about Nothing: Theories of Space and Vacuum from the Middle Ages to the Scientific Revolution*. Cambridge: Cambridge University Press, 1981.

Graverol, F. de. *Memories of the life of S. Sorbière*. London, 1709.

Groarke, Leo. *Greek Scepticism: Anti-realist Trends in Ancient Thought*. Montreal/Kingston: McGill-Queens University Press, 1990.

Groarke, Leo. *Scepticism: A Defense*. Ann Arbor: University Microfilms, 1982.

Grosholz, Emily R. "A Case Study in the Application of Mathematics to Physics: Descartes's *Principles of Philosophy*, Part II." *Philosophy of Science Association 1986*. Vol. 1.

Hahn, R. *The Anatomy of a Scientific Institution: The Paris Academy of Sciences, 1666–1803*. Berkeley: University of California Press, 1971.

Halkett, S., and J. Laing, *Dictionary of Anonymous and Pseudonymous English Literature*, ed. J. Kennedy, W. A. Smith, and A. F. Johnson. London, 1929.

Hall, Marie Boas. "The Establishment of the Mechanical Philosophy." *Osiris* 10 (1952): 412–541.

Hall, Roland. "'Idea' in Locke's Works." *Locke Newsletter* 21 (1990): 9–26.

Hare, R. M. *The Language of Morals*. New York: Oxford University Press, 1964. First published 1952.

Harrison, John. *The Library of Isaac Newton*. Cambridge: Cambridge University Press, 1978.

Harrison, John, and Peter Laslett. *The Library of John Locke*. 2d ed. Oxford: Clarendon Press, 1971.

Harvart, Daniel. *Op-en ondergang van cormandel, In zijn binnenste geheel open, en ten toon gesteld*. Amsterdam, 1693.

Heath, T. L. *The Thirteen Books of Euclid's Elements*. Cambridge, 1908.

Heimann, P. M., and J. E. McGuire "Newtonian Forces and Lockean Powers: Concepts of Matter in Eighteenth-Century Thought." *Historical Studies in the Physical Sciences* 3 (1971): 233–306.

Henry, Ch. "Pierre de Carcavy, intermédiaire de Fermat, de Pascal, et de Huygens, bibliothécaire de Colbert et du roi, directeur del'Académie des Sciences." *Bulletino Boncompagni* 17 (1884): 317–91.

Hermes Trismegistus. See *Corpus Hermeticum*

Heyd, M. "The New Experimental Philosophy: A Manifestation of 'Enthusiasm' or an Antidote to It." *Minerva* 25 (1987).

―――. "From Rationalist Theology to Cartesian Voluntarism." *Journal of the History of Ideas* 40 (1979): 527–42.

Hinckfuss, Ian. "Locke's Ideas, Abstraction, and Substance." In *Cause, Mind and Reality*, ed. John Heil. Dordrecht: Kluwer, 1989.

Hobbes, Thomas. *The English Works*, ed. W. Molesworth. London, 1839–45.

Hoffman, Paul. "The Unity of Descartes's Man." *Philosophical Review* 95 (1986): 160–80.

Horace. *Epistles, Satires . . .*, trans. H. R. Fairclough. Cambridge: Loeb Classical Library, 1961.

Horton, R. "African Traditional Thought and Western Science." *Africa* 37 (1967): 50–71, 155–87.

Huet, P.-D. *Censura philosophiae Cartesianae*. Paris, 1689.

Hume, David. *Enquiries . . .* , ed. L. A. Selby-Bigge, rev. P. H. Nidditch. Oxford: Clarendon Press, 1975.

―――. *A Treatise of Human Nature*, ed. L. A. Selby-Bigge. Oxford: Clarendon, 1960.

Hunter, Michael. *The Royal Society and Its Fellows 1660–1700*. Chalfont St. Giles: British Society for the History of Science, 1982.

Huygens, Chr. *Oeuvres. . . .* The Hague: Martinus Nijhoff, 1888–1910.

Iamblichus. *Life of Pythagoras*, trans. Thomas Taylor. Reprinted from edition of 1818; Rochester, Vt.: Inner Traditions International, 1986.

Iltis, C. "The Decline of Cartesianism in Mechanics: The Leibnizian-Cartesian Debates." *Isis* 64 (1973): 356–73.

Iorio, D. See Malebranche, *Dialogue . . .*

Jacob, Margaret C. *The Radical Enlightenment: Pantheists, Freemasons, and Republicans*. London: Allen and Unwin, 1981.

Jackson, R. "Locke's Distinction between Primary and Secondary Qualities"; "Locke's Version of the Doctrine of Representative Perception." In *Locke and Berkeley*, ed. C. B. Martin and D. M. Armstrong. Garden City, N.Y.: Doubleday, 1968.

Jammer, Max. *Concepts of Space: The History of Theories of Space in Physics*. Cambridge: Harvard University Press, 1954.

Johnston, Charlotte. "Locke's Examination of Malebranche and Norris." *Journal of the History of Ideas* 19 (1958): 551–58.

Jolley, Nicholas. *Leibniz and Locke: A Study of the New Essays on Human Understanding*. Oxford: Clarendon Press, 1984.

Jolley, N. *The Light of the Soul: Theories of Ideas in Leibniz, Malebranche, and Descartes*. Oxford: Clarendon Press, 1990.

Jones, H. *Pierre Gassendi, 1592–1655: An Intellectual Autobiography*. Nieuwkoop: B. DeGraaf, 1981.

Jovy, Ernest. *Le médecin Antoine Menjot*. Vitray-le-françois, 1914.

Joy, L. *Gassendi the Atomist: Advocate of History in an Age of Science*. Cambridge: Cambridge University Press, 1987.

Juppont. "L'oeuvre scientifique de Cyrano de Bergerac." *Mémoires de l'Académie de Toulouse*. 1906.

Kant, Immanuel. *Immanuel Kant's Critique of Pure Reason*, trans. Norman Kemp Smith. London: Macmillan, 1963. 1st ed. 1929.

Kargon, R. H. *Epicurean Atomism in England from Hariot to Newton*. Oxford; 1966.

———. "Walter Charleton, Robert Boyle and the Acceptance of Epicurean Atomism in England." *Isis* 55 (1964): 184–92.

Keeling, S. V. *Descartes*. Oxford University Press, 1968. First published 1934.

Kerviler, René. *Marin et Pierre Cureau de la Chambre: 1596–1693*. Le Mans, 1877.

King, James E. *Science and Rationalism in the Government of Louis XIV, 1661–1683*. Baltimore: Johns Hopkins University Press, 1949.

King, Lord. *The Life of John Locke*. London, 1929.

Kors, A. C. "'A First Being of Whom We Have No Proof': The Preamble of Atheism in Early-Modern France." In *Anticipations of the Enlightenment in England, France and Germany*, ed. A. C. Kors and P. J. Korshin. Philadelphia: University of Pennsylvania Press, 1987.

Koyré, Alexandre *From the Closed World to the Infinite Universe*. Baltimore: Johns Hopkins University Press, 1957.

———. "Gassendi et la science de son temps." *Actes du Congrès du tricentennaire de Pierre Gassendi* (1957): 173–190.

Kroll, Richard W. F. "The Question of Locke's Relation to Gassendi and Some Methodological Implications." *Journal of the History of Ideas* 45 (1984): 339–59.

Krook, Dorothea "Thomas Hobbes's Doctrine of Meaning and Truth." *Philosophy* 31 (1956): 3–22.

La Forge, Louis de. *Oeuvres Philosophiques*, ed. Pierre Clair. Paris: Presses Universitaires de France, 1974.

La Grange, Jean Baptiste de. *Les principes de la philosophie, contre les nouveaux philosophes Descartes, Rohault, Regius, Gassendi, le P. Maignan, & c*. Paris, 1675.

———. *Traité des elemens et des météores*. Paris, 1679.

Lai, Yuen-ting. "The Linking of Spinoza to Chinese Thought by Bayle and Malebranche." *Journal of the History of Philosophy* 23 (1985): 151–78.

Lamy, François. *Le nouvel athéisme renversé ou réfutation du système de Spinoza*. Paris, 1696.

Lamy, Guillaume. *De principiis rerum*. Paris, 1669.

Lange, F. A. *History of Materialism*, trans. E. C. Thomas. 3 vols. Reprinted, New York: Humanities Press, 1950.

Lasswitz, K. *Geschichte der Atomistik vom Mittelalter bis Newton*. Hamburg, 1890.

Laudan, L. *Progress and Its Problems*. Berkeley: University of California Press, 1977.

Launay, Gilles de. *La dialectique . . . contenant l'art de raisonner sur toute sorte de matières. . . .* Paris, 1673.

––––––. *Dissertation de la philosophie en general*. Paris, 1668.

––––––. *Les essais metaphysiques*. Paris, 1672.

––––––. *Les essais physiques*. Paris, 1667.

––––––. *Introduction à la philosophie*. 2d ed. Paris, 1675.

Launoy, J. de. *De varia Aristotelis. . . .* Paris, 1653.

Le Bossu, René. *Parallèle des principes de la philosophie d'Aristote & . . . Descartes*. Paris, 1674.

Lee, Henry. *Anti-scepticism*. London, 1702.

Le Gallois, Pierre. *Conversations de l'Académie de Monsieur l'Abbé Bordelot*. Paris, 1672.

Leibniz, G. W. *Selections*, ed. P. Wiener. New York: Charles Scribner's, 1951.

––––––. *New Essays on Human Understanding*, trans. P. Remnant and J. Bennett. Cambridge: Cambridge University Press, 1981.

––––––. *Philosophical Papers and Letters*, ed. Leroy E. Loemker. 2d ed. Dordrecht: D. Reidel, 1969.

––––––. *Sämtliche Schriften und Briefe*. Berlin: Academie-Verlag, 1923- .

Legrand, A. *An Entire Body of Philosophy*. London, 1694.

Lelevel, H. *La vraye et la fausse metaphysique, ou l'on refute les sentimens de M. Regis sur cette affaire*. Rotterdam, 1694.

Lemaire, C. *Paris ancien et nouveau*. Paris, 1685.

Lemoine, J., and A. Lichtenberger *Trois familiers du Grand Condé*. Paris, 1908.

Lennon, Thomas M. "The Inherence Pattern and Descartes' *Ideas*." *Journal of the History of Philosophy* (1974): 43–52.

––––––. "Jansenism and the *Crise* Pyrrhonienne." *Journal of the History of Ideas* 38 (1977): 297–306.

––––––. "Locke's Atomism." *Philosophy Research Archives* 9 (1983): 1–28.

––––––. "Occasionalism and the Cartesian Metaphysic of Motion." *Canadian Journal of Philosophy*, sup. vol. (1974): 29–40.

––––––. In N. Malebranche, *The Search After Truth: Philosophical Commentary*. Columbus: Ohio State University Press, 1980.

––––––. "Representationalism, Judgement and Perception of Distance: Further to Yolton and McRae." *Dialogue* 19 (1980): 151–62.

––––––. "Schüler und Anhänger von Gassendi (3. Bernier 4. Launay). In *Gundriss der geschichte der Philosophie begrundet von Friedrich Ueberweg*. Basel: Schwabe, forthcoming.

Lens, L. de. "Notice sommaire sur François Bernier." In M. C. Port, *Dictionnaire historique, géographique et biographique de l'Anjou*, November 21, 1872, pp. 1–4.

Le Valois, L. [Louis de La Ville]. *Sentiments de M. Descartes touchant l'essence . . . du corps*. Paris, 1680.

Locke, J. *The Correspondence*, ed. E. S. De Beer. Oxford: Clarendon Press, 1976–82.

––––––. *Drafts for The Essay Concerning Human Understanding, and Other Philosophical Writings*, ed. P. H. Nidditch and G. A. G. Rogers. Oxford: Clarendon Press, 1990.

_____. *An Essay Concerning Human Understanding*, ed. Peter H. Nidditch. Oxford: Clarendon Press, 1975; reprinted with corrections, 1979.

_____. *Essay Concerning Human Understanding*, ed. A. C. Fraser. New York: Dover reprint, 1959.

_____. *Essays on the Law and Nature . . . together with transcripts & Locke's shorthand in his journal for 1676*

_____. *Remarks upon some of Mr. Norris's books, . . . in Locke's Philosophical Works*, ed. J. A. St. John. Vol. 2. London, 1877. First published as *A Collection of several pieces of Mr. John Locke, . . .* , ed. P. Des Maiseaux London, 1720.

_____. *Two Treatises of Government*. Cambridge: Cambridge University Press, 1967.

_____. *The Works*. London, 1823.

Loeb, Louis *From Descartes to Hume: Continental Metaphysics and the Development of Modern Philosophy*. Ithaca: Cornell University Press, 1981.

Long, P. *A Summary Catalogue of the Lovelace Collection of the Papers of John Locke in the Bodleian Library*. Oxford: Oxford University Press for the Library, 1959.

Lough, John. "Locke's Reading During His Stay in France (1675–79)." *The Library* (1953): 229–58.

_____. *Locke's Travels in France 1675–1679: As Related in his Journals, Correspondence and Other Papers*. Cambridge: Cambridge University Press, 1953.

Loux, M. J. *Universals and Particulars: Readings in Ontology*. Garden City, N.Y.: Doubleday, 1970.

Lovejoy, A. O. *The Great Chain of Being: A Study in the History of an Idea*. New York: Harper and Row, 1960.

Luce, A. A. *Berkeley and Malebranche*. Oxford: Clarendon Press, 1967.

Lucretius. *De rerum natura*, trans. M. R. Smith. Cambridge: Loeb Classical Library, 1975.

Lycan, W., and G. Pappas. "What Is Eliminative Materialism".*Australasian Journal of Philosophy* (1972): 149–59.

McCann, Edwin. "Lockean Mechanism." In *Philosophy: Its History and Historiography*, ed. A. J. Holland. Dordrecht: D. Reidel, 1985.

McClaughlin, Trevor. "Censorship and Defenders of the Cartesian Faith in Mid-Seventeenth Century France." *Journal of the History of Ideas* 40 (1979): 563–81.

McCracken, Charles J. *Malebranche and British Philosophy*. Oxford: Clarendon Press, 1983.

McCullagh, C. Behan. *Justifying Historical Descriptions*. Cambridge: Cambridge University Press, 1984.

McGuire, J. E. *Certain Philosophical Questions: Newton's Trinity Notebook*. Cambridge: Cambridge University Press, 1983.

McIntosh, J. J. "Primary and Secondary Qualities." *Studia Leibniziana* 8 (1976): 88–104.

McKeon, Robert M. "Une lettre de Melchisédech Thévenot sur les débuts de l'Academie des Sciences." *Revue d'histoire des sciences* 18 (1965): 1–6.

McMullin, E. *Newton on Matter and Activity*. Notre Dame, Ind.: University of Notre Dame Press, 1978.

McRae, R. F. "'Idea' as Philosophical Term in the Seventeenth Century." *Journal of the History of Ideas* 26 (1965): 175–90.

––––––. "Innate Ideas." In R. J. Butler, *Cartesian Studies*. Oxford: Basil Blackwell, 1972.

––––––. "Reply [to Myles]." *Dialogue* 27 (1988): 25–27.

Mackie, J. L. "Locke's Anticipation of Kripke." *Analysis* 34 (1974): 177–80.

––––––. *Problems from Locke*. Oxford: Clarendon Press, 1976.

Maindron, E. *L'Académie des Sciences*. Paris, 1888.

––––––. *L'ancienne Académie des Sciences: Les Académiciens 1666–1793*. Paris, 1895.

Malebranche, N. *Conversations chrétiennes*, ed. A. Robinet. In *Oeuvres*, vol. 4.

––––––. *Correspondence et actes*, ed. A. Robinet. In *Oeuvres*, vols. 18, 19.

––––––. *Dialogue Between a Christian and a Chinese Philosopher*, trans. D. Iorio. Washington, D.C.: University Press of America, 1980.

––––––. *Dialogues on Metaphysics and on Religion*, trans. M. Ginsberg. London: Allen and Unwin, 1923.

––––––. *Eclaircissements sur la recherche de la verité*, ed. G. Rodis-Lewis. In *Oeuvres*, vol. 3.

––––––. *Elucidations of the Search After Truth*, trans. T. M. Lennon. In N. Malebranche, *The Search After Truth*. Columbus: Ohio State University Press, 1980).

––––––. *Entretien d'un philosophe Chrétien et Chinois*, ed. A. Robinet. In *Oeuvres*, vol. 15, trans. W. Doney. New York: Abaris, 1980; also London: M. Ginsberg, 1923.

––––––. *Entretiens sur la métaphysique et sur la mort*, ed. A. Robinet. In *Oeuvres*, vols. 12–13, trans. D. Iorio. Washington, D.C.: University Press of America, 1980.

––––––. *Méditations chrétiennes*, ed. H. Gouhier and A. Robinet. In *Oeuvres*, vol. 9.

––––––. *Oeuvres complètes*, ed. A. Robinet. Paris: Vrin, 1958–69.

––––––. *Pièces jointes et Ecrits divers*, ed. A. Cuvillier, A. Robinet, and P. Costable. In *Oeuvres*, vol. 17–1.

––––––. *Receuil de toutes les réponses à M. Arnauld*, ed. A. Robinet. In *Oeuvres*, vols. 6–9.

––––––. *De la recherche de la vérité*, ed. G. Rodis-Lewis. In *Oeuvres*, vols. 1–2.

––––––. *The Search After Truth*, trans. T. M. Lennon and P. J. Olscamp. Columbus: Ohio State University Press, 1980.

Mandelbaum, Maurice. *Philosophy, Science and Sense Perception*. Baltimore: Johns Hopkins University Press, 1964.

Mariotte, E. *Traitté de la percussion ou chocq des corps dans lequel les principales regles du mouvement, contraires à celles que Mr. Descartes, & quelques autres Modernes ont voulu establir, sont demonstrées par leurs veritables causes*. Paris, 1673.

––––––. *De la nature des couleurs*. Paris, 1681.

––––––. *Essay de logique*. Paris, 1678.

Martin, André. *Philosophia christiana*. . . . Paris, 1668.

Martin, C. B., and D. M. Armstrong, eds. *Locke and Berkeley*. Garden City, N.Y.: Doubleday, 1968.

Mattern, Ruth "Locke on Active Power and the Obscure Idea of Active Power from Bodies." *Studies in the History and Philosophy of Science* 11 (1980): 39–77.

Matthews, H. E. "Locke, Malebranche and the Representative Theory." *Locke Newsletter* 2 (1971): 12–21.

Maury, L.-F. *L'ancienne académie des sciences*. Paris, 1864.

Menjot, Antoine. *Opuscules posthumes*. Amsterdam, 1697.

Michael, Fred S. and Emily "The Theory of Ideas in Gassendi and Locke." *Journal of the History of Ideas* 51 (1990): 379–99.

Mijuskovic, Ben Lazare. *The Achilles of Rationalist Arguments: The Simplicity, Unity, and Identity of Thought and Soul from the Cambridge Platonists to Kant: A Study in the History of an Argument*. The Hague: Martinus Nijhoff, 1974.

Mill, J. S. *Utilitarianism*. In *Collected Works*, ed. J. M. Robson, 10:203–59. Toronto: University of Toronto Press, 1969.

Milton, J. R. "The Date and Significance of Two of Locke's Early Manuscripts." *Locke Newsletter* 19 (1988): 47–89.

————. "Locke and Gassendi: A Reappraisal." In *Studies in Seventeenth-Century Philosophy*, ed. M. A. Stewart. Oxford: Clarendon Press, forthcoming.

Monson, Charles H., Jr. "Locke's Political Theory and Its Interpreters." In *Locke and Berkeley*, ed. C. B. Martin and D. M. Armstrong. Garden City, N.Y.: Doubleday, 1968.

Montaigne, M. de. *Oeuvres complètes*. Paris: Editions du Seuil, 1967.

Moore, G. E. "The Refutation of Idealism." *Mind* N.S. 12, (1903); reprinted, in *Philosophical Studies*. London: Routledge and Kegan Paul, 1922.

More, H. *Conjectura Cabbalistica*. In *A Collection of Several Philosophical Writings*. London, 1662.

Moreau, J. "Le réalisme de Malebranche et la fonction de l'idée." *Revue de métaphysique et de morale* 56 (1946): 97–142.

Morin, J. B. *Vincentii Panurgi Epistola de tribus impostoribus.* . . . Paris,1654.

Mouy, P. *Le dévelopement de la physique cartésienne: 1646–1712*. Paris: Vrin, 1934.

Myles, M. "The Idea of Extension: Innate or Adventitious? On R. F. McRae's Interpretation of Descartes." *Dialogue* 27 (1988): 15–24.

Myles, M. "McRae on Innate Ideas: A Rejoinder." *Dialogue* 27 (1988): 29–30.

Nadler, Steven M. *Arnauld and the Cartesian Philosophy of Ideas*. Manchester: Manchester University Press, 1989.

Newton, I. *The Mathematical Principles of Natural Philosophy*, trans. A. Motte, and F. Cajori. Berkeley, 1934.

————. *Unpublished Scientific Papers of Isaac Newton*, ed. A. R. and M. B. Hall. Cambridge: Cambridge University Press, 1962.

Niceron, J.-P. *Mémoires pour servir a l'histoire des hommes illustres dans la république des lettres*. Paris, 1727–45.

Nock, A. D. See *Corpus Hermeticum*

Norris, J. *An Essay Towards the Theory of the Ideal or Intelligible World*. London, 1701–4.

Norton, David Fate. "The Myth of 'British Empiricism'" *History of European Ideas* 1 (1981): 331–44.

O'Neil, Brian E. *Epistemological Direct Realism in Descartes' Philosophy*. Albuquerque: University of New Mexico Press, 1974.

Osler, M. "Baptizing Epicurean Atomism." In, ed. M. Osler and P. L. Farber. *Religion, Science and Worldview* Cambridge: Cambridge University Press, 1985.

————. "Descartes and Charleton on Nature and God." *Journal of the History of Ideas* 40 (1979): 445–56.

————. "Providence and Divine Will in Gassendi's Views on Scientific Knowledge." *Journal of The History of Ideas* 44 (1983): 549–60.

Pardies, I.-G. *Discours de la connoissance des bestes*. Paris, 1672.

Pascal, B. *Expériences nouvelles touchant le vuide*. . . . Paris, 1657.

————. *Pensées*, ed. L. Lafuma. Paris: Ed. du Seuil, 1962.

————. *Pensées*, ed. Ph. Sellier. Paris: Mercure de France, 1976.

Patin, G. *Lettres*, ed. J.-A. Reveillé-Parise. Paris, 1846.

Perrault, Claude. *Essais de physique ou receuil de plusiers traitez touchant les choses naturelles*. Vol. 1, Paris, 1680.

Petit, Pierre (of Montluçon). *Dissertations academiques sur la nature du froid et du chaud*. Paris, 1676.

————. *Lettre . . . a monsieur de la Chambre*. Paris, 1666.

————. *Observation touchant le vuide faite pour la premiere fois en France: Conference ou une lettre écrite a Monsieur Chanut*. . . . Paris, 1647.

————. *L'usage ou le moyen de pratiquer par une règle toutes les opérations du compas de proportion*. Paris, 1634.

Petit, Pierre (of Paris). *De nova Renati Cartesii philosophia dissertationes*. Paris, 1670.

————. *De extensione animae et rerum incorporearum natura libri duo, ad novum animae systema*. Paris, 1665.

Pillon, F. "La critique de Bayle: critique de l'atomisme épicurien." *Année Philosophique* 8 (1897): 85–167.

Pintard, R. *Le libertinage érudit dans la première moitié du XIIe siècle*. Paris: Boivin, 1943.

————. "Autour de Pascal. L'Académie Bourdelot et le problème du vide." In *Mélanges . . . offerts à Daniel Mornet*. Paris, 1951.

Piobert. "Relations des savants entre eux avant la création de l'Académie des Sciences en 1666." Comptes-rendus, *Académie des Sciences*, 1 mars 1862.

Piobetta, J.-B. *Pierre Chanet*. Paris, 1937.

Plato. *The Collected Dialogues*, ed. E. Hamilton and H. Cairns. Bollingen Series 710 New York, 1963.

Poisson, N.-J. *Traité de méchanique*. Paris, 1668.

————. *Commentaire ou remarques sur la methode de René Descartes. Où on établit plusieurs principes generaux, necessaires pour entendre toutes ses oeuvres*. Vandosme, 1670.

Popkin, Richard H. *The History of Scepticism from Erasmus to Spinoza*. Berkeley: University of California Press, 1979.

————. "The Philosophy of Bishop Stillingfleet." *Journal of the History of Philosophy* 9 (1971): 303–19.

————. "Samuel Sorbière's Translation of Sextus Empiricus." *Journal of the History of Ideas* 14 (1953): 617–21.

Popper, K. *The Open Society and Its Enemies*. 4th ed. New York: Harper Torchbooks, 1962.

Poullain de la Barre, F. *De l'education des dames pour la conduite de l'esprit dans les sciences et dans les moeurs*. Paris, 1671.

Prost, Joseph *La philosophie protestante à l'Académie protestante de Saumur: 1606–85*. Paris, 1907.

_____. *Essai sur l'atomisme et l'occasionalisme dans la philosophie cartésienne.* Paris, 1907.

Radner, Daisie *Malebranche: A Study of a Cartesian System.* Assen: Van Gorcum, 1978.

Rand, Benjamin, ed. *An Essay Concerning the Understanding, Knowledge, Opinion, and Assent by John Locke.* Cambridge: Harvard University Press, 1931.

Régis, P.-S. *Réponse au livre . . . Censura [de Huet].* Paris, 1691.

_____. *Système de philosophie contenant la logique, la métaphysique, la physique, et la morale.* 3 vols. Paris, 1690.

Reid, Thomas. *Works*, ed. W. Hamilton. 8th ed. Edinburgh, 1880.

Reynier, G. *La femme au XVIIe siècle.* Paris, 1929.

Robinet, A. *Malebranche et Leibniz: relations personelles.* Paris: Vrin, 1955.

_____. *Système et existence dans l'oeuvre de Malebranche.* Paris: Vrin, 1965.

Robinson, J. M. *An Introduction to Early Greek Philosophy.* Boston: Houghton Mifflin, 1968.

Rochot, B. *Les travaux de Gassendi sur Epicure et sur l'atomisme 1619–1658.* Paris, 1944.

(Rodis-)Lewis, Geneviève. *L'individualité selon Descartes.* Paris: Vrin, 1950.

Rogerius (Roger), Abraham *De open-deure tot het verborgen leydendom, ofte Waerachtigh vertoogh van wet leven ende zeden; mits gaders de religie ende godsdienst der brahmins, op de cust Chormandel, ende de landern daar outrent, etc.* Leyden, 1651.

_____. *La porte ouverte, pour parvenir à la connoissance du paganisme caché ou la vraye representation . . . Traduite . . . Thomas La Grue.* Amsterdam, 1670.

Rogers, G. A. J. "Boyle, Locke and Reason." *Journal of the History of Ideas* 27 (1966): 205–16.

Rohault, Jacques *Entretiens sur la philosophie.* Paris, 1671.

_____. *Traité de physique.* Paris, 1671.

Rorty, R. "The Historiography of Philosophy: Four Genres." In *Philosophy in History*, ed. R. Rorty, J. B. Schneewind, and Q. Skinner. Cambridge: Cambridge University Press, 1884.

Rorty, R., J. B Schneewind, and Q. Skinner, eds. *Philosophy in History.* Cambridge: Cambridge University Press, 1984.

Rosenfield, Leonora Cohen. *From Beast-Machine to Man-Machine: Animal Soul in French Letters from Descartes to La Mettrie.* New York: Oxford University Press, 1941.

Saint-Evremond, C. de. *Oeuvres.* ed. P. Des Maizeaux. N.p., 1740.

Sallengre, Albert-Henry. *Memoires de litterature.* Paris, 1715.

Sambursky, S. "Place and Space in late Neo-platonism." *Studies in History and Philosophy of Science.* 8 (1977); 173–87.

Schouls, Peter A. *The Imposition of Method: A Study of Descartes and Locke.* Oxford: Clarendon Press, 1980.

Scott, J. F. *The Scientific Work of René Descartes (1596–1650).* London: Taylor and Francis, 1952.

Sebba, G. *Bibliographia Cartesiana: A Critical Guide to the Descartes Literature.* The Hague: Martinus Nijhoff, 1964.

Sennert, Daniel. *De origine et natura animarum in brutis.* . . . Frankfurt, 1638.

Sergeant, John. *Non ultra: or, a letter to a learned Cartesian; settling the rule of truth, and first principles, upon their deepest grounds.* London, 1698.

———. *The Method to Science* [by J. S.]. London, 1696.

———. *Solid philosophy asserted, against the ideists: or the method to science further illustrated.* London, 1697.

Sévigné, Marie de Rabutin-Chantal, Marquise de. *The Letters.* Philadelphia: Horn, 1927.

Shaftesbury, Anthony Ashley Cooper, Third Earl of. *Characteristics of Men, Manners, Opinions, Times.* London, 1711.

Shankula, H. A. S. "Locke, Descartes and the Science of Nature." *Journal of the History of Ideas* 41, no. 3 (1980):459–77.

Sharp, Lindsay. "Walter Charleton's Early Life 1620–1659, and Relationship to Natural Philosophy in Mid-Seventeenth Century England." *Annals of Science* 30 (1973): 311–40.

Shea, William R. *The Magic of Numbers and Motion: The Scientific Career of René Descartes.* Canton, Mass.: Science History Publications, 1991.

Sorabji, Richard. *Time, Creation and the Continuum.* London: Duckworth, 1983.

Sorbière, Samuel. *Relation d'un voyage en Angleterre.* Paris, 1664.

———. *A Voyage to England . . . also Observations on the same voyage by Dr. Thomas Sprat . . . with a letter of Monsieur Sorbières, . . . to all which is prefix'd his Life, . . .* London, 1709.

Sortais, Gaston. "Le Cartésianisme chez les Jésuites français au XVIIe et au XVIIIe siècle", *Archives de Philosophie* 6 (1929).

———. *La philosophie moderne.* Paris, 1922.

Spiller, Michael R. G. *"Concerning Natural Experimental Philosophie": Meric Casaubon and the Royal Society.* The Hague: Martinus Nijhoff, 1980.

Spink, J. S. *French Free-thought from Gassendi to Voltaire.* London: Athlone Press, 1960.

Spinoza, B. *The Collected Works*, ed. and trans. E. Curley. Princeton: Princeton University Press, 1985.

———. *Opera*, ed. G. Gebhardt. Heidelberg: C. Winter, 1925.

———. *Selections*, ed. John Wild. New York: Charles Scribner's Sons, 1930.

Sprat, Thomas. *The History of the Royal-Society of London, for the improving of natural knowledge.* London, 1667. See also Samuel Sorbière, *A Voyage to England . . .*

Squadrito, K. "The Ontological Status of Ideas in Locke's *Essay.*" *Indian Philosophy Quarterly* 10 (1983):173–82.

———. "Substance, Modification, and Ideas in Locke's *Essay.*" *Dialogos* 48 (1986): 145–50.

Stanley, Thomas. *History of Philosophy.* London, 1655–62, 1687, 1701.

Stewart, Dugald. *Collected Works*, ed. W. Hamilton. Edinburgh, 1854–58.

Stewart, M. A. "Locke's Professional Contacts with Robert Boyle." *Locke Newsletter* 12 (1981): 19–44.

Stillingfleet, E. *The Works.* London, 1710.

Strutt, Samuel. *A Defense of the Late Learned Dr. Clarke's Notion of Natural Liberty.* London, 1730.

————. *A Philosophical Enquiry into the Physical Spring of Human Actions and the Immediate cause of Thinking*. London, 1732.

Swift, Jonathan. *A Tale of a tub, to which is added, The Battle of the books, and the mechanical operation of the spirit*, ed. A. C. Guthkelch and D. Nichol Smith. 2d ed. Oxford: Clarendon Press, 1958. First published, London 1704, 5th ed. 1710.

Tannery, P. "A propos de la correspondence de Huygens." *Bulletin des sciences mathématiques*. 2, no. 16 (1892).

Taton, R. *Les origines de l'Académie Royale des Sciences*. Paris, 1966.

Taylor, A. E. *Plato: The Man and His Work*. Cleveland: World Publishing, 1956; reprinted from 6th ed.

Thomas Aquinas, Saint. *Commentary*. In *Aristotle's De Anima in the version of William of Moerbeke and the Commentary of St. Thomas Aquinas*, trans. Kenelm Foster and Silvester Humphries. New Haven: Yale University Press, 1951.

Toland, John *Christianity Not Mysterious: Or, a treatise showing, that there is nothing in the Gospel contrary to Reason, nor above it: and that no Christian doctrine can be properly call'd a mystery*. London, 1696.

Tolmer, Abbé Léon. *Pierre-Daniel Huet (1630–1721): Humaniste-Physicien*. Bayeux, 1949.

Trentman, John "Scholasticism in the Seventeenth Century." In *The Cambridge History of Later Medieval Philosophy*, ed. Norman Kretzman, Anthony Kenny, and Jan Pinborg. Cambridge: Cambridge University Press, 1982.

Urbain, Ch. *Sur un opuscule de P. Daniel Huet*. Paris, 1911.

Vissac, Raoul de *Anthoine du Roure et la révolte de 1670*. Paris, 1895.

Vlastos, G. "*Anamnesis* in The *Meno*." *Dialogue* 4 (1965): 143–67.

Waard, C. de "Les objections de Pierre Petit contre le discours et les essais de Descartes." *Revue de Métaphysique et Morale* (1925): 51–89.

Walton, C. *De la Recherche du Bien: A Study of Malebranche's Science of Ethics*. The Hague: Martinus Nijhoff, 1972.

Ware, Charlotte S. "The Influence of Descartes on Locke. A Bibliographical Study." *Revue Internationale de Philosophie* 4 (1950): 210–30.

Watkins, J. W. N. *Hobbes's System of Ideas: A Study in the Political Significance of Philosophical Theories*. 2d ed. London: Hutchinson, 1973.

Watson, R. A. *The Downfall of Cartesianism*. The Hague: Martinus Nijhoff, 1968.

Weinberg, J. *Abstraction, Relation and Induction: Three Essays in the History of Thought*. Madison: University of Wisconsin Press, 1965.

Westfall, Richard S. *The Construction of Modern Science: Mechanisms and Mechanics*. New York: John Wiley, 1971.

————. "The Foundations of Newton's Philosophy of Nature." *British Journal for the History of Science* 1 (1962): 171–82.

White, Hayden. *Tropics of Discourse: Essays in Cultural Criticism*. Baltimore: Johns Hopkins University Press, 1978.

Willis, Thomas. *De Anima Brutorum*. . . . Oxford, 1672.

Wilson, Fred. "The Lockean Revolution in the Theory of Science." In *Early Modern Philosophy: Metaphysics, Epistemology, and Poetics. Essays in honour of Robert F. McRae*, ed. G. Moyal and S. Tweyman. Delmar, N.Y.: Carhran Books, 1985.

Wilson, M. *Descartes*. London: Routledge and Kegan Paul, 1978.

_____. "Superadded Powers: The Limits of Mechanism in Locke." *American Philosophical Quarterly* 16 (1979): 143–50.

Windet, James A. Stromateus epistolikos *de vita functorum statu.* . . . 2d ed. London, 1664.

Witty, John. *The First Principles of Modern Deism Confuted*. London, 1707.

Yates, F. *Giordano Bruno and The Hermetic Tradition*. New York: Vintage, 1969.

_____. *The Rosicrucian Enlightenment*. Frogmore, St. Albans, Herts: Paladin, 1975.

Yolton, John. "On Being Present to the Mind: A Sketch for the History of an Idea." *Dialogue* 14 (1975): 378–88.

_____. "Ideas and Knowledge in Seventeenth-Century Philosophy." *Journal of the History of Philosophy* 13 (1975): 145–65.

_____. Review of François Duchesneau, *L'empirisme de Locke*. In *Journal of the History of Philosophy* 13 (1975): 410–13.

_____. *John Locke and the Way of Ideas*. Oxford: Oxford University Press, 1956.

_____. *Locke and the Compass of Human Understanding*. Cambridge: Cambridge University Press, 1970.

_____. *The Locke Reader: Selections from the Works of John Locke with a General Introduction and Commentary*. Cambridge: Cambridge University Press, 1977.

_____. "Locke's Unpublished Marginal Replies to John Sergeant." *Journal of the History of Ideas* 12 (1951): 528–59.

_____. "As in a Looking-Glass: Perceptual Acquaintance in Eighteenth-Century Britain." *Journal of the History of Ideas* 40 (1979): 207–34.

_____. *Perceptual Acquaintance from Descartes to Reid*. Oxford: Basil Blackwell, 1984.

_____. *Thinking Matter: Materialism in Eighteenth-Century Britain*. Oxford: Basil Blackwell, 1984.

Index